TRICKS OF THE WINDOWS GAME PROGRAMMING GURUS

SECOND EDITION

André LaMothe

SAMS

201 West 103rd Street,
Indianapolis, Indiana 46290

Tricks of the Windows Game Programming Gurus

Copyright © 2002 by Sams Publishing

International Standard Book Number: 0-672-32369-9

Library of Congress Catalog Card Number: 2001097517

Printed in the United States of America

First Printing: June 2002

05   04   03   02   4   3   2   1

Trademarks

Warning and Disclaimer

Executive Editor
Michael Stephens

Acquisitions Editor
Kim Spilker

Development Editor
Mark Renfrow

Managing Editor
Charlotte Clapp

Project Editor
George E. Nedeff

Copy Editor
Sean Medlock
Aaron Black
Howard Jones

Indexer
Erika Millen

Proofreader
Mike Henry

Technical Editor
David Franson

Team Coordinator
Lynn Williams

Multimedia Developer
Dan Scherf

Interior Designer
Gary Adair

Cover Designer
Gary Adair

Page Layout
Becky Harmon

Contents at a Glance

Table of Contents

Part III   Hardcore Game Programming   655

11   Algorithms, Data Structures, Memory Management, and Multithreading   657

Foreword

I remember first falling in love with computers back in 1983 while programming Logo on an Apple IIe (thanks, Woz!). The sense of power I got from that experience was very addicting and mind-shaping. The computer would do whatever I told it. It didn't get tired after countless repetitions or question my reasoning behind having it perform any particular task. The machine just did it. I owe much of my career to that experience, the movie *War Games*, and an author by the name of Andrè LaMothe.

I bought my first book by Andrè LaMothe, *Sams Teach Yourself Game Programming in 21 Days*, back in 1994. It had never occurred to me that people could make a career out of programming video games. It was then that I saw the connection between my love for programming and my addiction to video games. Who would have ever thought that all those hours of playing Galaga could now be considered research? Andrè's writing and teaching style inspired me and gave me the confidence to believe that I could program video games. I remember calling him up on the phone (I still can't believe he actually talks to people and gives out his phone number) and asking for his help with a simple program I was making for my physics class based on his gas model demo. I couldn't get the program to work. Well, he instantly reviewed my program and in seconds said something like, Rich, you're killing me, you need to put a semicolon at the end of each line! Well, that was it, and my first game program was up and running.

A few years later, I had the pleasure of working with Andrè on a video game called Rex Blade as the tools programmer and a level designer. It was a tremendous learning experience for me. We worked amazingly hard (Andrè is a slave driver), had a lot of fun (going to movies, gun shooting, skiing, and a lot more can anyone say, Desert Eagle 51 caliber? <GRIN>), and ended up with a 3D interactive video game trilogy. We took Rex Blade from the concept to the shelves in an unbelievable six months (Rex would make an interesting postmortem to be sure). Working on Rex taught me what really went into making a real video game, and working with Andrè showed me what it really meant to work around the clock—and I do mean around the clock. I thought he was kidding when he said he worked 100+ hours a week!

There are few areas of software engineering that push the limits of the hardware, the software, and the programmer himself as much as game programming does. There are so many intricate pieces that have to work together perfectly: math, physics, AI, graphics, sound, music, GUI, data structures, and so forth. This is where *Tricks of the Windows Game Programming Gurus* proves itself to be an essential tool in the art of programming the video games of today and tomorrow.

This book takes you to the next level in game programming technology. The artificial intelligence coverage alone is enough to make your mouth water—the demos are killer. Where else can you get detailed coverage of fuzzy logic, neural nets, and genetic algorithms and how to apply them to video games? The book also takes you through all the major components of DirectX, including DirectDraw, DirectInput (with force feedback coverage—Yes!), DirectSound, and the latest and greatest technology of DirectMusic.

Then there's the physics modeling coverage. Finally, someone who knows what he's talking about has taken the time to delve into full collision response, momentum transfer, and forward kinematics, and how to simulate them in real-time. Imagine creatures that learn, objects that collide like in the real world, and enemies who remember how you defeated them in your last encounter. These are the basics that will make the great games of tomorrow.

I really have to hand it to Andrè for writing this book. He always says that if he didn't, who would? It's true: For someone to give away 20+ years of hard work, secrets, and tricks to help others is really cool.

With technology advancing by leaps and bounds, I think it's a great time to be alive, especially if you're a game programmer. It seems like every few months there's a new CPU, video card, or other piece of hardware that pushes the boundaries of what we believe to be technologically possible. (I mean, it's crazy to think that Voodoo III does 70 billion operations a second.) This great gift of technology comes with a price, though. With it comes the expectation that the games we create will use this technology, which raises the bar on what's expected of tomorrow's video games. It seems as though in the very near future, the only limiting factors will be our knowledge and our imagination.

It excites me to know that the next generation of game programmers will have this book to inspire and educate them. And I think Andrè hopes that somewhere, someone will take his place in the 21st century and continue this work of disseminating the black magic, because he needs a vacation!

—Richard Benson
3D Game Programmer
DreamWorks Interactive/Electronic Arts

About the Author

Andrè LaMothe (a.k.a. Lord Necron) has been programming for over 24 years and holds degrees in mathematics, computer science, and electrical engineering. He has written numerous articles on the subjects of graphics, game programming, and artificial intelligence. He is the author of *Tricks of the Game Programming Gurus, Sams Teach Yourself Game Programming in 21 Days, The Game Programming Starter Kit, The Black Art of 3D Game Programming, and Windows Game Programming for Dummies*, all bestsellers. In addition, he coauthored Ciarcia's Circuit Cellar I and II. Mr. LaMothe has also taught at the University of Santa Cruz Extension Multimedia Department.

Last, but not least, Andre is the founder and CEO of Xtreme Games LLC (www.xgames3d.com) and the Xtreme Games Developers Conference (www.xgdc.com).

He can be reached at ceo@xgames3d.com.

Contributing Authors of Online Books in Digital Form

Location on CD: T3DGAME\ONLINEBOOKS

Matthew Ellis, author of *Direct3D Primer*

Matthew is a teenage 3D game programmer and author. He lives in Las Vegas, NV, and is interested in all aspects of 3D game programming and graphics. He is currently creating a new 3D engine, as well as publishing articles and working on a book of his own.

He can be reached at matt@magmagames.com.

Sergei Savchenko, author of *General 3D Graphics*

Sergei is a graduate student of computer science at McGill University in Montreal. Sergei hails from the city of Kharkov (XAPbKOB), Ukraine, in the former Soviet Union.

In addition to his computer science studies, Sergei also studied aircraft design at the Kharkov Aviation Institute. He also teaches computer science classes and performs active research in automated reasoning.

He can be reached at savs@cs.mcgill.ca or at his Web page, http://www.cs.mcgill.ca/~savs/3dgpl/.

David Dougher, author of *Genesis 3D Engine Reference, Tool, and API Function Manuals*

David has been programming and gaming for over 25 years, creating his first computer games on paper tape for use on the PDP-8 systems at Syracuse University in 1974. His collection of gaming magazines goes back to *Strategic Review*, Issue

Number 1 (the precursor to *Dragon* magazine). He is currently employed full-time as a release engineer by Parlance Corp. and loves Babylon 5, Myst, Riven, Obsidian, game design, teaching ballroom dancing, and his wife, although not in that order.

He can be reached at ddougher@ids.net.

Contributing Authors of Articles and Papers

Location on CD: T3DGAME\ARTICLES

Bernt Habermeier, author of *Internet Based Client/Server Network Traffic Reduction*. Email: bert@bolt.com. Web page: http://www.bolt.com.

Ivan Pocina, author of KD Trees. Email: ipocina@aol.com.

Nathan Papke, author of *Artificial Intelligence Voice Recognition and Beyond*. Email: nathan.papke@juno.com.

Semion S.Bezrukov, author of *Linking Up with DirectPlay*. Email: deltree@rocketmail.com.

Michael Tanczos, author of *The Art of Modeling Lens Flares*. Email: webmaster@logic-gate.com.

David Filip, author of *Multimedia Musical Content Fundamentals*. Email: grimlock@u.washington.edu.

Terje Mathisen, author of *Pentium Secrets*. Email: terjem@hda.hydro.com.

Greg Pisanich and Michelle Prevost, authors *of Representing Artificial Personalities* and *Representing Human Characters in Interactive Games*. Email: gp@garlic.com, prevost@sgi.com.

Zach Mortensen, author of Polygon Sorting Algorithms. Email: mortens1@nersc.gov.

James P. Abbott, author of *Web Games on a Shoestring*. Email: jabbott@longshot.com. Web page: http://www.longshot.com.

Mike Schmit, author of *Optimizing Code with MMX Technology*. Email: mschmit@zoran.com, mschmit@ix.netcom.com.

Alisa J. Baker, author of *Into the Grey Zone and Beyond*. Email: abaker@gcounsel.com.

Dan Royer, author of *3D Technical Article Series*. Email: aggravated@bigfoot.com. Web page: http://members.home.com/droyer/index.html.

Tom Hammersley, author of *Viewing Systems for 3D Engines*. Email: tomh@globalnet.co.uk.

Bruce Wilcox, author of *Applied AI*: Chess is Easy. Go is Hard. Email: brucewilcox@bigfoot.com.

Nathan Davies, author of *Transparency in D3D Immediate Mode*. Email: alamar@cgocable.net.

Bob Bates, author of *Designing the Puzzle*. Email: bbates@legendent.com.

Marcus Fisher, author of *Dynamic 3D Animation Though Traditional Animation Techniques*. Email: mfisher@avalanchesoftware.com.

Lorenzo Phillips, author of *Game Development Methodology for Small Development Teams*. Email: pain19@ix.netcom.com.

Jason McIntosh, author of *Tile Graphics Techniques 1.0.*

In addition, the CDs contain a number of selected articles from the Game Programming MegaSite at http://www.perplexed.com/. The articles are authored by *Matt Reiferson, *Geoff Howland, Mark Baldwin, John De Goes, *Jeff Weeks, Mirek, *Tom Hammersley, Jesse Aronson, Matthias Holitzer, Chris Palmer, Dominic Filion, JiiQ, Dhonn Lushine, David Brebner, Travis "Razorblade" Bemann, Jonathan Mak, Justin Hust, Steve King, Michael Bacarella II, Seumas McNally, Robin Ward, Dominic Filion, Dragun, Lynch Hung, Martin Weiner, Jon Wise, and Francois Dominic Larame.

*Contributed more than one article.

About the Technical Editor

David Franson been a professional in the field of networking, programming, and 2D and 3D graphic arts since 1990. In 2000, he resigned his position as Information Systems Director of one of the largest entertainment law firms in New York City to persue a full-time career in game development. Currently, he is authoring *2D Artwork and 3D Modeling for Game Artists*, set to be released July 2002.

Dedication

"I dedicate this book to the innocent men and women that suffer for the guilty"

Acknowledgments

I always hate writing acknowledgements because there are simply too many people involved in a book to mention everybody and give them proper thanks. However, here goes once again, in no particular order.

I would first like to thank my parents for having me late in life, causing me to have so many genetic mutations that I don't need to sleep and I can work continuously without a break. Thanks, Mom and Dad!

Next, I want to thank all the people at Sams Publishing for letting me have my way with the book. Making corporate America do anything different is surely a strain, and I am Mr. Nonconformist, but that's what it takes if you want to break new ground. Particularly, I want to thank the acquisitions editor, Kim Spilker, for listening to my artistic/marketing concepts and making them happen; George Nedeff, the project editor, for making sure that my policy of less editing is more was taken seriously; Dan Scherf, the media specialist, for making sure that all the programs made it to the CDs; and Mark Renfrow, the development editor, for making sure that the hundreds of figures and thousand-plus pages of manuscript didn't get mangled; and last but not least, I would like to thank David Franson, the tech editor.

And of course, thanks to all the other editors and formatters that worked on the book. It seemed like all of you were playing musical chairs during editing, but you all did a fantastic job. And of course, for this new revision of Tricks, Michael Stephens was instrumental in making it happen. The original book was on a really rushed schedule before, so there were a great many details that we never had time to address, but this revision will hopefully clear those issues up along with add some new content. At least that's the plan!

Next I want to thank the DirectX group at Microsoft, especially Kevin Bachus, and Stacey Tsurusaki for helping with the acquisition of the latest DirectX SDK stuff, along with making sure that I was sent to all the major DirectX parties. Very important to send me to parties; that's a good thing.

The next group I want to thank are all the companies that had something to do with this book in one way or another, whether it was a piece of software or whatever. The major players are Caligari Corporation for the use of TrueSpace, JASC for the use of Paint Shop Pro, and Sonic Foundry for the use of Sound Forge. I would also like to thank Matrox and Diamond Multimedia for demo 3D accelerators, Creative Labs for sound cards, Intel Corporation for VTune, Kinetics for 3D Studio Max, and Microsoft® and Borland® for their compiler products.

I'd like to thank all of my friends that I made contact with during this hellish production. To all the guys at Shamrock's Universal Submission Academy: Crazy Bob, Josh, Kelly, Javier, Big Papa, Liquid Rob, Brian, The Puppet, and everyone else. To Mike Perone, for always getting me that hard-to-find piece of software at a moment's notice. Oh yes, to my friend Mark Bell or as I like to think of him, Mr. Happy you still owe me $180 from that ski trip eight years ago! (And I can't stand always being right anymore; please try harder, Mark. I can't keep taking your money.)

Next I want to thank all the contributing editors who allowed me to put their articles on the CDs. If it weren't for you guys, these poor readers would have nothing more then my eccentric prose to read. A special thanks goes to Matthew Ellis, the author of the Direct3D book on the CDs, and to Richard Benson (Keebler) for doing the foreword to the book.

Thanks to everyone!

We Want to Hear from You!

As the reader of this book, *you* are our most important critic and commentator. We value your opinion and want to know what we're doing right, what we could do better, what areas you'd like to see us publish in, and any other words of wisdom you're willing to pass our way.

As an associate publisher for Sams Publishing, I welcome your comments. You can email or write me directly to let me know what you did or didn't like about this book—as well as what we can do to make our books better.

Please note that I cannot help you with technical problems related to the *topic* of this book. We do have a User Services group, however, where I will forward specific technical questions related to the book.

When you write, please be sure to include this book's title and author as well as your name, email address, and phone number. I will carefully review your comments and share them with the author and editors who worked on the book.

Email: feedback@samspublishing.com

Mail: Michael Stephens
          Sams Publishing
          201 West 103rd Street
          Indianapolis, IN 46290 USA

For more information about this book or another Sams title, visit our Web site at www.samspublishing.com. Type the ISBN (excluding hyphens) or the title of a book in the Search field to find the page you're looking for.

Introduction

"Dead or alive, you're coming with me."

—Robocop

A long time ago, in a galaxy far, far away, I wrote a book about game programming called *Tricks of the Game Programming Gurus*. For me, it was an opportunity to create something that I had always wanted—a book that taught the reader how to make games. Anyway, it's been a few years and I'm a little older and wiser, and I have definitely learned a lot of tricks <BG>. This book is going to continue where the old book left off. I'm going to cover every major topic in game programming that I can fit within the binding of this bad boy!

However, as usual, I'm not going to assume that you are already a master programmer or that you even know how to make games. This book is for beginners as well as advanced game programmers. Nonetheless, the tempo is going to be fierce, so don't blink!

Today is probably the coolest time in history to be in the game business. I mean, we now have the technology to create games that do look real! Imagine what will come next? But all this technology isn't easy to understand or trivial—it takes hard work. These days the bar has definitely been raised on the skill set needed to make games. But if you're reading this, you are probably one of those people who like a challenge, right? Well, you came to right place, because when you're done with this book you will be able to create a full 3D, texture-mapped, professionally lit video game for the PC. Moreover, you will understand the underlying principles of artificial intelligence, physics modeling, game algorithms, and 2D/3D graphics, and you'll be able to use 3D hardware today and in the future.

What You're Going to Learn

In this book you're going to learn about 100 teraquads of information! I'm going to fill your neural net so full of information that you might have synaptic leakage! Seriously, though, this volume covers all the elements necessary to create a Windows 9X/NT/XP/2000-based game for the PC:

- Win32 programming
- DirectX Foundation
- 2D graphics and algorithms
- Game programming techniques and data structures
- Multithreaded programming

- Artificial intelligence
- Physics modeling
- Using 3D acceleration hardware (on the CD)

And more…

This book is primarily about game programming. There are two cyber-books on the CD that cover Direct3D Immediate mode and General 3D.

What You Need to Know

This book assumes that you can program. You are going to be fairly lost if you can't write C code. However, the book uses some C++—enough to make a C coder just a little uneasy. But I will warn you if I'm doing anything weird. Also, there's a decent C++ primer in Appendix D, so check it out if you need a crash course. Basically, C++ is needed only here and there for examples when using DirectX.

Nevertheless, I've decided that I'm going to use C++ a little more on this book because there are so many things in game programming that are *object-oriented*, and it's sacrilege to force them to be C-like structures. Bottom line—if you can program in C, you should be fine. If you program in C/C++, you shouldn't trip out at all.

Everyone knows that a computer program is nothing more than logic and math. Well, 3D video games put the emphasis on the math part! 3D graphics is *all* math. Luckily for us, it's *cool* math! (Yes, math can be cool.) About the only thing you need to know is basic algebra and geometry. The vector and matrix stuff I will teach you along the way. Heck, if you can add, subtract, multiply, and divide, you will be able to understand 90 percent of what's going even though you may not be able to rederive it. As long as you can use the code, that's all the matters. (Well, that and if 7 of 9 is on *Voyager* tonight, but I think I'm switching to the Vulcan girl from *Enterprise*.)

That's really all you need to know. Of course, you'd better call all your friends and tell them that they won't see you for about two years, because you're going to be a little busy. But just think of all the movies you can rent when you're done with your training!

How This Book Is Organized

Tricks of the Windows Game Programming Gurus is divided into four parts, covering 15 chapters and 6 appendixes.

Part I: Windows Programming Foundations

Chapter 1   Journey into the Abyss

Chapter 2   The Windows Programming Model

Installing the CD-ROM

The CD-ROMs contains all the source, executables, sample programs, stock art, 3D modelers, sound effects, and bonus technical articles that make up the book. Here's the directory structure:

```
CD-DRIVE:\
```

```
T3DGAMER1\

SOURCE\
                T3DCHAP01\
                T3DCHAP02\
                    .
                    .
                T3DCHAP14\
                T3DCHAP15\

APPLICATIONS\

ARTWORK\
                  BITMAPS\
                  MODELS\

SOUND\
                WAVES\
                MIDI\

DIRECTX\

GAMES\


ARTICLES\

ONLINEBOOKS\

ENGINES\
```

Each main directory contains specific data that you'll need. Here's a more detailed breakdown:

T3DGAMER1—The root directory that contains all other directories. Be sure to read the README.TXT file within it for any last-minute changes.

SOURCE—Contains all the source directories for the book, in chapter order. Simply drag the entire SOURCE\ directory to your hard drive and work from there.

DEMOS—Contains demo programs that various companies have so graciously allowed me to place on the CD.

ARTWORK—Contains stock artwork that you may use royalty-free in your games.

SOUND—Contains stock sound effects and music that you may use royalty-free in your games.

DIRECTX—Contains the latest version of the DirectX SDK.

GAMES—Contains a number of 2D and 3D shareware games that I think are cool!

ARTICLES—Contains articles written by various experts in the field of game programming for your edification.

ONLINEBOOKS—Contains online digital books covering Direct3D Immediate mode and general 3D graphics.

ENGINES—Contains evaluation copies of various 3D engines.

There isn't any general installation program for the CD because there are so many different types of programs and data. I'll leave the installation to you. However, in most cases, you'll simply copy the SOURCE\ directory to your hard drive and work within it. As for the other programs and data, you'll probably install them as you need them.

Installing DirectX

About the only important part of the CD that you must install is the DirectX SDK and runtime files. The installation program is located within the DIRECTX\ directory, along with a README.TXT file explaining any last-minute changes.

> **NOTE**
> You must install DirectX 8.0 SDK or better to work with these CD-ROMs. If you're not sure that you have the latest files on your system, run the installation and it will tell you.

Compiling the Programs

I wrote the code for this book with Microsoft Visual C++ 5.0/6.0. However, in most cases the programs will work with any Win32-compliant compiler. Nevertheless, I suggest Microsoft VC++ because it works the best for this type of work.

If you are unfamiliar with your compiler's IDE, you are going to be wildly lost compiling Windows programs. Please take the time to learn your way around the compiler, and at least know how to compile a "Hello World" console program or something similar before you dive into compiling the programs.

To compile Windows Win32 .EXE programs, you just need to set the target of your program project to Win32 .EXE and compile. However, to create DirectX programs, you must include the DirectX import libraries in your project. You may think that you can simply add the DirectX libraries to your include path, but that won't work! Save yourself a headache and include the DirectX .LIB files in your project or workspace manually. You can find the .LIB files in the LIB\ directory, right under the main DirectX SDK directory that you installed under. That way there won't be any linker confusion. In most cases, you'll need the following:

DDRAW.LIB	DirectDraw import library
DINPUT.LIB	DirectInput import library
DINPUT8.LIB	DirectInput8 import library
DSOUND.LIB	DirectSound import library

D3DIM.LIB	Direct3D Immediate Mode import library
DXGUID.LIB	DirectX GUID library
WINMM.LIB	Windows Multimedia Extensions

I'll go into more detail on these files when you actually start working with them, but at least keep them in mind when you start getting "unresolved symbol" errors from your linker. I don't want any e-mails on this subject from rookies!

In addition to the DirectX .LIB files, you must include the DirectX .H header files in your header search path, so keep that in mind. Also, be sure to make the DirectX SDK directories first in the search path list, because many C++ compilers contain old versions of DirectX and the old headers might be found in the compiler's own INCLUDE\, which is wrong. The proper place is the DirectX SDK include directory, which is located in the main installation directory of the DirectX SDK in INCLUDE\.

Finally, if you use Borland products, make sure that you use the Borland versions of the DirectX .LIB files. They can be found in the BORLAND\ directory of the DirectX SDK installation.

About the Second Edition

This revision of *Tricks* basically updates the material from the first printing. The updates are in various areas, such as cleaning up the typos and technical errors, along with adding new content and enabling compilation using the latest version of DirectX (what was Microsoft thinking removing DirectDraw!). Additionally, this new edition covers more details about 16-bit RGB modes, will compile under DirectX 8.0, and has a new chapter on text parsing, along with added explanations throughout the book. In general, this is a much cleaner, more complete version of *Tricks*.

Additionally, this book is about game programming; hence, the coverage of DirectX is only what is needed to get the point across when discussing various game programming topics. In most cases, my philosophy is to keep things as simple as possible. The new merger of DirectDraw and Direct3D is great for 3D applications, but overkill for 2D games and, of course, for tutorial explanation. Thus, I have stuck to using DirectDraw 7.0 to keeps things easy while at the same time upgrading to DirectX 8.0 in other areas that are relatively the same. The point is that DirectX is a set of technologies, and you must pick and choose what you need for any particular application.

PART I

Windows Programming Foundations

CHAPTER 1

Journey into the Abyss

"Oh, you want some too?!?"

—Hudson, *Aliens*

Windows programming has been an ongoing war with a long history. Game programmers have resisted the Windows platform since the beginning of time, but like the Borg say, "Resistance is futile...." I tend to agree. In this chapter you're going to take a whirlwind tour of Windows:

- History of games
- Types of games
- The elements of game programming
- Using tools
- A sample game: FreakOut

A Little History

It all began sometime in the '60s, when the first mainframe computers came to be. Now, don't quote me on this, but one of the first computer games ever played was Core Wars on Unix machines. When the '70s rolled around, there were quite a number of text-based and crude graphic adventures running on mainframe computers and minicomputers all around the world.

The funny thing is, back then most games were networked! I mean, 90% of the game programs were MUDs (multiuser dungeons) or similar simulations, like Star Trek and war simulations. However, the masses never got a taste of computer games until the quintessential Pong came out. Designed by Nolan Bushnell, this single game really started the whole video game arcade business overnight, and Atari was born.

Then, around 1976–1978, the TRS-80, Apple, and Atari 800 all hit the market. They were the first computers that a consumer could buy. Of course, before then you could buy kits like the Altair 8000, but who wanted to put them together? In any case, these computers all had their pros and cons. The Atari 800 was by far the most powerful (I'm convinced I could write a version of Wolfenstein that would work on it), the TRS-80 was the most businesslike, and the Apple had the best marketing.

Slowly, games started to hit the market for these systems, and many teenage million-aires were made overnight. A good lunar lander or Pong-type game was all you needed to strike it rich! In those days, computer games looked like computer games, and only a handful of people knew how to make them. There were absolutely no books on the topic. Every now and then someone would publish a 50–100-page, semi-underground booklet that had a few pieces of the puzzle, and maybe there'd be a magazine article in *Byte,* but for the most part you were on your own.

The '80s are when things started to heat up. The first 16-bit computers were available, like the IBM PC (and compatibles), Mac, Atari ST, Amiga 500, and so on. This was the time when games started to look good. There were even some 3D games on the market such as Wing Commander and Flight Simulator, but the PC was definitely at the back of the line of game machines. By 1985, the Amiga 500 and Atari ST reigned supreme as the ultimate game-playing computers. However, the PC slowly gained popularity due to its low price and usefulness in the business sector. And the bottom line is that the computer with the largest market base, regardless of its technology or quality, will rule the world in the end.

By the early 1990s, the IBM PC-compatible was the leader. With the release of Microsoft Windows 3.0, it was all over for the Apple Macintosh. The PC was the "working person's computer." You could actually play with it, write programs for it, and open it up and connect stuff to it. I think that those are the reasons why so many hobbyists stuck to PCs rather than the sexier Mac stuff. Bottom line—you couldn't have fun with Macs!

But the PC was still lagging behind in the graphics and audio department. The PC seemed like it just didn't have enough horsepower to make a game that looked as good as something on an Amiga or a game console.

And then there was light....

In late 1993, Id Software released DOOM as a follow-up to Wolfenstein 3D (one of the first shareware 3D games, also by Id). The PC became the game-playing and programming platform of choice for the home computer market, and it has remained that way ever since. DOOM proved that if you're clever enough, you can make a PC do anything. This is a very important point. *Remember it.* There is no substitute for imagination and determination. If you believe it's possible, it is!

After the DOOM craze hit, Microsoft really started to reevaluate its position on gaming and game programming. It realized that the entertainment industry is huge and only getting bigger. It also realized that it wanted to be part of that industry, so big plans were drawn up to get Microsoft into the game.

The problem was that even Windows 95 had terrible real-time video and audio capabilities. So Microsoft created a piece of software called Win-G to address the video aspect of the problem. Win-G was heralded as the ultimate game programming and graphics subsystem. It turned out to be nothing more than a couple of graphics calls to draw bitmaps, and Microsoft literally denied its existence after about a year—no joke!

However, work had already begun on a new set of graphics, sound, input, networking, and 3D systems (a la the Rendermorphics acquisition). And DirectX was born. As usual, the marketing people at Microsoft got carried away, claiming that DirectX would solve all the world's game programming problems on the PC platform and Windows games would be as fast as or faster than DOS32 games. That didn't quite happen.

The first couple of iterations of DirectX were horrible failures as actual products, but not in technological terms. Microsoft simply underestimated the complexity of video game programming. (And of video game programmers!) But by DirectX 3.0, DirectX worked better than DOS! However, most game companies at this time (1996–1997) still were working with DOS32, and they didn't make the transition to DirectX for actual product releases until version 5.0.

Today, DirectX is coming up on version 9.0 (this book covers 7.0 and 8.0), and it's a killer API. True, you have to think a little differently—using COM (the Component Object Model), programming in Win32, and not having total control over the whole computer anymore—but that's life. I don't think that Geordi can take over the whole computer system on the Enterprise either, so if resource-sharing works on a Galaxy Class starship, it's good enough for me.

With DirectX technology, you can create a virtual, DOS-like machine with a 4GB address space (or more) and linear memory, and you can program as if you're in DOS (if that's what you like). More importantly, now you can leverage every new piece of graphics and sound technology instantly. This is due to DirectX's forward-looking design and technology. Anyway, that's enough about DirectX; you'll get the full treatment soon enough. Let's get back to history....

First, there was DOOM, which used software rasterization only. Take a look at Figure 1.1 to see a screenshot of Rex Blade, a DOOM-clone. The next generation of 3D games, like Quake I, Quake II, and Unreal, really were a quantum leap. Take a look at Figure 1.2 to see a screenshot of Unreal. This game and others like it are simply unbelievable. All of them contain software rasterizers along with hardware acceleration code to get the best of both worlds. And let me tell you, Unreal II or Quake III running on a Pentium IV 2.4GHz with GeForce IV TI acceleration is as sweet as it gets.

FIGURE 1.1
Rex Blade: The first generation in DOOM technology.

FIGURE 1.2
It's so good, it's Unreal!

So where does this leave us? In a world where technology is so advanced that the sky is the limit. However, there's always the next "big thing." Even though games like Quake and Unreal can take years to make, I'm hoping that you'll come up with something just as engaging!

The history lesson's over. Let's get to the core of the matter with design.

Designing Games

One of the hardest things about writing video games is designing them. Sure, 3D mathematics is hard, but thinking of a fun game and a design to go along with it is just as difficult, in a manner of speaking, and definitely as important. Who cares if you have the latest volumetric photon traces if the game sucks?

Now, thinking up a game idea isn't that hard. It's the details, final implementation, and visual look that make the difference between the bargain bin and the cover of *PC Gamer*. So let's outline some basic concepts and rules of thumb that have worked for me and paid for a Dodge Viper or two.

Types of Games

These days, there are as many game types as political promises (those that are made, not kept), but you can bunch them into a handful of genres:

DOOM-like first-person games—These games are full 3D, for the most part, and you view them from the character's perspective. DOOM, Hexen, Quake, Unreal, Duke Nukem 3D, and Dark Forces are all good examples of this type of game. Technologically, they're probably the most difficult to develop, and they require cutting-edge technology to be noticed.

Sports games—Sports games can be either 2D or 3D, but these days more and more are 3D. In any case, the sport can be one-man or team play. The graphics in sports games have come a long way. Maybe they're not as impressive as first-person games, but they're catching up. However, the artificial intelligence in sports games is some of the most advanced of all the game genres.

Fighting games—Fighting games are typically played by one or two players, and the action is viewed from the side or by a floating 3D camera. The game imagery can be 2D, 2.5D (multiple 2D bitmap images of 3D objects), or full 3D. Tekken for the Sony Playstation I is the game that really made the genre for the home console market. Fighting games aren't as popular on the PC, probably due to the interface problems with controllers and the two-player fun factor.

Arcade/shoot'em-up/platform—These games are your typical Asteroids, Pac Man, and Jazz Jackrabbit type stuff. They're basically old-school games that are primarily 2D, but they're being redefined and remade into 3D worlds. However, the gameplay is relatively the same as it was in 2D.

Mechanical simulations—These games encompass any kind of driving, flying, boating, racing, and tank-battle simulation, and any other kind that you can think of. For the most part, they are 3D and have always been (even though they didn't look good until recently).

Ecosystem simulations—These games are really new and have no real-world analogs—other than the real world itself. Here I'm talking about Populous, SimCity, SimAnt, and so on. These games allow you, the player, to be a god of sorts and control an artificial system of some kind, whether it's a city, a colony of ants, or a financial simulation like Gazzillonaire (very cool game, BTW).

Strategy or war games—These games have splintered into a number of subgenres. But I'm not religious about them, so suffice it to say we're talking about strategy, turn-based (sometimes), thinking types of games such as Warcraft, Diablo, Final Fantasy, and so on. Again, I'm being a little cavalier here since Diablo is real-time, but it still involves a great deal of strategy and thinking. On the other hand, Final Fantasy is turn-based and not real-time.

Interactive stories—This category includes Myst-like games. Basically, these games are prerendered or on "tracks," and you move through them by figuring out puzzles. Usually, these games don't allow free roaming and are like playing interactive books, for lack of a better definition. Moreover, they aren't really "to-the-metal" game programs because 99% of them are written using Director or a Director-like tool. Boring, Jules.

Retro games—This area of gaming has sprung up overnight. In a nutshell, there are people who want to play old games, but with more bells and whistles than the originals. For example, Atari has made about 1,000 versions of Tempest. Granted, they never sell, but you get the point. However, I have had a lot of luck remaking some of the old games like Dig Dug, Centipede, Frogger, and so on.

Pure puzzle and board games—There's not much to say here. These games can be 2D, 3D, prerendered, or whatever. Tetris, Monopoly, and Mahjong are a few games that fall into this category.

Brainstorming on Ideas

Once you have decided what kind of game you want to make—which is usually easy since we all know what we like—it's time to think up the game. This is where you're totally on your own. There's no way to come up with good game ideas consistently.

Basically, you have to think of a game that you would like to make and develop it into something that sounds cool, is doable, and that other people will like as well.

Of course, you can get help by using other games as models or starting points. Don't copy another product exactly, but loosely following successful products is fine. Also, read a lot of science fiction books and game magazines, see what is selling, and watch a lot of movies for cool story ideas, game ideas, or just visual motivation.

What I usually do is sit with a friend (or by myself) and just throw out ideas until something sounds cool. Then I develop the idea until it sounds plausible or it falls apart. This can be very frustrating. You may overthink all your ideas and throw your hands up after two or three hours. Don't despair—this is a good thing. If a game idea survives the night and into the next day and you still like it, chances are that you might have something.

WARNING

> I want to say something that's very important, so listen carefully—don't bite off more than you can chew! I've received thousands of e-mails from newbie game programmers who want to create something at the level of DOOM or Quake for their first game. It's simply not going to happen. You'll be lucky if you can finish an Asteroids clone in three to six months, so don't get crazy. Set a reasonable goal. Try to think up something you can do by yourself, because in the end you'll be working by yourself—people flake out. Again, try to keep your first game ideas simple.

Now let's move on to some details.

The Design Document and Storyboards

Once you have a game idea, you need to get it on paper. Now, when I do a big game product, I require myself to make a real design document, but for little games, a few pages of details will do. Basically, a design document is a roadmap or outline of a game. It should have as many details about the game, the levels, and the gameplay as you can think of. This way you know what you're making and can follow some kind of plan. Otherwise, you will keep changing things and your game will end up being incoherent.

Usually, I like to write down a simple story to begin with, maybe a page or two that describes what the game is about. Who is the main character? What is the idea of the game? And last, how do you win the game? Then I decide on the hard-core details of the game—the levels and the gameplay—and outline them as much as possible. When I'm done, I can always add or delete things, but at least I have a working plan. If I think of 100 cool new ideas, I can always add them and not forget them.

Obviously, the amount of detail is up to you, but write something down. At least make some sketches! For example, maybe you don't even want a full design document and are more comfortable with some crude sketches of the levels and gameplay. Figure 1.3 is a sample storyboard that you might make for a game. Nothing complicated, just something to look at and work from.

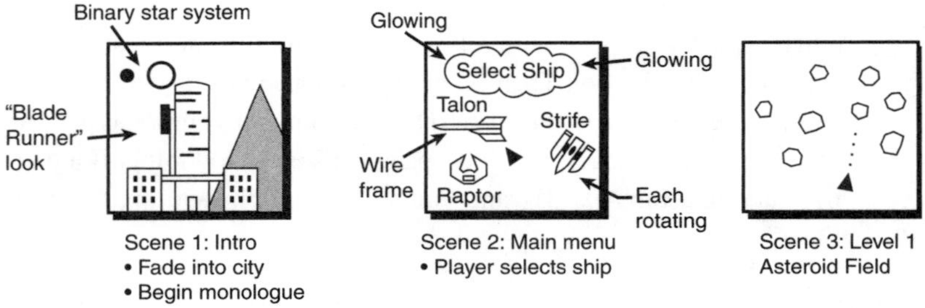

FIGURE 1.3
A basic storyboard.

Scene 1: Intro
• Fade into city
• Begin monologue

Scene 2: Main menu
• Player selects ship

Scene 3: Level 1
Asteroid Field

Making the Game Fun

The last part of designing a game is the reality check. Do you really think that the game will be fun and people will like it? Or are you lying to yourself? This is a serious question. There are about 10,000 games on the shelves and about 9,900 companies going out of business, so think about this. If you're totally excited about the game and can imagine wanting to play it more than anything, you're in the ballpark. But if you, as the designer, just get lukewarm about the idea, imagine how *other* people are going to feel about it!

The key here is to do a lot of thinking and beta testing of the game and add all kinds of cool features, because in the end it's the details that make a game fun. It's like fine workmanship on a piece of handcrafted oak furniture (I personally hate wood, but work with me). People appreciate the details.

The Components of a Game

Now it's time to look at what makes a video game program different from any other kind of program. Video games are extremely complex pieces of software. In fact, they are without a doubt the hardest programs to write. Sure, writing MS Word is harder than writing Asteroids, but writing Unreal is harder than writing any other program I can think of!

This means that you have to learn a new way of programming that's more conducive to real-time applications and simulation, rather than the single-line, event-driven, or sequential logic programs that you may be used to. A video game is basically a continuous loop that performs logic and draws an image on the screen, usually at a rate of 30 frames per second (fps) or more. This is similar to how a movie is displayed, except that you are creating the movie as you go.

Therefore, let's begin by taking a look at a simplified game loop, as shown in Figure 1.4. The following list describes each section.

FIGURE 1.4

General game loop architecture.

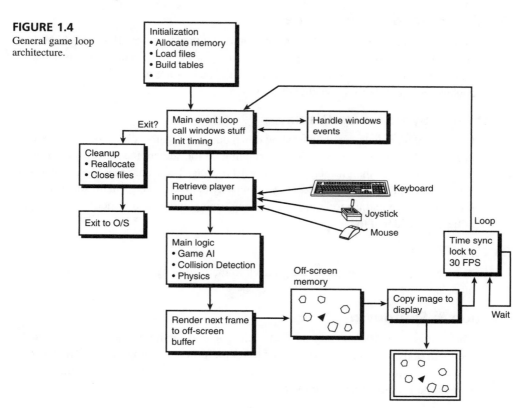

Section 1: Initialization

In this section, you perform the standard operations you would for any program, such as memory allocation, resource acquisition, loading data from disk, and so forth.

Section 2: Enter Game Loop

In this section, the code execution enters into the main game loop. This is where the action begins and continues until the user exits the main loop.

Section 3: Retrieve Player Input

In this section, the player's input is processed and/or buffered for later use in the AI and logic section.

Section 4: Perform AI and Game Logic

This section contains the majority of the game code. The artificial intelligence, physics systems, and general game logic are executed, and the results are used to draw the next frame on the screen.

Section 5: Render Next Frame

In this section, the results of the player's input and the execution of game AI and logic are used to generate the next frame of animation for the game. This image is usually drawn on an offscreen buffer area, so you can't see it being rendered. Then it is copied very quickly to the visible display.

Section 6: Synchronize Display

Many computers will speed up or slow down due to the game's level of complexity. For example, if there are 1,000 objects running on the screen, the CPU is going to have a higher load than if there were only 10 objects. The frame rate of the game will vary, which isn't acceptable. Hence, you must synchronize the game to some maximum frame rate and try to hold it there using timing and/or wait functions. Usually, 30fps is considered to be optimal.

Section 7: Loop

This section is fairly simple—just go back to the beginning of the game loop and do it all again.

Section 8: Shutdown

The shutdown phase indicates the end of the game, meaning that the user has exited the main body or game loop and wants to return to the operating system. However, before the user exits, you must release all resources and clean up the system, just as you would for any other piece of software.

You might be wondering about all the details of a real game loop. Granted, the preceding explanation is a little oversimplified, but it captures the essence of what's going on. In most cases, the game loop will be an FSM (finite state machine) that contains a number of states. Listing 1.1 is a more detailed version of what a C/C++ game loop might look like in real code.

LISTING 1.1   A Simple Game Event Loop

```
// defines for game loop states
#define GAME_INIT            // the game is initializing
#define GAME_MENU            // the game is in the menu mode
#define GAME_STARTING        // the game is about to run
#define GAME_RUN             // the game is now running
#define GAME_RESTART         // the game is going to restart
```

LISTING 1.1   Continued

```
#define GAME_EXIT        // the game is exiting

// game globals
int game_state = GAME_INIT; // start off in this state
int error      = 0;     // used to send errors back to OS


// main begins here

void main()
{
// implementation of main game loop

while (game_state!=GAME_EXIT)
    {
    // what state is game loop in
        switch(game_state)
    {
        case GAME_INIT: // the game is initializing
             {
             // allocate all memory and resources
             Init();

             // move to menu state
             game_state = GAME_MENU;
             } break;

        case GAME_MENU:  // the game is in the menu mode
             {
             // call the main menu function and let it switch states
             game_state = Menu();

             // note: we could force a RUN state here
             } break;

        case GAME_STARTING:   // the game is about to run
             {
             // this state is optional, but usually used to
             // set things up right before the game is run
             // you might do a little more housekeeping here
             Setup_For_Run();

             // switch to run state
             game_state = GAME_RUN;
             } break;

        case GAME_RUN:     // the game is now running
             {
             // this section contains the entire game logic loop
```

LISTING 1.1   Continued

```
                    // clear the display
                    Clear();

                    // get the input
                    Get_Input();

                    // perform logic and ai
                    Do_Logic();
                    // display the next frame of animation
                    Render_Frame();

                    // synchronize the display
                    Wait();

                    // the only way that state can be changed is
                    // thru user interaction in the
                    // input section or by maybe losing the game.
                    } break;

               case GAME_RESTART:  // the game is restarting
                    {
                    // this section is a cleanup state used to
                    // fix up any loose ends before
                    // running again
                    Fixup();
                    // switch states back to the menu
                    game_state = GAME_MENU;
                    } break;

               case GAME_EXIT:    // the game is exiting
                    {
                    // if the game is in this state then
                    // it's time to bail, kill everything
                    // and cross your fingers
                    Release_And_Cleanup();

                    // set the error word to whatever
                    error = 0;

                    // note: we don't have to switch states
                    // since we are already in this state
                    // on the next loop iteration the code
                    // will fall out of the main while and
                    // exit back to the OS
                    } break;

          default: break;
          } // end switch

     } // end while
```

LISTING 1.1   Continued

```
// return error code to operating system
return(error);

} // end main
```

Although Listing 1.1 is nonfunctional, I think that you can get a good idea of the structure of a real game loop by studying it. All game loops pretty much follow this structure in one way or another. Take a look at Figure 1.5, the state transition diagram for the game loop logic. As you can see, the state transitions are fairly sequential.

FIGURE 1.5
State transition diagram for a game loop.

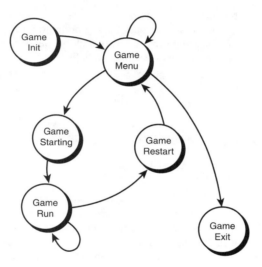

We'll talk more about game loops and finite state machines later in the chapter when we cover the FreakOut demo game.

General Game Programming Guidelines

Next I want to talk about some general game programming techniques and philosophies that you should think about and try to adopt (if you can) to make game programming much easier.

To begin with, video games are ultra-high-performance computer programs. No longer can you use high-level APIs for time-critical or memory-critical code sections. For the most part, you must write everything yourself that is related to the inner loop of your game code, or else your game will suffer terrible speed and performance problems. Obviously, this doesn't mean that you can't trust APIs like DirectX, since DirectX was written to be as high-performance and "thin" as possible. But in general, avoid high-level function calls.

With that in mind, take a look at a list of tricks to keep in mind as you're programming.

TRICK

Don't be afraid to use global variables. Many video games don't use parameters for a lot of time-critical functions, instead using a global parameter passing area. For example, say a function looks like this:

```
void Plot(int x, int y, int color)
{
// plots a pixel on the screen
video_buffer[x + y*MEMORY_PITCH] = color;
} // end Plot
```

Here the body of the function takes less time than the function call. This is due to the parameter pushing and popping on the stack. In this case a better method might be to create a global parameter passing area and then make assignments before a call, like this:

```
int gx,gy,gz,gcolor; // define some globals

void Plot_G(void)
{
// plot a pixel using globals
video_buffer[gx + gy*MEMORY_PITCH] = gcolor;

} // end Plot_G
```

TRICK

Use inline functions. You can improve the preceding trick even more by using the inline directive to get rid of the function call completely. The inline directive instructs the compiler to make its best attempt to put the code for the function right where it's called, rather than making the actual function call. Of course, this makes bigger programs, but speed is more important. Here's an example:

```
inline void Plot_I(int x, int y, int color)
{
// plots a pixel on the screen
video_buffer[x + y*MEMORY_PITCH] = color;
} // end Plot_I
```

Notice that I didn't use globals because the compiler will in effect perform the same type of data aliasing. However, globals would come in handy if only one or two of the parameters were changing between calls because the old values could be used without reloading.

TRICK

Always use 32-bit variables rather than 8- or 16-bit. The Pentium and later processors are totally 32-bit. This means that they don't like 8- or 16-bit data words, and in fact, smaller data can slow them down due to caching and other related memory addressing anomalies. For example, you might create a structure that looks something like this:

```
struct CPOINT
{
short x,y;
unsigned char c;
} // end CPOINT
```

Although creating this structure may seem like a good idea, it's not! First, the structure itself is now 5 bytes long—(2*sizeof(short) + sizeof(char)) = 5. This is really bad, and it's going to wreak havoc on the memory addressing. A better approach is the following structure:

```
struct CPOINT
{
int x,y;
int c;
} // end CPOINT
```

C++

Tip STRUCTs in C++ are just like CLASSes, except that they have default PUBLIC visibility.

This new structure is much better. For one thing, all the elements are the same size—that is, sizeof(int) = 4 bytes. Therefore, a single pointer can be incremented on a DWORD boundary to access any member. Of course, the new structure is now (3*sizeof(int)) = 12 bytes, but at least it's a multiple of 4 or on a DWORD boundary. This is definitely going to improve performance.

In fact, if you really want to make things rock, you can pad all structures to make them multiples of 32 bytes. This is the optimal length due to standard on-chip cache line sizes in the Pentium class processors. You can pad manually by adding dummy variables, or you can use a compiler directive (the easy way). Of course, padding may waste a lot of memory, but it may be worth it for the increase in speed.

TRICK

Comment the heck out of your code. Game programmers are notorious for not commenting their code. Don't make the same mistake. Clean, well-commented code is always worth the extra typing.

TRICK

Program in a RISC-like (reduced instruction set computer) manner. In other words, make your code simple rather than complex. Pentium and Pentium class processors in particular like simple instructions rather than complex ones. And making your code longer, with simpler instructions, makes it easier for the compiler. For example, don't do this:

```
if ((x+=(2*buffer[index++]))>10)
{
// do work
} // end if
```

Instead, do this:

```
x+=(2*buffer[index]);
index++;

if (x > 10)
{
// do work
} // end if
```

There are two reasons for coding like this. First, this approach allows a debugger to insert break points between code sections. Secondly, coding this way makes it easier for the compiler to send simplified code to the Pentium, which allows it to process more code in parallel using multiple execution units. Complex code is bad!

TRICK

Use binary shifts for simple multiplication of integers by powers of 2. Since all data in a computer is stored in binary form, shifting the bit pattern to the left or right is equivalent to multiplication or division, respectively. For example:

```
int y_pos = 10;

// multiply y_pos by 64
y_pos = (y_pos << 6);  // 2^6 = 64
```

Similarly,

```
// to divide y_pos by 8
y_pos = (y_pos >> 3); // 1/2^3 = 1/8
```

You'll see more tricks like this when you get to the optimization chapters. Cool, huh?

TRICK

Write efficient algorithms. All the assembly language in the world isn't going to make an n^2 algorithm go faster. It's better to use clean, efficient algorithms rather than brute force.

TRICK

Don't optimize your code as you program. This is usually a waste of time. Before you start heavy optimization, wait until you're done with a major code block or until you're done with the whole game. Working this way will save you time in the end because you won't have to deal with cryptic code or optimizations that aren't necessary. When the game is done, that's the time you should start profiling and finding problem areas to optimize. On the other hand, don't program sloppily.

TRICK

Don't write a lot of complex data structures for simple objects. Just because linked lists are cool doesn't mean you should use them for a fixed array that you know will always be around 256 items. Just allocate it statically and be done with it. Video game programming is 90% data manipulation. Keep your data as simple and visible as possible so you can access it quickly, do what you need to, and move on. Make sure the data structure fits the problem.

TRICK

Use C++ sparingly. If you're a seasoned professional, go ahead and do as you please, but don't go class crazy or overload everything to death. In the end, simple, straightforward code is the best and easiest to debug. And I never want to see multiple inheritance!

TRICK

If you see that you're going down a rocky road, stop, back up, and take a detour. I have seen many game programmers start down a bad programming line and bury themselves. It's better to realize you made a mistake and redo 500 lines of code than to have a generally undesirable code structure. So, if you see a problem with what you're doing, re-evaluate it and make sure that the time you're saving is worthwhile.

TRICK

Back up your work regularly. When you're writing game code, you're going to lock up the system fairly frequently. Redoing a sorting algorithm is one thing, but redoing the AI for a character and the collision detection is another.

TRICK Before you start on your game projects, be organized. Use reasonable filenames and directory names, come up with a consistent variable naming convention, and try to use separate directories for graphics and sound data rather than dumping everything in one directory.

Using Tools

In the past, writing video games required nothing more than a text editor and maybe a homemade paint program. However, today things are a little more complicated. At a minimum, you need a C/C++ compiler, a 2D paint program, and a sound processing program. In addition, you might need a 3D modeler if you're going to do a 3D game, along with a music sequencing program if you're going to use any MIDI.

Let's take a look at some of the more popular products and what they do.

C/C++ Compilers

For Windows 9X/NT development, there's simply no better compiler than MS VC++ 6.0+. It does everything you need it to, and more. The .EXEs generated are the fastest code available. The Borland compiler will also work fine (and is a lot cheaper), but it has a much smaller feature set. In either case, you don't need the full-blown version of either one. A student version that makes Win32 .EXEs is more than enough.

2D Art Software

Here you have paint programs, drawing programs, and image processing. Paint programs primarily allow you to draw images pixel by pixel with primitives and manipulate them. As far as I'm concerned, Paint Shop Pro by Jasc is the leader of the pack for price versus performance. ProCreate Painter (formerly Fractal Design Painter) is also great, but it's more for traditional artists, not to mention that it's very expensive. My favorite is Corel Photo-Paint, but that's definitely more firepower than most newbies need.

On the other hand, drawing programs allow you to create images that are mostly constructed from curves, lines, and 2D geometrical primitives. These types of programs aren't as useful, but if you need one, Adobe Illustrator is the way to go.

The final class of 2D art programs is the image processing type. These programs are more for post-production work than for art creation. Adobe Photoshop is the favorite in most circles, but I think Corel Photo-Paint is better. Decide for yourself.

Sound Processing Software

Ninety percent of all sound effects (SFX) used in games today are digitized samples. To work with sound data of this type, you're going to need a digital sound processing program. The best program in this genre is Sound Forge Xp. It has by far the most complex sound processing capabilities I have ever seen, and yet it's the simplest to use.

3D Modelers

Things get financially challenging when you consider 3D modelers, which can cost tens of thousands of dollars, but recently I've seen a number of low-cost modelers that have enough power to literally make a movie. The modeler that I primarily use for simple-to-medium-scale 3D models and animation is Caligari TrueSpace. It is the best 3D modeler for the price. It's a few hundred dollars and has the best interface there is.

If you want a little more firepower and absolute photorealism, 3D Studio Max is the way to go. It's around $2,500, though, so that might be something to think about. However, for the most part we're going to use these modelers just to create 3D meshes, not for rendering, so all the bells and whistles aren't really needed; thus, TrueSpace is the way to go.

Music and MIDI Sequencing Programs

There are two kinds of music in today's games: pure digital (like a CD) and MIDI (musical instrument digital interface), which is a synthesized performance based on note data. If you want to manipulate MIDI information and songs, you'll need a sequencing package. One of the best and most reasonably priced is called Cakewalk, so I suggest that you look into this program if you plan on recording and manipulating MIDI music. I'll talk about MIDI data when covering DirectMusic in Chapter 10, "Sounding Off with DirectSound and DirectMusic."

 TRICK And now for the cool part... A number of the software manufacturers listed here have allowed me to put shareware or evaluation versions on the CD, so make sure to check them out!

Setting Up to Get Down—Using the Compiler

One of the most frustrating parts of learning Windows game programming is learning how to use the compiler. In most cases, you're so excited to get started that you dive into the IDE and try to compile, and a million compiler and linker errors pop up! To help with this problem, let's cover a few basic compiler concepts here.

0. Read the entire compiler instructions—please, please, I beg you!

1. You must install the DirectX SDK on your system. All you need to do is navigate to the <DirectX SDK> directory on the CD, read README.TXT, and do what it says (which should be nothing more than "Click on the DirectX SDK INSTALL.EXE program").

2. We are going to make Win32 .EXE programs, not .DLLs, ActiveX components, and so on. So if you want to compile, the first thing you need to do with your compiler is create a new project or workspace and set the target output file to Win32 .EXE. This step is shown for the VC++ 6.0 compiler in Figure 1.6.

Windows Programming Foundations

FIGURE 1.6
Creating a Win32
.EXE with Visual C++
6.0.

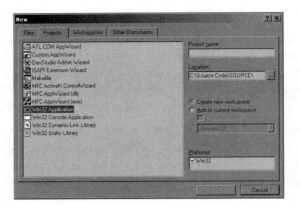

3. Add the source files to the project using the Add Files command from the main menu or from the project node itself. This is shown for the VC++ 6.0 compiler in Figure 1.7.

FIGURE 1.7
Adding files to a pro-
ject with VC++ 6.0.

4. When you get to the DirectX chapters, and from there on, you'll have to include most of the DirectX COM interface libraries listed here and shown in Figure 1.8.

- DDRAW.LIB

- DSOUND.LIB

- DINPUT.LIB

- DINPUT8.LIB

- DSETUP.LIB*

NOTE You will not need DSETUP.LIB unless you're using DirectSetup.

FIGURE 1.8
The resources needed
to create a Win32
DirectX application.

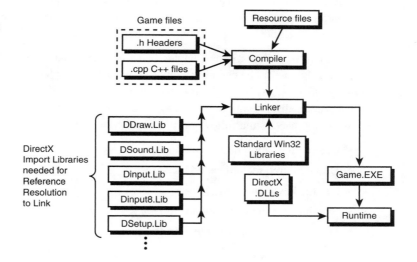

These DirectX .LIB files are located in the <LIB> directory wherever you installed the DirectX SDK. You *must* add these .LIB files to your project or workspace. You can't just add the search path, because the search engine will probably find old DirectX 3.0 .LIB files along with installation libraries of the compiler itself. While you're at it, you may have to add the Windows Multimedia Extensions library, WINMM.LIB, to your project. This file is located in the <LIB> directory of your compiler installation.

5. You're ready to compile your program.

WARNING If you're a Borland user, there is a separate Borland library directory within the DirectX SDK. So make sure to add those .LIB files—*not* the MS-compatible files higher up in the directory tree.

If you still have questions about this process, don't worry. I'll revisit these steps a number of times throughout the book when discussing Windows programming and your first contact with DirectX.

An Example: FreakOut

Before we both lose our minds with all this talk about Windows, DirectX, and 3D graphics, I would like to take a pause and show you a complete game—albeit a simple one, but a game nonetheless. This way you can see a real game loop and some graphics calls, and take a shot at compilation. Sound good? Alrighty, then!

The problem is, we're only on Chapter 1. It's not like I can use stuff from later chapters…that would be cheating, right? So what I've decided to do is get you used to using *black box* APIs for game programming. Based on that requirement, I asked, "What are the absolute minimum requirements for creating a 2D Breakout-like game?" All we really need is the following functionality:

- Change into any graphics mode.
- Draw colored rectangles on the screen.
- Get the keyboard input.
- Synchronize the game loop using some timing functions.
- Draw a string of colored text on the screen.

So I created a library called BLACKBOX.CPP|H. Within it is a DirectX (DirectDraw only) set of functions, along with support code that implements the required functionality. The beauty is, you don't need to look at the code; you just have to use the functions, based on their prototypes, and make sure to link with BLACKBOX.CPP|H to make an .EXE.

Based on the BLACKBOX library, I wrote a game called FreakOut that demonstrates a number of the concepts that we have discussed in this chapter. FreakOut contains all the major components of a real game, including a game loop, scoring, levels, and even a little baby physics model for the ball. And I do mean baby! Figure 1.9 is a screenshot of the game in action. Granted, it's not Arkanoid, but it's not bad for four hours of work!

FIGURE 1.9
A screenshot of
FreakOut.

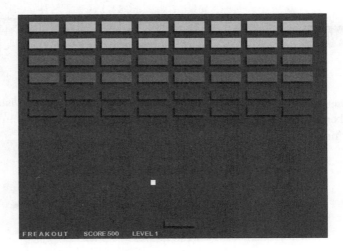

Before I show you the source code to the game, I want you to take a look at how the project and its various components fit together. Refer to Figure 1.10.

FIGURE 1.10
The structure of FreakOut.

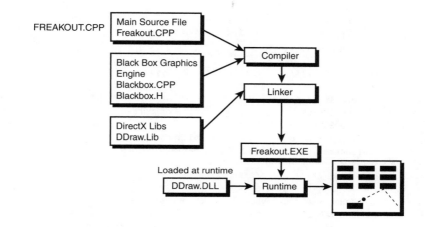

As you can see from the figure, the game is composed of the following files:

FREAKOUT.CPP—The main game logic that uses BLACKBOX.CPP and creates a minimum Win32 application.

BLACKBOX.CPP—The game library (don't peek).

BLACKBOX.H—The header file for the game library.

DDRAW.LIB—The DirectDraw import library needed to build the application. This doesn't contain the real DirectX code. It's more of an intermediary library that you make calls to, which in turn loads the dynamic link library DDRAW.DLL that does the real work. You can find this in the DirectX SDK installation under <LIB>.

DDRAW.DLL—The runtime DirectDraw library that actually contains the COM implementation of the DirectDraw interface functions that are called through the DDRAW.LIB import library. You don't need to worry about this per se; you just need to make sure that the DirectX runtime files are installed.

So, to compile, you need to include in your project the source files BLACKBOX.CPP and FREAKOUT.CPP, link to the library DDRAW.LIB, and make sure that BLACKBOX.H is in the search path or the working directory where you are compiling so that the compiler can find it.

Now that we have that all straight, let's take a look at the BLACKBOX.H header file and see what the functions are within it.

Windows Programming Foundations

LISTING 1.2 BLACKBOX.H Header File

```
// BLACKBOX.H - Header file for demo game engine library

// watch for multiple inclusions
#ifndef BLACKBOX
#define BLACKBOX

// DEFINES ///////////////////////////////////////////////////

// default screen size
#define SCREEN_WIDTH    640  // size of screen
#define SCREEN_HEIGHT   480
#define SCREEN_BPP      8    // bits per pixel
#define MAX_COLORS      256  // maximum colors

// MACROS ////////////////////////////////////////////////////

// these read the keyboard asynchronously
#define KEY_DOWN(vk_code) ((GetAsyncKeyState(vk_code) & 0x8000) ? 1 : 0)
#define KEY_UP(vk_code)   ((GetAsyncKeyState(vk_code) & 0x8000) ? 0 : 1)

// initializes a direct draw struct
#define DD_INIT_STRUCT(ddstruct) { memset(&ddstruct,0,sizeof(ddstruct));
ddstruct.dwSize=sizeof(ddstruct); }

// TYPES /////////////////////////////////////////////////////

// basic unsigned types
typedef unsigned short USHORT;
typedef unsigned short WORD;
typedef unsigned char  UCHAR;
typedef unsigned char  BYTE;

// EXTERNALS /////////////////////////////////////////////////

extern LPDIRECTDRAW7         lpdd;              // dd object
extern LPDIRECTDRAWSURFACE7  lpddsprimary;      // dd primary surface
extern LPDIRECTDRAWSURFACE7  lpddsback;         // dd back surface
extern LPDIRECTDRAWPALETTE   lpddpal;           // a pointer dd palette
extern LPDIRECTDRAWCLIPPER   lpddclipper;       // dd clipper
extern PALETTEENTRY          palette[256];      // color palette
extern PALETTEENTRY          save_palette[256]; // used to save palettes
extern DDSURFACEDESC2        ddsd;    // a ddraw surface description struct
extern DDBLTFX               ddbltfx;           // used to fill
extern DDSCAPS2              ddscaps; // a ddraw surface capabilities struct
extern HRESULT               ddrval;            // result back from dd calls
extern DWORD                 start_clock_count; // used for timing
```

LISTING 1.2   Continued

```
// these defined the general clipping rectangle
extern int min_clip_x,                            // clipping rectangle
           max_clip_x,
           min_clip_y,
           max_clip_y;

// these are overwritten globally by DD_Init()
extern int screen_width,                          // width of screen
           screen_height,                         // height of screen
           screen_bpp;                            // bits per pixel

// PROTOTYPES /////////////////////////////////////////////////////

// DirectDraw functions
int DD_Init(int width, int height, int bpp);
int DD_Shutdown(void);
LPDIRECTDRAWCLIPPER DD_Attach_Clipper(LPDIRECTDRAWSURFACE7 lpdds,
                                      int num_rects, LPRECT clip_list);
int DD_Flip(void);
int DD_Fill_Surface(LPDIRECTDRAWSURFACE7 lpdds,int color);

// general utility functions
DWORD Start_Clock(void);
DWORD Get_Clock(void);
DWORD Wait_Clock(DWORD count);

// graphics functions
int Draw_Rectangle(int x1, int y1, int x2, int y2,
                   int color,LPDIRECTDRAWSURFACE7 lpdds=lpddsback);

// gdi functions
int Draw_Text_GDI(char *text, int x,int y,COLORREF color,
                  LPDIRECTDRAWSURFACE7 lpdds=lpddsback);
int Draw_Text_GDI(char *text, int x,int y,int color,
                  LPDIRECTDRAWSURFACE7 lpdds=lpddsback);

#endif
```

Now, don't waste too much time straining your brain on the code and what all those
weird global variables are. Rather, just look at the functions themselves. As you can
see, there are functions to do everything that we needed for our little graphics interface. Based on that and a minimum Win32 application (the less Windows programming I have to do, the better), I have created the game FREAKOUT.CPP, which is shown
in Listing 1.3. Take a good look at it, especially the main game loop and the calls to
the game processing functions.

LISTING 1.3   The Source File `FREAKOUT.CPP`

```
// INCLUDES ///////////////////////////////////////////////

#define WIN32_LEAN_AND_MEAN // include all macros
#define INITGUID            // include all GUIDs

#include <windows.h>        // include important windows stuff
#include <windowsx.h>
#include <mmsystem.h>

#include <iostream.h>       // include important C/C++ stuff
#include <conio.h>
#include <stdlib.h>
#include <malloc.h>
#include <memory.h>
#include <string.h>
#include <stdarg.h>
#include <stdio.h>
#include <math.h>
#include <io.h>
#include <fcntl.h>

#include <ddraw.h>          // directX includes
#include "blackbox.h"       // game library includes

// DEFINES ///////////////////////////////////////////////

// defines for windows
#define WINDOW_CLASS_NAME "WIN3DCLASS"  // class name

#define WINDOW_WIDTH          640       // size of window
#define WINDOW_HEIGHT         480

// states for game loop
#define GAME_STATE_INIT         0
#define GAME_STATE_START_LEVEL  1
#define GAME_STATE_RUN          2
#define GAME_STATE_SHUTDOWN     3
#define GAME_STATE_EXIT         4

// block defines
#define NUM_BLOCK_ROWS          6
#define NUM_BLOCK_COLUMNS       8

#define BLOCK_WIDTH            64
#define BLOCK_HEIGHT          16
#define BLOCK_ORIGIN_X          8
#define BLOCK_ORIGIN_Y          8
#define BLOCK_X_GAP           80
#define BLOCK_Y_GAP           32
```

LISTING 1.3 Continued

```
// paddle defines
#define PADDLE_START_X          (SCREEN_WIDTH/2 - 16)
#define PADDLE_START_Y          (SCREEN_HEIGHT - 32);
#define PADDLE_WIDTH            32
#define PADDLE_HEIGHT           8
#define PADDLE_COLOR            191

// ball defines
#define BALL_START_Y            (SCREEN_HEIGHT/2)
#define BALL_SIZE                4

// PROTOTYPES //////////////////////////////////////////////

// game console
int Game_Init(void *parms=NULL);
int Game_Shutdown(void *parms=NULL);
int Game_Main(void *parms=NULL);

// GLOBALS //////////////////////////////////////////////////

HWND main_window_handle  = NULL; // save the window handle
HINSTANCE main_instance  = NULL; // save the instance
int game_state           = GAME_STATE_INIT; // starting state

int paddle_x = 0, paddle_y = 0; // tracks position of paddle
int ball_x   = 0, ball_y   = 0; // tracks position of ball
int ball_dx  = 0, ball_dy  = 0; // velocity of ball
int score    = 0;               // the score
int level    = 1;               // the current level
int blocks_hit = 0;             // tracks number of blocks hit

// this contains the game grid data

UCHAR blocks[NUM_BLOCK_ROWS][NUM_BLOCK_COLUMNS];

// FUNCTIONS ////////////////////////////////////////////////

LRESULT CALLBACK WindowProc(HWND hwnd,
                            UINT msg,
                            WPARAM wparam,
                            LPARAM lparam)
{
// this is the main message handler of the system
PAINTSTRUCT    ps;          // used in WM_PAINT
HDC            hdc;         // handle to a device context

// what is the message
switch(msg)
    {
    case WM_CREATE:
        {
```

LISTING 1.3 Continued

```c
        // do initialization stuff here
        return(0);
        } break;

    case WM_PAINT:
        {
        // start painting
        hdc = BeginPaint(hwnd,&ps);

        // the window is now validated

        // end painting
        EndPaint(hwnd,&ps);
        return(0);
        } break;

    case WM_DESTROY:
        {
        // kill the application
        PostQuitMessage(0);
        return(0);
        } break;

    default:break;

    } // end switch

// process any messages that we didn't take care of
return (DefWindowProc(hwnd, msg, wparam, lparam));

} // end WinProc

// WINMAIN ////////////////////////////////////////////////////

int WINAPI WinMain(HINSTANCE hinstance,
            HINSTANCE hprevinstance,
            LPSTR lpcmdline,
            int ncmdshow)
{
// this is the winmain function

WNDCLASS winclass;  // this will hold the class we create
HWND     hwnd;          // generic window handle
MSG      msg;          // generic message
HDC      hdc;         // generic dc
PAINTSTRUCT ps;      // generic paintstruct
// first fill in the window class structure
winclass.style     = CS_DBLCLKS | CS_OWNDC |
                CS_HREDRAW | CS_VREDRAW;
winclass.lpfnWndProc = WindowProc;
winclass.cbClsExtra      = 0;
```

LISTING 1.3   Continued

```c
winclass.cbWndExtra        = 0;
winclass.hInstance         = hinstance;
winclass.hIcon             = LoadIcon(NULL, IDI_APPLICATION);
winclass.hCursor           = LoadCursor(NULL, IDC_ARROW);
winclass.hbrBackground     = (HBRUSH)GetStockObject(BLACK_BRUSH);
winclass.lpszMenuName      = NULL;
winclass.lpszClassName     = WINDOW_CLASS_NAME;

// register the window class
if (!RegisterClass(&winclass))
    return(0);

// create the window, note the use of WS_POPUP
if (!(hwnd = CreateWindow(WINDOW_CLASS_NAME,    // class
        "WIN3D Game Console",    // title
        WS_POPUP | WS_VISIBLE,
        0,0,                     // initial x,y
        GetSystemMetrics(SM_CXSCREEN),  // initial width
        GetSystemMetrics(SM_CYSCREEN),  // initial height
        NULL,          // handle to parent
        NULL,          // handle to menu
        hinstance,     // instance
        NULL)))        // creation parms
return(0);

// hide mouse
ShowCursor(FALSE);

// save the window handle and instance in a global
main_window_handle = hwnd;
main_instance      = hinstance;

// perform all game console specific initialization
Game_Init();

// enter main event loop
while(1)
    {
    if (PeekMessage(&msg,NULL,0,0,PM_REMOVE))
    {
    // test if this is a quit
        if (msg.message == WM_QUIT)
            break;

    // translate any accelerator keys
    TranslateMessage(&msg);

    // send the message to the window proc
    DispatchMessage(&msg);
    } // end if
```

Windows Programming Foundations

LISTING 1.3   Continued

```
                // main game processing goes here
                Game_Main();

        } // end while

// shutdown game and release all resources
Game_Shutdown();

// show mouse
ShowCursor(TRUE);

// return to Windows like this
return(msg.wParam);

} // end WinMain

// T3DX GAME PROGRAMMING CONSOLE FUNCTIONS ////////////////////

int Game_Init(void *parms)
{
// this function is where you do all the initialization
// for your game

// return success
return(1);

} // end Game_Init

//////////////////////////////////////////////////////////////

int Game_Shutdown(void *parms)
{
// this function is where you shutdown your game and
// release all resources that you allocated

// return success
return(1);

} // end Game_Shutdown

//////////////////////////////////////////////////////////////

void Init_Blocks(void)
{
// initialize the block field
for (int row=0; row < NUM_BLOCK_ROWS; row++)
    for (int col=0; col < NUM_BLOCK_COLUMNS; col++)
        blocks[row][col] = row*16+col*3+16;

} // end Init_Blocks
```

LISTING 1.3   Continued

```
///////////////////////////////////////////////////////////

void Draw_Blocks(void)
{
// this function draws all the blocks in row major form
int x1 = BLOCK_ORIGIN_X, // used to track current position
    y1 = BLOCK_ORIGIN_Y;

// draw all the blocks
for (int row=0; row < NUM_BLOCK_ROWS; row++)
    {
    // reset column position
    x1 = BLOCK_ORIGIN_X;

    // draw this row of blocks
    for (int col=0; col < NUM_BLOCK_COLUMNS; col++)
        {
        // draw next block (if there is one)
        if (blocks[row][col]!=0)
            {
            // draw block
            Draw_Rectangle(x1-4,y1+4,
                x1+BLOCK_WIDTH-4,y1+BLOCK_HEIGHT+4,0);

            Draw_Rectangle(x1,y1,x1+BLOCK_WIDTH,
                y1+BLOCK_HEIGHT,blocks[row][col]);
            } // end if

        // advance column position
        x1+=BLOCK_X_GAP;
        } // end for col

    // advance to next row position
    y1+=BLOCK_Y_GAP;

    } // end for row

} // end Draw_Blocks

///////////////////////////////////////////////////////////

void Process_Ball(void)
{
// this function tests if the ball has hit a block or the paddle
// if so, the ball is bounced and the block is removed from
// the playfield note: very cheesy collision algorithm :)

// first test for ball block collisions

// the algorithm basically tests the ball against each
// block's bounding box this is inefficient, but easy to
```

LISTING 1.3   Continued

```
// implement, later we'll see a better way

int x1 = BLOCK_ORIGIN_X, // current rendering position
    y1 = BLOCK_ORIGIN_Y;

int ball_cx = ball_x+(BALL_SIZE/2),  // computer center of ball
    ball_cy = ball_y+(BALL_SIZE/2);

// test of the ball has hit the paddle
if (ball_y > (SCREEN_HEIGHT/2) && ball_dy > 0)
   {
   // extract leading edge of ball
   int x = ball_x+(BALL_SIZE/2);
   int y = ball_y+(BALL_SIZE/2);

   // test for collision with paddle
   if ((x >= paddle_x && x <= paddle_x+PADDLE_WIDTH) &&
       (y >= paddle_y && y <= paddle_y+PADDLE_HEIGHT))
      {
      // reflect ball
      ball_dy=-ball_dy;

      // push ball out of paddle since it made contact
      ball_y+=ball_dy;

      // add a little english to ball based on motion of paddle
      if (KEY_DOWN(VK_RIGHT))
         ball_dx-=(rand()%3);
      else
      if (KEY_DOWN(VK_LEFT))
         ball_dx+=(rand()%3);
      else
         ball_dx+=(-1+rand()%3);

      // test if there are no blocks, if so send a message
      // to game loop to start another level
      if (blocks_hit >= (NUM_BLOCK_ROWS*NUM_BLOCK_COLUMNS))
         {
         game_state = GAME_STATE_START_LEVEL;
         level++;
         } // end if

      // make a little noise
      MessageBeep(MB_OK);

      // return
      return;

      } // end if

   } // end if
```

LISTING 1.3   Continued

```
// now scan thru all the blocks and see if ball hit blocks
for (int row=0; row < NUM_BLOCK_ROWS; row++)
    {
    // reset column position
    x1 = BLOCK_ORIGIN_X;

    // scan this row of blocks
    for (int col=0; col < NUM_BLOCK_COLUMNS; col++)
        {
        // if there is a block here then test it against ball
        if (blocks[row][col]!=0)
            {
            // test ball against bounding box of block
            if ((ball_cx > x1) && (ball_cx < x1+BLOCK_WIDTH) &&
                (ball_cy > y1) && (ball_cy < y1+BLOCK_HEIGHT))
                {
                // remove the block
                blocks[row][col] = 0;

                // increment global block counter, so we know
                // when to start another level up
                blocks_hit++;

                // bounce the ball
                ball_dy=-ball_dy;

                // add a little english
                ball_dx+=(-1+rand()%3);

                // make a little noise
                MessageBeep(MB_OK);

                // add some points
                score+=5*(level+(abs(ball_dx)));

                // that's it -- no more block
                return;

                } // end if

            } // end if

        // advance column position
        x1+=BLOCK_X_GAP;
        } // end for col

    // advance to next row position
    y1+=BLOCK_Y_GAP;

    } // end for row
```

LISTING 1.3 Continued

```
} // end Process_Ball

/////////////////////////////////////////////////////////////////

int Game_Main(void *parms)
{
// this is the workhorse of your game it will be called
// continuously in real-time this is like main() in C
// all the calls for your game go here!

char buffer[80]; // used to print text

// what state is the game in?
if (game_state == GAME_STATE_INIT)
    {
    // initialize everything here graphics
    DD_Init(SCREEN_WIDTH, SCREEN_HEIGHT, SCREEN_BPP);

    // seed the random number generator
    // so game is different each play
    srand(Start_Clock());

    // set the paddle position here to the middle bottom
    paddle_x = PADDLE_START_X;
    paddle_y = PADDLE_START_Y;

    // set ball position and velocity
    ball_x = 8+rand()%(SCREEN_WIDTH-16);
    ball_y = BALL_START_Y;
    ball_dx = -4 + rand()%(8+1);
    ball_dy = 6 + rand()%2;

    // transition to start level state
    game_state = GAME_STATE_START_LEVEL;

    } // end if
/////////////////////////////////////////////////////////////////
else
if (game_state == GAME_STATE_START_LEVEL)
    {
    // get a new level ready to run

    // initialize the blocks
    Init_Blocks();

    // reset block counter
    blocks_hit = 0;

    // transition to run state
    game_state = GAME_STATE_RUN;
```

LISTING 1.3   Continued

```
    } // end if
/////////////////////////////////////////////////////////////
else
if (game_state == GAME_STATE_RUN)
    {
    // start the timing clock
    Start_Clock();

    // clear drawing surface for the next frame of animation
    Draw_Rectangle(0,0,SCREEN_WIDTH-1, SCREEN_HEIGHT-1,200);

    // move the paddle
    if (KEY_DOWN(VK_RIGHT))
        {
        // move paddle to right
        paddle_x+=8;

        // make sure paddle doesn't go off screen
        if (paddle_x > (SCREEN_WIDTH-PADDLE_WIDTH))
            paddle_x = SCREEN_WIDTH-PADDLE_WIDTH;

        } // end if
    else
    if (KEY_DOWN(VK_LEFT))
        {
        // move paddle to right
        paddle_x-=8;

        // make sure paddle doesn't go off screen
        if (paddle_x < 0)
            paddle_x = 0;

        } // end if

    // draw blocks
    Draw_Blocks();

    // move the ball
    ball_x+=ball_dx;
    ball_y+=ball_dy;

    // keep ball on screen, if the ball hits the edge of
    // screen then bounce it by reflecting its velocity
    if (ball_x > (SCREEN_WIDTH - BALL_SIZE) || ball_x < 0)
        {
        // reflect x-axis velocity
        ball_dx=-ball_dx;

        // update position
        ball_x+=ball_dx;
        } // end if
```

LISTING 1.3   Continued

```
// now y-axis
if (ball_y < 0)
    {
    // reflect y-axis velocity
    ball_dy=-ball_dy;

    // update position
    ball_y+=ball_dy;
    } // end if
else
// penalize player for missing the ball
if (ball_y > (SCREEN_HEIGHT - BALL_SIZE))
    {
    // reflect y-axis velocity
    ball_dy=-ball_dy;

    // update position
    ball_y+=ball_dy;

    // minus the score
    score-=100;

    } // end if

// next watch out for ball velocity getting out of hand
if (ball_dx > 8) ball_dx = 8;
else
if (ball_dx < -8) ball_dx = -8;

// test if ball hit any blocks or the paddle
Process_Ball();

// draw the paddle and shadow
Draw_Rectangle(paddle_x-8, paddle_y+8,
               paddle_x+PADDLE_WIDTH-8,
               paddle_y+PADDLE_HEIGHT+8,0);

Draw_Rectangle(paddle_x, paddle_y,
               paddle_x+PADDLE_WIDTH,
               paddle_y+PADDLE_HEIGHT,PADDLE_COLOR);

// draw the ball
Draw_Rectangle(ball_x-4, ball_y+4, ball_x+BALL_SIZE-4,
               ball_y+BALL_SIZE+4, 0);
Draw_Rectangle(ball_x, ball_y, ball_x+BALL_SIZE,
               ball_y+BALL_SIZE, 255);

// draw the info
sprintf(buffer,"F R E A K O U T          Score %d   //
    Level %d",score,level);
Draw_Text_GDI(buffer, 8,SCREEN_HEIGHT-16, 127);
```

Listing 1.3   Continued

```
    // flip the surfaces
    DD_Flip();

    // sync to 33ish fps
    Wait_Clock(30);

    // check if user is trying to exit
    if (KEY_DOWN(VK_ESCAPE))
       {
       // send message to windows to exit
       PostMessage(main_window_handle, WM_DESTROY,0,0);

       // set exit state
       game_state = GAME_STATE_SHUTDOWN;

       } // end if

    } // end if
/////////////////////////////////////////////////////////////
else
if (game_state == GAME_STATE_SHUTDOWN)
   {
   // in this state shut everything down and release resources
   DD_Shutdown();

   // switch to exit state
   game_state = GAME_STATE_EXIT;

   } // end if

// return success
return(1);

} // end Game_Main
```

Cool, huh? That's the entire Win32/DirectX game. Well, almost. There are a few hundred lines of code in the BLACKBOX.CPP source file, but we'll just pretend that it's like DirectX and someone else wrote it (me!). Anyway, let's take a quick look at the contents of Listing 1.3.

Basically, Windows needs to have what's called an *event loop*. This is standard for all Windows programs since Windows is, for the most part, event-driven. However, games aren't event-driven; they run at all times, whether the user does something or not. So we need to at least support a minimum event loop to make Windows happy. The code that implements this is in WinMain()—jeez, that's a surprise, huh?

WinMain() is the main entry point for all Windows programs, just like main() is the entry point for all DOS/Unix programs (please wash your mouth out if you said "Unix" out loud). In any case, the WinMain() for FreakOut creates a window and then enters right into the event loop. If Windows needs to do something, it does so. When all the basic event handling is over, Game_Main() is called. This is where the real action occurs for our game.

If you wanted to, you could loop in Game_Main() forever, never releasing it back to the main event loop in WinMain(). But this would be bad because Windows would never receive any messages and you would starve the system. Alas, what we need to do is perform one frame of animation and logic and then return back to WinMain(). This way, Windows will continue to function and process messages. If this all sounds a little hocus-pocus, don't worry—it gets worse in the next chapter <BG>.

Once in Game_Main(), the logic for FreakOut is executed. The game image is rendered into an offscreen workspace and then finally shown on the display at the end of the loop via the DD_FLIP() call. So what I want you to do is take a look at all the game states and try to follow each section of the game loop and what it does. To play the game, simply click on FREAKOUT.EXE. The program will launch immediately. The controls are

Right arrow—Move paddle right.

Left arrow—Move paddle left.

Esc—Exit back to Windows.

Also, there's a 100-point penalty if you miss the ball, so watch it!

When you feel comfortable with the game code and gameplay, try modifying the game and making changes to it. You could add different background colors (0–255 are valid colors), more balls, a paddle that changes size, and more sound effects (which I'm making right now with the Win32 API MessageBeep() function).

Summary

Well, I think that's about the quickest crash course in game programming I have ever given! We covered a lot of ground, but think of it as the "back of the box" version of the book. I just wanted to give you a feel for all the things that we are going to talk about and learn in this book. In addition, it's always good to take a look at a complete game because it generates a lot of questions for you to think about.

Now, before moving on to Chapter 2, which covers Windows programming, make sure that you feel comfortable with compiling the FreakOut game. If you aren't, open up the compiler book and RTFM! I'll be waiting.

CHAPTER 2

The Windows Programming Model

"Lilu Dallas Multipass!"
—Lilu, The 5th Element

Windows programming is like going to the dentist: You know it's good for you, but no one likes doing it. Am I right? In this chapter, I'm going to show you the basics of Windows programming using my "Zen" methodology—or, in other words, the easy way. I can't promise that you'll like going to the dentist after reading this chapter, but I can promise you that you'll like Windows programming a lot more than you ever did! Here's what you'll learn:

- The history of Windows
- Basic Windows architecture
- Windows' classes
- Creating Windows
- Windows event handlers
- Event-driven programming and event loops
- Opening multiple windows

The Genesis of Windows

To put you in the mood for the onslaught of horror that I'm about to unleash upon your mind (especially you DOS diehards), let's take a quick look at how Windows has shaped up over the past years and its relationship to the game development world—shall we?

Early Windows Versions

It all began with the release of Windows 1.0. This was Microsoft's first attempt at a commercial windowed operating system, and it was pretty much a failure. Windows 1.0 was based completely on DOS (big mistake), wasn't multitasking, ran really slow, and looked really bad. Its looks were probably the most important reason for its failure <BG>. Sarcasm aside, the problem was that Windows 1.0 needed much more hardware, graphics, and sound capabilities than the 80286 (or worst yet, 8086) machines of the time had to offer.

Nevertheless, Microsoft forged ahead, and shortly thereafter it released Windows 2.0. I actually remember working at Software Publishing Corporation when we got the beta of Windows 2.0. There was a boardroom filled with executives and the president of the company (as usual, he had a cocktail in his hand). We ran the Windows 2.0 beta demo and loaded multiple applications, and it seemed to work. However, at this time IBM Presentation Manager (PM) was out. PM simply looked a lot better, and it was based on OS/2, a vastly more advanced OS than Windows 2.0 (which was still a window manager simply overlaid on top of DOS). The verdict of the board that day: "Not bad, but not a viable OS for development. Let's stick to DOS, and can I have another cocktail?"

Windows 3.x

In 1990, the planets must have been in alignment, because Windows 3.0 was released and it was pretty damn good! It wasn't up to par with Mac OS yet, but who cared? (Real programmers hate Macs.) Finally, software developers could create sexy applications on the PC and start migrating away from DOS for business applications. This was the turning point for the PC and the thing that eventually put the Mac out of the running for business applications and later for desktop publishing. (That, along with Apple releasing new hardware every five minutes.)

Although Windows 3.0 worked well, it had a lot of problems, bugs, and so forth. Heck, it was a quantum leap ahead of Windows 2.0 in technology, so problems were to be expected. To fix these problems, Microsoft came out with Windows 3.1. The PR and marketing departments originally wanted to call it Windows 4.0, but Microsoft decided to simply call Windows 3.1 because it just didn't have enough features to qualify as a major revision upgrade. Nor did it live up to all the hype the marketing department had built up.

Windows 3.1 was very solid. It had multimedia extensions like sound and video support, and it was a good all-around OS that got work done for the user in a uniform manner. In addition, there was another version called Windows 3.11 (Windows for Workgroups) with network support. The only problem was that Windows 3.1 was still a DOS application, for the most part, and ran under a DOS Extender.

Windows 95

On the other side of the planet, the game programming community was still chanting "DOS TILL HELL FREEZES OVER!", and I was out in front burning a Windows 3.1 box myself! However, in 1995 hell did start to freeze over... Windows 95 was released, and it was a true 32-bit, multitasking, multithreaded operating system. Granted, it had some 16-bit code left in it, but for the most part, Windows 95 was the ultimate development and release platform for the PC.

(Of course, Windows NT 3.0 was also available. But NT just wasn't feasible for the average user, so I'm not even acknowledging it yet in my story.)

When Windows 95 was released, it was the first time ever that I actually liked programming for Windows. I always hated Windows 1.0, 2.0, 3.0, and 3.1 for programming, although I hated it less and less with each release. But when Windows 95 came out, there was one thing that changed my mind, as well as a lot of other people's—it looked cool! That's all I needed.

TIP	The most important thing in the game programming business is how the box looks and how the screen shots you send to magazines look. Sending the reviewers free stuff works too.

So almost overnight, Windows 95 changed the computing business. Sure, many companies today are *still* using Windows 3.1 (can you believe that?), but Windows 95 made the Intel-based PC the computer of choice for *all* applications—except games. Yes, DOS still had the hearts of game programmers, even though they knew it was only a matter of time.

In 1996, Microsoft released the Game SDK, which was basically the first version of DirectX. This technology worked on Windows 95 only, but it was simply too slow to compete with DOS games such as DOOM and Duke Nukem. Developers continued to develop for DOS32, but they knew it was only a matter of time before the DirectX technology would be fast enough to make games on the PC.

By version 3.0, DirectX was as fast as DOS32 on the same machines. By version 5.0, DirectX was very clean and the promises of the technology were coming true. Now, Microsoft is working on version 9.0, and version 8.1 is available. But, we'll talk more about that later when we cover DirectX in Chapter 5, "DirectX Fundamentals and the Dreaded COM." For now, just realize that Win32/DirectX is the *only* way to go on the PC for games. Back to the history lesson.

Windows 98

In mid-1998, Windows 98 was released. It's more of an evolutionary step than a revolutionary one, like Windows 95, but it's important nonetheless. Windows 98 is like a hot rod—it's sleek, fast, and kicks ass! It's totally 32-bit, has support for everything you can think of, and is open-ended for expansion. And it has DirectX, multimedia, 3D graphics, networking, and the Internet all integrated into it very nicely.

Windows 98 is also very robust compared to Windows 95. Sure, Windows 98 still crashes and tweaks out, but believe me, there is a lot less of that. Furthermore, plug-and-play actually works, and works well—it's about time!

Windows ME

In late 1999, early 2000 Windows ME (or Millennium) was released. ME is hard to explain, basically a 98 box, but with tighter and more integrated multimedia support and networking. ME really is targeted more at the consumer rather than a technical or business market. As far as functionality though, it's basically Windows 98. However, ME is tighter and because of this has much more trouble running certain applications, some hardware doesn't like it and in general is only good for very NEW machines, whereas you can run 98 on computers that were made in 1995 and it works great. This is definitely not the case with ME. But, on a new machine, this is a fairly stable and robust gaming OS.

Windows XP

At the time of this revision (late 2001), the new OS Windows XP was just released and I have to tell you I really like it! XP is like is the sexiest OS I have seen, it has the feel of 98 or ME, with the stability and robustness of Windows 2000 or NT. XP is truly the next step in operating systems for the consumer. But, there is a dark side to all this. XP is a true 32-bit, Win32-compliant operating system, and for years Microsoft has been telling hardware manufacturers, and software developers to not cheat and do things the wrong way in relation to their code. Well, finally, it's time to pay the fiddler, and XP simply will NOT run a lot of software that breaks rules. This is a really good thing though, since in the end, all the software companies will recompile their programs taking all the hacks and hardware specific coding out of their programs. This is one of the reasons that 95, and 98 are so unstable, it's all that bad code! Therefore, XP is like starting over again, and saying, here is the coolest, slickest, OS you have ever seen, but if you want to play, you must play fair, and by the rules.

However, to not be a complete disaster in reference to compatibility, XP has two things that help users get software running. First, the OS is continually updated via Microsoft update, and the companies are working around the clock to fix all their yucky software. And secondly, XP has what are called "compatibility" modes that you can run, "non-compliant" software with; in essence, you can turn on the "bugs" and the software will work. ☺ Aside from all that, I suggest migrating to XP for development without hesitation, I love it.

Windows NT/2000

Now we can talk about Windows NT. At the time of this writing, Windows NT is currently on release release 5 4.0, but has been renamed for intents and purposes to Windows 2000 which is really release 5.0 of NT. And as far as I can tell, ultimately it's going to replace Windows 9X as the OS of choice for everyone as Windows XP converges with it. 2000 is simply a lot tighter than Windows 9X; furthermore, most game programmers develop on NT and then release on Windows 9X/ME/XP. The cool thing about 2000 is that it has full plug-and-play support, along with Win32/DirectX, so applications written for Windows 9X with DirectX will work on 2000. This is great news, since now game developers who write PC games have the largest market potential in history.

So what's the bottom line? If you write a Win32 application with DirectX (or not), it will work on Windows 95, 98, ME, XP, and 2000. This is a good thing. Hence, everything you learn in this book is applicable to multiple operating systems. And don't forget Windows CE 3.0/Pocket PC 2002—DirectX and a subset of Win32 work on that system, too!

Basic Windows Architecture: Win9X/NT

Windows, unlike DOS, is a multitasking operating system designed to allow a number of applications and/or smaller processes to run at the same time, using the hardware to its fullest. This means that Windows is a shared environment—one application can't take over the entire system. Although Windows 95, 98, ME, XP, and 2000/NT are similar, there are a number of technical differences. However, as far as we are concerned here, we can generalize without too much drama. I will refer to the Windows machine as a Win 9X/NT or Windows box most of the time. So let's get started!

Multitasking and Multithreading

As I said, Windows allows a number of different applications to be executed simultaneously in a *round-robin* fashion, where each application gets a small time slice to run in and then the next application takes its turn. As you can see in Figure 2.1, the CPU is shared among a number of different applications in a circular manner. Figuring out the exact methodology that selects the next application, and the amount of time allotted to each application, is the job of the *scheduler*.

Windows Programming Foundations

FIGURE 2.1

Multiprocessing in action with a single processor.

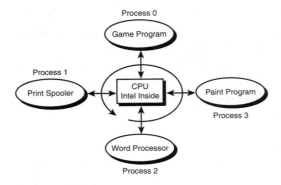

Execution Sequence: 0, 1, 2, 3, 0, 1, 2, 3, 0, 1, 2, 3, ...

The scheduler may be very simple, running each application for a fixed number of milliseconds, or it may be very complex, giving applications various levels of priority and preempting applications or events with lower priority. In the case of Win 9X/NT, the scheduler is priority-based with preemption. This means that some applications can have more processor time than others, but if an application needs the CPU, the current task can be blocked or preempted while another task runs.

However, you don't need to worry much about this unless you're writing OS or real-time code, where exact details matter. In most cases, Windows will run and schedule your application, and you will have nothing to do with it.

Taking a closer look at Windows, we see that not only is it multitasking, but it's *multi-threaded*. This means that programs are really composed of a number of simpler *threads of execution*. These threads are scheduled just like heavier-weight processes, such as programs. In fact, right now there are probably 30 to 50 threads running on your machine, performing various tasks. So in reality, you may have a single program running that consists of one or more threads of execution.

Take a look at Figure 2.2 to see a more realistic multithreaded view of Windows. As you can see, each program actually consists of a number of worker threads in addition to the main thread.

FIGURE 2.2

A more realistic multithreaded view of Windows.

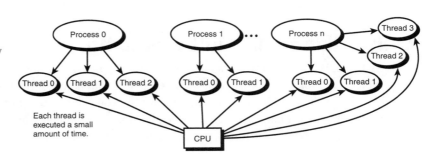

Each thread is executed a small amount of time.

Getting Info on the Threads

For some fun, let's see how many threads are running on your machine right now. On your Windows machine, press Ctrl+Alt+Delete to pop up the Active Program Task Manager, which displays all of the running tasks (or processes). This isn't exactly what we want, but it's close. What we really want is a tool or applet that displays the actual threads that are executing. A number of shareware and commercial utilities do this, but Windows comes with a couple of them built in.

Within the directory that Windows was installed in (WINDOWS\, in most cases), you will find an executable named SYSMON.EXE (not included with default Windows installation—user needs to add it through Control Panel / Add/Remove Programs / System Tools) (Windows 95/98) or PERFMON.EXE (Windows NT). Figure 2.3 depicts SYSMON.EXE running on my Windows 98 machine. As you can see, there is a wealth of information in addition to the number of threads running, such as memory use and processor load. In fact, I like to keep SYSMON.EXE running as I develop so I can see what's going on and how the system is loaded.

FIGURE 2.3
Running SYSM.

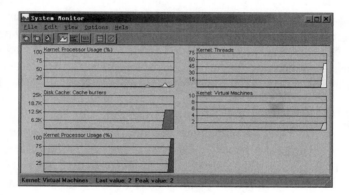

You might be wondering if you have any control over the creation of threads. The answer is yes!!! In fact, this is one of the most exciting things about Windows game programming—we can create as many threads as we want to perform other tasks in addition to our main game process.

> **NOTE**
>
> In Windows 98/NT, there is actually a new type of execution object called a *fiber*, which is even simpler than a thread. (Get it? Threads are made of fibers.)

This is much different than how a DOS game is written. DOS is a single-threaded OS, meaning that once your program runs, it's the only thing running (except for an interrupt handler from time to time). Therefore, if you want any kind of multitasking or multithreading, you must simulate it yourself (check out *Sams Teach Yourself Game Programming in 21 Days* for a complete DOS-based multitasking kernel). And this is exactly what game programmers have been doing over the years. Granted, simulating multitasking and multithreading is nowhere near as robust as having a complete OS that supports them, but for a single game, it works well enough.

Before we move into real Windows programming and the code that makes things happen, there is one detail that I want to mention. You might be thinking that Windows is a magical OS because it allows multiple tasks or programs to run at once. Remember, this is *not* true. If there is a single processor, only one execution stream, thread, program, or whatever you want to call it can run at a time. Windows just switches between them so quickly that it seems as if more than one program is running. On the other hand, if you have more than one processor, multiple programs can run. For example, I have a dual Pentium II computer, with two 400MHz Pentium II processors running Windows 2000. With this configuration, two instruction streams *can* be executed at the same time.

In the near future, I would expect that new microprocessor architectures for personal computers will allow multiple threads or fibers to be executed as part of the processors' design. For example, the Pentium has two execution units—the U pipe and V pipe. Hence, it can execute two instructions at once. However, these two instructions are always from the same thread. Similarly, the Pentium II, III, IV can execute multiple instructions at once, but again only from the same thread.

The Event Model

Windows is a multitasking/multithreaded OS, but it's also an *event-driven* OS. Unlike DOS programs, most Windows programs sit and wait for the user to do something, which fires an event, and then Windows responds to the event and takes action. Take a look at Figure 2.4 to see this graphically. It depicts a number of application windows, each sending their events or messages to Windows to be processed. Windows does some of the processing, but most of the messages or events are passed through to your application program for processing.

The good news is that you don't need to concern yourself with the other applications that are running. Windows will handle them for you. All you have to worry about is your own application and the processing of messages for your window(s). This wasn't the entire truth in Windows 3.0/3.1. Those versions of Windows weren't true multitasking operating systems, and each application had to yield to the next. This meant that applications running under these versions had a rather rough or sluggish feel. If other applications were hogging the system, there wasn't anything that the compliant applications could do. However, this isn't the case with Windows 9X/NT. The OS will pull the rug out from under your application whenever it feels like it—of course, it pulls it so quickly that you'll never notice!

FIGURE 2.4
Windows event
handling.

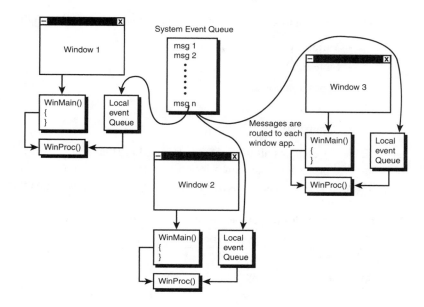

At this point, you know all you need to know about OS concepts. Luckily, Windows is such a nice OS to write games for these days that you won't have to worry about scheduling—all you need to worry about is the game code and pushing the machine to its limits.

Later in this chapter, we'll get into some actual programming so you can see just how easy Windows programming is. But (there's always a but) before we do that, we need to cover some conventions that Microsoft programmers like to use. This way, you won't be bewildered by all the weird function and variable naming.

Programming the Microsoft Way: Hungarian Notation

If you're running a company like Microsoft, with thousands of programmers working on various projects, at some point you have to come up with a standard way of writing code. Otherwise, chaos ensues. Therefore, a man named Charles Simonyi was put in charge of creating a specification for writing Microsoft code. This spec has been used ever since as a basic guideline for writing code. All Microsoft APIs, interfaces, technical articles, and so on use these conventions.

The specification is generally referred to as *Hungarian notation,* probably because creating it and working those late hours made him hungry. Or maybe it was because he was from Hungary. We'll never know. The point is, you have to learn it so you can read Microsoft code.

Windows Programming Foundations

Hungarian notation consists of a number of conventions relating to naming:

- Variables
- Functions
- Types and constants
- Classes
- Parameters

Table 2.1 contains all the prefix codes used in Hungarian notation. These codes are used to prefix variable names in most cases, along with other conventions depending on what is being named. Refer to the table for the remaining explanations.

TABLE 2.1   The Hungarian Notation Prefix Codes Specification

Prefix	Data Type (Base Type)
c	char
by	BYTE (unsigned char)
n	short or int (refers to a number)
i	int
x, y	short (used as x-coordinate or y-coordinate, generally)
cx, cy	short (used to denote x or y lengths; c stands for *count*)
b	BOOL (int)
w	UINT (unsigned int) or WORD (unsigned WORD)
l	LONG (long)
dw	DWORD (unsigned long)
fn	Function pointer
s	String
sz, str	String terminated by 0 byte
lp	32-bit long pointer
h	Handle (used to refer to Windows objects)
msg	Message

Variable Naming

With Hungarian notation, variables are prefixed by the codes in Table 2.1. In addition, if a variable name is made up of one or more subnames, each subname is capitalized. Here are some examples:

```
char *szFileName; // a null terminated string

int *lpiData;     // a 32-bit pointer to an int
```

```
BOOL bSemaphore;   // a boolean value

WORD dwMaxCount;   // a 32-bit unsigned WORD
```

Although I know of no specification for local variables of a function, there is a loose one for globals:

```
int g_iXPos;       // a global x-position

int g_iTimer;      // a global timer

char *g_szString;  // a global NULL terminated string
```

Basically, you begin the variable with g_, or sometimes just plain g. "When I grew up, I was a big G, lots of money…" Sorry, I had a rap attack <BG>.

Function Naming

Functions are named in the same way variables are, but without the prefixes. In other words, just capitalize all the first letters of subnames. Here are some examples:

```
int PlotPixel(int ix, int iy, int ic);

void *MemScan(char *szString);
```

Also, underscores are illegal. For example, the following wouldn't be a valid Hungarian-compliant function name:

```
int Get_Pixel(int ix, int iy);
```

Type and Constant Naming

All types and constants are in uppercase, but you're allowed to use underscores in the names. For example:

```
const LONG NUM_SECTORS = 100; // a C++ style constant

#define MAX_CELLS 64           // a C style constant

#define POWERUNIT 100          // a C style constant

typedef unsigned char UCHAR;   // a user defined type
```

Nothing too unusual here—fairly standard definitions. Although most Microsoft programmers don't use underscores, I prefer to use them because it makes the names more readable.

TIP

In C++, the const keyword has more than one meaning, but in the preceding code lines, it's used to create a constant variable. This is similar to #define, but it has the added property of retaining the type information. const is more like a variable than a simple preprocessed text replacement like #define. It allows compiler type-checking and casting to occur.

Class Naming

The naming conventions used for classes might bother you a bit. However, I have seen many people who use this convention and just made it up on their own. Anyway, all C++ classes must be prefixed by a capital C, and the first letter of each subname of the class name must be capitalized. Here is an example:

```
class CVector
{
public:
CVector() {ix=iy=iz=imagnitude = 0;}
CVector(int x, int y, int z) {ix=x; iy=y; iz=z;}
.
.
.

private:
int ix,iy,iz;   // the position of the vector
int imagnitude;  // the magnitude of the vector

};
```

Parameter Naming

Parameters to functions follow the same naming conventions that normal variables do. However, this is not a necessity. For example, you might see a function definition that looks like this:

```
UCHAR GetPixel(int x, int y);
```

In this case, the more Hungarian prototype would be

```
UCHAR GetPixel(int ix, int iy);
```

But I have seen it both ways.

And finally, you might not even see the variable names, but just the types, as in this example:

```
UCHAR GetPixel(int, int);
```

Of course, this would only be used for the prototype, and the real function declaration must have variable names to bind to, but you get the point.

> **NOTE** Just because you know how to read Hungarian notation doesn't mean that you have to use it! In fact, I have been programming for over 20 years, and I'm not going to change my programming style for anyone (well, maybe Pamela Anderson). Hence, the code in this book will use a Hungarian-like coding style where Win32 API functions are concerned, but it'll use my own style in other places. One thing is for certain—I'm not capitalizing each word of my variable names! And I'm using underscores, too!

The World's Simplest Windows Program

Now that you have a general overview of the Windows OS and some of its properties and underlying design issues, let's begin our journey into real Windows programming with our first Windows program.

It's customary to write a "Hello World" program in any new language or OS that you're learning, so let's try that. Listing 2.1 is the standard DOS-based "Hello World."

LISTING 2.1   A DOS-Based "Hello World" Program

```
// DEMO2_1.CPP - standard version
#include <stdio.h>

// main entry point for all standard DOS/console programs
void main(void)
{
printf("\nTHERE CAN BE ONLY ONE!!!\n");
} // end main
```

Now let's see how it's done with Windows.

> **TIP**
>
> By the way, if you want to compile DEMO2_1.CPP, you can actually create what's called a CONSOLE APPLICATION with the VC++ or Borland compilers. These are like DOS applications, but 32-bit. They run only in text mode, but they're great for testing out ideas and algorithms. To do this make sure to set the target .EXE as CONSOLE APPLICATION in the compiler NOT Win32 .EXE!

To compile the program, follow these steps:

1. Create a new CONSOLE Application .EXE project and include DEMO2_1.CPP from T3DCHAP02\ on the CD-ROM.

2. Compile and link the program.

3. Run it! (Or run the precompiled version, DEMO2_1.EXE, on the CD-ROM.)

It All Begins with WinMain()

As I mentioned before, all Windows programs begin execution at the function named WinMain(). This is equivalent to main() in a straight DOS program. What you do in WinMain() is up to you. If you want, you can create a window, start processing events, and draw things on the screen. On the other hand, you can just make a call to one of the hundreds (or are there thousands?) of Win32 API functions. This is what we're going to do.

I just want to print something on the screen in a little message box. There just so happens to be a Win32 API function that does this—MessageBox(). Listing 2.2 is a complete, compilable Windows program that creates and displays a message box that you can move around and close.

LISTING 2.2   Your First Windows Program

```cpp
// DEMO2_2.CPP - a simple message box
#define WIN32_LEAN_AND_MEAN

#include <windows.h>        // the main windows headers
#include <windowsx.h>       // a lot of cool macros

// main entry point for all windows programs
int WINAPI WinMain(HINSTANCE hinstance,
HINSTANCE hprevinstance,
LPSTR lpcmdline,
int ncmdshow)
{
// call message box api with NULL for parent window handle
MessageBox(NULL, "THERE CAN BE ONLY ONE!!!",
"MY FIRST WINDOWS PROGRAM",
MB_OK | MB_ICONEXCLAMATION);
// exit program
return(0);
} // end WinMain
```

To compile the program, follow these steps:

1. Create a new Win32 .EXE project and include DEMO2_2.CPP from T3DCHAP02\ on the CD-ROM.

2. Compile and link the program.

3. Run it! (Or run the precompiled version, DEMO2_2.EXE, on the CD-ROM.)

And you thought that a basic Windows program had hundreds of lines of code! Anyway, when you compile and run the program, you should see something like what's depicted in Figure 2.5.

FIGURE 2.5
Running DEMO2_2.EXE

Dissecting the Program

Now that you have a complete Windows program, let's take it apart line by line and see what's going on. The very first line of code is

```
#define WIN32_LEAN_AND_MEAN
```

This deserves a bit of explanation. There are two ways to create Windows programs—with the Microsoft Foundation Classes (MFC), or with the Software Development Kit (SDK). MFC is much more complex, totally based on C++ and classes, and 10 times more powerful and complicated than you will ever need for games. On the other hand, the SDK is manageable, can be learned in a week or two (at least the rudiments of it), and uses straight C. Hence, the SDK is what I'm going to use in this book.

So, `WIN32_LEAN_AND_MEAN` instructs the compiler (header file logic, actually) not to include extraneous MFC overhead. Now that we have that out of the way, let's move on.

Next, the following header files are included:

```
#include <windows.h>
#include <windowsx.h>
```

The first include of `"windows.h"` really includes all the Windows header files. There are a lot of them, so this is something like an inclusion macro to save you from manually including dozens of explicit header files.

The second include, `"windowsx.h"`, is a header that contains a number of important macros and constants that make Windows programming easier.

And now, for the important part—the main entry point of all Windows applications, `WinMain()`:

```
int WINAPI WinMain(HINSTANCE hinstance,
HINSTANCE hprevinstance,
LPSTR lpcmdline,
int ncmdshow);
```

First off, you should notice that weird WINAPI declarator. This is equivalent to the PASCAL function declarator, which forces the parameters to be passed from left to right, rather than the normal right-to-left order with the default CDECL. However, the PASCAL calling convention declarator is now obsolete, and WINAPI has taken its place. You must use WINAPI for the `WinMain()` function; otherwise, the startup code will end up passing the parameters incorrectly to the function!

Examining Parameters

Next, let's look at each of the parameters in detail:

- hinstance—This parameter is the instance handle that Windows generates for your application. Instances are pointers or numbers used to track resources. In this case, hinstance is used to track your application, like a name or address. When your application is executed, Windows will supply this parameter.

- hprevinstance—This parameter is no longer used, but in past versions of Windows, it tracked the previous instance of the application (in other words, the instance of the application that launched the current one). No wonder Microsoft got rid of it! It's like time travel—it gives me a headache thinking about it.

- lpcmdline—This is a null-terminated string, similar to the command-line parameters of the standard C/C++ main(int argc, char **argv) function, except that there isn't a separate parameter analogous to argc indicating the number of command-line parameters. For example, if you create a Windows application called TEST.EXE and launch it with the following parameters:

  ```
  TEST.EXE one two three
  ```

  lpcmdline will contain the following data:

  ```
  lpcmdline = "one two three"
  ```

  Notice that the name of the .EXE itself is *not* part of the command line.

- ncmdshow—This final parameter is simply an integer that is passed to the application during launch, indicating how the main application window is to be opened. Thus, the user has a little control over how the application starts up. Of course, as the programmer, you can disregard this if you want, but it's there if you want to use it. (You pass it to ShowWindow(), but we're getting ahead of ourselves.) Table 2.2 lists the most common values that ncmdshow can take on.

TABLE 2.2   Windows Codes for ncmdshow

Value	Function
SW_SHOWNORMAL	Activates and displays a window. If the window is minimized or maximized, Windows restores it to its original size and position. An application should specify this flag when displaying the window for the first time.
SW_SHOW	Activates the window and displays it in its current size and position.
SW_HIDE	Hides the window and activates another window.
SW_MAXIMIZE	Maximizes the specified window.
SW_MINIMIZE	Minimizes the specified window and activates the next top-level window in the Z order.
SW_RESTORE	Activates and displays the window. If the window is minimized or maximized, Windows restores it to its original size and position. An application should specify this flag when restoring a minimized window.
SW_SHOWMAXIMIZED	Activates the window and displays it as a maximized window.

TABLE 2.2   Continued

Value	Function
SW_SHOWMINIMIZED	Activates the window and displays it as a minimized window.
SW_SHOWMINNOACTIVE	Displays the window as a minimized window. The active window remains active.
SW_SHOWNA	Displays the window in its current state. The active window remains active.
SW_SHOWNOACTIVATE	Displays a window in its most recent size and position. The active window remains active.

As you can see from Table 2.2, there are a lot of settings for ncmdshow (many of which make no sense at this point). In reality, the majority of these settings will never be sent in ncmdshow. You will use them with another function, ShowWindow(), which actually displays a window once it's created. However, we will get to this a little later in the chapter.

The point I want to make is that Windows has a lot of options, flags, and so on that you will never use, but they're still there. It's like VCR programming options—more is always better, as long as you don't *need* to use them if you don't *want* to. Windows is designed this way. It has to make everybody happy, so that means including a lot of options. In fact, we will use SW_SHOW, SW_SHOWNORMAL, and SW_HIDE 99 percent of the time, but you need to know the other for that one percent!

Choosing a Message Box

Finally, let's talk about the actual function call to MessageBox() within WinMain(). MessageBox() is a Win32 API function that does something useful for us, so we don't have to do it. It is used to display messages with various icons, along with a button or two. You see, simply displaying messages is so common in Windows applications that a function was written just to save application programmers the half hour or so it would take to write one every time.

MessageBox() doesn't do much, but it does enough to get a window up on the screen, ask a question, and wait for the user's input. Here is the prototype for MessageBox():

```
int MessageBox( HWND    hwnd,     // handle of owner window
                LPCTSTR lptext,   // address of text in message box
LPCTSTR lpcaption,// address of title of message box
UINT    utype);   // style of message box
```

The parameters are defined as follows:

- hwnd—This is the handle of the window you want the message box to be attached to. At this point I haven't covered window handles yet, so just think of it as the parent of the message box. In the case of DEMO2_2.CPP, we are setting it to NULL, so use the Windows desktop as the parent window.

- lptext—This is a null-terminated string containing the text you want to display.
- lpcaption—This is a null-terminated string containing the caption for the message dialog box.
- utype—This is about the only exciting parameter of the bunch. It controls what kind of message box is displayed.

Take a look at Table 2.3 to see a (somewhat abridged) list of the various MessageBox() options.

TABLE 2.3 MessageBox() Options

Flag	Description
The following settings control the general style of the message box	
MB_OK	The message box contains one pushbutton: OK. This is the default.
MB_OKCANCEL	The message box contains two pushbuttons: OK and Cancel.
MB_RETRYCANCEL	The message box contains two pushbuttons: Retry and Cancel.
MB_YESNO	The message box contains two pushbuttons: Yes and No.
MB_YESNOCANCEL	The message box contains three pushbuttons: Yes, No, and Cancel.
MB_ABORTRETRYIGNORE	The message box contains three pushbuttons: Abort, Retry, and Ignore.
This group controls the addition of an icon to add a little "poor man's multimedia"	
MB_ICONEXCLAMATION	An exclamation-point icon appears in the message box.
MB_ICONINFORMATION	An icon consisting of a lowercase letter i in a circle appears in the message box.
MB_ICONQUESTION	A question-mark icon appears in the message box.
MB_ICONSTOP	A stop-sign icon appears in the message box.
This flag group controls which button is highlighted by default	
MB_DEFBUTTONn	Where n is a number (1...4) indicating which button is the default, numbered from left to right.

Note: There are additional advanced OS level flags, but we aren't concerned with them. You can always look them up in the online compiler Win32 SDK Help if you want to know more.

You can logically OR the values together in Table 2.3 to create the desired message box. Usually, you will OR only one flag from each group.

And of course, like all good Win32 API functions, MessageBox() returns a value to let you know what happened. In our case, who cares? But in general, you might want to know the return value if the message box was a yes/no question and so forth. Table 2.4 lists the possible return values.

TABLE 2.4   Return Values for `MessageBox()`

Value	Button Selected
IDABORT	Abort
IDCANCEL	Cancel
IDIGNORE	Ignore
IDNO	No
IDOK	OK
IDRETRY	Retry
IDYES	Yes

Finally, a table that can list all the values without defoliating an entire forest! Anyway, this completes the line-by-line analysis of our first Windows program—click!

> **TIP**
>
> Now I want you to get comfortable making changes to the program and compiling it in different ways. Try mucking with various compiler options, like optimization. Then try running the program through the debugger and see if you can figure that out. When you're done, come back.

If you want to hear a sound, a cheap trick is to use the `MessageBeep()` function. You can look it up in the Win32 SDK. It's similar to the `MessageBox()` function as far as simplicity of use. Here it is:

```
BOOL MessageBeep(UINT utype); // the sound to play
```

The different sounds can be from among the constants shown in Table 2.5.

TABLE 2.5   Sound Identifiers for `MessageBeep()`

Value	Sound
MB_ICONASTERISK	System asterisk
MB_ICONEXCLAMATION	System exclamation
MB_ICONHAND	System hand
MB_ICONQUESTION	System question
MB_OK	System default
0xFFFFFFFF	Standard beep using the computer speaker—yuck!

Note: If you have an MS-Plus theme installed, you're sure to get some interesting results.

See how cool the Win32 API is? There are literally hundreds of functions to play with. Granted, they aren't the fastest things in the world, but for general housekeeping, I/O, and GUI stuff, they're grrrreat! (I felt like Tony the Tiger for a second <BG>.)

Let's take a moment to summarize what we know at this point about Windows programming. The first thing is that Windows is multitasking/multithreaded, so multiple applications can run simultaneously. However, we don't have to do anything to make this happen. What does concern us is that Windows is event-driven. This means that we have to process events (which we have no idea how to do at this point) and respond to them. Okay, sounds good. And finally, all Windows programs start with the function WinMain(), which has a few more parameters than the normal DOS main() but is within the realm of logic and reason.

With all that in mind, it's time to write a real Windows application. (But before we start, you might want to grab something to drink. Normally I would say Mountain Dew, but these days I'm a *Red Bull* man. Tastes like crap, but it keeps the synapses going and the can looks cool.)

Real-World Windows Applications (Without Puck)

Even though the goal of this book is to write 3D games that run on Windows, you don't need to know much about Windows programming. Actually, all you need is a basic Windows program that opens a window, processes messages, calls the main game loop, and that's it. With that in mind, my goal in this section is to first show you how to create simple Windows programs, but at the same time to lay the groundwork for a game programming *shell* application that looks like a 32-bit DOS machine.

The main point of any Windows program is to open a window. A *window* is nothing more than a workspace that displays information, such as text and graphics, that the user can interact with. To create a fully functional Windows program, you only have to do a few things:

1. Create a Windows class.
2. Create an event handler or WinProc.
3. Register the Windows class with Windows.
4. Create a window with the previously created Windows class.
5. Create a main event loop that retrieves and dispatches Windows messages to the event handler.

Let's take a look at each step in detail.

The Windows Class

Windows is really an object-oriented OS, so a lot of concepts and procedures in Windows have their roots in C++. One of these concepts is *Windows classes*. Each window, control, list box, dialog box, gadget, and so forth in Windows is actually a window. What makes them all different is the *class* that defines them. A Windows class is a description of a window type that Windows can handle.

There are a number of predefined Window classes, such as buttons, list boxes, file selectors, and so on. However, you're free to create your own Windows classes. In fact, you will create at least one Windows class for each application you write. Otherwise, your program would be rather boring. So you can think of a Windows class as a template for Windows to follow when drawing your window, as well as processing messages for it.

Two data structures are available to hold Windows class information: WNDCLASS and WNDCLASSEX. WNDCLASS is the older of the two and will probably be obsolete soon, so we will use the new "extended" version, WNDCLASSEX. The structures are very similar, and if you are interested, you can look up the old WNDCLASS in the Win32 Help. Anyway, let's take a look at WNDCLASSEX as defined in the Windows header files:

```
typedef struct _WNDCLASSEX
        {
        UINT    cbSize;         // size of this structure
        UINT    style;          // style flags
        WNDPROC lpfnWndProc;    // function pointer to handler
        int     cbClsExtra;     // extra class info
        int     cbWndExtra;     // extra window info
        HANDLE  hInstance;      // the instance of the application
        HICON   hIcon;          // the main icon
        HCURSOR hCursor;        // the cursor for the window
HBRUSH  hbrBackground; // the background brush to paint the window
LPCTSTR lpszMenuName;  // the name of the menu to attach
LPCTSTR lpszClassName; // the name of the class itself
HICON   hIconSm;       // the handle of the small icon
} WNDCLASSEX;
```

So what you would do is create one of these structures and then fill in all the fields:

```
WNDCLASSEX winclass; // a blank windows class
```

The first field, cbSize, is very important (even Petzold forgot this in *Programming Windows 95*). It is the size of the WNDCLASSEX structure itself. You might be wondering why the structure needs to know how big it is. That's a good question. The reason is that if this structure is passed as a pointer, the receiver can always check the first field to decide how long the data chunk is at the very least. It's like a precaution and a little helper info so other functions don't have to compute the class size during runtime. Therefore, all you have to do is set it like this:

```
winclass.cbSize = sizeof(WNDCLASSEX);
```

The next field contains the style information flags that describe the general properties of the window. There are a lot of these flags, so I'm not going to show them all. Suffice it to say that you can create any type of window with them. Table 2.6 shows a good working subset of the possible flags. You can logically OR these values together to derive the type of window you want.

TABLE 2.6   Style Flags for Window Classes

Flag	Description
CS_HREDRAW	Redraws the entire window if a movement or size adjustment changes the width of the window.
CS_VREDRAW	Redraws the entire window if a movement or size adjustment changes the height of the window.
CS_OWNDC	Allocates a unique device context for each window in the class (more on this later in the chapter).
CS_DBLCLKS	Sends a double-click message to the window procedure when the user double-clicks the mouse while the cursor is in a window belonging to the class.
CS_PARENTDC	Sets the clipping region of the child window to that of the parent window so that the child can draw on the parent.
CS_SAVEBITS	Saves the client image in a window so you don't have to redraw it every time the window is obscured, moved, etc. However, this takes up more memory and is slower that doing it yourself.
CS_NOCLOSE	Disables the Close command on the system menu.

Note: The most commonly used flags are highlighted.

Table 2.6 contains a lot of flags, and I can't blame you if you're confused. For now, though, just set the style flags to indicate that you want the window to be redrawn if it is moved or resized, and you want a static *device context* along with the ability to handle double-click events.

I'm going to talk about device contexts in detail in Chapter 3, "Advanced Windows Programming," but basically they are used as data structures for graphics rendering into a window. Hence, if you want to do graphics, you need to request a device context for the particular window you are interested in. Alas, if you set the Windows class so that it has its own device context via CS_OWNDC, you can save some time since you don't have to request one each time you want to do graphics. Did that help at all, or did I make it worse? Windows is like that—the more you know, the more you don't. Anyway, here's how to set the style field:

```
winclass.style = CS_VREDRAW | CS_HREDRAW | CS_OWNDC | CS_DBLCLICKS;
```

The next field of the WNDCLASSEX structure, lpfnWndProc, is a function pointer to the event handler. Basically, what you are setting here is a *callback* function for the class. Callback functions are fairly common in Windows programming and work like this: When something happens, instead of you randomly polling for it, Windows notifies you by calling a callback function you've supplied. Then, within the callback function, you take whatever action needs to be taken.

This process is how the basic Window event loop and event handler work. You supply a callback function to the Windows class (with a specific prototype, of course). When an event occurs, Windows calls it for you, as Figure 2.6 shows. Again, we will cover this more in later sections. But for now, just set it to the event function that you'll write in a moment:

```
winclass.lpfnWndProc = WinProc; // this is our function
```

FIGURE 2.6
The Windows event handler callback in action.

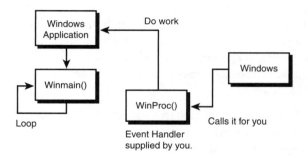

TIP

If you're not familiar with function pointers, they are like virtual functions in C++. If you're not familiar with virtual functions, I guess I have to explain them <BG>. Let's say you have two functions that operate on two numbers:

```
int Add(int op1, int op2) {return(op1+op2);}
int Sub(int op1, int op2) {return(op1-op2);}
```

You want to be able to call either function with the same call. You can do so with a function pointer, like this:

```
// define a function pointer that takes two int and
returns an int
int (Math*)(int, int);
```

Then you can assign the function pointer like this:

```
Math = Add;
int result = Math(1,2); // this really calls Add(1,2)
// result will be 3

Math = Sub;
int result = Math(1,2); // this really calls Sub(1,2)
// result will be -1
```

Cool, huh?

The next two fields, cbClsExtra and cbWndExtra, were originally designed to instruct Windows to save some extra space in the Windows class to hold extra runtime information. However, most people don't use these fields and simply set them to 0, like this:

```
winclass.cbClsExtra = 0; // extra class info space
winclass.cbWndExtra = 0; // extra window info space
```

Moving on, next is the hInstance field. This is simply the hinstance that is passed to the WinMain() function on startup, so just copy it in from WinMain():

```
winclass.hInstance = hinstance; // assign the application instance
```

The remaining fields relate to graphical aspects of the Windows class, but before I discuss them, I want to take a quick moment to review handles.

Again and again you're going to see handles in Windows programs and types: handles to bitmaps, handles to cursors, handles to everything. Remember, handles are just identifiers based on an internal Windows type. In fact, they are really integers. But Microsoft might change this, so it's a good idea to be safe and use the Microsoft types. In any case, you're going to see more and more "handles to [fill in the blank]," so don't trip out on me! And remember, any type prefixed by h is usually a handle. Okay, back to the chalkboard.

The next field sets the type of icon that will represent your application. You have the power to load your own custom icon, but for now you're going to use a system icon, which—you guessed it—you need a handle for. To retrieve a handle to a common system icon, you can use the LoadIcon() function, like this:

```
winclass.hIcon = LoadIcon(NULL, IDI_APPLICATION);
```

This code loads the standard application icon—boring, but simple. If you're interested in the LoadIcon() function, take a look at its prototype below, and see Table 2.7 for various icon options:

```
HICON LoadIcon(HINSTANCE hInstance,  // handle of application instance
LPCTSTR lpIconName);  // icon-name string or icon resource identifier
```

Here, hInstance is the instance of the application to load the icon resource from (more on this later), but for now just set it to NULL to load one of the standard icons. And lpIconName is a null-terminated string containing the name of the icon resource to be loaded. However, when hInstance is NULL, lpIconName can be one of the values in Table 2.7.

TABLE 2.7   Icon Identifiers for `LoadIcon()`

Value	Description
IDI_APPLICATION	Default application icon
IDI_ASTERISK	Asterisk
IDI_EXCLAMATION	Exclamation point
IDI_HAND	Hand-shaped icon
IDI_QUESTION	Question mark
IDI_WINLOGO	Windows logo

All right, we're about halfway through all the fields. Take another breath, and let's forge on to the next field: hCursor. This is similar to hIcon in that it's a handle to a graphics object. However, hCursor differs in that it's the handle to the cursor that will be displayed when the pointer enters the client region of the window. LoadCursor() is used to obtain a handle to a cursor that's a resource or a predefined system cursor. We will cover resources a bit later, but they are simply pieces of data, like bitmaps, cursors, icons, sounds, etc., that are compiled into your application and can be accessed at runtime. Anyway, here's how to set the cursor for the Windows class:

```
winclass.hCursor = LoadCursor(NULL, IDC_ARROW);
```

And here is the prototype for LoadCursor() (along with Table 2.8, which contains the various system cursor identifiers):

```
HCURSOR LoadCursor(HINSTANCE hInstance,// handle of application instance
LPCTSTR lpCursorName); // name string or cursor resource identifier
```

Again, hInstance is the application instance of your .EXE that contains the resource data to extract a custom cursor by name with. However, you aren't using this functionality yet and will set hInstance to NULL to allow default system cursors only.

lpCursorName identifies the resource name string or handle to the resource (which we aren't using at this point), or is a constant that identifies one of the system defaults shown in Table 2.8.

TABLE 2.8   Values for `LoadCursor()`

Value	Description
IDC_ARROW	Standard arrow
IDC_APPSTARTING	Standard arrow and small hourglass
IDC_CROSS	Crosshair
IDC_IBEAM	Text I-beam

TABLE 2.8   Continued

Value	Description
IDC_NO	Slashed circle
IDC_SIZEALL	Four-pointed arrow
IDC_SIZENESW	Double-pointed arrow pointing northeast and southwest
IDC_SIZENS	Double-pointed arrow pointing north and south
IDC_SIZENWSE	Double-pointed arrow pointing northwest and southeast
IDC_SIZEWE	Double-pointed arrow pointing west and east
IDC_UPARROW	Vertical arrow
IDC_WAIT	Hourglass

Now we're cooking! We're almost done—the remaining fields are a little more interesting. Let's move on to hbrBackground.

Whenever a window is drawn or refreshed, at the very least, Windows will repaint the background of the window's client area for you with a predefined color, or *brush* in Windows-speak. Hence, hbrBackground is a handle to the brush that you want the window to be refreshed with. Brushes, pens, colors, and graphics are all part of *GDI*— the Graphics Device Interface—and we will discuss them in detail in the next chapter. For now, I'm going to show you how to request a basic system brush to paint the window with. This is accomplished with the GetStockObject() function, as shown in the following line of code (notice the cast to (HBRUSH)):

```
winclass.hbrBackground = (HBRUSH)GetStockObject(WHITE_BRUSH);
```

GetStockObject() is a general function that retrieves a handle to one of the Windows stock brushes, pens, palettes, or fonts. GetStockObject() takes a single parameter indicating which one of these resources to load. Table 2.9 contains a list of possible stock objects for brushes and pens only.

TABLE 2.9   Stock Object Identifiers for GetStockObject()

Value	Description
BLACK_BRUSH	Black brush
WHITE_BRUSH	White brush
GRAY_BRUSH	Gray brush
LTGRAY_BRUSH	Light gray brush
DKGRAY_BRUSH	Dark gray brush
HOLLOW_BRUSH	Hollow brush

TABLE 2.9 Continued

Value	Description
NULL_BRUSH	Null brush
BLACK_PEN	Black pen
WHITE_PEN	White pen
NULL_PEN	Null pen

The next field in the WNDCLASS structure is the lpszMenuName. This is a null-terminated ASCII string of the menu resource's name to load and attach to the window. We will see how this works later in Chapter 3, "Advanced Windows Programming." For now, we'll just set it to NULL:

```
winclass.lpszMenuName = NULL;  // the name of the menu to attach
```

As I mentioned a while ago, each Windows class represents a different type of window that your application can create. Classes are like templates, in a manner of speaking, but Windows needs some way to track and identify them. Therefore, the next field, lpszClassName, is for just that. This field is filled with a null-terminated string that contains a text identifier for your class. I personally like using identifiers like "WINCLASS1", "WINCLASS2", and so forth. It's up to you, but it's better to keep it simple, like this:

```
winclass.lpszClassName = "WINCLASS1"; // the name of the class itself
```

After this assignment, you will refer to the new Windows class by its class name, "WINCLASS1"—kinda cool, huh?

Last but not least is the small application icon. This is a new addition to the Windows class WNDCLASSEX structure and wasn't available in the older WNDCLASS. Basically, this handle points to the icon you want to display on your window's title bar and on the Windows desktop taskbar. Usually you would load a custom resource, but for now let's just use one of the standard Windows icons via LoadIcon():

```
winclass.hIconSm =
LoadIcon(NULL, IDI_APPLICATION); // the handle of the small icon
```

That's it. Now let's take a look at the whole class definition at once:

```
WNDCLASSEX winclass; // this will hold the class we create
// first fill in the window class structure
winclass.cbSize = sizeof(WNDCLASSEX);
winclass.style        = CS_DBLCLKS | CS_OWNDC | CS_HREDRAW | CS_VREDRAW;
winclass.lpfnWndProc = WindowProc;
winclass.cbClsExtra   = 0;
winclass.cbWndExtra   = 0;
winclass.hInstance    = hinstance;
```

```
winclass.hIcon         = LoadIcon(NULL, IDI_APPLICATION);
winclass.hCursor       = LoadCursor(NULL, IDC_ARROW);
winclass.hbrBackground    = GetStockObject(BLACK_BRUSH);
winclass.lpszMenuName    = NULL;
winclass.lpszClassName    = "WINCLASS1";
winclass.hIconSm        = LoadIcon(NULL, IDI_APPLICATION);
```

And of course, if you want to save some typing, you could initialize the structure on-the-fly like this:

```
WNDCLASSEX winclass = {
winclass.cbSize = sizeof(WNDCLASSEX),
CS_DBLCLKS | CS_OWNDC | CS_HREDRAW | CS_VREDRAW,
WindowProc,
0,
0,
hinstance,
LoadIcon(NULL, IDI_APPLICATION),
LoadCursor(NULL, IDC_ARROW),
GetStockObject(BLACK_BRUSH),
NULL,
"WINCLASS1",
LoadIcon(NULL, IDI_APPLICATION)};
```

It saves typing!

Registering the Windows Class

Now that the Windows class is defined and stored in `winclass`, you must tell Windows about the new class. This is accomplished via the function `RegisterClassEx()`, which simply takes a pointer to the new class definition, like this:

```
RegisterClassEx(&winclass);
```

 WARNING   Notice that I'm not using the class name, which is "WINCLASS1" in the case of our example. For `RegisterClassEx()`, you must use the actual structure holding the class because at the point before the call to the function, Windows does not yet know of the existence of the new class. Get it?

Also, to be complete, there is the old `RegisterClass()` function, which is used to register a class based on the older structure `WNDCLASS`.

Once the class is registered, we are free to create the window with it. Let's see how to do that, and then revisit the details of the event handler and main event loop to see what kind of processing needs to be done for a Windows application to work.

Creating the Window

To create a window (or any window-like object), you use the `CreateWindow()` or `CreateWindowEx()` function. The latter is a little newer and supports an additional style parameter, so let's use it. This is where the Windows class comes in, which we took so long to dissect piece by piece. When you create a window, you must supply the text name of the window class—which in this case is `"WINCLASS1"`. This is what identifies your Windows class and differentiates it from other classes, along with the built-in types like buttons, text boxes, etc.

Here's the function prototype for `CreateWindowEx()`:

```
HWND CreateWindowEx(
DWORD dwExStyle,      // extended window style
LPCTSTR lpClassName,  // pointer to registered class name
LPCTSTR lpWindowName, // pointer to window name
     DWORD dwStyle,        // window style
     int x,                // horizontal position of window
     int y,                // vertical position of window
     int nWidth,           // window width
     int nHeight,          // window height
     HWND hWndParent,      // handle to parent or owner window
     HMENU hMenu,          // handle to menu, or child-window identifier
HINSTANCE hInstance,  // handle to application instance
LPVOID lpParam);      // pointer to window-creation data
```

If the function is successful, it returns a handle to the newly created window; other-wise, it returns `NULL`.

Most of the parameters are self-explanatory, but let's cover them anyway:

- `dwExStyle`—The extended styles flag is an advanced feature, and for most cases, you'll set it to `NULL`. However, if you're interested in all the possible values, take a look at the Win32 SDK Help—there are a lot of them. About the only one I ever use is `WS_EX_TOPMOST`, which makes the window stay on top.

- `lpClassName`—This is the name of the class you want to create a window based on—for example, `"WINCLASS1"`.

- `lpWindowName`—This is a null-terminated text string containing the title of the window—for example, `"My First Window"`.

- `dwStyle`—This is the general window flag that describes what the window looks like and how it behaves—very important! See Table 2.10 for a list of some of the more popular values. Of course, you can logically OR these values together to get the various features you want.

- `x,y`—This is the position of the upper left-hand corner of the window in pixel coordinates. If you don't care, use `CW_USEDEFAULT` and Windows will decide.

- nWidth, nHeight—This is the width and height of the window in pixels. If you don't care, use CW_USEDEFAULT and Windows will decide.
- hWndParent—This is the handle to the parent window, if there is one. Use NULL if there isn't a parent, and then the desktop will be the parent.
- hMenu—This is the handle to the menu to attach to the window. You'll learn more on this in the next chapter. Use NULL for now.
- hInstance—This is the instance of the application. Use hinstance from WinMain() here.
- lpParam—Advanced. Set to NULL.

Table 2.10 lists the various window flags settings.

TABLE 2.10 General Style Values for dwStyle

WS_POPUP	A pop-up window.
WS_OVERLAPPED	An overlapped window, which has a title bar and a border. Same as the WS_TILED style.
WS_OVERLAPPEDWINDOW	An overlapped window with the WS_OVERLAPPED, WS_CAPTION, WS_SYSMENU, WS_THICKFRAME, WS_MINIMIZEBOX, and WS_MAXI-MIZEBOX styles.
WS_VISIBLE	A window that is initially visible.
WS_SYSMENU	A window that has a window menu on its title bar. The WS_CAP-TION style must also be specified.
WS_BORDER	A window that has a thin-line border.
WS_CAPTION	A window that has a title bar (includes the WS_BORDER style).
WS_ICONIC	A window that is initially minimized. Same as the WS_MINIMIZE style.
WS_MAXIMIZE	A window that is initially maximized.
WS_MAXIMIZEBOX	A window that has a Maximize button. Cannot be combined with the WS_EX_CONTEXTHELP style. The WS_SYSMENU style must also be specified.
WS_MINIMIZE	A window that is initially minimized. Same as the WS_ICONIC style.
WS_MINIMIZEBOX	A window that has a Minimize button. Cannot be combined with the WS_EX_CONTEXTHELP style. The WS_SYSMENU style must also be specified.
WS_POPUPWINDOW	A pop-up window with WS_BORDER, WS_POPUP, and WS_SYSMENU styles. The WS_CAPTION and WS_POPUPWINDOW styles must be combined to make the window menu visible.

TABLE 2.10   Continued

WS_SIZEBOX	A window that has a sizing border. Same as the WS_THICKFRAME style.
WS_HSCROLL	A window that has a horizontal scrollbar.
WS_VSCROLL	A window that has a vertical scrollbar.

Note: I have highlighted commonly used values.

And here's how you would create a basic overlapped window with the standard controls at position 0,0 with a size of 400,400 pixels:

```
HWND hwnd; // window handle

// create the window, bail if problem
if (!(hwnd = CreateWindowEx(NULL, // extended style
            "WINCLASS1",          // class
            "Your Basic Window",  // title
            WS_OVERLAPPEDWINDOW | WS_VISIBLE,
            0,0,         // initial x,y
            400,400,     // initial width, height
            NULL,        // handle to parent
            NULL,        // handle to menu
            hinstance,   // instance of this application
            NULL)))      // extra creation parms
return(0);
```

Once the window has been created, it may or may not be visible. However, in this case, we added the style flag WS_VISIBLE, which does this automatically. If this flag isn't added, use the following function call to manually display the window:

```
// this shows the window
ShowWindow(hwnd, ncmdshow);
```

Remember the ncmdshow parameter of WinMain()? This is where it comes in handy. Although here you've overridden it by adding WS_VISIBLE, you would normally send it as the parameter to ShowWindow(). The next thing that you might want to do is force Windows to update your window's contents and generate a WM_PAINT message. This is accomplished with a call to UpdateWindow():

```
// this sends a WM_PAINT message to window and makes
// sure the contents are refreshed
UpdateWindow();
```

The Event Handler

I don't know about you, but I'm starting to get the hang of this Windows stuff! It's not that bad. It's like a mystery novel—except the mystery is figuring out what language the novel is written in! With that in mind, let's tackle the main event handler, or at least take a first look at it. Remember, I mentioned that the event handler is a callback function called by Windows from the main event loop whenever an event occurs that your window must handle. Take a look at Figure 2.6 again to refresh your memory about the general data flow.

This event handler is written by you, and it handles as many (or as few) events as you want to take care of. The rest you can pass on to Windows and let it deal with them. Of course, keep that in mind that the more events and messages your application handles, the more functionality it will have.

Before we get into some code, though, let's talk about some of the details of the event handler, exactly what it does, and how it works. First, for each Windows class that you create, you can have a separate event handler that I will refer to as *Windows' Procedure* or simply *WinProc* from now on. The WinProc is sent messages from the main event loop as messages are received from the user or Windows and placed in the main event queue. That's a mental tongue twister, so I'll say it in another way…

As the user and Windows perform tasks, events and messages are generated that are for your window and/or other applications' windows. All of these messages go into a queue, but the ones for your window are sent to your window's own private queue. Then the main event loop retrieves these messages and sends them to your window's WinProc to be processed.

There are literally hundreds of possible messages and variations, so we aren't going to cover them all. Luckily, you only have to handle very few of them to get a Windows application up and running.

So in a nutshell, the main event loop feeds the WinProc with messages and events, and the WinProc does something with them. Hence, not only do you have to worry about the WinProc, but also the main event loop. We will get to this shortly; for now, assume that the WinProc is simply going to be fed messages.

Now that you know what the WinProc does, let's take a look at the prototype for it:

```
LRESULT CALLBACK WindowProc(
HWND hwnd, // window handle of sender
UINT msg,  // the message id
WPARAM wparam,  // further defines message
LPARAM lparam); // further defines message
```

Of course, this is just a prototype for the callback. You can call the function anything you want because you are only going to assign the function's address as a function pointer to `winclass.lpfnWndProc`, like this:

```
winclass.lpfnWndProc = WindowProc;
```

Remember? Anyway, the parameters are fairly self-explanatory:

- hwnd—This is the window handle and is only important if you have multiple windows open with the same Windows class. In that case, hwnd is the only way you can tell which messages are coming from which window. Figure 2.7 shows this possibility.

FIGURE 2.7
Multiple windows based on the same class.

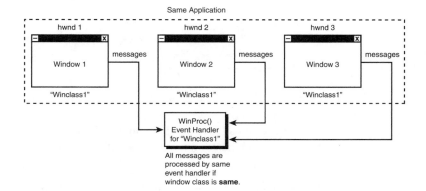

- msg—This is the actual message ID that the WinProc should handle. This ID may be one of dozens of main messages.

- wparam and lparam—These further qualify or subclass the message sent in the msg parameter.

And finally, the return type, LRESULT, and declaration specifier, CALLBACK, are of interest. These keywords are a must, so don't forget them!

So what most people do is switch() on the msg and then write code for each case. And based on msg, you will know if you need to further evaluate wparam and/or lparam. Cool? So let's take a look at some of the possible messages that might come through the WinProc, and then we'll see a bare-bones WinProc. Take a look at Table 2.11 to see a short list of some basic message IDs.

TABLE 2.11   A Short List of Message IDs

Value	Description
WM_ACTIVATE	Sent when a window is activated or becomes the focus.
WM_CLOSE	Sent when a window is closed.
WM_CREATE	Sent when a window is first created.
WM_DESTROY	Sent when a window is about to be destroyed.
WM_MOVE	Sent when a window has been moved.
WM_MOUSEMOVE	Sent when the mouse has been moved.

TABLE 2.11   Continued

Value	Description
WM_KEYUP	Sent when a key is released.
WM_KEYDOWN	Sent when a key is pressed.
WM_TIMER	Sent when a timer event occurs.
WM_USER	Allows you to send messages.
WM_PAINT	Sent when a window needs repainting.
WM_QUIT	Sent when a Windows application is finally terminating.
WM_SIZE	Sent when a window has changed size.

Take a good look at Table 2.11 and read what all those messages are for. Basically, the WinProc will be sent one or more of these messages as the application runs. The message ID itself will be in msg, and any remaining info is stored in wparam and lparam. Thus, it's always a good idea to reference the online Win32 SDK Help to see what all the parameters of a particular message do.

Fortunately, we are only interested in three messages right now:

- WM_CREATE—This message is sent when the window is first created and gives you a chance to do any setup, initialization, or resource allocation.

- WM_PAINT—This message is sent whenever your window's contents need repainting. This can occur for a number of reasons: the window was moved or resized by the user, another application popped up and obscured yours, and so on.

- WM_DESTROY—This message is sent to your window when the window is about to be destroyed. Usually, this is a direct result of the user clicking the window's close icon or closing from the window's system menu. Either way, this is where you should deallocate all the resources and tell Windows to terminate the application completely by sending a WM_QUIT message yourself—more on this later.

So without further ado, let's see a complete WinProc that handles all these messages:

```
LRESULT CALLBACK WindowProc(HWND hwnd,
                            UINT msg,
                            WPARAM wparam,
                            LPARAM lparam)
{
// this is the main message handler of the system
PAINTSTRUCT    ps;    // used in WM_PAINT
HDC         hdc;    // handle to a device context

// what is the message
switch(msg)
    {
```

```
    case WM_CREATE:
        {
// do initialization stuff here

    // return success
return(0);
} break;

    case WM_PAINT:
    {
// simply validate the window
hdc = BeginPaint(hwnd,&ps);
// you would do all your painting here
    EndPaint(hwnd,&ps);


    // return success
return(0);
} break;

    case WM_DESTROY:
    {
// kill the application, this sends a WM_QUIT message
PostQuitMessage(0);

    // return success
return(0);
} break;

    default:break;

    } // end switch

// process any messages that we didn't take care of
return (DefWindowProc(hwnd, msg, wparam, lparam));

} // end WinProc
```

As you can see, the function is composed of empty space for the most part—which is a good thing! Let's begin with the processing of WM_CREATE. Here, all the function does is return(0). This simply tells Windows that you handled it, so don't take any more actions. Of course, you could have done all kinds of initialization in the WM_CREATE message, but that's up to you.

The next message, WM_PAINT, is very important. This message is sent whenever your window needs repainting. This usually means that you have to do the repainting. For DirectX games, this isn't going to matter because you are going to redraw the screen 30 to 60 fps (frames per second). But for a normal Windows application, it does matter. I'm going to cover WM_PAINT in much more detail in the next chapter, but for now just tell Windows that you *did* repaint the window, so it can stop sending WM_PAINT messages.

To accomplish this feat, you must validate the client rectangle of the window. There are a number of ways to do this, but the simplest is to put a call to BeginPaint()— EndPaint(). This calling pair validates the window and fills the background with the background brush previously stored in the Windows class variable hbrBackground. Once again, here's the code for the validation:

```
// begin painting
hdc = BeginPaint(hwnd,&ps);
// you would do all your painting here
EndPaint(hwnd,&ps);
```

There are a couple of things going on here that I want to address. First, notice that the first parameter to each call is the window handle hwnd. This is necessary because the BeginPaint()—EndPaint() functions can potentially paint in any window of your application, so the window handle indicates which one you're interested in messing with. The second parameter is the address of a PAINTSTRUCT structure that contains the rectangle that you must redraw. Here's what a PAINTSTRUCT looks like:

```
typedef struct tagPAINTSTRUCT
        {
        HDC   hdc;
        BOOL  fErase;
        RECT  rcPaint;
        BOOL  fRestore;
        BOOL  fIncUpdate;
        BYTE  rgbReserved[32];
        } PAINTSTRUCT;
```

You don't really need to worry about this until later, when we talk about the Graphics Device Interface or GDI. But the most important field is rcPaint, which is a RECT structure that contains the minimum rectangle that needs to be repainted. Take a look at Figure 2.8 to see this. Notice that Windows tries to do the least amount of work possible, so when the contents of a window are mangled, Windows at least tries to tell you the smallest rectangle that you can repaint to restore the contents. And if you're interested in the RECT structure, it's nothing more than the four corners of a rectangle, as shown here:

```
typedef struct tagRECT
        {
        LONG left;      // left x-edge of rect
        LONG top;       // top y-edge of rect
        LONG right;     // right x-edge of rect
        LONG bottom;    // bottom y-edge of rect
        } RECT;
```

And the last thing that you'll notice about the call to BeginPaint() is that it returns a handle to a graphics context or hdc:

```
HDC hdc; // handle to graphics context
hdc = BeginPaint(hwnd,&ps);
```

FIGURE 2.8
Repainting the
invalid region only.

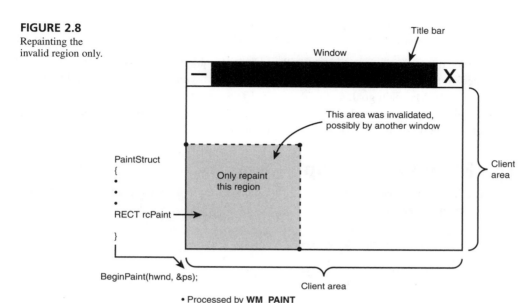

A *graphics context* is a data structure that describes the video system and drawing surface. It's magic, as far as we are concerned; you just have to retrieve one if you want to do any graphics. That's about it for the WM_PAINT message—for now.

The WM_DESTROY message is actually quite interesting. WM_DESTROY is sent when the user closes the window. However, this only closes the window, not the application. The application will continue to run, but without a window. You need to do something about this. In most cases, when the user kills the main window, he intends for the application to terminate. Thus, you must facilitate this by sending a message yourself! The message is called WM_QUIT. And since this message is so common, there's a function to send it for you, called PostQuitMessage().

All you need to do in the WM_DESTROY handler is clean up everything and then tell Windows to terminate your application with a call to PostQuitMessage(0). This, in turn, puts a WM_QUIT into the message queue, which at some point causes the main event loop to bail.

There are a couple of details you should know about in the WinProc handler we have been analyzing. First, I'm sure you have noticed the return(0) after each handler body. This serves two purposes: to exit the WinProc and to tell Windows that you handled the message. The second important detail is the *default message handler*, DefaultWindowProc(). This function is a *passthrough* that passes messages that you don't process onto Windows for default processing. Therefore, if you don't handle the message, make sure to always end all your event handler functions with a call like this:

```
// process any messages that we didn't take care of
return (DefWindowProc(hwnd, msg, wparam, lparam));
```

I know this may all seem like overkill and more trouble than it's worth. Nevertheless, once you have a basic Windows application skeleton, you just copy it and add your own code. My main goal, as I said, is to help you create a DOS32-looking game console that you can use and almost forget that any Windows stuff is going on. Anyway, let's move on to the last part—the main event loop.

The Main Event Loop

The hard part is over! The main event loop is so simple, I'm just going to blurt it out and then talk about it:

```
// enter main event loop
while(GetMessage(&msg,NULL,0,0))
     {
     // translate any accelerator keys
     TranslateMessage(&msg);

     // send the message to the window proc
     DispatchMessage(&msg);
     } // end while
```

That's it? Yup! Let's see what's going on here, shall we? The main `while()` is executed as long as `GetMessage()` returns a nonzero value. `GetMessage()` is the workhorse of the main event loop, and its sole purpose is to get the next message from the event queue and process it. You'll notice that there are four parameters to `GetMessage()`. The first one is important to us; however, the remaining parameters are set to `NULL` and 0. Here's the prototype, for reference:

```
BOOL GetMessage(
     LPMSG lpMsg,         // address of structure with message
     HWND hWnd,           // handle of window
     UINT wMsgFilterMin,  // first message
     UINT wMsgFilterMax); // last message
```

The `msg` parameter is (yes, you guessed it) the storage for Windows to place the next message in. However, unlike the `msg` parameter for `WinProc()`, this `msg` is a complex data structure rather than just an integer. Remember, by the time a message gets to the WinProc, it has been "cooked" and split apart into its constituent parts. Anyway, here is the `MSG` structure:

```
typedef struct tagMSG
        {
        HWND hwnd;      // window where message occurred
        UINT message;   // message id itself
        WPARAM wParam;  // sub qualifies message
        LPARAM lParam;  // sub qualifies message
```

```
DWORD  time;    // time of message event
POINT  pt;      // position of mouse
} MSG;
```

Starting to make sense, Jules? Notice that the parameters to WinProc() are all contained within this structure, along with some others, like the time and position of the mouse when the event occurred.

So GetMessage() retrieves the next message from the event queue, but then what? Well, TranslateMessage() is called next. TranslateMessage() is a virtual accelerator key translator—in other words, an input cooker. Just call it and don't worry about what it does. The final function, DispatchMessage(), is where all the action occurs. After the message is retrieved with GetMessage() and potentially processed and translated a bit with TranslateMessage(), the actual WinProc() is called by the call to DispatchMessage().

DispatchMessage() makes the call to the WinProc, sending the appropriate parameters from the original MSG structure. Figure 2.9 shows the whole process in its final glory.

FIGURE 2.9
The mechanics of event loop message processing.

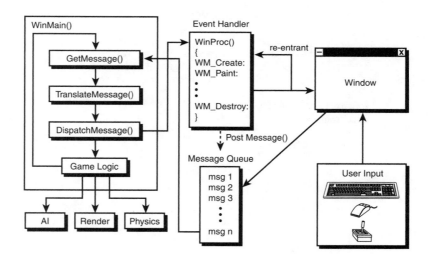

That's it, you're a Windows expert! If you grasp the concepts just covered and the importance of the event loop, event handler, and so on, that's 90 percent of the battle. The rest is just details.

With that in mind, take a look at Listing 2.3. It's a complete Windows program that creates a single window and waits for you to close it.

LISTING 2.3   A Basic Windows Program

```cpp
// DEMO2_3.CPP - A complete windows program

// INCLUDES ///////////////////////////////////////////////
#define WIN32_LEAN_AND_MEAN  // just say no to MFC

#include <windows.h>   // include all the windows headers
#include <windowsx.h>  // include useful macros
#include <stdio.h>
#include <math.h>

// DEFINES ////////////////////////////////////////////////

// defines for windows
#define WINDOW_CLASS_NAME "WINCLASS1"

// GLOBALS ////////////////////////////////////////////////

// FUNCTIONS //////////////////////////////////////////////
LRESULT CALLBACK WindowProc(HWND hwnd,
                     UINT msg,
                            WPARAM wparam,
                            LPARAM lparam)
{
// this is the main message handler of the system
PAINTSTRUCT    ps;    // used in WM_PAINT
HDC                 hdc;  // handle to a device context

// what is the message
switch(msg)
    {
    case WM_CREATE:
        {
    // do initialization stuff here

        // return success
    return(0);
    } break;

    case WM_PAINT:
    {
    // simply validate the window
    hdc = BeginPaint(hwnd,&ps);
    // you would do all your painting here
        EndPaint(hwnd,&ps);

        // return success
    return(0);
    } break;
```

LISTING 2.3 Continued

```
        case WM_DESTROY:
        {
        // kill the application, this sends a WM_QUIT message
        PostQuitMessage(0);

            // return success
        return(0);
        } break;

        default:break;

        } // end switch

    // process any messages that we didn't take care of
    return (DefWindowProc(hwnd, msg, wparam, lparam));

} // end WinProc

// WINMAIN ///////////////////////////////////////////////
int WINAPI WinMain(HINSTANCE hinstance,
                   HINSTANCE hprevinstance,
                   LPSTR lpcmdline,
                   int ncmdshow)
{

WNDCLASSEX winclass; // this will hold the class we create
HWND       hwnd;      // generic window handle
MSG        msg;       // generic message

// first fill in the window class structure
winclass.cbSize = sizeof(WNDCLASSEX);
winclass.style       = CS_DBLCLKS | CS_OWNDC |
                       CS_HREDRAW | CS_VREDRAW;
winclass.lpfnWndProc    = WindowProc;
winclass.cbClsExtra     = 0;
winclass.cbWndExtra     = 0;
winclass.hInstance      = hinstance;
winclass.hIcon          = LoadIcon(NULL, IDI_APPLICATION);
winclass.hCursor        = LoadCursor(NULL, IDC_ARROW);
winclass.hbrBackground  = GetStockObject(BLACK_BRUSH);
winclass.lpszMenuName   = NULL;
winclass.lpszClassName  = WINDOW_CLASS_NAME;
winclass.hIconSm        = LoadIcon(NULL, IDI_APPLICATION);

// register the window class
if (!RegisterClassEx(&winclass))
    return(0);

// create the window
if (!(hwnd = CreateWindowEx(NULL, // extended style
                WINDOW_CLASS_NAME,    // class
                "Your Basic Window", // title
```

LISTING 2.3   Continued

```
                    WS_OVERLAPPEDWINDOW | WS_VISIBLE,
                    0,0,          // initial x,y
                    400,400,  // initial width, height
                    NULL,         // handle to parent
                    NULL,         // handle to menu
                    hinstance,// instance of this application
                    NULL)))    // extra creation parms
return(0);

// enter main event loop
while(GetMessage(&msg,NULL,0,0))
      {
      // translate any accelerator keys
      TranslateMessage(&msg);

      // send the message to the window proc
      DispatchMessage(&msg);
      } // end while

// return to Windows like this
return(msg.wParam);

} // end WinMain

//////////////////////////////////////////////////////////
```

To compile DEMO2_3.CPP, simply create a Win32 .EXE application and add
DEMO2_3.CPP to the project. Or if you like, you can run the precompiled program,
DEMO2_3.EXE, off the CD-ROM. Figure 2.10 shows the program in action. It's not
much to look at, but what do you want? This is a paperback book!

FIGURE 2.10
DEMO2_3.EXE
in action.

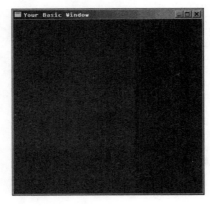

There are a couple of issues that I want to hit you with before moving on. First, if you take a close look at the event loop, it doesn't look all that real-time. Meaning that while the program waits for a message via `GetMessage()`, the main event loop is basically blocked. This is very true; you must somehow get around this, since you need to perform your game processing continuously and handle Windows events if and when they come.

Making a Real-Time Event Loop

This type of real-time nonwaiting event loop is easy to make. All you need is a way to test if there is a message in the message queue. If there is, you can process it; otherwise, continue processing other game logic and repeat. The function that performs this test is called `PeekMessage()`. Its prototype is almost identical to `GetMessage()`'s, as shown here:

```
BOOL PeekMessage(
    LPMSG lpMsg,          // pointer to structure for message
    HWND hWnd,            // handle to window
    UINT wMsgFilterMin,   // first message
    UINT wMsgFilterMax,   // last message
    UINT wRemoveMsg);     // removal flags
```

This returns nonzero if a message is available.

The difference is in the last parameter, which controls how the messages should be retrieved from the message queue. The valid flags for `wRemoveMsg` are

- `PM_NOREMOVE`—Messages are not removed from the queue after processing by `PeekMessage()`.

- `PM_REMOVE`—Messages are removed from the queue after processing by `PeekMessage()`.

Taking these two possibilities into consideration, you can do one of two things: Use `PeekMessage()` with `PM_NOREMOVE` and, if there is a message, call `GetMessage()`; or use `PM_REMOVE` and use `PeekMessage()` itself to retrieve a message if there is one. Use the latter. Here's the core logic, changed to reflect this new technique in the main event loop:

```
while(TRUE)
    {
    // test if there is a message in queue, if so get it
    if (PeekMessage(&msg,NULL,0,0,PM_REMOVE))
        {
        // test if this is a quit
        if (msg.message == WM_QUIT)
        break;
```

```
    // translate any accelerator keys
    TranslateMessage(&msg);

    // send the message to the window proc
    DispatchMessage(&msg);
    } // end if

    // main game processing goes here
    Game_Main();
} // end while
```

I've highlighted important points in the code. The first section in bold is

```
if (msg.message == WM_QUIT) break;
```

This is how you must detect to bail out of the infinite while(TRUE) loop. Remember, when a WM_DESTROY message is processed in the WinProc, it's your job to send a WM_QUIT message via the call to PostQuitMessage(). The WM_QUIT then trickles through the event queue, and you can detect it so you can bail out of the main loop.

The last section of highlighted code simply indicates where you would put the call to your main game code loop. But remember, the call to Game_Main()—or whatever you call it—must return after one frame of animation or game logic. Otherwise, messages won't be processed by the main Windows event loop.

For an example of this new real-time structure that is more appropriate for game logic processing, take a look at the source DEMO2_4.CPP and the associated DEMO2_4.EXE on the CD-ROM. This structure will in fact be our model for the remainder of the book.

Opening More Windows

Before finishing up this chapter, I want to cover one more quick topic that you might be wondering about—how do you open more than one window. Actually, this is trivial, and you already know how to do it. All you need to do is make two or more calls to CreateWindowEx() to create the windows, and that's it. However, there are some caveats to this.

First, remember that when you create a window, it's based on a Windows class. This class, among other things, defines the WinProc or event handler for the entire class. This is a very important detail, so pay attention. You can make as many windows as you want with the same class, but *all* the messages for them will be sent to the same WinProc, as defined by the event handler pointed to by the lpfnWndProc field of the WINCLASSEX structure. To see this, take a look at Figure 2.11. It depicts the message flow in this case.

FIGURE 2.11
The message flow for
multiple windows
with the same
Windows class.

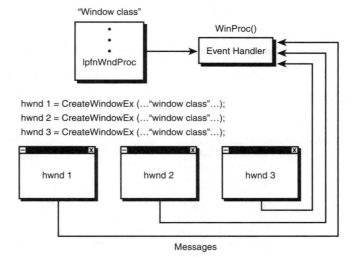

This may or may not be want you want. If you want a different WinProc for each window, you must create more than one Windows class and create each window with a different class. Hence, a different WinProc is sent messages for each class window. Figure 2.12 shows this setup.

FIGURE 2.12
Multiple Windows
classes with multiple
windows.

With that in mind, here's the code to create two windows based on the same class:

```
// create the first window
if (!(hwnd = CreateWindowEx(NULL,                     // extended style
            WINDOW_CLASS_NAME,                        // class
            "Window 1 Based on WINCLASS1",   // title
```

Windows Programming Foundations

```
                    WS_OVERLAPPEDWINDOW | WS_VISIBLE,
                    0,0,      // initial x,y
                    400,400,  // initial width, height
                    NULL,     // handle to parent
                    NULL,     // handle to menu
                    hinstance,// instance of this application
                    NULL)))   // extra creation parms
    return(0);

    // create the second window
    if (!(hwnd = CreateWindowEx(NULL,                 // extended style
                    WINDOW_CLASS_NAME,      // class
                    "Window 2 Also Based on WINCLASS1", // title
                    WS_OVERLAPPEDWINDOW | WS_VISIBLE,
                    100,100,  // initial x,y
                    400,400,  // initial width, height
                    NULL,     // handle to parent
                    NULL,     // handle to menu
                    hinstance,// instance of this application
                    NULL)))   // extra creation parms
    return(0);
```

Of course, you might want to track each window handle in different variables rather than
the same one, as is the case with hwnd, but you get the idea. For an example of opening
two windows at once, take a look at DEMO2_5.CPP and the associated executable,
DEMO2_5.EXE. When you run the .EXE, you should see something like Figure 2.13. Notice
that when you close either window, they both close and the application terminates. See if
you can figure out a way to close only one window at a time. (Hint: Create two Windows
classes, and don't send a WM_QUIT message until both windows have been closed.)

FIGURE 2.13
The multiple-window
program DEMO2_5.EXE.

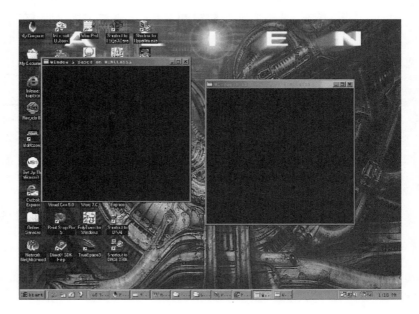

Summary

I don't know about you, but I'm really excited! At this point, you have everything you need to start understanding much more complex Windows programming. You know about the architecture of Windows and multitasking, and you know how to create Window classes, register classes, create windows, write event loops and handlers, and a lot more! So pat yourself on the back (or, for my alien readers, lick your eyeballs). You have done a most excellent job <BG>.

In the next chapter, we're going to cover some more Windows-related stuff, like using resources, creating menus, working with dialogs, and getting information.

CHAPTER 3

Advanced Windows Programming

"Are you sure this sweet machine isn't going to waste?"
—Dade, Hackers

It doesn't take a rocket scientist to realize that Windows programming is a huge subject. However, the cool thing about it is that you don't need to know much to get a lot done. With that in mind, this chapter supplies some of the most important pieces you need to make a complete Windows application. You'll learn about:

- Using resources such as icons, cursors, and sounds
- Menus
- Basic GDI and the video system
- Input devices
- Sending messages

Using Resources

One of the main design issues that the creators of Windows wanted to address was storing more than just the program code in a Windows application (even Mac programs do this). They reasoned that the data for a program should also reside within the program's .EXE file. This isn't a bad idea for a number of reasons:

- A single .EXE that contains both code and data is simpler to distribute.
- If you don't have external data files, you can't lose them.
- Outside forces can't easily access your data files—such as .BMPs, .WAVs, and so on—and hack, jack, and distribute them around the planet.

To facilitate this kind of database technology, Windows programs support what are called *resources*. These are simply pieces of data combined with your program code that can be loaded in later during runtime by the program itself. Figure 3.1 depicts this concept.

FIGURE 3.1
The relationship of resources to a Windows application.

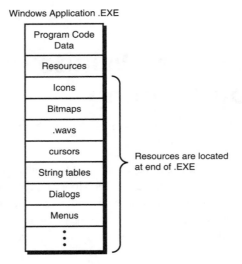

So what kind of resources are we talking about here? Well, in reality, there is no limit to the types of data you can compile into your program because Windows programs support *user-defined* resource types. However, there are some predefined types that should take care of most of your needs:

- Icons—Small bitmapped images used in a number of places, such as the image that you click on to run a program within a directory. Icons use the .ICO file extension.

- Cursor—A bitmap that represents the mouse pointer. Windows allows you to manipulate cursors in a number of ways. For example, you might want the cursor to change as it is moved from window to window. Cursors use the .CUR file extension.

- String—The string resource might not be so obvious a choice for a resource. You might say, "I usually put strings into my program anyway, or in a data file." I can see your point. Nevertheless, Windows allows you to place a table of strings in your program as a resource and to access them via IDs.

- Sound—Most Windows programs make at least minimal use of sounds via .WAV files. Hence, .WAV files can be added to your resources, too. This is a great way to keep people from hijacking your sound effects!

- Bitmap—These are the standard bitmaps that you would imagine: a rectangular matrix of pixels in monochrome or 4-, 8-, 16-, 24-, or 32-bit format. They are very common objects in graphical operating systems such as Windows, so they can be added as resources also. Bitmaps use the .BMP file extension.

- Dialog—Dialog boxes are so common in Windows that the designers decided to make them a resource rather than something that is loaded externally. Good idea! Therefore, you can either create dialog boxes on-the-fly with code, or design them with an editor and store them as a resource.

- Metafile—Metafiles are a bit advanced. They allow you to record a sequence of graphical operations in a file and then play the file back.

Now that you have an idea of what resources are and the types that exist, the next question is, how does it all go together? Well, there is a program called a *resource compiler.* It takes as input an ASCII text resource file with the extension .RC. This file is a C/English–like description of all the resources you want to compile into a single data file. The resource compiler then loads all the resources and places them into one big data file with the extension .RES.

This .RES file contains all the binary data making up whichever icons, cursors, bitmaps, sounds, and so forth that you may have defined in the .RC resource file. Then the .RES file is taken, along with your .CPP, .H, .LIB, .OBJ, and so on, and compiled into one .EXE, and that's it! Figure 3.2 illustrates the data flow possibilities of this process.

Putting Your Resources Together

Back in the old days, you would use an external resource compiler like RC.EXE to compile all your resources together. But these days, the compiler IDE does all this for you. Hence, if you want to add a resource to your program, you can simply add it by selecting New (in most cases) from the File menu in your IDE and then selecting the resource type you want to add (more on this later).

Windows Programming Foundations

FIGURE 3.2
The data flow
of resources during
compilation and
linking.

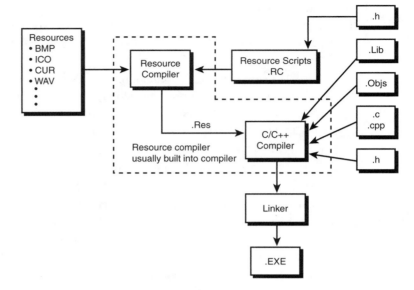

Let's review what the deal is with resources: You can add a number of data types and objects to your program, and they will reside as resources within the .EXE itself (somewhere at the end), along with the actual computer code. Then, during runtime, you can access this resource database and load resource data from your program itself instead of from the disk as separate files. Furthermore, to create the resource file, you must have a resource description file that is in ASCII text and named *.RC. This file is then fed to the compiler (along with access to the resources) and a *.RES file is generated. This .RES file is then linked together with all your other program objects to create a final .EXE. It's as simple as that! Yeah, right, and I'm a billionaire!

With all that in mind, let's cover a number of resource objects and see how to create them and load them into our programs. I'm not going to cover all the resources previously mentioned, but you should be able to figure out any others with the information here. They all work in the same manner, give or take a data type, handle, or psychotic episode of staying up all night and not sleeping.

Using Icon Resources

There are only two files that you need to create to work with resources: an .RC file and possibly an .H file, if you want to make references to symbolic identifiers in the .RC file. I'll cover this detail in the following pages. Of course, ultimately you need to generate an .RES file, but we'll let the compiler IDE do this.

As an example of creating an ICON resource, let's see how to change the icon that the application uses on the taskbar and the one next to the system menu on the window itself. If you recall, you set these icons during the creation of the Windows class with the following lines of code:

```
winclass.hIcon   = LoadIcon(NULL, IDI_APPLICATION);
winclass.hIconSm = LoadIcon(NULL, IDI_APPLICATION);
```

These lines of code load the default application icon for both the normal icon and the small version of the icon. However, you can load any icon you want into these slots by using icons that have been compiled into a resource file.

First, you need an icon to work with... I have created a cool icon to use for all the applications in this book. It's called T3DX.ICO and is shown in Figure 3.3. I created the icon using VC++ 6.0's Image Editor, which is shown in Figure 3.4. However, you can create icons, cursors, bitmaps, and so on with any program you want (as long as it supports the export type).

FIGURE 3.3
The T3DX.ICO
icon bitmap.

FIGURE 3.4
The VC++ 6.0
Image Editor.

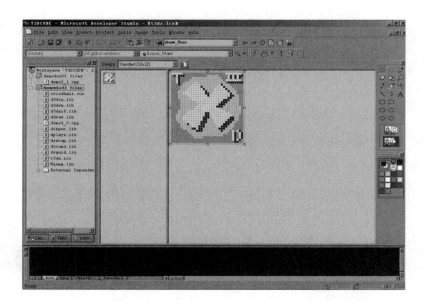

T3DX.ICO is 32 pixels x 32 pixels, with 16 colors. Icons can range in size from 16x16 to 64x64, with up to 256 colors. However, most icons are 32x32 with 16 colors, so let's stick to that for now.

Once you have the icon that you're interested in placing into a resource file, you need to create a resource file to place it in. To keep things simple, you're going to do everything by hand. (Remember that the compiler IDE will do all this stuff for you—but then you wouldn't learn anything, right?)

The .RC file contains all the resource definitions, meaning that you can have more than one resource in your program.

> **NOTE**
>
> Before I show you any code, I want to make a very important point about resources. Windows uses either ASCII text strings or integer IDs to refer to resources. In most cases, you can use both in your .RC files. However, some resources only allow you to use one or the other. In either case, the resources must be loaded in a slightly different way, and if IDs are involved, an extra .H file containing the symbolic cross-references must also be included in your project.

Here's how you would define an ICON resource in your .RC script file:

Method 1—By string name:

```
icon_name ICON FILENAME.ICO
```

Examples:

```
windowicon ICON star.ico
MyCoolIcon ICON cool.ico
```

or

Method 2—By integer ID:

```
icon_id ICON FILENAME.ICO
```

Examples:

```
windowicon ICON star.ico
124 ICON ship.ico
```

Here's the confusing part: Notice that there aren't any quotes at all in method 1. This is a bit of a problem and will cause you much grief, so listen up. You might have noticed that the first example in each method of the ICON definitions looks exactly the same. However, one of them is interpreted as "windowicon" and the other as the symbol windowicon. What makes this happen is an additional file that you literally include in the .RC file (and your application's .CPP file) that defines any symbolic constants. When the resource compiler parses the following line of code,

```
windowicon ICON star.ico
```

it takes a look at any symbols that have been defined via include header files. If the symbol exists, the resource compiler then refers to the resource numerically by the integer ID that the symbol resolves to. Otherwise, the resource compiler assumes it's a string and refers to the ICON by the string "windowicon".

Thus, if you want to define symbolic ICONs in your .RC resource script, you also need an .H file to resolve the symbolic references. To include the .H file in the .RC script, you use the standard C/C++ #include keyword.

For example, suppose that you want to define three symbolic ICONs in your .RC file, which we'll name RESOURCES.RC. You'll also need an .H file, which we'll name RESOURCES.H. Here's what the contents of each file would look like:

Contents of RESOURCES.H:

```
#define ID_ICON1      100 // these numbers are arbitrary
#define ID_ICON2      101
#define ID_ICON3      102
```

Contents of RESOURCES.RC:

```
#include "RESOURCES.H"

// here are the icon defines, note the use of C++ comments

ID_ICON1 ICON star.ico
ID_ICON2 ICON ball.ico
ID_ICON3 ICON cross.ico
```

That's it. Then you would add RESOURCES.RC to your project and make sure to #include RESOURCES.H in your application file, and you would be ready to rock and roll! Of course, the .ICO files must be in the working directory of your project so the resource compiler can find them.

Now, if you didn't #define the symbols for the icons and include an .H file, the resource compiler would just assume that the symbols ID_ICON1, ID_ICON2, and ID_ICON3 were literal strings. That's how you would refer to them in the program— "ID_ICON1", "ID_ICON2", and "ID_ICON3".

Now that I have completely upset the time/space continuum with all this stuff, let's back up to what you were trying to do—just load a simple icon!

To load an icon by string name, do the following:

In an .RC file:

```
your_icon_name ICON filename.ICO
```

In program code:

```
// Notice the use of hinstance instead of NULL.
winclass.hIcon    = LoadIcon(hinstance, "your_icon_name");
winclass.hIconSm = LoadIcon(hinstance, "your_icon_name");
```

And to load by symbolic reference, you would #include the header containing the references to the symbols, as in the preceding example:

In an .H file:

```
#define ID_ICON1    100 // these numbers are arbitrary
#define ID_ICON2    101
#define ID_ICON3    102
```

In an .RC file:

```
// here are the icon defines, note the use of C++ comments
ID_ICON1 ICON star.ico
ID_ICON2 ICON ball.ico
ID_ICON3 ICON cross.ico
```

And then the program code would look like this:

```
// Notice the use of hinstance instead of NULL.
// use the MAKEINTRESOURCE macro to reference
// symbolic constant resource properly
winclass.hIcon    = LoadIcon(hinstance,MAKEINTRESOURCE(ID_ICON1));
winclass.hIconSm = LoadIcon(hinstance,MAKEINTRESOURCE(ID_ICON1));
```

Notice the use of the macro MAKEINTRESOURCE(). This macro converts the integer into a string pointer, but don't worry about that—just use it when using #defined symbolic constants.

Using Cursor Resources

Cursor resources are almost identical to ICON resources. Cursor files are small bitmaps with the extension .CUR and can be created in most compiler IDEs or with separate image processing programs. Cursors are usually 32x32 with 16 colors, but they can be up to 64x64 with 256 colors and even animated!

Assuming that you have created a cursor file with your IDE or a separate paint program, the steps to add them to an .RC file and access them via your program are similar to the steps for ICONs. To define a cursor, use the CURSOR keyword in your .RC file.

Method 1—By string name:

```
cursor_name CURSOR FILENAME.CUR
```

Examples:

```
windowcursor CURSOR crosshair.cur

MyCoolCursor CURSOR greenarrow.cur
```

or

Method 2—By integer ID:

```
cursor_id CURSOR FILENAME.CUR
```

Examples:

```
windowcursor CURSOR bluearrow.cur

292 CURSOR redcross.cur
```

Of course, if you use symbolic IDs, you must create an .H file with the symbol's defines.

Contents of RESOURCES.H:

```
#define ID_CURSOR_CROSSHAIR   200 // these numbers are arbitrary
#define ID_CURSOR_GREENARROW  201
```

Contents of RESOURCES.RC:

```
#include "RESOURCES.H"

// here are the icon defines, note the use of C++ comments
ID_CURSOR_CROSSHAIR CURSOR crosshair.cur
ID_CURSOR_GREENARROW CURSOR greenarrow.cur
```

And there isn't any reason why a resource data file can't exist in another directory. For example, the greenarrow.cur might exist in the root directory in a CURSOR\ directory, like this:

```
ID_CURSOR_GREENARROW CURSOR C:\CURSOR\greenarrow.cur
```

> **TRICK**　I have created a few cursor .ICO files for this chapter. Try looking at them with your IDE, or just open up the directory and Windows will show the bitmap of each one by its filename!

Now that you know how to add a CURSOR resource to an .RC file, here's the code to load the resource from the application by string name only.

In an .RC file:

```
CrossHair CURSOR crosshair.CUR
```

In program code:

```
// Notice the use of hinstance instead of NULL.
winclass.hCursor = LoadCursor(hinstance, "CrossHair");
```

And to load a cursor with a symbolic ID defined in an .H file, here's what you would do:

In an .H file:

```
#define ID_CROSSHAIR   200
```

In an .RC file:

```
ID_CROSSHAIR CURSOR crosshair.CUR
```

In program code:

```
// Notice the use of hinstance instead of NULL.
winclass.hCursor = LoadCursor(hinstance, MAKEINTRESOURCE(ID_CROSSHAIR));
```

Again, you use the MAKEINTRESOURCE() macro to convert the symbolic integer ID into the form Windows wants.

All right, there's one little detail that may not have crossed your mind. So far you have only messed with the Windows class icon and cursor. But is it possible to manipulate the window icon and cursor at the window level? For example, you might want to create two windows and make the cursor change in each one. To do this, you *could* use this SetCursor() function:

```
HCURSOR SetCursor(HCURSOR hCursor);
```

Here, hCursor is the handle of the cursor retrieved by LoadCursor(). The only problem with this technique is that SetCursor() isn't that smart, so your application must do the tracking and change the cursor as the mouse moves from window to window. Here's an example of setting the cursor:

```
// load the cursor somewhere maybe in the WM_CREATE
HCURSOR hcrosshair = LoadCursor(hinstance, "CrossHair");

// later in program code to change the cursor…
SetCursor(hcrosshair);
```

For an example of both setting the window icon and the mouse cursor, take a look DEMO3_1.CPP on the CD-ROM. The following list contains excerpts of the important code sections that load the new icon and cursor:

```
// include resources
#include "DEMO3_1RES.H"
.
.
// changes to the window class definition
winclass.hIcon=
```

```
    LoadIcon(hinstance, MAKEINTRESOURCE(ICON_T3DX));
winclass.hCursor =
    LoadCursor(hinstance, MAKEINTRESOURCE(CURSOR_CROSSHAIR));
winclass.hIconSm = LoadIcon(hinstance, MAKEINTRESOURCE(ICON_T3DX));
```

Furthermore, the program uses the resource script named DEMO3_1.RC and the resource header named DEMO3_1RES.H.

Contents of DEMO3_1RES.H:

```
#define ICON_T3DX               100
#define CURSOR_CROSSHAIR        200
```

Contents of DEMO3_1.RC:

```
#include "DEMO3_1RES.H"

// note that this file has different types of resources
ICON_T3DX        ICON    t3dx.ico
CURSOR_CROSSHAIR CURSOR crosshair.cur
```

To build the application yourself, you'll need the following:

DEMO3_1.CPP—The main C/C++ file

DEMO3_1RES.H—The header with the symbols defined in it

DEMO3_1.RC—The resource script itself

T3DX.ICO—The bitmap data for the icon

CROSSHAIR.CUR—The bitmap data for the cursor

All these files should be in the same directory as your project. Otherwise, the compiler and linker will have trouble finding them. Once you create and run the program or use the precompiled DEMO3_1.EXE, you should see something like what's shown in Figure 3.5. Pretty cool, huh?

As an experiment, try opening the DEMO3_1.RC file with your IDE. Figure 3.6 shows what VC++ 6.0 does when I do this. However, you may get different results with your particular compiler, so don't tweak if it doesn't look the same. Alas, there is one point I want to make about the IDE before moving on. As I said, you can use the IDE to create both the .RC and .H file, but you'll have to read the manual on this yourself.

However, there is one problem with loading a handmade .RC file—if you save it with your IDE, it will undoubtedly be inflicted with a zillion comments, macros, #defines, and other garbage that Windows compilers like to see in .RC files. Thus, the moral of the story is that if you want to edit your handmade .RC files, do the editing by loading the .RC file as text. That way the compiler won't try to load it as an .RC, but just as plain ASCII text.

FIGURE 3.5

The output of
DEMO3_1.EXE
with custom ICON and
CURSOR.

FIGURE 3.6

The results of opening
the resource file
DEMO3_1.RC in
VC++ 6.0.

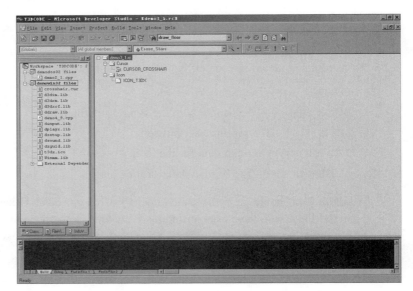

Creating String Table Resources

As I mentioned in the introduction, Windows supports string resources. Unlike
other resources, you can only have one string table that must contain all your strings.
Furthermore, string resources do *not* allow definition by string. Therefore, all string
tables defined in your .RC files must be accompanied by symbolic reference constants
and the associated .H header file to resolve the references.

I'm still not sure how I feel about string resources. Using them is equivalent to just
using header files, and in either case—string resources or plain header files—you
have to recompile. So I don't see the need for them! But if you really want to get
complicated, you can put string resources into .DLLs and the main program doesn't
have to be recompiled. However, I'm a scientist, not a philosopher, so who cares?

To create a string table in your .RC file, you must use the following syntax:

```
STRINGTABLE
{
ID_STRING1, "string 1"
ID_STRING2, "string 2"
.
.
.
}
```

Of course, the symbolic constants can be anything, as can the strings within the quotes. However, there is one rule: No line can be longer than 255 characters—including the constant itself.

Here's an example of an .H and .RC file containing a string table that you might use in a game for the main menu. The .H file contains

```
// the constant values are up to you
#define ID_STRING_START_GAME    16
#define ID_STRING_LOAD_GAME     17
#define ID_STRING_SAVE_GAME     18
#define ID_STRING_OPTIONS       19
#define ID_STRING_EXIT          20
```

The .RC file contains

```
// note the stringtable does not have a name since
// only one stringtable is allowed per .RC file
STRINGTABLE
{
ID_STRING_START_GAME,    "Kill Some Aliens"
ID_STRING_LOAD_GAME,     "Download Logs"
ID_STRING_SAVE_GAME,     "Upload Data"
ID_STRING_OPTIONS,       "Tweak The Settings"
ID_STRING_EXIT,          "Let's Bail!"
}
```

> **TIP**
> You can put almost anything you want in the strings, including printf() command specifiers like %d, %s, etc. You can't use escape sequences like "\n", but you can use octal sequences like \015 and so on.

Once you have created your resource files containing the string resources, you can use the LoadString() function to load in a particular string. Here's its prototype:

```
int LoadString(HINSTANCE hInstance,//handle of module withstring resource
               UINT uID,            //resource identifier
               LPTSTR lpBuffer,     //address of buffer for resource
               int nBufferMax);     //size of buffer
```

`LoadString()` returns the number of characters read, or 0 if the call was unsuccessful. Here's how you would use the function to load and save game strings during runtime:

```
// create some storage space
char load_string[80], // used to hold load game string
     save_string[80]; // used to hold save game string

// load in the first string and check for error
if (!LoadString(hinstance, ID_STRING_LOAD_GAME, load_string,80))
   {
   // there's an error!
   } // end if

// load in the second string and check for error
if (!LoadString(hinstance, ID_STRING_SAVE_GAME, save_string,80))
   {
   // there's an error!
   } // end if

// use the strings now
```

As usual, `hinstance` is the instance of your application as passed in `WinMain()`.

That wraps it up for string resources. If you can find a good use for them, email me at `ceo@xgames3d.com`!

Using Sound `.WAV` Resources

By now you're either getting very comfortable with resource scripting or you're so upset that you're about to hack into my Web site and destroy me. Remember, it wasn't me—it was Microsoft (`http://www.microsoft.com`) that invented all this stuff. I'm just trying to make sense of it too!

All right, dog. Now that I've given you my occasional disclaimer, let's continue by loading some sound resources!

Most games use one of two types of sounds:

- Digital `.WAV` files
- MIDI `.MID` music files

To my knowledge, the standard resources for Windows only support `.WAV` files, so I'm only going to show you how to create `.WAV` resources. However, even if `.MID`s aren't supported, you can always create a user-defined resource type. I'm not going to go into this, but the ability to do so is there.

The first thing you need is a `.WAV` file, which is simply a digital waveform of data that contains a number of 8- or 16-bit samples at some frequency. Typical sample frequencies for game sound effects are 11KHz, 22KHz, and 44KHz (for CD-level quality).

This stuff doesn't concern you yet, but I just wanted to give you a heads up. You'll learn all about digital sampling theory and .WAV files when we cover DirectSound. But for now, just know that sample size and rate are issues.

With that in mind, let's assume that you have a .WAV file on disk, and you want to add it to a resource file and be able to load and play it programmatically. Okay, let's go! The resource type for .WAV files is WAVE—there's a surprise. To add it to your .RC file, you would use the following syntax.

Method 1—By string name:

```
wave_name WAVE FILENAME.WAV
```

Examples:

```
BigExplosion WAVE expl1.wav

FireWeapons  WAVE fire.wav
```

Method 2—By integer ID:

```
ID_WAVE WAVE FILENAME.WAV
```

Examples:

```
DEATH_SOUND_ID WAVE die.wav
20             WAVE intro.wav
```

Of course, the symbolic constants would have to be defined elsewhere in an .H file, but you knew that!

At this point, we run into a little snag: WAVE resources are a little more complex than cursors, icons, and string tables. The problem is, to load them in takes a lot more programming than the other resources, so I'm going to hold off on showing you the way to load .WAV resources in a real game until later. For now, I'm just going to show you a trick to load and play a .WAV on-the-fly using the PlaySound() function. Here's its prototype:

```
BOOL PlaySound(LPCSTR pszSound, // string of sound to play
               HMODULE hmod,    // instance of application
               DWORD fdwSound); // flags parameter
```

Unlike LoadString(), PlaySound() is a little more complex, so let's take a closer look at each of the parameters:

- pszSound—This parameter is either the string name of the sound resource in the resource file or a filename on disk. Also, you can use the MAKEINTRESOURCE() and use a WAVE that is defined with a symbolic constant.

- hmod—The instance of the application to load the resource from. This is simply the hinstance of the application.

- fdwSound—This is the clincher. This parameter controls how the sound is loaded and played. Table 3.1 contains a list of the most useful values for fdwSound.

TABLE 3.1 Values for the fdwSound Parameter of PlaySound()

Value	Description
SND_FILENAME	The pszSound parameter is a filename.
SND_RESOURCE	The pszSound parameter is a resource identifier; hmod must identify the instance that contains the resource.
SND_MEMORY	A sound event's file is loaded in RAM. The parameter specified by pszSound must point to an image of a sound in memory.
SND_SYNC	Synchronous playback of a sound event. PlaySound() returns after the sound event is completed.
SND_ASYNC	The sound is played asynchronously, and PlaySound() returns immediately after beginning the sound. To terminate an asynchronously played waveform sound, call PlaySound() with pszSound set to NULL.
SND_LOOP	The sound plays repeatedly until PlaySound() is called again with the pszSound parameter set to NULL. You must also specify the SND_ASYNC flag to indicate an asynchronous sound event.
SND_NODEFAULT	No default sound event is used. If the sound cannot be found, PlaySound() returns silently without playing the default sound.
SND_PURGE	Sounds are to be stopped for the calling task. If pszSound is not NULL, all instances of the specified sound are stopped. If pszSound is NULL, all sounds that are playing on behalf of the calling task are stopped.
SND_NOSTOP	The specified sound event will yield to another sound event that is already playing. If a sound cannot be played because the resource needed to generate that sound is busy playing another sound, the function immediately returns FALSE without playing the requested sound.
SND_NOWAIT	If the driver is busy, the function returns immediately without playing the sound.

To play a WAVE sound resource with PlaySound(), there are four general steps:

1. Create the .WAV file itself and store it on disk.
2. Create the .RC resource script and associated H file.
3. Compile the resources along with your program code.
4. In your program, make a call to PlaySound() with either the WAVE resource name or the WAVE resource ID using the MAKEINTRESOURCE() macro.

Let's see some examples, shall we? Let's begin with a general RC file that has two sounds: one with a string name and the other with a symbolic constant. Let's name them RESOURCE.RC and RESOURCE.H. The files would look something like this:

The RESOURCE.H file would contain

```
#define SOUND_ID_ENERGIZE    1
```

The RESOURCE.RC file would contain

```
#include  "RESOURCE.H"

// first the string name defined sound resource
Telporter WAVE teleport.wav

// and now the symbolically defined sound
SOUND_ID_ENERGIZE WAVE energize.wav
```

Within your program, here's how you would play the sounds in different ways:

```
// to play the telport sound asynchronously
PlaySound("Teleporter", hinstance,
         SND_ASYNC | SND_RESOURCE);

// to play the telport sound asynchronously with looping
PlaySound("Teleporter", hinstance,
         SND_ASYNC | SND_LOOP | SND_RESOURCE);

// to play the energize sound asynchronously
PlaySound(MAKEINTRESOURCE(SOUND_ID_ENERGIZE), hinstance,
         SND_ASYNC | SND_RESOURCE);

// and if you simply wanted to play a sound off disk
// directly then you could do this
PlaySound("C:\path\filename.wav", hinstance,
         SND_ASYNC | SND_FILENAME);
```

And to stop all sounds, use the SND_PURGE flag with NULL as the sound name, like this:

```
// stop all sounds
PlaySound(NULL, hinstance, SND_PURGE);
```

Obviously, there are myriad flags options that you should feel free to experiment with. Anyway, you don't have any controls or menus yet, so it's hard to interact with the demo applications. However, as a simple demo of using sound resources, I have created DEMO3_2.CPP, which you can find on the disk. I would list it here, but 99 percent of it is just the standard template you have been using, and the sound code is nothing more than a couple lines of code identical to the earlier examples. The demo is pre-compiled, and you can run DEMO3_2.EXE yourself to see what it does.

However, I do want to show you the `.RC` and `.H` files that it uses. They are `DEMO3_2.RC` and `DEMO3_2RES.H`, respectively:

Contents of `DEMO3_2RES.H`:

```
// defines for sound ids
#define SOUND_ID_CREATE      1
#define SOUND_ID_MUSIC       2

// defines for icons
#define ICON_T3DX            500

// defines for cursors
#define CURSOR_CROSSHAIR     600
```

Contents of `DEMO3_2.RC`:

```
#include "DEMO3_2RES.H"


// the sound resources
SOUND_ID_CREATE    WAVE create.wav
SOUND_ID_MUSIC     WAVE techno.wav

// icon resources
ICON_T3DX ICON T3DX.ICO

// cursor resources
CURSOR_CROSSHAIR CURSOR CROSSHAIR.CUR
```

You'll notice that I have also included the `ICON` and `CURSOR` resources just to make things a little more exciting.

To make `DEMO3_2.CPP`, I took the standard Window demo we have been working with and added calls to sound code in two places: the `WM_CREATE` message and the `WM_DESTROY` message. In `WM_CREATE`, I start two sound effects. One of them says `Creating window` and stops, and the other is a short song in loop mode so it will continue to play. Then, in the `WM_DESTROY` section, I stop all sounds.

> **NOTE** I used the SND_SYNC flag as one of the flags for the first sound. This flag is needed because you are only allowed to play one sound at a time with PlaySound(), and I didn't want the second sound to stop the first one in midplay.

Here's the added code to the `WM_CREATE` and `WM_DESTROY` messages from `DEMO3_2.CPP`:

```
case WM_CREATE:
    {
    // do initialization stuff here
```

```
    // play the create sound once
    PlaySound(MAKEINTRESOURCE(SOUND_ID_CREATE),
            hinstance_app, SND_RESOURCE | SND_SYNC);

    // play the music in loop mode
    PlaySound(MAKEINTRESOURCE(SOUND_ID_MUSIC),
            hinstance_app, SND_RESOURCE | SND_ASYNC | SND_LOOP);

    // return success
    return(0);
    } break;


    case WM_DESTROY:
    {
        // stop the sounds first
        PlaySound(NULL, hinstance_app, SND_PURGE);

        // kill the application, this sends a WM_QUIT message
        PostQuitMessage(0);

        // return success
    return(0);
    } break;
```

Also, you'll notice that there is a variable, `hinstance_app`, used as the instance handle to the application in the `PlaySound()` calls. This is simply a global that saves the `hinstance` sent in `WinMain()`. It is coded right after the class definition in `WinMain()`, like this:

```
.
.
// save hinstance in global
hinstance_app = hinstance;

// register the window class
if (!RegisterClassEx(&winclass))
    return(0);
.
.
```

To build this application, you'll need the following files in your project:

DEMO3_2.CPP—The main source file.

DEMO3_2RES.H—The header file contains all the symbols.

DEMO3_2.RC—The resource script itself.

TECHNO.WAV—The music clip, which just needs to be in the working directory.

CREATE.WAV—The creating window vocalization, which needs to be the in working directory.

WINMM.LIB—The *Windows Multimedia Library Extensions*. This file is found in your compiler's LIB\ directory. You should add it to all projects from here on out.

MMSYSTEM.H—The header for WINMM.LIB. This is already included as part of DEMO3_2.CPP, and all my demos, for that matter. All you need to know is that you need it in your compiler's search path. It is part of the standard Win32 header file collection.

Last, But Not Least—Using the Compiler to Create .RC Files

Most compilers that generate Windows applications come with a quite extensive development environment, such as Microsoft's Visual Development Studio and so on. Each of these IDEs contains one or more tools to create various resources, resource scripts, and the associated headers automatically and/or with drag-and-drop technology.

The only problem with using these tools is that you have to learn them! Moreover, .RC files created with the IDE are in human-readable ASCII, but they have a great deal of added #defines and macros that the compiler adds to help automate and simplify the selection of constants and interfacing to MFC (wash your mouth out).

Since I'm a Microsoft VC++ 6.0 user these days, I'll briefly cover some key elements of using VC++ 6.0's resource manipulation support. First, there are two ways that you can add resources to your project:

Method 1—Using the File, New option from the main menu, you can add a number of resources to your project. Figure 3.7 is a screen shot of the dialog that comes up. When you add resources like icons, cursors, and bitmaps, the compiler IDE will automatically launch the Image Editor (as shown back in Figure 3.4). This is a crude image editing utility that you can use to draw your cursors and icons. If you add a menu resource (which we will get to in the next section), the menu editor will appear.

FIGURE 3.7
Adding resources
with File, New
in VC++ 6.0.

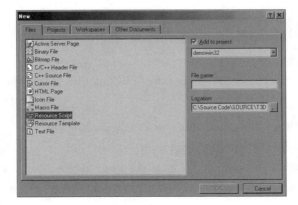

Method 2—This is a bit more flexible and contains all possible resource types, whereas method 1 only supports a few. To add any type of resource to your project, you can use the Insert, Resource option on the main menu. The dialog that appears is shown in Figure 3.8. However, this method does some stuff under the hood. Whenever you add a resource, you must add it to a resource script—right? Therefore, if your project doesn't already have a resource script, the compiler IDE will generate one for you and call it `SCRIPT*.RC`. In addition, both methods will end up generating (and/or modifying) a file named `RESOURCE.H`. This file contains the resource symbols, ID values, and so on that you define with the editor(s) in relation to resources.

FIGURE 3.8
Using Insert, Resource to add resources to your application.

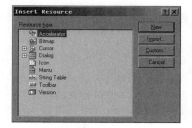

I would like to delve much more into the area of resource editing via the IDE, but it's really a topic for an entire chapter—if not a whole book. Please review your particular compiler's documentation on the subject. We aren't going to use many resources in this book, so the info I have already given you will suffice. Let's move on to a more complex type of resource—the menu.

Working with Menus

Menus are one of the coolest things about a Windows program and are ultimately the point of interaction between the user and your program (that is, if you're making a word processor <BG>). Knowing how to create and work with menus is very important because you might want to design simple tools to help create your game, or you might want to have a window-based front end to start up your game. And these tools will undoubtedly have menus—millions of them if you're making a 3D tool. Trust me! In either case, you need to know how to create, load, and respond to menus.

Creating a Menu

You can create an entire menu and all the associated files with the compiler's menu editor, but we'll do it manually because I can't be sure which compiler you're using. This way you'll learn what's in a menu description, too. But when you're writing a real application and creating a menu, most of the time you'll use the IDE editor because menus are just too complex to type in manually. It's like HTML code—when the Web started, it wasn't a big deal to make a home page with a text editor. Nowadays, it's nearly impossible to create a Web site without using a tool. (Speaking of Web site design, my friend needs work at `http://www.belmdesigngroup.com`—he has 15 kids to feed!)

Anyway, let's get started making menus! Menus are just like the other resources you have already worked with. They reside in an .RC resource script and must have an .H file to resolve any symbolic references, which are all IDs in the case of menus. (One exception: The name of the menu must be symbolic—no name strings.) Here's the basic syntax of a MENU description as you would see it in an .RC file:

```
MENU_NAME MENU DISCARDABLE
{ // you can use BEGIN instead of { if you wish

// menu definitions

} // you can use END instead of } if you wish
```

MENU_NAME can be a name string or a symbol, and the keyword DISCARDABLE is vestigial but necessary. Seems simple enough. Of course, the stuff in the middle is missing, but chill—I'm getting there!

Before I show you the code to define menu items and submenus, we need to get some terminology straight. For my little discussion, refer to the menu in Figure 3.9. It has two top-level menus, File and Help. The File menu contains four menu items: Open, Close, Save, and Exit. The Help menu contains only one menu item: About. So there are top-level menus and menu items within them. However, this is misleading because it's possible to also have menus within menus, or *cascading menus*. I'm not going to create any cascading menus, but the theory is simple: You just use a menu definition for one of the menu items itself. You can do this recursively, ad infinitum.

FIGURE 3.9
A menu bar with two submenus.

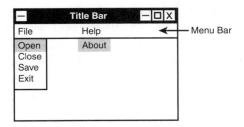

Now that we have the terminology straight, here's how you would implement the menu shown in Figure 3.9:

```
MainMenu MENU DISCARDABLE
{
POPUP "File"
```

```
    {
    MENUITEM "Open",   MENU_FILE_ID_OPEN
    MENUITEM "Close",  MENU_FILE_ID_CLOSE
    MENUITEM "Save",   MENU_FILE_ID_SAVE
    MENUITEM "Exit",   MENU_FILE_ID_EXIT
    } // end popup

POPUP "Help"
    {
    MENUITEM "About",   MENU_HELP_ABOUT
    } // end popup

} // end top level menu
```

Let's analyze the menu definition section by section. To begin with, the menu is named MainMenu. At this point we don't know if it's a name string or an ID, but since I usually capitalize all constants, it's a safe bet that it's a plain string. So that's what we'll make it. Moving on, there are two top-level menu definitions, beginning with the keyword POPUP—this is key. POPUP indicates that a menu is being defined with the following ASCII name and menu items.

The ASCII name must follow the keyword POPUP and be surrounded by quotes. The pop-up menu definition must be contained within { } or a BEGIN END block— whichever you like. (You Pascal people should be happy <BG>.)

Within the definition block, follow all of the menu items. To define a menu item, you use the keyword MENUITEM with the following syntax:

```
MENUITEM "name", MENU_ID
```

And that's it! Of course, in this example you haven't defined all the symbols, but you would do so in an .H file something like this:

```
// defines for the top level menu FILE
#define MENU_FILE_ID_OPEN          1000
#define MENU_FILE_ID_CLOSE         1001
#define MENU_FILE_ID_SAVE          1002
#define MENU_FILE_ID_EXIT          1003

// defines for the top level menu HELP
#define MENU_HELP_ABOUT            2000
```

TIP

Notice the values of the IDs. I have selected to start off the first top-level menu at 1000 and increment by 1 for each item. Then I increment by 1000 for the next top-level menu. Thus, each top-level menu differs by 1000, and each menu item within a menu differs by 1. This is a good convention that works well. And it's less filling.

I didn't define `"MainMenu"` because I want to refer to the menu by string rather than ID. This isn't the only way to do it. For example, if I put the single line of code

```
#define MainMenu 100
```

within the .H file with the other symbols, the resource compiler would automatically assume that I wanted to refer to the menu by ID. I would have to use `MAKEINTRESOURCE(MainMenu)` or `MAKEINTRESOURCE(100)` to refer to the menu resource. Get it? Alrighty, then!

TRICK

You'll notice that many menu items have hotkeys or shortcuts that you can use instead of manually selecting the top-level menu or menu item with the mouse. This is achieved by using the ampersand character (&). All you do is place the ampersand in front of the character that you want to be a shortcut or hotkey in a POPUP menu or a MENUITEM string. For example,

```
                MENUITEM "E&xit",  MENU_FILE_ID_EXIT
```

makes the x a hotkey, and

```
                POPUP "&File"
```

makes F a shortcut via Alt+F.

Now that you know how to create and define a menu, let's see how to load it into your application and attach it to a window.

Loading a Menu

There are a number of ways to attach a menu to a window. You can associate a single menu with all windows in a Windows class, or you can attach different menus to each window that you create. First, let's see how to associate a single menu with the Windows class itself.

In the definition of the Windows class, there is a line of code that defines what the menu is

```
winclass.lpszMenuName    = NULL;
```

All you need to do is assign it the name of the menu resource. Presto, that's it! Here's how

```
winclass.lpszMenuName    = "MainMenu";
```

And if `"MainMenu"` was a constant, you would do it this way:

```
winclass.lpszMenuName    = MAKEINTRESOURCE(MainMenu);
```

No problemo…almost. The only problem with this is that every window you create will have the same menu. To get around this, you can assign a menu to a window during creation by passing a menu handle. However, to get a menu handle, you must load the menu resource with `LoadMenu()`. Here's its prototype(s):

```
HMENU LoadMenu(HINSTANCE hInstance,// handle of application instance
 LPCTSTR lpMenuName);// menu name string or menu-resource identifier
```

If successful, `LoadMenu()` returns an `HMENU` handle to the menu resource, which you can then use.

Here's the normal `CreateWindow()` call you have been making, changed to load the menu `"MainMenu"` into the menu handle parameter:

```
// create the window
if (!(hwnd = CreateWindowEx(NULL,                    // extended style
                WINDOW_CLASS_NAME,    // class
                "Sound Resource Demo", // title
                WS_OVERLAPPEDWINDOW | WS_VISIBLE,
                0,0,       // initial x,y
                400,400,   // initial width, height
                NULL,      // handle to parent
                LoadMenu(hinstance, "MainMenu"),  // handle to menu
                hinstance,// instance of this application
                NULL)))    // extra creation parms
return(0);
```

Or if `MainMenu` was a symbolic constant, the call would look like this:

```
LoadMenu(instance, MAKEINTRESOURCE(MainMenu)),  // handle to menu
```

NOTE You may think I'm belaboring the difference between resources defined by string and by symbolic constant. However, taking into consideration that it's the number one cause of self-mutilation among Windows programmers, I think it's worth the extra work—don't you?

And of course, you can have many different menus defined in your `.RC` file, and thus you can attach a different one to each window.

The final method of attaching a menu to a window is by using the `SetMenu()` function, shown here:

```
BOOL SetMenu(HWND hWnd,     // handle of window to attach to
           HMENU hMenu); // handle of menu
```

SetMenu() takes the window handle, along with the handle to the menu (retrieved from LoadMenu()), and simply attaches the menu to the window. The new menu will override any menu previously attached. Here's an example listing, assuming that the Windows class defines the menu as NULL, as does the menu handle in the call to CreateWindow():

```cpp
// first fill in the window class structure
winclass.cbSize     = sizeof(WNDCLASSEX);
winclass.style      = CS_DBLCLKS | CS_OWNDC |
                              CS_HREDRAW | CS_VREDRAW;
winclass.lpfnWndProc    = WindowProc;
winclass.cbClsExtra     = 0;
winclass.cbWndExtra     = 0;
winclass.hInstance      = hinstance;
winclass.hIcon          = LoadIcon(hinstance,
                                MAKEINTRESOURCE(ICON_T3DX));
winclass.hCursor        = LoadCursor(hinstance,
                                MAKEINTRESOURCE(CURSOR_CROSSHAIR));
winclass.hbrBackground  = (HBRUSH)GetStockObject(BLACK_BRUSH);
winclass.lpszMenuName   = NULL; // note this is null
winclass.lpszClassName  = WINDOW_CLASS_NAME;
winclass.hIconSm        = LoadIcon(hinstance, MAKEINTRESOURCE(ICON_T3DX));

// register the window class
if (!RegisterClassEx(&winclass))
    return(0);

// create the window
if (!(hwnd = CreateWindowEx(NULL,                  // extended style
            WINDOW_CLASS_NAME,  // class
             "Menu Resource Demo", // title
             WS_OVERLAPPEDWINDOW | WS_VISIBLE,
             0,0,     // initial x,y
             400,400,  // initial width, height
             NULL,     // handle to parent
             NULL,     // handle to menu, note it's null
             hinstance,// instance of this application
             NULL)))   // extra creation parms
return(0);

// since the window has been created you can
// attach a new menu at any time

// load the menu resource
HMENU hmenuhandle = LoadMenu(hinstance, "MainMenu");

// attach the menu to the window
SetMenu(hwnd, hmenuhandle);
```

For an example of creating the menu and attaching it to the window using the second method (that is, during the window creation call), take a look at DEMO3_3.CPP on the CD-ROM and the associated executable, DEMO3_3.EXE, which is shown running in Figure 3.10.

FIGURE 3.10
Running
DEMO3_3.EXE.

The only two files of interest are the resource and header files, DEMO3_3RES.H and DEMO3_3.RC.

Contents of DEMO3_3RES.H:

```
// defines for the top level menu FILE
#define MENU_FILE_ID_OPEN               1000
#define MENU_FILE_ID_CLOSE              1001
#define MENU_FILE_ID_SAVE              1002
#define MENU_FILE_ID_EXIT              1003

// defines for the top level menu HELP
#define MENU_HELP_ABOUT               2000
```

Contents of DEMO3_3.RC:

```
#include "DEMO3_3RES.H"

MainMenu MENU DISCARDABLE
{
POPUP "File"
    {
    MENUITEM "Open",   MENU_FILE_ID_OPEN
    MENUITEM "Close", MENU_FILE_ID_CLOSE
    MENUITEM "Save",   MENU_FILE_ID_SAVE
    MENUITEM "Exit",   MENU_FILE_ID_EXIT
    } // end popup

POPUP "Help"
    {
    MENUITEM "About",   MENU_HELP_ABOUT
    } // end popup

} // end top level menu
```

To compile your own DEMO3_3.CPP executable, make sure to include

DEMO3_3.CPP—The main source.

DEMO3_3RES.H—The resource symbol header.

DEMO3_3.RC—The resource script file.

Try playing with DEMO3_3.EXE and the associated source. Change the menu items, add some more menus by adding more POPUP blocks to the .RC file, and get a good feel for it. Also, try making a cascading menu tree. (Hint: Just replace MENUITEM with a POPUP for one of the MENUITEMS making up a menu.)

Responding to Menu Event Messages

The only problem with DEMO3_3.EXE is that it doesn't do anything! True, my young Jedi. The problem is that you don't know how to detect the messages that menu item selections and manipulations generate. That is the topic of this section.

The Windows menu system generates a number of messages as you slide across top-level menu items as shown in Figure 3.11.

FIGURE 3.11
Window menu selection message flow.

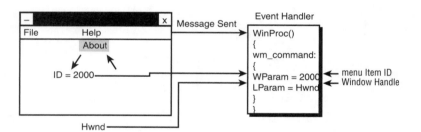

The message we are interested in is sent when a menu item is selected and then the mouse is released. This denotes a *selection*. Selections send a WM_COMMAND message to the WinProc() of the window that the menu is attached to. The particular menu item ID and various other data are stored in the wparam and lparam of the message, as shown here:

msg—WM_COMMAND

lparam—The window handle that the message was sent from

wparam—The ID of the menu item that was selected

TIP

Technically, you should extract the low-order WORD from wparam with the LOWORD() macro to be safe. This macro is part of the standard includes, so you have access to it.

So all you have to do is switch() on the wparam parameter, with the cases being the different MENUITEM IDs defined in your menu, and you're in business. For example, using the menu defined in DEMO3_3.RC, you would add the WM_COMMAND message handler and end up with something like this for your WinProc():

```
LRESULT CALLBACK WindowProc(HWND hwnd,
                            UINT msg,
                            WPARAM wparam,
                            LPARAM lparam)
{
// this is the main message handler of the system
PAINTSTRUCT        ps;    // used in WM_PAINT
HDC                      hdc;    // handle to a device context

// what is the message
switch(msg)
    {
    case WM_CREATE:
        {
    // do initialization stuff here

        // return success
        return(0);
    } break;

        case WM_COMMAND:
        {
        switch(LOWORD(wparam))
            {
            // handle the FILE menu
            case MENU_FILE_ID_OPEN:
            {
            // do work here
            } break;
            case MENU_FILE_ID_CLOSE:
            {
             // do work here
            } break;
            case MENU_FILE_ID_SAVE:
            {
            // do work here
            } break;
            case MENU_FILE_ID_EXIT:
            {
            // do work here
            } break;

            // handle the HELP menu
            case MENU_HELP_ABOUT:
            {
            // do work here
            } break;
```

```
        default: break;

        } // end switch wparam

      } break; // end WM_COMMAND

  case WM_PAINT:
  {
  // simply validate the window
  hdc = BeginPaint(hwnd,&ps);
  // you would do all your painting here
     EndPaint(hwnd,&ps);
     // return success
  return(0);
  } break;

  case WM_DESTROY:
  {
  // kill the application, this sends a WM_QUIT message
  PostQuitMessage(0);

     // return success
  return(0);
  } break;

     default:break;

  } // end switch

// process any messages that we didn't take care of
return (DefWindowProc(hwnd, msg, wparam, lparam));

} // end WinProc
```

It's so easy, it should be illegal! Of course, there are other messages that manipulate the top-level menus and menu items themselves, but you can look in your Win32 SDK Help for more info. (I rarely need to know more than if a menu item was clicked or not.)

As a solid example of doing something with menus, I have created a cool sound demo that allows you to exit the program via the main menu, play one of four different tele-porter sound effects, and finally pop up an About box via the Help menu. Also, the .RC file contains the sound, icon, and cursor resources. The program is DEMO3_4.CPP. Let's take a look at the resource script and header first.

Contents of DEMO3_4RES.H:

```
// defines for sounds resources
#define SOUND_ID_ENERGIZE   1
#define SOUND_ID_BEAM       2
#define SOUND_ID_TELEPORT   3
#define SOUND_ID_WARP       4
```

```
// defines for icon and cursor
#define ICON_T3DX        100
#define CURSOR_CROSSHAIR 200

// defines for the top level menu FILE
#define MENU_FILE_ID_EXIT              1000

// defines for play sound top level menu
#define MENU_PLAY_ID_ENERGIZE         2000
#define MENU_PLAY_ID_BEAM             2001
#define MENU_PLAY_ID_TELEPORT         2002
#define MENU_PLAY_ID_WARP             2003

// defines for the top level menu HELP
#define MENU_HELP_ABOUT               3000
```

Contents of DEMO3_4.RC:

```
#include "DEMO3_4RES.H"

// the icon and cursor resource
ICON_T3DX        ICON   t3dx.ico
CURSOR_CROSSHAIR CURSOR crosshair.cur

// the sound resources
SOUND_ID_ENERGIZE   WAVE energize.wav
SOUND_ID_BEAM       WAVE beam.wav
SOUND_ID_TELEPORT   WAVE teleport.wav
SOUND_ID_WARP       WAVE warp.wav

// the menu resource
SoundMenu MENU DISCARDABLE
{
POPUP "&File"
    {
    MENUITEM "E&xit",  MENU_FILE_ID_EXIT
    } // end popup

POPUP "&PlaySound"
    {
        MENUITEM   "Energize!",             MENU_PLAY_ID_ENERGIZE
        MENUITEM   "Beam Me Up",            MENU_PLAY_ID_BEAM
        MENUITEM   "Engage Teleporter",     MENU_PLAY_ID_TELEPORT
        MENUITEM   "Quantum Warp Teleport", MENU_PLAY_ID_WARP
    } // end popup

POPUP "Help"
    {
    MENUITEM "About",  MENU_HELP_ABOUT
    } // end popup

} // end top level menu
```

Based on the resource script and header file (which must be included in the main app), let's take a look at the code excerpts of DEMO3_4.CPP loading each resource. First, the loading of the main menu, icon, and cursor:

```
winclass.hCursor = LoadCursor(hinstance,
                       MAKEINTRESOURCE(CURSOR_CROSSHAIR));
winclass.lpszMenuName = "SoundMenu";
winclass.hIcon   = LoadIcon(hinstance, MAKEINTRESOURCE(ICON_T3DX));
winclass.hIconSm= LoadIcon(hinstance, MAKEINTRESOURCE(ICON_T3DX));
```

And now the fun part—the processing of the WM_COMMAND message that plays each sound, along with the handling of the Exit menu item and the display of the About box under Help. For brevity, I'll just show the WM_COMMAND message handler, since you've seen the entire WinProc() enough by now:

```
case WM_COMMAND:
     {
     switch(LOWORD(wparam))
          {
          // handle the FILE menu
          case MENU_FILE_ID_EXIT:
          {
          // terminate window
          PostQuitMessage(0);
          } break;

          // handle the HELP menu
          case MENU_HELP_ABOUT:
          {
          //  pop up a message box
          MessageBox(hwnd, "Menu Sound Demo",
                        "About Sound Menu",
                         MB_OK | MB_ICONEXCLAMATION);
          } break;
          // handle each of sounds
          case MENU_PLAY_ID_ENERGIZE:
          {
          // play the sound
          PlaySound(MAKEINTRESOURCE(SOUND_ID_ENERGIZE),
                   hinstance_app, SND_RESOURCE | SND_ASYNC);
          } break;
          case MENU_PLAY_ID_BEAM:
          {
          // play the sound
          PlaySound(MAKEINTRESOURCE(SOUND_ID_BEAM),
                   hinstance_app, SND_RESOURCE | SND_ASYNC);
          } break;
          case MENU_PLAY_ID_TELEPORT:
          {
          // play the sound
          PlaySound(MAKEINTRESOURCE(SOUND_ID_TELEPORT),
                     hinstance_app, SND_RESOURCE | SND_ASYNC);
```

```
            } break;
            case MENU_PLAY_ID_WARP:
            {
            // play the sound
            PlaySound(MAKEINTRESOURCE(SOUND_ID_WARP),
                        hinstance_app, SND_RESOURCE | SND_ASYNC);
            } break;

            default: break;
            } // end switch wparam
        } break; // end WM_COMMAND
```

And that's all I have to say about that.

As you can see, resources can do a lot and are fun to work with. Now let's take a break from resources and take an introductory crash course on the WM_PAINT message and basic GDI manipulation.

Introduction to GDI (Graphics Device Interface)

Thus far, the only experience you've had with GDI is the processing of the WM_PAINT message in the main event handler. Remember that GDI, or the Graphics Device Interface, is how all graphics are drawn under Windows when DirectX is not in use. Alas, you haven't yet learned how to actually draw anything on the screen with GDI, but this is very key because rendering on the screen is one of the most important parts of writing a video game. Basically, a game is just logic that drives a video display. In this section, I'm going to revisit the WM_PAINT message, cover some basic video concepts, and teach you how to draw text within your window. The next chapter will focus more heavily on GDI.

Understanding the WM_PAINT message is very important for standard GDI graphics and Windows programming because most Windows programs' displays revolve around this single message. In a DirectX game this isn't true, because DirectX, or more specifically DirectDraw or Direct3D, will do the drawing, but you still need to know GDI to write Windows applications.

The WM_PAINT Message Once Again

The WM_PAINT message is sent to your window's WinProc() whenever the window's client area needs repainting. Until now, you haven't done much processing on this event. Here's the standard WM_PAINT handler you have been using:

```
PAINTSTRUCT    ps;     // used in WM_PAINT
HDC            hdc;    // handle to a device context

case WM_PAINT:
    {
    // simply validate the window
```

```
hdc = BeginPaint(hwnd,&ps);
// you would do all your painting here
   EndPaint(hwnd,&ps);
   // return success
   return(0);
   } break;
```

Refer to Figure 3.12 for the following explanation. When a window is moved, resized, or in some way graphically obscured by another window or event, some or all of the window's client area must be redrawn. When this happens, a WM_PAINT message is sent and you must deal with it.

FIGURE 3.12

The WM_PAINT message.

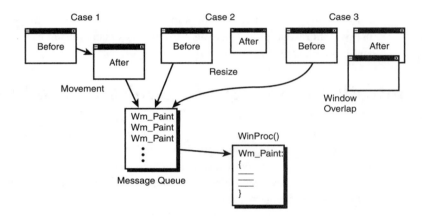

In the case of the preceding code example, the calls to BeginPaint() and EndPaint() accomplish a couple of tasks. First, they validate the client area, and second, they fill the background of your window with the background brush defined in the Windows class that the window was originally created with.

Now, if you want to do your own graphics within the BeginPaint()—EndPaint() call, you can. However, there is one problem: You will only have access to the portion of the window's client area that actually needs repainting. The coordinates of the invalid rectangle are stored in the rcPaint field of the ps (PAINTSTRUCT) returned by the call to BeginPaint():

```
typedef struct tagPAINTSTRUCT
        {
        HDC  hdc;        // graphics device context
        BOOL fErase;     // if TRUE then you must draw background
        RECT rcPaint;    // the RECT containing invalid region
        BOOL fRestore;   // internal
        BOOL fIncUpdate; // internal
        BYTE rgbReserved[32]; // internal
        } PAINTSTRUCT;
```

And to refresh your memory, here's the definition of RECT:

```
typedef struct _RECT
        {
        LONG left;    // left edge if rectangle
        LONG top;     // upper edge of rectangle
        LONG right;   // right edge of rectangle
        LONG bottom;  // bottom edge of rectangle
        } RECT;
```

In other words, referring back to Figure 3.12, the window is 400x400, but only the lower region of the window—300,300 to 400,400—needs repainting. Thus, the graphics device context returned by the call to BeginPaint() is only valid for this 100x100 region of your window! Obviously, this is a problem if you want to have access to the entire client area.

The solution to the problem has to do with gaining access to the graphics device context for the window directly without it being sent as part of a window update message via BeginPaint(). You can always get a graphics context for a window or hdc using the GetDC() function, as shown here:

```
HDC GetDC(HWND hWnd); // handle of window
```

You simply pass the window handle of the graphics device context you want to access, and the function returns a handle to it. If the function is unsuccessful, it returns NULL. When you're done with the graphics device context handle, you must give it back to Windows with a call to ReleaseDC(), as shown here:

```
int ReleaseDC(HWND hWnd, // handle of window
              HDC hDC);  // handle of device context
```

ReleaseDC() takes the window handle and the handle to the device context you previously acquired with GetDC().

NOTE   Windows-speak gets confusing when it comes to graphics device contexts. Technically, a handle to a device context can refer to more than one output device. For example, a device context could be a printer. Therefore, I usually refer to a graphics-only device context as a *graphics device context*. But the data type is HDC or *handle to device context*. So typically, I will define a graphics device context variable as HDC hdc, but sometimes I will also use HDC gdc because it makes more sense to me. In any case, just be aware that for this book, a *graphics device context* and a *device context* are interchangeable, and variables with the names hdc and gdc are of the same type.

Here's how you would use GetDC()—ReleaseDC() to do graphics:

```
HDC gdc = NULL; // this will hold the graphics device context

// get the graphics context for the window
if (!(gdc = GetDC(hwnd)))
    error();

// use the gdc here and do graphics - you don't know how yet!

// release the dc back to windows
ReleaseDC(hwnd, gdc);
```

Of course, you don't know how to do any graphics yet, but I'm getting there…. The important thing is that you now have another way to process a WM_PAINT message. However, there is one problem: When you make a call to GetDC()—ReleaseDC(), Windows has no idea that you have restored or validated the client area of your window. In other words, if you use GetDC()—ReleaseDC() in place of BeginPaint()—EndPaint(), you'll create another problem!

The problem is that BeginPaint()—EndPaint() sends a message to Windows indicating that the window contents have been restored (even if you don't make any graphics calls). Hence, Windows won't send any more WM_PAINT messages. On the other hand, if you replace BeginPaint()—EndPaint() with GetDC()—ReleaseDC() in the WM_PAINT handler, WM_PAINT messages will continue to be sent forever! Why? Because you must validate the window.

To validate the area of a window that needs repainting and tell Windows that you have restored the window, you *could* call BeginPaint()—EndPaint() after the call to GetDC()—ReleaseDC(), but this would be inefficient. Instead, use the call specifically designed for this, called ValidateRect():

```
BOOL ValidateRect(HWND hWnd,  // handle of window
 CONST RECT *lpRect); // address of validation rectangle coordinates
```

To validate a window, send the handle of the window along with the region you want to be validated in lpRect. In most cases, the region to validate would be the entire window. Thus, to use GetDC()—ReleaseDC() in the WM_PAINT handler, you would have to do something like this:

```
PAINTSTRUCT    ps;  // used in WM_PAINT
HDC         hdc; // handle to a device context
RECT           rect; // rectangle of window

case WM_PAINT:
    {
    // simply validate the window
    hdc = GetDC(hwnd);
    // you would do all your painting here
        ReleaseDC(hwnd,hdc);
```

```
// get client rectangle of window - use Win32 call
GetClientRect(hwnd,&rect);
// validate window
ValidateRect(hwnd,&rect);

// return success
return(0);
} break;
```

Notice the call to GetClientRect(). All this does is get the client rectangle coordinates for you. Remember, because a window can move around, it has two sets of coordinates: *window coordinates* and *client coordinates*. Window coordinates are relative to the screen, and client coordinates are relative to the upper left-hand corner of the window (0,0). Figure 3.13 shows this more clearly.

FIGURE 3.13
Window coordinates versus client coordinates.

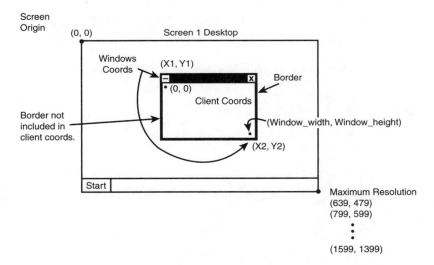

You must be saying, "Does it really need to be this hard?" Of course it does—it's Windows <BG>. Remember, the whole reason for all this drama in the WM_PAINT message handler is that you need to make sure that you can draw graphics anywhere you want in the client area of the window. This is only possible if you use GetDC()— ReleaseDC() or BeginPaint()—EndPaint() with a completely invalid window. However, we are trying to get the best of both worlds, and we're almost done. The final trick I want to show you is how to invalidate a window manually.

Consider this: If you could somehow invalidate the entire window within your WM_PAINT handler, you would be sure that the rcPaint field of the ps PAINTSTRUCT returned by BeginPaint() and the associated gdc would give you access to the entire client area of the window. To make this happen, you can manually enlarge the invalidated area of any window with a call to InvalidateRect(), as shown here:

```
BOOL InvalidateRect(HWND hWnd, // handle of window with
                               // changed update region
CONST RECT *lpRect,    // address of rectangle coordinates
BOOL bErase);          // erase-background flag
```

If bErase is TRUE, the call to BeginPaint() fills in the background brush; otherwise, it doesn't.

Simply call InvalidateRect() before the BeginPaint()—EndPaint() pair, and then, when you do call BeginPaint(), the invalid region will reflect the union of what it was and what you added to it with the InvalidatRect(). However, in most cases, you will use NULL as the lpRect parameter of InvalidateRect(), which will invalidate the entire window. Here's the code:

```
PAINTSTRUCT    ps;     // used in WM_PAINT
HDC            hdc;    // handle to a device context

case WM_PAINT:
  {
  // invalidate the entire window
  InvalidateRect(hwnd, NULL, FALSE);
  // begin painting
  hdc = BeginPaint(hwnd,&ps);
  // you would do all your painting here
  EndPaint(hwnd,&ps);
  // return success
  return(0);
  } break;
```

In most of the programs in this book, you'll use GetDC()—ReleaseDC() in places other than the WM_PAINT message, and BeginPaint()—EndPaint() solely in the WM_PAINT handler. Now let's move on to some simple graphics so you can at least print out text.

Video Display Basics and Color

At this point, I want to take time to discuss some concepts and terminology that relate to graphics and color on the PC. Let's start with some definitions:

- Pixel—A single addressable picture element on a raster display, such as a computer monitor.

- Resolution—The number of pixels that the display card supports, such as 640x480, 800x600, and so forth. The higher the resolution, the better the image, but the more memory required too. Table 3.2 lists some of the most common resolutions and their various memory requirements.

- Color depth—The number of bits or bytes that represent each pixel on the screen—bits per pixel (bpp). For example, if each pixel is represented by 8 bits (a single byte), the display can only support 256 colors because $2^8 = 256$. On the other hand, if each pixel is made of 16 bits (2 bytes), each pixel can support up to 16,384 colors or 2^{16}. Again, the greater the color depth, the greater the detail, but memory usage also goes up. Furthermore, 8-bit modes are usually palettized (which will be explained shortly), 16-bit modes are called high color, and 24- and 32-bit modes are called true and ultra-color respectively.

- Interlaced/noninterlaced displays—Computer displays are drawn by a scanning electron gun one line at a time—*rasterization.* Standard television draws two frames for each image. One frame consists of all the odd-numbered scan lines, and the other frame is all the even-numbered lines. When these two frames are drawn in quick succession, your eyes fuse them together and create a single image. This only looks acceptable for moving images and therefore is not acceptable for static imagery like a Windows display. However, some cards can only support high-resolution modes if they interlace. When interlacing occurs, you will usually see a flicker or shake in the display.

- Video RAM (VRAM)—The amount of onboard memory on a video card for representing the video image(s) on the screen or in texture memory.

- Refresh rate—The number of times per second the video image is refreshed, measured in Hz (hertz) or fps (frames per second). 60Hz is considered the minimum acceptable level these days, and some monitors and display cards go up to well over 100Hz for a rock-solid display.

- 2D acceleration—Hardware support on the video card that helps Windows and/or DirectX with 2D operations like bitmapped graphics, lines, circles, text, scaling, and so forth.

- 3D acceleration—Hardware support on the video card that helps Windows or DirectX/Direct3D with 3D graphics rendering.

These elements are shown in Figure 3.14.

TABLE 3.2   Video Resolutions and Memory Requirements

Resolution	Bits per Pixel	Memory (min-max)
320x200*	8	64KB
320x240*	8	64KB
640x480	8, 16, 24, 32	307KB–1.22MB
800x600	8, 16, 24, 32	480KB–1.92MB
1024x768	8, 16, 24, 32	786KB–3.14MB
1280x1024	8, 16, 24, 32	1.31MB–5.24MB
1600x1200	8, 16, 24, 32	1.92KB–7.68MB

These are considered to be Mode X modes and may not be supported by your video card.

Of course, Table 3.2 is only a sampling of possible video modes and color depths. Your card may support many more. The important thing is to understand that it's pretty easy to eat up 2MB to 4MB of video RAM. The good news is that most DirectX Windows games that you'll write will run in 320x240 or 640x480, which, depending on the color depth, a 2MB card can support.

FIGURE 3.14

The mechanics of a video display.

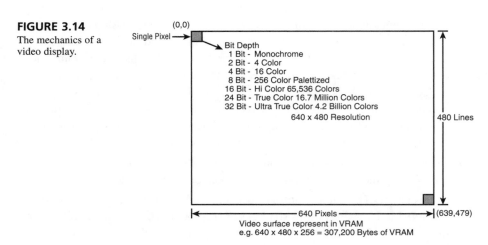

RGB and Palletized Modes

There are two ways to represent color on a video display: directly or indirectly. Direct color modes, or RGB modes, represent each pixel on the screen with either 16, 24, or 32 bits that represent the red, green, and blue components of the color (see Figure 3.15). This is possible due to the additive nature of the primary colors red, green, and blue.

Referring to Figure 3.15, you can see that for each possible color depth (16, 24, 32), there are a number of bits assigned to each color channel. Of course, with 16-bit and 32-bit color, these numbers aren't evenly divisible by 3; therefore, there might be an unequal amount of one of the color channels. For example, with 16-bit color modes, there are three different RGB encodings you might find:

- RGB (6.5.5)—Six bits of red, five bits of green, and five bits of blue.
- RGB (1.5.5.5)—One bit alpha and five bits each of red, green, and blue. Alpha is a transparency control.
- RGB (5.6.5)—Five bits of red, six bits of green, and five bits of blue. This is the most common, in my experience.

FIGURE 3.15

Color encoding for RGB modes.

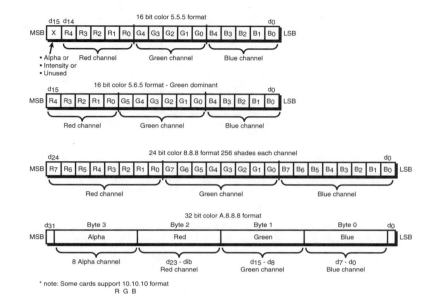

The 24-bit mode is almost always eight bits per channel. However, the 32-bit mode can be weird, and in most cases there are eight bits for alpha (transparency) and eight bits each for the red, green, and blue channels.

Basically, RGB modes give you control over the exact red, green, and blue components of each pixel on the screen. Palettized modes work on a principle called *indirection*. When there are only eight bits per pixel, you could decide to allocate the three bits for red, three bits for green, and maybe two bits for blue or some combination thereof. However, this would leave you with only a few shades of each of the primary colors, and that wouldn't be very exciting. Instead, 8-bit modes use a palette.

As shown in Figure 3.16, a *palette* is a table that has 256 entries, one for each possible value of a single byte—0 to 255. However, each of these entries is really composed of three 8-bit entries of red, green, and blue. In essence, it's a full RGB 24-bit descriptor. The *color lookup table (CLUT)* works like this: When a pixel in an 8-bit color mode is read from the screen, say value 26, the 26 is used as an index into the color table. Then the 24-bit RGB value for color descriptor index 26 is used to drive the red, green, and blue channels for the actual color that is sent to the display. In this way, you can have just 256 colors on the screen at once, but they can be from among 16.7 million colors or 24-bit RGB values. Figure 3.16 illustrates the lookup process.

FIGURE 3.16

How 256-color palettized modes work.

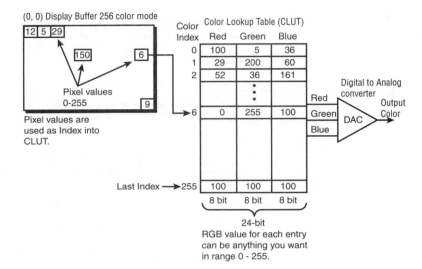

We are getting a little ahead of ourselves with all this color stuff, but I want to let you chew on the concepts a bit so that when you see them again during the DirectDraw discussion, it won't be for the first time. In fact, color is such a complex problem to work with in normal GDI-based Windows graphics that Windows has abstracted color to a 24-bit model no matter what. That way you don't have to worry about the details of color depth and such when you're programming. Of course, you will get better results if you *do* worry about them, but you don't *have* to.

Basic Text Printing

Windows has one of the most complex and robust text-rendering systems of any operating system I have ever seen. Of course, for most game programmers, printing the score is all we want to do, but it's nice to have nonetheless.

In reality, the GDI text engine is usually too slow to print text in a real-time game, so in the end you will need to design our own DirectX-based text engine. For now, though, let's learn how to print text with GDI. At the very least, it will help with debugging and output with demos.

There are two popular functions for printing text: TextOut() and DrawText(). TextOut() is the "ghetto ride" version of text output, and DrawText() is the Lexus. I usually use TextOut() because it's faster and I don't need all the bells and whistles of DrawText(), but we'll take a look at both. Here are their prototypes:

```
BOOL TextOut(HDC hdc, // handle of device context
     int nXStart,      // x-coordinate of starting position
     int nYStart,      // y-coordinate of starting position
     LPCTSTR lpString,// address of string
     int cbString);   // number of characters in string
```

```
int DrawText( HDC hDC,      // handle to device context
    LPCTSTR lpString,       // pointer to string to draw
    int nCount,             // string length, in characters
    LPRECT lpRect,          // ptr to bounding RECT
    UINT uFormat);          // text-drawing flags
```

Most of the parameters are self-explanatory. For TextOut(), you simply send the device context, the x,y coordinates to print to, and the ASCII string, along with the length of the string in bytes. DrawText(), on the other hand, is a little more complex. Because it does word wrapping and formatting, it takes a different approach to printing via a rendering RECT. Thus, DrawText() doesn't take an x,y for the place to start printing; instead, it takes a RECT that defines where the printing will take place within the window (see Figure 3.17). Along with the RECT of where to print it, you send some flags that describe *how* to print it (such as left-justified). Please refer to the Win32 documentation for all the flags, because there are a ton of them. I'll just stick to DT_LEFT, which is the most intuitive and justifies all text to the left.

FIGURE 3.17
The drawing RECT
of DrawText().

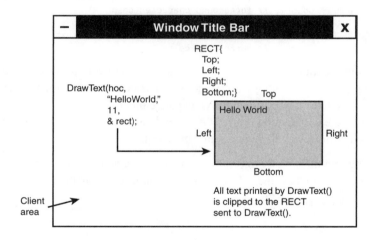

The only problem with both calls is that there's no mention of color. Hmmmm. That's almost as strange as *Boogie Nights,* but who cares? Anyway, thankfully there is a way to set both the foreground color of the text and the background color behind it, in addition to the transparency mode of the text.

The transparency mode of the text dictates how the characters will be drawn. Will the characters be stamped down with rectangular regions or drawn pixel by pixel as an overlay? Figure 3.18 illustrates transparency as it relates to printing. As you can see, when text is printed with transparency, it looks as if it was drawn right on top of the graphics. Without transparency, you can actually see that there is an opaque block surrounding each character, which obscures everything—very ugly.

FIGURE 3.18
Opaque and trans-
parent text printing.

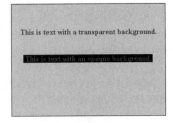

TIP	Rendering without transparency is faster, so if you're printing on a monochrome background and you can get away with it, do it!

Let's take a look at the functions to set the foreground and background colors of text:

```
COLORREF SetTextColor(HDC hdc, // handle of device context
 COLORREF Color); // foreground character color

COLORREF SetBkColor(HDC hdc, // handle of device context
 COLORREF color); // background color
```

Both functions take the graphics device context (from a call to GetDC() or BeginPaint()) along with the color to use in COLORREF format. Once you set these colors, they stay in flux until you change them. In addition, when you do set the colors, each function returns the current value so you can restore the old one when you're done or when your application exits.

You're almost ready to print, but this new COLORREF type has to be dealt with, don't you think? Okay, then! Here's the definition of COLORREF:

```
typedef struct tagCOLORREF
        {
        BYTE bRed;   // the red component
        BYTE bGreen; // the green component
        BYTE bBlue;  // the blue component
        BYTE bDummy; // unused
        } COLORREF;
```

So in memory, a COLORREF looks like 0x00bbggrr. Remember, PCs are *Little Endian*—that is, low BYTE to high BYTE. To create a valid COLORREF, you can use the RGB() macro, like this:

```
COLORREF red    = RGB(255,0,0);
COLORREF yellow = RGB(255,255,0);
```

And so forth. While we're looking at color descriptor structures, we might as well look at PALETTEENTRY because it is absolutely identical:

```
typedef struct tagPALETTEENTRY
        {
        BYTE peRed;      // red bits
        BYTE peGreen;    // green bits
        BYTE peBlue;     // blue bits
        BYTE peFlags;    // control flags
        } PALETTEENTRY;
```

peFlags can take on the values in Table 3.3. In most cases you will use PC_NOCOLLAPSE and PC_RESERVED, but for now just know they exist. The interesting thing that I wanted to point out, though, is the similarity between COLORREFs and PALETTEENTRYs. They are identical except for the interpretation of the last BYTE. Hence, in many cases they're interchangeable.

TABLE 3.3   PALLETTEENTRY Flags

Value	Description
PC_EXPLICIT	Specifies that the low-order word of the logical palette entry designates a hardware palette index. Advanced.
PC_NOCOLLAPSE	Specifies that the color be placed in an unused entry in the system palette instead of being matched to an existing color in the system palette.
PC_RESERVED	Specifies that the logical palette entry be used for palette animation. This flag prevents other windows from matching colors to the palette entry because the color frequently changes. If an unused system-palette entry is available, the color is placed in that entry. Otherwise, the color is not available for animation.

Now you're almost ready to print, but remember that there was the issue of transparency and how to set it. The function used to set the transparency mode is SetBkMode(), and here's its prototype:

```
int SetBkMode(HDC hdc,      // handle to device context
              int iBkMode); // transparency mode
```

The function takes the graphics device context along with the new transparency mode to switch to, which can be either TRANSPARENT or OPAQUE. The function returns the old mode so you can save it for later restoration.

Now you're ready to kick the tires and light the fires, big daddy. Here's how you would print some text:

```
COLORREF old_fcolor, // old foreground text color
         old_bcolor; // old background text color
```

```
int old_tmode; // old text transparency mode

// first get a graphics device context
HDC hdc = GetDC(hwnd);

// set the foreground color to green and save old one
old_fcolor = SetTextColor(hdc, RGB(0,255,0));

// set the background color to black and save old one
old_bcolor = SetBkColor(hdc, RGB(0,0,0));

// finally set the transparency mode to transparent
old_tmode = SetBkMode(hdc, TRANSPARENT);

// draw some text at (20,30)
TextOut(hdc, 20,30, "Hello",strlen("Hello"));

// now restore everything
SetTextColor(hwnd, old_fcolor);
SetBkColor(hwnd, old_bcolor);
SetBkMode(hwnd, old_tmode);

// release the device context
ReleaseDC(hwnd, hdc);
```

Of course, there is no law that you have to restore the old values, but I did it here just to show you how. Also, the color and transparency settings are valid as long as you have the handle to the device context. Let's say you wanted to draw some blue text in addition to the green text. You'd only have to change the text color to blue and then draw the text. You wouldn't have to set all three values again.

For an example of printing text using the preceding technique, take a look at DEMO3_5.CPP and the executable DEMO3_5.EXE. The demo creates a display of randomly positioned text strings in different colors all over the screen, as shown in Figure 3.19.

FIGURE 3.19
Random text output from DEMO3_5.EXE.

The following is an excerpt from the program's `WinMain()`, where all the action takes place:

```
// get the dc and hold it
HDC hdc = GetDC(hwnd);

// enter main event loop, but this time we use PeekMessage()
// instead of GetMessage() to retrieve messages
while(TRUE)
    {
    // test if there is a message in queue, if so get it
    if (PeekMessage(&msg,NULL,0,0,PM_REMOVE))
        {
        // test if this is a quit
        if (msg.message == WM_QUIT)
            break;

        // translate any accelerator keys
        TranslateMessage(&msg);

        // send the message to the window proc
        DispatchMessage(&msg);
        } // end if

    // main game processing goes here

    // set the foreground color to random
    SetTextColor(hdc, RGB(rand()%256,rand()%256,rand()%256));

    // set the background color to black
    SetBkColor(hdc, RGB(0,0,0));

    // finally set the transparency mode to transparent
    SetBkMode(hdc, TRANSPARENT);

    // draw some text at a random location
    TextOut(hdc,rand()%400,rand()%400,
    "GDI Text Demo!", strlen("GDI Text Demo!"));

    } // end while

// release the dc
ReleaseDC(hwnd,hdc);
```

As a second example of printing text, let's try doing something like updating a counter in response to the WM_PAINT message. Here's the code to do that:

```
char buffer[80]; // used to print string
static int wm_paint_count = 0; // track number of msg's


    case WM_PAINT:
    {
```

```
// simply validate the window
hdc = BeginPaint(hwnd,&ps);

    // set the foreground color to blue
    SetTextColor(hdc, RGB(0,0,255));
    // set the background color to black
    SetBkColor(hdc, RGB(0,0,0));
    // finally set the transparency mode to transparent
    SetBkMode(hdc, OPAQUE);

    // draw some text at (0,0) reflecting number of times
    // wm_paint has been called
    sprintf(buffer,"WM_PAINT called %d times    ", ++wm_paint_count);
    TextOut(hdc, 0,0, buffer, strlen(buffer));

    EndPaint(hwnd,&ps);
    // return success
return(0);
} break;
```

Take a look at DEMO3_6.CPP and the executable DEMO3_6.EXE on the CD-ROM to see the program in action. Notice that nothing will print until you move or overwrite the window. This is because WM_PAINT is generated only when there is some reason to restore or redraw the window, such as a movement or resize.

That's about it for basic printing. Of course, the DrawText() function does a lot more, but that's up to you. Also, you might want to look into fonts and that whole can of worms, but stuff like that is normally for full Windows GUI programming and is not really what we're trying to do in this book.

Handling Important Events

As you've been painfully learning, Windows is an event-based operating system. Responding to events is one of the most important aspects of a standard Windows program. This next section covers some of the more important events that have to do with window manipulation, input devices, and timing. If you can handle these basic events, you'll have more than you need in your Windows arsenal to handle anything that might come up as part of a DirectX game, which itself relies very little on events and the Windows operating system.

Window Manipulation

There are a number of messages that Windows sends to notify you that the user has manipulated your window. Table 3.4 contains a small list of some of the more interesting manipulation messages that Windows generates.

TABLE 3.4   Window Manipulation Messages

Value	Description
WM_ACTIVATE	Sent when a window is being activated or deactivated. This message is sent first to the window procedure of the top-level window being deactivated. It is then sent to the window procedure of the top-level window being activated.
WM_ACTIVATEAPP	Sent when a window belonging to an application other than the active window is about to be activated. The message is sent both to the application whose window is being activated and to the application whose window is being deactivated.
WM_CLOSE	Sent as a signal that a window or an application should terminate.
WM_MOVE	Sent after a window has been moved.
WM_MOVING	Sent to a window that the user is moving. By processing this message, an application can monitor the size and position of the drag rectangle and, if needed, change its size or position.
WM_SIZE	Sent to a window after its size has changed.
WM_SIZING	Sent to a window that the user is resizing. By processing this message, an application can monitor the size and position of the resizing rectangle and, if needed, change its size or position.

Let's take a look at WM_ACTIVATE, WM_CLOSE, WM_SIZE, and WM_MOVE and what they do. For each one of these messages, I'm going to list the message, wparam, lparam, and some comments, along with a short example WinProc() handler for the event.

Message: WM_ACTIVATE

Parameterization:

```
fActive       = LOWORD(wParam);        // activation flag
fMinimized    = (BOOL)HIWORD(wParam);  // minimized flag
hwndPrevious  = (HWND)lParam;          // window handle
```

The fActive parameter basically defines what is happening to the window—that is, is the window being activated or deactivated? This information is stored in the low-order word of wparam and can take on the values shown in Table 3.5.

TABLE 3.5   The Activation Flags for WM_ACTIVATE

Value	Description
WA_CLICKACTIVE	Activated by a mouse click.
WA_ACTIVE	The window has been activated by some means other than the mouse, such as the keyboard interface.
WA_INACTIVE	The window is being deactivated.

The fMinimized variable simply indicates if the window was minimized. This is true if the variable is nonzero. Lastly, the hwndPrevious value identifies the window being activated or deactivated, depending on the value of the fActive parameter. If the value of fActive is WA_INACTIVE, hwndPrevious is the handle of the window being activated. If the value of fActive is WA_ACTIVE or WA_CLICKACTIVE, hwndPrevious is the handle of the window being deactivated. This handle can be NULL. That makes sense, huh?

In essence, you use the WM_ACTIVATE message if you want to know when your application is being activated or deactivated. This might be useful if your application keeps track of every time the user Alt+Tabs away or selects another application with the mouse. On the other hand, when your application is reactivated, maybe you want to play a sound or do something. Whatever, it's up to you.

Here's how you code when your application is being activated in the main WinProc():

```
case WM_ACTIVATE:
{
// test if window is being activated
if (LOWORD(wparam)!=WA_INACTIVE)
    {
    // application is being activated
    } // end if
else
    {
    // application is being deactivated
    } // end else

} break;
```

Message: WM_CLOSE

Parameterization: None

The WM_CLOSE message is very cool. It is sent right before a WM_DESTROY and the following WM_QUIT are sent. The WM_CLOSE indicates that the user is trying to close your window. If you simply return(0) in your WinProc(), nothing will happen and the user won't be able to close your window! Take a look at DEMO3_7.CPP and the executable DEMO3_7.EXE to see this in action. Try killing the application—you won't be able to!

 Don't panic when you can't kill DEMO3_7.EXE. Simply press Ctrl+Alt+Del, and the Task Manager will come up. Then select and terminate the DEMO3_7.EXE application. It will cease to exist—just like service at electronics stores starting with "F" in Silicon Valley.

Here's the coding of the empty WM_CLOSE handler in the WinProc() as coded in
DEMO3_7.CPP:

```
case WM_CLOSE:
    {
    // kill message, so no further WM_DESTROY is sent
    return(0);
} break;
```

If making the user mad is your goal, the preceding code will do it. However, a better
use of trapping the WM_CLOSE message might be to include a message box that confirms
that the application is going to close or maybe do some housework. DEMO3_8.CPP and
the executable take this route. When you try to close the window, a message box asks
if you're certain. The logic flow for this is shown in Figure 3.20.

FIGURE 3.20
The logic flow for
WM_CLOSE.

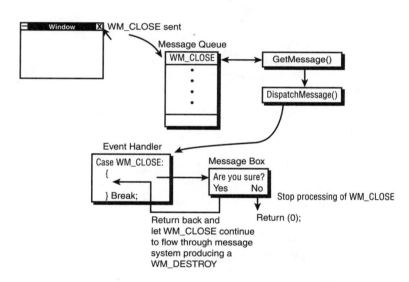

Here's the code from DEMO3_8.CPP that processes the WM_CLOSE message:

```
case WM_CLOSE:
{
// display message box
int result = MessageBox(hwnd,
    "Are you sure you want to close this application?",
            "WM_CLOSE Message Processor",
            MB_YESNO | MB_ICONQUESTION);

// does the user want to close?
if (result == IDYES)
    {
    // call default handler
    return (DefWindowProc(hwnd, msg, wparam, lparam));
```

```
    } // end if
else // throw message away
   return(0);

} break;
```

Cool, huh? Notice the call to the default message handler, DefWindowProc(). This occurs when the user answers Yes and you want the standard shutdown process to continue. If you knew how to, you could have sent a WM_DESTROY message instead, but since you haven't learned how to send messages yet, you just called the default handler. Either way is fine, though.

Next, let's take a look at the WM_SIZE message, which is an important message to process if you've written a windowed game and the user keeps resizing the view window!

Message: WM_SIZE

Parameterization:

```
fwSizeType = wParam;          // resizing flag
nWidth     = LOWORD(lParam);  // width of client area
nHeight    = HIWORD(lParam);  // height of client area
```

The fwSizeType flag indicates what kind of resizing just occurred, as shown in Table 3.6, and the low and high word of lParam indicate the new window client dimensions.

TABLE 3.6   Resizing Flags for WM_SIZE

Value	Description
SIZE_MAXHIDE	Message is sent to all pop-up windows when some other window is maximized.
SIZE_MAXIMIZED	Window has been maximized.
SIZE_MAXSHOW	Message is sent to all pop-up windows when some other window has been restored to its former size.
SIZE_MINIMIZED	Window has been minimized.
SIZE_RESTORED	Window has been resized, but neither the SIZE_MINIMIZED nor SIZE_MAXIMIZED value applies.

As I said, processing the WM_SIZE message can be very important for windowed games because when the window is resized, the graphics display must be scaled to fit. This will never happen if your game is running in full-screen, but in a windowed game, you can count on the user trying to make the window larger and smaller. When this happens, you must recenter the display and scale the universe or whatever to keep the image looking correct. As an example of tracking the WM_SIZE message, DEMO3_9.CPP prints out the new size of the window as it's resized. The code that tracks the WM_SIZE message in DEMO3_9.CPP is shown here:

```
case WM_SIZE:
        {
        // extract size info
        int width  = LOWORD(lparam);
        int height = HIWORD(lparam);

        // get a graphics context
        hdc = GetDC(hwnd);

        // set the foreground color to green
        SetTextColor(hdc, RGB(0,255,0));

        // set the background color to black
        SetBkColor(hdc, RGB(0,0,0));

        // set the transparency mode to OPAQUE
        SetBkMode(hdc, OPAQUE);

        // draw the size of the window
        sprintf(buffer,
        "WM_SIZE Called -  New Size = (%d,%d)", width, height);
        TextOut(hdc, 0,0, buffer, strlen(buffer));

        // release the dc back
        ReleaseDC(hwnd, hdc);

        } break;
```

WARNING

You should know that the code for the WM_SIZE message handler has a potential problem: When a window is resized, not only is a WM_SIZE message sent, but a WM_PAINT message is sent as well! Therefore, if the WM_PAINT message was sent after the WM_SIZE, the code in WM_PAINT could erase the background and thus the information just printed in WM_SIZE. Luckily, this isn't the case, but it's a good example of problems that can occur when messages are out of order or when they aren't sent in the order you think they are.

Last, but not least, let's take a look at the WM_MOVE message. It's almost identical to WM_SIZE, but it is sent when a window is moved rather than resized. Here are the details:

Message: WM_MOVE

Parameterization:

```
xPos = (int) LOWORD(lParam); // new horizontal position in screen coords
yPos = (int) HIWORD(lParam); // new vertical position in screen coords
```

WM_MOVE is sent whenever a window is moved to a new position, as shown in Figure 3.21. However, the message is sent *after* the window has been moved, not during the movement in real time. If you want to track the exact pixel-by-pixel movement of a window, you need to process the WM_MOVING message. However, in most cases, processing stops until the user is done moving your window.

FIGURE 3.21
Generation of the WM_MOVE message.

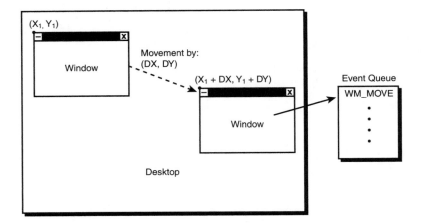

As an example of tracking the motion of a window, DEMO3_10.CPP and the associated executable DEMO3_10.EXE print out the new position of a window whenever it's moved. Here's the code that handles the WM_MOVE processing:

```
case WM_MOVE:
        {
        // extract the position
        int xpos = LOWORD(lparam);
        int ypos = HIWORD(lparam);

        // get a graphics context
        hdc = GetDC(hwnd);

        // set the foreground color to green
        SetTextColor(hdc, RGB(0,255,0));

        // set the background color to black
        SetBkColor(hdc, RGB(0,0,0));

        // set the transparency mode to OPAQUE
        SetBkMode(hdc, OPAQUE);

        // draw the size of the window
        sprintf(buffer,
        "WM_MOVE Called -  New Position = (%d,%d)", xpos, ypos);
        TextOut(hdc, 0,0, buffer, strlen(buffer));
```

```
// release the dc back
ReleaseDC(hwnd, hdc);

} break;
```

Well, that's it for window manipulation messages. There are a lot more, obviously, but you should have the hang of it now. The thing to remember is that there is a message for everything. If you want to track something, just look in the Win32 Help and sure enough, you'll find a message that works for you!

The next sections cover input devices so you can interact with the user (or yourself) and make much more interesting demos and experiments that will help you master Windows programming.

Banging on the Keyboard

Back in the old days, accessing the keyboard required sorcery. You had to write an interrupt handler, create a state table, and perform a number of other interesting feats to make it work. I'm a low-level programmer, but I can say without regret that I don't miss writing keyboard handlers anymore!

Ultimately you're going to use DirectInput to access the keyboard, mouse, joystick, and any other input devices. Nevertheless, you still need to learn how to use the Win32 library to access the keyboard and mouse. If for nothing else, you'll need them to respond to GUI interactions and/or to create more engaging demos throughout the book until we cover DirectInput. So without further ado, let's see how the keyboard works.

The keyboard consists of a number of keys, a microcontroller, and support electronics. When you press a key or keys on the keyboard, a serial stream of packets is sent to Windows describing the key(s) that you pressed. Windows then processes this stream and sends your window keyboard event messages. The beauty is that under Windows, you can access the keyboard messages in a number of ways:

- With the WM_CHAR message
- With the WM_KEYDOWN and WM_KEYUP messages
- With a call to GetAsyncKeyState()

Each one of these methods works in a slightly different manner. The WM_CHAR and WM_KEYDOWN messages are generated by Windows whenever a keyboard keypress or event occurs. However, there is a difference between the types of information encapsulated in the two messages. When you press a key on the keyboard, such as *A*, two pieces of data are generated:

- The scan code
- The ASCII code

The *scan code* is a unique code that is assigned to each key of the keyboard and has nothing to do with ASCII. In many cases, you just want to know if the *A* key was pressed; you're not interested in whether or not the Shift key was held down and so on. Basically, you just want to use the keyboard like a set of momentary switches. This is accomplished by using scan codes. The WM_KEYDOWN message is responsible for generating scan codes when keys are pressed.

The *ASCII code,* on the other hand, is *cooked* data. This means that if you press the *A* key on the keyboard but the Shift key is not pressed or the Caps Lock key is not engaged, you see an *a* character. Similarly, if you press Shift+A, you see an *A*. The WM_CHAR message sends these kinds of messages.

You can use either technique—it's up to you. For example, if you were writing a word processor, you would probably want to use the WM_CHAR message because the character case matters and you want ASCII codes, not virtual scan codes. On the other hand, if you're making a game and *F* is fire, *S* is thrust, and the Shift key is the shields, who cares what the ASCII code is? You just want to know if a particular button on the keyboard is up or down.

The final method of reading the keyboard is to use the Win32 function GetAsyncKeyState(), which tracks the last known keyboard state of the keys in a state table—like an array of Boolean switches. This is the method I prefer because you don't have to write a keyboard handler.

Now that you know a little about each method, let's cover the details of each one in order, starting with the WM_CHAR message.

The WM_CHAR message has the following parameterization:

Wparam—Contains the ASCII code of the key pressed.

Lparam—Contains a bit-encoded state vector that describes other special control keys that may be pressed. The bit encoding is shown in Table 3.7.

TABLE 3.7 Bit Encoding for the Key State Vector

Bits	Description
0–15	Contains the *repeat count*, which is the number of times the keystroke is repeated as a result of the user holding down the key.
16–23	Contains the scan code. The value depends on the *original equipment manufacturer (OEM)*.
24	Boolean; extended key flag. If it's 1, the key is an extended key, such as the right-hand Alt and Ctrl keys that appear on an enhanced 101- or 102-key keyboard.
29	Boolean; indicates whether the Alt key is down.

TABLE 3.7   Continued

Bits	Description
30	Boolean; indicates the previous key state. It's useless.
31	Boolean; indicates the key transition state. If the value is 1, the key is being released; otherwise, the key is being pressed.

To process the WM_CHAR message, all you have to do is write a message handle for it, like this:

```
case WM_CHAR:
{
// extract ascii code and state vector
int ascii_code = wparam;
int key_state  = lparam;

// take whatever action

} break;
```

And of course, you can test for various state information that might be of interest. For example, here's how you would test for the Alt key being pressed down:

```
// test the 29th bit of key_state to see if it's true

#define ALT_STATE_BIT 0x20000000
if (key_state & ALT_STATE_BIT)
    {
    // do something
    } // end if
```

And you can test for the other states with similar bitwise tests and manipulations.

As an example of processing the WM_CHAR message, I have created a demo that prints out the character and the state vector in hexadecimal form as you press keys. The program is called DEMO3_11.CPP, and the executable is of course DEMO3_11.EXE. Try pressing weird key combinations and see what happens. The code that processes and displays the WM_CHAR information is shown here, excerpted from the WinProc():

```
case WM_CHAR:
        {
        // get the character
        char ascii_code = wparam;
        unsigned int key_state = lparam;

        // get a graphics context
        hdc = GetDC(hwnd);

        // set the foreground color to green
        SetTextColor(hdc, RGB(0,255,0));
```

```
// set the background color to black
SetBkColor(hdc, RGB(0,0,0));

// set the transparency mode to OPAQUE
SetBkMode(hdc, OPAQUE);

// print the ascii code and key state
sprintf(buffer,"WM_CHAR: Character = %c   ",ascii_code);
TextOut(hdc, 0,0, buffer, strlen(buffer));

sprintf(buffer,"Key State = 0X%X   ",key_state);
TextOut(hdc, 0,16, buffer, strlen(buffer));

// release the dc back
ReleaseDC(hwnd, hdc);

} break;
```

The next keyboard event message, WM_KEYDOWN, is similar to WM_CHAR, except that the information is not "cooked." The key data sent during a WM_KEYDOWN message is the virtual scan code of the key rather than the ASCII code. The virtual scan codes are similar to the standard scan codes generated by any keyboard, except that virtual scan codes are guaranteed to be the same for any keyboard. For example, it's possible that the scan code for a particular key on your 101 AT–style keyboard is 67, but on another manufacturer's keyboard, it might be 69. See the problem?

The solution used in Windows was to virtualize the real scan codes to virtual scan code with a lookup table. As programmers, we use the virtual scan codes and let Windows do the translation. Thanks, Windows! With that in mind, here are the details of the WM_KEYDOWN message:

Message: WM_KEYDOWN

Wparam—Contains the virtual key code of the key pressed. Table 3.8 contains a list of the most common keys that you might be interested in.

lpara—Contains a bit-encoded state vector that describes other special control keys that may be pressed. The bit encoding is shown in Table 3.8.

TABLE 3.8 Virtual Key Codes

Symbol	Value (Hexadecimal)	Description
VK_BACK	08	Backspace key
VK_TAB	09	Tab key
VK_RETURN	0D	Enter key
VK_SHIFT	10	Shift key
VK_CONTROL	11	Ctrl key

TABLE 3.8   Continued

Symbol	Value (Hexadecimal)	Description
VK_PAUSE	13	Pause key
VK_ESCAPE	1B	Esc key
VK_SPACE	20	Spacebar
VK_PRIOR	21	Page Up key
VK_NEXT	22	Page Down key
VK_END	23	End key
VK_HOME	24	Home key
VK_LEFT	25	Left-arrow key
VK_UP	26	Up-arrow key
VK_RIGHT	27	Right-arrow key
VK_INSERT	2D	Ins key
VK_DELETE	2E	Del key
VK_HELP	2F	Help key
No VK_Code	30–39	0–9 keys
No VK_Code	41–5A	A–Z keys
VK_F1 - VK_F12	70–7B	F1–F12 keys

Note: The keys A–Z and 0–9 have no VK_ *codes. You must use the numeric constants or define your own.*

In addition to the WM_KEYDOWN message, there is WM_KEYUP. It has the same parameterization—that is, wparam contains the virtual key code, and lparam contains the key state vector. The only difference is that WM_KEYUP is sent when a key is released.

For example, if you're using the WM_KEYDOWN message to control something, take a look at the code here:

```
case WM_KEYDOWN:
    {
    // get virtual key code and data bits
    int virtual_code = (int)wparam;
    int key_state    = (int)lparam;

    // switch on the virtual_key code to be clean
    switch(virtual_code)
        {
        case VK_RIGHT:{ } break;
        case VK_LEFT: { } break;
        case VK_UP:   { } break;
        case VK_DOWN: { } break;
```

```
            // more cases…

            default: break;
            } // end switch

      // tell windows that you processed the message
      return(0);
      } break;
```

As an experiment, try modifying the code in DEMO3_11.CPP to support the WM_KEYDOWN message instead of WM_CHAR. When you're done, come back and we'll talk about the last method of reading the keyboard.

The final method of reading the keyboard is to make a call to one of the keyboard state functions: GetKeyboardState(), GetKeyState(), or GetAsyncKeyState(). We'll focus on GetAsyncKeyState() because it works for a single key, which is what you're usually interested in rather than the entire keyboard. If you're interested in the other functions, you can always look them up in the Win32 SDK. Anyway, GetAsyncKeyState() as the following prototype:

```
SHORT GetAsyncKeyState(int virtual_key);
```

You simply send the function the virtual key code that you want to test, and if the high bit of the return value is 1, the key is pressed. Otherwise, it's not. I have written some macros to make this easier:

```
#define KEYDOWN(vk_code) ((GetAsyncKeyState(vk_code) & 0x8000) ? 1 : 0)
#define KEYUP(vk_code)   ((GetAsyncKeyState(vk_code) & 0x8000) ? 0 : 1)
```

The beauty of using GetAsyncKeyState() is that it's not coupled to the event loop. You can test for keypresses anywhere you want. For example, say that you're writing a game and you want to track the arrow keys, spacebar, and maybe the Ctrl key. You don't want to have to deal with the WM_CHAR or WM_KEYDOWN messages; you just want to code something like this:

```
if (KEYDOWN(VK_DOWN))
   {
   // move ship down, whatever
   } // end if

if (KEYDOWN(VK_SPACE))
   {
   // fire weapons maybe?
   } // end if

// and so on
```

Similarly, you might want to detect when a key is released to turn something off. Here's an example:

```
if (KEYUP(VK_ENTER))
   {
   // disengage engines
   } // end if
```

As an example, I have created a demo that continually prints out the status of the
arrow keys in the `WinMain()`. It's called `DEMO3_12.CPP`, and the executable is
`DEMO3_12.EXE`. Here's the `WinMain()` from the program:

```
int WINAPI WinMain(HINSTANCE hinstance,
           HINSTANCE hprevinstance,
           LPSTR lpcmdline,
              int ncmdshow)
{
WNDCLASSEX winclass; // this will hold the class we create
HWND       hwnd;     // generic window handle
MSG        msg;      // generic message
HDC        hdc;      // graphics device context

// first fill in the window class stucture
winclass.cbSize       = sizeof(WNDCLASSEX);
winclass.style        = CS_DBLCLKS | CS_OWNDC |
                        CS_HREDRAW | CS_VREDRAW;
winclass.lpfnWndProc  = WindowProc;
winclass.cbClsExtra   = 0;
winclass.cbWndExtra   = 0;
winclass.hInstance    = hinstance;
winclass.hIcon        = LoadIcon(NULL, IDI_APPLICATION);
winclass.hCursor      = LoadCursor(NULL, IDC_ARROW);
winclass.hbrBackground    = (HBRUSH)GetStockObject(BLACK_BRUSH);
winclass.lpszMenuName    = NULL;
winclass.lpszClassName    = WINDOW_CLASS_NAME;
winclass.hIconSm       = LoadIcon(NULL, IDI_APPLICATION);

// save hinstance in global
hinstance_app = hinstance;

// register the window class
if (!RegisterClassEx(&winclass))
    return(0);

// create the window
if (!(hwnd = CreateWindowEx(NULL,                        // extended style
              WINDOW_CLASS_NAME,       // class
               "GetAsyncKeyState() Demo", // title
               WS_OVERLAPPEDWINDOW | WS_VISIBLE,
               0,0,      // initial x,y
               400,300,  // initial width, height
               NULL,       // handle to parent
               NULL,       // handle to menu
             hinstance,// instance of this application
               NULL)))    // extra creation parms
```

```
return(0);

// save main window handle
main_window_handle = hwnd;

// enter main event loop, but this time we use PeekMessage()
// instead of GetMessage() to retrieve messages
while(TRUE)
    {
    // test if there is a message in queue, if so get it
    if (PeekMessage(&msg,NULL,0,0,PM_REMOVE))
        {
        // test if this is a quit
        if (msg.message == WM_QUIT)
            break;

        // translate any accelerator keys
        TranslateMessage(&msg);

        // send the message to the window proc
        DispatchMessage(&msg);
        } // end if

    // main game processing goes here

    // get a graphics context
    hdc = GetDC(hwnd);

    // set the foreground color to green
    SetTextColor(hdc, RGB(0,255,0));

    // set the background color to black
    SetBkColor(hdc, RGB(0,0,0));

    // set the transparency mode to OPAQUE
    SetBkMode(hdc, OPAQUE);

    // print out the state of each arrow key
    sprintf(buffer,"Up Arrow: = %d    ",KEYDOWN(VK_UP));
    TextOut(hdc, 0,0, buffer, strlen(buffer));

    sprintf(buffer,"Down Arrow: = %d    ",KEYDOWN(VK_DOWN));
    TextOut(hdc, 0,16, buffer, strlen(buffer));

    sprintf(buffer,"Right Arrow: = %d    ",KEYDOWN(VK_RIGHT));
    TextOut(hdc, 0,32, buffer, strlen(buffer));

    sprintf(buffer,"Left Arrow: = %d    ",KEYDOWN(VK_LEFT));
    TextOut(hdc, 0,48, buffer, strlen(buffer));
```

```
        // release the dc back
        ReleaseDC(hwnd, hdc);

    } // end while

// return to Windows like this
return(msg.wParam);

} // end WinMain
```

Also, if you review the entire source on the CD-ROM, you'll notice that there aren't handlers for `WM_CHAR` or `WM_KEYDOWN` in the message handler for the window. The fewer messages that you have to handle in the `WinProc()`, the better! In addition, this is the first time you have seen action taking place in the `WinMain()`, which is the section that does all game processing. Notice that there isn't any timing delay or synchronization, so the redrawing of the information is free-running (in other words, working as fast as possible). In Chapter 4, "Windows GDI, Controls, and Last-Minute Gift Ideas," you'll learn about timing issues, how to keep processes locked to a certain frame rate, and so forth. But for now, let's move on to the mouse.

Squeezing the Mouse

The mouse is probably the most innovative computer input device ever created. You point and click, and the mouse pad is physically mapped to the screen surface—that's innovation! Anyway, as you guessed, Windows has a truckload of messages for the mouse, but we're going to look at only two classes of messages: `WM_MOUSEMOVE` and `WM_*BUTTON*`.

Let's start with the `WM_MOUSEMOVE` message. The first thing to remember about the mouse is that its position is relative to the client area of the window that it's in. Referring to Figure 3.22, the mouse sends coordinates relative to the upper-left corner of your window, which is 0,0.

Other than that, the `WM_MOUSEMOVE` message is fairly straightforward.

Message: `WM_MOUSEMOVE`

Parameterization:

```
int mouse_x = (int)LOWORD(lParam);
int mouse_y = (int)HIWORD(lParam);

int buttons = (int)wParam;
```

Basically, the position is encoded as 16-bit entries in the `lparam`, and the buttons are encoded in the `wparam`, as shown in Table 3.9.

FIGURE 3.22
The details of
mouse movement.

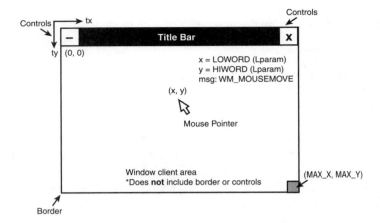

TABLE 3.9   Button Bit Encoding for WM_MOUSEMOVE

Value	Description
MK_LBUTTON	Set if the left mouse button is down.
MK_MBUTTON	Set if the middle mouse button is down.
MK_RBUTTON	Set if the right mouse button is down.
MK_CONTROL	Set if the Ctrl key is down.
MK_SHIFT	Set if the Shift key is down.

So all you have to do is logically AND one of the bit codes with the button state and
you can detect which mouse buttons are pressed. Here's an example of tracking the
x,y position of the mouse along with the left and right buttons:

```
case WM_MOUSEMOVE:
{
// get the position of the mouse
int mouse_x = (int)LOWORD(lParam);
int mouse_y = (int)HIWORD(lParam);

// get the button state
int buttons = (int)wParam;

// test if left button is down
if (buttons & MK_LBUTTON)
    {
    // do something
    } // end if
```

```
// test if right button is down
if (buttons & MK_RBUTTON)
    {
    // do something
    } // end if

} break;
```

Trivial, ooh, trivial! For an example of mouse tracking, take a look at DEMO3_13.CPP on the CD-ROM and the associated executable. The program prints out the position of the mouse and the state of the buttons using the preceding code as a starting point. Take note of how the button changes only when the mouse is moving. This is as you would expect because the message is sent when the mouse moves rather than when the buttons are pressed.

Now for some details. The WM_MOUSEMOVE is not guaranteed to be sent all the time. You may move the mouse too quickly for it to track. Therefore, don't assume that you'll be able to track individual mouse movements that well—for the most part, it's not a problem, but keep it in mind. Also, you should be scratching your head right now, wondering how to track if a mouse button was pressed *without* a mouse move. Of course, there is a whole set of messages just for that. Take a look at Table 3.10.

TABLE 3.10   Mouse Button Messages

Message	Description
WM_LBUTTONDBLCLK	The left mouse button was double-clicked.
WM_LBUTTONDOWN	The left mouse button was pressed.
WM_LBUTTONUP	The left mouse button was released.
WM_MBUTTONDBLCLK	The middle mouse button was double-clicked.
WM_MBUTTONDOWN	The middle mouse button was pressed.
WM_MBUTTONUP	The middle mouse button was released.
WM_RBUTTONDBLCLK	The right mouse button was double-clicked.
WM_RBUTTONDOWN	The right mouse button was pressed.
WM_RBUTTONUP	The right mouse button was released.

The button messages also have the position of the mouse encoded just as they were for the WM_MOUSEMOVE message—in the wparam and lparam. For example, to test for a left button double-click, you would do this:

```
case WM_LBUTTONDBLCLK:
    {
    // extract x,y and buttons
    int mouse_x = (int)LOWORD(lParam);
    int mouse_y = (int)HIWORD(lParam);
```

```
// do something intelligent

// tell windows you handled it
return(0);
} // break;
```

Killer! I feel powerful, don't you? Windows is almost at our feet!

Sending Messages Yourself

The last subject I want to talk about is sending messages yourself. There are two ways to do this:

SendMessage()—Sends a message to the window immediately for processing. The function returns after the WinProc() if the receiving window has processed the message.

PostMessage()—Sends a message to the window's message queue and returns immediately. Use this if you don't care if there's a delay until your message is processed, or your message is a low priority.

The prototypes for both functions are similar, as shown here:

```
LRESULT SendMessage(HWND hWnd,   // handle of destination window
                    UINT Msg,  // message to send
                    WPARAM wParam,  // first message parameter
                    LPARAM lParam); // second message parameter
```

The return value of SendMessage() is the value returned by the WinProc() of the window you sent it to.

```
BOOL PostMessage(HWND hWnd,   // handle of destination window
                 UINT Msg,  // message to post
                 WPARAM wParam,  // first message parameter
                 LPARAM lParam ); // second message parameter
```

If PostMessage() is successful, it returns a nonzero value. Notice that this is different than SendMessage(). Why? Because SendMessage() actually calls the WinProc(), whereas PostMessage() simply places a message in the message queue of the receiving window without any processing.

You might be wondering why you would ever want to send a message yourself. There are millions of reasons—literally. This is something that the designers of Windows want you to do, and it's how you make things happen in a windowed environment. For example, in the next chapter, when I talk about window controls like buttons, sending messages is the only way to talk to a control window! But if you're like me, you like something a little more concrete.

In all of the demos thus far, you've terminated them by double-clicking the close box or pressing Alt+F4. Wouldn't be nice if you could programmatically kill the window?

You know that either a WM_CLOSE or WM_DESTROY will do the job. If you use WM_CLOSE, it gives your application a little warning, whereas WM_DESTROY is a little tighter. But either way you go, you just do something like this:

```
SendMessage(hwnd, WM_DESTROY,0,0);
```

Or if you want a little delay and don't mind if your message is queued, use PostMessage():

```
PostMessage(hwnd, WM_DESTROY,0,0);
```

In both cases, the application will terminate—unless there is steering logic in the WM_DESTROY handler, of course. But the next question is when to launch the message. Well, that's up to you. In a game, you might track the Esc key and exit on that. Here's how you would do that using the KEYDOWN() macro in the main event loop:

```
if (KEYDOWN(VK_ESCAPE))
    SendMessage(hwnd,WM_CLOSE,0,0);
```

For an example of the preceding code in action, take a look at DEMO3_14.CPP and the executable DEMO3_14.EXE on the CD-ROM. The program implements the logic in the preceding code exactly. As an experiment, try changing the message to WM_DESTROY and using PostMessage(), too.

> **WARNING**
>
> Sending messages out of the main event loop can cause unforeseen problems. For example, in the preceding case, you're killing the window out of the main event loop by sending a message directly to the WinProc() with SendMessage(). However, if you normally assume that the event handling is done in the main event loop, you might create an *out-of-execution-order* bug. This means that you assume that event B happens after event A, but in some cases event B happens before event A. Whammo! This is a typical problem when you're sending messages, so make sure to think it out. PostMessage() is usually safer because it doesn't leapfrog the event queue.

Finally, there is also a way to send your own custom messages called WM_USER. Simply send a message with SendMessage() or PostMessage(), using WM_USER as the message type. You can put whatever you want in the wparam and lparam values. For example, you might want to use the WM_USER message to create a number of virtual messages for a memory management system that you have. Take a look:

```
// defines for memory manager
#define ALLOC_MEM      0
#define DEALLOC_MEM    1
```

```
// send WM_USER message, use the lparam as amount of memory
// and the wparam as the type of operation
SendMessage(hwnd, WM_USER, ALLOC_MEM, 1000);
```

Then, in your `WinProc()`, you might have

```
case WM_USER:
{
// what is the virtual message
switch(wparam)
     {
     case ALLOC_MEM: { } break;
     case DEALLOC_MEM: { } break;
     // .. more messages
     } // end switch
} break;
```

As you can see, you can encode whatever you want in the `wparam` and `lparam` and do something as stupid as I just did for this example, or something that is more interesting!

Summary

Thank God! I never thought I would finish this chapter—did you? We covered resources, menus, input devices, GDIs, and messaging—wow! A good Windows treatise is about 3,000 pages, so you can see my dilemma. But I think we covered a lot of good material that's useful. After the next chapter, you'll know everything you need to work with Windows.

CHAPTER 4

Windows GDI, Controls, and Last-Minute Gift Ideas

"Compuuuuterrr?"
—Scotty, Star Trek IV

This is the last chapter on pure Windows programming. Thank the gods! Anyway, we're going to cover more on using the Graphics Device Interface. Stuff like drawing pixels, lines, and simple shapes. Then we'll touch on timing and finish off with Windows' child controls. Finally, we'll take everything and create our first shot at the T3D Game Console template application that we'll use throughout the remainder of the book as a starting point for all demos. Here's a list of the main topics:

- Advanced GDI programming, pens, brushes, and rendering
- Child controls
- System timing functions
- Sending messages
- Getting information
- The T3D Game Console

Advanced GDI Graphics

As I've mentioned, GDI is horribly slow when compared to DirectX. However, GDI is good at everything and it's the native rendering engine for Windows itself. This means if you create any tools or standard GUI applications, knowing your way around GDI is an asset. Moreover, knowing how to mix GDI and DirectX is a way to leverage the power of GDI's functionality to emulate functions you haven't completed in your DirectX programming. Hence, GDI has utility as a slow software emulation for functions you might write down the road in your game design. Bottom line—you need to know it.

What I'm going to do now is cover a few basic GDI operations. You can always learn more by perusing the Win32 SDK, but the basic skill set you'll learn here will more than prepare you for figuring out any GDI function. It's like Comdex—if you've seen one, you've seen them all.

Under the Hood with the Graphics Device Context

In Chapter 3, "Advanced Windows Programming," you saw the type handle to device context, or *HDC,* a number of times. This of course is the data type that represents a handle to a device context. In our case, the device context has been a graphics device context type, but there are others like printer contexts. Anyway, you might be wondering what exactly a graphics device context is? What does it really mean? Both are good questions.

A graphics device context is really a description of the video graphics card installed in your system. Therefore, when you have access to a graphics device context or handle this really means that stuffed away somewhere is an actual description of the video card in your system and its resolution and color capabilities. This information is needed for any graphics call you might make to GDI. In essence, the HDC handle you supply to any GDI function is used to reference whatever important information about your video system that a function needs to operate with. And that's why you need a graphics device context.

Furthermore, the graphics device context tracks software settings that you may change throughout the life of your program. For example, GDI uses a number of graphics objects such as *pens*, *brushes*, *line styles*, and more. These basic data descriptions are used by GDI to draw any graphics primitives that you may request. Therefore, even though the current pen color is something that you might set and isn't intrinsic to your video card, the graphics device context still tracks it. In this way, the graphics device context is not only a hardware description of your video system, but a repository of information that records your settings and stores them for you, so that the GDI calls you make can use those settings rather than explicitly sending them along with the call. This way you can save a lot of parameters for GDI calls. With that in mind, let's take a look at how to render graphics with GDI.

Color, Pens, and Brushes

If you think about it, there aren't that many types of objects that you can draw on a computer screen. Sure, there are an unlimited number of shapes and colors you can draw them with, but the types of objects are very limited. There are *points*, *lines*, and *polygons*. Everything else is really a combination of these types of primitive objects.

The approach that GDI takes is something like that of a painter. A painter paints pictures with colors, pens, and brushes—work with me on this <BG>. GDI works in the same manner, with the following definitions:

- **Pens**—These are used to draw lines or contours. They have color, thickness, and a line style.

- **Brushes**—These are used to fill in any closed objects. They have color, style, and can even be bitmaps. Take a look at Figure 4.1 for a detailed labeling.

FIGURE 4.1
A brush, labeled in detail.

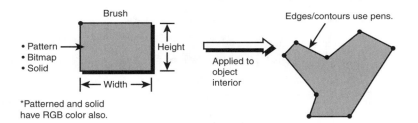

Before we get into pens and brushes and actually using them, I want to take a minute to look at the situation. GDI likes to use only one pen, and one brush at a time. Sure, you can have many pens and brushes at your disposal, but only one of each is active in the current graphics device context. This means that you must "select objects" into the graphics device context to use them.

Remember, the graphics device context is not only a description of the video card and its services, but a description of the current drawing tools. Pens and brushes are primary examples of tools that the context tracks and that you must select in and out of the graphics context. This process is called *selection*. As your program runs, you'll select in a new pen and then select it out later, and maybe select in and out different brushes and so on. The thing to remember is that once a drawing object is selected into the context it's used until it is changed.

Finally, whenever you create a new pen or brush, you must delete it when you're done. This is important because Windows GDI has only so many slots for pen and brush handles and you could run out! But we'll get to that in a minute. Okay, so let's cover pens first, and then brushes.

Working with Pens

The handle to a pen is called HPEN. Here's how you would create a NULL pen.

```
HPEN pen_1 = NULL;
```

pen_1 is just a handle to a pen, but pen_1 hasn't been filled in or defined yet with the desired information. This operation is accomplished in one of two ways:

- Using a stock object
- Creating a user-defined pen

Remember, *stock objects*, or stock anything, are just objects that Windows has a few default types for to get you started. In the case of pens, there are a couple of pen types already defined, but they are very limited. You can use the GetStockObject() function shown in the following line to retrieve a number of different object handles, including pen handles, brushes, and fonts.

```
HGDIOBJ GetStockObject(int fnObject); // type of stock object
```

The function simply takes the type of stock object you desire and returns a handle to it. The types of pens that are pre-defined stock objects are shown in Table 4.1.

TABLE 4.1   Stock Object Types

Value	Description
BLACK_PEN	Black pen.
NULL_PEN	Null pen.
WHITE_PEN	White pen.
BLACK_BRUSH	Black brush.
DKGRAY_BRUSH	Dark gray brush.
GRAY_BRUSH	Gray brush.
HOLLOW_BRUSH	Hollow brush (equivalent to NULL_BRUSH).
LTGRAY_BRUSH	Light gray brush.
NULL_BRUSH	Null brush (equivalent to HOLLOW_BRUSH).
WHITE_BRUSH	White brush.
ANSI_FIXED_FONT	Standard Windows fixed-pitch (monospace) system font.
ANSI_VAR_FONT	Standard Windows variable-pitch (proportional space) system font.
DEFAULT_GUI_FONT	Windows 95 only: Default font for user interface objects such as menus and dialog boxes.
OEM_FIXED_FONT	Original equipment manufacturer (OEM) dependent fixed-pitch (monospace) font.

TABLE 4.1 Continued

Value	Description
SYSTEM_FONT	The system font. By default, Windows uses the system font to draw menus, dialog box controls, and text. In Windows versions 3.0 and later, the system font is a proportionally spaced font; earlier versions of Windows used a monospace system font.
SYSTEM_FIXED_FONT	Fixed-pitch (monospace) system font used in Windows versions earlier than 3.0. This stock object is provided for compatibility with earlier versions of Windows.

As you can see from Table 4.1, there aren't a whole lot of pens to select from (that's a little GDI humor—get it?). Anyway, here's an example of how you would create a white pen:

```
HPEN white_pen = NULL;
white_pen = GetStockObject(WHITE_PEN);
```

Of course, GDI knows nothing about white_pen because it hasn't been selected into the graphics device context, but we're getting there.

A more interesting method of creating pens is to create them yourself by defining their color, line style, and width in pixels. The function used to create a pen is called CreatePen() and is shown here:

```
HPEN CreatePen(int fnPenStyle,    // style of the pen
               int nWidth,        // width of pen in pixels
               COLORREF crColor); // color of pen
```

The nWidth and crColor parameters are easy enough to understand, but the fnPenStyle needs a little explanation.

In most cases you probably want to draw solid lines, but in some cases you might need a dashed line to represent something in a charting program. You could draw a number of lines all separated by a little space to make a dashed line, but why not let GDI do it for you? The line style facilitates this functionality. GDI logically ANDs or masks a line style filter as it's rendering lines. This way, you can draw lines that are composed of dots and dashes, or solid pixels, or whatever one-dimensional entity you want. Table 4.2 contains the valid line styles that you can choose from.

TABLE 4.2 Line Styles for CreatePen()

Style	Description
PS_NULL	Pen is invisible.
PS_SOLID	Pen is solid.
PS_DASH	Pen is dashed.

TABLE 4.2 Continued

Style	Description
PS_DOT	Pen is dotted.
PS_DASHDOT	Pen has alternating dashes and dots.
PS_DASHDOTDOT	Pen has alternating dashes and double dots.

As an example, let's create three pens, each 1 pixel wide, with solid style:

```
// the red pen, notice the use of the RGB macro
HPEN red_pen = CreatePen(PS_SOLID, 1, RGB(255,0,0));

// the green pen, notice the use of the RGB macro
HPEN green_pen = CreatePen(PS_SOLID, 1, RGB(0,255,0));

// the blue pen, notice the use of the RGB macro
HPEN blue_pen = CreatePen(PS_SOLID, 1, RGB(0,0,255));
```

And let's also make a white dashed pen:

```
HPEN white_dashed_pen = CreatePen(PS_DASHED, 1, RGB(255,255,255));
```

Simple enough? Now, that we have a little to work with, let's take a look at how to select pens into the graphics device context. We still don't know how to draw anything, but now is a good time to see the concept.

To select any GDI object into the graphics device context use the SelectObject() function shown here:

```
HGDIOBJ SelectObject(HDC hdc,           // handle of device context
                     HGDIOBJ hgdiobj); // handle of object
```

SelectObject() takes the handle to the graphics context along with the object to be selected. Notice that SelectObject() is *polymorphic*, meaning that it can take many different handle types. The reason for this is that all handles to graphics objects are also subclasses of the data type *HGDIOBJs* (handles to GDI objects), so everything works out. Also, the function returns the current handle of the object you are de-selecting from the context. In other words, if you select a new pen into the context, obviously you must select the old one out. Therefore, you can save the old handle and restore it later if you wish. Here's an example of selecting a pen into the context and saving the old one:

```
HDC hdc; // the graphics context, assume valid

// create the blue
HPEN blue_pen = CreatePen(PS_SOLID, 1, RGB(0,0,255));

HPEN old_pen = NULL; // used to store old pen
```

```
// select the blue pen in and save the old pen
old_pen = SelectObject(hdc, blue_pen);

// do drawing...

// restore the old pen
SelectObject(hdc, old_pen);
```

And then finally, when you are done with pens that you have created either with `GetStockObject()` or `CreatePen()`, you must destroy them. This is accomplished with `DeleteObject()`, which, similar to `SelectObject()`, is polymorphic and can delete many object types. Here's its prototype:

```
BOOL DeleteObject(HGDIOBJ hObject); // handle to graphic object
```

WARNING Be careful when you destroy pens. If you delete an object that is currently selected or try to select an object that is currently deleted chances are you will cause an error and possibly a GP Fault.

NOTE I haven't been doing too much error checking, but obviously this is an issue. In a real program, you should always check the return type of your function calls to see if they are successful; otherwise, there could be trouble.

The next question is when to actually call `DeleteObject()` on graphics objects. Typically, you will do this at the end of the program. However, if you create hundreds of objects, use them, and won't use them for the remainder of the program, you should delete them then and there. This is because Windows GDI only has limited resources. As an example, here's how to release and destroy the group of pens we created in the earlier example:

```
DeleteObject(red_pen);
DeleteObject(green_pen);
DeleteObject(blue_pen);
DeleteObject(white_dashed_pen);
```

WARNING Try not to delete objects you have already deleted. It can cause unpredictable results.

Painting with Brushes

Let's talk more about brushes. Brushes are similar to pens in most ways except how they look. Brushes are used to fill in graphic objects, whereas pens are used to outline objects or draw simple lines. However, all the same principles are in flux. The handle to a brush is called an HBRUSH. And to define a blank brush object you would do something like:

```
HBRUSH brush_1 = NULL;
```

To actually make the brush look like something, you can either use a stock brush type from Table 4.1 via GetStockObject() or define one yourself. For example, here's how to create a light gray stock brush:

```
brush_1 = GetStockObject(LTGRAY_BRUSH);
```

Bam, baby! Too easy, huh? To create more interesting brushes you can select the fill pattern type and color just as you can for pens. Unfortunately GDI broke brushes up into two classes: *solid* and *hatched*. I think this is stupid—GDI should allow all brushes to be hatched and then simply have a solid type, but whatever! The function to create a solid fill brush is called CreateSolidBrush() and is shown here:

```
HBRUSH CreateSolidBrush(COLORREF crColor); // brush color
```

To create a green solid brush all you have to do is this:

```
HBRUSH green_brush = CreateSolidBrush(RGB(0,255,0));
```

To select it into the graphics device context, do this:

```
HBRUSH old_brush = NULL;

old_brush = SelectObject(hdc, green_brush);

// draw something with brush

// restore old brush
SelectObject(hdc, old_brush);
```

At the end of your program you would delete the brush object like this:

```
DeleteObject(green_brush);
```

Starting to all make sense? In a nutshell, you create an object, select it, use it, delete it. Okay, let's next see how to create patterned or hatched brushes.

To create a hatch brush, use the CreateHatchBrush() function shown here:

```
HBRUSH CreateHatchBrush(int fnStyle,      // hatch style
                        COLORREF clrref); // color value
```

The style of the brush can be one of the values listed in Table 4.3.

TABLE 4.3   Style Values for `CreateHatchBrush()`

Value	Description
HS_BDIAGONAL	45-degree downward left-to-right hatch
HS_CROSS	Horizontal and vertical crosshatch
HS_DIAGCROSS	45-degree crosshatch
HS_FDIAGONAL	45-degree upward left-to-right hatch
HS_HORIZONTAL	Horizontal hatch
HS_VERTICAL	Vertical hatch

As a final example of brushes, let's create a cross-hatched red brush:

```
HBRUSH red_hbrush = CreateHatchBrush(HS_CROSS, RGB(255,0,0));
```

Select it into the device context:

```
HBRUSH old_brush = SelectObject(hdc, red_hbrush);
```

Finally, restore the old brush and delete the red brush we created:

```
SelectObject(hdc, old_brush);
DeleteObject(red_hbrush);
```

Of course, we still aren't doing anything with the pens or brushes, but we will <BG>.

Points, Lines, Polygons, and Circles

Now that you have the concept of pens and brushes under your belt, it's time to see how these entities are used in real programs to draw objects. Let's start with the simplest of all graphic objects—the point.

Straight to the Point

Drawing points with GDI is trivial and doesn't require a pen or a brush. That's because a point is a single pixel and selecting a pen or brush wouldn't have much of an effect. To draw a point within the client area of your window, you need the HDC to your window along with the coordinates and the color you wish to draw it with. However, you don't need to select the color or anything like that—you simply make a function call to `SetPixel()` with all this information. Take a look:

```
COLORREF SetPixel(HDC hdc, // the graphics context
                  int x,   // x-coordinate
                  int y,   // y-coordinate
                  COLORREF crColor); // color of pixel
```

The function takes the HDC to the window along with the (x,y) coordinate and the color. The function then plots the pixel and returns the color actually plotted. You see,

if you are in a 256 color mode and request an RGB color that doesn't exist, GDI will
plot a closest match to the color for you, and either way return the RGB color that
was *actually* plotted. If you're a little uneasy about the exact meaning of the (x,y)
coordinates that you send the function, take a look at Figure 4.2. The figure depicts a
window and the coordinate system that Windows GDI uses, which is an inverted
Quadrant I *Cartesian* system—meaning that the x increases from left to right and y
increases from top to bottom.

FIGURE 4.2

Windows coordinates
in relation to standard
Cartesian coordinates.

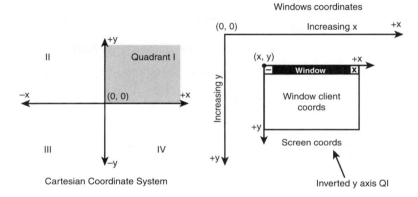

Technically, GDI has other mapping modes, but this is the default and the one to use
for all GDI and DirectX. Notice that the origin (0,0) is in the upper-left corner of the
window's client area. It's possible to get an HDC for the entire window with
GetWindowDC() rather than GetDC(). The difference is that if you use GetWindowDC()
to retrieve an HDC, the graphics device context is for the whole window. With an
HDC retrieved with GetWindowDC(), you can draw over everything including the window controls, not just the client area. Here's an example of drawing 1000 randomly
positioned and colored pixels on a window that we know is 400x400:

```
HWND hwnd; // assume this is valid
HDC hdc;   // used to access window

// get the dc for the window
hdc = GetDC(hwnd);

for (int index=0; index<1000; index++)
    {
    // get random position
    int x = rand()%400;
    int y = rand()%400;

    COLORREF color = RGB(rand()%255,rand()%255,rand()%255);
    SetPixel(hdc, x,y, color);

    } // end for index
```

As an example of plotting pixels, take a look at DEMO4_1.CPP and DEMO4_1.EXE. They illustrate the preceding code, but in a continuous loop. Figure 4.3 is a screen shot of the program running.

FIGURE 4.3
Demo of pixel-plotting program
DEMO4_1.EXE.

Getting a Line on Things

Now let's draw the next most primitive complex—the line. To draw a line, we need to create the pen, and then make a call to the line-drawing function. Under GDI, lines are little more complex than that. GDI likes to draw lines in a three-step process:

1. Create a pen and select it into the graphics device contexts. All lines will be drawn with this pen.
2. Set the initial position of the line.
3. Draw a line from the initial position to the destination position (the destination position becomes the initial position of the next segment).
4. Go to step 3 and draw more segments if desired.

In essence, GDI has a little invisible cursor that tracks the current starting position of a line to be drawn. This position must be set by you if you want to draw a line, but once it's set, GDI will update it with every segment you draw, facilitating drawing complex objects like polygons. The function to set the initial position of the line cursor is called MoveToEx():

```
BOOL MoveToEx(HDC hdc, // handle of device context
              int X,   // x-coordinate of new current position
              int Y,   // y-coordinate of new current position
              LPPOINT lpPoint ); // address of old current position
```

Suppose you wanted to draw a line from (10,10) to (50,60). You would first make a call to MoveToEx() like this:

```
// set current position
MoveToEx(hdc, 10,10,NULL);
```

Notice the NULL for the last position parameter. If you wanted to save the last position, do this:

```
POINT last_pos; // used to store last position

// set current position, but save last
MoveToEx(hdc, 10,10, &last_pos);
```

By the way, here's a POINT structure again just in case you forgot:

```
typedef struct tagPOINT
        { // pt
        LONG x;
        LONG y;
        } POINT;
```

Okay, once you have set the initial position of the line, you can draw a segment with a call to LineTo():

```
BOOL LineTo(HDC hdc,  // device context handle
            int xEnd, // destination x-coordinate
            int yEnd);// destination y-coordinate
```

As a complete example of drawing a line, here's how you would draw a solid green line from (10,10) to (50,60):

```
HWND hwnd; // assume this is valid

// get the dc first
HDC hdc = GetDc(hwnd);

// create the green pen
HPEN green_pen = CreatePen(PS_SOLID, 1, RGB(0,255,0));

// select the pen into the context
HPEN old_pen = SelectObject(hdc, green_pen);

// draw the line
MoveToEx(hdc, 10,10, NULL);
LineTo(hdc,50,60);

// restore old pen
SelectObject(hdc, old_pen);

// delete the green pen
DeleteObject(green_pen);

// release the dc
ReleaseDC(hwnd, hdc);
```

If you wanted to draw a triangle with the vertices (20,10), (30,20), (10,20), here's the line drawing code:

```
// start the triangle
MoveToEx(hdc, 20,10, NULL);

// draw first leg
LineTo(hdc,30,20);

// draw second leg
LineTo(hdc,10,20);

// close it up
LineTo(hdc,20,10);
```

You can see why using the `MoveToEx()`—`LineTo()` technique is useful.

As a working example of drawing lines, take a look at `DEMO4_2.CPP`. It draws randomly positioned lines at high speed. Its output is shown in Figure 4.4.

FIGURE 4.4
Line-drawing
program
`DEMO4_2.EXE`.

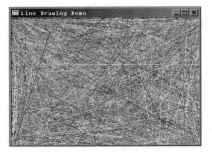

Getting Rectangular

The next step up in the food chain of GDI is *rectangles*. Rectangles are drawn with both a pen and a brush (if the interior is filled). Therefore, rectangles are the most complex GDI primitives thus far. To draw a rectangle, use the `Rectangle()` function that follows:

```
BOOL Rectangle(HDC hdc, // handle of device context
     int nLeftRect,     // x-coord. of bounding
                        // rectangle's upper-left corner
     int nTopRect,      // y-coord. of bounding
                        // rectangle's upper-left corner
     int nRightRect,    // x-coord. of bounding
                        // rectangle's lower-right corner
     int nBottomRect);  // y-coord. of bounding
                        // rectangle's lower-right corner
```

`Rectangle()` draws a rectangle with the current pen and brush as shown in Figure 4.5.

FIGURE 4.5
Using the
`DrawRectangle()`
function.

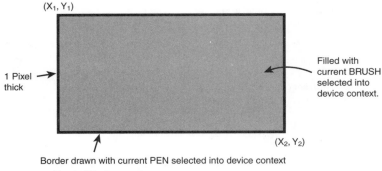

(X_1, Y_1)

1 Pixel
thick →

Filled with
current BRUSH
selected into
device context.

(X_2, Y_2)

↑
Border drawn with current PEN selected into device context

X_1: nLeftRect
X_2: nRightRect
Y_1: nTopRect
Y_2: nBottomRect

NOTE

I want to bring a very important detail to your attention. The coordinates you send `Rectangle()` are for the bounding box of the rectangle. This means that if the line style is NULL and you have a solid rectangle, it will be 1 pixel smaller on all four sides.

There are also two other more specific functions to draw rectangles `FillRect()` and `FrameRect()`, shown here:

```
int FillRect(HDC hDC,    // handle to device context
    CONST RECT *lprc,    // pointer to structure with rectangle
    HBRUSH hbr);         // handle to brush

int FrameRect( HDC hDC,// handle to device context
    CONST RECT *lprc,    // pointer to rectangle coordinates
    HBRUSH hbr);         // handle to brush
```

`FillRect()` draws a filled rectangle without a border pen and includes the upper-left corner, but not the lower-right corner. Therefore, if you want a rectangle to fill in (10,10) to (20,20) you must send (10,10) to (21,21) in the RECT structure. `FrameRect()` on the other hand, just draws a hollow rectangle with a border. Surprisingly, `FrameRect()` uses a brush rather than a pen. Any ideas? In any case, here's an example of drawing a solid filled rectangle with the `Rectangle()` function:

```
// create the pen and brush
HPEN blue_pen = CreatePen(PS_SOLID, 1, RGB(0,0,255));
HBRUSH red_brush = CreateSolidBrush(RGB(255,0,0));
```

```
// select the pen and brush into context
SelectObject(blue_pen);
SelectObject(red_brush);

// draw the rectangle
Rectangle(hdc, 10,10, 20,20);

// do house keeping...
```

Here's a similar example using the `FillRect()` function instead:

```
// define rectangle
RECT rect {10,10,20,20};


// draw rectangle
FillRect(hdc, &rect, CreateSolidBrush(RGB(255,0,0)));
```

Notice the slickness here! I defined the RECT on-the-fly as well as the brush. The brush doesn't need to be deleted because it was never selected into context; hence, it's transient.

 WARNING I'm being fairly loose about the HDC and other details in these examples, so I hope you're awake! Obviously, for any of these examples to work you must have a window, an HDC, and perform the appropriate prolog and epilog code to each segment. As the book continues, I will assume that you know this already.

As an example of using the `Rectangle()` function, take a look at DEMO4_3.CPP; it draws a slew of random rectangles in different sizes and colors on the window surface. However, as a change, I retrieved the handle to the entire window rather than just the client area, so the window looks like it's getting destroyed—cool, huh? Take a look at Figure 4.6 to see the output the program creates.

FIGURE 4.6
Rectangle program
DEMO4_3.EXE.

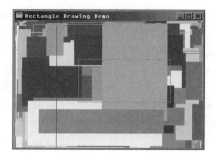

Round and Round She Goes—Circles

Back in the '80s if you could make your computer draw a circle, you were a master-mind. There were a number of ways to do it—with the explicit formula:

```
(x-x0)2 + (y-y0)2 = r2
```

Or maybe with the sine and cosine functions:

```
x=r*cos(angle)
y=r*sin(angle)
```

Or maybe with lookup tables! The point is that circles aren't the fastest things in the world to draw. This dilemma is no longer important since Pentium IIs, but it used to be. In any case, GDI has a circle-drawing function—well, sort of... GDI likes ellipses rather than circles.

If you recall from geometry, an ellipse is like a squished circle on either axis. An ellipse has both a major axis and a minor axis, as shown in the figure. The equation of an ellipse centered at (x0,y0) is shown in Figure 4.7.

FIGURE 4.7
The mathematics of circles and ellipses.

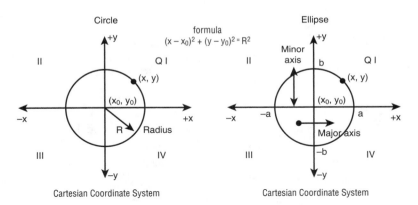

$$\frac{(x - x_0)^2}{a^2} + \frac{(y - y_0)^2}{b^2} = 1$$

You would think that GDI would use some of the same concepts—the major axis and minor axis to define an ellipse—but GDI took a slightly different approach to defining an ellipse. With GDI, you simply give a bounding rectangle and GDI draws the ellipse that's bounded by it. In essence, you're defining the origin of the ellipse while at the same time the major and minor axes—whatever!

The function that draws an ellipse is called `Ellipse()` and it draws with the current pen and brush. Here's the prototype:

```
BOOL Ellipse( HDC hdc,// handle to device context
    int nLeftRect,   // x-coord. of bounding
```

```
                        // rectangle's upper-left corner
    int nTopRect,       // y-coord. of bounding
                        // rectangle's upper-left corner
    int nRightRect,     // x-coord. of bounding
                        // rectangle's lower-right corner
    int nBottomRect );  // y-coord. bounding
                        // rectangle's f lower-right corner
```

So to draw a circle you would make sure that the bounding rectangle was square. For example, to draw a circle that had center (20,20) with a radius of 10, you would do this:

```
Ellipse(hdc,10,10,30,30);
```

Get it? And if you wanted to draw a real-life ellipse with major axis 100, minor axis 50, with an origin of (300,200), you would do this:

```
Ellipse(hdc,250,175,350,225);
```

For a working example of drawing ellipses, take a look at DEMO4_4.CPP on the CD and the associated executable. The program draws a moving ellipse in a simple animation loop of erase, move, draw. This type of animation loop is very similar to the technique we'll use later called *double buffering* or *page flipping*, but with those techniques we won't be able to see the update as shown in the demo, and hence there won't be a flicker! For fun, try messing with the demo and changing things around. See if you can figure out how to add more ellipses.

Polygon, Polygon, Wherefore Art Thou, Polygon?

The last little primitive I want to show you is the polygon primitive. Its purpose is to draw open or closed polygonal objects very quickly. The function that draws a polygon is called Polygon() and is shown here:

```
BOOL Polygon(HDC hdc,        // handle to device context
    CONST POINT *lpPoints,   // pointer to polygon's vertices
    int nCount );            // count of polygon's vertices
```

You simply send Polygon() a list of POINTs along with the number of them and it will draw a closed polygon with the current pen and brush. Take a look at Figure 4.8 to see this graphically.

FIGURE 4.8
Using the Polygon() function.

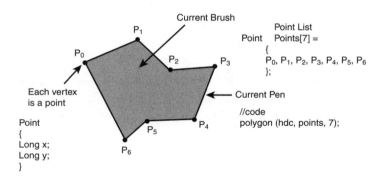

Here's an example:

```
// create the polygon shown in the figure
POINT poly[7] = {p0x, p0y, p1x, p1y, p2x, p2y,
p3x, p3y, p4x, p4y, p5x, p5y, p6x, p6y  };

// assume hdc is valid, and pen and brush are selected into
// graphics device context
Polygon(hdc, poly,7);
```

That was easy! Of course, if you send points that make a degenerate polygon, or a polygon that closes on itself, GDI will do its best to draw it, but no promises!

As an example of drawing filled polygons, DEMO4_5.CPP draws a collection of random 3–10 point polygons all over the screen with a little delay between each, so you can see the weird results that occur with degenerate polygon vertex lists. Figure 4.9 shows the output of the program in action. Notice that because the points are random, the polygons are almost always degenerate due to overlapping geometry. Can you find a way to make sure that all the points exist within a convex hull?

FIGURE 4.9
Output of polygon program
DEMO4_5.EXE.

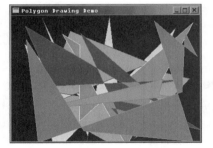

More on Text and Fonts

Working with fonts is an extremely complex subject and not really something that I want to get into. If you want an in-depth treatise on this subject, your best bet is to pick up Charles Petzold's *Programming Windows 95/98*. For products such as games under DirectX, you will in most cases render text yourself with your own font engine. The only time you might want to use GDI to draw text is in a GUI situation or a quick solution to drawing scores or other simple information during development of your game. However, in the end you *must* create your own font system to get any kind of speed.

To be somewhat complete I want to at least show you how to change fonts for the DrawText() and TextOut() functions. This is done by selecting a new font object into the current graphics device context just as you would a new pen or brush. Table 4.1

shows a number of font constants, such as SYSTEM_FIXED_FONT, which is a *monospaced* font. Monospaced means that each character is always the same width. Proportional fonts have different spacing. Anyway, to select a new font into the graphics context, you would do this:

```
SelectObject(hdc, GetStockObject(SYSTEM_FIXED_FONT));
```

Whatever GDI text you rendered with TextOut() or DrawText() is drawn in the new font. If you want a little more power over the selection of fonts, you can use one of the built-in TrueType fonts listed in Table 4.4.

TABLE 4.4   TrueType Font Typeface Names

Font Typeface String	Example
Courier New	Hello World
Courier New Bold	**Hello World**
Courier New Italic	*Hello World*
Courier New Bold Italic	***Hello World***
Times New Roman	Hello World
Times New Roman Bold	**Hello World**
Times New Roman Italic	*Hello World*
Times New Roman Bold Italic	***Hello World***
Arial	Hello World
Arial Bold	**Hello World**
Arial Italic	*Hello World*
Arial Bold Italic	***Hello World***
Symbol	Ηελλο Ωορλδ

To create one of these fonts, you can use the CreateFont() function:

```
HFONT CreateFont( int nHeight,      // logical height of font
      int nWidth,                   // logical average character width
      int nEscapement,              // angle of escapement
      int nOrientation,             // base-line orientation angle
      int fnWeight,                 // font weight
      DWORD fdwItalic,              // italic attribute flag
      DWORD fdwUnderline,           // underline attribute flag
      DWORD fdwStrikeOut,           // strikeout attribute flag
      DWORD fdwCharSet,             // character set identifier
      DWORD fdwOutputPrecision,     // output precision
      DWORD fdwClipPrecision,       // clipping precision
      DWORD fdwQuality,             // output quality
      DWORD fdwPitchAndFamily,      // pitch and family
      LPCTSTR lpszFace);            // pointer to typeface name string
                                    // as shown in table 4.4
```

The explanation of the function is far too long, so take a look at the Win32 SDK Help for details. Basically, you fill in all those ugly parameters and the results are a handle to a rasterized version of the font you requested. Then you can select the font into your device context and you're ready to rock.

Timing Is Everything

The next topic we're going to cover is timing. Although it may seem unimportant, timing is crucial in a video game. Without timing and proper delays a game can run too fast or too slow and the illusion of animation is completely lost.

If you recall, back in Chapter 1, "Journey into the Abyss," I mentioned that most games run about 30 fps (frames per second), but I never alluded to how to keep this timing constant. In this section you'll learn some techniques to track time and even send time-based messages. Later in the book you'll see how these ideas are used over and over to keep frame rate solid and you'll see how to augment parametric animation and physics on slow systems that can't sustain high frame rates. First, though, take a look at the WM_TIMER message.

The WM_TIMER Message

The PC has a built-in timer that can be very accurate (in the microsecond range), but because we're programming in Windows, it's not a good idea to muck with the timer ourselves. Instead, we'll use the timing functions built into Windows (which are built upon the actual hardware timer). The cool thing about this approach is that Windows virtualizes the timer into an almost infinite number of virtual timers. Thus, from your point of view, you can start and receive many messages from a number of timers, even though there's only one physical timer on most PCs.

FIGURE 4.10
Message flow for the
WM_TIMER message.

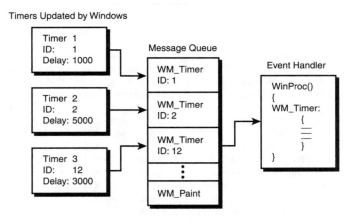

When you create a timer you set the ID of the timer along with the delay. The timer will begin to send messages to your WinProc() at the specified interval. Take a look at Figure 4.10 to see the data flow of some timers. Each timer sends WM_TIMER messages when its elapsed time has passed. You tell one timer from another when processing the WM_TIMER message with the timer ID (which you set when you create the timer). With that in mind, let's take a look at the function to create a timer—SetTimer():

```
UNIT SetTimer(HWND hWnd,      // handle to parent window
              UINT nIDevent, // timer id
              UINT nElapse,  // time delay in milliseconds
              TIMERPROC lpTimerFunc); // timer callback
```

To create a timer you need:

- The window handle
- ID of choice
- The time delay in milliseconds

With these three things, you're in business. However, the last parameter takes a little explanation. lpTimerFunc() is a callback function just like WinProc() is, hence, you can create a timer that calls a function at some specified interval instead of processing it in the WinProc() via WM_TIMER messages. It's up to you, but I usually use the WM_TIMER messages and leave the TIMERPROC set to NULL.

You can create as many timers as you wish, but remember that they all take up resources. If the function fails, it will return 0. Otherwise, SetTimer() returns the timer ID you sent to create the timer with.

The next question is how to tell one timer from another. The answer is that you interrogate the wparam when the WM_TIMER message is sent; it contains the timer ID that you originally created the timer with. As an example, here's how you would create two timers, one with a 1.0 second delay and the other with a 3.0-second delay:

```
#define TIMER_ID_1SEC   1
#define TIMER_ID_3SEC   2

// maybe do this in WM_CREATE
SetTimer(hwnd, TIMER_ID_1SEC, 1000,NULL);
SetTimer(hwnd, TIMER_ID_3SEC, 3000,NULL);
```

Notice that the delays are in milliseconds. In other words, 1000 milliseconds equals 1.0 seconds and so forth. Moving on, here's the code you would need to add to your WinProc() to process the timer messages:

```
case WM_TIMER:
    {
    // what timer fired?
    switch(wparam)
```

```
        {
        case TIMER_ID_1SEC:
              {
              // do processing here
              } break;

        case TIMER_ID_3SEC:
              {
              // do processing here
              } break;

        default:break;

        } // end switch

    // let windows know we handled the message
    return(0);

    } break;
```

Finally, when you're done with a timer, you can kill it with `KillTimer()`:

```
BOOL KillTimer(HWND hWnd,        // handle of window
               UINT uIDEvent ); // timer id
```

Continuing with the example, you might want to kill all the timers in the WM_DESTROY message, as shown here:

```
case WM_DESTROY:
    {
     // kill timers
    KillTimer(hwnd, TIMER_ID_1SEC);
    KillTimer(hwnd, TIMER_ID_3SEC);

    // terminate application or whatever...
    PostQuitMessage(0);

    } break;
```

> **WARNING**   Even though timers may seem free and abundant, PCs aren't Star Trek computers. Timers use resources and should be used sparingly. Make sure to kill any timer that you don't need anymore during run-time.

As a working example of using timers, take a look at DEMO4_6.CPP on the CD. It creates three timers with different times and then prints out when each timer changes. Finally, although timers take time delays in milliseconds, they are hardly millisecond-accurate. Don't expect your timers to be more accurate than 10–20 milliseconds. If you need more accuracy, there are methods, such as using the Win32 High Performance timers or using the Pentium Real-Time hardware counters based on the RDTSC assembly language instruction.

Low-Level Timing

Although creating timers is at least one way to keep track of time, the technique suffers from a few faults: First, timers send messages, and second, timers aren't that accurate. Finally, in most game loops you want to force the main body of the code to run at a specific frame rate and no higher; this is achieved by locking the frame rate via timing code. Timers aren't very good at this. What's really needed is a way to query a system clock of sorts and then perform differential tests to see how much time has elapsed. The Win32 API has such a function, and it's called `GetTickCount()`:

```
DWORD GetTickCount(void);
```

`GetTickCount()` returns the number of milliseconds since Windows was started. That may not seem useful as an absolute reference, because you have none, but it's perfect as a differential reference. All you have to do at the top of any code block that you want to time is query the current tick count and then at the end of the loop query again, and take the difference. Whammo, you have the time difference in milliseconds. For example, here's how you would make sure that a chunk of code runs at exactly 30 fps or with a delay of 1/30fps = 33.33 milliseconds:

```
// get the starting time
DWORD start_time = GetTickCount();

// do work, draw frame, whatever

// now wait until 33 milliseconds has elapsed
while ((GetTickCount() - start_time) < 33);
```

That's what I'm talking about, baby! Of course, sitting in a *busy loop* is a waste of time performing the `while()` logic, but you can always branch off and test every now and then, so you don't waste cycles. The point is that with this technique you can force time constraints on chunks of code.

> **NOTE**
>
> Obviously, if your PC can't run at 30 fps, the loop will take longer. However, if during a free run of your code the loop ran from 30–100 fps, the preceding code would lock it to 30 fps always. That's the point!

As an example, take a look at `DEMO4_7.CPP` on the CD. It basically locks the frame rate to 30 fps and updates a little screen saver with lines on each frame. Following is the code from the `WinMain()` that does the work:

```
// get the dc and hold onto it
hdc = GetDC(hwnd);

// seed random number generator
srand(GetTickCount());
```

```
// endpoints of line
int x1 = rand()%WINDOW_WIDTH;
int y1 = rand()%WINDOW_HEIGHT;
int x2 = rand()%WINDOW_WIDTH;
int y2 = rand()%WINDOW_HEIGHT;

// intial velocity of each end
int x1v = -4 + rand()%8;
int y1v = -4 + rand()%8;
int x2v = -4 + rand()%8;
int y2v = -4 + rand()%8;

// enter main event loop, but this time we use PeekMessage()
// instead of GetMessage() to retrieve messages
while(TRUE)
    {
    // get time reference
    DWORD start_time = GetTickCount();

    // test if there is a message in queue, if so get it
    if (PeekMessage(&msg,NULL,0,0,PM_REMOVE))
       {
       // test if this is a quit
       if (msg.message == WM_QUIT)
          break;

       // translate any accelerator keys
       TranslateMessage(&msg);

       // send the message to the window proc
       DispatchMessage(&msg);
       } // end if

    // is it time to change color
    if (++color_change_count >= 100)
       {
       // reset counter
       color_change_count = 0;

       // create a random colored pen
       if (pen)
          DeleteObject(pen);

       // create a new pen
       pen = CreatePen(PS_SOLID,1,
             RGB(rand()%256,rand()%256,rand()%256));

       // select the pen into context
       SelectObject(hdc,pen);

       } // end if
```

```
// move endpoints of line
x1+=x1v;
y1+=y1v;

x2+=x2v;
y2+=y2v;

// test if either end hit window edge
if (x1 < 0 || x1 >= WINDOW_WIDTH)
   {
   // invert velocity
   x1v=-x1v;

   // bum endpoint back
   x1+=x1v;
   } // end if

if (y1 < 0 || y1 >= WINDOW_HEIGHT)
   {
   // invert velocity
   y1v=-y1v;

   // bum endpoint back
   y1+=y1v;
   } // end if

// now test second endpoint
if (x2 < 0 || x2 >= WINDOW_WIDTH)
   {
   // invert velocity
   x2v=-x2v;

   // bum endpoint back
   x2+=x2v;
   } // end if

if (y2 < 0 || y2 >= WINDOW_HEIGHT)
   {
   // invert velocity
   y2v=-y2v;

   // bum endpoint back
   y2+=y2v;
   } // end if

// move to end one of line
MoveToEx(hdc, x1,y1, NULL);

// draw the line to other end
LineTo(hdc,x2,y2);

// lock time to 30 fps which is approx. 33 milliseconds
while((GetTickCount() - start_time) < 33);
```

```
                // main game processing goes here
                if (KEYDOWN(VK_ESCAPE))
                    SendMessage(hwnd, WM_CLOSE, 0,0);

            } // end while


    // release the device context
    ReleaseDC(hwnd,hdc);

    // return to Windows like this
    return(msg.wParam);

    } // end WinMain
```

Other than the timing aspect of the code, there is some other logic that you should
take some time to review: the collision logic. You'll notice that there are two ends of
the line segment, each with a position and velocity. As the segment moves, the code
tests whether it has collided with the edge of the window client area. If so, the segment is bounced off the edge, creating the illusion of a bouncing line.

TRICK   If you just want to delay your code, use a Win32 API function called
Sleep(). Just send it the time delay in milliseconds you wish to delay
and the function will. For example, to delay 1.0 second, you would say
Sleep(1000).

Playing with Controls

Window child controls are really little windows themselves. Here's a short list of some
of the more popular child controls:

- Static text boxes
- Edit boxes
- Buttons
- List boxes
- Scroll bars

In addition, there are a number of sub-button types, such as

- Push buttons
- Check boxes
- Radio buttons

There are even further sub-types of each. Nevertheless, most complex window controls
that you see are conglomerations of these basic types. For example, a file directory

control is just a few list boxes, some text edit boxes, and some buttons. If you can work with the basic controls listed here, you can handle anything. Once you have mastered one, they're all roughly the same, give or take a few details, so I'm just going to show you how to work with a few of the child controls, including buttons.

Buttons

There are a number of button types that Windows supports. If you're reading this book, hopefully you have used Windows and are at least familiar with push buttons, check boxes, and radio buttons, so I'm not go into the details of each. Rather, I'm going to show you how to create any type of button you want and respond to messages sent from it. The rest is up to you. Let's begin by taking a look at Table 4.5, which lists all the available button types.

TABLE 4.5 Button Styles

Value	Description
BS_PUSHBUTTON	Creates a push button that posts a WM_COMMAND message to the owner window when the user selects the button.
BS_RADIOBUTTON	Creates a small circle with text. By default, the text is displayed to the right of the circle.
BS_CHECKBOX	Creates a small empty check box with text. By default, the text is displayed to the right of the check box.
BS_3STATE	Creates a button that is the same as a check box, except that the box can be grayed as well as checked or unchecked.
BS_AUTO3STATE	Creates a button that is the same as a three-state check box, except that the box changes its state when the user selects it. The state cycles through checked, grayed, and unchecked.
BS_AUTOCHECKBOX	Creates a button that is the same as a check box, except that the check state automatically toggles between checked and unchecked each time the user selects the check box.
BS_AUTORADIOBUTTON	Creates a button that is the same as a radio button, except that when the user selects it, Windows automatically sets the button's check state to checked and automatically sets the check state for all other buttons in the same group to unchecked.
BS_OWNERDRAW	Creates an owner-drawn button. The owner window receives a WM_MEASUREITEM message when the button is created and a WM_DRAWITEM message when a visual aspect of the button has changed.

To create a child control button you simply create a window using "button" as the class string along with one of the button styles in Table 4.5. Then, when the button is manipulated, it sends `WM_COMMAND` messages to your window, as shown in Figure 4.11. You process the `wparam` and `lparam` as usual to see what child control sent the message and what the message was.

FIGURE 4.11
Child window
message passing.

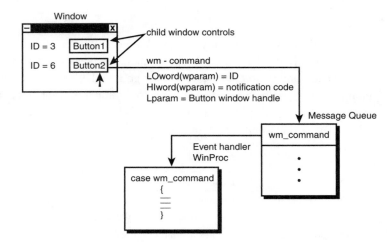

Let's begin by seeing the exact parameters you'll need to send to `CreateWindowEx()` to create a child button control. First, you need to set the class name to `"button"`. Then you need to set the style flags to `WS_CHILD | WS_VISIBLE` logically `ORed` with a button style from Table 4.5. Then in the place where you would normally put the handle to the menu or `HMENU`, you send the ID you want to refer to the button with (of course you must cast it to a `HMENU`). That's about it.

As an example, here's how you would create a push button with ID equal to 100 and the text "Push Me" on it:

```
CreateWindowEx(NULL,      // extended style
            "button",  // class
            "Push Me", // text on button
            WS_CHILD | WS_VISIBLE | BS_PUSHBUTTON,
            10,10,       // initial x,y
            100,24,      // initial width, height
            main_window_handle,    // handle to parent
            (HMENU)(100),          // id of button, notice cast to HMENU
            hinstance, // instance of this application
            NULL);     // extra creation parms
```

Simple, isn't it? When you press the button, a `WM_COMMAND` message is sent to the `WinProc()` of the parent window with the following paramaterization:

msg:	WM_COMMAND
LOWORD(wparam):	Child Window ID

HIWORD(wparam):   Notification Code

lparam: Child Window Handle

Seem reasonable? The only mystery is the *notification code*. Notification codes describe what happened to the button control and begin with BN_. Table 4.6 lists all the possible notification codes and values.

TABLE 4.6   Notification Codes for Buttons

Code	Value
BN_CLICKED	0
BN_PAINT	1
BN_HLITE	2
BN_UNHILITE	3
BN_DISABLE	4
BN_DOUBLECLICKED	5

The most important of the notification codes are of course BN_CLICKED and BN_DOUBLECLICKED. To process a button child control like a simple push button, you might do something like this in the WM_COMMAND event handler:

```
// assume a child button was created with id 100
case WM_COMMAND:
    {
    // test for id
    if (LOWORD(wparam) == 100)
    {
    // do whatever
    } // end if

    // process all other child controls, menus, etc.

    // we handled it
    return(0);

    } break;
```

As an example, take a look at DEMO4_8.CPP; it creates a list of all button types and then displays all the messages along with the wparam and lparam for each message as you click and manipulate the buttons. Figure 4.12 shows the program in action. By experimenting with it, you will get a much better idea of how button child controls work.

FIGURE 4.12

The DEMO4_8.EXE
child control program.

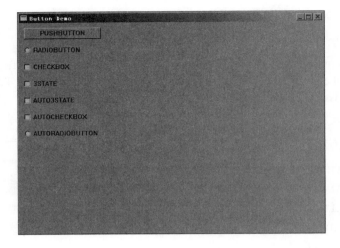

If you play with DEMO4_8.EXE, you'll quickly realize that although your WinProc() is sending messages indicating what the user (you) is doing to the controls, you don't know how to change or manipulate the controls programmatically. In essence, many of the controls don't seem to do anything when you click them. This is important, so let's briefly cover it.

Sending Messages to Child Controls

Because child controls are windows, they can receive messages just like any other window. But because they are children of a parent the messages are sent onto the parent in the case of the WM_COMMAND message. However, it's possible to send a child control (like a button) a message and it will itself process the message with its own default WinProc(). This is exactly how you change the state of any control—by sending messages to it.

In the case of buttons, there are a number of messages you can send button controls, using SendMessage() to change the state of the button and/or retrieve the state of the button. Remember that SendMessage() returns a value too. Here's a list of some of the more interesting messages for use with the parameterizations of wparam and lparam.

Purpose: To simulate clicking the button.

msg:	BM_CLICK
wparam:	0
lparam:	0

Example:

```
// this would make the button look like it was pressed
SendMessage(hwndbutton, BM_CLICK,0,0);
```

Purpose: Used to set the check on a check box or radio button.

msg:	BM_SETCHECK
wparam:	fCheck
lparam:	0

fCheck can be one of the following:

Value	Description
BST_CHECKED	Sets the button state to checked.
BST_INDETERMINATE	Sets the button state to grayed, indicating an indeterminate state. Use this value only if the button has the BS_3STATE or BS_AUTO3STATE style.
BST_UNCHECKED	Sets the button state to unchecked.

Example:

```
// this would check a check button
SendMessage(hwndbutton, BM_SETCHECK, BST_CHECKED, 0);
```

Purpose: Used to retrieve the current state of the button check. Possible return values are shown here.

msg:	BM_GETCHECK
wparam:	0
lparam:	0

Value	Description
BST_CHECKED	Button is checked.
BST_INDETERMINATE	Button is grayed, indicating an indeterminate state (applies only if the button has the BS_3STATE or BS_AUTO3STATE style).
BST_UNCHECKED	Button is unchecked.

Example:

```
// this would get the check state of a checkbox
if (SendMessage(hwndbutton,BM_GETCHECK,0,0) == BST_CHECKED)
   {
   // button is checked
   } // end if
else
   {
   // button is not checked
   } // end else
```

Purpose: Used to highlight the button as if it were selected by the user.

msg:	BM_SETSTATE
wparam:	fState
lparam:	0

Where fState is a TRUE for highlighted and FALSE otherwise.

Example:

```
// this would highlight the button control
SendMessage(hwndbutton, BM_SETSTATE, 1, 0);
```

Purpose: To get the general state of the button control. Possible return values are shown below.

msg:	BM_GETSTATE
wparam:	0
lparam:	0

Value	Description
BST_CHECKED	Indicates the button is checked.
BST_FOCUS	Specifies the focus state. A nonzero value indicates that the button has the keyboard focus.
BST_INDETERMINATE	Indicates the button is grayed because the state of the button is indeterminate. This value applies only if the button has the BS_3STATE or BS_AUTO3STATE style.
BST_PUSHED	Specifies the highlight state. A nonzero value indicates that the button is highlighted. A button is automatically highlighted when the user positions the cursor over it and presses and holds the left mouse button. The highlighting is removed when the user releases the mouse button.
BST_UNCHECKED	Indicates the button is unchecked.

Example:

```
// this code can be used to get the state of the button
switch(SendMessage(hwndbutton, BM_GETSTATE, 0, 0))
      {
      // what is the button state
      case BST_CHECKED:       { } break;
      case BST_FOCUS:         { } break;
      case BST_INDETERMINATE: { } break;
      case BST_PUSHED:        { } break;
      case BST_UNCHECKED:     { } break;
```

```
      default: break;
      } // end switch
```

Well, that's it for child controls. At least you have an idea of what they are and how to handle them. Now it's time to move onto querying information from Windows.

Getting Information

In the movie, *Wall Street,* Gordon Gekko once said: "Why don't you stop sending me information and start getting some?" These words are appropriate for this circumstance and many other things. Information about the system your game is running on is vital to making your game take advantage of all the resources that a system has to offer. As you would expect, Windows is full of information retrieval functions that acquire a myriad of details about Windows settings and the hardware itself.

Win32 supports a number of `Get*()` functions and DirectX supports a number of `GetCaps*()` functions. I'm only going to cover a few of the Win32 functions that I use from time to time. In the next part of the book you'll see more of the information retrieval functions that DirectX supports. Those functions are more geared toward the multimedia end of the spectrum.

The following paragraphs describe three functions that I like to use from time to time. (There are many more.) Basically, anything you want to know about Windows is there and can be queried with a `"Get"` class function. Simply type **`get`** into the Win32 SDK Search engine within your compiler Help and you should find whatever you need. We'll take a look at these three functions just to get a feel for using them.

The first function we'll look at is called `GetSystemInfo()`. It basically returns everything you would ever want to know about the processing hardware you're running on— things like the type of processor, how many processors, and so forth. Here's the function prototype:

```
VOID GetSystemInfo(
    LPSYSTEM_INFO lpSystemInfo);
    // address of system information structure
```

The function simply takes a pointer to a `SYSTEM_INFO` structure and fills in all the fields. Here's what a `SYSTEM_INFO` structure looks like:

```
typedef struct _SYSTEM_INFO
{ // sinf
union {
    DWORD dwOemId;
    struct {
            WORD wProcessorArchitecture;
            WORD wReserved;
            };
    };
```

```
DWORD   dwPageSize;
LPVOID  lpMinimumApplicationAddress;
LPVOID  lpMaximumApplicationAddress;
DWORD   dwActiveProcessorMask;
DWORD   dwNumberOfProcessors;
DWORD   dwProcessorType;
DWORD   dwAllocationGranularity;
WORD    wProcessorLevel;
WORD    wProcessorRevision;
} SYSTEM_INFO;
```

The details of all these fields are pages long and we don't have room to cover them, but obviously there are some interesting fields. For example, `dwNumberOfProcessors` is the number of processors on the motherboard of the PC. `dwProcessorType` is the actual type of the processor, which can be one of the following:

Value
PROCESSOR_INTEL_386
PROCESSOR_INTEL_486
PROCESSOR_INTEL_PENTIUM

The other fields are all self-explanatory—just take a look at the Win32 SDK for details. This is an amazing function, however, if you think about it. Can you imagine how hard it is to determine the type of processor installed, let alone how many of them? Where would you even start?

You would start by writing a very complex detection algorithm that knows things about 486s, Pentiums, Pentium IIs, and so on, and it would poke and pry with writes and reads until it figured out what processor was on the machine. Of course, Pentium class processors have ID strings and machine flags, but 486s are a lot harder to figure out. The point is that this is a great function to get system-level information.

The next function I want to show you is very general and can retrieve all kinds of cool information about Windows and the Desktop. It's called `GetSystemMetrics()`:

```
int GetSystemMetrics(int nIndex); // system metric or configuration setting to
retrieve
```

`GetSystemMetrics()` is very powerful. What you do is send it the index of the data you want retrieved, as shown in Table 4.7, and it is returned. By the way, Table 4.7 is the longest table in the book. I really hate looking it up in the Help, so I'm going to break down and add it to the book for your convenience <BG>.

TABLE 4.7 System Metric Constants for `GetSystemMetrics()`

Value	Description
SM_ARRANGE	Flags specifying how the system arranged minimized windows. For more information about minimized windows, see the following Remarks section.
SM_CLEANBOOT	Value that specifies how the system was started: 0 Normal boot 1 Fail-safe boot 2 Fail-safe with network boot
SM_CMOUSEBUTTONS	Number of buttons on mouse, or zero if no mouse is installed.
SM_CXBORDER, SM_CYBORDER	The width and height, in pixels, of a window border. This is equivalent to the SM_CXEDGE value for windows with the 3-D look.
SM_CXCURSOR, SM_CYCURSOR	Width and height, in pixels, of a cursor. These are the cursor dimensions supported by the current display driver. The system cannot create cursors of other sizes.
SM_CXDOUBLECLK, SM_CYDOUBLECLK	Width and height, in pixels, of the rectangle around the location of a first click in a double-click sequence. The second click must occur within this rectangle for the system to consider the two clicks a double-click. (The two clicks must also occur within a specified time.)
SM_CXDRAG, SM_CYDRAG	Width and height, in pixels, of a rectangle centered on a drag point to allow for limited movement of the mouse pointer before a drag operation begins. This enables the user to click and release the mouse button easily without unintentionally starting a drag operation.
SM_CXEDGE, SM_CYEDGE	Dimensions, in pixels, of a 3-D border. These are the 3-D counterparts of SM_CXBORDER and SM_CYBORDER.
SM_CXFIXEDFRAME, SM_CYFIXEDFRAME	Thickness, in pixels, of the frame around the perimeter of a window that has a caption but is not sizable. SM_CXFIXEDFRAME is the width of the horizontal border and SM_CYFIXEDFRAME is the height of the vertical border.

TABLE 4.7 Continued

Value	Description
SM_CXFULLSCREEN, SM_CYFULLSCREEN	Width and height of the client area for a full-screen window. To get the coordinates of the portion of the screen not obscured by the tray, call the SystemParametersInfo function with the SPI_GETWORKAREA value.
SM_CXHSCROLL, SM_CYHSCROLL	Width, in pixels, of the arrow bitmap on a horizontal scroll bar; and height, in pixels, of a horizontal scroll bar.
SM_CXHTHUMB	Width, in pixels, of the thumb box in a horizontal scroll bar.
SM_CXICON, SM_CYICON	The default width and height, in pixels, of an icon. These values are typically 32x32, but can vary depending on the installed display hardware.
SM_CXICONSPACING, SM_CYICONSPACING	Dimensions, in pixels, of a grid cell for items in large icon view. Each item fits into a rectangle of this size when arranged. These values are always greater than or equal to SM_CXICON and SM_CYICON.
SM_CXMAXIMIZED, SM_CYMAXIMIZED	Default dimensions, in pixels, of a maximized top-level window.
SM_CXMAXTRACK, SM_CYMAXTRACK	Default maximum dimensions, in pixels, of a window that has a caption and sizing borders. The user cannot drag the window frame to a size larger than these dimensions. A window can override these values by processing the WM_GETMINMAXINFO message.
SM_CXMENUCHECK, SM_CYMENUCHECK	Dimensions, in pixels, of the default menu check mark bitmap.
SM_CXMENUSIZE, SM_CYMENUSIZE	Dimensions, in pixels, of menu bar buttons, such as multiple document (MDI) child close.
SM_CXMIN, SM_CYMIN	Minimum width and height, in pixels, of a window.
SM_CXMINIMIZED, SM_CYMINIMIZED	Dimensions, in pixels, of a normal minimized window.
SM_CXMINSPACING, SM_CYMINSPACING	Dimensions, in pixels, of a grid cell for minimized windows. Each minimized window fits into a rectangle this size when arranged. These values are always greater than or equal to SM_CXMINIMIZED and SM_CYMINIMIZED.

Value	Description
SM_CXMINTRACK, SM_CYMINTRACK	Minimum tracking width and height, in pixels, of a window. The user cannot drag the window frame to a size smaller than these dimensions. A window can override these values by processing the WM_GETMINMAXINFO message.
SM_CXSCREEN, SM_CYSCREEN	Width and height, in pixels, of the screen.
SM_CXSIZE, SM_CYSIZE	Width and height, in pixels, of a button in a window's caption or title bar.
SM_CXSIZEFRAME, SM_CYSIZEFRAME	Thickness, in pixels, of the sizing border around the perimeter of a window that can be resized. SM_CXSIZEFRAME is the width of the horizontal border and SM_CYSIZEFRAME is the height of the vertical border.
SM_CXSMICON, SM_CYSMICON	Recommended dimensions, in pixels, of a small icon. Small icons typically appear in window captions and in small icon view.
SM_CXSMSIZE, SM_CYSMSIZE	Dimensions, in pixels, of small caption buttons.
SM_CXVSCROLL, SM_CYVSCROLL	Width, in pixels, of a vertical scroll bar; and height, in pixels, of the arrow bitmap on a vertical scroll bar.
SM_CYCAPTION	Height, in pixels, of the normal caption area.
SM_CYKANJIWINDOW	For double-byte character set versions of Windows, height, in pixels, of the Kanji window at the bottom of the screen.
SM_CYMENU	Height, in pixels, of single-line menu bar.
SM_CYSMCAPTION	Height, in pixels, of a small caption.
SM_CYVTHUMB	Height, in pixels, of the thumb box in a vertical scroll bar.
SM_DBCSENABLED	TRUE or nonzero if the double-byte character set (DBCS) version of USER.EXE is installed; FALSE or zero otherwise.
SM_DEBUG	TRUE or nonzero if the debugging version of USER.EXE is installed; FALSE or zero otherwise.
SM_MENUDROPALIGNMENT	TRUE or nonzero if drop-down menus are right-aligned relative to the corresponding menu-bar item; FALSE or zero if they are left-aligned.

TABLE 4.7 Continued

Value	Description
SM_MIDEASTENABLED	TRUE if the system is enabled for Hebrew/Arabic languages.
SM_MOUSEPRESENT	TRUE or nonzero if a mouse is installed; FALSE or zero otherwise.
SM_MOUSEWHEELPRESENT	Windows NT only: TRUE or nonzero if a mouse with a wheel is installed; FALSE or zero otherwise.
SM_NETWORK	The least significant bit is set if a network is present; otherwise, it is cleared. The other bits are reserved for future use.
SM_PENWINDOWS	TRUE or nonzero if the Microsoft Windows for Pen computing extensions are installed; zero or FALSE otherwise.
SM_SECURE	TRUE if security is present FALSE otherwise.
SM_SHOWSOUNDS	TRUE or nonzero if the user requires an application to present information visually in situations where it would otherwise present the information only in audible form; FALSE or zero otherwise.
SM_SLOWMACHINE	TRUE if the computer has a low-end (slow) processor; FALSE otherwise.
SM_SWAPBUTTON	TRUE or nonzero if the meanings of the left and right mouse buttons are swapped; FALSE or zero otherwise.

If it isn't in Table 4.7, you don't need to know! As an example, here's a cool way to create a window that's as large as the screen display:

```
// create the window
if (!(hwnd = CreateWindowEx(NULL,      // extended style
                WINDOW_CLASS_NAME,  // class
                "Button Demo",      // title
                WS_POPUP | WS_VISIBLE,
                0,0,      // initial x,y
                GetSystemMetrics(SM_CXSCREEN), // initial width
                GetSystemMetrics(SM_CYSCREEN), // initial height
                NULL,     // handle to parent
                NULL,     // handle to menu
                hinstance,   // instance of this application
                NULL)))     // extra creation parms
                return(0);
```

NOTE Notice the use of the WS_POPUP window style rather than the WM_OVERLAPPEDWINDOW. This creates a window without any borders or controls, resulting in a blank screen—the effect you would want for a full-screen game application.

As another example, you could use the following code to test for a mouse:

```
if (GetSystemMetrics(SM_MOUSEPRESENT))
    {
    // there's a mouse
    } // end if
else
    {
    // no mouse
    } // end else
```

Finally, when you're drawing text, you might want to know about the font that GDI is using—for example, how wide each character is and other related metrics. If you write some code to draw text and you know the font, you can position the text with some reasonable accuracy. The name of the function that retrieves text metrics is called GetTextMetrics():

```
BOOL GetTextMetrics(HDC hdc,  // handle of device context
    LPTEXTMETRIC lptm ); // address of text metrics structure
```

You may be wondering why the hdc is needed—it's because you may have multiple dc's with different fonts selected, so you have to tell the function which one to compute the metrics on. Smart little function! Anyway, lptm is a pointer to a TEXTMETRIC structure that is filled with the information. It looks like this:

```
typedef struct tagTEXTMETRIC {
  LONG tmHeight;          // the height of the font
  LONG tmAscent;          // the ascent of the font
  LONG tmDescent;         // the descent of the font
  LONG tmInternalLeading; // the internal leading
  LONG tmExternalLeading; // the external leading
  LONG tmAveCharWidth;    // the average width
  LONG tmMaxCharWidth;    // the maximum width
  LONG tmWeight;          // the weight of the font
  LONG tmOverhang;        // the overhang of the font
  LONG tmDigitizedAspectX; // the designed for x-aspect
  LONG tmDigitizedAspectY; // the designed for y-aspect
  BCHAR tmFirstChar;      // first character font defines
  BCHAR tmLastChar;       // last character font defines
  BCHAR tmDefaultChar;    // char used when desired not in set
  BCHAR tmBreakChar;      // the break character
  BYTE tmItalic;          // is this an italic font
  BYTE tmUnderlined;      // is this an underlined font
  BYTE tmStruckOut;       // is this a strikeout font
  BYTE tmPitchAndFamily;  //family and tech,truetype..
  BYTE tmCharSet;         // what is the character set
} TEXTMETRIC;
```

Because most of us haven't worked with a printing press our whole lives, a number of these fields are meaningless, but I have highlighted the ones that should make some sense. Take a look at the following list of terms and refer to Figure 4.13; it might help with some of the terminology.

- **Height**—This is the total height in pixels of the character.
- **Baseline**—This is a reference point, usually the bottom of an uppercase character.
- **Ascen**—This is the number of pixels from the baseline to the top of where an accent mark might be.
- **Descen**—This is the number of pixels from the baseline to the bottom of lower case extensions.
- **Internal leadin**—This is the number of pixels to allow for accent marks.
- **External leadin**—This is the number of pixels to allow for other characters above the character, so they don't run on top of each other.

FIGURE 4.13
The makeup of a character.

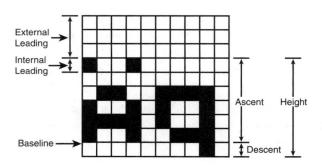

Here's an example of how you would center some text:

```
TEXTMETRIC tm; // holds the textmetric data

// get the textmetrics
GetTextMetrics(hdc,&tm);

// used tm data to center a string given the horizontal width
// assume width of window is WINDOW_WIDTH
int x_pos = WINDOW_WIDTH -
    strlen("Center This String")*tm.tmAveCharWidth/2;

// print the text at the centered position
TextOut(hdc,x_pos,0,"Center This String",
        strlen("Center This String"));
```

No matter what the font size is, this code will always center it.

The T3D Game Console

In the beginning of the book I mentioned that Win32/DirectX programming is almost like 32-bit DOS programming if you create a shell Windows application and then create a code structure that hides the details of the dull Windows stuff that's going on. Now you know enough to do this. In this section you'll see how to put together the T3D Game Console, which will be the basis for all the demos and games from here on.

At this point, you know that to create a Windows application you need a `WinProc()` and a `WinMain()` and that's about it. So we'll create a minimal Windows application that has these components and create a generic window. The application will then call out to three functions that perform the game logic. As a result, the details of handling Windows messages and other Win32-related drama won't be an issue (unless of course you want it to be). Take a look at Figure 4.14 to see the T3D Game Console architecture.

FIGURE 4.14
The architecture of the T3D Game Console.

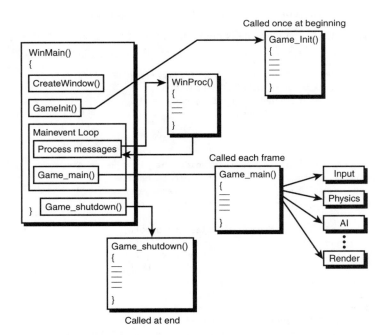

As you can see, there are only three functions that are needed to implement the console:

```
int Game_Init(void *parms = NULL, int num_parms = 0);

int Game_Main(void *parms = NULL, int num_parms = 0);

int Game_Shutdown(void *parms = NULL, int num_parms = 0);
```

- Game_Init() is called before the main event loop in WinMain() is entered and is called only once. Here is where you'll initialize everything for your game.

- Game_Main() is like main() in a normal C/C++ program except that it is called each cycle after any Windows message handling is performed by the main event loop. This is where the entire logic of your game will be. You'll do all the rendering, sound, AI, and so forth in Game_Main() or as calls out of Game_Main(). The only caveat about Game_Main() is that you must draw only one frame and then return, so you don't starve the WinMain() event handler. Also, because this function is entered and exited each cycle, remember that automatic variables are transient—if you want data to stick around, make it global or local static to Game_Main().

- Game_Shutdown() is called after the main event loop in WinMain() is exited, which is caused by a message sent from the user, ultimately causing a WM_QUIT message to be posted. In Game_Shutdown() you'll do all your housekeeping and cleanup of resources allocated during game play.

The T3D Game Console is contained in the file T3DCONSOLE.CPP. Below is the WinMain() section showing the calls to all the console functions:

```
// WINMAIN ////////////////////////////////////////////////
int WINAPI WinMain(HINSTANCE hinstance,
                   HINSTANCE hprevinstance,
                   LPSTR lpcmdline,
                   int ncmdshow)
{

WNDCLASSEX winclass; // this holds the class we create
HWND       hwnd;     // generic window handle
MSG        msg;      // generic message
HDC        hdc;      // graphics device context

// first fill in the window class structure
winclass.cbSize        = sizeof(WNDCLASSEX);
winclass.style         = CS_DBLCLKS | CS_OWNDC |
                                  CS_HREDRAW | CS_VREDRAW;
winclass.lpfnWndProc   = WindowProc;
winclass.cbClsExtra    = 0;
winclass.cbWndExtra    = 0;
winclass.hInstance     = hinstance;
winclass.hIcon         = LoadIcon(NULL, IDI_APPLICATION);
winclass.hCursor       = LoadCursor(NULL, IDC_ARROW);
winclass.hbrBackground = GetStockObject(BLACK_BRUSH);
winclass.lpszMenuName  = NULL;
winclass.lpszClassName = WINDOW_CLASS_NAME;
winclass.hIconSm       = LoadIcon(NULL, IDI_APPLICATION);

// save hinstance in global
hinstance_app = hinstance;
```

```
// register the window class
if (!RegisterClassEx(&winclass))
    return(0);

// create the window
if (!(hwnd = CreateWindowEx(NULL,                    // extended style
                            WINDOW_CLASS_NAME,       // class
                            "T3D Game Console Version 1.0", // title
                            WS_OVERLAPPEDWINDOW | WS_VISIBLE,
                            0,0,             // initial x,y
                            400,300,    // initial width, height
                            NULL,       // handle to parent
                            NULL,       // handle to menu
                            hinstance, // instance of this application
                            NULL)))     // extra creation parms
return(0);

// save main window handle
HWND main_window_handle = hwnd;

// initialize game here
Game_Init();

// enter main event loop
while(TRUE)
    {
    // test if there is a message in queue, if so get it
    if (PeekMessage(&msg,NULL,0,0,PM_REMOVE))
        {
        // test if this is a quit
        if (msg.message == WM_QUIT)
            break;

        // translate any accelerator keys
        TranslateMessage(&msg);

        // send the message to the window proc
        DispatchMessage(&msg);
        } // end if

        // main game processing goes here
        Game_Main();

    } // end while

// closedown game here
Game_Shutdown();

// return to Windows like this
return(msg.wParam);

} // end WinMain
```

Take a moment or two and review the WinMain(). It should look very generic because it's the one we have been using all along! The only differences, of course, are the calls to Game_Init(), Game_Main(), and Game_Shutdown(), which follow:

```
///////////////////////////////////////////////////////////

int Game_Main(void *parms = NULL)
{
// this is the main loop of the game, do all your processing
// here

// for now test if user is hitting ESC and send WM_CLOSE
if (KEYDOWN(VK_ESCAPE))
   SendMessage(main_window_handle,WM_CLOSE,0,0);

// return success or failure or your own return code here
return(1);

} // end Game_Main

///////////////////////////////////////////////////////////

int Game_Init(void *parms = NULL)
{
// this is called once after the initial window is created and
// before the main event loop is entered; do all your initialization
// here



// return success or failure or your own return code here
return(1);

} // end Game_Init

///////////////////////////////////////////////////////////

int Game_Shutdown(void *parms = NULL)
{
// this is called after the game is exited and the main event
// loop while is exited; do all you cleanup and shutdown here



// return success or failure or your own return code here
return(1);

} // end Game_Shutdown
```

The console functions don't do much! That's right—you're the one that's going to fill them in with code each time. However, I did put a little something in `Game_Main()` to test for the Esc key and send a `WM_CLOSE` message to kill the window. This way you don't always have to close the window with the mouse or Alt+F4 key combination. Also, I'm sure that you've noticed the parameter list of each function looks like the following:

```
Game_*(void *parms = NULL, int num_parms=0);
```

The `num_parms` is just a convenience for you if you want to send parameters to any of the functions along with the number of parameters sent. The type is `void`, so it's flexible. Again, this isn't in stone and you can surely change it, but it's something to start with.

Finally, you might think that I should have forced the window to be full screen without any controls by using the `WS_POPUP` style. I could have done this, but I'm thinking of making them windowed for a number of demos so that they're easier to debug. We can also change to full screen on a demo-by-demo basis, so let's leave it windowed for now.

> **C++**
>
> If you're a C programmer, the syntax `Game_Main(void *parms = NULL, int num_parms=0)` might look a little alien. The assignment on-the-fly is called default parameters. All it does is assign the parameters the listed default values so you don't have to type in parameters if you know that they are the same as the default values. For example, if you don't want to use the parameter list and don't care if `*parms ==` `NULL` and `num_parms == 0`, you can call `Game_Main()` just like that—without parameters. On the other hand, if you want to send parameters, you would have to use `Game_Main(&list, 12)`, or something similar. Take a look at Appendix D for a short tutorial on C++ if it still seems fuzzy.

If you run `T3DCONSOLE.EXE` on the CD, you won't see much other than a blank window. The cool thing is that all you have to do is fill in `Game_Init()`, `Game_Main()`, and `Game_Shutdown()` with your 3D game code and you have a million dollars! Of course, we have a little ways to go, but we're getting there <BG>.

As a final demo of using the T3D Game Console, I have created an application based on it called `DEMO4_9.CPP`. It's a 3D star field demo—not bad for GDI. Check it out and see if you can make it speed up and slow down. The program once again illustrates the erase, move, draw animation cycle. It also locks the frame rate to 30 fps with our timing code.

Summary

Well, my young Jedi, you are now a master of Windows—at least enough to take on the evil empire of game programming. In this chapter, you saw a number of topics, including GDI, controls, timing, getting information. In the end, you saw a real template application—the T3D Game Console. With it, you can get started on some serious Windows applications. Beginning with the next chapter, you're going to embark on the wonderful world of DirectX. It's cooler than cool—definitely a NexTGeN topic!

PART II

DirectX and 2D Fundamentals

CHAPTER 5

DirectX Fundamentals and the Dreaded COM

"Louie, Louie, Louie... I've had to listen to that for centuries!"
—Lestat, Interview With the Vampire

In this chapter, we're going to get a gargoyle's-eye view of DirectX and all the underlying components that make up this incredible technology. In addition, we're going to take a detailed look at COM (Component Object Model), which all the DirectX components are made of. If you're a straight C programmer, you should pay close attention. But not to worry, I'll keep it chill.

However, a word of warning on this material—read the whole chapter before you decide you don't get it. DirectX and COM are circularly related, so it's hard to explain one without the other. As an example, try to think how you would explain the concept of zero without using the word itself in the definition. If you think it's easy, it's not!

Here's a list of the main topics we'll touch upon:

- An introduction to DirectX
- The Component Object Model (COM)

- A working example of a COM implementation
- How DirectX and COM fit together
- The future of COM

DirectX Primer

I'm starting to feel like an evangelist for Microsoft these days (hint to Microsoft: Send me money), trying to turn all my friends to the dark side. But the bad guys always have better technology! Am I right? What would you rather ride around in, one of the Empire's Super Star Destroyers or some half-converted Rebel transport? See what I'm saying?

DirectX may take a bit more control from you as a programmer, but in truth it's worth its weight in gold. It's basically a system of software that abstracts video, audio, input, networking, installation, and more, so no matter what a particular PC's hardware configuration is, you can use the same code. In addition, DirectX technology is many times faster and more robust than GDI and/or MCI (the Media Control Interface), which is native to Windows.

Figure 5.1 illustrates how you would make a Windows game with and without DirectX. Notice how clean and elegant the DirectX solution is.

FIGURE 5.1
DirectX versus GDI/MCI.

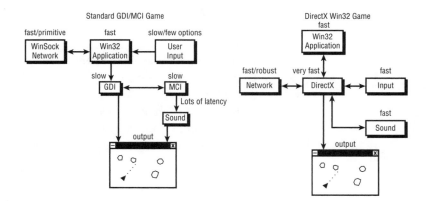

So how does DirectX work? Well, it gives you almost hardware-level control of all devices. This is possible through a technology called Component Object Model (COM) and a set of drivers and libraries written by both Microsoft and the hardware vendors themselves. Microsoft came up with a set of conventions—functions, variables, data structures, and so on—that must be used by the hardware vendors when implementing drivers to talk to the hardware.

As long as these conventions are followed, you don't need to worry about the details of the hardware. You just make calls to DirectX and it handles the details for you. No matter the video card, sound card, input device, network card, or whatever, as long as there's DirectX support, your program will be able to use it without you knowing anything about it!

Currently there are a number of DirectX components. They are listed here and shown graphically in Figure 5.2.

FIGURE 5.2
The architecture of DirectX and its relationship to Win32.

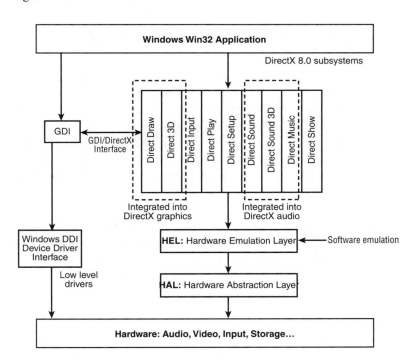

- DirectDraw (not available in DirectX 8.0+)
- DirectSound
- DirectSound3D
- DirectMusic
- DirectInput
- DirectPlay
- DirectSetup
- Direct3DRM
- Direct3DIM

- DirectX Graphics (merged DirectDraw/Direct3D)
- DirectX Audio (merged DirectSound/DirectMusic)
- DirectShow

With the release of DirectX 8.0, Microsoft decided to tightly integrate DirectDraw and Direct3D together and refer to it as DirectX Graphics. The results are the removal of DirectDraw from version 8.0; however, you can still use DirectDraw, there's simply not an upgrade of it in DirectX 8.0. Additionally, DirectSound and DirectMusic are more tightly integrated and now called DirectX Audio. Finally, DirectShow (formerly from DirectMedia) has been integrated into DirectX. Those guys at Microsoft really are busy little beavers!

All this may seem a bit overwhelming and confusing, but the cool thing about DirectX is if we want we could just use DirectX 3.0, or 5.0, or 6.0, or whatever. It's up to us since with COM (which we will get to) we can work with whatever version we like that suits our needs. And in our case, version 7.0 and some of 8.0 is more than enough. Furthermore, if you know one version of DirectX you know them all, the syntax may change a little, the interfaces do more, but all in all it's roughly the same. The only thing that really changes quickly is Direct3D, and we aren't going to be talking about that in this book, per se, we are going to be talking about game programming. True, on the CD there are two books on 3D and one is on Direct3D, but within the book we are going to try and keep the monster of DirectX under control, so you learn it well enough to use to make games. But, your entire game programming life is not connected to it, and if you were to use another API, you would still understand the fundamental techniques of game programming, that's the ultimate goal of this book.

The HEL and HAL

In Figure 5.2, you may notice that there are two layers under DirectX called the *HEL (Hardware Emulation Layer)* and the *HAL (Hardware Abstraction Layer)*. Here's the deal: DirectX is a very forward-looking design, so it assumes that advanced features are implemented by the hardware. However, if the hardware doesn't support some feature, what happens? This is the basis of the dual-mode HAL and HEL design.

The HAL, or Hardware Abstraction Layer, is the "to the metal" layer. It talks directly to the hardware. This layer is usually the device driver from the vendor, and you communicate to it directly through generic DirectX calls. The bottom line is that HAL is used when the feature you're requesting is supported directly by the hardware and thus is accelerated. For example, when you request a bitmap to be drawn, the hardware blitter does the work rather than a software loop.

The HEL, or Hardware Emulation Layer, is used when the hardware doesn't support the feature that you're requesting. Let's say that you ask the video card to rotate a bitmap. If the hardware doesn't support rotation, the HEL kicks in and software algorithms take over. Obviously, this is slower, but the point is that it does *not* break your program. It will still work—just slower. In addition, the switching between the HAL and HEL is transparent to you. If you ask DirectX to do something and the HAL does it directly, the hardware will do it. Otherwise, a software emulation will be called to get the job done with HEL.

Now, you might be thinking that there are a lot of layers of software here. That's a concern, but the truth is that DirectX is so clean that the only penalty you take for using it is maybe an extra function call or two. That's a small price to pay for 2D/3D graphics, network, and audio acceleration. Can you imagine writing drivers to control all the video accelerators on the market? Trust me, it would take literally thousands of man-years—it just can't be done. DirectX is really a massively distributed engineering effort by Microsoft and all the hardware vendors to bring you an ultra-high-performance standard.

The DirectX Foundation Classes in Depth

Now let's take a quick look at each DirectX component and what each does:

DirectDraw—This is the primary rendering and 2D bitmap engine that controls the video display. It's the conduit that all graphics must go through and probably the most important of all the DirectX components. The DirectDraw object represents more or less the video card(s) in your system. This is no longer available in DirectX 8.0 though, so we must use DirectX 7.0 interfaces for this one.

DirectSound—This is the sound component of DirectX. It only supports digital sound, not MIDI. However, this component makes your life 100 times easier because no longer do you have to license a third-party sound system to do your sound. Sound programming is a black art, and in the past no one wanted to keep up with writing all the drivers for all the sound cards. Hence, a couple of vendors cornered the market on sound libraries: Miles Sound System and DiamondWare Sound Toolkit. Both were very capable systems that allowed you to simply load and play digital and MIDI sounds from your DOS or Win32 programs. However, with DirectSound, DirectSound3D, and the latest DirectMusic components, there's obviously less use for third-party libraries.

DirectSound3—This is the 3D sound component of DirectSound. It allows you to position 3D sounds in space as if objects were floating around the room! This technology is relatively new, but it's maturing quickly. Today, most sound cards support hardware-accelerated 3D effects, including Doppler shift, refraction, reflection, and more. However, if software emulation is used, all this stuff comes to a halt!

DirectMusic—The newest addition to DirectX. Thank God! DirectMusic is the missing MIDI technology that DirectSound didn't support. But more than that, DirectMusic has a new *DLS* (Downloadable Sounds) system that allows you to create digital representations of instruments and then play them back with MIDI control. It's much like a Wave Table synthesizer, but in software. Also, DirectMusic has a new Performance Engine that is an artificial intelligence system of sorts. In real-time, it can make changes to your music based on templates you supply it with. In essence, the system can create new music on-the-fly. Wild, huh?

DirectInput—This system handles all input devices, including the mouse, keyboard, joystick, paddles, space balls, and so forth. Moreover, DirectInput now supports Force Feedback devices, which have electromechanical actuators and force sensors that allow you to physically manifest forces so the user can feel them. It's going to really put the cybersex industry into overdrive!

DirectPlay—This is the networking aspect of DirectX. It allows you to make abstract connections using the Internet, modems, direct connect, or any other kind of medium that might come up. The cool thing about DirectPlay is that it allows you to make these connections without knowing anything about networking. You don't have to write drivers, use sockets, or anything like that. In addition, DirectPlay supports the concepts of *sessions*, which are games in progress, and *lobbies*, which are places for gamers to congregate and play. Also, DirectPlay doesn't force you into any kind of multiplayer network architecture. All it does is send and receive packets for you. What they contain and if they are reliable is up to you.

Direct3DRM—This is Direct3D Retained Mode, which is a high-level, object- and frame-based 3D system that you can use to create basic 3D programs. It takes advantage of 3D acceleration, but it isn't the fastest thing in the world. It's great for making walkthrough programs, model displayers, or extremely slow demos.

Direct3DIM—This is Direct3D Immediate Mode, which is the low-level 3D support for DirectX. Originally, this was incredibly hard to work with and was the cause for many flamewars with OpenGL. The old Immediate Mode used what are called *execute buffers*, basically arrays of data and instructions that you created that described the scene to be drawn—very ugly. However, since DirectX 5.0, Immediate Mode now supports a much more OpenGL-like interface through the `DrawPrimitive()` functions. This allows you to send triangle strips, fans, and so on to the rendering engine and make state changes with function calls rather than execute buffers. Hence, I now like Direct3D Immediate Mode! Even though this volume and Volume II are software-based 3D game books, to be complete, we're going to cover D3D IM at the end of Volume II. In fact, there is an entire cyber-book on Direct3D Immediate Mode on the CD of Volume II.

DirectSetup/AutoPlay—These are quasi-DirectX components that allow a program to install DirectX from your application on the user's machine and start your game up directly when the CD is placed in the system. DirectSetup is a small set of functions that load the run-time DirectX files on a user's machine and register them in the registry. AutoPlay is the standard CD subsystem that looks for the AUTOPLAY.INF file on the CD root. If the file is found, AutoPlay executes the batch command functions in the file.

DirectX Graphics—Microsoft decided to merge the functionality of DirectDraw and Direct3D here to increase performance and allow 3D effects in a 2D domain. I personally don't think that DirectDraw should have been removed. Not only is there a lot of software that uses it, but using Direct3D to do 2D is a pain for the most part, it's overkill in many applications that are 2D in nature for example GUI applications or other simple games. In any case, we won't need to worry about it since we are going to use DirectX 7.0 interfaces for DirectDraw.

DirectX Audio—This merger is far less destructive than that of DirectX Graphics, here DirectSound and DirectMusic have been more tightly integrated—that's about it, nothing has been removed. In DirectX 7.0 DirectMusic was still a little on its own, totally COM based, and not accessible from DirectSound. With DirectX Audio this has changed, and you can work with them together if you wish.

DirectShow—This component is used to stream media on the Windows platform. DirectShow provides for high-quality capture and playback of multimedia streams. It supports a wide variety of formats, including Advanced Streaming Format (ASF), Motion Picture Experts Group (MPEG), Audio-Video Interleaved (AVI), MPEG Audio Layer-3 (MP3), and WAV files. It supports capture using Windows Driver Model (WDM) devices or older Video for Windows devices. DirectShow is integrated with other DirectX technologies. It automatically detects and uses video and audio acceleration hardware when available, but also supports systems without acceleration hardware. This makes life really easy, since before when you wanted to play some video in a game you either had to use a 3rd party library or write one yourself. This is REALLY nice since it's integrated into DirectX. The only problem is it's rather advanced, and takes quite a bit to set up and use.

Finally, you might be wondering what the deal is with all the versions of DirectX. It seems to be revised on a six-month basis. This is true, for the most part. It's a hazard of the business we're in—graphics and game technology move very fast. However, since DirectX is based on COM technology, programs that you write for, say, DirectX version 3.0 are guaranteed to work on DirectX version 8.0. Let's see how that works...

COM: Is It the Work of Microsoft... or Demons?

Computer programs today are easily reaching multimillion-line sizes, and large systems will soon reach to billions of lines of code. With programs this large, abstraction and hierarchy are of utmost importance. Otherwise, complete chaos would ensue. Kinda like customer service when you call the phone company.

The two most recent attempts at computer languages that foster more object-oriented programming techniques are, of course, C++ and Java. C++ is really an evolution (or maybe more a regurgitation) of C, with object-oriented hooks built into it. On the other hand, Java is based on C++ but is fully object-oriented and much cleaner. In addition, Java is more of a platform while C++ is simply a language.

Anyway, languages are great, but it's how you use them that counts in the long run. Alas, even though C++ is chock full of cool OO (object-oriented) features, many people don't use them or use them the wrong way. Thus, large-scale programs are still a bit of a problem. This is one of the difficulties that the COM model addresses.

COM was invented many years back as a simple white paper on a new software paradigm, which was similar to how computer chips or Lego blocks work. You simply plug them together and they work. Computer chips and Lego blocks know how to be computer chips and Lego blocks (since their interfaces are well defined), so everything works out. To implement this kind of technology with software, you need a very generic interface that can take on the form of any type of function set you can imagine. This is what COM does.

One of the cool things about computer chips is that when you add more of them to a design, you don't have to tell all the other chips that you've changed something. However, as you know, this is a little harder with software programs. You at least have to recompile to make an executable. Fixing this problem is another goal of COM. You should be able to add new features to a COM object without breaking the software that uses the old COM object. In addition, COM objects can be changed without recompiling the original program, which is very cool.

Since you can upgrade COM objects without recompiling your program, that means you can upgrade your software without patches and new versions. For example, say you have a program that uses three COM objects: one that implements graphics, one for sound, and one for networking (see Figure 5.3). Now imagine that you sell 100,000 copies of this program, but you don't want to send out 100,000 upgrades! To update the graphics COM object, all you do is give the users the new COM object for graphics and the program will automatically use it. No recompiling, no linking, no nothing. Easy. Of course, all this technology is very complex at the low level, and writing your own COM objects is a bit challenging, but using them is easy.

FIGURE 5.3
An overview of
COM.

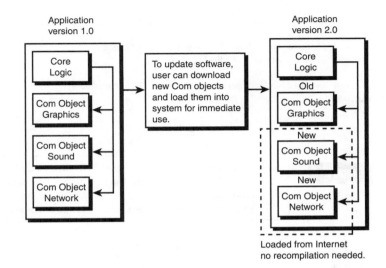

The next question is, how are COM objects distributed or contained, given their plug-and-play nature? The answer is that there are no rules about this, but in most cases COM objects are DLLs, or Dynamic Link Libraries, that can be downloaded or supplied with the program that uses them. This way they can be easily upgraded and changed. The only problem with this is that the program that uses the COM object must know how to load it from a DLL. But we'll get to that in the "Building a Quasi-COM Object" section later in this chapter.

What Exactly Is a COM Object?

A COM object is really a C++ class or a set of C++ classes that implement a number of *interfaces*. (Basically, an interface is a set of functions.) These interfaces are used to communicate with the COM object. Take a look at Figure 5.4. Here we see a single COM object that has three interfaces named IGRAPHICS, ISOUND, and IINPUT.

Each one of these interfaces has a number of functions that you can call (when you know how) to do work. So a single COM object can have one or more interfaces, and you may have one or more COM objects. Moreover, the COM specification states that all interfaces you create must be derived from a special base class interface called IUnknown. For you C programmers, all this means is that IUnknown is like a starting point to build the interface from.

Let's take a look at the IUnknown class definition:

```
struct  IUnknown
{

// this function is used to retrieve other interfaces
```

```
virtual HRESULT __stdcall QueryInterface(const IID &iid, (void **)ip) = 0;

// this is used to increment interfaces reference count
virtual ULONG __stdcall AddRef() = 0;

// this is used to decrement interfaces reference count
virtual ULONG __stdcall Release() = 0;


};
```

NOTE
Notice that all methods are pure and virtual. In addition, the methods use __stdcall in deference to the standard C/C++ calling convention. If you remember from Chapter 2, "The Windows Programming Model," __stdcall pushes the parameters on the stack from right to left.

FIGURE 5.4
The interfaces of a COM object.

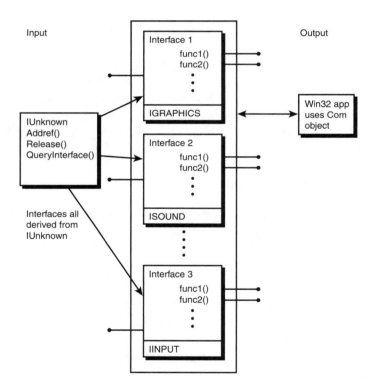

Even if you're a C++ programmer, this class definition may look a bit bizarre if you're rusty on virtual functions. Anyway, let's dissect IUnknown and see what's up. All interfaces derived from IUnknown must implement, at very minimum, each of the methods QueryInterface(), AddRef(), and Release().

QueryInterface() is the key to COM. It's used to request a pointer to the interface functions that you desire. To make the request happen, you must have an *interface ID*. This is a unique number, 128 bits long, that you assign to your interface. There are 2^{128} different possible interface IDs, and I guarantee that we wouldn't run out in a billion years even if everybody on this planet did nothing but make COM objects 24 hours a day! More on the interface ID when we get to a real example a little later in the chapter.

Furthermore, one of the rules of COM is that if you have an interface, you can always request any other interface from it as long as it's from the same COM object. Basically, this means that you can get anywhere from anywhere else. Take a look at Figure 5.5 to see this graphically.

TIP	Usually, you don't have to call AddRef() yourself on interfaces or COM objects. It's done internally by the QueryInterface() function. But sometimes you may have to, if you want to increase the reference count to trick the COM object into thinking that there are more references to it than there really are.

FIGURE 5.5
Navigating the interfaces of a COM object.

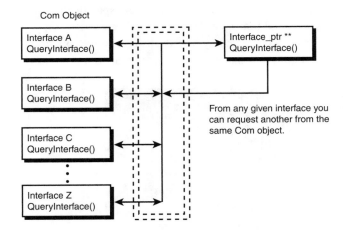

AddRef() is a curious function. COM objects use a technique called reference counting to track their life. This is due to one of the specifications of COM: It's not language-specific. Hence, AddRef() is called when a COM object is created and when interfaces are created to track how many references there are to the objects. If a COM object were to use malloc() or new[], that would be C/C++-specific. When the reference count drops to 0, the objects are destroyed internally.

This brings us to a problem—if COM objects are C++ classes, how can they be created or used in Visual Basic, Java, ActiveX, and so on? It just so happens that the designers of COM used virtual C++ classes to implement COM, but you don't need to use C++

to access them or even to create them. As long as you create the same binary image that a Microsoft C++ compiler would when creating a virtual C++ class, the COM object will be COM-compliant. Of course, most compiler products have extras or tools to help make COM objects, so that's not too much of a problem. The cool thing about this is that you can write a COM object in C++, Visual Basic, or Delphi, and then that COM object can be used by any of those languages! A binary image in memory is a binary image in memory.

`Release()` is used to decrement the reference count of a COM object or interface. In most cases, you must call this function yourself when you're done with an interface. However, sometimes if you create an object and then create another object from that object, calling `Release()` on the parent will trickle down and `Release()` the child or derived object. But either way, it's a good idea to `Release()` in the opposite order that you queried.

More on Interface IDs and GUIDs

As I mentioned earlier, every COM object and interface thereof must have a unique 128-bit identifier that you use to request or access it. These numbers are called *GUIDs (Globally Unique Identifiers)* in general. More specifically, when defining COM interfaces they're called *Interface IDs* or *IIDs*. To generate them, you must use a program called `GUIDGEN.EXE` created by Microsoft (or a similar program that uses the same algorithm). Figure 5.6 shows `GUIDGEN.EXE` in action.

FIGURE 5.6
The GUID generator
GUIDGEN.EXE
in action.

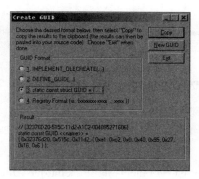

What you do is select what kind of ID you want (there are four different formats), and then the program generates a 128-bit vector that is guaranteed to never be generated again on any machine at any time. Seem impossible? It's not. It's just math and probability theory. The bottom line is that it works, so don't get a headache asking why.

After you generate the GUID or IID, it's placed on the Clipboard and you can paste it into your programs by pressing Ctrl+V. Here's an example of an IID I just made while writing this paragraph:

```
// {C1BCE961-3E98-11d2-A1C2-004095271606}
static const <<name>> =
{ 0xc1bce961, 0x3e98, 0x11d2,
{ 0xa1, 0xc2, 0x0, 0x40, 0x95, 0x27, 0x16, 0x6 } };
```

Of course, you would replace <<name>> with the name you choose for the GUID in your program, but you get the idea.

GUIDs and IIDs are used to reference COM objects and their interfaces. So whenever you make a new COM object and a set of interfaces, these are the only numbers that you have to give to programmers to work with your COM objects. Once they have the IIDs, they can create COM objects and interfaces.

Building a Quasi-COM Object

Creating a full-fledged COM object is well beyond the scope of this book. You only need to know how to use them. However, if you're like me, you like to have some idea of what's going on. So what we're going to do is build up a very basic COM example to help you answer some of the questions that I'm sure I've created for you.

All right, you know that all COM objects contain a number of interfaces, but all COM objects must be derived from the IUnknown class to begin with. Then, once you have all your interfaces built, you put them all in a container class and implement everything. As an example, let's create a COM object that has three interfaces: ISound, IGraphics, and IInput. Here's how you might define them:

```
// the graphics interface
struct IGraphics : IUnknown
{
virtual int InitGraphics(int mode)=0;
virtual int SetPixel(int x, int y, int c)=0;
// more methods...
};

// the sound interface
struct ISound : IUnknown
{
virtual int InitSound(int driver)=0;
virtual int PlaySound(int note, int vol)=0;
// more methods...
};


// the input interface
struct IInput: IUnknown
{
virtual int InitInput(int device)=0;
virtual int ReadStick(int stick)=0;
// more methods...
};
```

Now that you have all your interfaces, let's create your container class, which is really the heart of the COM object:

```
class CT3D_Engine: public IGraphics, ISound, IInput
{
public:

// implement IUnknown here
virtual HRESULT __stdcall QueryInterface(const IID &iid,
                                         (void **)ip)
{ /* real implementation */ }

// this method increases the interfaces reference count
virtual ULONG __stdcall Addref()
                    { /* real implementation */}

// this method decreases the interfaces reference count
virtual ULONG __stdcall Release()
                    { /* real implementation */}

// note there still isn't a method to create one of these
// objects...

// implement each interface now

// IGraphics
virtual int InitGraphics(int mode)
                    { /*implementation */}
virtual int SetPixel(int x, int y, int c)
                    {/*implementation */}


// ISound
virtual int InitSound(int driver)
                    { /*implementation */}
virtual int PlaySound(int note, int vol)
                    { /*implementation */}

// IInput
virtual int InitInput(int device)
                    { /*implementation */}

virtual int ReadStick(int stick)
                    { /*implementation */}

private:

// .. locals

};
```

> **NOTE**
>
> You're still missing a generic way to create a COM object. This is a problem, no doubt. The COM specification states that there are a number of ways to do it, but none of them can tie the implementation to a specific platform or language. One of the simpler ways to do it is to create a function called `CoCreateInstance()` or `ComCreate()` to create the initial `IUnknown` instance of the object. The function usually loads a DLL that contains the COM code and works from there. Again, this technology is beyond what you need to know, but I just want to throw it out there for you. However, we're going to cheat a little to continue with the example.

As you can see from the example, COM interfaces and coding are nothing really more than slightly advanced C++ virtual classes with some conventions. However, true COM objects must be created properly and registered in the registry, and a number of other rules must be adhered to. But at the lowest level, they are simply classes with methods (or for you C programmers, *structs*) with function pointers, more or less. Anyway, let's take a brief step back and review what you know about COM.

A Quick Recap of COM

COM is a new way of writing component software that allows you to create reusable software modules that are dynamically linked at run-time. Each of these COM objects has one or more interfaces that do the actual work. These interfaces are nothing more than collections of methods or functions that are referenced through a virtual function table pointer (more on this in the next section).

Each COM object and interface is unique from the others due to the use of GUIDs, or Globally Unique Identifiers, that you must generate for your COM objects and interfaces. You use the GUIDs or IIDs to refer to COM objects and interfaces and share them with other programmers.

If you create a new COM object that upgrades an old one, you must still implement the old interfaces along with any new ones you might add. This is a very important rule: All programs based on COM objects should still work, without recompilation, with new versions of the COM object(s).

COM is a general specification that can be followed with any language on any machine. The only rule is that the binary image of the COM object must be that of a virtual class generated by a Microsoft VC compiler—it just worked out that way. However, COM can be used on other machines, like Mac, SGI, and so on, as long as they follow the rules for using and creating COM objects.

Finally, COM opens up the possibility of creating massive computer programs (in the multibillion-line range) by means of its component-level generic architecture. And of course, DirectX, OLE, and ActiveX are all based on COM, so you need to understand it!

A Working COM Program

As a complete example of creating a COM object and a couple of interfaces, I I
have created DEMO5_1.CPP for you. The program implements a COM object called
CCOM_OBJECT that is composed of two interfaces, IX and IY. The program is a decent
implementation of a COM object, but of course it's missing some of the high-level
details like being a DLL, loading dynamically, and so on. But the COM object is fully
implemented as far as all the methods and the IUnknown class are concerned.

What I want you to do is look at it very carefully, play with the code, and see how it
works. Listing 5.1 contains the entire source for the COM object and a simple C/C++
main() test bed to run it in.

LISTING 5.1 A Complete COM Object Program

```
// DEMO5_1.CPP - A ultra minimal working COM example
// NOTE: not fully COM compliant

// INCLUDES //////////////////////////////////////////////////

#include <stdio.h>
#include <malloc.h>
#include <iostream.h>
#include <objbase.h> // note: you must include this header it
                     // contains important constants
                     // you must use in COM programs

// GUIDS /////////////////////////////////////////////////////

// these were all generated with GUIDGEN.EXE

// {B9B8ACE1-CE14-11d0-AE58-444553540000}
const IID IID_IX =
{ 0xb9b8ace1, 0xce14, 0x11d0,
{ 0xae, 0x58, 0x44, 0x45, 0x53, 0x54, 0x0, 0x0 } };


// {B9B8ACE2-CE14-11d0-AE58-444553540000}
const IID IID_IY =
{ 0xb9b8ace2, 0xce14, 0x11d0,
{ 0xae, 0x58, 0x44, 0x45, 0x53, 0x54, 0x0, 0x0 } };

// {B9B8ACE3-CE14-11d0-AE58-444553540000}
const IID IID_IZ =
{ 0xb9b8ace3, 0xce14, 0x11d0,
{ 0xae, 0x58, 0x44, 0x45, 0x53, 0x54, 0x0, 0x0 } };


// INTERFACES ////////////////////////////////////////////////

// define the IX interface
```

LISTING 5.1   Continued

```
interface IX: IUnknown
{

virtual void __stdcall fx(void)=0;

};

// define the IY interface
interface IY: IUnknown
{

virtual void __stdcall fy(void)=0;

};


// CLASSES AND COMPONENTS /////////////////////////////////////

// define the COM object
class CCOM_OBJECT :     public IX,
                    public IY
{
public:

    CCOM_OBJECT() : ref_count(0) {}
    ~CCOM_OBJECT() {}

private:

virtual HRESULT __stdcall QueryInterface(const IID &iid, void **iface);
virtual ULONG __stdcall AddRef();
virtual ULONG __stdcall Release();

virtual    void __stdcall fx(void)
            {cout << "Function fx has been called." << endl; }
virtual void __stdcall fy(void)
            {cout << "Function fy has been called." << endl; }

int ref_count;

};

// CLASS METHODS /////////////////////////////////////////////

HRESULT __stdcall CCOM_OBJECT::QueryInterface(const IID &iid,
                                            void **iface)
{
// this function basically casts the this pointer or the IUnknown
// pointer into the interface requested, notice the comparison with
// the GUIDs generated and defined in the beginning of the program

// requesting the IUnknown base interface
if (iid==IID_IUnknown)
```

DirectX and 2D Fundamentals

LISTING 5.1 Continued

```
    {
    cout << "Requesting IUnknown interface" << endl;
    *iface = (IX*)this;

    } // end if

// maybe IX?
if (iid==IID_IX)
    {
    cout << "Requesting IX interface" << endl;
    *iface = (IX*)this;

    } // end if
else  // maybe IY
if (iid==IID_IY)
    {
    cout << "Requesting IY interface" << endl;
    *iface = (IY*)this;

    } // end if
else
    { // cant find it!
    cout << "Requesting unknown interface!" << endl;
    *iface = NULL;
    return(E_NOINTERFACE);
    } // end else

// if everything went well cast pointer to
// IUnknown and call addref()
((IUnknown *)(*iface))->AddRef();

return(S_OK);

} // end QueryInterface

//////////////////////////////////////////////////////////////

ULONG __stdcall CCOM_OBJECT::AddRef()
{
// increments reference count
cout << "Adding a reference" << endl;
return(++ref_count);

} // end AddRef

//////////////////////////////////////////////////////////////

ULONG __stdcall CCOM_OBJECT::Release()
{
// decrements reference count
cout << "Deleting a reference" << endl;
if (—ref_count==0)
```

LISTING 5.1 Continued

```
    {
    delete this;
    return(0);
    } // end if
else
    return(ref_count);

} // end Release

///////////////////////////////////////////////////////////

IUnknown *CoCreateInstance(void)
{
// this is a very basic implementation of CoCreateInstance()
// it creates an instance of the COM object, in this case
// I decided to start with a pointer to IX — IY would have
// done just as well

IUnknown *comm_obj = (IX *)new(CCOM_OBJECT);

cout << "Creating Comm object" << endl;

// update reference count
comm_obj->AddRef();

return(comm_obj);

} // end CoCreateInstance

///////////////////////////////////////////////////////////

void main(void)
{

// create the main COM object
IUnknown *punknown = CoCreateInstance();

// create two NULL pointers the IX and IY interfaces
IX *pix=NULL;
IY *piy=NULL;

// from the original COM object query for interface IX
punknown->QueryInterface(IID_IX, (void **)&pix);

// try some of the methods of IX
pix->fx();

// release the interface
pix->Release();
```

DirectX and 2D Fundamentals

LISTING 5.1   Continued

```
// now query for the IY interface
punknown->QueryInterface(IID_IY, (void **)&piy);

// try some of the methods
piy->fy();

// release the interface
piy->Release();

// release the COM object itself
punknown->Release();

} // end main
```

I have already precompiled the program for you into the executable DEMO5_1.EXE.
However, if you want to experiment and compile DEMO5_1.CPP, remember to create a
Win32 Console Application because the demo uses main() rather than WinMain() and
is, of course, a text-based program.

Working with DirectX COM Objects

Now that you have an idea what DirectX is and how COM works, let's take a closer
look at how they actually work together. Like I said, there are a number of COM
objects that make up DirectX. These COM objects are contained within your system
as DLLs when you load the run-time version of DirectX. When you run a third-party
DirectX game, what happens is that one or more of these DLLs are loaded by the
DirectX application, and then interfaces are requested and the methods (functions) of
the interfaces are used to get the work done. That's the run-time side of things.

The compile-time angle is a little different. The designers of DirectX knew that they
were dealing with us game programmers, and assumed that most of us hate Windows
programming—very true. Alas, they knew that they better keep the COM stuff to a
minimum, or else game programmers would really hate using DirectX. Thus, 90%
of the DirectX COM objects are wrapped in nice little function calls that take care of
the COM stuff. So, you don't have to call CoCreateInstance(), do COM initialization, and stuff like that. However, you may have to query for a new interface with
QueryInterface(), but we'll get to that in a bit. The point is, DirectX really tries to
hide the tedium of working with COM from you so you can work with the core functionality of DirectX.

With all that said, to compile a DirectX program, you must include a number of
import libraries that have the COM wrappers within them so you can make calls to
DirectX using those wrapper functions to create the COM objects. For the most part,
the libraries you need are

```
DDRAW.LIB
DSOUND.LIB
DINPUT.LIB
DINPUT8.LIB
DSETUP.LIB
DPLAYX.LIB
D3DIM.LIB
D3DRM.LIB
```

But remember, these libraries don't contain the COM objects themselves. These are only wrapper libraries and hooks that make calls to load the DirectX DLLs themselves, which are the COM objects. Finally, when you do call one of the DirectX COM objects, the result is usually just an interface pointer. This is where are the action occurs. Just like in the example of DEMO5_1.CPP, once you have the interface pointer, you're free to make function calls—or more correctly in C++ speak, method calls. However, if you're a C programmer, take a quick look at the next section if you feel uncomfortable with function pointers. If you're a C++ programmer, you can skip ahead to the next section if you want.

COM and Function Pointers

Once you have created a COM object and retrieved an interface pointer, what you really have is a *VTABLE (Virtual Function Table)* pointer. Take a look at Figure 5.7 to see this graphically. Virtual functions are used so that you can code with function calls that are not bound until run-time. This is the key to COM and virtual functions. In essence, C++ has this built in, but you can do the same thing with C by using straight function pointers.

FIGURE 5.7
Virtual Function
Table architecture.

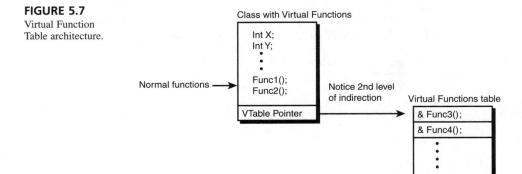

A function pointer is a type of pointer used to make calls to a function. But instead of the function being hard-bound to some code, you can move it around as long as the prototype of the function pointer is the same as the function(s) you point it to. For example, say that you want to write a graphics driver function to plot a pixel on the

DirectX and 2D Fundamentals

screen. But also suppose that you have dozens of different video cards to support and they all work differently, as shown in Figure 5.8.

FIGURE 5.8
Software design needed to support different video cards.

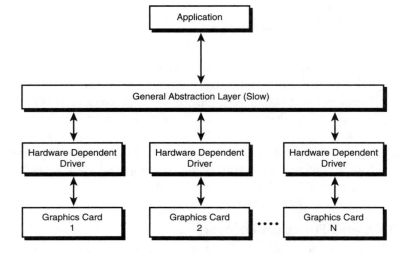

You want to call the plot pixel function the same way for all these video cards, but the internal code is different depending on what card is plugged in. Here's a typical C programmer's solution:

```
int SetPixel(int x, int y, int color, int card)
{
// what video card do we have?
switch(card)
      {
      case ATI:    { /* hardware specific code */ } break;
      case VOODOO: { /* hardware specific code */ } break;
      case SIII:   { /* hardware specific code */ } break;
      .
      .
      .
      default:     { /* standard VGA code */  } break;

      } // end switch

// return success
return(1);

} // end SetPixel
```

Do you see the problem with this? First, the `switch` statement sucks. It's slow, long, prone to errors, and you might break the function while adding support for another card. A better solution for straight C is to use function pointers like this:

```
// function pointer declaration, weird huh?
int (* SetPixel)(int x, int y, int color);
```

```
// now here's all our set pixel functions

int SetPixel_ATI(int x, int y, int color)
{
// code for ATI

} // end SetPixel_ATI

////////////////////////////////////////////////////////////

int SetPixel_VOODOO(int x, int y, int color)
{
// code for VOODOO

} // end SetPixel_VOODOO

////////////////////////////////////////////////////////////

int SetPixel_SIII(int x, int y, int color)
{
// code for SIII

} // end SetPixel_SIII
```

Now you're ready to rock. When the system starts up, it checks what kind of card is installed and then, once and *only* once, sets the generic function pointer to point to the correct card's function. For example, if you wanted `SetPixel()` to point to the ATI version, you would code it like this:

```
// assigning a function pointer
SetPixel = SetPixel_ATI;
```

Isn't that easy? Figure 5.9 shows what this looks like graphically.

FIGURE 5.9
Using function pointers to enable different code blocks.

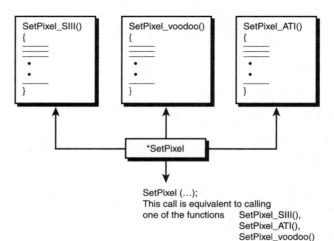

Notice that SetPixel() is, in a way, an alias for SetPixel_ATI(). This is the key to function pointers. Now, to call SetPixel() you make a normal call, but instead of calling the empty SetPixel(), the call really calls SetPixel_ATI():

```
// this really calls SetPixel_ATI(10,20,4);
SetPixel(10,20,4);
```

The point is that your code always looks the same, but it does different things based on how you assign the function pointer. This is such a cool technology that much of C++ and virtual functions are based on it. That's all virtual functions really are—late binding of function pointers, but nicely built into the language and then built up as you've done here.

With that in mind, let's see how you would finish your generic video driver link-up… All you have to do is test to see which card is installed, set the SetPixel() function pointer once to the proper SetPixel*() function, and that's it. Take a look:

```
int SetCard(int card)
{
// assign the function pointer based on the card
switch(card)
    {
    case ATI:
        {
        SetPixel = SetPixel_ATI;

        } break;

    case VOODOO:
        {
        SetPixel = SetPixel_VOODOO;
        } break;

    case SIII:
        {
        SetPixel = SetPixel_SIII;
        } break;

    default: break;

    } // end switch

} // end SetCard
```

At the beginning of your code, you would make a call to the set up function like this:

```
SetCard(card);
```

And from then on, you're good to go. This is how function pointers and virtual functions are used in C++, so now let's see how these techniques are used with DirectX.

Creating and Using DirectX Interfaces

At this point, I think you understand that COM objects are collections of interfaces, which are simply function pointers (and more specifically, VTABLEs). Hence, all you need to do to work with a DirectX COM object is create it, retrieve an interface pointer, and then make calls to the interface using the proper syntax. As an example, I'll use the main DirectDraw interface to show how this is done.

First off, you need three things to experiment with DirectDraw:

- The DirectDraw run-time COM object(s) and DLLs must be loaded and registered. This is what the DirectX installer does.
- You must include the DDRAW.LIB import library in your Win32 programs so that the wrapper functions you call are linked in.
- You need to include DDRAW.H in your program so the compiler can see the header information, prototypes, and data types for DirectDraw.

With that in mind, here's the data type for a DirectDraw 1.0 interface pointer:

```
LPDIRECTDRAW lpdd = NULL;
```

and here is the interface pointer type for DirectDraw 4.0:

```
LPDIRECTDRAW4 lpdd = NULL;
```

and for DirectDraw 7.0:

```
LPDIRECTDRAW7 lpdd = NULL;
```

And for 8.0 there isn't any!

Now, to create a DirectDraw COM object and retrieve an interface pointer to the DirectDraw object (which represents the video card), all you need to do is use the wrapper function DirectDrawCreate() like this:

```
DirectDrawCreate(NULL, &lpdd, NULL);
```

This will return the basic DirectDraw interface 1.0. In Chapter 6, "First Contact: DirectDraw," I go into the parameters in detail. But for now, just be aware that this call creates a DirectDraw object and assigns the interface pointer to lpdd.

Now you're in business and can make calls to DirectDraw. But wait a minute! You don't know the methods or functions that are available—that's why you're reading this book <BG>. As an example, here's how you would set the video mode to 640x480 with 256 colors:

```
lpdd->SetVideoMode(640, 480, 256);
```

Is that simple or what? About the only extra work is the pointer dereference from the DirectDraw interface pointer `lpdd`—that's it. Of course, what's really happening is a lookup in the virtual table of the interface, but don't be concerned about that.

In essence, any call to DirectX takes the following form:

```
interface_pointer->method_name(parameter list);
```

Also, you can get any other interfaces that you might want to work with (for example, Direct3D) from the original DirectDraw interface by using `QueryInterface()`. Moreover, since there are multiple versions of DirectX floating around, a while ago Microsoft stopped writing wrapped functions to retrieve the latest interface for everything, so sometimes you have to manually retrieve the latest DirectX interface yourself with `QueryInterface()`. Let's take a look at that.

Querying for Interfaces

The weird thing about DirectX is that all the version numbers are out of sync. This is a bit of a problem, and definitely a cause for confusion. Here's the deal: When the first version of DirectX came out, the DirectDraw interface was named like this:

```
IDIRECTDRAW
```

Then, when DirectX 2.0 came out, DirectDraw was upgraded to version 2.0, so we had this:

```
IDIRECTDRAW
IDIRECTDRAW2
```

Now, at version 6.0, we have something like this:

```
IDIRECTDRAW
IDIRECTDRAW2
IDIRECTDRAW4
```

Then with version 7.0, we have something like this:

```
IDIRECTDRAW
IDIRECTDRAW2
IDIRECTDRAW4

IDIRECTDRAW7
```

And now with version 8.0 there is no support for DirectDraw, so you still only have `IDIRECTDRAW7` as the latest interface —get it?

Wait a minute—what happened to interfaces 3 and 5? I have no idea, but this is the problem. Hence, the idea is that even though you're using DirectX 8.0, it doesn't mean that the interfaces are up to that version. Moreover, they can all be out of sync. DirectX 6.0 may have DirectDraw interfaces up to `IDIRECTDRAW4`, but DirectSound is only up to interface version 1.0, which is simply called `IDIRECTSOUND`. You can see the mess we're in! The moral of the story is that whenever you use a DirectX interface, you should make sure that you're using the latest version. If you're not sure, use the revision 1.0 interface pointer from the generic create function to get the latest version.

Here's an example of what I'm talking about: `DirectDrawCreate()` returns a revision 1.0 interface pointer, but DirectDraw is really up to `IDIRECTDRAW7`. So how do you take advantage of this new functionality?

There are two ways to do this: with low-level COM functions or with `QueryInterfaced()`. Let's use the latter. The process goes like this: First, you create the DirectDraw COM interface with a call to `DirectDrawCreate()`. This returns a boring `IDIRECTDRAW` interface pointer. Then, you make a call to `QueryInterface()` using this pointer and you retrieve it using the Interface ID (or GUID) for `IDIRECT-DRAW7`. Here's an example:

```
LPDIRECTDRAW  lpdd;   // version 1.0
LPDIRECTDRAW7 lpdd7;  // version 7.0

// create version 1.0 DirectDraw object interface
DirectDrawCreate(NULL, &lpdd, NULL);

// now look in DDRAW.H header, find IDIRECTDRAW7 interface
// ID and use it to query for the interface
lpdd->QueryInterface(IID_IDirectDraw7, &lpdd7);
```

At this point, you have two interface pointers. But you don't need the pointer to `IDIRECTDRAW`, so you should release it:

```
// release, decrement reference count
lpdd->Release();

// set to NULL to be safe
lpdd = NULL;
```

Remember this? You should release an interface when you're done with it. Hence, when your program terminates, you would also release the `IDIRECTDRAW7` interface like this:

```
// release, decrement reference count
lpdd7->Release();

// set to NULL to be safe
lpdd7 = NULL;
```

Ok, now that you see how to get one interface from another, there is a ray of light—in DirectX 7.0 Microsoft added a new `DirectDrawCreateEx()` function that actually returns the `IDIRECTDRAW7` interface! Amazing huh? Then they killed DirectDraw in version 8.0, but who cares? We can still use the function:

```
HRESULT WINAPI DirectDrawCreateEx(
```

```
GUID FAR *lpGUID,  // the GUID of the driver, NULL for active display
LPVOID *lplpDD,    // receiver of the interface
REFIID iid,        // the interface ID of the interface you are requesting
IUnknown FAR *pUnkOuter  // advanced COM, NULL
);
```

This new function allows you to send the requested DirectDraw version in *iid* and the function will create the COM object for you, thus, we just call the function like this:

```
LPDIRECTDRAW7 lpdd;  // version 7.0

// create version 7.0 DirectDraw object interface
DirectDrawCreateEx(NULL, (void **)&lpdd, IID_IDirectDraw7, NULL);
```

Basically, the call to `DirectDrawCreateEx()` creates the requested interface directly, so you don't have to go thru the intermediary of DirectDraw 1.0. Well, that's all there is to using DirectX and COM. Of course, you haven't seen all the hundreds of functions that DirectX components have or all the interfaces—but you will <BG>.

The Future of COM

Currently, there are a number of distributed object technologies similar to COM, such as CORBA (Common Object Request Broker Architecture). However, since you're worried about Windows games, these other technologies aren't as important.

The latest version of COM is called COM++, and it's a much more robust implementation, with better rules and a more thought-out set of implementation details. COM++ will make distributed component software even easier to create. Granted, COM++ is a bit more complex than COM, but hey, that's life.

In addition to COM and COM++, there's also the full Internet/intranet version of COM called DCOM—Distributed COM. With DCOM technology, the COM objects don't even need to be on your machine. They can be served from other machines on the network. Is that cool or what? Imagine having massive DCOM servers that your programs basically act as clients to. Incredible technology, if I do say so myself.

Summary

This chapter has covered some pretty technical material and concepts. COM is not simple to understand, and it does take a bit of studying to really get a good hold on it. However, using COM is ten times easier than understanding it, as you'll see in the next chapter. Anyway, you also took a look at DirectX and all of its components. So once you've seen the details of each component and how to use it in the following chapters, you'll have a good idea of how they fit together.

CHAPTER 6

First Contact: DirectDraw

"Are you sure you don't want to come upstairs?"
—*John Milton, The Devil's Advocate*

In this chapter you're going to take your first look at one of the
most important components of DirectX: *DirectDraw*. This is
perhaps the most enabling technology in DirectX because it's
the conduit through which 2D graphics are performed and the
frame buffer layer that Direct3D is built upon. And of course in
DirectX version 8.0 DirectDraw is completely integrated into
Direct3D. Furthermore, if you understand DirectDraw alone, you
have more than enough power to create any kind of graphical
application that you might have written under DOS16/32.
DirectDraw is the key to understanding a number of concepts
indigenous to DirectX, so listen up!

Here's your hit list for this chapter:

- The interfaces of DirectDraw
- Creating a DirectDraw object
- Cooperating with Windows
- Getting into the mode of things
- The subtleties of color
- Building a display surface

The Interfaces of DirectDraw

DirectDraw is composed of a number of *interfaces*. If you recall from the discussion on the Component Object Model (COM) in Chapter 5, "DirectX Fundamentals and the Dreaded COM," interfaces are nothing more than collections of functions and/or methods that you use to communicate with components. Take a look at Figure 6.1 for a graphical illustration of the DirectDraw interfaces. And keep in mind, I am not going to put the version numbers on each of the interfaces; for now, let's talk in the abstract. For example, IDirectDraw is really up to version 7.0, so when we actually use it, we would be talking about IDirectDraw7, but for now, I just want to show basics and relationships.

FIGURE 6.1
The interfaces of
DirectDraw.

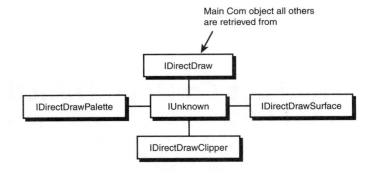

Interface Characteristics

As you can see, there are only five interfaces that make up DirectDraw:

IUnknown—All COM objects must be derived from this base interface, and DirectDraw is no exception. IUnknown doesn't contain much more than the Addref(), Release(), and QueryInterface() functions that are overridden by each of the other interfaces.

IDirectDraw—This is the main interface object that must be created to start working with DirectDraw. IDirectDraw literally represents the video card and support hardware. Interestingly enough, with MMS (Multiple Monitor Support) and Windows 98/ME/XP/NT2000, now you can have more than one video card installed in your system and hence more than one DirectDraw object. However, in this book we'll assume that there is only one video card in the computer and always select the default card to represent the DirectDraw object, even if there is more than one card in the system.

IDirectDrawSurface—This represents the actual display surface(s) that you will create, manipulate, and display using DirectDraw. A DirectDraw surface can exist on the video card itself using *VRAM (Video RAM)* or within system memory. There are basically two types of surfaces: *primary surfaces* and *secondary surfaces*.

Primary surfaces usually represent the actual video buffer that is currently being ras-terized and displayed by the video card. Secondary surfaces, on the other hand, are usually offscreen. In most cases, you will create a single primary surface to represent the actual video display, and then one or more secondary surfaces to represent object bitmaps and/or *back buffers* to represent offscreen drawing areas where you'll build up the next frame of animation. We'll get to the details of surfaces later in the chapter, but for now, take a look at Figure 6.2 for a little graphical elaboration.

FIGURE 6.2

DirectDraw surfaces.

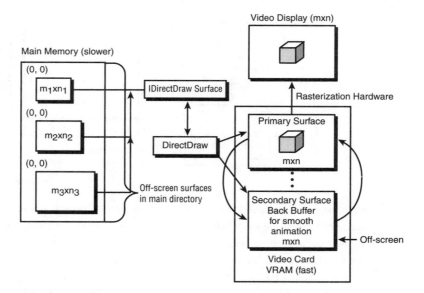

IDirectDrawPalette—DirectDraw is equipped to deal with any color space, from 1-bit monochrome to 32-bit Ultra-True Color. Thus, DirectDraw supports the IDirectDrawPalette interface to deal with color palettes in video modes that use 256 or fewer colors. In this case, you will use the 256-color mode extensively in a number of demos because it's the fastest mode for a software rasterizer. In the discussion of Direct3D Immediate Mode in Volume II, you'll switch over to 24-bit color because that's the native mode that D3D likes to work in. In any case, the IDirectDrawPalette interface is used to create, load, and manipulate palettes, and to attach palettes to drawing surfaces, such as the primary or secondary surfaces that you might create for your DirectDraw applications. Take a look at Figure 6.3 to see the relationship between a drawing surface and a DirectDraw palette.

IDirectDrawClipper—This is used to help with clipping DirectDraw raster and bitmap operations to some subset of the visible display surface. In most cases, you'll only use DirectDraw clippers for windowed DirectX applications and/or to clip bitmap operations to the extents of your display surface, whether it be a primary or secondary surface. The cool thing about the `IDirectDrawClipper` interface is that it takes advantage of hardware acceleration if it's available, and the costly pixel-by-pixel or sub-image processing that is normally needed to clip bitmaps to the screen extents is done for you.

FIGURE 6.3

The relationship between DirectDraw surfaces and palettes.

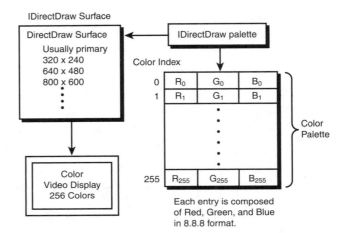

Now, before you move on to creating a DirectDraw object, I want to refresh your memory with some tasty tidbits of information that we touched upon in the previous chapter when dealing with COM. DirectDraw and all DirectX components are in constant flux, and thus the interfaces are always being upgraded. Alas, even though so far in this chapter I have referred to the interfaces of DirectDraw generically as `IDirectDraw`, `IDirectDrawSurface`, `IDirectDrawPalette`, and `IDirectDrawClipper`, for the most part these interfaces have all been updated and newer versions exist. For example as mentioned before, `IDirectDraw` is up to `IDirectDraw7` as of DirectX version 7.0.

All this means is that if you want the very latest software and hardware performance, you should always `IUnknown::QueryInterface()` for the latest interface revision. However, to find this out you'll have to take a look at the DirectX SDK docs. Of course, in this book you're using DirectX 8.0, so you already know what's up, but keep in mind that when you upgrade to DirectX 9.0 you might have some newer interfaces that you want to use. However, both volumes of this book are about writing your own rasterization and 3D software, so I want to cheat as little as possible. In most cases, you're going to be using very few of the bells and whistles of all the new revisions. Cool, home slice?

Using the Interfaces Together

Next, I want to briefly run down how all the interfaces are used together to create a DirectDraw application:

1. Create the main DirectDraw object and retrieve a `IDirectDraw7` interface using `QueryInterface()` or create an `IDirectDraw7` interface directly with `DirectDrawCreateEx()`. Using this interface, set both the cooperation level and video mode.

2. Using the `IDirectDrawSurface7` interface, create at least a primary surface to draw on. Based on the color depth of the surface and the video mode itself, a palette will be needed if the video mode is 8 bits per pixel or less.

3. Create a palette using the `IDirectDrawPalette` interface, initialize it with RGB triples, and attach it to the surface of interest.

4. If the DirectDraw application is going to be windowed, or if you're going to render bitmaps that could potentially go out of bounds of the visible DirectDraw surface, at least create a single clipper and size it to the extents of the visible window. See Figure 6.4.

FIGURE 6.4
DirectDraw clippers.

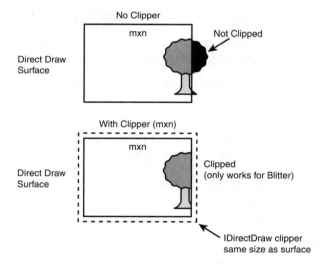

5. Draw on the primary surface.

Of course, there are about a bazillion (yes, that's a technical term) little details I've left out, but that's the gist of using the different interfaces. With that in mind, let's get down to details and really make these interfaces work...

DirectX and 2D Fundamentals

 TIP You might want to have both the DDRAW.H header file and the DirectX SDK Help system open for reference during the remainder of the chapter.

Creating a DirectDraw Object

To create a DirectDraw 1.0 object with C++, all you need to do is call DirectDrawCreate(), shown here:

```
HRESULT WINAPI DirectDrawCreate(GUID FAR *lpGUID,    // guid of object
                 LPDIRECTDRAW FAR *lplpDD, // receives interface
                 IUnknown     FAR *pUnkOuter ); // com stuff
```

LpGUID—This is the *GUID (Globally Unique Identifier)* of the display driver that you want to use. In most cases, you'll simply send NULL to represent the default hardware.

lplpDD—This is a pointer to a pointer that receives the IDirectDraw interface pointer if the call is successful. Note that the function returns a IDirectDraw interface, *not* a IDirectDraw7 interface!

pUnkOuter—Advanced feature; always send NULL.

Here's how you would use the function to create a default DirectDraw object based on the IDirectDraw interface:

```
LPDIRECTDRAW lpdd = NULL; // storage for IDirectDraw

// create the DirectDraw object
DirectDrawCreate(NULL, &lpdd, NULL);
```

If the function is successful, lpdd will be a valid IDirectDraw 1.0 object interface. However, you still would like that latest interface, IDirectDraw7. But before you learn how to do that—what about error handling?

Error Handling with DirectDraw

Error handling in DirectX is very clean. There are a number of macros that can test the results of any function for general success or failure. The Microsoft-endorsed way of testing for errors with DirectX functions is to use these two macros:

FAILED()—Tests for failure.

SUCCEEDED()—Tests for success.

Based on this new information, you could do something smart by adding the following error handling code:

```
if (FAILED(DirectDrawCreate(NULL, &lpdd, NULL)))
   {
```

```
// error
} // end if
```

Or similarly, you could test for success:

```
if (SUCCEEDED(DirectDrawCreate(NULL, &lpdd, NULL)))
    {
    // move onto next step
    } // end if
else
    {
    // error
    } // end else
```

I usually use the `FAILED()` macro because I don't like having two different logic paths, but whatever lights your fusion reactor... The only problem with the macros is that they don't tell you much; they are more to detect a general problem. If you want to know the exact problem, you can always take a look at the return code for the function. In this case, Table 6.1 lists the possible return codes for DirectX version 6.0 `DirectDrawCreate()`.

TABLE 6.1   Return Codes for `DirectDrawCreate()`

Return Code	Description
DD_OK	Total Success.
DDERR_DIRECTDRAWALREADYCREATED	DirectDraw object has already been created.
DDERR_GENERIC	DirectDraw has no idea what's wrong.
DDERR_INVALIDDIRECTDRAWGUID	The device GUID is unknown.
DDERR_INVALIDPARAMS	Something is wrong with the parameters you sent.
DDERR_NODIRECTDRAWHW	There isn't any hardware.
DDERR_OUTOFMEMORY	Take a wild guess?

The only problem with using the constants along with conditional logic is that Microsoft doesn't guarantee that they won't completely change all the error codes. However, I think that you'll be pretty safe with

```
if (DirectDrawCreate(...)!=DD_OK)
    {
    // error
    } // end if
```

in all cases. Moreover, `DD_OK` is defined for all DirectDraw functions, so you can use it safely without worrying.

Getting an Interface Lift

As I said, you can use the basic IDirectDraw interface stored in lpdd from the call to DirectDrawCreate(). Or you can upgrade it to the latest version (whatever it may be) by querying for a new interface via the IUnknown interface method QueryInterface(), which is part of every DirectDraw interface implementation. The latest DirectDraw interface as of DirectX version 7.0 is IDirectDraw7, so here's how you retrieve the interface pointer:

```
LPDIRECTDRAW lpdd  = NULL; // standard DirectDraw 1.0
LPDIRECTDRAW lpdd7 = NULL; // DirectDraw 7.0 interface 7

// first create base IDirectDraw interface
if (FAILED(DirectDrawCreate(NULL, &lpdd, NULL)))
   {
   // error
   } // end if

// now query for IDirectDraw7
if (FAILED(lpdd->QueryInterface(IID_IDirectDraw7,
                                (LPVOID *)&lpdd7)))
   {
   // error
   } // end if
```

Now, here are the important things to pay attention to:

- The way that QueryInterface() is called.
- The constant used to request the IDirectDraw7 interface, which is IID_IDirectDraw7.

In general, all calls from an interface are in the form

```
interface_pointer->method(parms...);
```

And all interface identifiers are in the form

```
IID_IDirectCD
```

Here, C refers to the component: Draw for DirectDraw, Sound for DirectSound, Input for DirectInput, and so on. D is a number, from 2 to *n*, indicating the interface you desire. In addition, you can find all these constants within the DDRAW.H file.

Moving on with this example, you now have a bit of a dilemma—you have both a IDirectDraw interface and a IDirectDraw7 interface. What to do? Simply blow the old interface away since you don't need it, like this:

```
lpdd->Release();
lpdd = NULL; // set to NULL for safety
```

And from this point on, do all method calls using the new interface IDirectDraw7.

WARNING

Along with the new functionality of IDirectDraw7 comes a little housekeeping and responsibility. The problem is that not only is the IDirectDraw7 interface more sophisticated and advanced, but in many cases it needs and returns new data structures rather than the base structures defined for DirectX 1.0. The only way to be sure about these anomalies is to take a look at the DirectX SDK documentation and verify the version of the data structure that any specific function needs and/or returns. However, this is just a warning in general. I'll show you the correct structures for all the examples that you work through in this book—because I'm that kind of guy! By the way, my birthday is on June 14th.

In addition to using the QueryInterface() function from the initial IDirectDraw interface pointer (lpdd), there is a more direct "COM way" of getting the IDirectDraw7 interface directly. Under COM, you can retrieve an interface pointer to any interface as long as you have the *Interface ID*, or *IID*, that represents the interface that you desire. In most cases, I personally prefer not to use low-level COM functions because I already have enough drama in my life. Nevertheless, when you get to DirectMusic there will be no way around using low-level COM stuff, so this is a good place to at least introduce the process to you. Here's how you would directly obtain an IDirectDraw7 interface:

```
// first initialize COM, this will load the COM libraries
// if they aren't already loaded
if (FAILED(CoInitialize(NULL)))
    {
    // error
    } // end if

// Create the DirectDraw object by using the
// CoCreateInstance() function
if (FAILED(CoCreateInstance(&CLSID_DirectDraw,
                           NULL,
                           CLSCTX_ALL,
                           &IID_IDirectDraw7,
                           &lpdd7)))
    {
    // error
    } // end if


// now before using the DirectDraw object, it must
// be initialized using the initialize method

if (FAILED(IDirectDraw7_Initialize(lpdd7, NULL)))
    {
    // error
    } // end if
```

```
// now that we're done with COM, uninitialize it
CoUninitialize();
```

The preceding code is the Microsoft-recommended way to create a DirectDraw object. However, the technique does cheat a bit and use one macro:

```
IDirectDraw7_Initialize(lpdd7, NULL);
```

You can get rid of this and be totally COM by replacing it with

```
lpdd7->Initialize(NULL);
```

where the NULL in both calls is the video device, which in this case is the default driver. (That's why it's been left NULL.) In any case, it's not hard to see how the macro expands out into the code in the preceding line. Just makes life easier, I guess? Now, for the good news, Microsoft has created a function call that will actually create an IDirectDraw7 interface without the intermediate steps. Usually, this was not the case, but in DirectX version 7.0 they created a new function called DirectDrawCreateEx() which I mentioned before in the last chapter. Its prototype looks like this

```
'HRESULT WINAPI DirectDrawCreateEx(
   GUID FAR *lpGUID,    // the GUID of the driver, NULL for active display
   LPVOID *lplpDD,      // receiver of the interface
   REFIID iid,          // the interface ID of the interface you are requesting
   IUnknown FAR *pUnkOuter  // advanced COM, NULL
);
```

It's very similar to the simpler DirectDrawCreate(), but takes more parameters and allows you to create any DirectDraw interface. In any case, the call to create the IDirectDraw7 interaface would look like this:

```
LPDIRECTDRAW7 lpdd;  // version 7.0

// create version 7.0 DirectDraw object interface
DirectDrawCreateEx(NULL, (void **)&lpdd, IID_IDirectDraw7, NULL);
```

The only tricky part is the casting of the interface pointer, note the (void **) and you must send the requested interface in the parameter iid. Other than that, it's pretty simple and just works!

Let's take a minute to reiterate everything here. Ok, we need an IDirectDraw7 interface if we want to work with the latest version of DirectDraw which is version 7.0 (since in version 8.0 Microsoft removed DirectDraw). We can use the basic DirectDrawCreate() function and get an IDirectDraw 1.0 interface, and then from there use QueryInterface() to get IDirectDraw7. On the other hand, we can use low

level COM and get `IDirectDraw7` directly, or we can use the function
`DirectDrawCreateEx()` that is available since the release of DirectX 7.0 to create the
interface directly. Nice, huh? DirectX is starting to sound like X Windows, about
5,000 ways to do everything <BG>.

Now that you know how to create a DirectDraw object and obtain the latest interface,
let's move on to the next step in the sequence of getting DirectDraw working, which
is setting the cooperation level.

Cooperating with Windows

As you know, Windows is a cooperative, shared environment. At least that's the idea,
although as a programmer I still haven't figured out how to make it cooperate with
my code! Anyway, DirectX is similar to any Win32 system, and at the very least, it
must inform Windows that it's going to use various resources so that other Windows
applications don't try to request (and get) resources that DirectX has control over.
Basically, DirectX can be a complete resource hog as long is it tells Windows what
it's doing—seems fair to me <BG>.

In the case of DirectDraw, about the only thing that you should be interested in is the
video display hardware. There are two cases that you must concern yourselves with:

- Full-screen mode
- Windowed mode

In *full-screen* mode, DirectDraw acts much like an old DOS program. That is, the entire
screen surface is allocated to your game, and you write directly to the video hardware.
No other application can touch the hardware. *Windowed mode* is a little different. In
windowed mode, DirectDraw must cooperate much more with Windows because other
applications may need to update their own client window areas (which may be visible
to the user). Hence, in windowed mode your control and monopolization of the video
hardware is much more restrained. However, you still have full access to 2D and 3D
acceleration, so that's a good thing. But then, so were bell-bottoms at first…

Chapter 7, "Advanced DirectDraw and Bitmapped Graphics," will talk more about
windowed DirectX applications, but they are a little more complex to handle. Most of
this chapter will deal with full-screen modes because they are easier to work with, so
keep that in mind.

Now that you know a little bit about why there needs to be cooperation between
Windows and DirectX, let's see how to tell Windows how you want to cooperate.
To set the cooperation level of DirectDraw, use the `IDirectDraw7::`
`SetCooperativeLevel()` function, which is a method of `IDirectDraw7`.

For you C programmers, the syntax IDirectDraw7::SetCooperative Level() may be a little cryptic. The :: operator is called the *scope resolution operator*, and the syntax simply means that SetCooperativeLevel() is a method (or member function) of the IDirectDraw7 interface. This is basically a class that is nothing more than a structure with data and a virtual function table. In some cases, I may forgo using the interface to prefix the method and write it like SetCooperativeLevel(). However, be advised that all DirectX functions are part of an interface and thus must be called using a function pointer style call, like lpdd->function(...).

Here's the prototype of IDirectDraw7::SetCooperativeLevel():

```
HRESULT SetCooperativeLevel(HWND hWnd,      // window handle
                            DWORD dwFlags);// control flags
```

This returns DD_OK if successful, and an error code if not.

Interestingly enough, this is the first time that the window handle has entered into the DirectX equation. The hWnd parameter is needed so that DirectX (or more specifically, DirectDraw) has something to anchor to. Simply use your main window handle in all cases.

The second and last parameter to SetCoopertiveLevel() is dwFlags, which is the control flags parameter and directly influences the way that DirectDraw works with Windows. Table 6.2 lists the most commonly used values that can be logically ORed together to obtain the desired cooperation level.

TABLE 6.2   Control Flags for SetCooperativeLevel()

Value	Description
DDSCL_ALLOWMODEX	Allows the use of Mode X (320x200,240,400) display modes. Can be used only if the DDSCL_EXCLUSIVE and DDSCL_FULLSCREEN flags are present.
DDSCL_ALLOWREBOOT	Allows Ctrl+Alt+Del to be detected while in exclusive (full-screen) mode.
DDSCL_EXCLUSIVE	Requests the exclusive level. This flag must be used with the DDSCL_FULLSCREEN flag.
DDSCL_FPUSETUP	Indicates that the calling application is likely to keep the FPU set up for optimal Direct3D performance (single precision and exceptions disabled) so Direct3D does not need to explicitly set the FPU each time. For more information, look up "DirectDraw Cooperative Levels and FPU Precision" in the DirectX SDK.

TABLE 6.2   Continued

Value	Description
DDSCL_FULLSCREEN	Indicates full-screen mode will be used. GDI from other applications will not be able to draw on the screen. This flag must be used with the DDSCL_EXCLUSIVE flag.
DDSCL_MULTITHREADED	Requests multithread-safe DirectDraw behavior. Don't worry about this for now.
DDSCL_NORMAL	Indicates that the application will function as a regular Windows application. This flag cannot be used with the DDSCL_ALLOWMODEX, DDSCL_EXCLUSIVE, or DDSCL_FULLSCREEN flags.
DDSCL_NOWINDOWCHANGES	Indicates that DirectDraw is not allowed to minimize or restore the application window on activation.

If you take a good look at the various flags, it may seem that some of them are redundant—very true. Basically, DDSCL_FULLSCREEN and DDSCL_EXCLUSIVE must be used together, and if you decide to use any Mode X modes, you must use DDSCL_FULLSCREEN, DDSCL_EXCLUSIVE, and DDSCL_ALLOWMODEX all together. Other than that, the flags pretty much do what they would seem to from their definitions. In most cases, you'll set full-screen applications like this:

```
lpdd7->SetCooperativeLevel(hwnd,
                           DDSCL_FULLSCREEN |
                           DDSCL_ALLOWMODEX |
                           DDSCL_EXCLUSIVE |
                           DDSCL_ALLOWREBOOT);
```

and normal windowed applications like this:

```
lpdd7->SetCooperativeLevel(hwnd, DDSCL_NORMAL);
```

Of course, when you get to multithreaded programming techniques later in the book, you might want to add the multithreading flag DDSCL_MULTITHREADED to play it safe. Anyway, let's see how you would create a DirectDraw object and set the cooperation level together:

```
LPDIRECTDRAW lpdd  = NULL; // standard DirectDraw 1.0
LPDIRECTDRAW7 lpdd7 = NULL; // DirectDraw 7.0 interface 7

// first create base IDirectDraw interface
if (FAILED(DirectDrawCreateEx(NULL, (void **)&lpdd7, IID_IDirectDraw7, NULL)))
    {
    // error
    } // end if
```

```
// now set the cooperation level for windowed DirectDraw
// since we aren't going to do any drawing yet
if (FAILED(lpdd7->SetCooperativeLevel(hwnd, DDSCL_NORMAL)))
   {
   // error
   } // end if
```

NOTE I may start leaving out the error handling calls to FAILED() and/or SUCCEEDED() to save space, but remember that you should always check for errors!

At this point, you have enough information to create a complete DirectX application that creates a window, starts up DirectDraw, and sets the cooperation level. Although you don't know how to draw, it's a start. As an example, take a look at DEMO6_1.CPP on the CD, along with its executable DEMO6_1.EXE. When you run the program, you'll see something like what's shown in Figure 6.5. I based the program on the T3D Game Console template, so the only changes I made were in the Game_Init() and Game_Shutdown() to create and set the cooperation level for DirectDraw.

FIGURE 6.5
DEMO6_1.EXE
in action.

Here are those functions with the added DirectDraw code from DEMO6_1.CPP, so you can see how simple DirectDraw is to set up:

```
int Game_Init(void *parms = NULL, int num_parms = 0)
{
// this is called once after the initial window is created and
// before the main event loop is entered, do all your initialization
// here

// first create base IDirectDraw interface
if (FAILED(DirectDrawCreateEx(NULL, (void **)&lpdd, IID_IDirectDraw7, NULL)))
   {
   // error
   return(0);
   } // end if
```

```
// set cooperation to normal since this will be a windowed app
lpdd->SetCooperativeLevel(main_window_handle, DDSCL_NORMAL);

// return success or failure or your own return code here
return(1);

} // end Game_Init

///////////////////////////////////////////////////////////////

int Game_Shutdown(void *parms = NULL, int num_parms = 0)
{
// this is called after the game is exited and the main event
// loop while is exited, do all you cleanup and shutdown here

// simply blow away the IDirectDraw interface
if (lpdd)
   {
   lpdd->Release();
   lpdd = NULL;
   } // end if

// return success or failure or your own return code here
return(1);

} // end Game_Shutdown
```

> **TIP**
>
> If you're about to jump in head-first and try to compile DEMO6_1.CPP, please remember to manually include DDRAW.LIB from the DirectX 8.0 SDK LIB\ directory, along with adding the DirectX header paths to your compiler's .H search directories as the *first* directory! And of course, you should build a Win32 .EXE. I get at least 10 emails a day from rookie compiler users who forget to include the .LIB files, so don't be another statistic...

Getting into the Mode of Things

The next step in setting up DirectDraw is probably the coolest of all. Normally, in DOS setting the video mode is fairly reasonable for the basic ROM BIOS modes, but in Windows it's nearly impossible due to the aftershocks of the mode switch. However, with DirectX, it's a snap. One of the main goals of DirectDraw was to make video mode switching trivial and transparent to the programmer. No more VGA/CRT control register programming just to make a single call. Presto—the mode will be set to whatever you desire (if the card can do it, of course).

The function to set the video mode is called SetDisplayMode() and is a method of the IDirectDraw7 interface, or, in C++-speak, IDirectDraw7::SetDisplayMode(). Here's its prototype:

```
HRESULT SetDisplayMode(DWORD dwWidth,  // width of mode in pixels
                DWORD dwHeight, // height if mode in pixels
                DWORD dwBPP,     // bits per pixel, 8,16,24, etc.
                DWORD dwRefreshRate, // desired refresh, 0 for default
                DWORD dwFlags); // extra flags (advanced) 0 for default
```

As usual, the function returns DD_OK if successful.

All you should be saying is, "Wow, this is too good to be true!" Have you ever tried to set up a Mode X mode like 320x400 or 800x600 mode? Even if you're successful, good luck trying to render to the video buffer! With this DirectDraw function, you just send the width, height, and color depth, and bam! DirectDraw handles all the idiosyncrasies of whichever video card is plugged in, and if the requested mode can be built, it is. Moreover, the mode is guaranteed to have a linear memory buffer...but more on that later. Take a look at Table 6.3 for a brief refresher on the most commonly used video modes and their color depths.

TABLE 6.3   Common Video Mode Resolutions

Width	Height	BPP	Mode X
320	200	8	*
320	240	8	*
320	400	8	*
512	512	8,16,24,32	
640	480	8,16,24,32	
800	600	8,16,24,32	
1024	768	8,16,24,32	
1280	1024	8,16,24,32	

Higher resolution modes are available on many cards.

Interestingly enough, you can request any mode you wish. For example, you can choose 400x400, and if the video driver can build it, it will work. However, it's best to stick to the modes listed in Table 6.3 because they are the most common.

> **TRICK**   Actually, there is a Win32 API function to set the video mode that I have used before, but it wreaks havoc on the system and really messes things up.

Referring back to the function, the first three parameters are straightforward, but the last two need a bit of explanation. dwRefreshRate is used to override the video driver's default refresh for the mode you request. Hence, if you request a 320x200 mode, chances are the refresh will be at 70Hz. But with this parameter, you could force it to 60Hz if you wanted to. I would leave the refresh rate alone, to tell you the truth, and simply set the bit to 0 (which indicates to the driver to use the default).

The last parameter, dwFlags, is an extra flags WORD that is a catchall and is of very little use. Currently, it's used as an override so you can use VGA mode 13h for 320x200 instead of Mode X 320x200 via the flag DDSDM_STANDARDVGAMODE. Again, I wouldn't worry about it. If you do write a game that uses 320x200, you can try experimenting with this flag and using VGA mode 13h or Mode X for 320x200 to see which is faster, but the performance difference will be almost negligible. For now, just set dwFlags to 0.

That's enough of the preliminaries. Let's get to switching modes! To switch modes, you must create the DirectDraw object, set the cooperation level, and finally set the display mode, like this:

```
lpdd->SetDisplayMode(width,height,bpp,0,0);
```

For example, to create a 640x480 mode in 256 (8-bit) color, you would do this:

```
lpdd->SetDisplayMode(640,480,8,0,0);
```

And to set a 800x600 with 16-bit color, you would do this:

```
lpdd->SetDisplayMode(800,600,16,0,0);
```

Now, there's a big difference between these two modes that extends further than the mere difference in resolution: *the color depth.* An 8-bit mode works completely differently than 16-bit, 24-bit, or 32-bit modes. If you'll recall, the previous chapters on Win32/GDI programming covered the topic of palettes extensively (Chapter 3, "Advanced Windows Programming," and Chapter 4, "Windows GDI, Controls, and Last-Minute Gift Ideas"), and the same theory is in force with DirectDraw. That is, when you create an 8-bit mode, you are requesting a palletized mode, and you must also create a palette and fill it with 8.8.8 RGB entries.

On the other hand, if you create a straight RGB mode with color depth 16, 24, or 32 bpp (bits per pixel), you don't have to worry about this step. You can write encoded data directly to the video buffer (when you learn how). At very least, you must learn how to work with DirectDraw palettes (which will be the next topic of discussion). However, before moving on, let's take a look at a complete example of creating a full-screen DirectX application with a resolution of 640x480x8.

DEMO6_2.CPP on the CD and the associated executable do just that. I would show you a figure, but all you would see is a black rectangle because the demo is a full-screen application. However, I can surely show you the code that makes it happen. As usual, I have based the demo on your game console, with the appropriate modifications, and made the DirectX-related changes to the `Game_Init()` and `Game_Shutdown()` sections, which are listed here from `DEMO6_2.CPP`. Take a close look at them and be amazed by the simplicity...

```
int Game_Init(void *parms = NULL, int num_parms = 0)
{
// this is called once after the initial window is created and
// before the main event loop is entered, do all your initialization
// here

// first create base IDirectDraw interface
if (FAILED(DirectDrawCreateEx(NULL, (void **)&lpdd, IID_IDirectDraw7, NULL)))
   {
   // error
   return(0);
   } // end if




// set cooperation to full screen
if (FAILED(lpdd->SetCooperativeLevel(main_window_handle,
                  DDSCL_FULLSCREEN | DDSCL_ALLOWMODEX |
                  DDSCL_EXCLUSIVE | DDSCL_ALLOWREBOOT)))
   {
   // error
   return(0);
   } // end if

// set display mode to 640x480x8
if (FAILED(lpdd->SetDisplayMode(SCREEN_WIDTH,
                  SCREEN_HEIGHT, SCREEN_BPP,0,0)))
   {
   // error
   return(0);
   } // end if


// return success or failure or your own return code here
return(1);

} // end Game_Init

//////////////////////////////////////////////////////////////

int Game_Shutdown(void *parms = NULL, int num_parms = 0)
{
// this is called after the game is exited and the main event
// loop while is exited, do all your cleanup and shutdown here

// simply blow away the IDirectDraw7 interface
if (lpdd)
   {
```

```
        lpdd->Release();
        lpdd = NULL;
        } // end if

// return success or failure or your own return code here
return(1);

} // end Game_Shutdown
```

At this point, there are two things that you're still missing: controlling the palette (in 256-color modes) and accessing the display buffers. Let's take care of the color problem first.

The Subtleties of Color

DirectDraw supports a number of different color depths, including 1, 2, 4, 8, 16, 24, and 32 bpp. Obviously, 1, 2, and 4 bits per pixel are a little outdated, so don't concern yourself with these color depths. On the other hand, the 8-, 16-, 24-, and 32-bit modes are of utmost interest. Most games you write, you'll write to run in either 8-bit palletized mode for speed reasons (also it's a good mode to learn with), or 16- or 24-bit mode for full RGB color utilization. The RGB modes work by writing similar-sized WORDs into the frame buffer, as shown in Figure 6.6. The palletized mode works by using a look-up table that is indexed by each individual pixel value in the frame buffer, which is always a single byte. Thus, there are 256 different values—*you have seen all this before, so it should look familiar.*

What you need to learn to do is create a 256-color palette and then tell DirectDraw that you want to use it. So let's see the steps involved:

1. Create one or more palette data structures as arrays of 256 PALETTENTRY's.

2. Create a DirectDraw palette interface IDirectDrawPalette object from the DirectDraw object itself. In many cases, this will be directly mapped to the hardware VGA palette registers.

3. Attach the palette object to a drawing surface, such as the primary surface, so all data rendered to it is displayed in the appropriate colors.

4. (Optional) If you desire, you can change the palette entries or the entire palette. You will need to take this step if you sent a NULL palette during step 2 and opted to omit step 1. Basically, what I'm trying to say is that when you create a palette interface, you can send it a palette of color also. But if you don't, you can always do it later. Therefore, step 2 can be step 1 if you remember to fill up the palette entries at a later time.

DirectX and 2D Fundamentals

FIGURE 6.6

Comparison of various color depths.

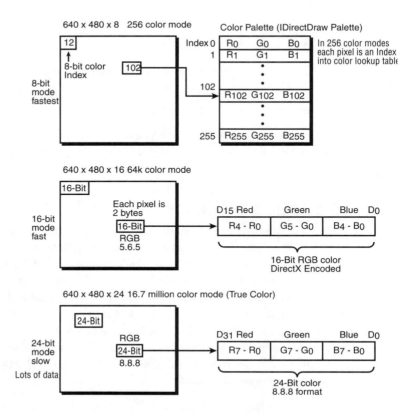

Let's begin by creating the palette data structure. It's nothing more than an array of 256 palette entries based on the PALETTENTRY Win32 structure, shown here:

```
typedef struct tagPALETTEENTRY
        {
        BYTE peRed;      // red component 8-bits
        BYTE peGreen;    // green component 8-bits
        BYTE peBlue;     // blue component 8-bits
        BYTE peFlags;    // control flags: set to PC_NOCOLLAPSE
        } PALETTEENTRY;
```

Look familiar? It better! Anyway, to create a palette, you simply create an array of these structures, like this:

```
PALETTEENTRY palette[256];
```

And then you fill them up in any way you desire. However, there is one rule: You must set the peFlags field to PC_NOCOLLAPSE. This is necessary because you don't want Win32/DirectX optimizing your palette for you. With that in mind, here's an example of creating a random palette with black in position 0 and white in position 255:

```
PALETTEENTRY palette[256]; // palette storage

// fill em up with color!
for (int color=1; color < 255; color++)
    {
    // fill with random RGB values
    palette[color].peRed   = rand()%256;
    palette[color].peGreen = rand()%256;
    palette[color].peBlue  = rand()%256;

    // set flags field to PC_NOCOLLAPSE
    palette[color].peFlags = PC_NOCOLLAPSE;
    } // end for color

// now fill in entry 0 and 255 with black and white
palette[0].peRed   = 0;
palette[0].peGreen = 0;
palette[0].peBlue  = 0;
palette[0].peFlags = PC_NOCOLLAPSE;

palette[255].peRed   = 255;
palette[255].peGreen = 255;
palette[255].peBlue  = 255;
palette[255].peFlags = PC_NOCOLLAPSE;
```

That's all there is to it! Of course, you can create multiple palettes and fill them with whatever you want; it's up to you.

Moving on, the next step is to create the actual `IDirectDrawPalette` interface. Luckily for you, the interface hasn't changed as of DirectX 6.0, so you don't need to use `QueryInterface()` or anything. Here's the prototype for `IDirectDraw7::CreatePalette()`, which creates a palette object:

```
HRESULT CreatePalette(DWORD dwFlags,    // control flags
LPPALETTEENTRY lpColorTable,  // palette data or NULL
LPDIRECTDRAWPALETTE FAR *lplpDDPalette,  // received palette interface
        IUnknown FAR *pUnkOuter);   // advanced, make NULL
```

The function returns `DD_OK` if successful.

Let's take a look at the parameters. The first parameter is `dwFlags`, which controls the various properties of the palette—more on this in a minute. The next parameter is a pointer to the initial palette, or `NULL` if you don't want to send one. Next you have the actual `IDirectDrawPalette` interface storage pointer that receives the interface if the function is successful. Finally, `pUnkOuter` is for advanced COM stuff, so simply send `NULL`.

The only interesting parameter of the bunch is, of course, the flags parameter `dwFlags`. Let's take a more in-depth look at what your options are. Refer to Table 6.4 for the possible values you can logically `OR` to create the flags `WORD`.

TABLE 6.4 Control Flags for `CreatePalette()`

Value	Description
DDPCAPS_1BIT	1-bit color. There are two entries in the color table.
DDPCAPS_2BIT	2-bit color. There are four entries in the color table.
DDPCAPS_4BIT	4-bit color. There are 16 entries in the color table.
DDPCAPS_8BIT	8-bit color. The most common. There are 256 entries in the color table.
DDPCAPS_8BITENTRIES	This is for an advanced feature referred to as *indexed palettes* and is used for 1-, 2-, and 4-bit palettes. Just say no.
DDPCAPS_ALPHA	Indicates that the `peFlags` member of the associated PALET-TEENTRY structure is to be interpreted as a single _8-bit alpha value controlling the transparency. A palette created with this flag can only be attached to a D3D texture surface created with the DDSCAPS_TEXTURE capability flag. Again, this is advanced and for big G's.
DDPCAPS_ALLOW256	Indicates that this palette can have all 256 entries defined. Normally, entries 0 and 255 are reserved for black and white, respectively, and on some systems like NT you can't write to these entries under any circumstances. However, in most cases you don't need this flag because 0 is usually black anyway, and most palettes can live with entry 255 being white. It's up to you.
DDPCAPS_INITIALIZE	Initialize this palette with the colors in the color array passed at `lpDDColorArray`. This is used to enable the palette data sent to be downloaded into the hardware palette.
DDPCAPS_PRIMARYSURFACE	This palette is attached to the primary surface. Changing this palette's color table immediately affects the display unless DDPSETPAL_VSYNC is specified and supported.
DDPCAPS_VSYNC	Forces palette updates to be performed only during the vertical blank period. This minimizes color anomalies and sparkling. Not fully supported yet, though.

A lot of confusing control words, if you ask me. Basically, you only need to work with 8-bit palettes, so the control flags you need to OR together are

```
DDPCAPS_8BIT | DDPCAPS_ALLOW256 | DDPCAPS_INITIALIZE
```

And if you don't care about setting color entries 0 and 256, you can omit DDPCAPS_ALLOW256. Furthermore, if you're not sending a palette during the CreatePalette() call, you can omit DDPCAPS_INITIALIZE.

Sucking all that down into your brain, here's how you would create a palette object with your random palette:

```
LPDIRECTDRAWPALETTE lpddpal = NULL; // palette interface

if (FAILED(lpdd->CreatePalette(DDPCAPS_8BIT |
                               DDPCAPS_ALLOW256 |
                               DDPCAPS_INITIALIZE,
                               palette,
                               &lpddpal,
                               NULL)))
   {
   // error
   } // end if
```

If the function call is successful, `lpddpal` will return with a valid `IDirectDrawPalette` interface. Also, the hardware color palette will instantly be updated with the sent palette, which in this case is a collection of 256 random colors.

Normally, at this point I would drop a demo on you, but unfortunately we're at one of those "chicken and the egg" points in DirectDraw. That is, you can't see the colors until you can draw on the screen. So that's what's next!

Building a Display Surface

As you know, the image displayed on the screen is nothing more than a matrix of colored pixels represented in memory for some format, either palletized or RGB. In either case, to make anything happen, you need to know how to draw into this memory. However, under DirectDraw the designers decided to abstract the concept of video memory just a little bit so that no matter how weird the video card in your system (or someone else's) is, accessing the video surfaces will be the same for you (the programmer's point of view). Thus, DirectDraw supports what are called *surfaces*.

Referring to Figure 6.7, surfaces are rectangular regions of memory that can hold bitmap data. Furthermore, there are two kinds of surfaces: primary and secondary.

A primary surface directly corresponds to the actual video memory being rasterized by the video card and is visible at all times. Hence, you will have only one primary surface in any DirectDraw program, and it refers directly to the screen image and usually resides in VRAM. When you manipulate it, you see the results instantly on the screen. For example, if you set the video mode to 640x480x256, you must create a primary surface that is also 640x480x256 and then attach it to the display device—the `IDirectDraw7` object.

FIGURE 6.7
Surfaces can be
any size.

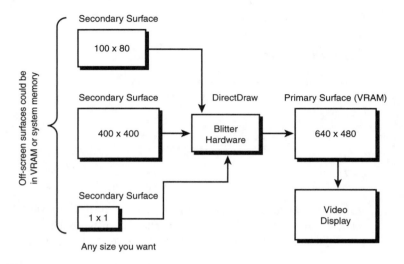

Secondary surfaces, on the other hand, are much more flexible. They can be any size, can reside in either VRAM or system memory, and you can create as many of them as memory will allow. In most cases, you will create one or two secondary surfaces (back buffers) for smooth animation. These will always have the same color depth and geometry as the primary surface. Then you update these offscreen surfaces with the next frame of animation, and then quickly copy or *page flip* the offscreen surface into the primary surface for smooth animation. This is called *double* or *triple buffering*. You'll learn more on this in the next chapter, but that's one use for secondary surfaces.

The second use for secondary surfaces is to hold your bitmap images and animations that represent objects in the game. This is a very important feature of DirectDraw because only by using DirectDraw surfaces can you invoke hardware acceleration on bitmap data. If you write your own bit blitting (bitmap image transferring) software to write bitmaps, you lose all acceleration.

Now, I'm getting a little ahead of myself here, so I want to come out of warp and back down to sub-light speed. I just wanted to get you thinking a bit. For now, let's just see how to create a simple primary surface that's the same size as your display mode, and then you'll learn to write data to it and plot pixels on the screen.

Creating a Primary Surface

All right, to create any surface, you must follow these steps:

1. Fill out a DDSURFACEDESC2 data structure that describes the surface you want to create.

2. Call IDirectDraw7::CreateSurface() to create the surface.

Here's the prototype for `CreateSurface()`:

```
HRESULT CreateSurface(
        LPDDSURFACEDESC2 lpDDSurfaceDesc2,
        LPDIRECTDRAWSURFACE4 FAR *lplpDDSurface,
        IUnknown FAR *pUnkOuter);
```

Basically, the function takes a DirectDraw surface description of the surface you want to create, a pointer to receive the interface, and finally NULL for the advanced COM feature `pUnkOuter`. Huh? Filling out the data structure can be a bit bewildering, but I'll step you through it. First, let's take a look at the DDSURFACEDESC2:

```
typedef struct _DDSURFACEDESC2
        {
        DWORD dwSize;   // size of this structure
        DWORD dwFlags;  // control flags
        DWORD dwHeight; // height of surface in pixels
        DWORD dwWidth;  // width of surface in pixels
        union
        {
        LONG  lPitch;         // memory pitch per row
        DWORD dwLinearSize;   // size of the buffer in bytes
        } DUMMYUNIONNAMEN(1);
        DWORD dwBackBufferCount;  // number of back buffers chained
        union
        {
        DWORD dwMipMapCount;               // number of mip-map levels
        DWORD dwRefreshRate;               // refresh rate
        } DUMMYUNIONNAMEN(2);
        DWORD   dwAlphaBitDepth;           // number of alpha bits
        DWORD   dwReserved;                // reserved
        LPVOID  lpSurface;                 // pointer to surface memory
        DDCOLORKEY ddckCKDestOverlay; // dest overlay color key
        DDCOLORKEY ddckCKDestBlt;     // destination color key
        DDCOLORKEY ddckCKSrcOverlay;  // source overlay color key
        DDCOLORKEY ddckCKSrcBlt;      // source color key
        DDPIXELFORMAT ddpfPixelFormat; // pixel format of surface
        DDSCAPS2    ddsCaps;           // surface capabilities
        DWORD       dwTextureStage;    // used to bind a texture
                                       // to specific stage of D3D
        } DDSURFACEDESC2, FAR* LPDDSURFACEDESC2;
```

As you can see, this is a complicated structure. Moreover, 75 percent of the fields are more than cryptic. Luckily, you only need to know about the ones that I've bolded. Let's take a look at their functions in detail, one by one:

dwSize—This is one of the most important fields in any DirectX data structure. Many DirectX data structures are sent by address, so the receiving function or method doesn't know the size of the data structure. However, if the first 32-bit value is always the size of the data structure, the receiving function will always know how much data is there just by dereferencing the first DWORD. Hence, DirectDraw and DirectX data structures in general have the size specifier as the first element of all structures. It may seem redundant, but it's a good design—trust me. All you need to do is fill it in like this:

```
DDSURFACEDESC2 ddsd;
ddsd.dwSize = sizeof(DDSURFACEDESC2);
```

dwFlags—This field is used to indicate to DirectDraw which fields you'll be filling in with valid info or, if you're using this structure in a query operation, which fields you want to retrieve. Take a look at Table 6.5 for the possible values that the flags word can take on. For example, if you were going to place valid data in the dwWidth and dwHeight fields, you would set the dwFlags field like this:

```
ddsd.dwFlags = DDSD_WIDTH | DDSD_HEIGHT;
```

Then DirectDraw would know to look in the dwHeight and dwWidth fields and that the data would be valid. Think of dwFlags as a valid data specifier.

TABLE 6.5   The Various Flags for the dwFlags Field of DDSURFACEDESC2

Value	Description
DDSD_ALPHABITDEPTH	Indicates that the dwAlphaBitDepth member is valid.
DDSD_BACKBUFFERCOUNT	Indicates that the dwBackBufferCount member is valid.
DDSD_CAPS	Indicates that the ddsCaps member is valid.
DDSD_CKDESTBLT	Indicates that the ddckCKDestBlt member is valid.
DDSD_CKDESTOVERLAY	Indicates that the ddckCKDestOverlay member is valid.
DDSD_CKSRCBLT	Indicates that the ddckCKSrcBlt member is valid.
DDSD_CKSRCOVERLAY	Indicates that the ddckCKSrcOverlay member is valid.
DDSD_HEIGHT	Indicates that the dwHeight member is valid.
DDSD_LINEARSIZE	Indicates that the dwLinearSize member is valid.
DDSD_LPSURFACE	Indicates that the lpSurface member is valid.
DDSD_MIPMAPCOUNT	Indicates that the dwMipMapCount member is valid.
DDSD_PITCH	Indicates that the lPitch member is valid.
DDSD_PIXELFORMAT	Indicates that the ddpfPixelFormat member is valid.
DDSD_REFRESHRATE	Indicates that the dwRefreshRate member is valid.
DDSD_TEXTURESTAGE	Indicates that the dwTextureStage member is valid.
DDSD_WIDTH	Indicates that the dwWidth member is valid.

dwWidth—Indicates the width of the surface in pixels. When you create a surface, this is where you set the width—320, 640, and so on. In addition, if you query the properties of a surface, this field will return the width of the surface (if you requested it).

dwHeight—Indicates the height of the surface in pixels. Similarly to dwWidth, this is where you set the height of the surface you are creating—200, 240, 480, and so on.

lPitch—This is an interesting field. It's basically the horizontal memory pitch of the display mode that you're in. Referring to Figure 6.8, the lPitch is the number of bytes per line for the video mode, also referred to as the *stride* or *memory width*. However you pronounce it, the bottom line is that this is a very important piece of data for the following reason: When you request a video mode like 640x480x8, you know that there are 640 pixels per line and each pixel is 8 bits (or 1 byte). Therefore, there should be exactly 640 bytes per line, and hence lPitch should be 640. Right? Not necessarily.

> **TIP**
>
> lPitch could be anything due to the layout of VRAM and thus when you advance line to line to access the memory in a DirectDraw surface you must use the lPitch to move to the next line rather than the width times the number of bytes per pixel, this is VERY important!

FIGURE 6.8
Accessing a surface.

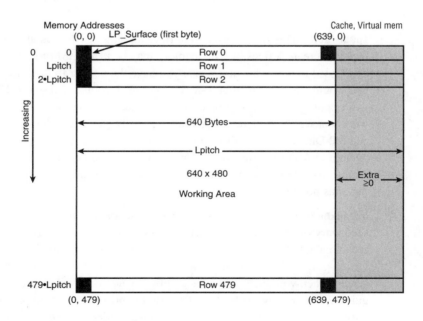

Most new video boards support what are called *linear memory modes* and have addressing hardware, so this property holds true, but it's not guaranteed. Therefore, you can't assume that a 640x480x8 video mode has 640 bytes per line. This is what the lPitch field is for. You must refer to it to make your memory addressing calculations correct, so that you can move from line to line. For example, to access any pixel in a 640x480x8 (256-color) display mode, you can use the following code, assuming you've already requested DirectDraw to give you `lPitch` and `lpSurface` is pointing to the surface memory (which I'll explain next):

```
ddsd.lpSurface[x + y*ddsd.lPitch] = color;
```

Simple, isn't it? In most cases, `ddsd.lPitch` would be 640 for a 640x480x8 mode, and for a 640x480x16 mode, `ddsd.lPitch` would be 1280 (two bytes per pixel = 640x2). But for some cards, this may not be the case due to the way memory is stored on the card, the internal cache for the card, or whatever... The moral of the story is: Always use `lPitch` for your memory calculations and you'll always be safe.

TRICK

> Even though `lPitch` may not equal the horizontal resolution of the mode that you set, it may be worth it to test for it so that you can switch to more optimized functions. For example, during the initialization of your code, you might get `lPitch` and compare it to the selected horizontal resolution. If they are equal, you might switch to highly optimized code that hard-codes the number of bytes per line.

lpSurface—This field is used to retrieve a pointer to the actual memory that the surface you create resides in. The memory may be in VRAM or system memory, but you don't need to worry about it. Once you have the pointer to it, you can manipulate it as you would any other memory—write to it, read from it, and so on. This is exactly how you're going to implement pixel plotting. Alas, making this pointer valid takes a little work, but we'll get there in a minute. Basically, you must "lock" the surface memory and tell DirectX that you're going to muck with it and that no other process should attempt to read or write from it. Furthermore, when you do get this pointer, depending on the color depth—8, 16, 24, 32 bpp—you will usually cast and assign it to a working alias pointer.

dwBackBufferCount—This field is used to set or read the number of back buffers or secondary offscreen flipping buffers that are chained to the primary surface. If you'll recall, back buffers are used to implement smooth animation by creating one or more virtual primary buffers (buffers with the same geometry and color depth) that are off-screen. Then you draw on the back buffer, which is invisible to the user, and then quickly flip or copy the back buffer(s) to the primary buffer for display. If you have only one back buffer, the technique is called *double buffering*. Using two back buffers is called *triple buffering*, which is a little better but memory-intensive. To keep things simple, in most cases you'll create flipping chains that contain a single primary surface and one back buffer.

ddckCKDestBlt—This field is used to control the destination color key, which is used in blitting operations to control the color(s) that can be written to. More on this later in the Chapter 7, "Advanced DirectDraw and Bitmapped Graphics."

ddckCKSrcBlt—This field is used to indicate the source color key, which is basically the colors that you don't want to be blitted when you're performing bitmapping operations. This is how you set the transparent colors for your bitmaps. More on this in Chapter 7.

ddpfPixelFormat—This field is used to retrieve the pixel format of a surface, which is quite important if you're trying to figure out what the properties of a surface are. The following is the general structure, but you'll have to look at the DirectX SDK for all the details because they're lengthy and not really relevant right now:

```
typedef struct _DDPIXELFORMAT
        {
        DWORD dwSize;
        DWORD dwFlags;
        DWORD dwFourCC;
        union
        {
        DWORD dwRGBBitCount;
        DWORD dwYUVBitCount;
        DWORD dwZBufferBitDepth;
        DWORD dwAlphaBitDepth;
        DWORD dwLuminanceBitCount;  // new for DirectX 6.0
        DWORD dwBumpBitCount;       // new for DirectX 6.0
        } DUMMYUNIONNAMEN(1);
        union
        {
        DWORD dwRBitMask;
        DWORD dwYBitMask;
        DWORD dwStencilBitDepth;    // new for DirectX 6.0
        DWORD dwLuminanceBitMask;   // new for DirectX 6.0
        DWORD dwBumpDuBitMask;      // new for DirectX 6.0
        } DUMMYUNIONNAMEN(2);
        union
        {
        DWORD dwGBitMask;
        DWORD dwUBitMask;
        DWORD dwZBitMask;           // new for DirectX 6.0
        DWORD dwBumpDvBitMask;      // new for DirectX 6.0
        } DUMMYUNIONNAMEN(3);
        union
        {
        DWORD dwBBitMask;
        DWORD dwVBitMask;
        DWORD dwStencilBitMask;     // new for DirectX 6.0
        DWORD dwBumpLuminanceBitMask;  // new for DirectX 6.0
        } DUMMYUNIONNAMEN(4);
```

DirectX and 2D Fundamentals

```
union
{
DWORD dwRGBAlphaBitMask;
DWORD dwYUVAlphaBitMask;
DWORD dwLuminanceAlphaBitMask; // new for DirectX 6.0
DWORD dwRGBZBitMask;
DWORD dwYUVZBitMask;
} DUMMYUNIONNAMEN(5);
} DDPIXELFORMAT, FAR* LPDDPIXELFORMAT;
```

> **NOTE**   I have bolded some of the more commonly used fields.

ddsCaps—This field is used to indicate the requested properties of the surface that haven't been defined elsewhere. In reality, this field is another data structure. DDSCAPS2 is shown here:

```
typedef struct _DDSCAPS2
        {
        DWORD    dwCaps;    // Surface capabilities
        DWORD    dwCaps2;   // More surface capabilities
        DWORD    dwCaps3;   // future expansion
        DWORD    dwCaps4;   // future expansion
        } DDSCAPS2, FAR* LPDDSCAPS2;
```

In 99.9 percent of all cases, you will set only the first field, dwCaps. dwCaps2 is for 3D stuff, and the remaining fields, dwCaps3 and dwCaps4, are future expansion and unused. In any case, a partial list of the possible flag settings for the dwCaps are shown in Table 6.6. For a complete listing, take a look at the DirectX SDK.

For example, when creating a primary surface you would set ddsd.ddsCaps like this:

```
ddsd.ddsCaps.dwCaps = DDSCAPS_PRIMARYSURFACE;
```

I know this may seem overly complex, and in some ways it is. Having doubly nested control flags is a bit of a pain, but oh well…

TABLE 6.6   Capabilities Control Settings for DirectDraw Surfaces

Value	Description
DDSCAPS_BACKBUFFER	Indicates that this surface is the back buffer of a surface flipping structure.
DDSCAPS_COMPLEX	Indicates that a complex surface is being described. A complex surface is a surface with a primary surface and one or more back buffers to create a flipping chain.

TABLE 6.6   Continued

Value	Description
DDSCAPS_FLIP	Indicates that this surface is a part of a surface flipping structure. When this capability is passed to the CreateSurface() method, a front buffer and one or more back buffers are created.
DDSCAPS_LOCALVIDMEM	Indicates that this surface exists in true, local video memory rather than non-local video memory. If this flag is specified, DDSCAPS_VIDEOMEMORY must be specified as well.
DDSCAPS_MODEX	Indicates that this surface is a 320x200 or 320x240 Mode X surface.
DDSCAPS_NONLOCALVIDMEM	Indicates that this surface exists in non-local video memory rather than true, local video memory. If this flag is specified, DDSCAPS_VIDEOMEMORY flag must be specified as well.
DDSCAPS_OFFSCREENPLAIN	Indicates that this surface is an offscreen surface that is not a special surface such as an overlay, texture, z-buffer, front-buffer, back-buffer, or alpha surface. Usually used for sprites.
DDSCAPS_OWNDC	Indicates that this surface will have a device context association for a long period.
DDSCAPS_PRIMARYSURFACE	Indicates that this surface is the primary surface. It represents what is visible to the user at the moment.
DDSCAPS_STANDARDVGAMODE	Indicates that this surface is a standard VGA mode surface, and not a Mode X surface. This flag cannot be used in combination with the DDSCAPS_MODEX flag.
DDSCAPS_SYSTEMMEMORY	Indicates that this surface memory was allocated in system memory.
DDSCAPS_VIDEOMEMORY	Indicates that this surface exists in display memory.

Now that you have an idea of the complexity and power that DirectDraw gives you when you're creating surfaces, let's put the knowledge to work and create a simple primary surface that's the same size and color depth as the display mode (default behavior). Here's the code to create a primary surface:

```
// interface pointer to hold primary surface, note that
// it's the 7th revision of the interface
LPDIRECTDRAWSURFACE7  lpddsprimary = NULL;

DDSURFACEDESC2 ddsd; // the DirectDraw surface description

// MS recommends clearing out the structure
memset(&ddsd,0,sizeof(ddsd)); // could use ZeroMemory()
```

```
// now fill in size of structure
ddsd.dwSize = sizeof(ddsd);

// enable data fields with values from table 6.5 that we
// will send valid data in
// in this case only the ddsCaps field is enabled, we
// could have enabled the width, height etc., but they
// aren't needed since primary surfaces take on the
// dimensions of the display mode by default
ddsd.dwFlags = DDSD_CAPS;


// now set the capabilities that we want from table 6.6
ddsd.ddsCaps.dwCaps = DDSCAPS_PRIMARYSURFACE;

// now create the primary surface
if (FAILED(lpdd->CreateSurface(&ddsd, &lpddsprimary, NULL)))
    {
    // error
    } // end if
```

If the function was successful, lpddsprimary will point to the new surface interface
and you can call methods on it (of which there are quite a few, such as attaching the
palette in 256-color modes). Let's take a look at this to bring the palette example back
full-circle.

Attaching the Palette

In the previous section on palettes, you did everything except attach the palette to a
surface. You created the palette and filled it with entries, but you couldn't attach the
palette to a surface because you didn't have one yet. Now that you have a surface (the
primary), you can complete this step.

To attach a palette to any surface, all you need to do is use the
IDirectDrawSurface7::SetPalette() function, which is shown here:

```
HRESULT SetPalette(LPDIRECTDRAWPALETTE lpDDPalette);
```

This function simply takes a pointer to the palette that you want to be attached. Using
the same palette that you created in the previous palette section, here's how you
would associate the palette with the primary surface:

```
if (FAILED(lpddsprimary->SetPalette(lpddpal)))
    {
    // error
    } // end if
```

Not too bad, huh? At this point, you have everything you need to emulate the entire
power of a DOS32 game. You can switch video modes, set the palette, and create a
primary drawing surface that represents the active video image. However, there are

still some details that you have to learn about, like actually locking the primary surface memory and gaining access to the VRAM and plotting a pixel. Let's take a look
at that now.

Plotting Pixels

To plot a pixel (or pixels) in a full-screen DirectDraw mode, you first must set up
DirectDraw, set the cooperation level, set a display mode, and create at least a primary
surface. Then you have to gain access to the primary surface and write to the video
memory. However, before you learn how to do this, let's take another look at how
video surfaces work.

If you'll recall, all DirectDraw video modes and surfaces are linear, as shown in
Figure 6.9. This means that memory increases from left to right and from top to
bottom as you move from row to row.

FIGURE 6.9

DirectDraw surfaces
are linear.

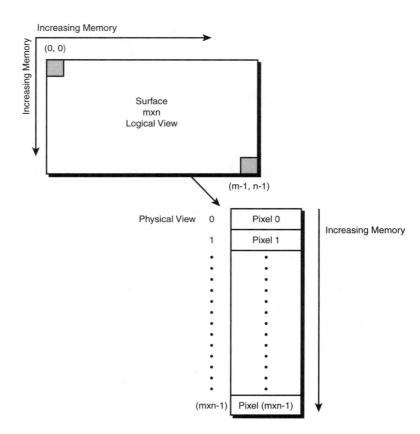

TIP	You may be wondering how DirectDraw can magically turn a nonlinear video mode into a linear one if the video card itself doesn't support it. For example, Mode X is totally nonlinear and bank-switched. Well, the truth is this—when DirectDraw detects that a mode is nonlinear in hardware, a driver called VFLATD.VXD is invoked, which creates a software layer between you and the VRAM and makes the VRAM look linear. Keep in mind that this is going to be slow.

In addition, to locate any position in the video buffer, you need only two pieces of information: the memory pitch per line (that is, how many bytes make up each row) and the size of each pixel (8-bit, 16-bit, 24-bit, 32-bit). You can use the following formula:

```
// assume this points to VRAM or the surface memory
UCHAR *video_buffer8;

video_buffer8[x + y*memory_pitchB] = pixel_color_8;
```

Of course, this is not exactly true because this formula works only for 8-bit modes, or modes that have one BYTE per pixel. For a 16-bit mode, or two BYTEs per pixel, you would have to do something like this:

```
// assume this points to VRAM or the surface memory
USHORT *video_buffer16;

video_buffer16[x + y*(memory_pitchB >> 1)] = pixel_color_16;
```

There's a lot going on here, so let's take a look at the code carefully. Since we're in a 16-bit mode, I'm using a USHORT pointer to the VRAM. What this does is let me use array access, but with 16-bit pointer arithmetic. Hence, when I say

```
video_buffer16[1]
```

this really accesses the second SHORT or byte pair 2,3. In addition, because memory_pitchB is in bytes, you must divide it by two by shifting right one bit so that it's in SHORT or 16-bit memory pitch. Finally, the assignment of pixel_color16 is also misleading because now a complete 16-bit USHORT will be written into the video buffer, rather than a single 8-bit value as in the previous example. Moreover, the 8-bit value would be a color index, whereas a 16-bit value must be a RGB value, usually encoded in $R_5G_6B_5$ format or five bits for red, six bits for green, and five bits for blue, as shown in Figure 6.10.

Here's a macro to make up a 16-bit RGB word in 5.5.5 and 5.6.5 format:

```
// this builds a 16 bit color value in 5.5.5 format (1-bit alpha mode)
#define _RGB16BIT555(r,g,b) ((b & 31) + ((g & 31) << 5) + ((r & 31) << 10))

// this builds a 16 bit color value in 5.6.5 format (green dominate mode)
#define _RGB16BIT565(r,g,b) ((b & 31) + ((g & 63) << 5) + ((r & 31) << 11))
```

FIGURE 6.10
Possible 16-bit RGB encodings, including 5.6.5 format.

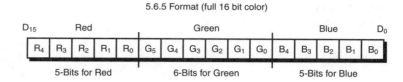

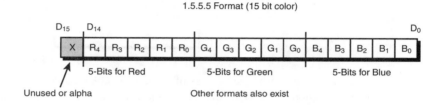

As you can see, 16-bit modes and RGB modes in general have a little more complex addressing and manipulation than do the 256-color 8-bit modes, so let's begin there.

To gain access to any surface—primary, secondary, and so on—you must lock and unlock the memory. This lock and unlock sequence is necessary for two reasons: First, to tell DirectDraw that you are in control of the memory (that is, it shouldn't be accessed by other processes), and second, to indicate to the video hardware that it shouldn't move any cache or virtual memory buffers around while you're messing with the locked memory. Remember, there is no guarantee that VRAM will stay in the same place. It could be virtual, but when you lock it, the memory will stay in the same address space for the duration of the lock so you can manipulate it. The function to lock memory is called `IDirectDrawSurface7::Lock()` and is shown here:

```
HRESULT Lock(LPRECT      lpDestRect,     // destination RECT to lock
    LPDDSURFACEDESC2 lpDDSurfaceDesc, // address of struct to receive info
    DWORD           dwFlags,        // request flags
    HANDLE          hEvent);        // advanced, make NULL
```

The parameters aren't that bad, but there are some new players. Let's step through them. The first parameter is the `RECT` of the region of surface memory that you want to lock; take a look at Figure 6.11. DirectDraw allows you to lock only a certain portion of surface memory so that, if another process is accessing a region that you aren't, processing can continue. This is great if you know that you're going to update only a certain part of the surface and don't need a full lock on the entire surface. However, in most cases you'll just lock the entire surface to keeps things simple. This is accomplished by passing `NULL`.

DirectX and 2D Fundamentals

FIGURE 6.11
IDirectDrawSurface
7->Lock(...)

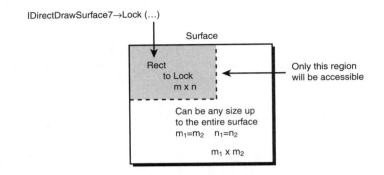

The second parameter is the address of a DDSURFACEDESC2 that will be filled with information about the surface that you request. Basically, just send a blank DDSURFACEDESC2 and that's it. The next parameter, dwFlags, tells Lock() what you want to do. Table 6.7 contains a list of the most commonly used values.

TABLE 6.7   The Control Flags for the Lock() Method

Value	Description
DDLOCK_READONLY	Indicates that the surface being locked will be read-only.
DDLOCK_SURFACEMEMORYPTR	Indicates that a valid memory pointer to the top of the specified RECT should be returned. If no rectangle is specified, a pointer to the top of the surface is returned. This is the default.
DDLOCK_WAIT	If a lock cannot be obtained because a blit operation is in progress, the method retries until a lock is obtained or another error occurs, such as DDERR_SURFACEBUSY.
DDLOCK_WRITEONLY	Indicates that the surface being locked will be write-enabled.

> **NOTE**
> I have bolded the most commonly used flags.

The last parameter is to facilitate an advanced feature that Win32 supports called *events*. Set it to NULL.

Locking the primary surface is really easy. What you want to do is request the memory pointer to the surface, along with requesting DirectDraw to wait for the surface to become available. Here's the code:

```
DDSURFACEDESC2 ddsd; // this will hold the results of the lock

// clear the surface description out always
```

```
memset(&ddsd, 0, sizeof(ddsd));

// set the size field always
ddsd.dwSize = sizeof(ddsd);

// lock the surface
if (FAILED(lpddsprimary->Lock(NULL,
           &ddsd,
           DDLOCK_SURFACEMEMORYPTR | DDLOCK_WAIT,NULL)))
 {
 // error

 } // end if

// ****** at this point there are two fields that we are
// concerned with: ddsd.lPitch which contains the memory
// pitch in bytes per line and ddsd.lpSurface which is a
// pointer to the top left corner of the locked surface
```

Once you've locked the surface, you're free to manipulate the surface memory as you wish. The memory pitch per line is stored in ddsd.lPitch, and the pointer to the actual surface is ddsd.lpSurface. Therefore, if you're in any 8-bit mode (1 byte per pixel), the following function can be used to plot a pixel anywhere on the primary surface:

```
inline void Plot8(int x, int y,  // position of pixel
           UCHAR color,   // color index of pixel
           UCHAR *buffer, // pointer to surface memory
           int mempitch)  // memory pitch per line
{
// this function plots a single pixel
buffer[x+y*mempitch] = color;

} // end Plot8
```

Here's how you would call it to plot a pixel at (100,20) with color index 26:

```
Plot8(100,20,26, (UCHAR *)ddsd.lpSurface,(int)ddsd.lPitch);
```

Similarly, here's a 16-bit 5.6.5 RGB mode plot function:

```
inline void Plot16(int x, int y,  // position of pixel
           UCHAR red,
           UCHAR green,
           UCHAR, blue  // RGB color of pixel
           USHORT *buffer, // pointer to surface memory
           int mempitch)   // memory pitch bytes per line
{
// this function plots a single pixel
buffer[x+y*(mempitch>>1)] = __RGB16BIT565(red,green,blue);

} // end Plot16
```

And here's how you would plot a pixel at (300,100) with RGB value (10,14,30):

```
Plot16(300,100,10,14,30,(USHORT *)ddsd.lpSurface,(int)ddsd.lPitch);
```

Now, once you're done with all your video surface access for the current frame of animation, you need to unlock the surface. This is accomplished with the `IDirectDrawSurface7::Unlock()` method shown here:

```
HRESULT Unlock(LPRECT lpRect);
```

You send `Unlock()` the original RECT that you used in the lock command, or NULL if you locked the entire surface. In this case, here's all you would do to unlock the surface:

```
if (FAILED(lpddsprimary->Unlock(NULL)))
    {
    // error
    } // end if
```

That's all there is to it. Now, let's see all the steps put together to plot random pixels on the screen (without error detection):

```
LPDIRECTDRAW7 lpdd = NULL; // DirectDraw 7.0 interface 7
LPDIRECTDRAWSURFACE7 lpddsprimary = NULL; // surface ptr
DDSURFACEDESC2      ddsd;      // surface description
LPDIRECTDRAWPALETTE lpddpal = NULL; // palette interface
PALETTEENTRY palette[256]; // palette storage

// first create base IDirectDraw 7.0 interface
DirectDrawCreateEx(NULL, (void **)&lpdd, IID_IDirectDraw7, NULL);


// set the cooperative level for full-screen mode
lpdd->SetCooperativeLevel(hwnd,
                          DDSCL_FULLSCREEN |
                          DDSCL_ALLOWMODEX |
                          DDSCL_EXCLUSIVE |
                          DDSCL_ALLOWREBOOT);

// set the display mode to 640x480x256
lpdd->SetDisplayMode(640,480,8,0,0);

// clear ddsd and set size
memset(&ddsd,0,sizeof(ddsd));
ddsd.dwSize = sizeof(ddsd);

// enable valid fields
ddsd.dwFlags = DDSD_CAPS;

// request primary surface
ddsd.ddsCaps.dwCaps = DDSCAPS_PRIMARYSURFACE;
```

```
// create the primary surface
lpdd->CreateSurface(&ddsd, &lpddsprimary, NULL);


// build up the palette data array
for (int color=1; color < 255; color++)
    {
    // fill with random RGB values
    palette[color].peRed   = rand()%256;
    palette[color].peGreen = rand()%256;
    palette[color].peBlue  = rand()%256;

    // set flags field to PC_NOCOLLAPSE
    palette[color].peFlags = PC_NOCOLLAPSE;
    } // end for color

// now fill in entry 0 and 255 with black and white
palette[0].peRed   = 0;
palette[0].peGreen = 0;
palette[0].peBlue  = 0;
palette[0].peFlags = PC_NOCOLLAPSE;

palette[255].peRed   = 255;
palette[255].peGreen = 255;
palette[255].peBlue  = 255;
palette[255].peFlags = PC_NOCOLLAPSE;

// create the palette object
lpdd->CreatePalette(DDPCAPS_8BIT |DDPCAPS_ALLOW256 |
                    DDPCAPS_INITIALIZE,
                    palette,&lpddpal, NULL);

// finally attach the palette to the primary surface
lpddsprimary->SetPalette(lpddpal);

// and you're ready to rock n roll!
// lock the surface first and retrieve memory pointer
// and memory pitch

// clear ddsd and set size, never assume it's clean
memset(&ddsd,0,sizeof(ddsd));
ddsd.dwSize = sizeof(ddsd);

lpddsprimary->Lock(NULL, &ddsd,
             DDLOCK_SURFACEMEMORYPTR | DDLOCK_WAIT, NULL);

// now ddsd.lPitch is valid and so is ddsd.lpSurface

// make a couple aliases to make code cleaner, so we don't
// have to cast
int mempitch        = ddsd.lPitch;
UCHAR *video_buffer = ddsd.lpSurface;
```

DirectX and 2D Fundamentals

```
// plot 1000 random pixels with random colors on the
// primary surface, they will be instantly visible
for (int index=0; index<1000; index++)
    {
    // select random position and color for 640x480x8
    UCHAR color = rand()%256;
    int x = rand()%640;
    int y = rand()%480;

    // plot the pixel
    video_buffer[x+y*mempitch] = color;

    } // end for index

// now unlock the primary surface
lpddsprimary->Unlock(NULL);
```

Of course, I'm leaving out all the Windows initialization and event loop stuff, but that never changes. However, to be complete, take a look at DEMO6_3.CPP and the associated executable DEMO6_3.EXE on the CD. They contain the preceding code injected into your Game Console's Game_Main() function, shown in the following listing along with the updated Game_Init(). Figure 6.12 is a screen shot of the program in action.

FIGURE 6.12
DEMO6_3.EXE
in action.

```
int Game_Main(void *parms = NULL, int num_parms = 0)
{
// this is the main loop of the game, do all your processing
// here

// for now test if user is hitting ESC and send WM_CLOSE
if (KEYDOWN(VK_ESCAPE))
    SendMessage(main_window_handle,WM_CLOSE,0,0);
```

```
// plot 1000 random pixels to the primary surface and return
// clear ddsd and set size, never assume it's clean
memset(&ddsd,0,sizeof(ddsd));
ddsd.dwSize = sizeof(ddsd);

if (FAILED(lpddsprimary->Lock(NULL, &ddsd,
                     DDLOCK_SURFACEMEMORYPTR | DDLOCK_WAIT,
                     NULL)))
   {
   // error
   return(0);
   } // end if

// now ddsd.lPitch is valid and so is ddsd.lpSurface

// make a couple aliases to make code cleaner, so we don't
// have to cast
int mempitch        = (int)ddsd.lPitch;
UCHAR *video_buffer = (UCHAR *)ddsd.lpSurface;

// plot 1000 random pixels with random colors on the
// primary surface, they will be instantly visible
for (int index=0; index < 1000; index++)
    {
    // select random position and color for 640x480x8
    UCHAR color = rand()%256;
    int x = rand()%640;
    int y = rand()%480;

    // plot the pixel
    video_buffer[x+y*mempitch] = color;

    } // end for index

// now unlock the primary surface
if (FAILED(lpddsprimary->Unlock(NULL)))
   return(0);

// sleep a bit
Sleep(30);

// return success or failure or your own return code here
return(1);

} // end Game_Main

///////////////////////////////////////////////////////////

int Game_Init(void *parms = NULL, int num_parms = 0)
{
// this is called once after the initial window is created and
// before the main event loop is entered, do all your initialization
```

DirectX and 2D Fundamentals

```
// here

// first create base IDirectDraw interface
if (FAILED(DirectDrawCreateEx(NULL, (void **)&lpdd, IID_IDirectDraw7, NULL)))
   {
   // error
   return(0);
   } // end if



// set cooperation to full screen
if (FAILED(lpdd->SetCooperativeLevel(main_window_handle,
                   DDSCL_FULLSCREEN | DDSCL_ALLOWMODEX |
                   DDSCL_EXCLUSIVE | DDSCL_ALLOWREBOOT)))
   {
   // error
   return(0);
   } // end if

// set display mode to 640x480x8
if (FAILED(lpdd->SetDisplayMode(SCREEN_WIDTH,
                   SCREEN_HEIGHT, SCREEN_BPP,0,0)))
   {
   // error
   return(0);
   } // end if


// clear ddsd and set size
memset(&ddsd,0,sizeof(ddsd));
ddsd.dwSize = sizeof(ddsd);

// enable valid fields
ddsd.dwFlags = DDSD_CAPS;

// request primary surface
ddsd.ddsCaps.dwCaps = DDSCAPS_PRIMARYSURFACE;

// create the primary surface
if (FAILED(lpdd->CreateSurface(&ddsd, &lpddsprimary, NULL)))
   {
   // error
   return(0);
   } // end if

// build up the palette data array
for (int color=1; color < 255; color++)
   {
   // fill with random RGB values
   palette[color].peRed   = rand()%256;
   palette[color].peGreen = rand()%256;
   palette[color].peBlue  = rand()%256;
```

```
    // set flags field to PC_NOCOLLAPSE
    palette[color].peFlags = PC_NOCOLLAPSE;
    } // end for color

// now fill in entry 0 and 255 with black and white
palette[0].peRed   = 0;
palette[0].peGreen = 0;
palette[0].peBlue  = 0;
palette[0].peFlags = PC_NOCOLLAPSE;

palette[255].peRed   = 255;
palette[255].peGreen = 255;
palette[255].peBlue  = 255;
palette[255].peFlags = PC_NOCOLLAPSE;

// create the palette object
if (FAILED(lpdd->CreatePalette(DDPCAPS_8BIT | DDPCAPS_ALLOW256 |
                               DDPCAPS_INITIALIZE,
                               palette,&lpddpal, NULL)))
{
// error
return(0);
} // end if

// finally attach the palette to the primary surface
if (FAILED(lpddsprimary->SetPalette(lpddpal)))
    {
    // error
    return(0);
    } // end if

// return success or failure or your own return code here
return(1);

} // end Game_Init
```

The only other detail I want to bring to your attention about the demo program code is the creation of the main window, shown here:

```
// create the window
if (!(hwnd = CreateWindowEx(NULL,                    // extended style
                            WINDOW_CLASS_NAME,       // class
                            "T3D DirectX Pixel Demo", // title
                                          WS_POPUP | WS_VISIBLE,
                    0,0,    // initial x,y
                    640,480,  // initial width, height
                    NULL,   // handle to parent
                    NULL,   // handle to menu
                    hinstance, // instance of this application
                    NULL)))    // extra creation parms
return(0);
```

Notice that instead of using the WS_OVERLAPPEDWINDOW window style, the demo uses WS_POPUP. If you'll recall, this style is devoid of all controls and Windows GUI stuff, which is what you want for a full-screen DirectX application.

Cleaning Up

Before moving on to the end of the chapter, I want to bring up a topic that I've been putting off for a while—resource management. Yuck! Anyway, this seemingly un-fun concept simply means making sure that you Release() DirectDraw or DirectX objects in general when you're done with them. For example, if you take a look at the source code in DEMO6_3.CPP, in the Game_Shutdown() function you'll see a number of Release() calls to release all the DirectDraw objects back to the operating system, and DirectDraw itself, shown here:

```
int Game_Shutdown(void *parms = NULL, int num_parms = 0)
{
// this is called after the game is exited and the main event
// loop while is exited, do all you cleanup and shutdown here

// first the palette
if (lpddpal)
   {
   lpddpal->Release();
   lpddpal = NULL;
   } // end if

// now the primary surface
if (lpddsprimary)
   {
   lpddsprimary->Release();
   lpddsprimary = NULL;
   } // end if

// now blow away the IDirectDraw7 interface
if (lpdd)
   {
   lpdd->Release();
   lpdd = NULL;
   } // end if

// return success or failure or your own return code here
return(1);

} // end Game_Shutdown
```

In general, you should Release() objects only when you're done with them, and you should do so in reverse order of creation. For example, you created the DirectDraw object, the primary surface, and the palette, in that order, so a good rule of thumb would be to release the palette, surface, and then DirectDraw, like this:

```
// first kill the palette
if (lpddpal)
    {
    lpddpal->Release();
    lpddpal = NULL;
    } // end if

// now the primary surface
if (lpddsprimary)
    lpddsprimary->Release();


// and finally the directdraw object itself
if (lpdd)
    {
    lpdd->Release();
    lpdd = NULL;
    } // end if
```

  WARNING Before you make a call to Release(), notice the testing to see if the interface is non-NULL. This is absolutely necessary because the interface pointer may be NULL, and releasing on a NULL pointer may cause problems if the implementers of the interface haven't thought of it.

Summary

In this chapter you learned the basics of DirectDraw—how to get it up and running in full-screen mode, for the most part. Also, we touched upon palettes, display surfaces, and the differences between full-screen and windowed applications. In the next chapter, I'm going to put on the gas and we're going to cover a lot of ground, so strap on your seat belt, baby!

CHAPTER 7

Advanced DirectDraw and Bitmapped Graphics

"There are a lot of decaffeinated brands on the market that are just as tasty as the real thing…"
—Chris Knight, Real Genius

In this chapter I'm going to show you the guts of DirectDraw and start working on the first module of the graphics library (T3DLIB1.CPP|H), which will be the basis of all demos and games created in this book. A lot of material will be covered in this chapter, in addition to me throwing a graphics library at you that I'll write through the course of this chapter. However, I promise that everything will be reasonably simple, while still complex enough to do something cool with. Here's what this chapter will cover:

- High-color modes
- Page flipping and double buffering
- The blitter
- Clipping
- Loading bitmaps

- Color animation
- Windowed DirectX
- Getting information from DirectX

Working with High-Color Modes

High-color modes (modes that require more than eight bits per pixel) are of course more visually pleasing to the eye than the 256-color modes. However, they usually aren't used in software-based 3D engines for a number of reasons. The biggest reasons are as follows:

- **Computational speed**—A standard 640x480 pixel frame buffer consists of 307,200 pixels. If each pixel is 8-bit, that means that most calculations can be done using a single byte per pixel and rasterization is simpler. On the other hand, in 16-bit or 24-bit modes, full RGB space calculations are usually employed (or very large lookup tables) and the speed is cut at least in half. Furthermore, two or three bytes per pixel must be written to the frame buffer instead of one as in 8-bit modes.

  Of course, with acceleration hardware, this isn't as much of a problem for bitmapping or 3D (in fact, most 3D cards work in 24/32-bit color), but for software rasterization (which is what you're learning in this book), it's a big deal. You want to write the least amount of data per pixel as possible, and 8-bit mode meets this requirement (although it's not as pretty as 16-bit). However, with 8-bit mode, you can rest assured that someone with a Pentium 133-233 might be able to play your game, and you won't have to worry about your audience having a P4 2.4GHz with 3D acceleration at a minimum.

- **Memory bandwidth**—This is something that people hardly ever take into consideration. Your PC has either an ISA (Industry Standard Architecture), VLB (VESA Local Bus), PCI (Peripheral Component Interconnect), or PCI/AGP (Accelerated Graphics Port) hybrid bus system. The bottom line is that everything but the AGP port is relatively slow compared to video clock rates. This means that although you may have a 500+ MHz Pentium III, it's not going to do you any good if you have a PCI bus that's bottlenecking your access to video RAM and/or acceleration hardware. Of course, a number of hardware optimizations can help in this area, such as caching, multi-port VRAM, and so forth, but there's always a fill rate limit that you can never exceed no matter what you do. The moral of the story is that as you move to higher and higher resolutions and color depths, in many cases the memory bandwidth is more of a limiting factor than the processor's speed. However, with AGP 2x and 4x this will become less of an issue.

However, today, computers are sufficiently fast that you can do 16-bit and even 24-bit software engines and they are fast enough (not nearly as fast as hardware of course). So just something to think about if you are making simpler games that target a large audience, 8-bit is also easier to understand for beginners to program. Working with high-color modes is conceptually similar to working with palletized modes, with the single caveat that you aren't writing color indices into the frame buffer, but instead full RGB-encoded pixel values. This means that you must know how to create an RGB pixel encoding for the high-color modes that you want to work with. Figure 7.1 depicts a number of various 16-bit pixel encodings.

FIGURE 7.1
16-Bit RGB pixel encodings.

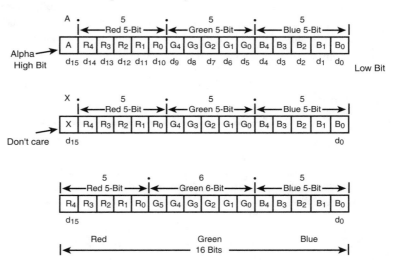

16-Bit High-Color Mode

Referring to Figure 7.1, there are a number of possible bit encodings for 16-bit modes:

Alpha.5.5.5—This mode uses a single bit at position D_{15} to represent a possible Alpha component (transparency), and the remaining 15 bits are equally distributed with five bits for red, five bits for green, and five bits for blue. This makes a total of $2^5 = 32$ shades for each color and a palette of 32x32x32 = 32,768 colors.

X.5.5.5—This mode is similar to the Alpha.5.5.5 mode, except the MSB (most significant bit) is unused and can be anything. The color range is still 32 shades of each primary color (red, green, and blue), with a total of 32x32x32 = 32,768 colors.

5.6.5—This is the most common mode and uses all 16 bits of the WORD to define the color. The format is, of course, five bits for red, six bits for green, and five bits for blue, for a total of 32x64x32 = 65536 color. Now, you may ask, "Why six bits for green?" Well, my little leprechaun, the answer is that human eyes are more sensitive to green, and therefore the increased range for green is the most logical choice of the three primaries.

Now that you know the RGB bit-encoding formats, the question is how to build them up. You accomplish this task with simple bit shifting and masking operations, as shown in the following macros:

```
// this builds a 16 bit color value in 5.5.5 format (1-bit alpha mode)
#define _RGB16BIT555(r,g,b) ((b & 31) + ((g & 31) << 5) + ((r & 31) << 10))

// this builds a 16 bit color value in 5.6.5 format (green dominate mode)
#define _RGB16BIT565(r,g,b) ((b & 31) + ((g & 63) << 5) + ((r & 31) << 11))
```

You'll notice from the macros and Figure 7.2 that the red bits are located in the high-order bits of the color WORD, the green bits are in the middle bits, and the blue bits are located in the low-order bits of the color WORD. This may seem backwards because PCs are *little-endian* and place data in low-to-high order, but in this case the bits are in *big-endian* format, which is much better because they follow RGB order from MSB to LSB.

FIGURE 7.2
Color WORDs are big-endian.

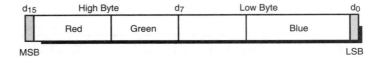

WARNING

Before you build a quick demo of 16-bit mode, there's one more little detail that I must address—how on Earth do you detect if the video mode is 5.5.5 or 5.6.5? This is important because it's not under your control. You can tell DirectDraw to create a 16-bit mode, but the bit encoding is up to the hardware. You must know this detail because the green channel will be all jacked up if you don't take it into consideration! What you need to know is the pixel format.

Getting the Pixel Format

To figure out the pixel format of any surface, all you need to do is call the function `IDIRECTDRAWSURFACE7:GetPixelFormat()`, shown here:

```
HRESULT GetPixelFormat(LPDDPIXELFORMAT lpDDPixelFormat);
```

You already saw the `DDPIXELFORMAT` structure in the previous chapter, but the fields you're interested in are

```
DWORD dwSize;        // the size of the structure, must be set by you
DWORD dwFlags;       // flags describing the surface, refer to Table 7.1
DWORD dwRGBBitCount; // number of bits for Red, Green, and Blue
```

The `dwSize` field must be set before you make the call to the size of a `DDPIXELFORMAT` structure. After the call, both the `dwFlags` field and the `dwRGBBitCount` fields will be valid and contain the informational flags, along with the number of RGB bits for the surface in question. Table 7.1 lists a subset of the possible flags contained in `dwFlags`.

TABLE 7.1 Valid Flags for `DDPIXELFORMAT.dwFlags`

Value	Description
DDPF_ALPHA	The pixel format describes an alpha-only surface.
DDPF_ALPHAPIXELS	The surface has alpha channel information in the pixel format.
DDPF_LUMINANCE	The pixel format describes a luminance-only or luminance-alpha surface.
DDPF_PALETTEINDEXED1	The surface is 1-bit color indexed.
DDPF_PALETTEINDEXED2	The surface is 2-bit color indexed.
DDPF_PALETTEINDEXED4	The surface is 4-bit color indexed.
DDPF_PALETTEINDEXED8	The surface is 8-bit color indexed. Most common.
DDPF_PALETTEINDEXEDTO8	The surface is 1-, 2-, or 4-bit color indexed to an 8-bit palette.
DDPF_RGB	The RGB data in the pixel format structure is valid.
DDPF_ZBUFFER	The pixel format describes a z-buffer surface.
DDPF_ZPIXELS	The surface contains z information in the pixels.

Note that there are a lot more flags especially for D3D-related properties. Please refer to the DirectX SDK for more information.

The fields that matter the most right now are

DDPF_PALETTEINDEXED8—This indicates that the surface is an 8-bit palettized mode.

DDPF_RGB—This indicates that the surface is an RGB mode and the format can be queried by testing the value in `dwRGBBitCount`.

So all you need to do is write a test that looks something like this:

```
DDPIXELFORMAT ddpixel; // used to hold info

LPDIRECTDRAWSURFACE7 lpdds_primary; // assume this is valid

// clear our structure
memset(&ddpixel, 0, sizeof(ddpixel));

// set length
ddpixel.dwSize = sizeof(ddpixel);

// make call off surface (assume primary this time)
lpdds_primary->GetPixelFormat(&ddpixel);

// now perform tests
// check if this is an RGB mode or palettized
if (ddpixel.dwFlags & DDPF_RGB)
   {
   // RGB mode
   // what's the RGB mode
```

```
switch(ddpixel.dwRGBBitCount)
    {
    case 15: // must be 5.5.5 mode
        {
        // use the _RGB16BIT555(r,g,b) macro
        } break;

    case 16: // must be 5.6.5 mode
        {
        // use the _RGB16BIT565(r,g,b) macro
        } break;

    case 24: // must be 8.8.8 mode
        {
        } break;

    case 32: // must be alpha(8).8.8.8 mode
        {
        } break;

    default: break;

    } // end switch

    } // end if
else
if (ddpixel.dwFlags & DDPF_PALETTEINDEXED8)
    {
    // 256 color palettized mode
    } // end if
else
    {
    // something else??? more tests
    } // end else
```

Fairly simple code, huh? A bit ugly granted, but that comes with the territory, baby! The real power of GetPixelFormat() comes into play when you don't set the video mode and you simply create a primary surface in a windowed mode. In that case, you'll have no idea about the properties of the video system and you must query the system. Otherwise, you won't know the color depth, pixel format, or even the resolution of the system.

Now that you're a 16-bit expert, here's a demo! There's nothing to creating a 16-bit application—just make the call to SetDisplayMode() with 16 bits for the color depth, and that's it. As an example, here are the steps you would take to create a full-screen, 16-bit color mode in DirectDraw:

```
LPDIRECTDRAW7  lpdd      = NULL; // used to get directdraw7
DDSURFACEDESC2 ddsd;             // surface description
LPDIRECTDRAWSURFACE7 lpddsprimary = NULL; // primary surface
```

```
// create IDirectDraw7and test for error
if (FAILED(DirectDrawCreateEx(NULL, (void **)&lpdd, IID_IDirectDraw7, NULL)))
    return(0);



// set cooperation level to requested mode
if (FAILED(lpdd->SetCooperativeLevel(main_window_handle,
            DDSCL_ALLOWMODEX | DDSCL_FULLSCREEN |
            DDSCL_EXCLUSIVE | DDSCL_ALLOWREBOOT)))
    return(0);

// set the display mode to 16 bit color mode
if (FAILED(lpdd->SetDisplayMode(640,480,16,0,0)))
    return(0);

// Create the primary surface
memset(&ddsd,0,sizeof(ddsd));
ddsd.dwSize = sizeof(ddsd);
ddsd.dwFlags = DDSD_CAPS;

// set caps for primary surface
ddsd.ddsCaps.dwCaps = DDSCAPS_PRIMARYSURFACE;

// create the primary surface
lpdd->CreateSurface(&ddsd,&lpddsprimary,NULL);
```

And that's all there is to it. At this point, you would see a black screen (possibly garbage if the primary buffer memory has data in it).

To simplify the discussion, assume that you already tested the pixel format and found that it's RGB 16-bit 5.6.5 mode—which is correct, because you set the mode! In the worst-case scenario, however, it could have been the 5.5.5 format. Anyway, to write a pixel to the screen, you must

1. Lock the surface. In this example, that means locking the primary surface with a call to Lock().

2. Build the RGB WORD for 16-bit mode. This entails using one of the macros or doing it yourself. Basically, you're going to send the pixel-plotting function red, green, and blue values. They must be scaled and then combined into the 16-bit 5.6.5 format that the primary surface needs.

3. Write the pixel. This means addressing the primary buffer using a USHORT pointer and writing the pixel into the VRAM buffer.

4. Unlock the primary surface. A call to Unlock() is made.

Here's the code for a rough 16-bit plot pixel function:

```
void Plot_Pixel16(int x, int y, int red, int green, int blue,
                LPDIRECTDRAWSURFACE7 lpdds)
```

```
{
// this function plots a pixel in 16-bit color mode
// very inefficient...

DDSURFACEDESC2 ddsd; // directdraw surface description

// first build up color WORD
USHORT pixel = __RGB16BIT565(red,green,blue);

// now lock video buffer
DDRAW_INIT_STRUCT(ddsd);

lpdds->Lock(NULL,&ddsd,DDLOCK_WAIT |
            DDLOCK_SURFACEMEMORYPTR,NULL);

// write the pixel

// alias the surface memory pointer to a USHORT ptr
USHORT *video_buffer = ddsd.lpSurface;

// write the data
video_buffer[x + y*(ddsd.lPitch >> 1)] = pixel;

// unlock the surface
lpdds->Unlock(NULL);

} // end Plot_Pixel16
```

Notice the use of DDRAW_INIT_STRUCT(ddsd), which is a simple macro that zeros out the structure and sets its dwSize field. I'm getting tired of doing it the long way. Here's the macro definition:

```
// this macro should be on one line
#define DDRAW_INIT_STRUCT(ddstruct)
{ memset(&ddstruct,0,sizeof(ddstruct));
  ddstruct.dwSize=sizeof(ddstruct); }
```

For example, to plot a pixel on the primary surface at (10,30) with RGB values (255,0,0), you would do something like this:

```
Plot_Pixel16(10,30,   // x,y
             255,0,0, // rgb
             lpddsprimary); // surface to draw on
```

Although the function seems reasonably simple, it's extremely inefficient. There are a number of optimizations that you can take advantage of. The first problem is that the function locks and unlocks the sent surface each time. This is totally unacceptable. Locking/unlocking can take hundreds of microseconds on some video cards, and maybe even longer. The bottom line is that in a game loop, you should lock a surface once, do all the manipulation you're going to do with it, and unlock it when you're done, as shown in Figure 7.3. That way you don't have to keep locking/unlocking, zeroing out memory, etc. For example, the memory fill of the DDSURFACEDESC2 structure probably takes longer than the pixel plot! Not to mention that the function isn't inline and the function overhead is probably killing you.

FIGURE 7.3
DirectDraw surfaces should be locked as little as possible.

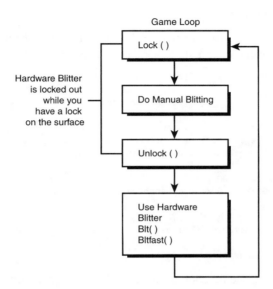

These are the types of things that a game programmer needs to keep in mind. You aren't writing a word processor program here—you need speed! Here's another version of the function with a little bit of optimization, but it can still be 10 times faster:

```
inline void Plot_Pixel_Fast16(int x, int y,
                              int red, int green, int blue,
                              USHORT *video_buffer, int lpitch)
{
// this function plots a pixel in 16-bit color mode
// assuming that the caller already locked the surface
// and is sending a pointer and byte pitch to it

// first build up color WORD
USHORT pixel = __RGB16BIT565(red,green,blue);

// write the data
video_buffer[x + y*(lpitch >> 1)] = pixel;

} // end Plot_Pixel_Fast16
```

I still don't like the multiply and shift, but this new version isn't bad. You can get rid of both the multiply and shift with a couple of tricks. First, the shift is needed because lPitch is memory width in bytes. However, because you're assuming that the caller already locked the surface and queried the memory pointer and pitch from the surface, it's a no-brainer to add one more step to the process to compute a WORD or 16-bit strided version of lpitch, like this:

```
int lpitch16 = (lpitch >> 1);
```

Basically, lpitch16 is now the number of 16-bit WORDs that make up a video line. With this new value, you can rewrite the functions once again, like this:

```
inline void Plot_Pixel_Faster16(int x, int y,
                                int red, int green, int blue,
                                USHORT *video_buffer, int lpitch16)
{
// this function plots a pixel in 16-bit color mode
// assuming that the caller already locked the surface
// and is sending a pointer and byte pitch to it

// first build up color WORD
USHORT pixel = _RGB16BIT565(red,green,blue);

// write the data
video_buffer[x + y*lpitch16] = pixel;

} // end Plot_Pixel_Faster16
```

That's getting there! The function is inline and has a single multiply, addition, and memory access. Not bad, but it could be better! The final optimization is to use a huge lookup table to get rid of the multiply, but this may not be needed because integer multiplies are getting down to single cycles on newer Pentium X architectures. It is a way to speed things up, however.

On the other hand, you can get rid of the multiply by using a number of shift-adds. For example, assuming a perfectly linear memory mode (without any extra stride per line), you know that it's exactly 1,280 bytes from one video line to another in a 640x480 16-bit mode. Therefore, you need to multiply y by 640 because the array access will use automatic pointer arithmetic and scale anything in the [ ] array operator by a factor of 2 (2 bytes per USHORT WORD). Anyway, here's the math:

```
y*640 = y*512 + y*128
```

512 is equal to 2^9, and 128 is equal to 2^7. Therefore, if you were to shift y to the left 9 times and then add that to y shifted to the left 7 times, the result should be equivalent to y*640, or mathematically:

```
y*640 = y*512 + y*128
      = (y << 9) + (y << 7)
```

That's it! If you aren't familiar with this trick, take a look at Figure 7.4. Basically, shifting any binary-encoded number to the right is the same as dividing by 2 and shifting to the left is the same as multiplying by 2. Furthermore, multiple shifts accumulate. Hence, you can use this property to perform very fast multiplication on numbers that are powers of 2. However, if the numbers aren't powers of 2, you can always break them into a sum of products that are—as in the previous case. Now, optimizations like these aren't really important on Pentium II+ processors since they can usually multiply in a single clock, but on older processors or other platforms like the Game Boy Advance, etc. knowing tricks always come in handy.

FIGURE 7.4
Using binary shifting to multiply and divide.

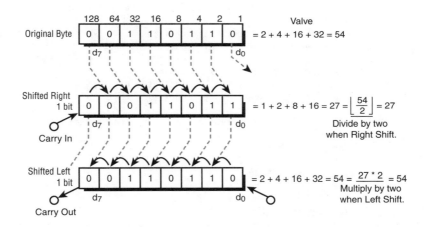

NOTE

You'll see a lot more of these tricks when you get to the Chapter 11, "Algorithms, Data Structures, Memory Management, and Multithreading."

For an example of using the 16-bit modes to write pixels to the screen, take a look at DEMO7_1.CPP|EXE on the CD. The program basically implements what you've done here and blasts random pixels to the screen. Take a look at the code and note that you don't need a palette anymore, which is kind of nice <BG>. By the way, the code is in the standard T3D Game Engine template, so the only things you need to really look at are Game_Init() and Game_Main(). The contents of Game_Main() are shown here:

```
int Game_Main(void *parms = NULL, int num_parms = 0)
{
// this is the main loop of the game, do all your processing
// here

// for now test if user is hitting ESC and send WM_CLOSE
if (KEYDOWN(VK_ESCAPE))
   SendMessage(main_window_handle,WM_CLOSE,0,0);
```

DirectX and 2D Fundamentals

```
// plot 1000 random pixels to the primary surface and return
// clear ddsd and set size, never assume it's clean
DDRAW_INIT_STRUCT(ddsd);

// lock the primary surface
if (FAILED(lpddsprimary->Lock(NULL, &ddsd,
                  DDLOCK_SURFACEMEMORYPTR | DDLOCK_WAIT,
                  NULL)))
   return(0);

// now ddsd.lPitch is valid and so is ddsd.lpSurface

// make a couple aliases to make code cleaner, so we don't
// have to cast
int lpitch16 = (int)(ddsd.lPitch >> 1);
USHORT *video_buffer = (USHORT *)ddsd.lpSurface;

// plot 1000 random pixels with random colors on the
// primary surface, they will be instantly visible
for (int index=0; index < 1000; index++)
    {
    // select random position and color for 640x480x16
    int red   = rand()%256;
    int green = rand()%256;
    int blue  = rand()%256;
    int x = rand()%640;
    int y = rand()%480;

    // plot the pixel
    Plot_Pixel_Faster16(x,y,red,green,blue,video_buffer,lpitch16);

    } // end for index


// now unlock the primary surface
if (FAILED(lpddsprimary->Unlock(NULL)))
   return(0);

// return success or failure or your own return code here
return(1);

} // end Game_Main
```

24/32-Bit High-Color Mode

Once you've mastered 16-bit mode, 24-bit and 32-bit modes are trivial. I'll begin with 24-bit mode because it's simpler than 32-bit mode—which is not a surprise! 24-bit mode uses exactly one byte per channel of RGB blue. Thus, there's no loss and a total of 256 shades per channel, giving a total possible number of colors of 256x256x256 = 16.7 million. The bits for red, green, and blue are encoded just as they were in 16-bit mode, except that you don't have to worry about one channel using more bits than another.

Because there's one byte per channel and three channels, there are three bytes per pixel. This makes for really ugly addressing, as shown in Figure 7.5. Alas, writing pixels in pure 24-bit mode is rather contrived, as shown in the following 24-bit version of the pixel-writing function:

```
inline void Plot_Pixel_24(int x, int y,
                          int red, int green, int blue,
                          UCHAR *video_buffer, int lpitch)
{
// this function plots a pixel in 24-bit color mode
// assuming that the caller already locked the surface
// and is sending a pointer and byte pitch to it

// in byte or 8-bit math the proper address is: 3*x + y*lpitch
// this is the address of the low order byte which is the Blue channel
// since the data is in RGB order
DWORD pixel_addr = (x+x+x) + y*lpitch;

// write the data, first blue
video_buffer[pixel_addr]   = blue;

// now red
video_buffer[pixel_addr+1] = green;

// finally green
video_buffer[pixel_addr+2] = red;

} // end Plot_Pixel_24
```

FIGURE 7.5
Three-byte RGB
addressing is ugly.

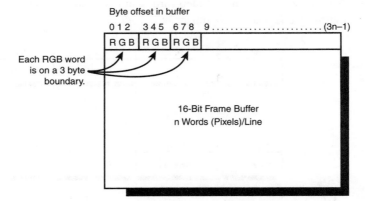

> **WARNING**
>
> Many video cards don't support 24-bit color mode. They support only 32-bit color, which is usually 8 bits of alpha transparency and then 24 bits of color. This is due to addressing constraints. So DEMO7_2.EXE may not work on your system.

The function takes as parameters the x,y, along with the RGB color, and finally the video buffer starting address and the memory pitch in bytes. There's no point in sending the memory pitch or the video buffer in some WORD length because there isn't any data type that's three bytes long. Hence, the function basically starts addressing the video buffer at the requested pixel location and then writes the blue, green, and red bits for the pixel. Here's a macro to build an RGB 24-bit word:

```
// this builds a 24 bit color value in 8.8.8 format
#define _RGB24BIT(r,g,b) ((b) + ((g) << 8) + ((r) << 16) )
```

For an example of 24-bit mode, take a look at DEMO7_2.CPP|EXE on the CD. It basically mimics the functionality of DEMO7_1.CPP, but in 24-bit mode.

Moving on to 32-bit color, the pixel setup is a little different, as shown in Figure 7.6. In 32-bit mode, the pixel data is arranged in the following two formats:

Alpha(8).8.8.8—This format uses eight bits for alpha or transparency information (or sometimes other information) and then eight bits for each channel: red, green, and blue. However, where simple bitmapping is concerned, you can usually disregard the alpha information and simply write eights to it. The nice thing about this mode is that it's 32 bits per pixel, which is the fastest possible memory addressing mode for a Pentium.

X(8).8.8.—Similar to the preceding mode, except in this mode the upper eight bits of the color WORD are "don't care's" or irrelevant. However, I still suggest setting them to zeroes to be safe. You may say, "This mode seems like a 24-bit mode, so why have it?" The answer is that many video cards can't address on three-byte boundaries, so the fourth byte is just for alignment.

FIGURE 7.6
32-bit RGB pixel encodings.

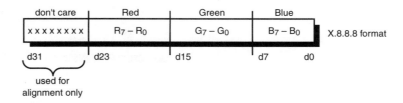

Now, take a look at a macro to create a 32-bit color WORD:

```
// this builds a 32 bit color value in A.8.8.8 format (8-bit alpha mode)
#define _RGB32BIT(a,r,g,b) ((b) + ((g) << 8) + ((r) << 16) + ((a) << 24))
```

Then all you need to do is change your pixel-plotting function to use the new macro and take advantage of the four-byte-per-pixel data size. Here it is

```
inline void Plot_Pixel_32(int x, int y,
                          int alpha,int red, int green, int blue,
                          UINT *video_buffer, int lpitch32)
{
// this function plots a pixel in 32-bit color mode
// assuming that the caller already locked the surface
// and is sending a pointer and DWORD aligned pitch to it

// first build up color WORD
UINT pixel = __RGB32BIT(alpha,red,green,blue);

// write the data
video_buffer[x + y*lpitch32] = pixel;

} // end Plot_Pixel_32
```

This should look familiar. The only thing hidden is the fact that lpitch32 is the byte pitch divided by four, so it's a DWORD or 32-bit WORD stride. With that all in mind, check out DEMO7_3.CPP|EXE. It's the same pixel-plotting demo, but in 32-bit mode. It should work on your machine because more video cards support 32-bit mode than pure 24-bit mode.

All righty, then! I think I've belabored high-color modes enough that you can work with them and convert any 8-bit color code that you want. Remember, I can't assume that everyone has a Pentium IV 2.0GHz with a GeForce III 3D Accelerator. Sticking to 8-bit color is a good way to get your programs running then you can move to 16-bit or higher modes.

Double Buffering

Thus far you've directly modified the contents of the primary surface, which is directly rasterized each frame by the video controller. This is fine for demos and static imagery, but what if you want to perform smooth animation? This is a definite problem; let me explain. As I alluded to earlier in the book, most computer animation is achieved by drawing each frame of animation in an offscreen buffer area and then blasting the image to the visible display surface very quickly, as shown in Figure 7.7.

This way the user can't see you erase images, generate the display, or anything else you might do in each frame. As long as the copying of the offscreen image to the visible surface is very quick, you could theoretically do it 15 times a second, or 15 fps, and still have a reasonably smooth game. However, the standard these days is at least 30 fps, so that has become the minimum to get high-quality animation.

FIGURE 7.7

Performing animation
with double buffering.

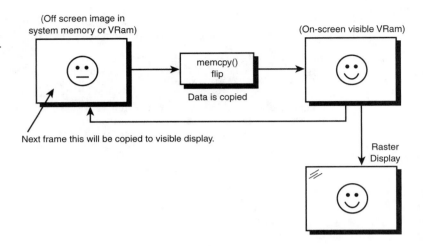

The process of drawing an image in an offscreen area and then copying it to the display surface is called *double buffering,* and it's how 99 percent of all games perform animation. However, in the past (under DOS especially), there wasn't special hardware to help with this process. This obviously changed with the introduction of DirectX/DirectDraw.

If acceleration hardware is present (and enough **VRAM** memory is on the video card), a process that's similar to double buffering, called *page flipping*, can be employed. Page flipping is roughly the same idea as double buffering, except that you draw to one of two potentially visible surfaces and then direct the hardware to make the other surface the active display surface. This basically removes the "copy" step because the hardware addressing system is used to point the video rasterizer to a different portion of memory. The end result is an instantaneous page flip and update of the visual on the screen (hence the term *page flipping*).

Of course, page flipping has always been possible, and many game programmers used it when programming Mode X modes (320x200, 320x240, 320x400). However, it's a down-low-and-direct technique. Assembly language and video controller programming was usually needed to accomplish the task. But with DirectDraw it's a snap. You'll get to it in the next section. I just wanted you to have an idea of where this chapter is going before I show you double buffering in detail.

Implementing double buffering is trivial. All you need to do is allocate a portion of memory that has the same geometry as the primary DirectDraw surface, draw each frame of animation on it, and then copy the double buffer memory to the primary display surface. Unfortunately, there's a problem with this scheme....

Let's say you've decided to create a 640x480x8 DirectDraw mode. Hence, you would need to allocate a double buffer that was 640x480 or a linear array of 307,200 bytes. And keep in mind that the data is mapped in a row-order form, one row for each row on the screen. This is no problem, though. Here's the code to create the double buffer:

```
UCHAR *double_buffer  = (UCHAR *)malloc(640*480);
```

Or, using the new operator in C++:

```
UCHAR *double_buffer = new UCHAR[640*480];
```

Either way you do it, you have an array of 307,200 bytes linearly addressable in memory that `double_buffer` points to. To address a single pixel at position (x,y), you would use the following code:

```
double_buffer[x + 640*y] = ...
```

Seems reasonable because there are 640 bytes per virtual line and you're assuming a rectangular mapping of 640 bytes per line and 480 lines. Okay, here's the problem: Assume that you've also locked a pointer to the primary display surface and it's in `primary_buffer`. In addition, assume that during the lock you've extracted the memory pitch and stored it in `mempitch`, as shown in Figure 7.8. If `mempitch` is equal to 640, you can use the following code to copy the `double_buffer` to the `primary_buffer`:

```
memcpy((void *)primary_buffer, (void *)double_buffer,640*480);
```

And almost instantly, the `double_buffer` will show up in the primary buffer.

TRICK

> There's a potential optimization here. Notice, I'm using `memcpy()`. This function is rather slow because it only copies bytes (on some compilers). A better method would be to write your own DWORD or 32-bit copy function to move more data per cycle. You can do this with inline or external assembly language. You'll see how when you get to optimization theory, but this is a good example if you're taking advantage of the largest data chunk that the Pentium can process, which is a 32-bit value.

FIGURE 7.8
Primary display sur-
faces may have extra
memory per line,
causing addressing
problems.

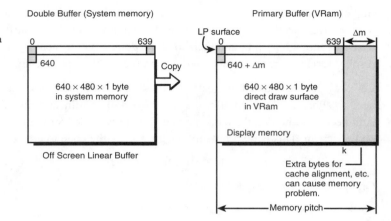

Everything seems fine, right? Wrong! The preceding memcpy() code will work only if
mempitch or the primary surface stride is exactly 640 bytes per line. This may or may
not be true. Alas, the preceding memcpy() code may fail terribly. A better way to write
the double buffer copy function is to add a little function that tests if the memory pitch
of the primary surface is 640. If so, the memcpy() is employed; if not, a line-by-line
copy is used. A little slower, but the best you can do…. Here's the code for that:

```
// can we use a straight memory copy?
if (mempitch==640)
{
memcpy((void *)primary_buffer, (void *)double_buffer,640*480);
} // end if
else
{
// copy line by line, bummer!
for (int y=0; y<480; y++)
    {
    // copy next line of 640 bytes
    memcpy((void *)primary_buffer, (void
    *)double_buffer,640);

    // now for the tricky part...
    // advance each pointer ahead to next line

    // advance to next line which is mempitch bytes away
    primary_buffer+=mempitch;

    // we know that we need to advance 640 bytes per line
    double_buffer+=640;

    } // end for y

} // end else
```

Figure 7.9 shows the process graphically. As you can see, this is one of the times that you have to do the work—no cheating! However, at least you can optimize the code with 4-byte or 32-bit copy code later. That makes me feel a little better.

FIGURE 7.9
Copying the double buffer line by line.

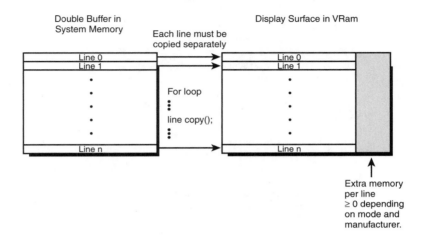

As an example, I have created a demo that draws a set of random pixels on a double buffer and then copies the double buffer to the primary buffer in 640x480x8 mode. There's a long delay between copies, so you can see that the image is entirely different. The name of the program is DEMO7_4.CPP|EXE and it's on the CD. Remember to compile it yourself to add DDRAW.LIB to your project and have the header file paths set to the DirectX include directory. Here's the Game_Main() from the program, which is where all the action occurs:

```
int Game_Main(void *parms = NULL, int num_parms = 0)
{
// this is the main loop of the game, do all your processing
// here

UCHAR *primary_buffer = NULL; // used as alias to primary surface buffer

// make sure this isn't executed again
if (window_closed)
   return(0);

// for now test if user is hitting ESC and send WM_CLOSE
if (KEYDOWN(VK_ESCAPE))
   {
   PostMessage(main_window_handle,WM_CLOSE,0,0);
   window_closed = 1;
   } // end if

// erase double buffer
memset((void *)double_buffer,0, SCREEN_WIDTH*SCREEN_HEIGHT);
```

DirectX and 2D Fundamentals

```
// you would perform game logic...

// draw the next frame into the double buffer
// plot 5000 random pixels
for (int index=0; index < 5000; index++)
    {
    int  x   = rand()%SCREEN_WIDTH;
    int  y   = rand()%SCREEN_HEIGHT;
    UCHAR col = rand()%256;
    double_buffer[x+y*SCREEN_WIDTH] = col;
    } // end for index

// copy the double buffer into the primary buffer
DDRAW_INIT_STRUCT(ddsd);

// lock the primary surface
lpddsprimary->Lock(NULL,&ddsd,
                   DDLOCK_SURFACEMEMORYPTR | DDLOCK_WAIT,NULL);

// get video pointer to primary surfce
primary_buffer = (UCHAR *)ddsd.lpSurface;

// test if memory is linear
if (ddsd.lPitch == SCREEN_WIDTH)
   {
   // copy memory from double buffer to primary buffer
   memcpy((void *)primary_buffer, (void *)double_buffer,
         SCREEN_WIDTH*SCREEN_HEIGHT);
   } // end if
else
   { // non-linear

   // make copy of source and destination addresses
   UCHAR *dest_ptr = primary_buffer;
   UCHAR *src_ptr  = double_buffer;

   // memory is non-linear, copy line by line
   for (int y=0; y < SCREEN_HEIGHT; y++)
       {
       // copy line
       memcpy((void *)dest_ptr, (void *)src_ptr, SCREEN_WIDTH);

       // advance pointers to next line
       dest_ptr+=ddsd.lPitch;
       src_ptr +=SCREEN_WIDTH;

       // note: the above code can be replaced with the simpler
       // memcpy(&primary_buffer[y*ddsd.lPitch],
       //        double_buffer[y*SCREEN_WIDTH], SCREEN_WIDTH);
       // but it is much slower due to the recalculation
       // and multiplication each cycle

       } // end for
```

```
    } // end else

// now unlock the primary surface
if (FAILED(lpddsprimary->Unlock(NULL)))
    return(0);

// wait a sec
Sleep(500);

// return success or failure or your own return code here
return(1);

} // end Game_Main
```

Surface Dynamics

Throughout the book I've mentioned that you can create a number of different types of surfaces, but up to this point you've only seen how to work with primary surfaces. Now I want to talk about offscreen surfaces. Basically, there are two types of offscreen surfaces. The first kind is the *back buffer.*

Back buffers are surfaces used in an animation chain that have the same geometry and color depth as the primary surface. Back buffer surfaces are unique because you create them as you create the primary surface. They're part of the primary surface's flipping chain. In other words, when you request one or more secondary surfaces to be back buffers, by default DirectDraw assumes that you'll be using them in an animation loop. Figure 7.10 shows the relationship between the primary surface and secondary surfaces that are back buffers.

FIGURE 7.10
The primary surface and back buffer(s).

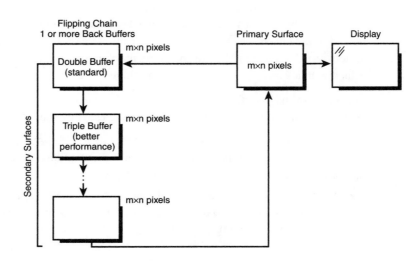

The reason you would create a back buffer is to emulate the functionality of double buffering, but in a more DirectDraw kind of way. If you create a DirectDraw back buffer, usually it will be in VRAM and thus will be very fast. Moreover, you'll be able to page flip it with the primary surface, which is much faster than the memory copy needed for a double buffering scheme.

Technically, you can have as many back buffers as you want in a flipping chain. However, at some point you'll run out of VRAM and the surface will have to be created in system memory, which is much slower. In general, if you create an (m x n) mode with a color depth of one byte, the amount of memory for the primary buffer is of course m*n bytes (unless there's memory pitch alignment). Therefore, if you have one extra back buffer secondary surface, you would multiply this by 2 because back buffers have the same geometry and color depth. So 2*m*n bytes would be the memory required. Finally, if the color depth is 16-bit, you would have to scale all the calculations by two bytes, and similarly for 32-bit buffers you would scale by 4. For example, the primary buffer for a 640x480x16-bit mode would take

```
Width * Height * Number of bytes per pixel
```

```
640 * 480 * 2 = 614,400 bytes
```

And if you want one extra back buffer, you need to multiply that result by 2 so the final number of bytes is

```
614,400 * 2 = 1,228,800 bytes
```

Roughly 1.2MB of VRAM! Hence, if you have only a 1MB card, you can forget having a VRAM back buffer in 640x480x16-bit color mode. Most cards have at least 2MB these days, so you're usually safe, but it's always good to test for the amount of memory available on the card. You can do so with a `GetCaps` class function. We'll cover that at the end of the chapter. Now, most video cards these days have 8–64 megs of VRAM, but lots of value computers have shared memory and you can easily find yourself out of luck with a 2–4 meg card on a value machine.

To create a primary surface that has a back buffer surface attached to it, you have to create what DirectDraw calls a *complex surface*. Here are the steps:

1. First, you have to add `DDSD_BACKBUFFERCOUNT` to the `dwFlags` flag field to indicate to DirectDraw that the `dwBackBufferCount` field of the `DDSURFACEDESC2` structure will be valid and contain the number of back buffers (one in this case).

2. Second, you must add the control flags `DDSCAPS_COMPLEX` and `DDSCAPS_FLIP` to the capabilities `WORD` of the `DDSURFACEDESC2` structure contained in the `ddsCaps.dwCaps` field.

3. Finally, create the primary surface as usual. From it, request the attached back buffer with a call to `IDIRECTDRAWSURFACE7::GetAttachedSurface()`, shown below, and you're in business.

```
HRESULT GetAttachedSurface(  LPDDSCAPS2 lpDDSCaps,
   LPDIRECTDRAWSURFACE7 FAR *lplpDDAttachedSurface  );
```

`lpDDSCaps` is a `DDSCAPS2` structure containing the requested surface capabilities. In your case, you're requesting a back buffer, so you'll set it like this:

```
DDSCAPS2 ddscaps.dwCaps = DDSCAPS_BACKBUFFER;
```

Or just use the `DDSCAPS2` field of the `DDSURFACEDESC2` structure to save another variable, like this:

```
ddsd.ddsCaps.dwCaps = DDSCAPS_BACKBUFFER;
```

Here's the code to create a primary surface and a single back buffer flipping chain:

```
// assume we already have the directdraw object etc...

DDSURFACEDESC2 ddsd; // directdraw surface description
LPDIRECTDRAWSURFACE7 lpddsprimary = NULL; // primary surface
LPDIRECTDRAWSURFACE7 lpddsback    = NULL; // back buffer

// clear ddsd and set size
DDRAW_INIT_STRUCT(ddsd);

// enable valid fields
ddsd.dwFlags = DDSD_CAPS | DDSD_BACKBUFFERCOUNT;

// set the backbuffer count field to 1
ddsd.dwBackBufferCount = 1;

// request a complex, flippable
ddsd.ddsCaps.dwCaps = DDSCAPS_PRIMARYSURFACE |
                      DDSCAPS_COMPLEX | DDSCAPS_FLIP;

// create the primary surface
if (FAILED(lpdd->CreateSurface(&ddsd, &lpddsprimary, NULL)))
   return(0);

// now query for attached surface from the primary surface

// this line is needed by the call
ddsd.ddsCaps.dwCaps = DDSCAPS_BACKBUFFER;

if (FAILED(lpddsprimary->GetAttachedSurface(&ddsd.ddsCaps, &lpddsback)))

return(0);
```

At this point, `lpddsprimary` points to the primary surface, which is currently visible, and `lpddsback` points to the back buffer surface, which is not. Take a look at Figure 7.11 to see this graphically. To access the back buffer, you can lock/unlock it just like the primary surface.

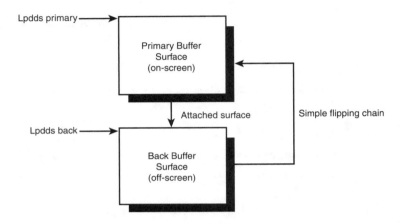

FIGURE 7.11
A true complex surface.

So, if you wanted to manipulate the information in the back buffer, you could do this:

```
// copy the double buffer into the primary buffer
DDRAW_INIT_STRUCT(ddsd);

// lock the back buffer surface
lpddsback->Lock(NULL,&ddsd, DDLOCK_SURFACEMEMORYPTR | DDLOCK_WAIT,NULL);

// now ddsd.lpSurface and ddsd.lPitch are valid
// do whatever...

// unlock the back buffer, so hardware can work with it
lpddsback->Unlock(NULL);
```

Now, the only problem is that you don't know how to flip the pages, or, in other words, make the back buffer surface the primary surface and hence animate the two pages. Let me show you how that's done!

Page Flipping

Once you've created a complex surface with a primary surface and a back buffer surface, you're ready to page flip. The standard animation loop requires these steps (see Figure 7.12):

1. Clear back buffer.
2. Render scene to back buffer.

3. Flip primary surface with back buffer surface.

4. Lock to frame rate (30 fps, for example).

5. Repeat step 1.

FIGURE 7.12
A page flipped
animation system.

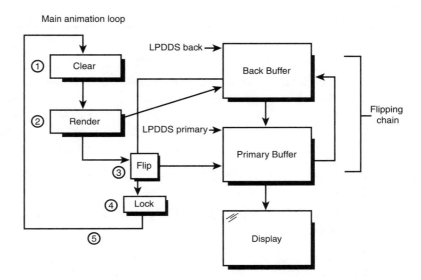

Main animation loop

There are a few details that may confuse you. First, if the back buffer is flipped with the primary buffer, won't the back buffer become the primary buffer, and vice versa? If so, won't you need to draw on the primary surface every other frame? Although this may seem to make sense, it's not what really happens. In reality, pointers to VRAM are switched by the hardware, and from your point of view and DirectDraw's, the back buffer surface is always offscreen and the primary is always onscreen. Therefore, you always draw to the back buffer and flip with the primary surface each frame.

To flip the primary surface with the next attached surface in the flipping chain, you use the function IDIRECTDRAWSURFACE7::Flip(), shown here:

```
HRESULT Flip(LPDIRECTDRAWSURFACE7 lpDDSurfaceTargetOverride,  // override surface
             DWORD dwFlags); // control flags
```

This returns DD_OK if successful and an error code if not.

The parameters are simple. lpDDSurfaceTargetOverride is basically an advanced parameter used to override the flipping chain and flip to another surface other than the back buffer attached to the primary surface; just send NULL here. The dwFlags parameter, however, might be of interest to you. Table 7.2 contains the various settings for it.

TABLE 7.2   Control Flags for Flip()

Value	Description
DDFLIP_INTERVAL2	Flip after two vertical retraces.
DDFLIP_INTERVAL3	Flip after three vertical retraces.
DDFLIP_INTERVAL4	Flip after four vertical retraces.

(Note that the default is one vertical retrace.)

These flags indicate how many vertical retraces to wait between each flip. The default is one. DirectDraw will return DERR_WASSTILLDRAWING for each surface involved in the flip until the specified number of vertical retraces has occurred. If DDFLIP_INTERVAL2 is set, DirectDraw will flip on every second vertical sync; if DDFLIP_INTERVAL3, on every third sync; and if DDFLIP_INTERVAL4, on every fourth sync.

These flags are effective only if DDCAPS2_FLIPINTERVAL is set in the DDCAPS structure returned for the device.

DDFLIP_NOVSYNC—This flag causes DirectDraw to perform the physical flip as close as possible to the next scan line.

DDFLIP_WAIT—This flag forces the hardware to wait until a flip is possible rather than returning back immediately if there's a problem.

TRICK

It's possible to create a complex surface with two back buffers or a flipping chain that has a total of three surfaces, including the primary surface. This is called *triple buffering,* and it gives the ultimate in performance. The reason is obvious: If you have a single back buffer, the video hardware may be bottlenecked by your accessing it along with the video hardware and so on. But with two extra surfaces in the flipping chain, the hardware never has to wait. The beauty of triple buffering with DirectDraw is that you simply use Flip() and the hardware flips the surfaces in a cyclic manner, but you still only render to a single back buffer, so it's transparent to you.

Typically, you'll set the flags for DDFLIP_WAIT and that's it. Also, you must call Flip() as a method from the primary surface, not the back buffer. This should make sense because the primary surface is the "parent" of the back buffer surface, and the back buffer is part of the parent's flipping chain. Anyway, here's how you would make the call to flip pages:

```
lpddsprimary->Flip(NULL, DDFLIP_WAIT);
```

And I've found that adding a little logic like this helps if the function errors out for some stupid reason:

```
while (FAILED(lpddsprimary->Flip(NULL, DDFLIP_WAIT)));
```

 Both the back buffer surface and the primary surface must be unlocked to perform the flip, so make sure you've unlocked them both before trying a call to Flip().

For an example of page flipping, check out DEM07_5.CPP|EXE. I took DEM07_4.CPP and changed the double buffering to page flipping, and of course I updated the Game_Init() code to create a complex surface with a single back buffer. Here are Game_Init() and Game_Main() for your review:

```
int Game_Init(void *parms = NULL, int num_parms = 0)
{
// this is called once after the initial window is created and
// before the main event loop is entered, do all your initialization
// here

LPDIRECTDRAW7 lpdd;

// first create base IDirectDraw interface
if (FAILED(DirectDrawCreate(NULL, (void **)&lpdd, IID_IDirectDraw7, NULL)))
   return(0);


// set cooperation to full screen
if (FAILED(lpdd->SetCooperativeLevel(main_window_handle,
               DDSCL_FULLSCREEN | DDSCL_ALLOWMODEX |
               DDSCL_EXCLUSIVE | DDSCL_ALLOWREBOOT)))
   return(0);

// set display mode to 640x480x8
if (FAILED(lpdd->SetDisplayMode(SCREEN_WIDTH, SCREEN_HEIGHT,
                               SCREEN_BPP,0,0)))
   return(0);


// clear ddsd and set size
DDRAW_INIT_STRUCT(ddsd);

// enable valid fields
ddsd.dwFlags = DDSD_CAPS | DDSD_BACKBUFFERCOUNT;

// set the backbuffer count field to 1, use 2 for triple buffering
ddsd.dwBackBufferCount = 1;

// request a complex, flippable
ddsd.ddsCaps.dwCaps = DDSCAPS_PRIMARYSURFACE |
                      DDSCAPS_COMPLEX | DDSCAPS_FLIP;
```

DirectX and 2D Fundamentals

```
    // create the primary surface
    if (FAILED(lpdd->CreateSurface(&ddsd, &lpddsprimary, NULL)))
        return(0);

    // now query for attached surface from the primary surface

    // this line is needed by the call
    ddsd.ddsCaps.dwCaps = DDSCAPS_BACKBUFFER;

    // get the attached back buffer surface
    if (FAILED(lpddsprimary->GetAttachedSurface(&ddsd.ddsCaps, &lpddsback)));

    // build up the palette data array
    for (int color=1; color < 255; color++)
        {
        // fill with random RGB values
        palette[color].peRed   = rand()%256;
        palette[color].peGreen = rand()%256;
        palette[color].peBlue  = rand()%256;

        // set flags field to PC_NOCOLLAPSE
        palette[color].peFlags = PC_NOCOLLAPSE;
        } // end for color

    // now fill in entry 0 and 255 with black and white
    palette[0].peRed     = 0;
    palette[0].peGreen   = 0;
    palette[0].peBlue    = 0;
    palette[0].peFlags   = PC_NOCOLLAPSE;

    palette[255].peRed   = 255;
    palette[255].peGreen = 255;
    palette[255].peBlue  = 255;
    palette[255].peFlags = PC_NOCOLLAPSE;

    // create the palette object
    if (FAILED(lpdd->CreatePalette(DDPCAPS_8BIT | DDPCAPS_ALLOW256 |
                                   DDPCAPS_INITIALIZE,
                                   palette,&lpddpal, NULL)))
    return(0);

    // finally attach the palette to the primary surface
    if (FAILED(lpddsprimary->SetPalette(lpddpal)))
        return(0);

    // return success or failure or your own return code here
    return(1);

} // end Game_Init

//////////////////////////////////////////////////////////
////

int Game_Main(void *parms = NULL, int num_parms = 0)
```

```
{
// this is the main loop of the game, do all your processing
// here

// make sure this isn't executed again
if (window_closed)
   return(0);

// for now test if user is hitting ESC and send WM_CLOSE
if (KEYDOWN(VK_ESCAPE))
   {
   PostMessage(main_window_handle,WM_CLOSE,0,0);
   window_closed = 1;
   } // end if

// lock the back buffer
DDRAW_INIT_STRUCT(ddsd);
lpddsback->Lock(NULL,&ddsd, DDLOCK_SURFACEMEMORYPTR | DDLOCK_WAIT,NULL);

// alias pointer to back buffer surface
UCHAR *back_buffer = (UCHAR *)ddsd.lpSurface;

// now clear the back buffer out

// linear memory?
if (ddsd.lPitch == SCREEN_WIDTH)
    memset(back_buffer,0,SCREEN_WIDTH*SCREEN_HEIGHT);
else
    {
    // non-linear memory

    // make copy of video pointer
    UCHAR *dest_ptr = back_buffer;

    // clear out memory one line at a time
    for (int y=0; y<SCREEN_HEIGHT; y++)
        {
        // clear next line
        memset(dest_ptr,0,SCREEN_WIDTH);

        // advance pointer to next line
        dest_ptr+=ddsd.lPitch;

        } // end for y

    } // end else


// you would perform game logic...

// draw the next frame into the back buffer, notice that we
// must use the lpitch since it's a surface and may not be linear

// plot 5000 random pixels
```

```
for (int index=0; index < 5000; index++)
    {
    int  x   = rand()%SCREEN_WIDTH;
    int  y   = rand()%SCREEN_HEIGHT;
    UCHAR col = rand()%256;
    back_buffer[x+y*ddsd.lPitch] = col;
    } // end for index

// unlock the back buffer
if (FAILED(lpddsback->Unlock(NULL)))
   return(0);

// perform the flip
while (FAILED(lpddsprimary->Flip(NULL, DDFLIP_WAIT)));

// wait a sec
Sleep(500);

// return success or failure or your own return code here
return(1);

} // end Game_Main
```

Also, note the boldfaced code from `Game_Main()` that deals with the lock `window_closed`, reprinted here:

```
// make sure this isn't executed again
if (window_closed)
   return(0);

// for now test if user is hitting ESC and send WM_CLOSE
if (KEYDOWN(VK_ESCAPE))
    {
    PostMessage(main_window_handle,WM_CLOSE,0,0);
    window_closed = 1;
    } // end if
```

TRICK

I needed to add the exit state in the preceding code because it's possible that `Game_Main()` will be called one extra time even though the window was destroyed. This will cause an error, of course, because DirectDraw anchors to the window handle. Hence, I have created a locking variable (or binary *semaphore* if you will) that's set once the window is closed, and the gate keeps the `Game_Main()` function from any future entry. This is a very important detail that I should have mentioned in the last program, but I didn't. Of course, I could have rewritten the text, but I just wanted to show you how easy it is to make a mistake with DirectX/Win32 asynchronous programming.

That's about all there is to page flipping. DirectDraw does most of the work, but I want to leave you with some last details about it. First, when you create a back buffer, there is the possibility that DirectDraw will create it in system memory rather than VRAM (if there isn't any left). In that case, you don't have to do anything; DirectDraw will emulate the functionality of page flipping with double buffering and copy the back buffer to the primary surface when you make a call to `Flip()`. However, it will be slower. The cool thing is that your code will work no matter what. So that's pretty killer and drama-free, baby!

> **NOTE**
>
> In general, when you create the primary and secondary back buffer, you want them both in VRAM. The primary is always in VRAM, but it's possible to get stuck with a system memory back buffer. However, always remember that there's only so much VRAM, and you might want to forgo the use of a VRAM back buffer in exchange for putting all your game graphics in VRAM to speed the blitting of images. Using the hardware blitter to move bitmaps from VRAM to VRAM is much faster than moving them from system memory to VRAM. Alas, you might decide to make a system memory back buffer in cases where you have a lot of small sprites or bitmaps and you're going to do a lot of blitting. In this case, you're doing so much blitting, the speed loss of a double buffer scheme in deference to page flipping with a VRAM animation system is far outweighed by the performance gain of having all your game bitmaps in VRAM.

Using the Blitter

If you've been programming in DOS, not only have you been stuck in a quasi-32-bit world (even with a DOS extender), but I'll bet you've never been able to use hardware acceleration for 2D/3D graphics without a driver from the manufacturer or a fat third-party library. Hardware acceleration has been around since way before *DOOM*, but game programmers could rarely use it because it was more of a Windows thing. However, with DirectX you can take total advantage of all acceleration—graphics, sound, input, networking, etc. But the coolest thing is finally being able to use the hardware blitter to move bitmaps and do fills! Let me show you how it works…

Normally, when you want to draw a bitmap or fill a video surface, you have to do it manually, pixel by pixel and so forth. For example, take a look at Figure 7.13, which depicts an 8x8, 256-color bitmap. Imagine that you want to copy this image to a video or off-screen buffer at position (x,y) that's 640x480 with linear pitch. Here's the code to do it:

```
UCHAR *video_buffer; // points to VRAM or offscreen surface

UCHAR bitmap[8*8];  // holds our bitmap in row major form

// crude bitmap copy
```

```
// outer loop is for each row
for (int index_y=0; index_y<8; index_y++)
    {
    // inner loop for each pixel of each row
    for (int index_x=0; index_x<8; index_x++)
        {
        // copy the pixel without transparency
        video_buffer[x+index_x + (y+index_y)*640] =
                    bitmap[index_x + index_y*8];
        } // end for index_x

    } // end for index_y
```

FIGURE 7.13

An 8×8, 256-color bitmap.

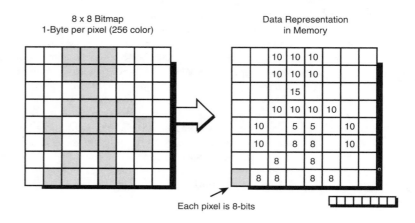

8 x 8 Bitmap
1-Byte per pixel (256 color)

Data Representation in Memory

Each pixel is 8-bits

Now take a few minutes (or seconds, if you're a cyborg) and make sure you completely understand what's going on and could write this yourself without looking. Refer back to Figure 7.13 to help visualize it. Basically, you're simply copying a rectangular bitmap of pixels from one place in memory to another. There are obviously a number of optimizations and problems with this function. First, I'll talk about the problems:

Problem 1: The function is incredibly slow.

Problem 2: The function doesn't take into consideration transparency, meaning that if you have a game object in the bitmap that has black around it, the black will be copied. This problem is shown in Figure 7.14. You need to add code for this.

As far as optimizations go, you can do the following:

Optimization 1: Get rid of all the multiplication and most of the addition by pre-computing starting addresses in the source and destination buffers and then increment pointers for each pixel.

Optimization 2: Use memory fills for nontransparent runs of pixels (advanced).

FIGURE 7.14
Transparent pixels aren't copied to the destination surface during blitting.

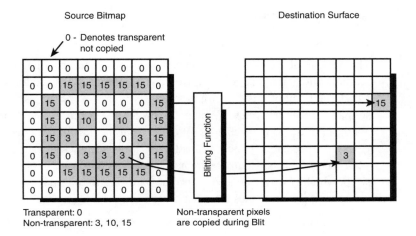

Let's start with making a real function that takes transparency into consideration (use color 0), and that uses better addressing to speed things up and get rid of the multiplies. Here's one example:

```
void Blit8x8(int x, int y,
             UCHAR *video_buffer,
             UCHAR *bitmap)
{
// this function blits the image sent in bitmap to the
// destination surface pointed to by video_buffer
// the function assumes a 640x480x8 mode with linear pitch

// compute starting point into video buffer
// video_buffer = video_buffer + (x + y*640)
video_buffer+= (x + (y << 9) + (y << 7));

UCHAR pixel; // used to read/write pixels

// main loop
for (int index_y=0; index_y < 8; index_y++)
    {
    // inner loop, this is where it counts!
    for (int index_x=0; index_x < 8; index_x++)
        {
        // copy pixel, test for transparent though
        if (pixel = bitmap[index_x])
            video_buffer[index_x] = pixel;
        } // end for index_x

    // advance pointers
    bitmap+=8;            // next line in bitmap
    video_buffer+=640;   // next line in video_buffer
```

```
    } // end for index_y

} // end Blit8x8
```

This version of the blitter function is many times faster than the previous one with multiplication, and this one even works with bitmaps that have transparent pixels—wow! The point of this exercise is to show you how something so simple can take up so many processor cycles. If you count cycles, the function is still crap. There's the overhead of the loop mechanics, of course, but the guts of the function are still ugly. A test for transparency must be made, two array accesses, a write to memory... yuck, yuck, yuck! This is why there are accelerators. A hardware blitter can do this in its sleep, which is why you need to use the hardware to blit images down. That way you can save processor cycles for other things, like AI and physics!

Not to mention that the blitter function just shown is really stupid. It is hard-coded to 640x480x256, doesn't do any clipping (more logic), and only works for 8-bit images.

Now that I've shown you the old way to draw bitmaps, here's the first look at the blitter and how to use it to do memory fills. Then you'll see how to copy images from one surface to another. Later in the chapter, you'll use the blitter to draw game objects, but take your time.

Using the Blitter for Memory Filling

Although accessing the blitter under DirectDraw is trivial compared to programming it manually, it's still a reasonably complex piece of hardware. Therefore, whenever I get my hands on a new piece of video hardware, I always like to try something simple first before I try pushing the envelope. So let me show you how to do something that's very useful—memory fills.

Memory filling simply means filling a region of VRAM with some value. You've done this a number of times by locking a surface and then using memset() or memcpy() to manipulate and fill the surface memory, but there are a number of problems with this approach. First, you're using the main CPU to do the memory fill, so the main bus is part of the transfer. Second, the VRAM that makes up a surface may not be totally linear. In that case, you'll have to do a line-by-line fill or move. However, with the hardware blitter you can directly fill or move chunks of VRAM or DirectDraw surfaces instantly!

The two functions that DirectDraw supports for blitting are IDIRECTDRAWSURFACE7:: Blt() and IDIRECTDRAWSURFACE7::BltFast(). Their prototypes are shown here:

```
HRESULT Blt(LPRECT lpDestRect, // dest RECT
    LPDIRECTDRAWSURFACE7 lpDDSrcSurface, // dest surface
    LPRECT lpSrcRect,  // source RECT
    DWORD dwFlags,     // control flags
    LPDDBLTFX lpDDBltFx); // special fx (very cool!)
```

The parameters are defined here and illustrated graphically in Figure 7.15:

FIGURE 7.15
Blitting from source
to destination.

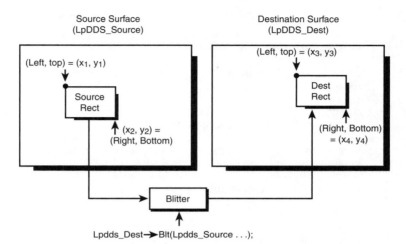

Source Surface
(LpDDS_Source)

Destination Surface
(LpDDS_Dest)

(Left, top) = (x_1, y_1)

Source
Rect

$(x_2, y_2) =$
(Right, Bottom)

(Left, top) = (x_3, y_3)

Dest
Rect

(Right, Bottom)
$= (x_4, y_4)$

Blitter

Lpdds_Dest → Blt(Lpdds_Source . . .);

lpDestRect is the address of a RECT structure that defines the upper-left and lower-right points of the rectangle to blit to on the destination surface. If this parameter is NULL, the entire destination surface will be used.

lpDDSrcSurface is the address of an IDIRECTDRAWSURFACE7 interface for the DirectDraw surface to be used as the source of the blit.

lpSrcRect is the address of a RECT structure that defines the upper-left and lower-right points of the rectangle to blit from on the source surface. If this parameter is NULL, the entire source surface will be used.

dwFlags determines the valid members of the next parameter, which is a DDBLTFX structure. Within DDBLTFX, special behaviors such as scaling, rotation, and so on can be controlled, as well as color key information. The valid flags for dwFlags are shown in Table 7.3.

lpDDBltFx is a structure containing special blitter-relating information about the blit you're requesting. The data structure follows:

```
typedef struct _DDBLTFX
  {
 DWORD dwSize;  // the size of this structure in bytes
 DWORD dwDDFX;  // type of blitter fx
 DWORD dwROP;   // Win32 raster ops that are supported
 DWORD dwDDROP; // DirectDraw raster ops that are supported
 DWORD dwRotationAngle; // angle for rotations
 DWORD dwZBufferOpCode;    // z-buffer fields (advanced)
 DWORD dwZBufferLow;       // advanced..
 DWORD dwZBufferHigh;      // advanced..
```

```
DWORD dwZBufferBaseDest;    // advanced..
DWORD dwZDestConstBitDepth; // advanced..
union
{
DWORD              dwZDestConst;      // advanced..
LPDIRECTDRAWSURFACE lpDDSZBufferDest;  // advanced..
};
DWORD dwZSrcConstBitDepth;            // advanced..
union
{
DWORD              dwZSrcConst;       // advanced..
LPDIRECTDRAWSURFACE lpDDSZBufferSrc;   // advanced..
};
DWORD dwAlphaEdgeBlendBitDepth;  // alpha stuff (advanced)
DWORD dwAlphaEdgeBlend;          // advanced..
DWORD dwReserved;                // advanced..
DWORD dwAlphaDestConstBitDepth;  // advanced..
union
{
DWORD              dwAlphaDestConst;  // advanced..
LPDIRECTDRAWSURFACE lpDDSAlphaDest;    // advanced..
};
DWORD dwAlphaSrcConstBitDepth;        // advanced..
union
{
DWORD              dwAlphaSrcConst;   // advanced..
LPDIRECTDRAWSURFACE lpDDSAlphaSrc;     // advanced..
};
union // these are very important
{
DWORD dwFillColor; // color word used for fill
DWORD dwFillDepth; // z filling (advanced)
DWORD dwFillPixel; // color fill word for RGB(alpha) fills
LPDIRECTDRAWSURFACE lpDDSPattern;
};
// these are very important
DDCOLORKEY ddckDestColorkey; // destination color key
DDCOLORKEY ddckSrcColorkey;  // source color key
} DDBLTFX,FAR* LPDDBLTFX;
```

(Note that I've boldfaced useful fields.)

TABLE 7.3 Control Flags for dwFlags Parameter of Blt()

Value	Description
	General Flags
DDBLT_COLORFILL	Uses the dwFillColor member of the DDBLTFX structure as the RGB color that fills the destination rectangle on the destination surface.
DDBLT_DDFX	Uses the dwDDFX member of the DDBLTFX structure to specify the effects to use for this blit.

TABLE 7.3   continued

Value	Description
DDBLT_DDROPS	Uses the dwDDROP member of the DDBLTFX structure to specify the raster operations (ROPs) that are not part of the Win32 API.
DDBLT_DEPTHFILL	Uses the dwFillDepth member of the DDBLTFX structure as the depth value with which to fill the destination rectangle on the destination z-buffer surface.
DDBLT_KEYDESTOVERRIDE	Uses the ddckDestColorkey member of the DDBLTFX structure as the color key for the destination surface.
DDBLT_KEYSRCOVERRIDE	Uses the ddckSrcColorkey member of the DDBLTFX structure as the color key for the source surface.
DDBLT_ROP	Uses the dwROP member of the DDBLTFX structure for the ROP for this blit. These ROPs are the same as those defined in the Win32 API.
DDBLT_ROTATIONANGLE	Uses the dwRotationAngle member of the DDBLTFX structure as the rotation angle (specified in 1/100ths of a degree) for the surface. This only works with hardware support. The HEL (Hardware Emulation Layer) can't do rotation—bummer!
Color Key Flags	
DDBLT_KEYDEST	Uses the color key associated with the destination surface.
DDBLT_KEYSRC	Uses the color key associated with the source surface.
Behavior Flags	
DDBLT_ASYNC	Performs this blit asynchronously through the FIFO (First In, First Out) in the order received. If no room is available in the FIFO hardware, the call fails. Fast, but risky; error logic is needed to use this flag properly.
DDBLT_WAIT	Waits until the blit can be performed and doesn't return the error DDERR_WASSTILLDRAWING if the blitter was busy.

(Note that I've boldfaced the most useful flags.)

If you're losing your mind, that's fantastic—it shows that you're following me <BG>. Now, take a look at BltFast():

```
HRESULT BltFast(
  DWORD dwX, // x-position of blit on destination
  DWORD dwY, // y-position of blit on destination
  LPDIRECTDRAWSURFACE7 lpDDSrcSurface, // source surface
  LPRECT lpSrcRect, // source RECT to blit from
  DWORD dwTrans);   // type of transfer
```

dwX and dwY are the (x,y) coordinates to blit to on the destination surface.

`lpDDSrcSurface` is the address of the `IDIRECTDRAWSURFACE7` interface for the DirectDraw surface to be used as the source of blit.

`lpSrcRect` is the address of the source `RECT` that defines the upper-left and lower-right points of the rectangle to blit from on the source surface.

`dwTrans` is the type of blitter operation. Table 7.4 shows the possible values.

TABLE 7.4 Control Flags for `BltFast()` Blitter Operation

Value	Description
DDBLTFAST_SRCCOLORKEY	Specifies a transparent blit that uses the source's color key.
DDBLTFAST_DESTCOLORKEY	Specifies a transparent blit that uses the destination's color key.
DDBLTFAST_NOCOLORKEY	Specifies a normal copy blit with no transparency. Could be faster on some hardware; definitely faster in HEL.
DDBLTFAST_WAIT	Forces the blitter to wait while busy and not send back the `DDERR_WASSTILLDRAWING` message. `BltFast()` returns as soon as the blit can be performed, or a serious error occurs.

(Note that I've boldfaced the most useful flags.)

All right, the first question is, "Why are there two different blitter functions?" The answer should be apparent from the functions themselves: `Blt()` is the full-blown kitchen sink model, while `BltFast()` is simpler but has fewer options. Furthermore, `Blt()` uses DirectDraw clippers while `BltFast()` doesn't. This means that `BltFast()` is faster than `Blt()` in the HEL by about 10%, and may even be faster in hardware (if the hardware is crappy and sucks at clipping). The point is, use `Blt()` if you need clipping, and use `BltFast()` if you don't.

Let me show you how to use the `Blt()` function to fill a surface. This will be reasonably simple because there isn't a source surface (only a destination surface). A lot of the parameters, therefore, can be `NULL`. To do a memory fill, you must perform the following steps:

1. Place the color index or RGB-encoded color you want to fill the surface with in the `dwFillColor` field of a `DDBLTFX` structure.

2. Set up a `RECT` structure with the area that you want to fill on your destination surface.

3. Make a call to `Blt()` from the destination surface's `IDIRECTDRAWSURFACE7` interface pointer with the control flags `DDBLT_COLORFILL | DDBLT_WAIT`. This is very important; `Blt()` and `BltFast()` are both called from the destination surface's interface, not the source!

Here's the code to fill a region of an 8-bit surface with a color:

```
DDBLTFX ddbltfx; // the blitter fx structure
RECT dest_rect;  // used to hold the destination RECT

// first initialize the DDBLTFX structure
DDRAW_INIT_STRUCT(ddbltfx);

// now set the color word info to the color we desire
// in this case, we are assuming an 8-bit mode, hence,
// we'll use a color index from 0-255, but if this was a
// 16/24/32 bit example then we would fill the WORD with
// the RGB encoding for the pixel - remember!
ddbltfx.dwFillColor = color_index; // or RGB for 16+ modes!

// now set up the RECT structure to fill the region from
// (x1,y1) to (x2,y2) on the destination surface
dest_rect.left   = x1;
dest_rect.top    = y1;
dest_rect.right  = x2;
dest_rect.bottom = y2;

// make the blitter call
lpddsprimary->Blt(&dest_rect, // pointer to dest RECT
            NULL, // pointer to source surface
            NULL, // pointer to source RECT
            DDBLT_COLORFILL | DDBLT_WAIT,
            // do a color fill and wait if you have to
            &ddbltfx); // pointer to DDBLTFX holding info
```

> **NOTE**
>
> There's one little detail with any of the RECT structures that you send to most DirectDraw functions: In general, they're upper-left inclusive, but lower-right exclusive. In other words, if you send a RECT that's (0,0) to (10,10), the actual rectangle scanned will be (0,0) to (9,9) inclusive. So keep that in mind. Basically, if you want to fill the entire 640×480 screen, you would send upper-left as (0,0) and lower-right as (640, 480).

The important things to notice are the setup and that both the source surface and RECT are NULL. This makes sense because you're using the blitter to fill with a color, not to copy data from one surface to another. Okay, let's move on, my little leprechaun.

The preceding example was for an 8-bit surface; the only change you need to make for a high-color mode in 16/24/32-bit mode is to simply change the value in ddbltfx.dwFillColor to reflect the pixel value that you want the fill to be performed in, that is you would build the actual RGB value of the pixel you want transparent. Isn't that cool?

For example, if the display happened to be a 16-bit mode and you wanted to fill the screen with green, the following code would work:

```
ddbltfx.dwFillColor = __RGB16BIT565(0,255,0);
```

Everything else in the preceding 8-bit example would stay the same. DirectDraw isn't that bad, huh?

To see the blitter hardware in action, I've created a little psychedelic demo for you called DEMO7_6.CPP|EXE. It puts the system into 640x480x16-bit mode and then fills different regions of the screen with random color. You'll see about a zillion colored rectangles per second getting blitted to the screen (try turning the lights off and tripping out on it). Take a look at the Game_Main(); it's almost trivial:

```
int Game_Main(void *parms = NULL, int num_parms = 0)
{
// this is the main loop of the game, do all your processing
// here

DDBLTFX ddbltfx; // the blitter fx structure
RECT dest_rect;  // used to hold the destination RECT

// make sure this isn't executed again
if (window_closed)
   return(0);

// for now test if user is hitting ESC and send WM_CLOSE
if (KEYDOWN(VK_ESCAPE))
   {
   PostMessage(main_window_handle,WM_CLOSE,0,0);
   window_closed = 1;
   } // end if

// first initialize the DDBLTFX structure
DDRAW_INIT_STRUCT(ddbltfx);

// now set the color word info to the color we desire
// in this case, we are assuming an 8-bit mode, hence,
// we'll use a color index from 0-255, but if this was a
// 16/24/32 bit example then we would fill the WORD with
// the RGB encoding for the pixel - remember!
ddbltfx.dwFillColor = __RGB16BIT565(rand()%256, rand()%256, rand()%256);

// get a random rectangle
int x1 = rand()%SCREEN_WIDTH;
int y1 = rand()%SCREEN_HEIGHT;
int x2 = rand()%SCREEN_WIDTH;
int y2 = rand()%SCREEN_HEIGHT;

// now set up the RECT structure to fill the region from
// (x1,y1) to (x2,y2) on the destination surface
dest_rect.left   = x1;
dest_rect.top    = y1;
```

```
                    dest_rect.right  = x2;
                    dest_rect.bottom = y2;

                    // make the blitter call
                    if (FAILED(lpddsprimary->Blt(&dest_rect, // pointer to dest RECT
                                        NULL, // pointer to source surface
                                        NULL, // pointer to source RECT
                                        DDBLT_COLORFILL | DDBLT_WAIT,
                                        // do a color fill and wait if you have to
                                        &ddbltfx))) // pointer to DDBLTFX holding info
                        return(0);

                    // return success or failure or your own return code here
                    return(1);

                    } // end Game_Main
```

Now that you know how to use the blitter to fill, let me show you how to use it to
copy data from surface to surface. This is where the real power of the blitter comes
into play. It's the foundation for the sprite or blitter object engine that you're going to
make in a little while.

Copying Bitmaps from Surface to Surface

The whole point of the blitter is to copy rectangular bitmaps from some source memory
to destination memory. This may involve copying the entire screen, or small bitmaps
that represent game objects. In either case, you need to learn how to instruct the blitter
to copy data from one surface to another. Actually, you already know how to do this
and may not realize it. The blitter fill demo will do the job with a couple of changes.

When you're using the Blt() function, you basically send a source RECT and surface
and a destination RECT and surface to perform the blit. The blitter will then copy the
pixels from the source RECT to the destination RECT. The source and destination surface
can be the same (surface to surface copy or move), but they're usually different. In
general, the latter is the basis for most sprite engines. (A *sprite* is a bitmap game
image that moves around the screen.)

At this point you know how to create a primary surface and secondary surface that
serves as a back buffer, but you don't know how to create plain offscreen surfaces that
aren't related to the primary surface. You can't blit them if you can't make them. Thus,
I'm going to hold off on showing you the general blitting case of any surface to the
primary surface until I've shown you how to blit from the back buffer to the primary
surface. Then the transition from generic surface to primary or back buffer will be
trivial.

All you need to do to make a blit from any two surfaces (the back buffer to the primary
surface, for example) is set the RECTs up correctly and make a call to Blt() with the
right parameterization. Take a look at Figure 7.15. Imagine that you want to copy the

RECT defined by (x1,y1) to (x2,y2) on the source surface (the back buffer in this case) to (x3,y3) to (x4,y4) on the destination surface (the primary surface in this case). Here's the code:

```
RECT source_rect, // used to hold source RECT
     dest_rect;   // used to hold the destination RECT

// set up the RECT structure to fill the region from
// (x1,y1) to (x2,y2) on the destination surface
source_rect.left   = x1;
source_rect.top    = y1;
source_rect.right  = x2;
source_rect.bottom = y2;

// now set up the RECT structure to fill the region from
// (x3,y3) to (x4,y4) on the destination surface
dest_rect.left   = x3;
dest_rect.top    = y3;
dest_rect.right  = x4;
dest_rect.bottom = y4;

// make the blitter call
lpddsprimary->Blt(&dest_rect, // pointer to dest RECT
                  lpddsback,   // pointer to source surface
                  &source_rect, // pointer to source RECT
                  DDBLT_WAIT,  // control flags
                  NULL); // pointer to DDBLTFX holding info
```

That was easy, huh? Of course, there are still a few details I'm leaving out, such as clipping and transparency. I'll talk about clipping first. Take a look at Figure 7.16, which depicts a bitmap that's drawn to a surface with and without clipping. Blitting without clipping is obviously a problem if the bitmap extends past the rectangle of the destination surface. Memory may be overwritten and so forth, so DirectDraw supports clipping via the IDirectDrawClipper interface. Or, if you wrote your own bitmap rasterizer, as you did in the example Blit8x8(), you could always add clipping code. That will slow things down, however. The second issue pertaining to blitting is transparency.

When you draw a bitmap, the image is always within a rectangular matrix of pixels. However, you don't want all those pixels copied when you blit. In many cases, you select a color, such as black, blue, green, or whatever, to serve as a transparent color that isn't copied (you saw this implemented in Blit8x8()). DirectDraw also has support for this called *color keys,* which I will also talk about shortly.

FIGURE 7.16
The basic bitmap clipping problem.

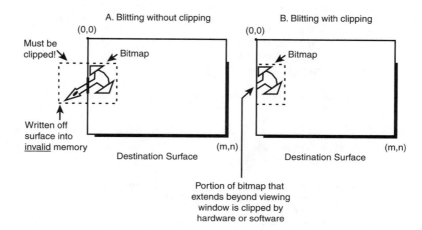

Before you move on to clipping, I'd like to show you a demo of blitting from the back buffer to the primary surface. Take a look at DEMO7_7.CPP|EXE on the CD. The only problem is that I haven't shown you how to load bitmaps from disk yet, so I can't really blit anything cool—bummer! So what I did was draw a gradient of green in 16-bit color mode from top to bottom on the back buffer, and then use this as the source data. You'll see a bunch of gradient rectangles copied to the primary surface at warp speed. Here's the source from Game_Main() for your review:

```
int Game_Main(void *parms = NULL, int num_parms = 0)
{
// this is the main loop of the game, do all your processing
// here

RECT source_rect, // used to hold the destination RECT
     dest_rect;   // used to hold the destination RECT

// make sure this isn't executed again
if (window_closed)
   return(0);

// for now test if user is hitting ESC and send WM_CLOSE
if (KEYDOWN(VK_ESCAPE))
   {
   PostMessage(main_window_handle,WM_CLOSE,0,0);
   window_closed = 1;
   } // end if

// get a random rectangle for source
int x1 = rand()%SCREEN_WIDTH;
int y1 = rand()%SCREEN_HEIGHT;
int x2 = rand()%SCREEN_WIDTH;
int y2 = rand()%SCREEN_HEIGHT;
```

```
// get a random rectangle for destination
int x3 = rand()%SCREEN_WIDTH;
int y3 = rand()%SCREEN_HEIGHT;
int x4 = rand()%SCREEN_WIDTH;
int y4 = rand()%SCREEN_HEIGHT;

// now set up the RECT structure to fill the region from
// (x1,y1) to (x2,y2) on the source surface
source_rect.left   = x1;
source_rect.top    = y1;
source_rect.right  = x2;
source_rect.bottom = y2;

// now set up the RECT structure to fill the region from
// (x3,y3) to (x4,y4) on the destination surface
dest_rect.left   = x3;
dest_rect.top    = y3;
dest_rect.right  = x4;
dest_rect.bottom = y4;

// make the blitter call
if (FAILED(lpddsprimary->Blt(&dest_rect,  // pointer to dest RECT
                lpddsback,   // pointer to source surface
                &source_rect,// pointer to source RECT
                DDBLT_WAIT,  // control flags
                NULL)))      // pointer to DDBLTFX holding info
    return(0);

// return success or failure or your own return code here
return(1);

} // end Game_Main
```

Also, in `Game_Init()` I used a little inline assembly to do a DWORD or 32-bit line of two 16-bit pixels at once in RGB.RGB format instead of a slower 8-bit fill. Here's that code:

```
_asm
    {
    CLD                         ; clear direction of copy to forward
    MOV EAX, color              ; color goes here
    MOV ECX, (SCREEN_WIDTH/2)   ; number of DWORDS goes here
    MOV EDI, video_buffer       ; address of line to move data
    REP STOSD                   ; send the Pentium X on its way…
    } // end asm
```

Basically, the preceding code implements the following C/C++ loop:

```
for (DWORD ecx = 0, DWORD *edi = video_buffer;
    ecx < (SCREEN_WIDTH/2); ecx++)
    edi[ecx] = color;
```

If you don't know assembly language, don't freak out. I just like to use it now and then for little things like this. Also, it's good practice to use the inline assembler; it keeps you on your toes!

As an exercise, see if you can make the program work only on the primary surface. Simply delete the back buffer code, draw the image on the primary surface, and then run the blitter with the source and destination as the same surface. Watch what happens...

Clipper Fundamentals

I'm going to talk about clipping over and over in this book. Pixel clipping, bitmap clipping, 2D clipping, and I'm sure I'll think of some more <BG>. Right now, though, the theme is DirectDraw. I want to focus on pixel clipping and bitmap clipping to help you ease into the subject, which I guarantee is going to get very complex when you do it in 3D!

Clipping is generally defined as "not drawing pixels or image elements that are out of bounds of the view port or window." Just like Windows clips anything you draw to the client area of your window, you need to do this in a game that runs under DirectX. Now, as far as 2D graphics go, the only thing that DirectDraw accelerates are bitmaps and bit blitting. Sure, many cards know how to draw lines, circles, and other conic sections, but DirectDraw doesn't support these primitives, so you don't get access to them (hopefully you will soon, though).

What this all means is that if you write a graphics engine that draws pixels, lines, and bitmaps, you have to do the clipping yourself for the pixel and line drawing algorithms. However, DirectDraw can help with the bitmaps—as long as the bitmaps are in the form of DirectDraw surfaces, or IDirectDrawSurface(s) to be exact.

The help that DirectDraw gives is in the form of DirectDraw clippers under the IDirectDrawClipper interface. What you do is create an IDirectDrawClipper, give it valid regions to clip to, and then attach it to a surface. Then, when you use the *blitter* function, Blt(), it will clip to the clipping regions and you won't have any out-of-bounds blitting or performance hits—if you have the proper hardware, of course. But first, take a look at how to clip pixels and do a rewrite of the Blit8x8() function that does clip.

Clipping Pixels to a Viewport

Figure 7.17 gives you a visual of the problem. You want to clip a pixel with coordinates (x,y) to a viewport located at (x1,y1) to (x2,y2). If (x,y) is within the rectangle defined by (x1,y1) to (x2,y2), render it; otherwise, don't. Simple enough?

Here's the code for a 640x480 linear 8-bit mode:

```
// assume clipping rectangle is global
int x1,y1,x2,y2; // these are defined somewhere


void Plot_Pixel_Clip8(int x, int y,
                      UCHAR color,
                      UCHAR *video_buffer)
```

DirectX and 2D Fundamentals

```
{
// test the pixel to see if it's in range
if (x>=x1 && x<=x2 && y>=y1 && y<=y2)
    video_buffer[x+y*640] = color;

} // end if
```

FIGURE 7.17
A detailed view of the
clipping region.

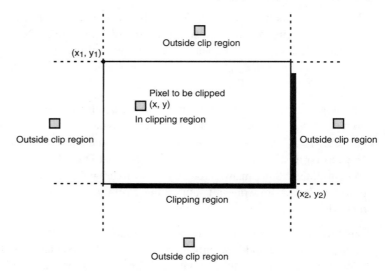

Of course, there's a lot of room for optimization, but you get the point—you've created a software filter on the pixel coordinates. Only pixel coordinate values that satisfy the if statement pass through the filter—interesting concept, huh? Now, the preceding clipper is very general, but in many cases, the window or viewport is located at (0,0) and has dimensions (win_width, win_height). This simplifies your code a little:

```
// assume clipping rectangle is global
int x1,y1,x2,y2; // these are defined somewhere


void Plot_Pixel2_Clip8(int x, int y,
                       UCHAR color,
                       UCHAR *video_buffer)
{
// test the pixel to see if it's in range
if (x>=0 && x<win_width && y>=0 && y<=win_height)
    video_buffer[x+y*640] = color;

} // end if
```

See? In addition, more optimizations can be made whenever zeros are around. Now that you get the point of clipping and know how to do it, I'll show you how to clip an entire bitmap.

Clipping Bitmaps the Hard Way

Clipping bitmaps is as simple as clipping pixels. There are two ways to approach it:

- **Method 1:** Clip each pixel of the bitmap on a independent basis as it's generated. Simple, but slow.

- **Method 2:** Clip the bounding rectangle of the bitmap to the viewport, and then only draw the portion of the bitmap that's within the viewport. More complex, but very fast, with almost no performance loss and no hit at all in the inner loop.

Obviously, you're going to use Method 2, which is shown graphically in Figure 7.18. Also, I'm going to generalize a little and assume that the screen extends from (0,0) to (SCREEN_WIDTH-1, SCREEN_HEIGHT-1), that your bitmap has its upper-left corner at (x,y), and that it's exactly so many widthxheight pixels in dimension—or in other words, the bitmap extends from (x,y) to (x+width-1, y+height-1). Please take a minute and make sure you see the reasoning for the "-1" factors. Basically, if a bitmap is 1x1, it has a width of 1 and a height of 1. Therefore, if the origin of the bitmap is at (x,y), the bitmap extends from (x,y) to (x+1-1,y+1-1) or (x,y). This is because it's only 1x1 pixels, so the "-1" factor is needed, as shown by this base case.

FIGURE 7.18
How to clip the
bounding box
of a bitmap.

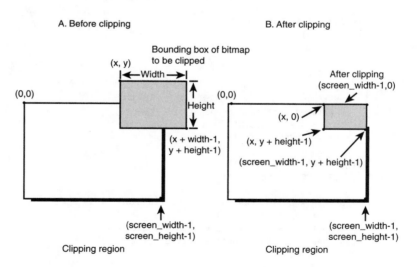

The plan of attack for clipping is simple—you just clip the virtual rectangle of the bitmap to the viewport and then draw only the portions of the bitmap that are in the clipped bitmap. Here's the code for a 640x480x8 linear mode:

```
// dimensions of window or viewport (0,0) is origin
#define SCREEN_WIDTH   640
#define SCREEN_HEIGHT  480
```

v

DirectX and 2D Fundamentals

```
            void Blit_Clipped(int x, int y,              // position to draw bitmap
                              int width, int height, // size of bitmap in pixels
                              UCHAR *bitmap,           // pointer to bitmap data
                              UCHAR *video_buffer,     // pointer to video buffer surface
                              int   mempitch)          // video pitch per line
            {
            // this function blits and clips the image sent in bitmap to the
            // destination surface pointed to by video_buffer
            // the function assumes a 640x480x8 mode
            // this function is slightly different than the one in the book
            // ie, it doesn't assume linear pitch

            // first do trivial rejections of bitmap, is it totally invisible?
            if ((x >= SCREEN_WIDTH) || (y>= SCREEN_HEIGHT) ||
                ((x + width) <= 0) || ((y + height) <= 0))
            return;

            // clip source rectangle
            // pre-compute the bounding rect to make life easy
            int x1 = x;
            int y1 = y;
            int x2 = x1 + width - 1;
            int y2 = y1 + height -1;

            // upper left hand corner first
            if (x1 < 0)
               x1 = 0;

            if (y1 < 0)
               y1 = 0;

            // now lower left hand corner
            if (x2 >= SCREEN_WIDTH)
                x2 = SCREEN_WIDTH-1;

            if (y2 >= SCREEN_HEIGHT)
                y2 = SCREEN_HEIGHT-1;

            // now we know to draw only the portions of
            // the bitmap from (x1,y1) to (x2,y2)
            // compute offsets into bitmap on x,y axes,
            // we need this to compute starting point
            // to rasterize from
            int x_off = x1 - x;
            int y_off = y1 - y;

            // compute number of columns and rows to blit
            int dx = x2 - x1 + 1;
            int dy = y2 - y1 + 1;

            // compute starting address in video_buffer
            video_buffer += (x1 + y1*mempitch);
```

```
// compute starting address in bitmap to scan data from
bitmap += (x_off + y_off*width);

// at this point bitmap is pointing to the first
// pixel in the bitmap that needs to
// be blitted, and video_buffer is pointing to
// the memory location on the destination
// buffer to put it, so now enter rasterizer loop

UCHAR pixel; // used to read/write pixels

for (int index_y = 0; index_y < dy; index_y++)
    {
    // inner loop, where the action takes place
    for (int index_x = 0; index_x < dx; index_x++)
        {
        // read pixel from source bitmap
        // test for transparency and plot
        if ((pixel = bitmap[index_x]))
            video_buffer[index_x] = pixel;

        } // end for index_x

        // advance pointers
        video_buffer+=mempitch;  // bytes per scanline
        bitmap      +=width;     // bytes per bitmap row

    } // end for index_y

} // end Blit_Clipped
```

As a demo of this little software clipper, I've written the crudest bitmap engine you've ever seen. Basically, I created an array of 64 bytes to hold a little happy face. Here's the declaration:

```
UCHAR happy_bitmap[64] = {0,0,0,0,0,0,0,0,
                          0,0,1,1,1,1,0,0,
                          0,1,0,1,1,0,1,0,
                          0,1,1,1,1,1,1,0,
                          0,1,0,1,1,0,1,0,
                          0,1,1,0,0,1,1,0,
                          0,0,1,1,1,1,0,0,
                          0,0,0,0,0,0,0,0};
```

Then I put the system into 320x240x8 back buffer mode and made color index RGB(255,255,0), which is yellow. Then I made the little happy face move around the screen by moving it on a constant random velocity and then wrapping the face around when it goes too far off any of the four screen edges. It goes out of the window just far enough for you to see the clipping function work. Then I got carried away and made 100 happy faces! The final program is DEMO7_8.CPP|EXE, and Figure 7.19 is a screen shot of the program in action.

DirectX and 2D Fundamentals

FIGURE 7.19
DEMO7_8.EXE
in action.

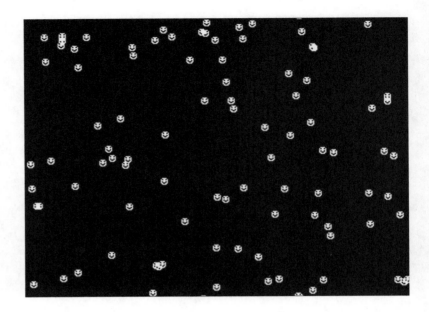

Here's the Game_Main() function for your review:

```
int Game_Main(void *parms = NULL, int num_parms = 0)
{
// this is the main loop of the game, do all your processing
// here

DDBLTFX ddbltfx; // the blitter fx structure

// make sure this isn't executed again
if (window_closed)
   return(0);

// for now test if user is hitting ESC and send WM_CLOSE
if (KEYDOWN(VK_ESCAPE))
   {
   PostMessage(main_window_handle,WM_CLOSE,0,0);
   window_closed = 1;
   } // end if

// use the blitter to erase the back buffer
// first initialize the DDBLTFX structure
DDRAW_INIT_STRUCT(ddbltfx);

// now set the color word info to the color we desire
ddbltfx.dwFillColor = 0;

// make the blitter call
if (FAILED(lpddsback->Blt(NULL, // ptr to dest RECT, NULL means all
                          NULL, // pointer to source surface
                          NULL, // pointer to source RECT
```

```
                    DDBLT_COLORFILL | DDBLT_WAIT,
                    // do a color fill and wait if you have to
                    &ddbltfx))) // pointer to DDBLTFX holding info
return(0);

// initialize ddsd
DDRAW_INIT_STRUCT(ddsd);

// lock the back buffer surface
if (FAILED(lpddsback->Lock(NULL,&ddsd,
                           DDLOCK_WAIT | DDLOCK_SURFACEMEMORYPTR,
                           NULL)))
    return(0);


// draw all the happy faces
for (int face=0; face < 100; face++)
    {
    Blit_Clipped(happy_faces[face].x,
                 happy_faces[face].y,
                 8,8,
                 happy_bitmap,
                 (UCHAR *)ddsd.lpSurface,
                 ddsd.lPitch);
    } // end face

// move all happy faces
for (face=0; face < 100; face++)
    {
    // move
    happy_faces[face].x+=happy_faces[face].xv;
    happy_faces[face].y+=happy_faces[face].yv;

    // check for off screen, if so wrap
    if (happy_faces[face].x > SCREEN_WIDTH)
        happy_faces[face].x = -8;
    else
    if (happy_faces[face].x < -8)
        happy_faces[face].x = SCREEN_WIDTH;

    if (happy_faces[face].y > SCREEN_HEIGHT)
        happy_faces[face].y = -8;
    else
    if (happy_faces[face].y < -8)
        happy_faces[face].y = SCREEN_HEIGHT;

    } // end face

// unlock surface
if (FAILED(lpddsback->Unlock(NULL)))
    return(0);

// flip the pages
while (FAILED(lpddsprimary->Flip(NULL, DDFLIP_WAIT)));
```

```
// wait a sec
Sleep(30);

// return success or failure or your own return code here
return(1);

} // end Game_Main
```

> **NOTE**   Make sure to look at the code for `Blit_Clipped()` in the demo program,
> because I slightly modified it to work with a variable memory pitch. No
> big deal, but I thought you might want to know. Also, you may be won-
> dering why I decided to use 320×240 mode. Well, the little 8×8 bitmap
> in 640×480 was so small, I was going blind <BG>.

Making a DirectDraw Clip with `IDirectDrawClipper`

Now that you see the work it takes to perform clipping via software, it's time to look at
how easy it is with DirectDraw. DirectDraw has an interface called `IDirectDrawClipper`
that's used for all 2D blitter clipping, as well as 3D rasterization under Direct3D. In
essence, the buck stops here. Right now, however, you're only interested in using the
clipper to clip bitmaps that are blitted using the `Blt()` function and the associated blitter hardware.

To set up DirectDraw clipping, you must do the following:

1. Create a DirectDraw clipper object.
2. Create a clipping list.
3. Send the clipping list data to the clipper with
   `IDIRECTDRAWCLIPPER::SetClipList()`.
4. Attach the clipper to a window and/or surface with
   `IDIRECTDRAWSURFACE7::SetClipper()`.

I'll begin with step 1. The function to create an `IDirectDrawClipper` interface is
called `IDIRECTDRAW7::CreateClipper()` and is shown here:

```
HRESULT CreateClipper(DWORD dwFlags, // control flags
        LPDIRECTDRAWCLIPPER FAR *lplpDDClipper, // address of interface pointer
        IUnknown FAR *pUnkOuter); // COM stuff
```

The function returns `DD_OK` if successful.

The parameters are pretty easy. `dwFlags` is currently unused and must be 0.
`lplpDDClipper` is the address of an `IDirectDrawClipper` interface that will point
to a valid DirectDraw clipper after the function succeeds. Finally, `pUnkOuter` is for
COM aggregation, which is something you don't care about—make it `NULL`. To
create a clipper object, just enter this:

```
LPDIRECTDRAWCLIPPER lpddclipper = NULL; // hold the clipper

if (FAILED(lpdd->CreateClipper(0,&lpddclipper,NULL)))
    return(0);
```

If the function succeeds, `lpddclipper` will point to a valid `IDirectDrawClipper` interface and you can call the methods on it.

That's great, but how do you create the clipping list, and what does it represent? Under DirectDraw, the clipping list is a list of rectangles stored in `RECT` structures that indicate the valid regions that can be blitted to, as shown in Figure 7.20. As you can see, there are a number of rectangles on the display surface, but DirectDraw's blitter system can blit only within these rectangles. You can draw anywhere you want with `Lock()/Unlock()`, but the blitter hardware will be able to draw *only* within the clipping regions, more commonly called the *clip list*.

FIGURE 7.20

The relationship between the clip list and the blitter.

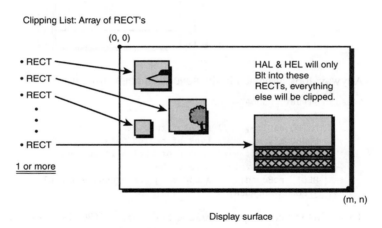

To create a clip list, you must fill in a rather ugly data structure called `RGNDATA` (Region Data), which is shown here:

```
typedef struct _RGNDATA
        { /* rgnd */
        RGNDATAHEADER rdh; // header info
        char Buffer[1];    // the actual RECT list
        } RGNDATA;
```

This is a very odd data structure. Basically, it's a variant size structure, which means that the `Buffer[]` part of it can be any length. The structure is generated dynamically rather than statically, and its true length is stored in the `RGNDATAHEADER`. What you're seeing here is the old version of the new DirectX data structure technique that sets the `dwSize` field of every structure. Maybe a better approach would have been to make `Buffer[]` a pointer rather than storage for a single byte?

Whatever the thinking was, here's the deal: All you have to do is allocate enough memory for a RGNDATAHEADER structure, along with memory to hold an array of one or more RECT structures that are contiguous in memory, as shown in Figure 7.21. Then you'll just cast it to a RGNDATA type and pass it.

FIGURE 7.21
The memory footprint of the RGNDATA clipping structure.

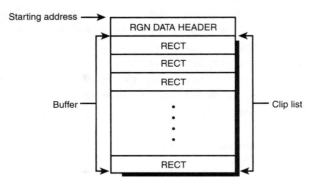

Anyway, look at what's in the RGNDATAHEADER structure:

```
typedef struct _RGNDATAHEADER
         { // rgndh
         DWORD dwSize;    // size of this header in bytes
         DWORD iType;     // type of region data
         DWORD nCount;    // number of RECT'S in Buffer[]
         DWORD nRgnSize;  // size of Buffer[]
         RECT  rcBound;   // a bounding box around all RECTS
         } RGNDATAHEADER;
```

To set this structure up, set dwSize to the sizeof(RGNDATAHEADER), set iType to RDH_RECTANGLES, set nCount to the number of rectangles or RECTS in your clipping list, set nRgnSize to the size in bytes of your Buffer[] (which is equal to sizeof(RECT)*nCount), create a bounding box around all your RECTs, and store this box in rcBound. Once you've generated the RGNDATA structure, you send it to your clipper with a call to IDIRECTDRAWCLIPPER::SetClipList(), shown here:

```
HRESULT SetClipList(LPRGNDATA lpClipList, // ptr to RGNDATA
                    DWORD dwFlags);  // flags, always 0
```

There's not much more to say about this. Assuming you've already generated the RGNDATA structure for your clipping list, here's how you would set the clipping list:

```
if (FAILED(lpddclipper->SetClipList(&rgndata,0)))
    return(0);
```

Once the clip list is set, you can finally attach the clipper to the surface you want it to be associated with using `IDIRECTDRAWSURFACE7::SetClipper()`, which is shown here:

```
HRESULT SetClipper(LPDIRECTDRAWCLIPPER lpDDClipper);
```

And here's the function in action:

```
if (FAILED(lpddsurface->SetClipper(&lpddcliper)))
    return(0);
```

In most cases, `lpddsurface` would be your offscreen rendering surface, such as the back buffer surface. Usually, you don't attach a clipper to the primary surface.

Okay, I know you're probably turning purple with frustration because I've hedged about the details of creating the `RGNDATA` structure and setting it up. The reason is that it's too hard to explain detail by detail; it's easier to just look at the code. Hence, I've created a function called `DDraw_Attach_Clipper()` (part of the graphics library) that creates a clipper and a clip list, and attaches them to any surface. Here's the code:

```
LPDIRECTDRAWCLIPPER DDraw_Attach_Clipper(LPDIRECTDRAWSURFACE7 lpdds,
                                         int num_rects,
                                         LPRECT clip_list)

{
// this function creates a clipper from the sent clip list and attaches
// it to the sent surface

int index;                           // looping var
LPDIRECTDRAWCLIPPER lpddclipper;     // pointer to the newly
                                     // created dd clipper
LPRGNDATA region_data;               // pointer to the region
                                     // data that contains
                                     // the header and clip list

// first create the direct draw clipper
if (FAILED(lpdd->CreateClipper(0,&lpddclipper,NULL)))
   return(NULL);

// now create the clip list from the sent data

// first allocate memory for region data
region_data = (LPRGNDATA)malloc(sizeof(RGNDATAHEADER)+
              num_rects*sizeof(RECT));

// now copy the rects into region data
memcpy(region_data->Buffer, clip_list, sizeof(RECT)*num_rects);

// set up fields of header
region_data->rdh.dwSize        = sizeof(RGNDATAHEADER);
region_data->rdh.iType         = RDH_RECTANGLES;
region_data->rdh.nCount        = num_rects;
region_data->rdh.nRgnSize      = num_rects*sizeof(RECT);
```

```
region_data->rdh.rcBound.left   =  64000;
region_data->rdh.rcBound.top    =  64000;
region_data->rdh.rcBound.right  = -64000;
region_data->rdh.rcBound.bottom = -64000;

// find bounds of all clipping regions
for (index=0; index<num_rects; index++)
    {
    // test if the next rectangle unioned with
    // the current bound is larger
    if (clip_list[index].left < region_data->rdh.rcBound.left)
       region_data->rdh.rcBound.left = clip_list[index].left;

    if (clip_list[index].right > region_data->rdh.rcBound.right)
       region_data->rdh.rcBound.right = clip_list[index].right;

    if (clip_list[index].top < region_data->rdh.rcBound.top)
       region_data->rdh.rcBound.top = clip_list[index].top;

    if (clip_list[index].bottom > region_data->rdh.rcBound.bottom)
       region_data->rdh.rcBound.bottom = clip_list[index].bottom;

    } // end for index

// now we have computed the bounding rectangle region and set up the data
// now let's set the clipping list

if (FAILED(lpddclipper->SetClipList(region_data, 0)))
    {
    // release memory and return error
    free(region_data);
    return(NULL);
    } // end if

// now attach the clipper to the surface
if (FAILED(lpdds->SetClipper(lpddclipper)))
    {
    // release memory and return error
    free(region_data);
    return(NULL);
    } // end if

// all is well, so release memory and
// send back the pointer to the new clipper
free(region_data);
return(lpddclipper);

} // end DDraw_Attach_Clipper
```

The function is almost trivial to use. Let's say you have an animation system with a primary surface called lpddsprimary and a secondary back buffer called lpddsback, to which you want to attach a clipper with the following RECT list:

```
RECT rect_list[3] = {{10,10,50,50},
                     {100,100,200,200},
                     {300,300, 500, 450}};
```

Here's the call to do it:

```
LPDIRECTDRAWCLIPPER lpddclipper =
                    DDraw_Attach_Clipper(lpddsback,3,rect_list);
```

Cool, huh? If you made this call, only portions of bitmaps that were within the rectangles (10,10) to (50,50), (100,100) to (200,200), and (300,300) to (500, 450) would be visible. Also, just to let you know, this function is part of a library that I'm working on as I write this chapter. Later, I'm going to show you all the functions in it so you don't have to write all this tedious DirectDraw code yourself and you can focus on game programming, my little spawn <BG>.

Anyway, based on the preceding code, I've created a demo called DEMO7_9.CPP|EXE. Basically, I took the blitter demo program DEMO7_7.CPP, converted it to 8-bit color, and added the clipper function so that only blits within the current clipping regions are displayed on the primary surface. Furthermore, to be consistent, the clipping regions are the same ones listed in the preceding paragraph. Figure 7.22 is a screen shot of the program in action. Notice that it looks like a bunch of little windows that the clipper allows bitmaps to be rendered to.

FIGURE 7.22
DEMO7_9.EXE
in action.

Here's the code that sets up the clipper in the `Game_Main()` of `DEMO7_9.CPP`:

```
// now create and attach clipper
RECT rect_list[3] = {{10,10,50,50},
                     {100,100,200,200},
                     {300,300, 500, 450}};

if (FAILED(lpddclipper = DDraw_Attach_Clipper(lpddsprimary,3,rect_list)))
    return(0);
```

And of course, there's no difference when attaching a clipper in 16-bit or higher modes, you make the call the exact same way. The clipper doesn't care what the mode is since clipping is performed at a different level, more abstractly that is, so the bits per pixel is irrelevant.

Coolio! At this point, I'm extremely bored with gradient fills and colored rectangles. If I don't see some bitmaps, I'm going to lose my mind! Next I'll show you how to load bitmaps with Windows.

Working with Bitmaps

There are about a trillion different bitmap file formats, but I only use a few for game programming: `.PCX` (PC Paint), `.TGA` (Targa), and `.BMP` (Windows native format). They all have their pros and cons, but you're using Windows, so you might as well use the native format `.BMP` to make life easier. (I'm already in DirectX API revision hell, so I'm a bit unstable at this point. If I see one more Don Lapre commercial, I think I'm going to go postal!)

The other formats all work in similar ways, so once you learn how to deal with one file format, figuring out another involves nothing more than getting hold of the header structure format and reading some bytes off the disk. For example, lots of people are really starting to like the `.PNG` (Portable Network Graphics) format.

Loading `.BMP` Files

There are a number of ways to read a `.BMP` file—you can write a reader yourself, use a Win32 API function, or a mixture of the two. Because figuring out Win32 functions is usually as hard as writing your own, you might as well write a `.BMP` loader yourself. A `.BMP` file consists of three parts, as shown in Figure 7.23.

The three parts are as follows:

Bitmap file header—This holds general information about the bitmap and is contained in the Win32 data structure `BITMAPFILEHEADER`:

```
typedef struct tagBITMAPFILEHEADER
        { // bmfh
        WORD    bfType; // Specifies the file type.
```

```
                        // Must be 0x4D42 for .BMP
      DWORD   bfSize; // Specifies the size in bytes of
                        // the bitmap file.
      WORD    bfReserved1; //Reserved; must be zero.
      WORD    bfReserved2; // Reserved; must be zero.
      DWORD   bfOffBits;   // Specifies the offset, in
                            // bytes, from the
                            // BITMAPFILEHEADER structure
                            // to the bitmap bits.
      } BITMAPFILEHEADER;
```

FIGURE 7.23

The structure of a
.BMP file on disk.

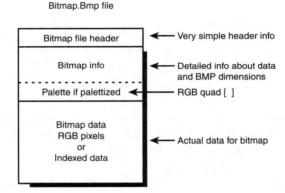

Bitmap.Bmp file

Bitmap file header ← Very simple header info

Bitmap info ← Detailed info about data and BMP dimensions

Palette if palettized ← RGB quad [ ]

Bitmap data
RGB pixels
or
Indexed data
← Actual data for bitmap

Bitmap info section—This is composed of two other data structures, the
BITMAPINFOHEADER section and the palette information (if there is one):

```
typedef struct tagBITMAPINFO
        { // bmi
        BITMAPINFOHEADER bmiHeader; // the info header
        RGBQUAD bmiColors[1];  // palette (if there is one)
        } BITMAPINFO;
```

And here's the BITMAPINFOHEADER structure:

```
typedef struct tagBITMAPINFOHEADER{ // bmih
   DWORD biSize;   // Specifies the number of
                    // bytes required by the structure.
   LONG  biWidth;  // Specifies the width of the bitmap, in pixels.
   LONG  biHeight; // Specifies the height of the bitmap, in pixels.
                    // If biHeight is positive, the bitmap is a
                    // bottom-up DIB and its
                    // origin is the lower left corner
                    // If biHeight is negative, the bitmap
                    // is a top-down DIB and its origin is the upper left corner.
   WORD  biPlanes;   // Specifies the number of color planes, must be 1.
   WORD  biBitCount  // Specifies the number of bits per pixel.
                    // This value must be 1, 4, 8, 16, 24, or 32.
   DWORD biCompression;   // specifies type of compression (advanced)
                            // it will always be
```

```
                             // BI_RGB for uncompressed .BMPs
                             // which is what we're going to use
        DWORD biSizeImage;   // size of image in bytes
        LONG  biXPelsPerMeter; // specifies the number of
                             // pixels per meter in X-axis
        LONG  biYPelsPerMeter; // specifies the number of
                             // pixels per meter in Y-axis
        DWORD biClrUsed;     // specifies the number of
                             // colors used by the bitmap
        DWORD biClrImportant; // specifies the number of
                             // colors that are important
        } BITMAPINFOHEADER;
```

> **NOTE**
>
> 8-bit images will usually have the `biClrUsed` and `biClrImportant` fields both set to 256, while 16 and 24-bit images will set them to 0. Hence, always test the `biBitCount` to find out how many bits per pixel are used and go from there.

Bitmap data area—This is a byte stream that describes the pixels of the image (this may or may not be in compressed form) in 1-, 4-, 8-, 16-, or 24-bit format. The data is in line-by-line order, but it may be upside-down so that the first line of data is the last line of the image, as shown in Figure 7.24. You can detect this by looking at the sign of `biHeight`—a positive sign means the bitmap is upside-down, and a negative sign means the bitmap is normal.

FIGURE 7.24
The image data in a .BMP file is sometimes inverted on the y-axis.

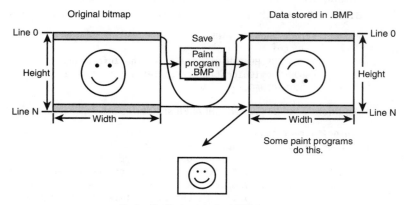

During the file load, re-invert the image.

To read a .BMP file manually, you first open the file (with any file I/O technique you like) and then read in the BITMAPFILEHEADER. Next, read in the BITMAPINFO section, which is really just a BITMAPINFOHEADER plus palette (if 256 color), so really you're just reading in the BITMAPINFOHEADER structure. From this, you determine the size of the bitmap (biWidth, biHeight) and its color depth (biBitCount, biClrUsed). Here you also read in the bitmap data along with the palette (if there is one). Of course, there are a lot of details, such as allocating buffers to read the data and moving file pointers around. Also, the palette entries are RGBQUAD, which are in reverse order of normal PALETTEENTRYs, so you have to convert them like this:

```
typedef struct tagRGBQUAD
        { // rgbq
        BYTE     rgbBlue;      // blue
        BYTE     rgbGreen;     // green
        BYTE     rgbRed;       // red
        BYTE     rgbReserved;  // unused
        } RGBQUAD;
```

Back in Chapter 4, "Windows GDI, Controls, and Last-Minute Gift Ideas," you may recall the LoadBitmap() function that's used to load bitmap resources from disk. You could use this function, but then you would always have to compile all your game bitmaps into your .EXE as a resource. Although this is cool for a complete product, it's not something you want to do when developing. Basically, you want to be able to tweak your graphics with a paint or modeling program, dump the bitmaps in a directory, and run your game to see what's up. Hence, you need a more general disk file-based bitmap reading function, which you'll write in a moment. Before you do, take a look at the Win32 API function to load bitmaps. Run LoadImage():

```
HANDLE LoadImage(
  HINSTANCE hinst, // handle of the instance that contains
                   // the image
  LPCTSTR lpszName,  // name or identifier of image
  UINT    uType,     // type of image
  int     cxDesired, // desired width
  int     cyDesired, // desired height
  UINT    fuLoad );  // load flags
```

This function is rather general, but you only want to use it to load .BMP files from the disk, so you don't have to worry about all the other stuff it does. Simply set the parameters to the following values to load a .BMP from disk:

hinst—This is the instance handle. Set it to NULL.

lpszName—This is the name of the .BMP file on disk. Send a standard NULL-terminated filename like ANDRE.BMP, C:/images/ship.bmp, and so forth.

uType—This is the type of image to load. Set it to IMAGE_BITMAP.

cxDesired, cyDesired—These are the desired width and height of the bitmap. If you set these to any number other than 0, LoadImage() will scale the bitmap to fit. Therefore, if you know the size of the image, set them. Otherwise, leave them at 0 and read the size of the image later.

fuLoad—This is a load control flag. Set it to (LR_LOADFROMFILE | LR_CREATEDIBSECTION). This instructs LoadImage() to load the data from disk using the name in `lpszName` and to not translate the bitmap data to the current display device's color characteristics.

The only problem with this function is that it's so general that getting to the damn data is difficult. You have to use more functions to access the header information, and if there's a palette, more trouble arises. Instead, I just created my own `Load_Bitmap_File()` function that loads a bitmap from disk in any format (including palettized) and stuffs the information into this structure:

```
typedef struct BITMAP_FILE_TAG
        {
        BITMAPFILEHEADER bitmapfileheader;  // this contains the
                                            // bitmapfile header
        BITMAPINFOHEADER bitmapinfoheader;  // this is all the info
                                            // including the palette
        PALETTEENTRY     palette[256];// we will store the palette here
        UCHAR            *buffer;  // this is a pointer to the data

        } BITMAP_FILE, *BITMAP_FILE_PTR;
```

Notice that I've basically put the `BITMAPINFOHEADER` and the exploded `BITMAPINFO` all together in one structure. This is much easier to work with. Now for the `Load_Bitmap_File()` function:

```
int Load_Bitmap_File(BITMAP_FILE_PTR bitmap, char *filename)
{
// this function opens a bitmap file and loads the data into bitmap

int file_handle,  // the file handle
    index;        // looping index

UCHAR   *temp_buffer = NULL; // used to convert 24 bit images to 16 bit
OFSTRUCT file_data;          // the file data information

// open the file if it exists
if ((file_handle = OpenFile(filename,&file_data,OF_READ))==-1)
   return(0);

// now load the bitmap file header
_lread(file_handle, &bitmap->bitmapfileheader,sizeof(BITMAPFILEHEADER));

// test if this is a bitmap file
if (bitmap->bitmapfileheader.bfType!=BITMAP_ID)
   {
   // close the file
   _lclose(file_handle);

   // return error
   return(0);
   } // end if

// now we know this is a bitmap, so read in all the sections
```

```
// first the bitmap infoheader

// now load the bitmap file header
_lread(file_handle, &bitmap->bitmapinfoheader,sizeof(BITMAPINFOHEADER));

// now load the color palette if there is one
if (bitmap->bitmapinfoheader.biBitCount == 8)
   {
   _lread(file_handle, &bitmap->palette,
          MAX_COLORS_PALETTE*sizeof(PALETTEENTRY));

   // now set all the flags in the palette correctly
   // and fix the reversed
   // BGR RGBQUAD data format
   for (index=0; index < MAX_COLORS_PALETTE; index++)
       {
       // reverse the red and green fields
       int temp_color                = bitmap->palette[index].peRed;
       bitmap->palette[index].peRed  = bitmap->palette[index].peBlue;
       bitmap->palette[index].peBlue = temp_color;

       // always set the flags word to this
       bitmap->palette[index].peFlags = PC_NOCOLLAPSE;
       } // end for index

   } // end if

// finally the image data itself
_lseek(file_handle,
       -(int)(bitmap->bitmapinfoheader.biSizeImage),SEEK_END);

// now read in the image

if (bitmap->bitmapinfoheader.biBitCount==8 ||
    bitmap->bitmapinfoheader.biBitCount==16 ||
    bitmap->bitmapinfoheader.biBitCount==24)
   {
   // delete the last image if there was one
   if (bitmap->buffer)
       free(bitmap->buffer);

   // allocate the memory for the image
   if (!(bitmap->buffer =
       (UCHAR *)malloc(bitmap->bitmapinfoheader.biSizeImage)))
       {
       // close the file
       _lclose(file_handle);

       // return error
       return(0);
       } // end if

   // now read it in
   _lread(file_handle,bitmap->buffer,
```

```
                    bitmap->bitmapinfoheader.biSizeImage);

    } // end if
else
    {
    // serious problem
    return(0);

    } // end else

// close the file
_lclose(file_handle);

// flip the bitmap
Flip_Bitmap(bitmap->buffer,
            bitmap->bitmapinfoheader.biWidth*
            (bitmap->bitmapinfoheader.biBitCount/8),
            bitmap->bitmapinfoheader.biHeight);

// return success
return(1);

} // end Load_Bitmap_File
```

The function isn't really that long or that complex; it's just a pain to write, that's all.

> **NOTE**
>
> There's a call to `Flip_Bitmap()` at the end of the function. This simply inverts the image because most `.BMP` files are in bottom-up format. `Flip_Bitmap()` is part of the library I'm building, and it's copied into the demos that will come shortly so you can review it at any time.

It opens the bitmap file, loads in the headers, and then loads in the image and palette (if the image is a 256-color bitmap). The function works on 8-, 16-, and 24-bit color images. However, regardless of the image format, the buffer that holds the image UCHAR buffer is just a byte pointer, so you must do any casting or pointer arithmetic if the image is 16- or 24-bit. In addition, the function allocates a buffer for the image, so the buffer must be released back to the operating system when you're done mucking with the image bits. This is accomplished with a call to `Unload_Bitmap_File()`, shown here:

```
int Unload_Bitmap_File(BITMAP_FILE_PTR bitmap)
{
// this function releases all memory associated with the bitmap
if (bitmap->buffer)
    {
    // release memory
    free(bitmap->buffer);

    // reset pointer
    bitmap->buffer = NULL;
```

```
    } // end if

// return success
return(1);

} // end Unload_Bitmap_File
```

In a moment, I'll show you how to load bitmap files into memory and display them, but first I want to describe what you'll do with these images in the general context of a game.

Working with Bitmaps

Most games have a lot of artwork, which consists of 2D sprites, 2D textures, 3D models, and so forth. In most cases, 2D art is loaded a frame at a time as single images (as shown in Figure 7.25), or as templates—that is, as a number of similar images all together in a rectangular matrix (as shown in Figure 7.26). Both methods have their pros and cons. The cool thing about loading single images, or one image per file, is that if you make a change to the image with an image processor, you can use the data immediately. However, there may be hundreds of frames of animation that make up a 2D game character. This means hundreds or thousands of separate image .BMP files!

FIGURE 7.25
A standard set of bitmaps without templating.

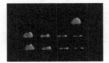

FIGURE 7.26
Bitmap images templated for easy access and extraction.

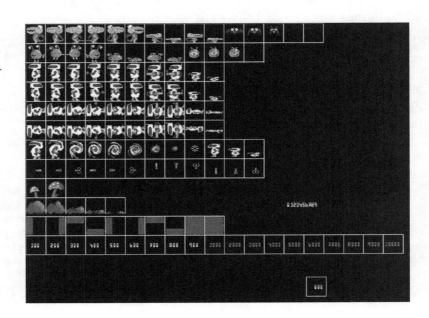

Templated images, as shown in Figure 7.26, are great because the template holds all the animation for a single character, and hence all the data is in one file. The only downfall is that someone has to template the data! This can be very time-consuming, not to mention that there's an alignment problem because you must create a template of cells, where each cell is mxn (usually m and n are powers of 2) with a one-pixel border around each cell. Next, you write some software to extract an image from a particular cell, because you now know the size of the cell and so forth. You might use both techniques, depending on the type of game and how much artwork it uses. In any case, later you're going to have to write software that can extract images from loaded bitmaps in single-image or templated format, and then load the data into DirectDraw surfaces. This allows you to use the blitter, but I'll get to that later. For now, just use the `Load_Bitmap_Function()` to load an 8-, 16-, and 24-bit bitmap and display it in the primary buffer to get a feel for the function.

> **NOTE**
>
> I created most of the art for these demos myself, using various paint or 3D modeling programs and writing the art out as .BMP files (some of the art was done by other artists). This is where a good 2D paint program with support for lots of image formats comes in handy. I usually use Paint Shop Pro, the best all-around 2D paint program as far as price and performance go—it's on this book's CD, too!

Loading an 8-Bit Bitmap

To load an 8-bit image, this all you need to do:

```
BITMAP_FILE bitmap; // this will hold the bitmap

if (!(Load_Bitmap_File(&bitmap,"path:\filename.bmp")))
   { /* error */ }

// do what you will with the data stored in bitmap.buffer

// in addition, the palette is stored in bitmap.palette

// when done, you must release the buffer holding the bitmap
Unload_Bitmap(&bitmap);
```

> **WARNING**
>
> You can have only 256 colors on the screen at once, so when you're generating your artwork, remember to find a 256-color palette that looks good when all the artwork is converted to 256 colors (Debabelizer is a great tool for this). In many cases you'll need multiple palettes—one for each level of the game—but no matter what, all the bitmaps that are going to be used for the same level and could be visible must be in the same palette!

The only interesting thing about loading an 8-bit bitmap is that the palette information in the BITMAP_FILE structure is valid. You can use the data to change the DirectDraw palette, save it, or whatever. This brings us to a little detail about writing 8-bit games.

Now is a good time to bring up something that I haven't had a good reason to show you yet—changing palette entries after the palette has already been created and attached to an 8-bit DirectDraw surface. As you know, most of the demos that you've written for 8-bit mode usually create a random or gradient palette and leave it at that. But this time, you're loading an image that has its own palette, and you want to update the DirectDraw palette object with the new palette entries. When you copy the image to the primary buffer, it looks right. To do this, all you need is the IDIRECTDRAWPALETTE:SetEntries() function, as shown here:

```
BITMAP_FILE bitmap; // holds the 8-bit image

// given that the 8-bit image has been loaded

if (FAILED(lpddpal->SetEntries(0,0,MAX_COLORS_PALETTE,
    bitmap.palette)))
{ /* error */ }
```

That's so easy it's sickening!

For an illustration of loading an 8-bit image and displaying it, take a look at DEMO7_10.CPP|EXE. It loads an 8-bit image in 640x480 and dumps it to the primary buffer.

Loading a 16-Bit Bitmap

Loading a 16-bit bitmap is almost identical to loading an 8-bit image. However, you don't need to worry about the palette because there isn't one. Also, very few paint programs can generate 16-bit .BMP files, so if you want to use a 16-bit DirectDraw mode, you may have to load a 24-bit bitmap and then manually convert the bits to 16-bit by using a color-scaling algorithm. In general, you would perform the following operations to convert a 24-bit image to a 16-bit image:

1. Create a buffer that's mxn WORDs, where each WORD is 16-bit. This will hold your 16-bit final image.

2. Access the image buffer after loading the 24-bit image into your BITMAP_FILE structure, and convert each 24-bit pixel to 16-bit by using the following crude color transform:

```
// each pixel in BITMAP_FILE.buffer[] is encoded as 3-bytes
// in BGR order, or BLUE, GREEN, RED

// assuming index is pointing to the next pixel...
UCHAR blue  = (bitmap.buffer[index*3 + 0]) >> 3,
      green = (bitmap.buffer[index*3 + 1]) >> 2,
      red   = (bitmap.buffer[index*3 + 2]) >> 3;
```

```
// build up 16 bit color word
USHORT color = __RGB16BIT565(red,green,blue);
```

And then you write **color** into your destination 16-bit buffer. Later in the book, when you see all the library functions, I'll be sure to write a 24-bit to 16-bit bitmap converter for you (because I'm that kind of guy).

Anyway, assuming that the bitmap is actually in 16-bit format and you don't need to do this operation, the bitmap load should be identical to the 8-bit load. For example, DEMO7_11.CPP|EXE loads a 24-bit image, converts it to 16-bit, and dumps it into the primary buffer.

Loading a 24-Bit Bitmap

Loading a 24-bit bitmap is the simplest of all. Just create a 24-bit bitmap file and then load it with the Load_Bitmap_File() function. Then BITMAP_FILE.buffer[] will hold the data in 3-byte pixels left to right, row by row, but in BGR (blue, green, red) format. Remember this, because it matters when you extract the data. Furthermore, many graphics cards don't support 24-bit graphics; they support 32-bit because they don't like the odd byte addressing (multiples of 3). So an extra byte is used for padding or alpha channeling. In either case, when you read out each pixel from BITMAP_FILE.buffer[] and write it to the primary surface or an offscreen DirectDraw surface that's 32-bit, you'll have to do this padding yourself. Here's an example:

```
// each pixel in BITMAP_FILE.buffer[] is encoded as 3-bytes
// in BGR order, or BLUE, GREEN, RED

// assuming index is pointing to the next pixel...
UCHAR blue  = (bitmap.buffer[index*3 + 0]),
      green = (bitmap.buffer[index*3 + 1]),
      red   = (bitmap.buffer[index*3 + 2]);

// this builds a 32 bit color value in A.8.8.8 format (8-bit alpha mode)
_RGB32BIT(0,red,green,blue);
```

And you've seen this macro, so don't freak out. Here it is again to refresh your memory:

```
// this builds a 32 bit color value in A.8.8.8 format (8-bit alpha mode)
#define _RGB32BIT(a,r,g,b)  ((B) + ((g) << 8) + ((r) << 16) + ((a) << 24))
```

For an example of loading and displaying a nice 24-bit image, take a look at DEMO7_12.CPP|EXE. It loads a full 24-bit image, sets the display mode for 32-bit color, and copies the image to the primary surface. Looks sweet, huh?

Last Word on Bitmaps

Well, that's it for loading bitmaps in 8-, 16-, or 24-bit format. However, you can see that a lot of utility functions will have to be written here! I'll do the dirty work, so don't worry. In addition, you might want to be able to load Targa files with the .TGA extension, because a number of 3D modelers can render animation sequences only to files with the name filename*nnnn*.tga, where *nnnn* varies from 0000 to 9999. You're probably going to need to be able to load animation sequences like this, so when I dump the library functions on you, I'll show you a .TGA load. It's much easier than the .BMP format.

Offscreen Surfaces

The whole point of DirectDraw is to take advantage of hardware acceleration. Alas, you can't do that unless you use DirectDraw data structures and objects to hold bitmaps. DirectDraw surfaces are the key to using the blitter. You've already seen how to create a primary surface along with a secondary back buffer to create a page flipping animation chain, but you still need to learn how to create general mxn offscreen surfaces in either system memory or VRAM. With surfaces like this, you can stuff bitmaps into them and then blit the surfaces to the screen using the blitter.

At this point in the game, you can load bitmaps and get the bits out of them, so that problem is solved (minus some cell extraction software). The only piece missing is how to create a general offscreen DirectDraw surface that's neither a primary surface nor a back buffer.

Creating Offscreen Surfaces

Creating an offscreen surface is almost identical to creating the primary buffer except for the following:

1. You must set the DDSURFACEDESC2.dwFlags to (DDSD_CAPS | DDSD_WIDTH | DDSD_HEIGHT).

2. You must set dimensions of the requested surface in DDSURFACEDESC2.dwWidth and DDSURFACEDESC2.dwHeight.

3. You must set the DDSURFACEDESC2.ddsCaps.dwCaps to DDSCAPS_ OFFSCREENPLAIN | memory_flags, where memory_flags determines where you want the surface to be created. If you set it to DDSCAPS_VIDEOMEMORY, the surface will be created in VRAM (if there's any space). If you set memory_flags equal to DDSCAPS_SYSTEMMEMORY, the surface will be created in system memory, and so the blitter will be almost unused because the bitmap data will have to be transferred over the system bus.

As an example, here's a function that creates any type of surface you request:

```
LPDIRECTDRAWSURFACE7 DDraw_Create_Surface(int width, int height,
                                          int mem_flags)
{
// this function creates an offscreen plain surface
```

```
DDSURFACEDESC2 ddsd;          // working description
LPDIRECTDRAWSURFACE7 lpdds;   // temporary surface

// initialize structure
DDRAW_INIT_STRUCT(ddsd);

// set to access caps, width, and height
ddsd.dwFlags = DDSD_CAPS | DDSD_WIDTH | DDSD_HEIGHT;

// set dimensions of the new bitmap surface
ddsd.dwWidth  =  width;
ddsd.dwHeight =  height;

// set surface to offscreen plain
ddsd.ddsCaps.dwCaps = DDSCAPS_OFFSCREENPLAIN | mem_flags;

// create the surface
if (FAILED(lpdd->CreateSurface(&ddsd,&lpdds,NULL)))
   return(NULL);

// set color key to color 0
DDCOLORKEY color_key; // used to set color key
color_key.dwColorSpaceLowValue  = 0;
color_key.dwColorSpaceHighValue = 0;

// now set the color key for source blitting
lpdds->SetColorKey(DDCKEY_SRCBLT, &color_key);

// return surface
return(lpdds);

} // end DDraw_Create_Surface
```

Now, if you look at the code, you won't find any mention of the pixel or color depth? Weird huh? Not really... The reason, of course, is that the surfaces you create are always compatible with the primary surface, thus the color depth matches, hence it would be redundant to send that information. Therefore, the above function can be used to create 8, 16, 24, or 32-bit surfaces.

For example, if you wanted to create a 64x64 pixel surface in VRAM, you'd make the following call:

```
LPDIRECTDRAWSURFACE7 space_ship = NULL; // used to hold surface

// create surface
if (!(space_ship = DDraw_Create_Surface(64,64,DDSCAPS_VIDEOMEMORY)))
   { /* error */ }
```

TRICK   When you're creating surfaces to hold bitmaps, only create VRAM surfaces of bitmaps that you're going to draw a lot. Moreover, create them in order from largest to smallest.

Now you can do whatever you want with the surface. For example, you might want to lock it so you can copy a bitmap to it. Here's how you would do that:

```
DDSURFACEDESC2 ddsd; // directdraw surface description

// initialize the structure
DDRAW_INIT_STRUCT();

// lock the surface, check for error in RL (real-life)
space_ship->Lock(NULL, &ddsd,
                 DDLOCK_WAIT | DDLOCK_SURFACEMEMORYPTR,
                 NULL);

// do what you will to ddsd.lpSurface and ddsd.lPitch

// unlock
space_ship->Unlock(NULL);
```

Then when you're done with the surface (the game is over, whatever) you must release the surface back to DirectDraw as usual with `Release()`:

```
if (space_ship)
    space_ship->Release();
```

That's all there is to creating an offscreen surface with DirectDraw! Now let me show you how to blit it to another surface, such as the back buffer or primary surface.

Blitting Offscreen Surfaces

Now that you know how to load bitmaps, create surfaces, and use the blitter, it's time to put it all together and do some real animation! The goal of this section is to load bitmaps that contain the frames of animation for some object (ship, creature, whatever), create a number of small surfaces to hold each frame of animation, and then load the images into each of the surfaces. Once all the surfaces are loaded with bitmap data, you want to blit the surfaces on the screen and animate the object!

Actually, you already know how to accomplish all these steps. About the only thing you haven't done is use the blitter to blit from a surface other than the back buffer to the primary buffer, but there's no difference. Referring to Figure 7.27, you see a number of small surfaces, each with a different frame of animation. In addition, you see both a primary surface and a back buffer surface. The plan is to load all the bitmaps into the small surfaces (the object to animate), use the blitter to blit the small surfaces onto the back buffer, and page flip to see the results. Every so often, you'll blit a different image and move the destination of the blit slightly to animate and move the object.

FIGURE 7.27

Blitting offscreen
surfaces to the
back buffer.

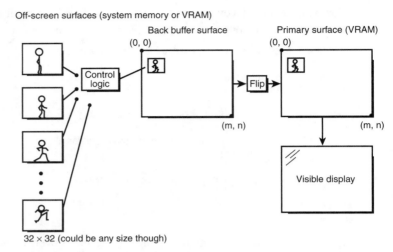

Frames of animation

Setting Up the Blitter

To set up the blitter, you need to do the following:

1. Set up the source RECT to blit from. This will be the small surface (8x8, 16x16, 64x64, etc.) containing the image of interest. Usually the coordinates will be (0,0) to (width–1, height–1)—that is, the whole surface.

2. Set up the destination RECT, which will usually be the back buffer. This part is a little tricky because you want to copy the source image at some location (x,y), so the RECT should be set with this in mind: (x,y) to (x+width-1,y+height-1).

3. Make a call to IDIRECTDRAWSURFACE7::Blt() with the proper parameters—which you'll see shortly.

 NOTE   If you make the destination RECT larger or smaller than the source RECT (the image), the blitter will scale the image appropriately to fit—this is the basis of 2.5D sprite-scaled games.

There's one problem that I must address before you see the call to the Blt() function—color keying.

Color Keys

Color keys are a bit hard to explain, probably because of their naming convention under DirectDraw. Let me give it a try. When you're performing bitmap operations, in most cases you're blitting bitmap objects that are contained in rectangular cells. However, when you draw the bitmap of a little creature, you usually don't want to copy the contents of the entire cell. You want only to copy the bits that relate to the creature, so you need to select a color (or colors) as transparent. Figure 7.28 shows a transparent blit vs. a nontransparent blit. I've discussed this before, and you've even implemented it in your software blitter for the exercise.

FIGURE 7.28
Transparent blit (top) versus nontransparent blit (bottom).

DirectDraw has a much more sophisticated color keying system than just selecting a simple transparent color. It can do much more than just perform blits with basic transparency. Let's take a quick look at the different types of color keys, and then I'll show you how to set up color keying for the type of operation you're interested in.

Source Color Keying

Source color keying is the color keying that you want to use and is the easiest to understand. Basically, you select a single color index (in 256-color modes) or a range of RGB color values that will act as transparent for your source image. Then, when you blit the source to the destination, the pixels that have the same value as the transparent color(s) will not be copied. Figure 7.14 shows this process. You can set the color key for a surface while creating the surface, or do it after the fact with IDIRECTDRAWSURFACE7::SetColorKey(). I'll show you both methods in a moment, but first look at the data structure that holds the color key. It's called DDCOLORKEY:

```
typedef struct _DDCOLORKEY
        {
        DWORD dwColorSpaceLowValue;  // low value (inclusive)
        DWORD dwColorSpaceHighValue; // high value (inclusive)
        } DDCOLORKEY,FAR* LPDDCOLORKEY;
```

The low- and high-color key values are a bit tricky, so listen up. If you're using 8-bit surfaces, the values should be color indices. If you're using 16-, 24-, or 32-bit surfaces, you actually use the RGB-encoded WORDs for the particular surface format as the values to store in the low- and high-color keywords. For example, let's say you're running in an 8-bit mode and you want color index 0 to be transparent. Here's how you would set up the color key:

```
DDCOLORKEY key;

key.dwColorSpaceLowValue  = 0;
key.dwColorSpaceHighValue = 0;
```

And if you wanted the range from color index 10–20 (inclusive) to be transparent:

```
key.dwColorSpaceLowValue  = 10;
key.dwColorSpaceHighValue = 20;
```

Next, let's say you're running in a 16-bit 5.6.5 mode and want pure blue to be transparent:

```
key.dwColorSpaceLowValue  = __RGB16BIT565(0,0,32);
key.dwColorSpaceHighValue = __RGB16BIT565(0,0,32);
```

Similarly, let's say you want the range of colors from black to half-intensity red to be transparent in the same 16-bit mode:

```
key.dwColorSpaceLowValue  = _RGB16BIT565(0,0,0);
key.dwColorSpaceHighValue = _RGB16BIT565(16,0,0);
```

Get the idea? Now let's take a look at how to set a DirectDraw surface's color key during creation. All you need to do is add the flag DDSD_CKSRCBLT (other valid settings shown in Table 7.5) to the dwFlags WORD of the surface descriptor, and then assign the low- and high-color keywords in the DDSURFACEDESC2.ddckCKSrcBlt, member.dwColorSpaceLowValue, and DDSURFACEDESC2.ddckCKSrcBlt.

dwColorSpaceHighValue fields (there are also members for destination and overlay color key information).

TABLE 7.5 Color Key Surface Flags

Value	Description
DDSD_CKSRCBLT	Indicates that the ddckCKSrcBlt member of the DDSURFACEDESC2 is valid and contains color key information for source color keying.
DDSD_CKDESTBLT	Indicates that the ddckCKDestBlt member of the DDSURFACEDESC2 is valid and contains color key information for destination color keying.
DDSD_CKDESTOVERLAY	Indicates that the ddckCKDestOverlay member of the DDSURFACEDESC2 is valid and contains color key information for destination overlay color keying.
DDSD_CKSRCBLT	Indicates that the ddckCKSrcBlt member of the DSURFACEDESC2 is valid and contains color key information for source color keying.
DDSD_CKSRCOVERLAY	Indicates that the ddckCKSrcOverlay member of the DSURFACEDESC2 is valid and contains color key information for source overlay color keying.

Here's an example:

```
DDSURFACEDESC2 ddsd;        // working description
LPDIRECTDRAWSURFACE7 lpdds; // temporary surface

// initialize structure
DDRAW_INIT_STRUCT(ddsd);

// set to access caps, width, and height
ddsd.dwFlags = DDSD_CAPS | DDSD_WIDTH | DDSD_HEIGHT | DDSD_CKSRCBLT;

// set dimensions of the new bitmap surface
ddsd.dwWidth  =  width;
ddsd.dwHeight =  height;

// set surface to offscreen plain
ddsd.ddsCaps.dwCaps = DDSCAPS_OFFSCREENPLAIN | mem_flags;

// set the color key fields
ddsd.ddckCKSrcBlt.dwColorSpaceLowValue  = low_color;
ddsd.ddckCKSrcBlt.dwColorSpaceHighValue = high_color;

// create the surface
if (FAILED(lpdd->CreateSurface(&ddsd,&lpdds,NULL)))
   return(NULL);
```

And once you've created a surface with or without a color key, you can always set it after the fact using the function `IDIRECTDRAWSURFACE7:SetColorKey()`:

```
HRESULT SetColorKey(DWORD dwFlags,
                    LPDDCOLORKEY lpDDColorKey);
```

The valid flags are listed in Table 7.6.

TABLE 7.6 Valid Flags for `SetColorKey()`

Value	Description
DDCKEY_COLORSPACE	Indicates that the structure contains a color space. You must set this if you're setting a range of colors.
DDCKEY_SRCBLT	Indicates that the structure specifies a color key or color space to be used as a source color key for blit operations.
DDCKEY_DESTBLT	Indicates that the structure specifies a color key or color space to be used as a destination color key for blit operations.
DDCKEY_DESTOVERLAY	Set if the structure specifies a color key or color space to be used as a destination color key for overlay operations. (Advanced)
DDCKEY_SRCOVERLAY	Set if the structure specifies a color key or color space to be used as a source color key for overlay operations. (Advanced)

Here's an example:

```
// assume lpdds points to a valid surface

// set color key
DDCOLORKEY color_key; // used to set color key
color_key.dwColorSpaceLowValue  = low_value;
color_key.dwColorSpaceHighValue = high_value;

// now set the color key for source blitting, notice
// the use of DDCKEY_SRCBLT
lpdds->SetColorKey(DDCKEY_SRCBLT, &color_key);
```

> **NOTE**
>
> If you set a range of colors for the source key, you must add the flag DDCKEY_COLORSPACE in the call to `SetColorKey()`. For example:
>
> ```
> lpdds->SetColorKey(DDCKEY_SRCBLT | DDCKEY_COLORSPACE,
>                    &color_key);
> ```
>
> Otherwise, DirectDraw will collapse the range to one value.

Destination Color Keying

Destination color keying is great in theory, but it never seems to get used. The basic concept of destination color keying is shown in Figure 7.29. The idea is as follows: You set a color or range of colors in the destination surface that can be blitted to. In essence, you're creating a mask of sorts. This way you can simulate windows, fences, etc.

FIGURE 7.29
Destination color
keying.

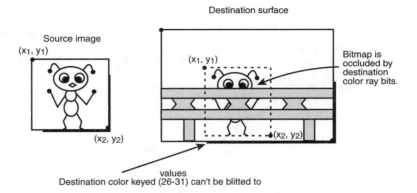

Destination surface

Source image
(x_1, y_1)

(x_1, y_1)

Bitmap is
occluded by
destination
color ray bits.

(x_2, y_2)

(x_2, y_2)

values
Destination color keyed (26–31) can't be blitted to

You can set a destination color key the exact same way you did for a source. Just change a couple of the flags. For example, to set a destination color key during creation of a surface, you set the exchange DDSD_CKSRCBLT for DDSD_CKDESTBLT when setting up the DDRAWSURFACEDESC2.dwFlags, and of course the key values will go into ddsd.ddckCKDestBlt rather than ddsd.ddckCKSrcBlt:

```
// set the color key fields
ddsd.ddckCKDestBlt.dwColorSpaceLowValue  = low_color;
ddsd.ddckCKDestBlt.dwColorSpaceHighValue = high_color;
```

If you want to set a destination color key after a surface is created, you do everything the same except during the call to SetColorKey(), where you must switch the DDCKEY_SRCBLT flag to DDCKEY_DESTBLT, like this:

```
lpdds->SetColorKey(DDCKEY_DESTBLT, &color_key);
```

WARNING

Destination color keying is currently only available in the HAL (Hardware Abstraction Layer), not the HEL. Hence, if there isn't hardware support for destination color keying, it won't work. This will probably change for future versions of DirectX.

Finally, there are two more types of keys: source overlays and destination overlays. They're useless for your purposes, but they come in handy for video processing. If you're interested, take a look at the DirectX SDK.

Using the Blitter (Finally!)

Now that you have the preliminaries out of the way, blitting an offscreen surface to any other surface is a snap. Here's how. Assume that you've created a 64x64-pixel 8-bit color surface image with color index 0 as the transparent color, or something like this:

```
DDSURFACEDESC2 ddsd;               // working description
LPDIRECTDRAWSURFACE7 lpdds_image;  // temporary surface
```

DirectX and 2D Fundamentals

```
// initialize structure
DDRAW_INIT_STRUCT(ddsd);

// set to access caps, width, and height
ddsd.dwFlags = DDSD_CAPS | DDSD_WIDTH | DDSD_HEIGHT | DDSD_CKSRCBLT;

// set dimensions of the new bitmap surface
ddsd.dwWidth  = 64;
ddsd.dwHeight = 64;

// set surface to offscreen plain
ddsd.ddsCaps.dwCaps = DDSCAPS_OFFSCREENPLAIN | mem_flags;

// set the color key fields
ddsd.ddckCKSrcBlt.dwColorSpaceLowValue  = 0;
ddsd.ddckCKSrcBlt.dwColorSpaceHighValue = 0;

// create the surface
if (FAILED(lpdd->CreateSurface(&ddsd,&lpdds_image,NULL)))
   return(NULL);
```

Next, imagine that you have both a primary surface, lpddsprimary, and a back buffer surface, lpddsback, and that you want to blit the surface lpdds_image to the back buffer at location (x,y) with the source color key you set. Here's how:

```
// fill in the destination rect
dest_rect.left   = x;
dest_rect.top    = x;
dest_rect.right  = x+64-1;
dest_rect.bottom = y+64-1;

// fill in the source rect
source_rect.left   = 0;
source_rect.top    = 0;
source_rect.right  = 64-1;
source_rect.bottom = 64-1;

// blt to destination surface
if (FAILED(lpddsback->Blt(&dest_rect, lpdds_image,
        &source_rect,
        (DDBLT_WAIT | DDBLT_KEYSRC),
        NULL)))
   return(0);
```

That's it, baby! Notice the flag DDBLT_KEYSRC. You must have this in the blit call, or else the color key won't work even though there is one defined by the surface.

WARNING
When you're blitting remember to watch out for clipping. Not setting a clipping region to the destination surface and blitting beyond it would be very bad. But all you have to do is make a call to your function DDraw_Attach_Clipper() and set a single clipping RECT that's identical to the bounds of the screen.

At long last, you're ready for a reasonably cool demo. Figure 7.30 is a screen shot of DEMO7_13.CPP|EXE. Looks cool, huh? What I've decided to do is add a little game programming so you can get more out of this demo than just some moving bitmaps. Basically, the demo loads in a large background bitmap and a number of frames of animation for an alien. The large background is copied to the back buffer each frame, along with a number of replicated and animated copies of the alien (which are surfaces). The aliens are then animated and moved at various velocities. See if you can add a player that's controlled by the keyboard to the demo!

FIGURE 7.30
DEMO7 13.EXE
in action.

Bitmap Rotation and Scaling

DirectDraw supports both bitmap rotation and scaling, as shown in Figure 7.31. However, only the HAL supports rotation. This means that if there isn't hardware support for rotation, you're out of luck. You might ask, "Why does the HEL support scaling and not rotation?" The answer is that bitmap rotation is about 10–100 times slower than a scaling operation, and Microsoft found that no matter how well they wrote software rotation code, it was just too slow! So the long and the short of it is that you can always count on scaling, but not rotation. You can always write your own bitmap rotation function, but this is rather complex and not really necessary for 3D polygon games. I'm not going to cover it in this book. However, this is one of the reasons Microsoft merged DirectDraw with Direct3D. If you just use 3D polygons for everything, and texture map onto them your 2D bitmap and place the camera in an aerial view then you end up being able to rotate, shear, do transparency, lighting effects, everything. However, this comes at the cost of having to use 3D hardware to do 2D graphics which is fine, but if you don't want to then it's not!

FIGURE 7.31
Bitmap scaling
and rotation.

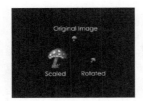

Performing bitmap scaling is easy. All you need to do is change the size of the destination RECT to make it different from the source RECT image, and the image will be
scaled. For example, let's say that you have an image that's 64x64, and you want to
scale it to a size mxn and position it at (x,y). Here's the code:

```
// fill in the destination rect
dest_rect.left   = x;
dest_rect.top    = x;
dest_rect.right  = x+m-1;
dest_rect.bottom = y+n-1;

// fill in the source rect
source_rect.left   = 0;
source_rect.top    = 0;
source_rect.right  = 64-1;
source_rect.bottom = 64-1;

// blt to destination surface
if (FAILED(lpddsback->Blt(&dest_rect, lpdds_image,
        &source_rect,
        (DDBLT_WAIT | DDBLT_KEYSRC),
        NULL)))
    return(0);
```

That's easy enough! Rotation is a little harder, though, because you have to set up a
DDBLTFX structure. To perform a rotation operation on a bitmap. you must have
hardware acceleration that supports it (very rare) and then set up a DDBLTFX structure,
as follows:

```
DDBLTFX ddbltfx; // this holds our data

// initialize the structure
DDRAW_INIT_STRUCT(ddbltfx);

// set rotation angle, note that each unit is in 1/100
// of a degree rotation
ddbltfx.dwRotationAngle = angle; // each unit is
```

Then you make the call to Blt() as you normally would, but you add the flag
DDBLT_ROTATIONANGLE to the flags parameter and add the ddbltfx parameter like this:

```
// blt to destination surface
if (FAILED(lpddsback->Blt(&dest_rect, lpdds_image,
    &source_rect,
    (DDBLT_WAIT | DDBLT_KEYSRC | DDBLT_ROTATIONANGLE),
    &ddbltfx)))
    return(0);
```

You can determine if your hardware has rotation support by querying the surface capabilities of the DDSCAPS structure of a surface and looking at the DDFXCAPS_BLTROTATION* caps flags in the dwFxCaps member of DDSCAPS. You can query the capabilities of a surface with the IDIRECTDRAWSURFACE7::GetCaps() function, which I'll cover at the end of the chapter.

And if you have hardware-accelerated rotation, the bitmap will rotate!

Before moving on to demos of DirectDraw scaling and rotation, I want to talk a little about sampling theory and how you would go about implementing scaling, at the very least, in software.

Discrete Sampling Theory

This is going to be brief: I'll turn your brain to mush with this stuff when you get to 3D texture mapping in Volume II, but for now, this is just a little teaser.

When you work with bitmaps, you're really working with signals; it's just that these signals are discrete 2D image data rather than continuous analog data like a radio signal. In either case, you can use signal processing, or more correctly digital signal processing concepts, on images. One of the areas of interest to us is data sampling and mapping.

Within the realm of 2D and 3D graphics, there will be numerous times when you want to sample a bitmap image and then perform some operation on it, such as scaling, rotation, or texture mapping. There are two types of general mappings: *forward mappings* and *inverse mappings*. Figures 7.32 and 7.33 show these graphically.

FIGURE 7.32
Sampling theory:
forward mapping.

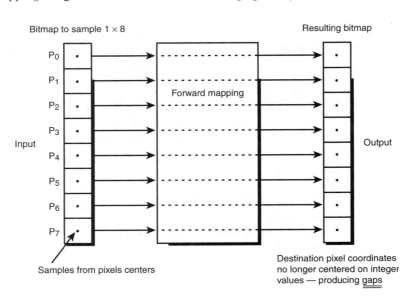

Bitmap to sample 1 × 8

Resulting bitmap

P_0
P_1
P_2
P_3
P_4
P_5
P_6
P_7

Input

Forward mapping

Output

Samples from pixels centers

Destination pixel coordinates no longer centered on integer values — producing gaps

FIGURE 7.33
Sampling theory:
inverse mapping.

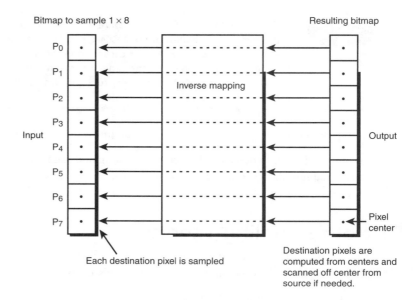

In general, a forward mapping takes pixels from the source and maps them or deposits them on the destination. The only problem with this is that during the mapping, some pixels on the destination may not get mapped from the source due to the mapping function selected.

Inverse mapping, on the other hand, is much better. It takes every pixel on the destination and finds what its source pixel should have been. Of course, there's a problem with this too—some pixels in the destination may have to be replicated because the source doesn't have enough data to fill up the destination. This problem creates aliasing. In a case where there's too much data, aliasing can also occur, but this can be minimized by averaging or using various mathematical filters. The point is, it's better to have too much data than not enough.

Scaling is an operation that lends itself to either forward or inverse mapping, but inverse mapping is the way to go. Let me show you how to scale a one-dimensional bitmap, and then you can generalize the algorithm to two dimensions. This is an important point: Many image processing algorithms are separable, meaning that images can be processed in multiple dimensions simultaneously. The results of one axis don't affect another—sort of.

- **Example 1:** Let's say you have a 1x4-pixel bitmap and you want to scale it to 1x8. Figure 7.34 shows the results. Basically, I just copied each pixel from the source to the destination twice.

FIGURE 7.34
Scaling a 1×4-pixel
bitmap to 1×8 pixels.

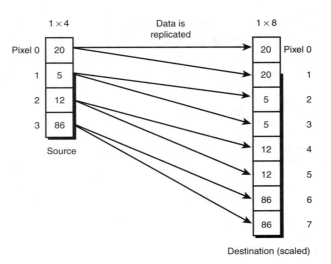

- **Example 2:** Let's say you have a 1x4-pixel bitmap and you want to scale it to 1x2. Figure 7.35 shows the results. Basically, I threw away two pixels from the source. This brings up a problem: You've thrown away information. Is this correct? Yes and no. "No" in the sense that data has been lost, but "yes" in the sense that it works and works quickly.

FIGURE 7.35
Scaling a 1×4-pixel
bitmap to 1×2 pixels.

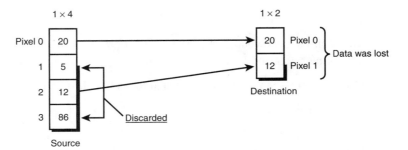

A better strategy in both examples would be to use a filter during the process. For example, in Example 1 you copied the pixels, but you could have taken the average of the two pixels above and below every extra pixel and used that value. This would have made the stretching look better. This is where the graphics term *bi-linear filtering* comes from; it's based on this idea, but just in the 2D case. In Example 2, you could have used a filter also and done the same thing—average the pixel values so that even though you throw away two pixels, you accumulate some of their information into the remaining pixels to make the results look more natural.

I'm not going to show you how to do filtering until later in the book, so you're just going to do scaling by brute force. Reviewing the examples, you should be able to pick up that we are sampling the source at some rate—call that the sample rate—and then, based on this sample rate, filling in the destination. Mathematically, this is what you're doing:

```
// the source height of the 1D bitmap.
float source_height;

// the destination height of the desired scaled 1D bitmap.
float dest_height;

// the sample rate
float sample_rate = source_height/destination_height;

// used to index source data
float sample_index = 0;

// generate scaled destination bitmap
for (index = 0; index < dest_height; index++)
    {
    // write pixel
    dest_bitmap[index] =
    source_bitmap[(int)sample_index];

    // advance source index
    sample_index+=sample_rate;

} // end for index
```

That's all the code you need for scaling a bitmap. Of course, you have to add the other dimension, and I would lose the floating point math, but it works.

Given that the source bitmap is 1x4 and looks like this:

1x4 Pixel Values

source_bitmap[0] = 12

source_bitmap[1] = 34

source_bitmap[2] = 56

source_bitmap[3] = 90

Now let's scale the 1x4 image data to 1x8:

Set source_height   = 4

dest_height   = 8

sample_rate   = 4/8 = 0.5

Algorithm Run (with rounding)

index	sample_index	dest_bitmap[index]
0	0	12
1	0.5	12
2	1.0	34
3	1.5	34
4	2.0	56
5	2.5	56
6	3.0	90
7	3.5	90

Not bad—it exactly replicated each pixel twice. Now, try a compressive scale to three pixels high:

Set source_height	= 4
dest_height	= 3
sample_rate	= 4/3 = 1.333

Algorithm Run (with rounding)

index	sample_index	dest_bitmap[index]
0	0	12
1	1.333	34
2	2.666	56

Notice that you missed the last pixel in the source—the 9—altogether. You may or may not like this; maybe you always want to see the top and bottom pixel in the scaling operation for scales 1x2 and greater and would rather throw away some in-between pixels. This is where rounding and biasing the sample_rate and sample_index come into play—think about it...

Now that you know how to scale an image, let DirectDraw do it for you. DEMO7_14.CPP|EXE is a remake of DEMO7_13.CPP|EXE, but I've added some code to arbitrarily scale the aliens so that they seem to be different sizes. If you have hardware scaling, the demo will run very smoothly, but if you don't, you may notice some degradation. Again, you'll see how to use IDIRECTDRAWSURFACE7::GetCaps() to detect this later in the chapter.

Color Effects

The next subject I want to discuss is color animation and tricks. In the past, 256-color palettized modes were the only bit depths available, and a lot of tricks and techniques were invented to take advantage of the instantaneous nature of color changes—that is, a change to one or more of the palette registers is instantly visible on the screen. These days 256-color modes are fading away due to faster hardware and acceleration. However, learning these techniques is still crucial to understanding other related concepts, not to mention that it will be many years until all games are totally RGB. There are a lot of 486 machines and even slower-MHz Pentiums still around that can handle only 256-color modes at any sort of reasonable speed!

Color Animation in 256-Color Modes

Color animation basically refers to any operation of modifying or shifting around color palette entries on-the-fly. For example, glowing objects, blinking lights, and many other effects can be created simply by manipulating the entries of the color table on-the-fly. The cool thing is that any object on the screen that has pixels with the values that you're manipulating in the color table will be affected.

Imagine how hard it would be to do this with bitmaps. For example, let's say you had a little ship with running lights on it, and you wanted them to blink. You would need a bitmap for each frame of animation. But with color animation, all you need to do is draw a single bitmap, make the lights a specific color index, and then animate the color index. Figure 7.36 illustrates this indirection graphically.

FIGURE 7.36
Color animation using palette indirection.

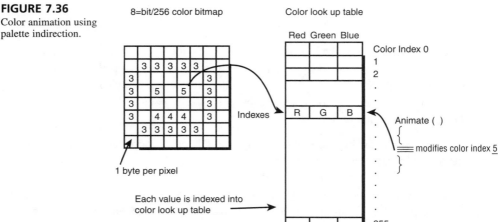

Two of my favorite effects are blinking and glowing colors. Let's begin with a blinking light function. Here's the functionality you want:

- Creating up to 256 blinking lights.
- Each light has an on and off color, in addition to a time delay measured in cycles for the on and off state.
- Turning on or off any blinking light at any time with an ID, and/or resetting its parameters.
- Terminating any blinking light and reusing its data storage.

This is a perfect example for showing some persistent data techniques and showing how to update DirectDraw palette entries. My strategy will be to create a single function that's called to create and destroy the lights as well as to perform the animation. The function will use static data arrays that are local and the function will have a number of operation modes:

BLINKER_ADD—Used to add a blinking color to the database. When called, the function returns an ID number used to reference the blinking light. System holds up to 256 lights.

BLINKER_DELETE—Deletes a blinking light of the sent ID.

BLINKER_UPDATE—Updates the on/off parameters of the sent ID's light.

BLINKER_RUN—Processes all the lights through one cycle.

The data structure used to hold a single light and also to create one is called BLINKER and is shown here:

```
// blinking light structure
typedef struct BLINKER_TYP
            {
            // user sets these
            int color_index;          // index of color to blink
            PALETTEENTRY on_color;    // RGB value of "on" color
            PALETTEENTRY off_color;   // RGB value of "off" color
            int on_time;              // number of frames to keep "on"
            int off_time;             // number of frames to keep "off"

            // internal member
            int counter;              // counter for state transitions
            int state;                // state of light,
                                      // -1 off, 1 on, 0 dead
            } BLINKER, *BLINKER_PTR;
```

Basically, you fill in the "user" fields and then call the function with a BLINKER_ADD command. Anyway, the general operation is as follows: You call the function at any time to add, delete, or update, but only once per frame with the run command. Here's the code for the function:

DirectX and 2D Fundamentals

```
int Blink_Colors(int command, BLINKER_PTR new_light, int id)
{
// this function blinks a set of lights

static BLINKER lights[256]; // supports up to 256 blinking lights
static int initialized = 0; // tracks if function has initialized

// test if this is the first time function has run
if (!initialized)
    {
    // set initialized
    initialized = 1;

    // clear out all structures
    memset((void *)lights,0, sizeof(lights));

    } // end if

// now test what command user is sending
switch (command)
        {
        case BLINKER_ADD: // add a light to the database
            {
            // run thru database and find an open light
            for (int index=0; index < 256; index++)
                {
                // is this light available?
                if (lights[index].state == 0)
                    {
                    // set light up
                    lights[index] = *new_light;

                    // set internal fields up
                    lights[index].counter =  0;
                    lights[index].state   = -1; // off

                    // update palette entry
                    lpddpal->SetEntries(0,lights[index].color_index,
                                        1,&lights[index].off_color);

                    // return id to caller
                    return(index);

                    } // end if

                } // end for index

            } break;

        case BLINKER_DELETE: // delete the light indicated by id
            {
            // delete the light sent in id
```

```
        if (lights[id].state != 0)
           {
           // kill the light
           memset((void *)&lights[id],0,sizeof(BLINKER));

           // return id
           return(id);

           } // end if
        else
            return(-1); // problem


        } break;

case BLINKER_UPDATE: // update the light indicated by id
        {
        // make sure light is active
        if (lights[id].state != 0)
           {
           // update on/off parms only
           lights[id].on_color  = new_light->on_color;
           lights[id].off_color = new_light->off_color;
           lights[id].on_time   = new_light->on_time;
           lights[id].off_time  = new_light->off_time;

           // update palette entry
           if (lights[id].state == -1)
              lpddpal->SetEntries(0,lights[id].color_index,
                                  1,&lights[id].off_color);
           else
              lpddpal->SetEntries(0,lights[id].color_index,
                                  1,&lights[id].on_color);

           // return id
           return(id);

           } // end if
        else
            return(-1); // problem

        } break;

case BLINKER_RUN: // run the algorithm
        {
        // run thru database and process each light
        for (int index=0; index < 256; index++)
            {
            // is this active?
            if (lights[index].state == -1)
               {
               // update counter
```

```
                        if (++lights[index].counter >= lights[index].off_time)
                           {
                           // reset counter
                           lights[index].counter = 0;

                           // change states
                           lights[index].state = -lights[index].state;

                           // update color
                           lpddpal->SetEntries(0,lights[index].color_index,
                                              1,&lights[index].on_color);

                           } // end if

                        } // end if
                     else
                     if (lights[index].state == 1)
                        {
                        // update counter
                        if (++lights[index].counter >= lights[index].on_time)
                           {
                           // reset counter
                           lights[index].counter = 0;

                           // change states
                           lights[index].state = -lights[index].state;
                           // update color
                           lpddpal->SetEntries(0,lights[index].color_index,
                                              1,&lights[index].off_color);

                           } // end if
                        } // end else if

                     } // end for index

              } break;

           default: break;

           } // end switch

      // return success
      return(1);

      } // end Blink_Colors
```

> **NOTE**
> I've boldfaced the sections that update the DirectDraw palette entries. I assume that there's a global palette interface lpddpal.

The function has three main sections: initialization, updating, and run logic. When the function is called for the first time, it initializes itself. Then the next code segment tests for updating commands or the run command. If an update-type command is requested, logic is performed to add, delete, or update a blinking light. If the run mode is requested, the lights are all processed through one cycle. In general, you would use the function after first adding one or more lights, which you'd do by setting up a generic BLINKER structure and then passing the structure to the function with the BLINKER_ADD command. The function would then return the ID of your blinking light, which you'd save—you'll need the ID if you want to delete or update a blinking light.

After you've created all the lights you want, you can call the function with all NULLs except for the command, which is BLINKER_RUN. You do this for each frame of your game loop. For example, let's say you have a game that runs at 30fps, and you want a red light to blink with a 50-50 duty cycle—one second on, one second off—along with a green light with a 50-50 duty cycle of two seconds on and two seconds off. Furthermore, you want to use palette entries 250 and 251 for the red and green light, respectively. Here's the code you need:

```
BLINKER temp; // used to hold temp info

PALETTEENTRY red   = {255,0,0,PC_NOCOLLAPSE};
PALETTEENTRY green = {0,255,0,PC_NOCOLLAPSE};
PALETTEENTRY black = {0,0,0,PC_NOCOLLAPSE};

// add red light
temp.color_index = 250;
temp.on_color    = red;
temp.off_color   = black;
temp.on_time     = 30; // 30 cycles at 30fps = 1 sec
temp.off_time    = 30;

// make call
int red_id = Blink_Colors(BLINKER_ADD, &temp, 0);

// now create green light
temp.color_index = 251;
temp.on_color    = green;
temp.off_color   = black;
temp.on_time     = 60; // 30 cycles at 30fps = 2 secs
temp.off_time    = 60;

// make call
int green_id = Blink_Colors(BLINKER_ADD, &temp, 0);
```

Now you're ready to rock and roll! In the main part of your game loop, you would make a call to Blink_Colors() each cycle, something like this:

```
// enter main event loop
while(TRUE)
```

DirectX and 2D Fundamentals

```
             {
// test if there is a message in queue, if so get it
   if (PeekMessage(&msg,NULL,0,0,PM_REMOVE))
      {
      // test if this is a quit
   if (msg.message == WM_QUIT)
      break;

      // translate any accelerator keys
      TranslateMessage(&msg);

      // send the message to the window proc
      DispatchMessage(&msg);
      } // end if

   // main game processing goes here
   Game_Main();

   // blink all the colors
   // could put this into Game_Main() also - better idea
   Blink_Colors(BLINKER_RUN, NULL, 0);

   } // end while
```

Of course, you can delete a blinker with its ID at any time, and it won't be processed anymore. For example, if you want to kill the red light:

```
Blink_Colors(BLINKER_DELETE, NULL, red_id);
```

It's as simple as that. And of course, you can update a blinker's on/off time and color values by setting up another BLINKER structure and then making the call with BLINKER_UPDATE. For example, if you want to alter the green blinker's parameters:

```
// set new parms
temp.on_time   = 100;
temp.off_time  = 200;
temp.on_color  = {255,255,0,PC_NOCOLLAPSE};
temp.off_color = {0,0,0,PC_NOCOLLAPSE};

// update blinker
Blink_Colors(BLINKER_UPDATE, temp, green_id);
```

That's enough of that! Check out DEMO7_15.CPP|EXE, which uses the Blink_Colors() function to make some of the lights on the starship image blink.

Color Rotation in 256-Color Modes

The next interesting color animation effect is called *color rotation* or *color shifting*. Basically, it's the process of taking a collection of adjacent color entries or registers and shifting them in a circular manner, as shown in Figure 7.37. Using this technique, you can make objects seem as if they're moving or shifting without writing a single pixel to the screen. It's great for simulating water or the motion of fluids. In addition, you can draw a number of images at different positions, each with a different color index. Then, if you rotate the colors, it will look like the object is moving. Great 3D *Star Wars* trenches can be created like this.

FIGURE 7.37
Color rotation.

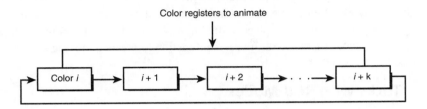

Color registers to animate

Each RGB Triple in the palette is
shifted into the next within
the range of rotation.

The code for color rotation is fairly trivial. Algorithmically, to rotate `color[c1]` to `color[c2]`, use the following code:

```
temp = color[c1];

for (int index = c1; index < c2; index++)
    color[c1] = color[c1+1];

// finish the cycle, close the loop
color[index] = temp;
```

Here's a function that implements the algorithm that I'm using for our library:

```
int Rotate_Colors(int start_index, int end_index)
{
// this function rotates the color between start and end

int colors = end_index - start_index + 1;

PALETTEENTRY work_pal[MAX_COLORS_PALETTE]; // working palette

// get the color palette
lpddpal->GetEntries(0,start_index,colors,work_pal);

// shift the colors
lpddpal->SetEntries(0,start_index+1,colors-1,work_pal);

// fix up the last color
lpddpal->SetEntries(0,start_index,1,&work_pal[colors - 1]);

// update shadow palette
lpddpal->GetEntries(0,0,MAX_COLORS_PALETTE,palette);

// return success
return(1);

} // end Rotate_Colors
```

Basically, the algorithm takes the starting and ending color index that you want to rotate and performs the rotation. Don't worry about the "shadow palettes" stuff; this is a library thing, so just focus on the logic. The interesting thing is how the algorithm works. It does the same thing as the FOR loop version, but in a different way. This is possible via an in-place shift. Anyway, for a demo of the function, take a look at DEMO7_16.CPP|EXE. It uses the function to create a moving stream of acid—water is for wimps!

Tricks with RGB Modes

The problem with RGB modes is that there isn't any color indirection. In other words, every pixel on the screen has its own RGB values, so there's no way to make a single change that affects the entire image. However, there are two ways to perform color-related processing:

- Using manual color transformations or lookup tables.
- Using the new DirectX color and gamma correction subsystems that perform real-time color manipulation on the primary surface.

TRICK	*Gamma correction* deals with the nonlinear response of a computer monitor to the input drive. In most cases, gamma correction allows you to modify the intensity or the brightness of the video signal. However, gamma correction can be performed separately on each red, green, and blue channel to obtain interesting effects.

Manual Color Transforms and Lookup Tables

At the very least, you can use the gamma correction system to perform filter operations on the entire image on the screen. Anyway, I'll talk about lookup tables in RGB modes first, and then discuss the DirectX gamma correction system.

When dealing with pixels that are encoded as RGB WORDs, there's really no way out of doing the work if you want to perform color animation. Not only must you write each pixel for which you want to change the color, but you may also have to read it. Hence, in the worst case you might have to perform a read, transform, and write cycle for each pixel you want to manipulate. There's simply no way around this.

However, help is available. In most cases, performing mathematical transformation in RGB space is very computationally expensive. For example, let's say that you want to simulate a square-shaped spotlight with a 16-bit graphics mode at location (x,y) with size (width, height). What would you do?

Well, you would begin by scanning out the rectangle of pixels that made up the spot-light area and storing them into a bitmap. Then, for each pixel in the bitmap, you would perform a color transform that looked something like this:

```
I*pixel(r,g,b) = pixel(I*r, I*g, I*b)
```

Three multiplies to modulate the intensity. Not to mention that you would have to first extract out the RGB components of the 16-bit WORD and then put the 16-bit RGB WORD back together after the transform. The trick here is to use a lookup table.

Instead of using all 65,536 colors available in 16-bit mode, you only draw objects that can possibly be illuminated with, say, 1,024 colors that are equally distributed throughout the 64KB color space. Then you create a lookup table that contains a 2D array that's 1,024 times however many levels of intensity you want, such as 64. Then you take the RGB level of each real color, compute 64 shades of it, and store each of them in the table. Then, when you create the spotlight, you use the 16-bit WORD as the index into the table, along with the light level as the second index, and the resulting 16-bit in the table is the RGB value premodulated! Hence, the lighting operation is a simple lookup.

This technique can be used for transparency, alpha-blending, lighting, darkening, and so on. I'm not going to show you a demo of it until the next chapter, but if you want to use lighting or color effects in 16-, 24-, or 32-bit color modes with any kind of speed, using lookup tables is the only way to go.

The New DirectX Color and Gamma Controls Interface

In DirectX 5.0, two new interfaces were added to help game programmers and video programmers gain more control over the color properties of the screen image without resorting to complex software algorithms. For example, it would seem to be a simple thing to add a little red to the image on the screen, change the tint, etc. But operations like these, which require nothing more than a turn of a knob on a television, are rather complex to perform with digital data in software. Thankfully, the two new interfaces IDirectDrawGammaControl and IDirectDrawColorControl let programmers make these changes with some very simple calls.

IDirectDrawColorControl is very similar to a TV interface and gives you control over the brightness, contrast, hue, saturation, sharpness, and general gamma. To use the interface, you must query for it from the primary surface pointer with the IID_IDirectDrawColorControl identifier. Once you have the interface, set up a DDCOLORCONTROL structure, shown here:

```
typedef struct _DDCOLORCONTROL
        {
        DWORD   dwSize;    // size of this struct
```

```
DWORD    dwFlags;    // indicates which fields are valid
LONG     lBrightness;
LONG     lContrast;
LONG     lHue;
LONG     lSaturation;
LONG     lSharpness;
LONG     lGamma;
LONG     lColorEnable;
DWORD    dwReserved1;
} DDCOLORCONTROL, FAR *LPDDCOLORCONTROL;
```

Next you make a call to IDIRECTDRAWCOLORCONTROL::SetColorControl(), and the primary surface will be immediately modified. The changes will remain in effect until you make another call.

```
HRESULT SetColorControl(LPDDCOLORCONTROL lpColorControl);
```

The gamma control is a little different. Instead of you setting all the TV-like settings, the gamma correction control gives you control over the red, green, and blue color ramps of the primary surface. In essence, the shape of the ramps you define determines the color response of red, green, and blue. The setup of an IDirectDrawGammaControl is similar to the color control, so I'm not going to cover it (as if I really covered the color control). Take a look at the DirectX SDK for more information on these subjects, because they can make a number of effects very easy to do, such as underwater scenes, screen flashes, lightness, darkness, and so on. The only problem is that they only work with hardware that supports them, and very few cards do—not one of mine does, so I can't make a demo!

Mixing GDI and DirectX

AAHAHAHAHAHAAHAHAHAHAH! Sorry, I just needed some tension relief. Now back to business. GDI, or the Graphics Device Interface, is the Win32 graphics subsystem responsible for all Windows rendering. You've already seen how to work with GDI in the previous sections on Windows programming, so I'm not going to reiterate device contexts and such.

To use GDI with DirectDraw, all you need to do is retrieve a compatible DC from DirectDraw and then use it like you'd use the DC from the standard GetDC() call. The cool thing is that once you retrieve a GDI-compatible DC from DirectDraw, there's really no difference in how you use the GDI functions. In fact, all of your code will work almost without change!

Now, you may be wondering how GDI can work with DirectDraw if DirectDraw takes over the graphics system, as it does in full-screen mode. Well, Windows can't use GDI to draw on any of your DirectDraw surfaces while in exclusive mode, but *you* can. This is the important detail that confuses many newbies to DirectX. In general, Windows sends messages to its subsystems like GDI, MCI, and so on. If DirectX has control of the hardware systems and is sharing them exclusively, the messages won't be processed. For example, a GDI graphics call to draw something while in full-screen mode will be dumped.

However, you can always use the software of the subsystems to do work for you because you're the one in charge. It's like a plasma blaster that's encoded to your DNA; if I pick it up it won't fire, but it will if you pick it up. So the user dictates when the blaster works, but the blaster is always functional. Weird example, huh? You try not sleeping for weeks—it's going to get weirder <BG>.

Because you do all your drawing on surfaces, you would assume that there's a way to get a GDI-compatible DC from a DirectDraw surface, and there is. The name of the function is `IDIRECTDRAWSURFACE7::GetDC()` and it's shown here:

```
HRESULT GetDC(HDC FAR *lphDC);
```

All you do is make a call with some storage for the DC, and you're good to go. Here's an example:

```
LPDIRECTDRAWSURFACE7 lpdds; // assume this is valid

HDC xdc; // I like calling DirectX DC XDC's

if (FAILED(lpdds->GetDC(&xdc)))
    { /* error */ }

// do what you will with the DC...
```

Once you're done with the DirectDraw-compatible DC, you must release it just as you would a normal GDI DC. The function is `IDIRECTDRAWSURFACE7::ReleaseDC()` and is shown here:

```
HRESULT ReleaseDC(HDC hDC);

Basically, just send it the DC you retrieved like this:

if (FAILED(lpdds->ReleaseDC(xdc)))
    { /* error */ }
```

WARNING If a surface is locked, `GetDC()` won't work on it because `GetDC()` also locks the surface. In addition, once you get the DC from a surface, make sure you `ReleaseDC()` as soon as you're done because `GetDC()` creates an internal lock on the surface, and you won't be able to access it. In essence, only GDI or DirectDraw can write to a surface at any time, not both.

For an example of using GDI, take a look at DEMO7_17.CPP|EXE. It creates a full-screen DirectDraw application in 640x480x256 and then prints GDI text at random locations. The code that prints the text is shown here:

```
int Draw_Text_GDI(char *text, int x,int y,
                  COLORREF color, LPDIRECTDRAWSURFACE7 lpdds)
{
// this function draws the sent text on the sent surface
// using color index as the color in the palette

HDC xdc; // the working dc

// get the dc from surface
if (FAILED(lpdds->GetDC(&xdc)))
   return(0);

// set the colors for the text up
SetTextColor(xdc,color);

// set background mode to transparent so black isn't copied
SetBkMode(xdc, TRANSPARENT);

// draw the text a
TextOut(xdc,x,y,text,strlen(text));

// release the dc
lpdds->ReleaseDC(xdc);

// return success
return(1);
} // end Draw_Text_GDI
```

TRICK

Please note that color is in the form of a COLORREF. This is a very important performance issue. COLORREFs are 24-bit RGB-encoded structures, meaning that the requested color is always in 24-bit RGB form. The problem with this is that when DirectX is in palettized mode, it must hunt for the nearest match to the requested color. This is in addition to the slow speed of GDI in general, which makes text printing using GDI very slow. I highly recommend writing your own text blitter for any speed-intensive text printing.

The function does all the manipulation of the DC itself, so all you have to do is call it. For example, to print out "You da Man!" at (100,100) in pure green on the primary surface, you would write

```
Draw_Text_GDI("You da Man!",
              100,100,
              RGB(0,255,0),
              lpddsprimary);
```

Before moving on, I want to talk a little about when to use GDI. In general, GDI is slow. I usually use it during development to print text, draw GUI stuff, and so on. Also, it's very useful for slow emulation during development. For example, let's say that you're planning to write a really fast line-drawing algorithm called `Draw_Line()`. You might not have time to do it yet, but you can always emulate `Draw_Line()` with GDI calls. That way at least you get something on the screen, and later you can write the fast line-drawing algorithm.

Getting the Lowdown on DirectDraw

As you've been learning, DirectDraw is a rather complex graphics system. It has a number of interfaces, each with numerous functions. The main point of DirectDraw is the utilization of hardware in a uniform manner. Therefore, it pays for game programmers to be able to query various DirectDraw interfaces for their states and/or capabilities so that the proper action can be taken. For example, when you're creating surfaces, you might want to first find out how much VRAM is available so you can optimize the creation order. Or maybe you want to use hardware rotation, but first you need to make sure it's available. The list of details that you might be interested in adding to the system your game is running goes on and on. Hence, there are a number of capability-testing functions, named `GetCaps()` or `Get*()` in general, available on each of the main interfaces. Let's take a look at the most useful `GetCaps()` functions.

The Main DirectDraw Object

The DirectDraw object itself represents the video card and describes the HEL and HAL. The function of interest is called `IDIRECTDRAW7::GetCaps()`:

```
HRESULT GetCaps(
  LPDDCAPS lpDDDriverCaps,   // ptr to storage for HAL caps
  LPDDCAPS lpDDHELCaps);     // ptr to storage for HEL caps
```

This function can be used to retrieve both the HEL and HAL capabilities. Then you can review the `DDCAPS` structures returned for the data of interest. For example, here's how you would query for both the HAL and HEL:

```
DDCAPS hel_caps, hal_caps;

// initialize the structures
DDRAW_INIT_STRUCT(hel_caps);
DDRAW_INIT_STRUCT(hal_caps);

// make the call
if (FAILED(lpdd->GetCaps(&hal_caps, &hel_caps)))
    return(0);
```

At this point you would index into either `hel_caps` or `hal_caps` and check things out. Here's what DDCAPS looks like:

```
typedef struct _DDCAPS
    {
    DWORD    dwSize;
    DWORD    dwCaps;                            // driver-specific caps
    DWORD    dwCaps2;                           // more driver-specific caps
    DWORD    dwCKeyCaps;                        // color key caps
    DWORD    dwFXCaps;                          // stretching and effects caps
    DWORD    dwFXAlphaCaps;                     // alpha caps
    DWORD    dwPalCaps;                         // palette caps
    DWORD    dwSVCaps;                          // stereo vision caps
    DWORD    dwAlphaBltConstBitDepths;          // alpha bit-depth members
    DWORD    dwAlphaBltPixelBitDepths;          //  .
    DWORD    dwAlphaBltSurfaceBitDepths;        //  .
    DWORD    dwAlphaOverlayConstBitDepths;      //  .
    DWORD    dwAlphaOverlayPixelBitDepths;      //  .
    DWORD    dwAlphaOverlaySurfaceBitDepths;    //  .
    DWORD    dwZBufferBitDepths;                // Z-buffer bit depth
    DWORD    dwVidMemTotal;                     // total video memory
    DWORD    dwVidMemFree;                      // total free video memory
    DWORD    dwMaxVisibleOverlays;              // maximum visible overlays
    DWORD    dwCurrVisibleOverlays;             // overlays currently visible
    DWORD    dwNumFourCCCodes;                  // number of supported FOURCC codes
    DWORD    dwAlignBoundarySrc;                // overlay alignment restrictions
    DWORD    dwAlignSizeSrc;                    //  .
    DWORD    dwAlignBoundaryDest;               //  .
    DWORD    dwAlignSizeDest;                   //  .
    DWORD    dwAlignStrideAlign;                // stride alignment
    DWORD    dwRops[DD_ROP_SPACE];              // supported raster ops
    DWORD    dwReservedCaps;                    // reserved
    DWORD    dwMinOverlayStretch;               // overlay stretch factors
    DWORD    dwMaxOverlayStretch;               //  .
    DWORD    dwMinLiveVideoStretch;             // obsolete
    DWORD    dwMaxLiveVideoStretch;             //  .
    DWORD    dwMinHwCodecStretch;               //  .
    DWORD    dwMaxHwCodecStretch;               //  .
    DWORD    dwReserved1;                       // reserved
    DWORD    dwReserved2;                       //  .
    DWORD    dwReserved3;                       //  .
    DWORD    dwSVBCaps;                         // system-to-video
                                               // blit related caps
    DWORD    dwSVBCKeyCaps;                     //  .
    DWORD    dwSVBFXCaps;                       //  .
    DWORD    dwSVBRops[DD_ROP_SPACE];           //  .
    DWORD    dwVSBCaps;                         // video-to-system
                                               // blit related caps
    DWORD    dwVSBCKeyCaps;                     //  .
    DWORD    dwVSBFXCaps;                       //  .
    DWORD    dwVSBRops[DD_ROP_SPACE];           //  .
    DWORD    dwSSBCaps;                         // system-to-system
                                               // blit related caps
```

```
    DWORD      dwSSBCKeyCaps;             //  .
    DWORD      dwSSBCFXCaps;              //  .
    DWORD      dwSSBRops[DD_ROP_SPACE];   //  .
    DWORD      dwMaxVideoPorts;           // maximum number of
                                          // live video ports
    DWORD      dwCurrVideoPorts;          // current number of
                                          // live video ports
    DWORD      dwSVBCaps2;                // additional
                                          // system-to-video blit caps
    DWORD      dwNLVBCaps;                // nonlocal-to-local
                                          // video memory blit caps
    DWORD      dwNLVBCaps2;               //  .
    DWORD      dwNLVBCKeyCaps;            //  .
    DWORD      dwNLVBFXCaps;              //  .
    DWORD      dwNLVBRops[DD_ROP_SPACE];  //  .
    DDSCAPS2 ddsCaps;                     // general surface caps
    } DDCAPS,FAR* LPDDCAPS;
```

Describing each field would require another book, so look it up in the SDK. Most of them are fairly obvious. For example, DDCAPS.dwVidMemFree is one of my favorite members because it indicates the amount of real VRAM that's available for use as surfaces.

There's also another function that I like to use, called GetDisplayMode(). It's useful in figuring out the mode that the system is in when running in windowed mode. Here's the prototype:

```
HRESULT GetDisplayMode(LPDDSURFACEDESC2 lpDDSurfaceDesc2);
```

And you've seen a DDSURFACEDESC2 structure before, so you know what to do there.

> **NOTE**
>
> In most cases, all DirectX data structures are used to write as well as to read. In other words, you may set up a data structure to create an object, but when you want to know about an object via a GetCaps() call, the object will fill in the same data structure with the data of object.

Surfing on Surfaces

Most of the time, you couldn't care less about finding out the properties of a surface that you've created because you already know (you did create the darn thing)! However, the properties of the primary and back buffer surfaces are of utmost importance because they give you insight into the hardware properties of each. The function (or "method," if you're anal-retentive) that tells you about the general surface capabilities is IDIRECTDRAWSURFACE7::GetCaps():

```
HRESULT GetCaps(LPDDSCAPS2 lpDDSCaps);
```

This function returns a standard DDSCAPS2 structure, which you've seen before. Just open it up and pour it out!

The next surface-related function of interest is called `IDIRECTDRAWSURFACE7::` `GetSurfaceDesc()`. It returns a `DDSURFACEDESC2` structure, which has a little more detail about the surface itself. Here's the prototype:

```
HRESULT GetSurfaceDesc(LPDDSURFACEDESC2 lpDDSurfaceDesc);
```

There's also a `IDIRECTDRAWSURFACE7::GetPixelFormat()` method, but I've talked about this before, and `GetSurfaceDesc()` returns the pixel format in `DDSURFACEDESC2.` `ddpfPixelFormat` anyway.

Playing with Palettes

There's not much to talk about when it comes to palettes. DirectDraw only gives you a bit-encoded `WORD` that describes the abilities of any given palette. The function is called `IDIRECTDRAWPALETTE::GetCaps()` and is shown here:

```
HRESULT GetCaps(LPDWORD lpdwCaps);
```

`lpdwCaps` is a bit-encoded `WORD` with the values in Table 7.7.

TABLE 7.7 Possible Flags for Palette Capabilities

Value	Description
DDPCAPS_1BIT	Supports 1-bit color palettes.
DDPCAPS_2BIT	Supports 2-bit color palettes.
DDPCAPS_4BIT	Supports 4-bit color palettes.
DDPCAPS_8BIT	Supports 8-bit color palettes.
DDPCAPS_8BITENTRIES	Palette is an index palette.
DDPCAPS_ALPHA	Supports an alpha component with each palette entry.
DDPCAPS_ALLOW256	All 256 colors can be defined.
DDPCAPS_PRIMARYSURFACE	Palette is attached to primary surface.
DDPCAPS_VSYNC	Palette can be modified synchronously with monitor's refresh.

Using DirectDraw in Windowed Modes

The last subject that I want to touch upon is using DirectDraw in windowed mode. The problem with windowed mode, as far as games go, is that you have very little control over the initial setting of the color depth and resolution. Writing DirectDraw applications that run full-screen is hard enough, but generalizing to a windowed mode is much more complex. You have to take into consideration that the user may start your application at any resolution and/or color depth. This means that the performance of your application may suffer. Not only that, but your game may be designed to work solely for 8- or 16-bit modes, and your code could fall apart completely if the user is in a higher color depth.

Although writing games that work in both windowed mode and full-screen mode is the best of both worlds, I'm going to stick to full-screen mode to simplify most of the work and demos. However, I may create a number of windowed applications that run specifically in 800x600 or higher resolutions with a color depth of 8 bits. This way you can more easily debug your DirectX application and/or have other output windows, including the graphics output. In any case, let's take a look at how to write a windowed DirectX application and how to manipulate the primary surface.

The first thing to know about windowed DirectDraw applications is that the primary surface is the entire screen display, not just your window! Take a look at Figure 7.38 to see this graphically. What this means is that you can't just write to the screen display blindly, or you'll end up mangling the client areas of other application windows. Of course, this may be your intent if you're writing a screen saver or other screen manipulation program. However, in most cases, you'll only want to write to the client area of your application's window. That means that somehow you must find the exact coordinates of your client window and then make sure only to draw in that area.

FIGURE 7.38
In windowed modes, the entire desktop is mapped to the DirectDraw primary surface.

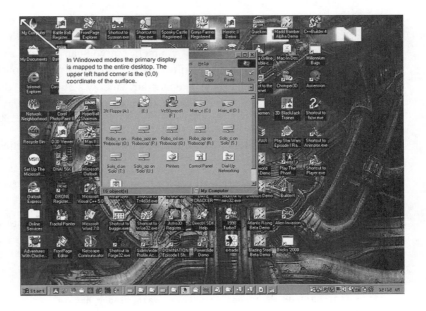

The second problem is with clipping. If you intend to use the Blt() function, it has no idea about your client window and will blit over the edges of the client window. This means that somehow you must tell the DirectDraw clipping system that you have a window on the screen so that it will make sure to clip to the window no matter where it's moved to or how it's sized.

This brings us to yet another problem—what if the window is moved or resized by the user? True, you can at least force the window to stay the same size, but movement is an absolute must. Otherwise, why even have a windowed application? To handle this, you must track the WM_SIZE and WM_MOVE messages.

The next problem is 8-bit palettes. If the video mode is 8-bit mode and you want to change the palette, you're in for trouble. Windows has a Palette Manager that you must appease if you're going to mess with the 8-bit palette, because you'll probably make all other Windows applications look ugly. In most cases, you can change the palette, but it's a good idea to leave about 20 of the palette entries alone (the Windows and system colors) so the Palette Manager can make the other applications look something like what they're supposed to.

Finally, the most obvious problems are those of bit blitting and pixel manipulation based on varying modes. Hence, you have to write code that handles all color depths if you really want to be robust.

So I'll begin with the details of getting into a windowed mode. You already know how to do this! The only difference is that you don't set the video mode or create a secondary back buffer. You're not allowed to page flip in windowed modes. You must either use the blitter to double buffer or do it yourself, but you can't set up a complex surface chain and then call Flip(). It won't work. No problem, really; you'll just create another surface that's the same size as your window's client area, draw on it, and blit it to the client area of your window on the primary buffer. That way you can avoid screen flicker.

Let me show you the code to create a windowed DirectDraw application. First, the DirectDraw initialization:

```
LPDIRECTDRAW7 lpdd = NULL; // used to hold the IDIRECTDRAW7 interface

// create the IDirectDraw7 interface
if (FAILED(DirectDrawCreateEx(NULL, (void **)&lpdd, IID_IDirectDraw7, NULL)))
   return(0);



// set cooperation to full screen
if (FAILED(lpdd->SetCooperativeLevel(main_window_handle, DDSCL_NORMAL)))
   return(0);

// clear ddsd and set size
DDRAW_INIT_STRUCT(ddsd);

// enable valid fields
ddsd.dwFlags = DDSD_CAPS;

// request primary surface
ddsd.ddsCaps.dwCaps = DDSCAPS_PRIMARYSURFACE;
```

```
// create the primary surface
if (FAILED(lpdd->CreateSurface(&ddsd, &lpddsprimary, NULL)))
   return(0);
```

The key thing here is the cooperation level setting. Notice that it's DDSCL_NORMAL, rather than the usual (DDSCL_FULLSCREEN | DDSCL_ALLOWMODEX | DDSCL_EXCLUSIVE | DDSCL_ALLOWREBOOT) that you've been using for full-screen modes.

Also, when you're creating the application window, you'll want to use WS_OVERLAPPED or maybe WS_OVERLAPPEDWINDOW rather than WS_POPUP. The WS_POPUP style creates a window without any title, controls, and so on. WS_OVERLAPPED creates a window with a title, but it can't be resized, and the WS_OVERLAPPEDWINDOW style creates a fully functional window with all the controls. However, in most cases I like to use WS_OVERLAPPED because I don't want to deal with the resizing problem—it's up to you.

For an example of what you know so far, take a look at DEMO7_18.CPP|EXE. It basically creates a windowed DirectX application with a client window that's 400x400, along with a primary surface.

Drawing Pixels in a Window

Okay, now let's move on to accessing the client area of the window. There are two things to remember: The primary surface is the entire screen, and you don't know the color depth. Let's look at the first problem—finding the client area of the window.

Because the user can move a window anywhere on the screen, the client coordinates are always changing—that is, if you think in terms of absolute coordinates. You need to find a way to figure out the upper-left corner of the client area in screen coordinates and then use that as your origin for pixel plotting. The function you need to use (which I've mentioned before) is GetWindowRect():

```
BOOL GetWindowRect(HWND hWnd,   // handle of window
                   LPRECT lpRect);  // address of structure
                                    // for window coordinates
```

> **WARNING** GetWindowRect() actually retrieves the coordinates of your entire window, including the controls and border. I'll show you how to figure out the exact client coordinates in a bit, but keep that in mind...

When you send the window handle of your application window, the function returns the screen coordinates of the client area of your window in lpRect. So all you need to do is call this function to retrieve the upper-left corner of your window in screen coordinates. Of course, every time the window moves, the coordinates change, so you must call GetWindowRect() every frame or when you receive a WM_MOVE message. I prefer calling the function once a frame since there's no reason to process more Window's messages then you have to!

Now that you know the screen coordinates of your window's client area, you're ready to manipulate the pixels. But wait a minute—what's the pixel format?

I'm glad you asked, because you know the answer! That's right, you need to use the `GetPixelFormat()` function at the beginning of your program to determine the color depth and then, based on this, make calls to different pixel plotting functions. So somewhere in your program, maybe in `Game_Init()` after setting up DirectDraw, you should make a call to `GetPixelFormat()` from the primary surface, like this:

```
int pixel_format = 0;        // global to hold the bpp
DDPIXELFORMAT ddpixelformat; // hold the pixel format

// clean out the structure and set it up
DDRAW_INIT_STRUCT(ddpixelformat);

// get the pixel format
lpddsprimary->GetPixelFormat(&ddpixelformat);

// set global pixel format
pixel_format = ddpixelformat.dwRGBBitCount;
```

Then, once you know the pixel format, you can use some conditional logic, function pointers, or virtual functions to set the pixel plotting function to the correct color depth. To keep things simple, you'll just use some conditional logic that tests the global `pixel_format` variable before plotting. Here's some code that plots random pixels at random locations in the client area of the window:

```
DDSURFACEDESC2 ddsd;    // directdraw surface description
RECT           client;  // used to hold client rectangle

// get the window's client rectangle in screen coordinates
GetWindowRect(main_window_handle, &client);

// initialize structure
DDRAW_INIT_STRUCT(ddsd);

// lock the primary surface
lpddsprimary->Lock(NULL,&ddsd,
               DDLOCK_SURFACEMEMORYPTR | DDLOCK_WAIT,NULL);

// get video pointer to primary surface
// cast to UCHAR * since we don't know what we are
// dealing with yet and I like bytes :)
UCHAR *primary_buffer = (UCHAR *)ddsd.lpSurface;

// what is the color depth?
if (pixel_format == 32)
   {
   // draw 10 random pixels in 32 bit mode
   for (int index=0; index<10; index++)
       {
```

```
                int x=rand()%(client.right - client.left) + client.left;
                int y=rand()%(client.bottom - client.top) + client.top;
                DWORD color = __RGB32BIT(0,rand()%256, rand()%256, rand()%256);
                *((DWORD *)(primary_buffer + x*4 + y*ddsd.lPitch)) = color;
                } // end for index
        } // end if 24 bit

    else
    if (pixel_format == 24)
        {
        // draw 10 random pixels in 24 bit mode (very rare???)
        for (int index=0; index<10; index++)
            {
            int x=rand()%(client.right - client.left) + client.left;
            int y=rand()%(client.bottom - client.top) + client.top;
            ((primary_buffer + x*3 + y*ddsd.lPitch))[0] = rand()%256;
            ((primary_buffer + x*3 + y*ddsd.lPitch))[1] = rand()%256;
            ((primary_buffer + x*3 + y*ddsd.lPitch))[2] = rand()%256;
            } // end for index
        } // end if 24 bit
    else
    if (pixel_format == 16)
        {
        // draw 10 random pixels in 16 bit mode
        for (int index=0; index<10; index++)
            {
            int x=rand()%(client.right - client.left) + client.left;
            int y=rand()%(client.bottom - client.top) + client.top;
            USHORT color = __RGB16BIT565(rand()%256, rand()%256, rand()%256);
            *((USHORT *)(primary_buffer + x*2 + y*ddsd.lPitch)) = color;
            } // end for index
        } // end if 16 bit
    else
        {// assume 8 bits per pixel
        // draw 10 random pixels in 8 bit mode
        for (int index=0; index<10; index++)
            {
            int x=rand()%(client.right - client.left) + client.left;
            int y=rand()%(client.bottom - client.top) + client.top;
            UCHAR color = rand()%256;
            primary_buffer[x + y*ddsd.lPitch] = color;
            } // end for index
        } // end else

// unlock primary buffer
lpddsprimary->Unlock(NULL);
```

TRICK   Of course, this code is an optimization nightmare, and it hurts me to even show you such slow, crude, troglodyte code, but it's easy to understand. In real life, you would use function pointers or a virtual function, completely remove all multiplies and mods, and use incremental addressing. Anyway, just wanted to indemnify myself <BG>.

For an example of plotting pixels in any color depth, take a look at `DEMO7_19.CPP|EXE`. It creates a 400x400 window and then plots pixels in the client area (well, almost). Try running the program with different color depths, and notice that it still works! When you're done, come back and I'll talk about rendering more accurately to the actual interior client area…

Finding the Real Client Area (51)

The problem with windows is that when you create a window using `CreateWindow()` or `CreateWindowEx()`, you're specifying the total width and size of the window, including any controls. Hence, if you create a blank `WS_POPUP` window without any controls, the size of the window is exactly the size of the client area. Presto—no drama. On the other hand, the second you add controls, menus, borders, whatever, and make the call to `CreateWindowEx()`, Windows shrinks the interior client area so that it can fit in all the controls. The result: a working area that's less than what you desired. Figure 7.39 illustrates this cosmic dilemma. The solution is to resize your window taking into consideration the border, controls, etc.

FIGURE 7.39
A window's client area is smaller than the window surrounding it.

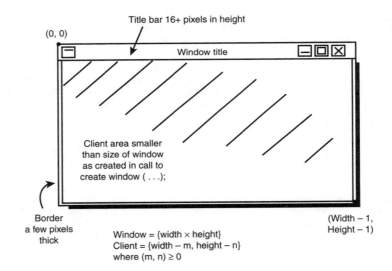

For example, let's say you want a window that has a working area of 640x480, but you want to also have a border, a menu, and standard window controls. What you need to do is calculate how many pixels all the extra Windows gadgetry takes in the X and Y direction, and then simply increase the size of your window until the working client area is the desired size. The magical function that computes the size of a window with various styles is called `AdjustWindowRectEx()` and is shown here:

```
BOOL AdjustWindowRectEx(
    LPRECT lpRect,     // pointer to client-rectangle structure
    DWORD  dwStyle,    // window styles
```

```
    BOOL    bMenu,      // menu-present flag
    DWORD   dwExStyle);// extended style
```

You fill in all the parameters, and the function resizes the structure data sent in `lpRect` to take into consideration all the extra styles and flags for the window. To use the function, you first set up a `RECT` structure with the desired client area size, say, 640x480. Then you make the call, along with all the proper parameters you created the original window with. However, I never can remember what I set the window to, or the exact names of the flags, so you can ask Windows to tell you what you did and save some neurons. Here's the call, along with the window's helper functions that query the styles based on the `HWND` that you send:

```
// the client size we desire
RECT window_rect = {0,0,640,480};

// make the call to adjust window_rect
AdjustWindowRectEx(&window_rect,
    GetWindowStyle(main_window_handle),
    GetMenu(main_window_handle) != NULL,
    GetWindowExStyle(main_window_handle));

// now resize the window with a call to MoveWindow()
MoveWindow(main_window_handle,
        CW_USEDEFAULT, // x position
        CW_USEDEFAULT, // y position
        window_rect.right - window_rect.left, // width
        window_rect.bottom - window_rect.top, // height
        FALSE);
```

And that's it, baby! The above code will be very crucial when we create the 16-bit library for the engine, since when we request a 640x480 or whatever size window, we mean the client area needs to be that big, thus the window *MUST* always be resized if it has any controls taking up client area.

Clipping a DirectX Window

Now we're getting somewhere! The next piece of the DirectDraw windowed mode conundrum is to get the clipping working. Make sure that you understand that clipping only matters to the blitter; it has no effect on what you do directly with the primary surface since the primary surface is actually the *entire* video screen, yes that's how you draw all over the Windows desktop.

You've seen the `IDIRECTDRAWCLIPPER` interface before, so I'm not going to belabor it anymore. (I still have the shakes from figuring out the exact nature of the coordinates in a `RECT` structure.) The first thing you need to do is create a DirectDraw clipper, like this:

```
LPDIRECTDRAWCLIPPER lpddclipper = NULL; // hold the clipper

if (FAILED(lpdd->CreateClipper(0,&lpddclipper,NULL)))
    return(0);
```

Next, you must attach the clipper to your application's window with
IDIRECTDRAWCLIPPER::SetHWnd(). This associates the clipper to your window and
handles all the details for sizing and movement for you. In fact, you don't even have
to send a clipping list at all; it's all automatic. The function is so simple. Here's the
prototype:

```
HRESULT SetHWnd(DWORD dwFlags, // unused, set to 0
                HWND hWnd);     // app window handle
```

Here's the call to associate the clipper with your main window:

```
if (FAILED(lpddclipper->SetHWnd(0, main_window_handle)))
    return(0);
```

Next you have to associate the clipper with the surface you want to clip—in this case,
the primary surface. To do this, you use SetClipper(), which you've already seen:

```
if (FAILED(lpddsprimary->SetClipper(lpddclipper)))
    return(0);
```

WARNING

Now you're ready to rock. There's one little DirectX problem, though.
The reference count on the clipper is now at 2—1 for the creation, 2 for
the call to SetClipper(). This is fine, but destroying the surface won't
kill the clipper. You must make another call to lpddclipper->Release()
to kill it, after releasing the surface with a call to lpddsprimary-
>Release(). The bottom line is you might think that you killed the clip-
per with a call to lpddclipper->Release(), but that only reduces the
reference count to 1. Alas, Microsoft recommends that you make a call
to lpddclipper->Release() right after the preceding code sequence, so
that the reference count of lpddclipper is 1 as it should be—Whatever!

Remember that the clipping that's attached to the window only matters for blits to the
primary surface—that is, the contents of the window. But in most cases, you'll create
an offscreen surface to simulate a double buffer, blit to that, and then copy the offscreen
surface to the primary buffer using the blitter—a crude form of page flipping. Alas,
attaching the blitter to the primary buffer only helps if the blits you make to it (the
offscreen buffer) go out of bounds. And this will only occur if the user resizes.

Working with 8-Bit Windowed Modes

The last topic I want to touch upon is 8-bit windowed mode and the palette. To make
a long story short, you can't just create a palette, do anything you want with it, and
then attach it to the primary surface. You must work a little with the Windows Palette
Manager. Window palette management under GDI is beyond the scope of this book (I
always wanted to say that), and I don't feel like boring you with all the stupid details.
The bottom line is, if you run your game in windowed 256-color mode, you're going
to have fewer than 256 colors at your disposal.

Each application running on the desktop has a logical palette that contains the desired colors of the application. However, the *physical* palette is the one that really matters. The physical palette reflects the actual hardware palette, and this is the compromise that Windows works with. When your application gets the focus, your logical palette is *realized*—in other words, the Windows Palette Manager starts mapping your colors to the physical palette as best it can. Sometimes it does a good job, and sometimes it doesn't.

Moreover, the way you set up your logical palette's flags determines how much slack Windows has to work with. Finally, at the very least, Windows needs 20 colors out of the palette: the first and last 10. These are reserved for Windows colors and are the bare minimum to make Windows applications look reasonable. The trick to creating a 256-color mode windowed application is restraining your artwork to 236 colors or less—so you have room for the Windows colors—and then setting the palette flags of your logical palette appropriately. Windows will then leave them alone when your palette is realized.

Here's the code that creates a generic palette. You can change the code to use your own RGB value for the entries from 10 to 245, inclusive. This code simply makes them all gray:

```
LPDIRECTDRAW7          lpdd;  // this is already setup
PALETTEENTRY           palette[256]; // holds palette data
LPDIRECTDRAWPALETTE    lpddpal = NULL; // palette interface

// first set up the windows static entries
// note it's irrelevant what we make them
for (int index = 0; index < 10 ; index++)
    {
    // the first 10 static entries
    palette[index].peFlags = PC_EXPLICIT;
    palette[index].peRed   = index;
    palette[index].peGreen = 0;
    palette[index].peBlue  = 0;

    // The last 10 static entries:
    palette[index+246].peFlags = PC_EXPLICIT;
    palette[index+246].peRed   = index+246;
    palette[index+246].peGreen = 0;
    palette[index+246].peBlue  = 0;
    }   // end for index

// Now set up our entries. You would load these from
// a file etc., but for now we'll make them grey
for (index = 10; index < 246; index ++)
    {
    palette[index].peFlags = PC_NOCOLLAPSE;
    palette[index].peRed   = 64;
    palette[index].peGreen = 64;
    palette[index].peBlue  = 64;
```

```
    }  // end for index

// Create the palette.
if (FAILED(lpdd->CreatePalette(DDPCAPS_8BIT, palette,
    &lpddpal,NULL)))
{ /* error */ }

// attach the palette to the primary surface...
```

Notice the use of PC_EXPLICIT and PC_NOCOLLAPSE. PC_EXPLICIT means "these colors map to hardware," and PC_NOCOLLAPSE means "don't try to map these colors to other entries; leave them as they are." If you wanted to animate some color registers, you would also logically OR the flag PC_RESERVED. This tells the palette manager not to map other Windows applications colors to the entry because it may change at any time.

Summary

Without a doubt, this has been one of the longest chapters in the book. Hey, sue me! There was just a lot of material to cover. I could still keep going, but I want to leave some trees in the rain forest!

I've covered all kinds of stuff, including high-color modes, the blitter, clipping, color keys, sampling theory, windowed DirectDraw, GDI, and querying information from DirectDraw. Also, I'm done with the T3DLIB1.CPP|H library. You can check it out now if you want, or you can wait until the end of the next chapter when I go through each function.

In the next chapter, I'm going to take a break from DirectDraw for a bit (although it returns at the end of the chapter) and I'm going to cover some vector-based 2D geometry, transformations, and rasterization theory.

CHAPTER 8

Vector Rasterization and 2D Transformations

"There are a lot worse things out than vampires tonight"
—Blade

This chapter will cover vector topics, such as how to draw lines and polygons, and will show you how to finish off the first module of the T3DLIB game library. This is the first chapter that pours on the math, but if you take your time, there shouldn't be anything you can't handle with a little effort. About the hardest thing I'm going to talk about is matrices. (It's just an introduction so that when you get to the 3D material on the CD, matrix math won't look totally alien.) Also, by popular request, I'm going to give you some ideas on how to do scrolling and even isometric 3D engines. Here's the hit list for this chapter:

- Drawing lines
- Clipping
- Matrices
- 2D transformation
- Drawing polygons

- Scrolling and ISO 3D engines
- Timing
- The T3DLIB version 1.1

Drawing Lines

Up to this point, you've drawn all of your graphical objects with either single points or bitmaps. Both of these entities are considered non-vector entities. A vector entity is something like a line or a polygon, as shown in Figure 8.1. So your first problem is figuring out how to draw a line.

FIGURE 8.1

A vector/line-based object.

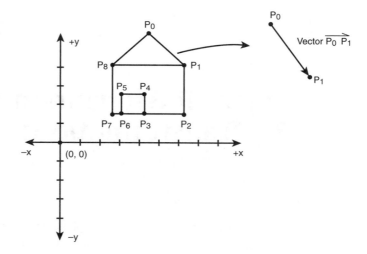

You may think that drawing a line is trivial, but I assure you it's not. Drawing a line on a computer screen has a number of problems associated with it, such as finite resolution, mapping real numbers onto an integer grid, speed issues, and so forth. In many cases, a 2D or 3D image is composed of a number of points that define the polygons or faces that make up an object or scene. These points are usually in the form of real numbers, such as (10.5, 120.3) and so on.

The first problem is that a computer screen is represented by a 2D grid of whole numbers, so plotting (10.5, 120.3) is almost impossible. You can only approximate it. You might decide to truncate the coordinates and plot (10,120), or you might decide to round them and plot (11,120). Finally, you might go high-tech and decide to perform a weighted pixel plotting function that plots a number of pixels of differing intensities centered at the pixel center (10.5, 120.3), as shown in Figure 8.2.

FIGURE 8.2
Area filtering a single
pixel.

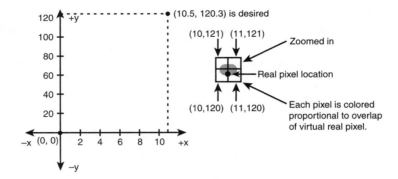

Basically, an area filter computes how much the original pixel overlaps into the other
pixel positions and then draws those pixels in the same color as the desired pixel, but
with decreased intensity. This creates a much rounder-looking pixel that looks anti-
aliased, but in general you have lowered your maximum resolution.

Instead of me jabbering on about line-drawing algorithms, filtering, and such, let's get
to the cream pie and see a couple of really good line-drawing algorithms that you can
use to compute the integer coordinates of a line from $(x0,y0)$ to $(x1,y1)$.

Bresenham's Algorithm

The first algorithm I want to present you with is called *Bresenham's algorithm*, named
after the man who invented it in 1965. Originally, the algorithm was designed to draw
lines on plotters, but it was later adapted to computer graphics. Let's take a quick look
at how the algorithm works and then see some code. Figure 8.3 shows the general
problem you're trying to solve. You want to fill in the pixels from point p1 to p2 with
the pixels that most closely fit to the real line. This process is called *rasterization*.

FIGURE 8.3
Rasterizing a line.

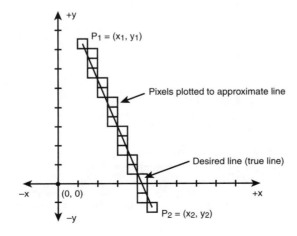

If you're a little rusty on lines, let me refresh your memory. The slope of a line is related to the angle that the line makes with the x-axis. Hence, a line with slope 0 is totally horizontal, while a line with infinite slope is totally vertical. A line with slope 1.0 is diagonal or 45 degrees. Slope is defined as rise over run, or, mathematically:

```
        Rise      Change in y    dy        (y1-y0)
Slope = ------ = ------------- ---- = m = ---------
        Run       Change in x    dx        (x1-x0)
```

For example, if you have a line with coordinates p0(1,2) and p1(5,22), the slope or m is

```
(y2-y1)/(x2-x1) = (22-2)/(5-1) = 20/4 = 5.0
```

So what does the slope really mean? It means that if you increment the x-coordinate by 1.0 unit, the y-coordinate will change by 5.0 units. Okay, this is the beginning of a rasterization algorithm. At this point, you have a rough idea of how to draw a line:

1. Compute the slope m.

2. Plot (x0,y0).

3. Advance x by 1.0 and then advance y by the slope m. Add this value to (x0,y0).

4. Repeat steps 2–4 until done.

Figure 8.4 shows this example for the previous values of p0 and p1.

FIGURE 8.4
A first attempt at rasterization.

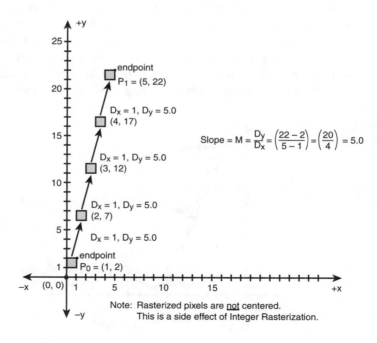

$$\text{Slope} = M = \frac{D_y}{D_x} = \left(\frac{22-2}{5-1}\right) = \left(\frac{20}{4}\right) = 5.0$$

Note: Rasterized pixels are not centered.
This is a side effect of Integer Rasterization.

Do you see the problem? Every time you step one pixel in x, you step 5.0 pixels in y. Therefore, you're drawing a line that has a lot of holes in it! The mistake you're making is not tracing a line, but plotting pixels as integer intervals; that is, whenever x is a whole number. In essence, you're plugging whole numbers into the equation of a line:

```
(y-y0) = m*(x-x0)
```

Here, (x,y) are the current values or pixel locations, (x0,y0) is the starting point, and m is the slope. Rearranging this a little, you have

```
y = m*(x-x0)+y0
```

So, if you let (x0,y0) be (1,2) and m be 5 as in the example, you get the following results:

```
x          y = 5*(x-1)+2
- - - - - - - - - - - - - - - - - - - - - - - - - -
1          2 (starting point)
2          7
3          12
4          17
5          22 (ending point)
```

Now, you might ask if the slope-intercept form of a line can help:

```
y = m*x + b
```

Here, b is the point where the line intercepts the y-axis. Again, though, this doesn't do you any good. The fundamental problem is that you're moving x by 1.0 each cycle. You have to move it by a much smaller amount, such as 0.01, so that you catch all the pixels and don't skip any, or else you have to try a different approach. Astute readers will realize that now matter how small you step x, you can always find a slope that will make it skip. You need to try something else—this is the basis of Bresenham's algorithm.

In a nutshell, Bresenham's algorithm starts at (x0,y0), but instead of using the slope to move, it moves x by one pixel and then decides which way to move the y component so that the line it's tracing out matches the true line as closely as possible. This is accomplished with an error term that tracks the closeness of the line being rasterized to the true line. The algorithm continually updates the error term and tries to keep the digital rasterized line as close as possible.

The algorithm basically works in quadrant I of the Cartesian plane, and the other quadrants are derived with reflections. In addition, the algorithm considers two kinds of lines: lines with slope less than 45 degrees, or m < 1, and lines with slope greater than 45 degrees, or m > 1. I like to call these x-dominate and y-dominate, respectively. Here's some pseudocode for an x-dominate line p0(x0,y0) and p1(x1, y1):

```
// initialize starting point
x = x0;
y = y0;

// compute deltas
dx = x1 - x0;
dy = y1 - y0;

// initialize error term
error = 0;

// draw line
for (int index = 0; index < dx; index++)
    {
    // plot the pixel
    Plot_Pixel(x,y,color);

    // adjust the error
    error+=dy;

    // test the error
    if (error > dx)
        {
        // adjust error
        error-=dx;

        // move up to next line
        y--;

        } // end if

    } // end for index
```

That's it! Of course, this is only for the first octant, but all the others are taken care of simply by checking signs and switching values. The algorithm is the same.

There's one point I want to make before I show you the code, and it's about accuracy. The algorithm continually minimizes the error between the rasterized line and the true line, but the starting conditions could be a little better. You see, you're starting the error term at 0.0. This is actually incorrect. It would be better to somehow take into consideration the first pixel position and then set the error a little better so that it straddles the minimum and maximum error. This can be done by setting the error term to 0.5, but because you're using integers you must scale this by 2 and then add in the contribution from dx and dy. The bottom line is, you're going to change the final algorithm to set the error to something like this:

```
// x-dominate
error = 2*dy - dx

// y-dominate
error = 2*dx - dy
```

And then you're going to scale the error accumulation by two accordingly. Here's the final algorithm, implemented as a function from your library called Draw_Line(). Notice that it takes both of the endpoints, color, video buffer, and video pitch and draws the line:

```
int Draw_Line(int x0, int y0, // starting position
              int x1, int y1, // ending position
              UCHAR color,    // color index
              UCHAR *vb_start,
              int lpitch) // video buffer and memory pitch
{
// this function draws a line from xo,yo to x1,y1
// using differential error
// terms (based on Bresenhams work)

int dx,         // difference in x's
    dy,         // difference in y's
    dx2,        // dx,dy * 2
    dy2,
    x_inc,      // amount in pixel space to move during drawing
    y_inc,      // amount in pixel space to move during drawing
    error,      // the discriminant i.e. error i.e. decision variable
    index;      // used for looping

// precompute first pixel address in video buffer
vb_start = vb_start + x0 + y0*lpitch;

// compute horizontal and vertical deltas
dx = x1-x0;
dy = y1-y0;

// test which direction the line is going in i.e. slope angle
if (dx>=0)
   {
   x_inc = 1;

   } // end if line is moving right
else
   {
   x_inc = -1;
   dx    = -dx;  // need absolute value

   } // end else moving left

// test y component of slope

if (dy>=0)
   {
   y_inc = lpitch;
   } // end if line is moving down
else
   {
```

```
        y_inc = -lpitch;
        dy    = -dy;  // need absolute value

        } // end else moving up

// compute (dx,dy) * 2
dx2 = dx << 1;
dy2 = dy << 1;

// now based on which delta is greater we can draw the line
if (dx > dy)
    {
    // initialize error term
    error = dy2 - dx;

    // draw the line
    for (index=0; index <= dx; index++)
        {
        // set the pixel
        *vb_start = color;

        // test if error has overflowed
        if (error >= 0)
            {
            error-=dx2;

            // move to next line
            vb_start+=y_inc;

            } // end if error overflowed

        // adjust the error term
        error+=dy2;

        // move to the next pixel
        vb_start+=x_inc;

        } // end for

    } // end if |slope| <= 1
else
    {
    // initialize error term
    error = dx2 - dy;

    // draw the line
    for (index=0; index <= dy; index++)
        {
        // set the pixel
        *vb_start = color;

        // test if error overflowed
```

```
        if (error >= 0)
            {
            error-=dy2;

            // move to next line
            vb_start+=x_inc;

            } // end if error overflowed

        // adjust the error term
        error+=dx2;

        // move to the next pixel
        vb_start+=y_inc;

        } // end for

    } // end else |slope| > 1

// return success
return(1);

} // end Draw_Line
```

NOTE This function works in 8-bit modes only. However, the library has a 16-bit version as well, with the name `Draw_Line16()`.

The function basically has three main sections. The first section does all the sign and endpoint swapping and computes the x and y axes' deltas. Then based on the dominance of the line, that is, if dx > dy, or dx <= dy, one of two main loops draws the line.

Speeding Up the Algorithm

Looking at the code, you might think that it's fairly tight and there's no room for optimization. However, there are a couple of ways to speed up the algorithm. The first way is to take into consideration that all lines are symmetrical about their midpoints, as shown in Figure 8.5, so there's no need to run the algorithm for the whole line. All you have to do is halve the line and copy the other half. In theory this is solid, but implementing it is a pain because you have to worry about lines that have an odd number of pixels and then decide to draw one extra pixel at either end. Not that it's hard—just *ugly*.

The other optimizations have been discovered by a number of people (including myself), including Michael Abrash's algorithm Run-Slicing, Xialon Wu's Symmetric Double Step, and Rokne's Quadruple Step. Basically, all these algorithms take advantage of the consistency of the pixel patterns that make up a line. The Run-Slicing algorithm takes advantage of the fact that sometimes large runs of pixels exist, such as the line (0,0) to (100,1). The line should consist of two runs of 50 pixels. One runs from (0-49,0) and the other runs from (50-100,1), as shown in Figure 8.6.

FIGURE 8.5
Lines are symmetrical
about their midpoints.

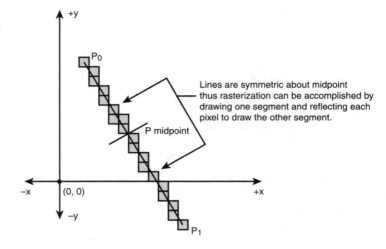

FIGURE 8.6
The Run-Slicing line
drawing optimization.

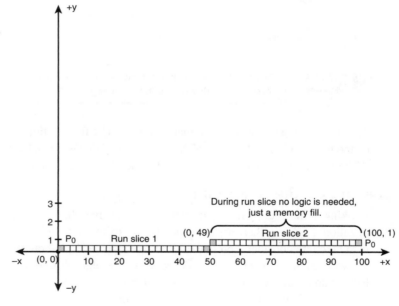

So what's the point in doing the line algorithm on each pixel? The problem is that the setup and the innards of the algorithm are very complex, but they work for lines with very large or very small slopes.

Wu's Symmetric Double Step algorithm works on a similar premise, but instead of considering runs, it notes that for every two pixels there are only four different patterns that can occur, as shown in Figure 8.7. It's fairly easy to compute the next pattern by looking at the error term and then plotting the entire pattern, in essence moving at twice normal speed. This, coupled with symmetry, gives you a speed increase of four times over the basic Bresenham algorithm. That's the story.

FIGURE 8.7
Drawing lines using raster patterns.

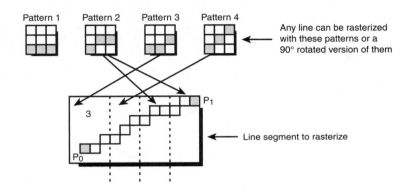

For a demo of the line drawing function, take a look at `DEM08_1.CPP|EXE`, which draws random lines in 640x480 mode.

NOTE If I decide you need a faster line, I'll write it. But for now I'd like to keep things simple, so let's move on to clipping.

Basic 2D Clipping

There are two ways to clip computer images: at the image space level and at the object space level. *Image space* really means at the pixel level. When the image is being rasterized, there is a clipping filter that determines if a pixel is within the viewport. This is appropriate for plotting single pixels, but not for large objects such as bitmaps, lines, or polygons. For objects like those that have some geometry to them, you might as well take advantage of the extra information.

For example, if you're writing a bitmap clipper, all you have to do is clip one rectangle against another; that is, clip your bitmap's bounding rectangle to the viewport. The intersection of the two is the area that you need to blit.

Although you wouldn't think so, lines are a little more difficult to clip. Take a look at Figure 8.8 to see the general problem of clipping a line to a rectangular viewport.

As you can see, there are four general cases:

- Case 1—The line is completely outside the clipping region. This is the trivial rejection case, which is good!

- Case 2—The line is completely inside the clipping region. In this case, no clipping is needed and the line can be passed to the rasterizer as is.
- Case 3—One end of the line segment is outside the clipping region and must be clipped.
- Case 4—Both ends of the line are outside the clipping region and must be clipped.

FIGURE 8.8
The general line clipping problem.

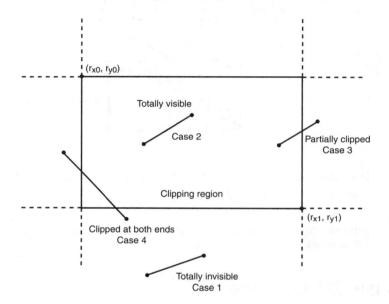

There are a number of known algorithms to clip lines, such as Cohen-Sutherland, Cyrus-Beck, and so on. But before you take a look at any full clipping algorithms, let's see if you can figure it out yourself!

Given that you have a line (x0,y0) to (x1,y1) in 2D space, along with a viewport defined by the rectangle (rx0, ry0) to (rx1, ry1), you want to clip all lines to this region. So what you need is a preprocessor—or clipping filter, if you will—that takes the input values (x0,y0), (x1,y1), (rx0,ry0), and (rx1,ry1) and outputs a new line segment, (x0',y0') to (x1',y1'), that represents the new line. This process is shown in Figure 8.9. Looking at this problem, the first thing you should notice is that at some point you're going to have to compute the intersection of two lines. Alas, this is a fundamental problem you need to figure out right off the bat, so you might as well start there.

Basically, the line segment from (x0,y0) to (x1,y1) will intersect either the left, right, top, or bottom edge of the clipping rectangle. This means that at least you don't have to find the intersection of two arbitrarily oriented lines since the line being rasterized will always intersect either a vertical or horizontal line. Knowing this may or may not help, but it's worth noting. To compute the intersection of two lines, there are a number of methods, but they are all based on the mathematical form of the lines.

FIGURE 8.9
The clipping process diagrammed.

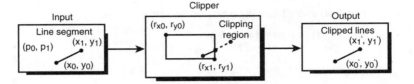

In general, lines can take these general forms:

```
Y-Intercept Form:     y=m*x+b
Point Slope:          (y-y0)=m*(x-x0)
Two Point Form:       (y-y0)=(x-x0)*(y1-y0)/(x1-x0)
General Form:         a*x+b*y=c
*Parametric Form:     P=p0+V*t
```

TIP	If you're uneasy with the parametric form, don't worry. I'll explain parametric equations shortly. In addition, note that the Point Slope form and the Two Point form are really the same because in both cases $m = (y1 - y0)/(x1 - x0)$.

Computing the Intersection of Two Lines Using the Point Slope Form

Off the top of my head, I like both the Point Slope form and the general form. As a good example of algebra, let's work through the intersection of two lines, p0 and p1, using each type of representation. This should warm you up a little for the really gnarly math that's ahead in later chapters <BG>. Let's do the general Point Slope version first (see Figure 8.10).

FIGURE 8.10
Computing the intersection of two lines.

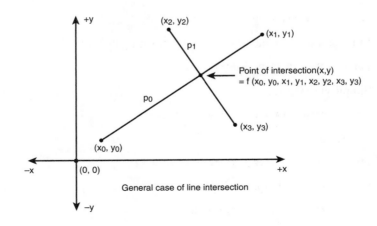

General case of line intersection

Referring to Figure 8.10:

```
Let the first line segment p0 be (x0,y0) to (x1,y1)
Let the second line segment p1 be (x2,y2) to (x3,y3)
```

Here, p0 and p1 can have any orientation:

```
Eq.1 - Point Slope form of p0:
m0 = (y1 - y0)/(x1 - x0)
```

and,

```
(x - x0) = m0*(y - y0)
Eq.2 - Point Slope form of p1:

m1 = (y3 - y2)/(x3 - x2)
```

and,

```
(x - x2) = m1*(y - y2)
```

Now you have two equations in two unknowns:

```
Eq.1: (x - x0) = m0*(y - y0)
Eq.2: (x - x2) = m1*(y - y2)
```

There are two primary ways to solve for (x,y): substitution or matrix operations. Let's try substitution first. The idea here is to find one variable in terms of the other and then plug it into the other equation. Let's try finding x in terms of y for Equation 1 and then plug it into Equation 2:

Equation 1—x in terms of y:

```
(x - x0) = m0*(y - y0)

x = m0*(y-y0) + x0
```

That was easy. Now let's plug it into Equation 2 for x.

Equation 2 is

```
(x - x2) = m1*(y - y2)
```

In Equation 1, x = m0*(y-y0) + x0. Let's plug that into x:

```
(m0*(y-y0) + x0 - x2) = m1*(y - y2)
```

Simplifying for y:

```
m0*y - m0*y0 + x0 - x2 = m1*y - m1*y2
```

Collect terms:

```
m0*y - m1*y = - m1*y2 - (- m0*y0 + x0 - x2)
```

Pull out y and multiply all signs:

```
y*(m0 - m1) = m0*y0 - m1*y2 + x2 - x0
```

And finally, divide both sides by (m0 – m1):

```
y = (m0*y0 - m1*y2 + x2 - x0)/(m0 - m1)
```

At this point you could plug this back into Equation 1 and solve for x, or you could rewrite Equation 2 in terms of x and plug that into y of Equation 1. The results will be the same and are shown here.

Equation 3:

```
x = (-m0/(m1 - m0))*x2 + m0*(y2 - y0) + x0
```

Equation 4:

```
y = (m0*y0 - m1*y2 + x2 - x0)/(m0 - m1)
```

Now, there are some things here that you must consider. First, are there any situations where the previous equations will have problems? Yes! In advanced mathematics, infinity isn't a problem to work with, but in computer graphics, it is! In Equations 3 and 4, the term (m1 – m0) and (m0 – m1) could be 0.0 if the slope of the two lines is the same—in other words, when the lines are parallel.

In this case, they can't possibly intersect and you get a 0.0 in the denominators, driving the quotients of both Equation 3 and 4 to infinity. Of course, this means that at infinity the lines touch, but because you're only working with screens that have a resolution of 1024x768 or so, it's not something you need to consider <BG>.

The bottom line is that this tells you that the intersection equations only work for lines that intersect! If they can't possibly intersect, the math will fail. This is easy to test. Simply check m0 and m1 before doing the math. If m0 == m1, there isn't an intersection. Anyway, let's move on…

If you take a look at Equations 3 and 4 and count up the operations, you're doing about four divides, four multiplies, and eight additions (subtractions count as additions). If you count computing the slopes m0 and m1, that adds four more additions and two divisions. Not too bad.

Computing the Intersection of Two Lines Using the General Form

The general form of any linear equation is

```
a*x + b*y = c
```

Or, if you like the canonical form:

```
a*x + b*y + c = 0
```

In reality, both the Point Slope form and Y-Intercept form can be put into the general form. For example, if you look at the Y-Intercept form:

```
y = m*x+b
```

```
m*x - 1*y = b
```

Or a = m, b = -1, and c = b (the intercept). But what if you don't have the intercept? How can you find the values of (a,b,c) if you only have the coordinates (x0,y1) and (x2,y2)? Well, let's see if the Point Slope form can help out…

```
(y - y0) = m*(x - x0)
```

Multiplying by m:

```
y - y0 = m*x - m*x0
```

Collecting x and y on the LHS (left-hand side):

```
-m*x + y = y0 + m*x0
```

Multiplying by –1:

```
m*x + (-1)*y = (-m)*x0 + (-1)*y0
```

 | The (-1) and the associated multiplies aren't necessary. They just make the extraction of (a,b,c) easier to see.

Computing the Intersection of Two Lines Using the Matrix Form

So it looks like a = m, b = -1, and c = (-m*x0 – y0). Now that you know how to transform the Point Slope form into the general form, you can move on to yet another method of solutions based on matrices. Let's take a look.

Given two general linear equations in this form:

```
a1*x + b1*y = c1
a2*x + b2*y = c2
```

You want to find (x,y) such that both equations are simultaneously solved. In the previous example, you used substitution, but there's another method based on matrices. I'm not going to go into the theory too much because I'm going to give you a crash course in vector/matrix math when you get to 3D. For now, I'm just going to show you the results and tell you how to find (x,y) using matrix operations. Take a look.

Let the matrix A equal

```
|a1    b1|
|a2    b2|
```

and X (the unknowns) equal

```
|x|
|y|
```

and finally, Y (the constants) equals

```
|c1|
|c2|
```

Therefore, you can write the matrix equation:

```
A*X = Y
```

Multiplying both sides by the inverse of A, or A^{-1}, you get

```
A-1*A*X = A-1*Y
```

Simplifying:

```
X = A-1*Y
```

That's it! Of course, you have to know how to find the inverse of a matrix and then perform the matrix multiplication to extract (x,y), but I'll give you some help here and show the final results:

```
x = Det(A1)/Det
y = Det(A2)/Det
```

where A1 equals

```
|c1 b1|
|c2 b2|
```

and A2 equals

```
|a1 c1|
|a2 c2|
```

In essence, you have replaced the first and second column of A with Y to create A1 and A2, respectively. Det(M) means the *determinate* of M and is computed as follows (in general).

Given a general 2x2 matrix M:

```
M = |a b|
    |c d|

Det(M) = (a*d - c*b)
```

With all that in mind, here's a real example:

```
A*X        = Y

5*x - 2*y = -1
2*x + 3*y = 3

A = |5 -2|
    |2  3|
```

```
X = |x|
    |y|

Y = |-1|
    | 3|
```

Therefore:

```
A1 = |-1  -2|
     |3    3|

A2 = |5   -1|
     |2    3|
```

Solving for x,y:

```
      Det |-1 -2|
          | 3  3|        (-1*3 - 3*(-2))
x =   ----------  =  ----------------  = 3/19
      Det |5  -2|      (5*3 - 2*(-2))
          |2   3|


      Det |5  -1|
          |2   3|        (5*3 - 2*(-1))
y =   ----------  =  ----------------  = 17/19
      Det |5  -2|      (5*3 - 2*(-2))
          |2   3|
```

Wow! Seems like a lot of drama, huh? Well, that's what game programming is all about—math! Especially these days. Luckily, once you write the math code, you don't have to worry about it. But it's good to understand it, which is why I have given you a brief refresher on it.

Now that you've taken a little mathematical detour, let's get back to the reason for all this—clipping.

Clipping the Line

As you can see, the concept of clipping is trivial, but the actual implementation can be a bit complex because linear algebra comes into play. At the very least, you have to understand how to deal with linear equations and compute their intersection. However, as I mentioned before, you can always take advantage of *a priori* knowledge about the geometry of the problem to help simplify the math, and this is one of those times.

Ultimately, you still have a long way to go to clip a line against a general rectangle, but we'll get to that. Right now, let's take a look at the problem and see if it can help to know that you're always going to clip a general line against either a vertical line or horizontal line. Take a look at Figure 8.11.

You see in Figure 8.11 that you only need to consider one variable at a time here, either the x or the y. This greatly simplifies the math. Basically, instead of doing all the hard math (which you need to know once you get to 3D), you can use the Point

Slope form of the line itself to find the intersection point by plugging in the known value for either a line of the form X = constant or Y = constant. For example, let's say that your clipping region is (x1,y1) to (x2,y2). If you want to find where your line intersects the left edge, you know that at the point of intersection the x-coordinate must be x1! Thus, all you have to do is find the y coordinate and you're done.

FIGURE 8.11
Clipping against a rectangle is much easier than t he general case.

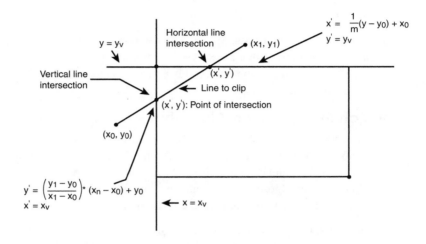

FIGURE 8.11
Clipping against a rectangle is much easier than t he general case.

Conversely, if you want to find the point of intersection on a horizontal line such as the bottom of the clipping rectangle, y2 in this case, you know that the y-coordinate is y2 and you just have to find the x—get it? Here's the math for computing the (x,y) intersections of a line, (x0,y0) to (x1,y1), with a horizontal line with value Y = Yh, and for a vertical line X = Xv.

Horizontal Line Intersection—(x,Yh):

```
We want x...

Start with Point-Slope, m =(y1 - y0)/(x1 - x0)

(y - y0)              = m*(x - x0)

(y - y0)              = m*x - m*x0
(y - y0)  + m*x0      = m*x
((y - y0) + m*x0)/m = x

x = ((y - y0) + m*x0)/m

or

x = 1/m * (y - y0) + x0
```

Vertical Line Intersection—(Xv, y):

```
We want y...

Start with Point-Slope, m =(y - y0)/(x - x0)

(y - y0)             = m*(x - x0)

y                    = m*(x - x0) + y0
```

And that's how that goes. So now you can compute the intersection of a line with an arbitrary line and with a purely vertical or horizontal line (the important one in the case of rectangular clipping). At this point, we can talk about the rest of the clipping problem.

The Cohen-Sutherland Algorithm

In general, you need to figure out if a line is totally visible, partially visible, partially clipped (one end), or totally clipped (both ends). This turns out to be quite an undertaking, and a number of algorithms have been invented to deal with all the cases. However, one algorithm is the most widely used: Cohen-Sutherland. It's reasonably fast, not too bad to implement, and well published.

Basically, it's a brute-force algorithm. But instead of using millions of if statements to figure out where the line is, the algorithm breaks the clipping region into a number of sectors and then assigns a bit code to each of the endpoints of the line segment being clipped. Then, using only a few if statements or a case statement, it figures out what the situation is. Figure 8.12 shows the plan of attack graphically.

FIGURE 8.12
Using clipping codes for efficient line endpoint determination.

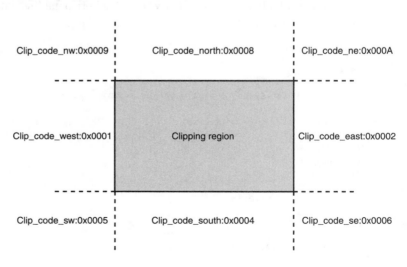

Clip_code_nw:0x0009   Clip_code_north:0x0008   Clip_code_ne:0x000A

Clip_code_west:0x0001   Clipping region   Clip_code_east:0x0002

Clip_code_sw:0x0005   Clip_code_south:0x0004   Clip_code_se:0x0006

The following function is a version of the Cohen-Sutherland I wrote that works on the same premise:

```
int Clip_Line(int &x1,int &y1,int &x2, int &y2)
{
// this function clips the sent line using the globally defined clipping
// region

// internal clipping codes
#define CLIP_CODE_C  0x0000
#define CLIP_CODE_N  0x0008
#define CLIP_CODE_S  0x0004
#define CLIP_CODE_E  0x0002
#define CLIP_CODE_W  0x0001

#define CLIP_CODE_NE 0x000a
#define CLIP_CODE_SE 0x0006
#define CLIP_CODE_NW 0x0009
#define CLIP_CODE_SW 0x0005

int xc1=x1,
    yc1=y1,
    xc2=x2,
    yc2=y2;

int p1_code=0,
    p2_code=0;

// determine codes for p1 and p2
if (y1 < min_clip_y)
    p1_code|=CLIP_CODE_N;
else
if (y1 > max_clip_y)
    p1_code|=CLIP_CODE_S;

if (x1 < min_clip_x)
    p1_code|=CLIP_CODE_W;
else
if (x1 > max_clip_x)
    p1_code|=CLIP_CODE_E;

if (y2 < min_clip_y)
    p2_code|=CLIP_CODE_N;
else
if (y2 > max_clip_y)
    p2_code|=CLIP_CODE_S;

if (x2 < min_clip_x)
    p2_code|=CLIP_CODE_W;
else
if (x2 > max_clip_x)
    p2_code|=CLIP_CODE_E;
```

```
// try and trivially reject
if ((p1_code & p2_code))
    return(0);

// test for totally visible, if so leave points untouched
if (p1_code==0 && p2_code==0)
    return(1);

// determine end clip point for p1
switch(p1_code)
    {
    case CLIP_CODE_C: break;

    case CLIP_CODE_N:
        {
        yc1 = min_clip_y;
        xc1 = x1 + 0.5+(min_clip_y-y1)*(x2-x1)/(y2-y1);
        } break;
    case CLIP_CODE_S:
        {
        yc1 = max_clip_y;
        xc1 = x1 + 0.5+(max_clip_y-y1)*(x2-x1)/(y2-y1);
        } break;

    case CLIP_CODE_W:
        {
        xc1 = min_clip_x;
        yc1 = y1 + 0.5+(min_clip_x-x1)*(y2-y1)/(x2-x1);
        } break;

    case CLIP_CODE_E:
        {
        xc1 = max_clip_x;
        yc1 = y1 + 0.5+(max_clip_x-x1)*(y2-y1)/(x2-x1);
        } break;

// these cases are more complex, must compute 2 intersections
    case CLIP_CODE_NE:
        {
        // north hline intersection
        yc1 = min_clip_y;
        xc1 = x1 + 0.5+(min_clip_y-y1)*(x2-x1)/(y2-y1);

        // test if intersection is valid,
        // if so then done, else compute next
        if (xc1 < min_clip_x || xc1 > max_clip_x)
            {
            // east vline intersection
            xc1 = max_clip_x;
            yc1 = y1 + 0.5+(max_clip_x-x1)*(y2-y1)/(x2-x1);
            } // end if

        } break;
```

```
case CLIP_CODE_SE:
     {
    // south hline intersection
    yc1 = max_clip_y;
    xc1 = x1 + 0.5+(max_clip_y-y1)*(x2-x1)/(y2-y1);

    // test if intersection is valid,
    // if so then done, else compute next
    if (xc1 < min_clip_x || xc1 > max_clip_x)
        {
        // east vline intersection
        xc1 = max_clip_x;
        yc1 = y1 + 0.5+(max_clip_x-x1)*(y2-y1)/(x2-x1);
        } // end if

    } break;

case CLIP_CODE_NW:
     {
    // north hline intersection
    yc1 = min_clip_y;
    xc1 = x1 + 0.5+(min_clip_y-y1)*(x2-x1)/(y2-y1);

    // test if intersection is valid,
    // if so then done, else compute next
    if (xc1 < min_clip_x || xc1 > max_clip_x)
        {
        xc1 = min_clip_x;
        yc1 = y1 + 0.5+(min_clip_x-x1)*(y2-y1)/(x2-x1);
        } // end if

    } break;

case CLIP_CODE_SW:
     {
    // south hline intersection
    yc1 = max_clip_y;
    xc1 = x1 + 0.5+(max_clip_y-y1)*(x2-x1)/(y2-y1);

    // test if intersection is valid,
    // if so then done, else compute next
    if (xc1 < min_clip_x || xc1 > max_clip_x)
        {
        xc1 = min_clip_x;
        yc1 = y1 + 0.5+(min_clip_x-x1)*(y2-y1)/(x2-x1);
        } // end if

    } break;

default:break;

} // end switch
```

```
        // determine clip point for p2
    switch(p2_code)
        {
        case CLIP_CODE_C: break;

        case CLIP_CODE_N:
            {
            yc2 = min_clip_y;
            xc2 = x2 + (min_clip_y-y2)*(x1-x2)/(y1-y2);
            } break;

        case CLIP_CODE_S:
            {
            yc2 = max_clip_y;
            xc2 = x2 + (max_clip_y-y2)*(x1-x2)/(y1-y2);
            } break;

        case CLIP_CODE_W:
            {
            xc2 = min_clip_x;
            yc2 = y2 + (min_clip_x-x2)*(y1-y2)/(x1-x2);
            } break;

        case CLIP_CODE_E:
            {
            xc2 = max_clip_x;
            yc2 = y2 + (max_clip_x-x2)*(y1-y2)/(x1-x2);
            } break;

        // these cases are more complex, must compute 2 intersections
        case CLIP_CODE_NE:
            {
            // north hline intersection
            yc2 = min_clip_y;
            xc2 = x2 + 0.5+(min_clip_y-y2)*(x1-x2)/(y1-y2);

            // test if intersection is valid,
            // if so then done, else compute next
             if (xc2 < min_clip_x || xc2 > max_clip_x)
                 {
                 // east vline intersection
                 xc2 = max_clip_x;
                 yc2 = y2 + 0.5+(max_clip_x-x2)*(y1-y2)/(x1-x2);
                 } // end if

            } break;

        case CLIP_CODE_SE:
             {
            // south hline intersection
            yc2 = max_clip_y;
            xc2 = x2 + 0.5+(max_clip_y-y2)*(x1-x2)/(y1-y2);
```

```
            // test if intersection is valid,
            // if so then done, else compute next
            if (xc2 < min_clip_x || xc2 > max_clip_x)
               {
               // east vline intersection
               xc2 = max_clip_x;
               yc2 = y2 + 0.5+(max_clip_x-x2)*(y1-y2)/(x1-x2);
               } // end if

            } break;

      case CLIP_CODE_NW:
            {
            // north hline intersection
            yc2 = min_clip_y;
            xc2 = x2 + 0.5+(min_clip_y-y2)*(x1-x2)/(y1-y2);

            // test if intersection is valid,
            // if so then done, else compute next
            if (xc2 < min_clip_x || xc2 > max_clip_x)
               {
               xc2 = min_clip_x;
               yc2 = y2 + 0.5+(min_clip_x-x2)*(y1-y2)/(x1-x2);
               } // end if

            } break;

      case CLIP_CODE_SW:
            {
            // south hline intersection
            yc2 = max_clip_y;
            xc2 = x2 + 0.5+(max_clip_y-y2)*(x1-x2)/(y1-y2);

            // test if intersection is valid,
            // if so then done, else compute next
            if (xc2 < min_clip_x || xc2 > max_clip_x)
                {
                xc2 = min_clip_x;
                yc2 = y2 + 0.5+(min_clip_x-x2)*(y1-y2)/(x1-x2);
                } // end if

            } break;

      default:break;

      } // end switch

// do bounds check
if ((xc1 < min_clip_x) || (xc1 > max_clip_x) ||
    (yc1 < min_clip_y) || (yc1 > max_clip_y) ||
    (xc2 < min_clip_x) || (xc2 > max_clip_x) ||
    (yc2 < min_clip_y) || (yc2 > max_clip_y) )
    {
```

```
        return(0);
        } // end if

// store vars back
x1 = xc1;
y1 = yc1;
x2 = xc2;
y2 = yc2;

return(1);

} // end Clip_Line
```

All you do is send the function the endpoints of the line, and it clips them to the clipping rectangle defined by the globals:

```
int min_clip_x = 0,      // clipping rectangle
    max_clip_x = SCREEN_WIDTH-1,
    min_clip_y = 0,
    max_clip_y = SCREEN_HEIGHT-1;
```

I usually set these globals to the size of the screen. The only detail about the function is that it takes the parameters as a call by the reference, so the variables can be modified. Make copies if you don't want the variables to be changed. Here's an example of the function in use:

```
// clip the line (x1,y1) to (x2,y2)

// make copies
int clipped_x1 = x1,
    clipped_y1 = y1,
    clipped_x2 = x2,
    clipped_y2 = y2;

// clip the line
Clip_Line(clipped_x1, clipped_y1,
          clipped_x2, clipped_y2);
```

When the function returns the `clipped_*` variables, they will have new clipped values based on the clipping rectangle stored in the globals.

The demo, `DEMO8_2.CPP|EXE`, creates a 200x200 clipping region that is centered on the screen and then draws random lines within it. Notice how they're clipped <BG>.

Wireframe Polygons

Now that you know how to draw lines and clip them to a rectangle, you're ready to move on to higher order objects such as polygons. Figure 8.13 illustrates a number of different polygons: a triangle, a square, and a pentagon. A polygon consists of three or more connected points and is closed. Also, polygons can be either convex or concave.

There is a mathematical definition and proof to prove that a polygon is convex or concave, but in general a convex polygon has no "dents" in it, while a concave polygon does.

Now I want to give you some ideas about how you might represent 2D polygonal objects and manipulate them.

FIGURE 8.13
Some general
polygons.

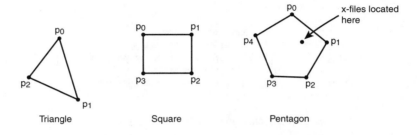

Triangle   Square   Pentagon

No concavities

MATH | One way to test for concavity is the following: If you can draw a line from any two edges of a polygon and the line falls outside the polygon, the polygon is concave.

Polygon Data Structures

In a game, the selection of data structures is of the utmost importance. Forget everything you ever learned about using complex data structures and concentrate on one thing—speed! In a game, you must access data all the time because the game is being rendered based on it. You must consider the ease of access, the size of the data, and the relative size the data is accessed by the processor cache, as well as the second-level cache and so forth. The bottom line is that having a 1000Mhz processor isn't going to help much if you can't get to your data effectively and quickly.

My rules of thumb when designing data structures are these:

- Keep it simple.
- Use static arrays for small structures that you know the size of, within 25 percent.
- Use linked lists when it makes sense.
- Use trees and other exotic data structures only if it's going to make the code run faster, not just because it's cool!
- Finally, think ahead when you're designing data structures. Don't corner yourself into not allowing new features or inventing some absurd limit on objects.

Anyway, enough preaching. Let's take a look at a very basic structure for a polygon.
Assume that a polygon can have a large number of vertices. That limits the static
array to hold the vertices, so the storage will have to be dynamic for the actual vertices. Other than that, you'll need the polygon's (x,y) position, its velocity (more on
this later), its color, and maybe some state information to track attributes that you may
not think of. Here's my first hack at it:

```
typedef struct POLYGON2D_TYP
{
int state;          // state of polygon
int num_verts;      // number of vertices
int x0,y0;          // position of center of polygon
int xv,yv;          // initial velocity
DWORD color;        // could be index or PALETTENTRY
VERTEX2DI *vlist;   // pointer to vertex list

} POLYGON2D, *POLYGON2D_PTR;
```

This is a perfect place for C++ and a class, but I want to keep it simple in
case you're a straight C user. However, as an exercise, I would like all
C++ programmers to convert all this polygon stuff into a nice class.

Not bad, but you're missing something here: the definition of VERTEX2DI. Again, this
is typical when you're designing data structures. You haven't defined everything, but
know you need something. Let's define VERTEX2DI now. Basically, it's just an integer-
accurate 2D vertex:

```
typedef struct VERTEX2DI_TYP
{
int x,y;

} VERTEX2DI, *VERTEX2DI_PTR;
```

MATH

In many 2D/3D engines, all vertices are only accurate to whole numbers.
Of course, this makes all scaling and rotation transformations less than
accurate. The problem with floating-point numbers is that they're slow
to convert to integers. Even though the Pentium can perform floating-
point math as fast or faster than integer math, the conversion to integer
at the end of rasterization kills you. This isn't an issue as long as the
conversion happens at the *very* end, but if you keep going back and
forth, you will kill your performance. The bottom line is that if you can
hang with integer accuracy, do so exclusively. Otherwise, go to floating-
point, but keep the conversions down!

At this point, you have nice data structure to hold a vertex and a polygon. Figure 8.14 depicts the structure abstractly in relationship to a real polygon.

FIGURE 8.14
The polygon data structure.

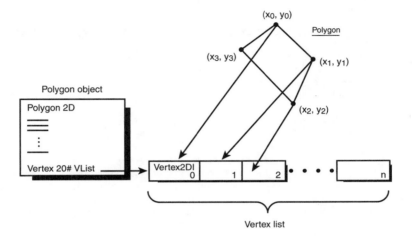

About the only thing you need to do to the POLYGON structure to use it is allocate the memory for the actual vertex storage, which you would do with something like this:

```
POLYGON2D triangle; // our polygon

// initialize the triangle
triangle.state      = 1; // turn it on
triangle.num_verts  = 3; // triangle
triangle.x0         = 100; // position it
triangle.y0         = 100;
triangle.xv         = 0; // initial velocity
triangle.yv         = 0;
triangle.color      = 50;  // assume 8-bit mode index 50
triangle.vlist      = new VERTEX2DI[triangle.num_verts];
```

Note that I've used the C++ new operator to allocate the memory. Thus, I'll have to use the delete operator to delete it. In straight C, the allocation would look like
(VERTEX2DI_PTR)malloc(triangle.num_verts*sizeof(VERTEX2DI)).

Fantabulous! Now let's see how to draw one of these things.

Drawing and Clipping Polygons

Drawing a polygon is as simple as drawing n connected line segments. You already know how to draw a line, so all you have to do to draw a polygon is loop on the vertices and connect the dots. Of course, if you want the polygon clipped, you

should call the clipping function, which I've put a little wrapper around called
`Draw_Clip_Line()`. It has the same parameterization as `Draw_Line()`, except it clips
to the globally defined clipping region. Here's a general function to draw a `POLYGON2D`
structure:

```
int Draw_Polygon2D(POLYGON2D_PTR poly, UCHAR *vbuffer, int lpitch)
{
// this function draws a POLYGON2D based on

// test if the polygon is visible
if (poly->state)
    {
    // loop thru and draw a line from vertices 1 to n
    for (int index=0; index < poly->num_verts-1; index++)
        {
        // draw line from ith to ith+1 vertex
        Draw_Clip_Line(poly->vlist[index].x+poly->x0,
                       poly->vlist[index].y+poly->y0,
                       poly->vlist[index+1].x+poly->x0,
                       poly->vlist[index+1].y+poly->y0,
                       poly->color,
                       vbuffer, lpitch);

        } // end for

        // now close up polygon
        // draw line from last vertex to 0th
        Draw_Clip_Line(poly->vlist[0].x+poly->x0,
                       poly->vlist[0].y+poly->y0,
                       poly->vlist[index].x+poly->x0,
                       poly->vlist[index].y+poly->y0,
                       poly->color,
                       vbuffer, lpitch);

    // return success
    return(1);
    } // end if
else
    return(0);

} // end Draw_Polygon2D
```

The only weird thing about the function is the use of (x0,y0) as the center of the polygon. This is so you can move the polygon around without messing with the individual
vertices. Furthermore, defining the polygon in a relative manner from its center allows
you to use what are called *local coordinates* rather than *world coordinates*. Take a
look at Figure 8.15 to see the relationship between the two.

FIGURE 8.15

Local coordinates in relation to world coordinates.

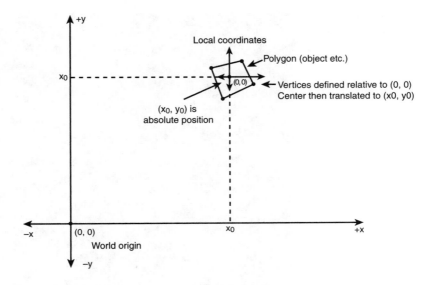

Local coordinates in relation to world coordinates. It's always much better to define polygons relative to the center of (0,0) (local coordinates) and then later transform the polygon out to a position (x,y) (world coordinates). You'll learn about local, world, and camera (the point relative to the viewpoint) coordinates in detail when you get to 3D, but for now, just take note that they exist.

As a demo, I have created DEM08_3.CPP|EXE. It first creates an array of polygon objects, each with eight points. These polygons look like little asteroids. Then the program randomly positions these asteroids and moves (translates) them around the screen. The program works in 640x480x8 and uses page flipping to accomplish the animation. Figure 8.16 is a screen shot from the program.

All right, Mr. Spock, now you can define a polygon and draw it. The next topic I want to cover is 2D transformations—translating, rotating, and scaling polygons.

Transformations in the 2D Plane

As I'm sure you can tell, you're slipping into the world of mathematics—I've been sneaking up on you <BG>. Nevertheless, this stuff is fun, and if you understand the basics, there's really nothing in 3D game programming that you won't be able to tackle! So let's hit it!

FIGURE 8.16

DEMO8_3.EXE in action.

You've seen translation a number of times up to this point, but you haven't really looked at a mathematical description of it, or for that matter any other transformations, like rotation and scaling. Let's take a look at each one of these concepts and how they relate to 2D vector images. Then, when you make the leap to 3D graphics, all you'll need to do is add a variable or two and take into consideration the z-axis—but we'll get to that.

Translation

Translation is nothing more than moving an object or point from one position to another. Let's assume that you have a single point, (x,y), that you want to translate by some amount, (dx,dy). The process of translation is shown in Figure 8.17.

Basically, you add the translation factors to the (x,y) coordinate, come up with a new position, and call it (xt,yt). Here's the math:

```
xt = x + dx;
yt = y + dy;
```

Here, dx,dy can be either positive or negative. If we're taking about translation with standard display coordinates, where $(0,0)$ is in the upper-left corner, positive translations in the x-axis move an object to the right. Positive translations in the y-axis move an object down. Negative translations in the x-axis move an object to the left. And finally, negative translations in the y-axis move an object up.

FIGURE 8.17

Translating a
single point.

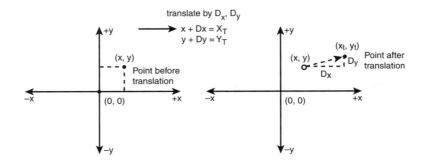

To translate an entire object, you simply apply the translation transformation to the center of the object, if the object has an x,y position that all points are relative to (as does the polygon structure). If the object doesn't have a general x,y position, you must apply the formula to every point that makes up the polygon. This brings us to the concept of local and world coordinates.

Generally, in 2D/3D computer graphics you want to define all objects to have at least local and world coordinates. The local coordinates of an object are those relative to (0,0) or (0,0,0) in 3D. Then the world coordinates are found by adding the world position (x0,y0) to each of the local coordinates, in essence translating the local coordinates each by (x0,y0) to place the object. This is shown in Figure 8.18.

In light of this, in the future you may decide to add more data storage to your polygon so that you can store both local and world coordinates. In fact, you will do this later. Moreover, you'll add storage for camera coordinates. The reasoning for the added storage is that once you transform an object to world coordinates and are ready to draw it, you don't want to have to do it each frame. As long as the object doesn't move or transform, you won't have to. You can just save the last calculated world coordinates.

With that all in your little neural net, let's take a look at a general polygon translation function. It's so simple, it should be illegal <BG>.

```
int Translate_Polygon2D(POLYGON2D_PTR poly, int dx, int dy)
{
// this function translates the center of a polygon

// test for valid pointer
if (!poly)
    return(0);

// translate
poly->x0+=dx;
poly->y0+=dy;
```

```
// return success
return(1);

} // end Translate_Polygon2D
```

FIGURE 8.18

Translation of
an object and the
resulting vertices.

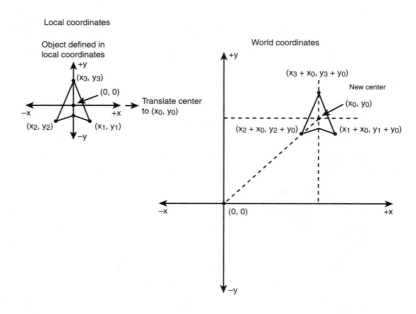

I think that deserves a Pentium.II.AGP double snap!!!

Rotation

Rotation of bitmaps is rather complex, but rotation of single points in the plane
is almost trivial—or at least the actual rotation is. *Deriving* the rotation is a bit
more complex, but I have a new derivation that I think is very cool. However,
before I show it to you, let's take a look at what you want to do. Referring to
Figure 8.19, you can see the point p0 with coordinates (x,y). You want to rotate
this point an angle theta about the z-axis (which is running through the paper)
to find the rotated coordinates p0[1] with coordinates (xr,yr).

Trigonometry Review

Obviously, you're going to need to use some trigonometry here. If you're rusty,
here's a quick review of some basic facts.

Most trigonometry is based on the analysis of a right triangle, as shown in
Figure 8.20.

FIGURE 8.19
The rotation of
a point.

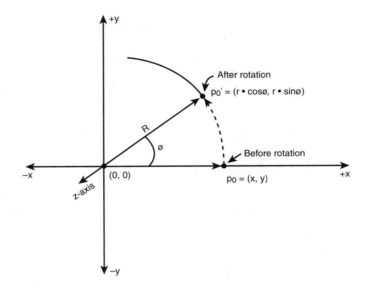

FIGURE 8.20
The right triangle.

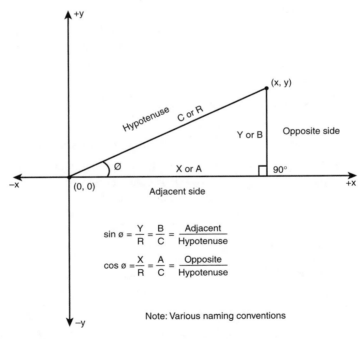

Table 8.1 shows the differences between radians and degrees.

TABLE 8.1 Radians Versus Degrees

Degrees	Radians (pi)	Radians (Numerically)
360	2*pi	6.28
180	1*pi	3.14159
90	pi/2	1.57
57.295	pi/pi	1.0
1	pi/180	0.0175

Here are some trigonometric facts:

- There are 360 degrees in a complete circle, or 2*pi radians. Hence, there are pi radians in 180 degrees. The computer functions `sin()` and `cos()` work in radians, *not* degrees—remember that! Table 8.1 lists the values.

- The sum of the interior angles theta1 + theta2 + theta3 = 180 degrees or pi radians.

- Referring to the right triangle in Figure 8.20, the side opposite theta1 is called the *opposite side*, the side below it is called the *adjacent side*, and the long side is called the *hypotenuse*.

- The sum of the squares of the sides of a right triangle equal the square of the hypotenuse. This is called the *Pythagorean theorem*. Mathematically, you write it like this:

`hypotenuse`^{2} `= adjacent`^{2} `+ opposite`^{2}

Or sometimes you can use a, b, and c for dummy variables:

`c`^{2} `= a`^{2} `+ b`^{2}

Therefore, if you have two sides of a triangle, you can find the third.

- There are three main trigonometric ratios that mathematicians like to use, called the *sine*, *cosine*, and *tangent*. They're defined as

```
                   adjacent side      x
cos(theta)  =   ----------------  =  -------
                   hypotenuse         r
```

Domain: 0 <= theta <= 2*pi

Range: -1 to 1

```
                 opposite side       y
sin(theta)   = ----------------  =  -------
                 hypotenuse          r
```

Domain: 0 <= theta <= 2*pi

Range: -1 to 1

```
                 sin(theta)         opposite/hypotenuse
tan(theta)   = -------------   =  ----------------------
                 cos(theta)         adjacent/hypotenuse
```

```
       opposite        y
   = ------------- = --- = slope = M
       adjacent        x
```

Domain: -pi/2 <= theta <= pi/2

Range: -infinity to +infinity

MATH   Note the use of the terms *domain* and *range*. These simply mean the input and the output, respectively.

Figure 8.21 shows graphs of all the functions. Notice that all the functions are periodic (repeating) and that sin(theta) and cos(theta) have periodicity of 2*pi, while the tangent has periodicity of pi. Also, notice that tan(theta) goes to +-infinity whenever theta mod pi is pi/2.

FIGURE 8.21
Graphs of basic trigonometric functions.

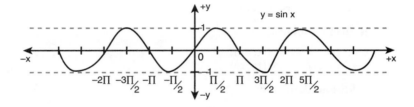

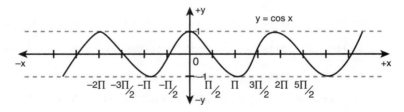

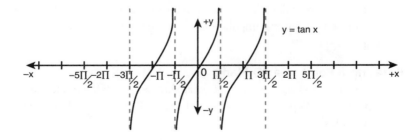

Now, there are about a bazillion trigonometric identities and tricks, and it would take a math book to prove them all. I'm just going to give you a table of the ones that a game programmer should know. Table 8.2 lists some other trigonometric ratios, as well as some neat identities.

TABLE 8.2 Useful Trigonometric Identities

Cosecant	`csc(theta) = 1/sin(theta)`
Secant	`sec(theta) = 1/cos(theta)`
Cotangent	`cot(theta) = 1/tan(theta)`

Pythagorean theorem in terms of trig functions:

```
sin(theta)2 + cos(theta)2 = 1
```

Conversion identity:

```
sin(theta1) = cos(theta1 - PI/2)
```

Reflection identities:

```
sin(-theta) = -sin(theta)
cos(-theta) =  cos(theta)
```

Addition identities:

```
sin(theta1 + theta2) = sin(theta1)*cos(theta2) + cos(theta1)*sin(theta2)

cos(theta1 + theta2) = cos(theta1)*cos(theta2) - sin(theta1)*sin(theta2)

sin(theta1 - theta2) = sin(theta1)*cos(theta2) - cos(theta1)*sin(theta2)

cos(theta1 - theta2) = cos(theta1)*cos(theta2) + sin(theta1)*sin(theta2)
```

Of course, you could derive identities until you turned many shades of blue. In general, identities help you simplify complex trigonometric formulas so you don't have to do the math. Hence, when you come up with an algorithm based on sin, cos, tan, and so on, always take a look in a trigonometry book and see if you can simplify your math so that fewer computations are needed to get the result. Remember, speed, speed, speed!!!

Rotating a Point in a 2D Plane

Now that you have an idea of what sin, cos, and tan are, let's use them to rotate a point in a 2D plane. Take a look at Figure 8.22, which shows the setup for the rotation formulas.

Start off by showing that any point on a circle of radius R is computed as

```
xr = r*cos(theta)
yr = r*sin(theta)
```

FIGURE 8.22
Derivation of the
rotation equations.

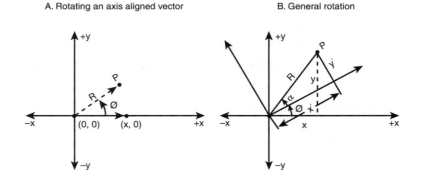

A. Rotating an axis aligned vector   B. General rotation

Hence, if you always wanted to rotate a point that had coordinates (x,0), you could use this equation. However, you need to generalize a little. You want to rotate a point (x,y) about an angle theta, as shown in Figure 8.22. You can think of this in two ways: as rotating the point P, or as rotating the axes themselves. If you think of it as rotating the axes themselves, you have two coordinate systems: one before the rotation, and one after.

In the coordinate system before the rotation, you have

```
xr = r*cos(theta)
yr = r*sin(theta)
```

But after the rotation, you have

Equations 1:

```
xr = r*cos(theta + alpha)
yr = r*sin(theta + alpha)
```

Equations 2:

```
x = r*cos(alpha)
y = r*sin(alpha)
```

Here, `alpha` is basically the angle created from the x-axis of the new system and the position vector from the origin to P.

If you're confused, let me explain what you're doing here in another way. You always know how to find the point (x,0) rotated about theta, and if you rotate the axes by theta, you can compute P in both the old axes and the new. Then, based on these two formulas, you can come up with the rotation equations. If you take Equations 1 and use the addition identities, you'll get the following results.

Equations 3:

```
xr = r*cos(theta)*sin(alpha) - r*sin(theta)*sin(alpha)
yr = r*sin(theta)*cos(alpha) + r*sin(theta)*cos(alpha)
```

Wait a minute, let me put some boom in it. You know that x,y are also equal to

```
x = r*cos(alpha)
y = r*sin(alpha)
```

Substituting these values into the bolded parts of Equations 3 gives you the results you desire.

Equations 4, the rotation formulas:

```
xr = x*cos(theta) - y*sin(theta)
yr = x*sin(theta) + y*cos(theta)
Q.E.D.
```

MATH

> For you math-heads, this derivation is very similar to a polar-only rotation with conversion to Cartesian coordinates at the end. That's how I came up with it.

Back to reality. You now know that to rotate a point (x,y) by an angle theta, you can use Equations 4. However, there is one detail to remember: The equations rotate a point in the counterclockwise direction for positive theta and in the clockwise direction for negative theta. However, there is one more problem… you did the derivation for quadrant I of the normal Cartesian coordinate system. Thus, the y-axis is inverted on the display screen and the roles of positive and negative are reversed.

Later, when you do 3D graphics, you'll transform all screen coordinates so that the x,y-axes are centered in the middle and are both pointing in the positive directions, just like quadrant I of the 2D Cartesian system. But for now, who cares?

Rotating a Polygon

Taking all of your immense knowledge, let's write a rotation function that rotates a polygon:

```
int Rotate_Polygon2D(POLYGON2D_PTR poly, float theta)
{
// this function rotates the local coordinates of the polygon

// test for valid pointer
if (!poly)
   return(0);

// loop and rotate each point, very crude, no lookup!!!
for (int curr_vert = 0; curr_vert < poly->num_verts; curr_vert++)
    {
    // perform rotation
    float xr =  poly->vlist[curr_vert].x*cos(theta) -
                poly->vlist[curr_vert].y*sin(theta);

    float yr = poly->vlist[curr_vert].x*sin(theta) +
               poly->vlist[curr_vert].y*cos(theta);
```

```
    // store result back
    poly->vlist[curr_vert].x = xr;
    poly->vlist[curr_vert].y = yr;

    } // end for curr_vert

// return success
return(1);

} // end Rotate_Polygon2D
```

There are a few things you should note. First, the math is performed in floating-point and then the results are stored as integers, so there's loss of precision.

Next, the function takes the angle in radians rather than degrees because the function uses the math libraries' `sin()` and `cos()` functions, which use radians. The loss of accuracy isn't a huge problem, but the use of trig functions in a real-time program is just about as ugly as it gets. What you need to do is create a lookup table that has the sine and cosine values for, say, 0–360 degrees already precomputed, and then replace the library function calls to `sin()` and `cos()` with table lookups.

The question is, how do you design the table? This really depends on the situation. Some programmers might want to use a single BYTE to index into the table. Thus, it would have 256 virtual degrees that made up a circle, as shown in Figure 8.23.

FIGURE 8.23
Breaking a circle into 256 virtual degrees.

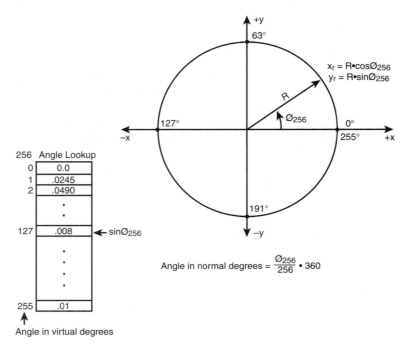

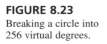
Angle in virtual degrees

It's up to you and the situation, but usually I like to make the table hold the angles from 0–359 degrees. Here's how you might create such tables:

```
// storage for our tables
float cos_look[360];
float sin_look[360];


// generate the tables
for (int ang = 0; ang < 360; ang++)
    {
    // convert ang to radians
    float theta = (float)ang*3.14159/180;

    // insert next entry into table
    cos_look[ang] = cos(theta);
    sin_look[ang] = sin(theta);

    } // end for ang
```

Then we can rewrite our rotation function to take an angle from 0–359 and use the tables by replacing the sin() and cos() with sin_look[] and cos_look[], respectively:

```
int Rotate_Polygon2D(POLYGON2D_PTR poly, int theta)
{
// this function rotates the local coordinates of the polygon

// test for valid pointer
if (!poly)
   return(0);

// loop and rotate each point, very crude, no lookup!!!
for (int curr_vert = 0; curr_vert < poly->num_verts; curr_vert++)
    {
    // perform rotation
    float xr = poly->vlist[curr_vert].x*cos_look[theta] -
               poly->vlist[curr_vert].y*sin_look[theta];

    float yr = poly->vlist[curr_vert].x*sin_look[theta] +
               poly->vlist[curr_vert].y*cos_look[theta];

    // store result back
    poly->vlist[curr_vert].x = xr;
    poly->vlist[curr_vert].y = yr;

    } // end for curr_vert

// return success
return(1);

} // end Rotate_Polygon2D
```

To rotate a `POLYGON2D` object 10 degrees, you would make the call

```
Rotate_Polygon2D(&object, 10);
```

> **NOTE**
>
> Note that all this rotation stuff mangles the original polygon's coordinates. Sure, if you rotate 10 degrees, you can then rotate –10 degrees to get back to the original vertices, but you will slowly lose your original vertex coordinates due to integer truncation and rounding. This is the reason for having a second set of coordinates stored in the polygon structure. It can hold transformations, and you always keep the originals too, so you can refresh your data if need be. More on this later.

A Word on Accuracy

I originally wrote this demo with integers to hold the local vertices. But to my dismay, the values degraded into fuzz within just a few rotations. Thus, I had to rewrite the demo to use `FLOAT`s. You must redefine your `POLYGON2D` structure to contain a floating-point-accurate vertex rather than an integer-accurate vertex.

There are two ways around this. One is to have a local and transformed (world) set of coordinates that are both integers, convert the local coordinates to floats, perform the transformation, store the result in the transformed coordinates, and then render. Then, on the next frame, use the local coordinates again. That way, no error creeps into the local coordinates.

Or you can just keep one set of local/transformed coordinates in floating-point. This is what I did. Hence, you have two new data structures for a vertex and for a polygon:

```
// a 2D vertex
typedef struct VERTEX2DF_TYP
        {
        float x,y; // the vertex
        } VERTEX2DF, *VERTEX2DF_PTR;


// a 2D polygon
typedef struct POLYGON2D_TYP
        {
        int state;       // state of polygon
        int num_verts;   // number of vertices
        int x0,y0;       // position of center of polygon
        int xv,yv;       // initial velocity
        DWORD color;     // could be index or PALETTENTRY
        VERTEX2DF *vlist; // pointer to vertex list

        } POLYGON2D, *POLYGON2D_PTR;
```

I just replaced the vertex list with the new floating-point vertex so I wouldn't have to rewrite everything. Now, both the translation and rotation work, although translation is still integer-based. Of course, I could have done this before writing about it, but I want you to see the process in action, the give and take of game programming. You hope that things will work out, but if they don't, you take a step back and try again <BG>.

For an example of using both the translation and rotation functions, I have taken DEMO8_3.CPP and modified it into DEMO8_4.CPP|EXE. It rotates all the asteroids at various rates. The program also uses the lookup tables. Take a look!

Scaling

After all that, anything should be easy. Scaling is almost as simple as translation. Take a look at Figure 8.24. All you need to do to scale an object is multiply each coordinate by the scaling factor.

FIGURE 8.24
The math of scaling.

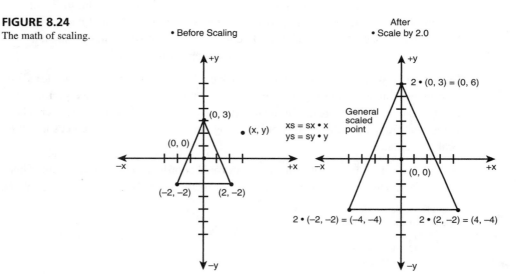

Scaling factors that are greater than 1.0 will make the object bigger, while scaling factors less that 1.0 will make the object smaller. A scaling factor of 1.0 will do nothing. The math to scale a point (x,y) by scaling factor s, resulting in (xs,ys), is

```
xs = s*x
ys = s*y
```

Also, you can scale each axis non-uniformly—that is, with different scaling factors for the x and y coordinates, like this:

```
xs = sx*x
ys = sy*y
```

Most of the time, you want to scale equally. But you might want to make an object grow in one axis, so who knows? Here's a function that scales a polygon. It takes both an x- and a y-axis scaling factor, just in case:

```
int Scale_Polygon2D(POLYGON2D_PTR poly, float sx, float sy)
{
// this function scales the local coordinates of the polygon

// test for valid pointer
if (!poly)
   return(0);

// loop and scale each point
for (int curr_vert = 0; curr_vert < poly->num_verts; curr_vert++)
    {
    // scale and store result back
    poly->vlist[curr_vert].x *= sx;
    poly->vlist[curr_vert].y *= sy;

    } // end for curr_vert

// return success
return(1);

} // end Scale_Polygon2D
```

That one was easy, huh, hot rocks?

To scale a polygon to 1/10 its size, you would make the call

```
Scale_Polygon2D(&polygon, 0.1, 0.1);
```

Notice that the x- and y-axis scale factors are both equal to 0.1. Thus, the scaling will be uniform on each axis.

As a demo of scaling, I have created DEMO8_5.CPP|EXE. It creates a single rotating asteroid. When you press the A key, the object gets bigger by 10 percent; when you press the S key, it gets smaller by 10 percent.

> **NOTE**
>
> You may notice that the mouse pointer is visible on most demos. If you want to make it disappear (which is a good idea for games in general), you can make a call to the Win32 function ShowCursor(BOOL bshow). If you send TRUE, the internal display count is incremented, and FALSE decrements it. When the system starts, the display count is 0. If the display count is greater than or equal to 0, the mouse pointer is displayed. Hence, the call ShowCursor(FALSE) will make the cursor disappear, and the call ShowCursor(TRUE) will make it appear again at some later time. Remember, though, that ShowCursor() accumulates your calls to it, so if you call ShowCursor(FALSE) five times, you must call ShowCursor(TRUE) five times to "unwind" the counter.

Introduction to Matrices

When we start talking about 3D graphics, I'm really going to drown you in vectors, matrices, and other mathematical concepts. However, at this point, I just want to show you a few things about matrices and how they can be used in relation to the simple 2D transformations you've been doing the longhand way. Sound like a plan?

A matrix is nothing more than a rectangular array of numbers with a given number of rows and columns. We usually say that a matrix is *mxn*, meaning it has *m* rows and *n* columns. The *mxn* is also referred to as the *dimension* of the matrix. For example, here's a matrix *A* that is 2x2:

```
A = |1   4|
    |9  -1|
```

Notice that I use the capital letter *A* to denote the matrix. In general, most people use capital letters to denote matrices and bold letters for vectors. In the previous example, the first row is <1 4> and the second row is <9 –1>. Here's a 3x2 matrix:

```
    |5    6|
B = |2    3|
    |100 -7|
```

And here's a 2x3 matrix:

```
C = | 3   5 0 |
    |-8  12 4 |
```

To locate the $<i,j>$th element in the matrix, you simply go to the *i*th row and the *j*th column and look up the value. However, there *is* a gotcha...most math books start counting matrix elements with 1, rather than 0 as you do in computer programs, so keep that in mind. You're going to start counting with 0 because this will make using C/C++ matrices work more naturally. For example, here's the labeling of a 3x3 matrix:

```
    |a₀₀ a₀₁ a₀₂|
A = |a₁₀ a₁₁ a₁₂|
    |a₂₀ a₂₁ a₂₂|
```

Easy enough. So that's all there is to the actual matrix itself and the labeling conventions. But you might ask, "Where do matrices come from?" Matrices are simply mathematical tools for lazy mathematicians, I kid you not. Basically, if you have a system of equations like

```
3*x + 2*y = 1
4*x - 9*y = 9
```

then that's a lot of work writing all the variables down. You know that they're (x,y), so why keep writing them? Why not just create a compact format that contains only the stuff you want to work with? This is how matrices came to be. In the previous example, there are three different sets of values that you can dump into matrices. You can work with these values together or separately.

Here are the coefficients:

```
3*x + 2*y = 1
4*x - 9*y = 9

A = |3    2|
    |4   -9|

Dimension is 2x2
```

Here are the variables themselves:

```
3*x + 2*y = 1
4*x - 9*y = 9

X = |x|
    |y|

Dimension is 2x1
```

And finally, here are the constants to the right:

```
3*x + 2*y = 1
4*x - 9*y = 9

B = |1|
    |9|

Dimension is 2x1
```

With all these nice matrices, you can focus on, say, the coefficient matrix *A* without all the other stuff. Moreover, you can write matrix equations like

```
A*X = B
```

If you perform the math, you get

```
3*x + 2*y = 1
4*x - 9*y = 9
```

But how to perform the math? That's our next topic.

The Identity Matrix

The first thing you need to define in any mathematical system is 1 and 0. In matrix mathematics, there are analogs of both of the values. The analog of 1 is called the *identity matrix* and is created by placing all 1s in the main diagonal of the matrix and 0s everywhere else. Furthermore, because matrices can be any size, there are obviously an infinite number of identity matrices. However, there is one constraint: All identity matrices must be square, or in other words *mxm*, where *m* >= 1. Here are a couple of examples:

$$I_2 = \begin{vmatrix} 1 & 0 \\ 0 & 1 \end{vmatrix}$$

Dimension 2x2

$$I_3 = \begin{vmatrix} 1 & 0 & 0 \\ 0 & 1 & 0 \\ 0 & 0 & 1 \end{vmatrix}$$

Dimension 3x3

Ironically, the identity matrix isn't exactly the analog of 1, but is under matrix multiplication (which we'll get to in a second).

The second type of fundamental matrix is called the *zero matrix*, and it's 0 under both addition and multiplication. It's nothing more than a matrix of dimension *mxn* with all entries 0. Other than that, there are no special constraints:

$$Z_{3x3} = \begin{vmatrix} 0 & 0 & 0 \\ 0 & 0 & 0 \\ 0 & 0 & 0 \end{vmatrix}$$

$$Z_{1x2} = \begin{vmatrix} 0 & 0 \end{vmatrix}$$

The only interesting thing about the zero matrix is that it has the standard properties of scalar 0 for both matrix addition and multiplication. Other than that, it's pretty useless.

Matrix Addition

Addition and subtraction of matrices is performed by adding or subtracting each element in two matrices and coming up with a result for each entry. The only rule to addition and subtraction is that the matrices that the operation is being performed on must be of the same dimension. Here are two examples:

$$A = \begin{vmatrix} 1 & 5 \\ -2 & 0 \end{vmatrix} \qquad B = \begin{vmatrix} 13 & 7 \\ 5 & -10 \end{vmatrix}$$

$$A + B = \begin{vmatrix} 1 & 5 \\ -2 & 0 \end{vmatrix} + \begin{vmatrix} 13 & 7 \\ 5 & -10 \end{vmatrix} = \begin{vmatrix} (1+13) & (5+7) \\ (-2+5) & (0-10) \end{vmatrix} = \begin{vmatrix} 14 & 12 \\ 3 & -10 \end{vmatrix}$$

$$A - B = \begin{vmatrix} 1 & 5 \\ -2 & 0 \end{vmatrix} + \begin{vmatrix} 13 & 7 \\ 5 & -10 \end{vmatrix} = \begin{vmatrix} (1-13) & (5-7) \\ (-2-5) & (0-(-10)) \end{vmatrix} = \begin{vmatrix} -12 & -2 \\ -7 & 10 \end{vmatrix}$$

Note that both addition and subtraction are associative; that is, A + (B + C) = (A + B) + C. However, they're not commutative under subtraction. (A − B) may not equal (B − A).

Matrix Multiplication

There are two forms of matrix multiplication: *scalar* and *matrix*. Scalar matrix multiplication is simply the multiplication of a matrix by a scalar number. You simply multiply each element of the matrix by the number. The matrix can be *mxn* at any size.

Here's a general description for a 3x3 matrix. Let *k* be any real constant:

$$\text{Let } A = \begin{vmatrix} a_{00} & a_{01} & a_{02} \\ a_{10} & a_{11} & a_{12} \\ a_{20} & a_{21} & a_{22} \end{vmatrix}$$

$$\text{Then } k*A = k* \begin{vmatrix} a_{00} & a_{01} & a_{02} \\ a_{10} & a_{11} & a_{12} \\ a_{20} & a_{21} & a_{22} \end{vmatrix} = \begin{vmatrix} k*a_{00} & k*a_{01} & k*a_{02} \\ k*a_{10} & k*a_{11} & k*a_{12} \\ k*a_{20} & k*a_{21} & k*a_{22} \end{vmatrix}$$

Here's an example:

$$3* \begin{vmatrix} 1 & 4 \\ -2 & 6 \end{vmatrix} = \begin{vmatrix} (3*1) & (3*4) \\ (3*(-2)) & (3*6) \end{vmatrix} = \begin{vmatrix} 3 & 12 \\ -6 & 18 \end{vmatrix}$$

MATH — Scalar multiplication is also valid for matrix equations, as long as you perform the multiplication on both sides. This is true because you can always multiply the coefficients of any system by a constant as long as you do so to both the RHS (right hand side) and LHS (left hand side) of the system.

The second type of multiplication is true matrix multiplication. Its mathematical basis is a bit complex, but you can think of a matrix as an "operator" that operates on another matrix. Given two matrices, *A* and *B*, that you want to multiply, they must have the same inner dimension. In other words, if *A* is *mxn*, *B* must be *nxr. m* and *r* may or may not be equal, but the inner dimension must be. For example, you can multiply a 2x2 by a 2x2, a 3x2 by a 2x3, and a 4x4 by a 4x5, but you can't multiply a 3x**3** by a **2x**4 because the inner dimensions aren't equal. The resulting matrix will have a size that is equal to the outer dimension of the multiplier and multiplicand matrix. For example, a **2x**3 multiplying a 3x**4** would have dimension 2x4.

Matrix multiplication is one of those things that's very hard to describe with words. I always end up waving my hands a lot to show what I'm saying, so take a look at Figure 8.25 while I give you the technical description of the multiplication algorithm.

Given a matrix *A* and *B*, or *AxB*, and to multiply them together to compute each element of the result matrix *C*, you must take a row of *A* and multiply it by a column in *B*. To perform the multiplication, you sum the products of each element, which is also called the *dot product*. Here's an example for a 2x2 multiplying a 2x3—order counts!

$$\text{Let } A = \begin{vmatrix} 1 & 2 \\ 3 & 4 \end{vmatrix} \quad B = \begin{vmatrix} 1 & 3 & 5 \\ 6 & 0 & 4 \end{vmatrix}$$

```
C = A x B = |(1*1 + 2*6) (1*3 + 2*0) (1*5 +2*4)|
            |(3*1 + 4*6) (3*3 + 4*0) (3*5 +4*4)|

          = |13 3 13|
            |27 9 31|
```

FIGURE 8.25

The mechanics of matrix multiplication.

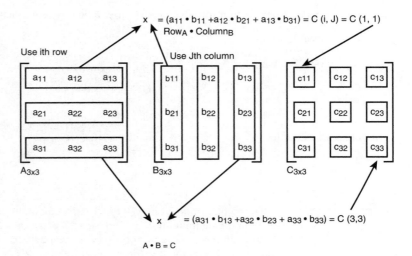

$A \cdot B = C$

As an aside, I want to bring your attention to the bolded sum of products $(1*1 + 2*6)$. This product and all the others are really vector dot products (a *vector* is just a collection of values, like a matrix with one row). A dot product has a very explicit mathematical meaning, which we'll get to later, but in general, you can compute the dot product of two vectors that are each $1 \times n$ by simply summing up the products of the independent components. Or, mathematically:

```
Let a = [1 2 3] b = [4 5 6]

a.b = [(1*4) + (2*5) + (3*6)]
    = [32]
      1x1
```

Or, if you want to be a little wet 'n' wild, it's just a *scalar*.

> **WARNING**
>
> I'm being a little cavalier right now with dot products; technically, they're only valid for vectors, but a column or row of a matrix is really a vector. Basically, I'm in a transitional period and I don't want to kill you. I want to *help* you...

So that's how you multiply matrices. Another way to think of it is that if you want to compute the product of *AxB*, call it *C*. You can do this element by element. Hence, if you want the c_{ij}th element (where both i and j are zero-based), you can find it by taking the ith row of A and doting (summing the products) with the jth column of B.

At this point, I think you get the general idea of what's going on. Let's take a look at some code that performs matrix multiplication. First, let's define a matrix type:

```
// here's a 3x3, useful for 2D stuff and some 3D
typedef struct MATRIX3X3_TYP
      {
      float M[3][3]; // data storage
      } MATRIX3X3, *MATRIX3X3_PTR;


int Mat_Mul_3X3(MATRIX3X3_PTR ma,
             MATRIX3X3_PTR mb,
             MATRIX3X3_PTR mprod)
{
// this function multiplies two matrices together and
// stores the result

for (int row=0; row<3; row++)
    {
    for (int col=0; col<3; col++)
        {
        // compute dot product from row of ma
        // and column of mb

        float sum = 0; // used to hold result

        for (int index=0; index<3; index++)
            {
            // add in next product pair
            sum+=(ma->M[row][index]*mb->M[index][col]);
            } // end for index

        // insert resulting row,col element
        mprod->M[row][col] = sum;

        } // end for col

    } // end for row

return(1);

} // end Mat_Mul_3X3
```

You'll notice that there's a lot of math going on. In general, matrix multiplication is an N^3 operation, meaning that there are three nested loops. However, a number of optimizations can be used, such as testing either the multiplier or multiplicand for 0 and not performing the multiplication.

Transformations Using Matrices

Using matrices to perform 2D/3D transformations is a snap. Basically, what you're going to do is multiply the point you want to be transformed against the desired transformation matrix. Or, mathematically:

```
p' = p*M
```

where p' is the transformed point, p is the original point, and M is the transformation matrix. If I haven't mentioned that matrix multiplication is *not* commutative, let me do so now:

```
(A*B) NOT EQUAL (B*A)
```

This statement is generally true unless A or B is the identity matrix or the zero matrix, or they're the same matrix. Order counts when you're matrix multiplying.

In this case, you're going to convert a single (x,y) point into a single row matrix with dimension 1x3, and then pre-multiply it by a 3x3 transformation matrix. The result will also be a 1x3 row matrix, and you can pick off the first two components as the transformed x',y'. Alas, you should have a slight problem with all this—what is the last component of the initial matrix p there for, if only two pieces of data, x and y, are needed?

In general, you're going to represent all points like this:

```
[x y 1.0]
```

The factor 1.0 is to make the matrix into what are called *homogenous coordinates*. This allows any transformed point to be scaled, and it also allows for translations in transformations. Other than that, the mathematical basis for it is unimportant. Just think of it as a dummy variable that you need. Hence, you're going to create a matrix that's 1x3 to hold your input point and then post-multiply it by the transformation matrix. Here are the data structures for the point or 1x3 matrix:

```
typedef struct MATRIX1X3_TYP
        {
        float M[3]; // data storage
        } MATRIX1X3, *MATRIX1X3_PTR;
```

And here's a function to multiply a point against a 3x3 matrix:

```
int Mat_Mul_1X3_3X3(MATRIX1X3_PTR ma,
                    MATRIX3X3_PTR mb,
                    MATRIX1X3_PTR mprod)
{
// this function multiplies a 1x3 matrix against a
// 3x3 matrix - ma*mb and stores the result
```

```
        for (int col=0; col<3; col++)
            {
            // compute dot product from row of ma
            // and column of mb

            float sum = 0; // used to hold result

            for (int index=0; index<3; index++)
                {
                // add in next product pair
                sum+=(ma->M[index]*mb->M[index][col]);
                } // end for index

            // insert resulting col element
            mprod->M[col] = sum;

            } // end for col
return(1);

} // end Mat_Mul_1X3_3X3
```

And to create a point *p* with components *x* and *y*, you would do the following:

```
MATRIX1X3 p = {x,y,1};
```

With all that in mind, let's take a look at the transformation matrices for all the operations you've performed manually.

Translation

To perform translation, you want to leave the *x,y* components alone while adding the translation factors to *x,y*. This matrix will do the job:

```
        |1  0  0 |
Mt =|0   1  0 |
        |dx dy 0 |
```

Example:

```
p = [x y 1]

                        |1  0  0 |
p' = p*Mt = [x y 1] * |0   1  0 | = [(x+1*dx) (y+1*dy) 1]
                        |dx dy 1 |
```

| **MATH** | Notice the necessity of the 1.0 factor in the left-hand matrix representing the point. Without it, there would be no way to perform translation. |

And if you pull out the first two elements, you get

```
x' = x+dx
y' = y+dy
```

This is exactly what you wanted.

Scaling

To scale a point relative to the origin, you want to multiply the *x,y* components by scaling factors *sx* and *sy*, respectively. In addition, you want no translation during the scaling operation. Here's the matrix you want:

```
     |sx  0   0|
Ms =|0   sy  0|
     |0   0   1|

Eg. p = [x y 1]

                   |sx  0   0|
p' = p*Ms = [x y 1] * |0   sy  0| = [(x*sx) (y*sy) 1]
                   |0   0   1|
```

Again, this is the desired result for scaling; that is

```
x' = sx*x
y' = sy*y
```

MATH

> Note the 1 in the lower-right corner of the transformation matrix. Technically, it's not necessary because you're never going to use the result from the third column. Hence, you're wasting math cycles. The question is, can you remove the last column of all the transformation matrices and use a 3×2 instead? Let's see the rotation matrix before you answer that...

Rotation

The rotation matrix is the most complex of all the transformations because it's full of trig functions. Basically, you want to rotate the input point by using the rotation equations. To achieve this, you must look at the rotation equations, pick the operators, and then push them into a matrix. In addition, you don't want any translation, so the bottom row in positions 0 and 1 will be 0. Here's the matrix that does the job:

```
     | cos  θ   sin θ  0|
Mr = |-sin  θ   cos θ  0|
     | 0        0      1 |
Eg. p = [x y 1]
                   | cos  θ   sin θ  0 |
p' = p*Mr = [x y 1] * |-sin  θ   cos θ  0 | =
                   | 0        0      1 |
p' = [(x*cos θ – y*sin θ) (x*sin θ + y*cos θ) 1]
```

Which is correct!

Before moving on to polygons, let's discuss the question that was posed before in reference to using a 3x2 post-multiplication matrix rather than a 3x3. It looks as if the last term in all the matrix multiplications is completely discarded, in addition to always being 1.0. Both of these statements are true.

Therefore, for the transformations that you've performed thus far, you *can* use a 3x2. However, I wanted to use a 3x3 to make a point about homogenous matrices and coordinates. The significance of the last 1.0 is this (in reality, let's refer to it as q): To convert the coordinates to their final correct form after the transformation is complete, you would divide by the factor q, or in other words:

```
p' =[x y q]

x' = x/q
y' = y/q
```

However, because $q = 1$ in this case, the divisions are unnecessary, as is the computation of q. Nonetheless, this factor will have importance later in the discussion of 3D graphics, so keep it in mind.

In any case, with this new information, you can change a couple of data structures and store all points in a 1x2 and all transformation matrices in a 3x2, using the following data structures and transform function:

```
// the transformation matrix

typedef struct MATRIX3X2_TYP
        {
        float M[3][2]; // data storage
        } MATRIX3X2, *MATRIX3X2_PTR;

// our 2D point
typedef struct MATRIX1X2_TYP
        {
        float M[2]; // data storage
        } MATRIX1X2, *MATRIX1X2_PTR;


int Mat_Mul_1X2_3X2(MATRIX1X2_PTR ma,
                    MATRIX3X2_PTR mb,
                    MATRIX1X2_PTR mprod)
{
// this function multiplies a 1x2 matrix against a
// 3x2 matrix - ma*mb and stores the result
// using a dummy element for the 3rd element of the 1x2
// to make the matrix multiply valid i.e. 1x3 X 3x2

    for (int col=0; col<2; col++)
        {
        // compute dot product from row of ma
```

```
        // and column of mb

        float sum = 0; // used to hold result

        for (int index=0; index<2; index++)
            {
            // add in next product pair
            sum+=(ma->M[index]*mb->M[index][col]);
            } // end for index

        // add in last element * 1
        sum+= mb[index][col];

        // insert resulting col element
        mprod->M[col] = sum;

        } // end for col

return(1);

} // end Mat_Mul_1X2_3X2
```

For a demo of using matrices in a program, check out DEMO8_6.CPP|EXE. I've created a polygon that resembles a little spaceship in wire frame, and you can scale, rotate, and translate it. Take a look at Figure 8.26 for a screen shot.

> **NOTE**
>
> You must always multiply a $m \times r$ matrix by an $r \times n$ matrix. In other words, the inner dimension must be equal. Obviously, 1×2 and 3×2 don't work because 2 is not equal to 3. However, in the code, you can add a dummy element 1.0 to each of the 1×2's, making them into 1×3's, just for the math to work out.

Here are the control keys for this demo:

Esc	Exits the demo.
A	Scales up 10%.
S	Scales down 10%.
Z	Rotates counterclockwise.
X	Rotates clockwise.
Arrow keys	Translates in x and y.

FIGURE 8.26

DEM08_6.EXE in action.

Solid Filled Polygons

Let's take a break from all the math and get back to something a little more tangible, shall we? One of the most basic requirements of a 3D engine, and many 2D engines, is to draw a solid or filled polygon, as shown in Figure 8.27. This is the next problem you're going to tackle.

FIGURE 8.27

Filling a polygon.

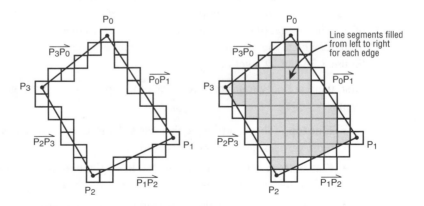

A. Vector or wire frame version   B. Filled version

There are a number of ways to draw filled polygons. However, because the point of all this is to create 2D/3D games, you want to be able to draw a filled polygon that can be a single color or texture-mapped, as shown in Figure 8.28. For now let's leave texture mapping alone until we get to the 3D stuff and just figure out how to draw a solid polygon of any color.

Before you solve the problem, you must clearly define what it is that you're trying to solve. The first constraint is that all polygons must be convex, so no holes or weird shapes are allowed. Then you have to decide how complex the polygon can be. Can it have three sides, four sides, or any number of sides? This is a definite issue, and you must employ a different algorithm for polygons that have more than three sides (four-sided polygons or quadrilaterals can be broken into two triangles).

FIGURE 8.28
A solid shaded polygon versus a texture-mapped polygon.

Thus, I'm going to show you how to fill both general polygons and triangles (which will be the basis of the final 3D engine you create).

Types of Triangles and Quadrilaterals

First off, let's take a look at a general quadrilateral, shown in Figure 8.29. The quadrilateral can be decomposed into two triangles, *ta* and *tb*, which simplifies the problem of drawing a quadrilateral. Therefore, you can now concentrate on drawing a single triangle, which you can then use to draw either a triangle or a quadrilateral. Refer to Figure 8.30 and let's get busy.

First, there are only four possible types of triangles that you can generate. Let's label them:

- **Flat top**—This is a triangle that has a flat top, or in other words, the two topmost vertices have the same *y* coordinate.
- **Flat bottom**—This is a triangle that has a flat bottom, or in other words, the two bottommost vertices have the same *y* coordinate.
- **Right side major**—This is a triangle in which all three vertices have different *y* coordinates, but the longest side of the triangle slopes to the right.
- **Left side major**—This is a triangle in which all three vertices have different *y* coordinates, but the longest side of the triangle slopes to the left.

FIGURE 8.29
A general four-sided quadrilateral.

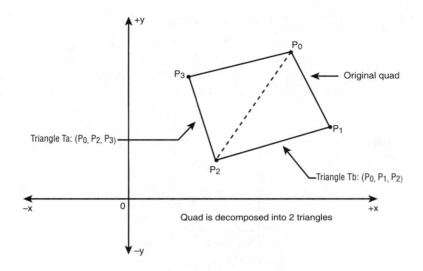

FIGURE 8.30
General triangle types.

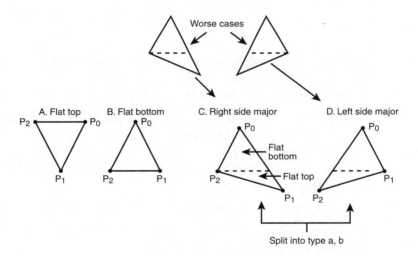

The first two types are the easiest to rasterize because each triangle leg is the same length (you'll see why that's important shortly). However, the latter two types are just as easy if you first decompose them into a pair of flat bottom and flat top triangles. You may or may not want to do this, but I usually do. If you don't, your rasterizer will need to contain steering logic to help with the slope changes on the side of the triangle with the two sides. Anyway, this will be much clearer once you see some examples.

Drawing Triangles and Quadrilaterals

Drawing a triangle is much like drawing a line, in that you must trace out the pixels of the edges to be drawn and then fill the triangle line by line. This is shown in Figure 8.31 for a flat bottom triangle. As you can see, once the slope of each edge is computed, you can simply move down each scanline, adjust the *x* endpoints *xs* and *xe* based on the slope (or more accurately 1/slope), and then draw a connecting line.

FIGURE 8.31
Rasterization of a triangle.

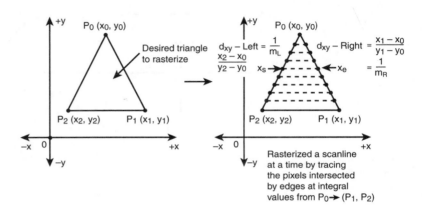

You don't need to use Bresenham's algorithm because you aren't interested in drawing a line. You're only interested in seeing where the line intersects the pixel centers at each integer interval. Here's the algorithm for the flat bottom triangle fill:

1. First, compute the ratio *dx/dy* for the left side and the right side. Basically, this is 1/slope. You need it because you're going to use a vertically oriented approach. Thus, you want to know the change in *x* for each *y*, which is simply *dx/dy* or *1/M*. Call these values `dxy_left` and `dxy_right` for the left and right side, respectively.

2. Starting at the topmost vertex (x0,y0), set *xs=xe=x0* and *y=y0*.

3. Add `dxy_left` to *xs* and `dxy_right` to *xe*. This will trace the endpoints to fill.

4. Draw a line from (*xs,y*) to (*xe,y*).

5. Go back to step 3 until the height of the triangle from the top to the bottom has been rasterized.

Of course, the initial conditions and boundary conditions for the algorithm take a little care to get right, but that's all there is to it, more or less—fairly simple. Now, before I show you anything else, let's talk about optimization for a minute.

At first glance, you might be tempted to use floating-point math for the edge tracing, which would work fine. However, the problem isn't that floating-point math is slower than integer math on a Pentium; the problem is that at some point, you'll have to convert the floating-point number into an integer.

If you let the compiler do it, you're looking at around 60 cycles. If you do it manually with FPU code, you can make it happen in about 10-20 cycles (remember, you need to convert to integers and then store). In any case, I refuse to lose 40 cycles on each raster line just to find my endpoints! Thus, you're going to create a floating-point version to show you the algorithm, but the final production model will use fixed-point math (which I'll brief you on in a moment).

Let's implement the flat bottom triangle rasterizer based on floating-point. First, let's label as shown in Figure 8.31. Here's the algorithm:

```
// compute deltas
float dxy_left  = (x2-x0)/(y2-y0);
float dxy_right = (x1-x0)/(y1-y0);

// set starting and ending points for edge trace
float xs = x0;
float xe = x0;

// draw each scanline
for (int y=y0; y <= y1; y++)
    {
    // draw a line from xs to xe at y in color c
    Draw_Line((int)xs, (int)xe, y, c);

    // move down one scanline
    xs+=dxy_left;
    xe+=dxy_right;

    } // end for y
```

Now, let's talk about some of the details of the algorithm and what's missing. First off, the algorithm truncates the endpoints each scanline. This is probably a bad thing because you're throwing away information. A better approach would be to round the value of each endpoint by adding 0.5 before converting to integer. Another problem has to do with the initial conditions. On the first iteration, the algorithm draws a line that's a single pixel wide. This works, but it's definitely a place for optimization.

Now, let's see if you can write the algorithm for a flat top triangle based on what you know. All you need to do is label the vertices, as shown in Figure 8.31, and then change the algorithm's initial conditions slightly so that the left and right interpolants are correctly computed. Here are the changes:

```
// compute deltas
float dxy_left  = (x2-x0)/(y2-y0);
float dxy_right = (x2-x1)/(y2-y1);

// set starting and ending points for edge trace
float xs = x0;
float xe = x1;

// draw each scanline
for (int y=y0; y <= y2; y++)
    {
    // draw a line from xs to xe at y in color c
    Draw_Line((int)(xs+0.5), (int)(xe+0.5), y, c);

    // move down one scanline
    xs+=dxy_left;
    xe+=dxy_right;

    } // end for y
```

Who's baaaaddd? Anyway, back to reality—you're halfway there. At this point, you can draw a triangle that has a flat top or a flat bottom, and you know that a triangle that doesn't have a flat top or bottom can be decomposed into one that does. Let's take a look at that problem and how to handle it.

Figure 8.32 shows a right side major triangle. Without proof, if you can rasterize a right side major triangle, the left side major is trivial. The first thing to notice is that you can start the algorithm off the same way you do for a flat bottom—that is, by starting the edge interpolators from the same starting point. The problem occurs when the left interpolator gets to the second vertex. This is where you need to make some changes. In essence, you must recompute the left side interpolant and continue rasterizing.

FIGURE 8.32
Rasterization of a
right side major
triangle.

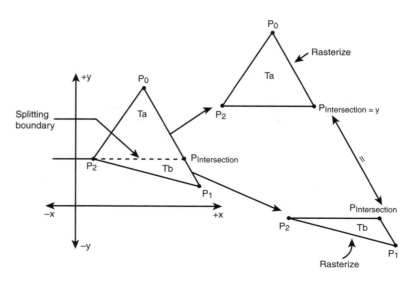

There are a number of ways to solve the problem. In the inner loop, you could draw the first part of the triangle up to the slope change, recompute the left side interpolant, and continue. Or you could do some triangular decomposition and break the triangle into two triangles (flat top and flat bottom) and then call the code you already have that draws a flat top and flat bottom triangle.

The latter is the technique you'll employ at this point. If you later find that this technique is inadequate in the 3D arena, change up and try the other method.

Triangular Deconstruction Details

Before I show you the code that draws a complete 8-bit colored triangle, I want to talk about a few more details involved in writing the algorithm correctly.

To decompose the triangle into a two triangles, one with a flat bottom and the other with a flat top, is a bit tricky. In essence, you need to take the height of the short side up until the first point where the slope changes, and then use this to find the point on the long side you'll use to partition the triangle. Basically, you take the vertical span from the top of the triangle and then, instead of interpolating one scanline on the long side, you interpolate n scanlines all at once by multiplying.

The result is equivalent to manually walking down the long edge of the triangle scanline by scanline. Then, once you have the correct point where you want to split the triangles, you simply make a call to your top and bottom triangle rasterizer and the triangle is drawn! Figure 8.32 showed the details of the splitting algorithm.

In addition to making the split, there comes another little problem—*overdraw*. If you send common vertices for the top triangle and the bottom triangle, the single scanline that is common to both will be rasterized twice. This isn't a big deal, but it's something to think about. You might want to step down on the bottom triangle one scanline to avoid the overdraw of the common scanline.

Almost ready… let's see, what else? Yes, what about clipping? If you recall, there are two ways to clip: *object space* and *image space*. Object space is great, but if you clip your triangle to the rectangle of the screen, in the very worst case you could add four more vertices! Take a look at Figure 8.33 to see this illustrated.

Instead you'll take the easy route and clip in image space as the polygon is being drawn, but you'll at least clip each scanline rather than each pixel. Moreover, you'll do some trivial rejection tests to determine if clipping is needed at all. If not, you'll jump to a part of the code that runs without clipping tests to run faster. Sound good?

Finally, while we're on the subject of trivial rejection and tests, we need to address all the degenerate cases of a triangle, such as a single point and a straight horizontal or vertical line. The code should test for these cases without blowing up! And of course, you can't assume that the vertices are in the correct order when sent to the function, so you'll sort them top to bottom, left to right. That way you'll have a known starting point. With all that in mind, here are the three functions that make up your 8-bit triangle drawing engine.

FIGURE 8.33

Worst-case scenario when clipping a triangle.

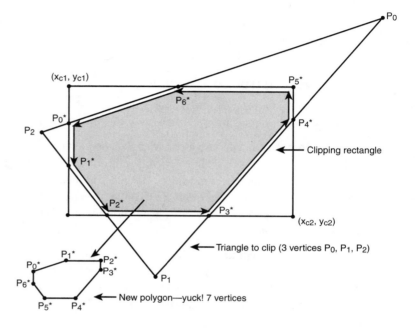

This function draws a triangle with a flat top:

```
void Draw_Top_Tri(int x1,int y1,
                  int x2,int y2,
                  int x3,int y3,
                  int color,
                  UCHAR *dest_buffer, int mempitch)
{
// this function draws a triangle that has a flat top

float dx_right,    // the dx/dy ratio of the right edge of line
      dx_left,     // the dx/dy ratio of the left edge of line
      xs,xe,       // the starting and ending points of the edges
      height;      // the height of the triangle

int temp_x,        // used during sorting as temps
    temp_y,
    right,         // used by clipping
    left;

// destination address of next scanline
UCHAR  *dest_addr = NULL;
```

```
// test order of x1 and x2
if (x2 < x1)
    {
    temp_x = x2;
    x2      = x1;
    x1      = temp_x;
    } // end if swap

// compute delta's
height = y3-y1;

dx_left  = (x3-x1)/height;
dx_right = (x3-x2)/height;

// set starting points
xs = (float)x1;
xe = (float)x2+(float)0.5;

// perform y clipping
if (y1 < min_clip_y)
    {
    // compute new xs and ys
    xs = xs+dx_left*(float)(-y1+min_clip_y);
    xe = xe+dx_right*(float)(-y1+min_clip_y);

    // reset y1
    y1=min_clip_y;

    } // end if top is off screen

if (y3>max_clip_y)
    y3=max_clip_y;

// compute starting address in video memory
dest_addr = dest_buffer+y1*mempitch;

// test if x clipping is needed
if (x1>=min_clip_x && x1<=max_clip_x &&
    x2>=min_clip_x && x2<=max_clip_x &&
    x3>=min_clip_x && x3<=max_clip_x)
    {
    // draw the triangle
    for (temp_y=y1; temp_y<=y3; temp_y++,dest_addr+=mempitch)
        {
        memset((UCHAR *)dest_addr+(unsigned int)xs,
                color,(unsigned int)(xe-xs+1));

        // adjust starting point and ending point
        xs+=dx_left;
        xe+=dx_right;

        } // end for
```

```
        } // end if no x clipping needed
    else
        {
        // clip x axis with slower version

        // draw the triangle
        for (temp_y=y1; temp_y<=y3; temp_y++,dest_addr+=mempitch)
            {
            // do x clip
            left  = (int)xs;
            right = (int)xe;

            // adjust starting point and ending point
            xs+=dx_left;
            xe+=dx_right;
            // clip line
            if (left < min_clip_x)
                {
                left = min_clip_x;

                if (right < min_clip_x)
                    continue;
                }

            if (right > max_clip_x)
                {
                right = max_clip_x;

                if (left > max_clip_x)
                    continue;
                }

            memset((UCHAR  *)dest_addr+(unsigned int)left,
                    color,(unsigned int)(right-left+1));

            } // end for

        } // end else x clipping needed

} // end Draw_Top_Tri
```

This function draws a triangle with a flat bottom:

```
void Draw_Bottom_Tri(int x1,int y1,
                     int x2,int y2,
                     int x3,int y3,
                     int color,
                     UCHAR *dest_buffer, int mempitch)
{
// this function draws a triangle that has a flat bottom

float dx_right,    // the dx/dy ratio of the right edge of line
      dx_left,     // the dx/dy ratio of the left edge of line
```

```
        xs,xe,        // the starting and ending points of the edges
        height;       // the height of the triangle

int temp_x,           // used during sorting as temps
    temp_y,
    right,            // used by clipping
    left;

// destination address of next scanline
UCHAR   *dest_addr;

// test order of x1 and x2
if (x3 < x2)
   {
   temp_x = x2;
   x2     = x3;
   x3     = temp_x;
   } // end if swap

// compute delta's
height = y3-y1;

dx_left  = (x2-x1)/height;
dx_right = (x3-x1)/height;

// set starting points
xs = (float)x1;
xe = (float)x1; // +(float)0.5;

// perform y clipping
if (y1<min_clip_y)
   {
   // compute new xs and ys
   xs = xs+dx_left*(float)(-y1+min_clip_y);
   xe = xe+dx_right*(float)(-y1+min_clip_y);

   // reset y1
   y1=min_clip_y;

   } // end if top is off screen

if (y3>max_clip_y)
   y3=max_clip_y;

// compute starting address in video memory
dest_addr = dest_buffer+y1*mempitch;

// test if x clipping is needed
if (x1>=min_clip_x && x1<=max_clip_x &&
    x2>=min_clip_x && x2<=max_clip_x &&
    x3>=min_clip_x && x3<=max_clip_x)
    {
    // draw the triangle
```

```
        for (temp_y=y1; temp_y<=y3; temp_y++,dest_addr+=mempitch)
          {
          memset((UCHAR  *)dest_addr+(unsigned int)xs,
                  color,(unsigned int)(xe-xs+1));

          // adjust starting point and ending point
          xs+=dx_left;
          xe+=dx_right;

          } // end for

      } // end if no x clipping needed
    else
      {
      // clip x axis with slower version

      // draw the triangle

      for (temp_y=y1; temp_y<=y3; temp_y++,dest_addr+=mempitch)
          {
          // do x clip
          left  = (int)xs;
          right = (int)xe;

          // adjust starting point and ending point
          xs+=dx_left;
          xe+=dx_right;

          // clip line
          if (left < min_clip_x)
             {
             left = min_clip_x;

             if (right < min_clip_x)
                continue;
             }

          if (right > max_clip_x)
             {
             right = max_clip_x;

             if (left > max_clip_x)
                continue;
             }

          memset((UCHAR  *)dest_addr+(unsigned int)left,
                 color,(unsigned int)(right-left+1));

          } // end for

      } // end else x clipping needed

   } // end Draw_Bottom_Tri
```

And finally, this function draws a general triangle by splitting it into a flat top and flat bottom if needed:

```
void Draw_Triangle_2D(int x1,int y1,
                      int x2,int y2,
                      int x3,int y3,
                      int color,
                 UCHAR *dest_buffer, int mempitch)
{
// this function draws a triangle on the destination buffer
// it decomposes all triangles into a pair of flat top, flat bottom

int temp_x, // used for sorting
    temp_y,
    new_x;

// test for h lines and v lines
if ((x1==x2 && x2==x3)  ||  (y1==y2 && y2==y3))
   return;

// sort p1,p2,p3 in ascending y order
if (y2<y1)
   {
   temp_x = x2;
   temp_y = y2;
   x2     = x1;
   y2     = y1;
   x1     = temp_x;
   y1     = temp_y;
   } // end if

// now we know that p1 and p2 are in order
if (y3<y1)
   {
   temp_x = x3;
   temp_y = y3;
   x3     = x1;
   y3     = y1;
   x1     = temp_x;
   y1     = temp_y;
   } // end if

// finally test y3 against y2
if (y3<y2)
   {
   temp_x = x3;
   temp_y = y3;
   x3     = x2;
   y3     = y2;
   x2     = temp_x;
   y2     = temp_y;

   } // end if
```

```
// do trivial rejection tests for clipping
if ( y3<min_clip_y || y1>max_clip_y ||
    (x1<min_clip_x && x2<min_clip_x && x3<min_clip_x) ||
    (x1>max_clip_x && x2>max_clip_x && x3>max_clip_x) )
    return;

// test if top of triangle is flat
if (y1==y2)
    {
    Draw_Top_Tri(x1,y1,x2,y2,x3,y3,color, dest_buffer, mempitch);
    } // end if
else
if (y2==y3)
    {
    Draw_Bottom_Tri(x1,y1,x2,y2,x3,y3,color, dest_buffer, mempitch);
    } // end if bottom is flat
else
    {
    // general triangle that's needs to be broken up along long edge
    new_x = x1 + (int)(0.5+(float)(y2-y1)*(float)(x3-x1)/(float)(y3-y1));

    // draw each sub-triangle
    Draw_Bottom_Tri(x1,y1,new_x,y2,x2,y2,color, dest_buffer, mempitch);
    Draw_Top_Tri(x2,y2,new_x,y2,x3,y3,color, dest_buffer, mempitch);

    } // end else

} // end Draw_Triangle_2D
```

To use the function, you need only call the last function because it internally calls the other support functions. Here's an example of calling the function to draw a triangle with the coordinates (100,100), (200,150), (40,200) in color 30:

```
Draw_Triangle_2D(100,100, 200,150, 40,200, 30, back_buffer, back_pitch);
```

In general, you should send the coordinates in counterclockwise as they wind around the triangle. At this point it doesn't matter, but when you get to 3D, this detail becomes very important because a number of the 3D algorithms look at the vertex order to determine the front- or back-facing property of the polygon.

TRICK	In addition to the preceding functions for drawing polygons, I've also created fixed-point versions of the functions that run a bit faster during the rasterization phase. These are also in the library file T3DLIB1.CPP. They're named with FP appended to each function name, but they all work the same. Basically, the only one you need to call is Draw_TriangleFP_2D(...). The function generates the same image as Draw_Triangle_2D(...) does, but it works a bit faster. If you're interested in fixed-point math, skip ahead to the Chapter 11, "Algorithms, Data Structures, Memory Management, and Multithreading," which covers optimization.

For an example of the polygon function in action, take a look at DEMO8_7.CPP|EXE. It draws randomly clipped triangles in 8-bit mode. Note that the global clipping region is defined by the general rectangular clipping variables:

```
int min_clip_x = 0,                              // clipping rectangle
    max_clip_x = (SCREEN_WIDTH-1),
    min_clip_y = 0,
    max_clip_y = (SCREEN_HEIGHT-1);
```

Now, let's move on to more complex rasterization techniques used for polygons with more than three vertices.

The General Case of Rasterizing a Quadrilateral

As you can see, rasterizing a simple triangle isn't the easiest thing in the world. Hence, you could assume that rasterizing polygons with more than three vertices is even harder. Guess what? It is!

Rasterizing a quadrilateral isn't bad if you split it into two triangles. For example, take a look back at Figure 8.29, where you see a quad being split into two triangles. Essentially, you can use this simple deterministic algorithm to split any quad into a two triangles:

> Given that the polygon vertices are labeled 0, 1, 2, 3 in some order, such as CW (clockwise)…
>
> Triangle 1 is composed of vertices 0, 1, 3
>
> Triangle 2 is composed of vertices 1, 2, 3

That's it, home slice <BG>.

With that in mind, to create a quad rasterizer, you can simply implement the previous code into a function that does the splitting. I've done this for you in a function called Draw_QuadFP_2D(...). There isn't a floating-point version. Anyway, here's the code for it:

```
inline void Draw_QuadFP_2D(int x0,int y0,
                           int x1,int y1,
                           int x2,int y2,
                           int x3, int y3,
                           int color,
                           UCHAR *dest_buffer, int mempitch)
{
// this function draws a 2D quadrilateral

// simply call the triangle function 2x, let it do all the work
Draw_TriangleFP_2D(x0,y0,x1,y1,x3,y3,color,dest_buffer,mempitch);
Draw_TriangleFP_2D(x1,y1,x2,y2,x3,y3,color,dest_buffer,mempitch);

} // end Draw_QuadFP_2D
```

The function is identical to the triangle function, except that it takes one more vertex. For an example of this function in use, take a look at `DEMO8_8.CPP|EXE`. It creates a number of random quads and draws them on the screen.

> **NOTE**   I'm getting sloppy with the parameters here. You could probably do a lot better by defining a polygon structure here and then passing an address rather than an entire set of vertices. I'm going to leave the code "as is" for now, but keep that in mind because you'll get to it when you do the 3D stuff.

Triangulating Quads

So let's see… you can draw a triangle and a quad, but how do you draw a polygon with more than four vertices? You could triangulate the polygon, as shown in Figure 8.34. Although this is a good approach, and many graphics engines do just this (especially hardware), it's a bit too complex of a problem to solve in general.

However, if the polygon is constrained to be convex (as yours are), it's much simpler. There are many algorithms to do this, but the one I generally use is recursive in nature and very simple. Figure 8.35 shows the steps of a five-sided convex polygon being triangulated.

FIGURE 8.34
Triangulating a large, multisided polygon.

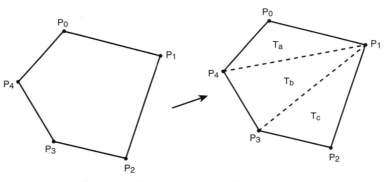

A. Polygon before triangulation

B. Polygon after triangulation

Note: There are other possible triangulations, e.g.

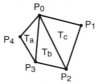

Note in Figure 8.35 that there are several possible valid triangulations. Thus, there may be heuristics and/or some kind of evaluation function applied to optimize the triangulation. For example, it may be a good idea to triangulate with the triangles that have nearly the same area, or first you might want to try to create very large triangles.

Whatever the case, it's something to think about in relation to your final engine. Anyway, here's a general algorithm that gets the job done.

Given a convex polygon with n vertices (n can be even or odd) in CC or CW order to triangulate...

1. If the number of vertices left to process is greater than three, continue to step 2; otherwise, stop.

2. Take the first three vertices and create a triangle with them.

3. Split off the new triangle and recursively process step 2 with the remaining $(n-1)$ vertices.

In essence, the algorithm keeps "peeling" off triangles and then resubmitting the remaining vertices back to the algorithm. It's very stupid and it doesn't do any preprocessing or testing, but it works. And of course, once you're done converting the polygon into triangles, you can send each one down the rasterization pipeline to the triangle renderer.

FIGURE 8.35

A possible triangulation algorithm visualized.

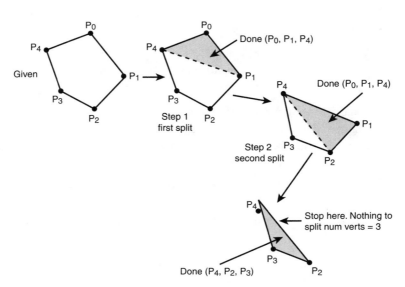

Okay, that's enough of that boooorrrrrriiinnnggg algorithm. Now let's look at another approach to rasterizing a general convex polygon the hard way. If you think in terms of how you rasterized a triangle, it's simply a matter of housekeeping to rasterize an n-sided convex polygon.

Take a look at Figure 8.36 to see the algorithm in action. In general, what you're going to do is sort the vertices from top to bottom and left to right so you have a sorted array of vertices in CW order this time. Then, starting from the topmost vertex, you're going to start rasterizing the two edges (left and right) emanating from the top vertex. When one of the edges comes to the point where it hits another vertex on the right or left side, you'll recompute the rasterization interpolants—that is, the `dx_left` or `dx_right` values—and continue until the polygon is rasterized.

That's really all there is to it. A flow chart for the algorithm is shown in Figure 8.37. Again, there are a number of boundary details to worry about, such as being careful not to put one of the edge interpolators out of sync during a vertex transition, but that's about it. And again, you can clip using image space or object space. Let's talk about this for a moment.

When you're rasterizing triangles, you don't want to clip in image space because you could end up with a six-sided polygon if all vertices are clipped. This would be bad because you'd have to convert the new polygon back into triangles. However, because your new algorithm likes general polygons, who cares about adding vertices?

Nevertheless, you need to consider one point—can a convex polygon be turned concave during a clipping operation? Absolutely, but (there's always a "but," and this time it's a good one) only if the clipping region is itself concave. Thus, clipping the convex polygon to the rectangle of the screen will at worst add one vertex per vertex that falls out of the clipping region.

This is usually the best approach when you're rasterizing an n-sided polygon—that is, to clip in object space and then rasterize the polygon without internal scanline clipping code. This is the approach you'll take here.

The following function takes a standard POLYGON2D_PTR, along with the frame buffer address and memory pitch, and then rasterizes the sent polygon. Of course, the polygon must be convex, and all vertex points must be within the clipping region because the function doesn't clip. Here's the function prototype:

```
void Draw_Filled_Polygon2D(POLYGON2D_PTR poly,
                           UCHAR *vbuffer, int mempitch);
```

To draw a square centered at 320,240 with sides 100x100, here's what you would do:

```
POLYGON2D square; // used to hold the square

// define points of object (must be convex)
VERTEX2DF square_vertices[4]
            = {-50,-50, 50,-50, 50,50,-50, 50};
```

```
// initialize square
object.state       = 1;   // turn it on
object.num_verts   = 4;
object.x0          = 320;
object.y0          = 240;
object.xv          = 0;
object.yv          = 0;
object.color       = 255; // white
object.vlist       = new VERTEX2DF [square.num_verts];

// copy the vertices into polygon
for (int index = 0; index < square.num_verts; index++)
    square.vlist[index] = square_vertices[index];



// .. in the main game loop
Draw_Filled_Polygon2D(&square, (UCHAR *)ddsd.lpSurface, ddsd.lPitch);
```

FIGURE 8.36

Rasterizing an *n*-sided convex polygon without triangulation.

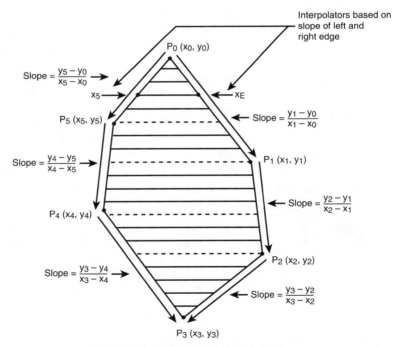

At each <u>vertex</u>, there is an interpolate change for the left and right edges.

DirectX and 2D Fundamentals

FIGURE 8.37
A flowchart of the
general *n*-sided
convex polygon-
rendering algorithm.

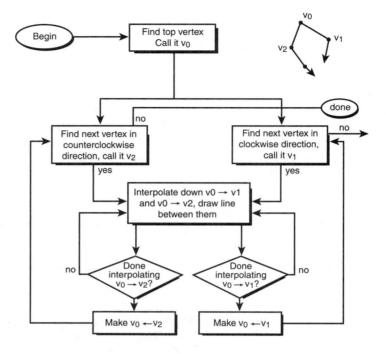

UHHHH! Can you feel that, baby? Anyway, I would show you the listing of the function, but it's rather large. However, you can see the code for yourself in DEMO8_9.CPP|EXE, which illustrates the use of the function by rotating around a four-sided polygon (a square) and then calling the fill function to draw the polygon. But instead of drawing the square using two triangles, the function rasterizes the polygon directly—without clipping.

> **TIP**
>
> Whenever you write a rasterization function, it's always a good idea to test if it can successfully render an object as it rotates. Many times when you test a rasterization function, you end up sending it "easy" coordinates. However, by rotating an object, you get all kinds of tweaked-out values. If the function can hang through a complete 360-degree rotation, you *know* it's good to go!

Collision Detection with Polygons

Thank Zeus that we're through all that material. I've about had it with rasterizing and transforming polygons! Let's take a bit of a break and talk about some game-related topics, such as collision detection and how to make such determinations with polygon objects. With that in mind, I'm going to show you three different ways to look at the problem. By using these techniques (or hybrids thereof), you should be able to handle all your polygon collision-detection needs.

Proximity AKA Bounding Sphere/Circle

The first method of testing two polygons for collision is to simply assume that the objects have an average radius and then test if the radii overlap. This can be accomplished with a simple distance calculation, as shown in Figure 8.38.

FIGURE 8.38
Using bounding circles (spheres in 3D) to detect collisions.

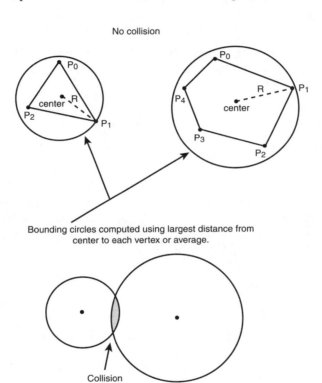

Of course, you're putting circular bounding boxes around each polygon. When tested by the preceding method, this results in collisions when there are none, as well as missed collisions (depending on how the average radius is computed).

To implement the algorithm, first you must compute a radius value for each polygon. This can be done in a number of ways. You might take the distance from the center of the polygon to each vertex and then average the radius values of each, use the largest value, or some other heuristic. I usually like to use a value that's midway between the average and the farthest vertex. In any case, this computation can be done out of the game loop, so there are no worries about CPU cycles. However, the actual test during runtime is a problem.

> **MATH** To compute the distance between two points, *(x1,y1)* and *(x2,y2)*, in a 2D space, use the formula $d = sqrt((x1-x2)^2 + (y1-y2)^2)$. For a 3D space, just add the *(z1-z2)²* term within the square root radical.

Given that you have two polygons—*poly1*, located at *(x1,y1)*, and *poly2*, located at *(x2,y2)*, with radius *r1* and *r2*, respectively (calculated in whatever way)—to test if the polygon's radii are overlapping, you can use the following pseudo-code:

```
// compute the distance between the center of each polygon
dist = sqrt((x1-x2)*(x1-x2) + (y1-y2)*(y1-y2));

// test the distance
if (dist <= (r1+r2)
    {
     // collision!
    } // end if
```

This works just as you'd expect, but there's one problem…it's freakin' slow! The square root function takes about a month in CPU cycles, so you know you need to get rid of that. But let's start with the simpler optimizations just to warm up. First, there's no need to compute the difference twice, (x1-x2) and (y1-y2). You can compute it once and then use the result in the computation, like this:

```
float dx = (x1-x2);
float dy = (y1-y2);

dist = sqrt(dx*dx + dy*dy);
```

That helps a bit, but the `sqrt()` function takes about 70 times longer than a floating-point multiply. That is, an FMUL takes about 1-3 cycles on a standard Pentium, and the FSQRT takes about 70 cycles. In either case, it's unacceptable. Let's see what you can do. One trick is to compute the distance using a mathematical trick based on a Taylor/Maclaurin series expansion.

> **MATH** Taylor/Maclaurin series are mathematical tools used to approximate complex functions by summing up simpler terms based on evaluating the function at constant intervals, along with taking the function's derivative into consideration. In general, the Maclaurin series expansion of *f(x)* is
>
> *f(0) + f'(0)*x1/1! + f''(0)*x2/2! + .. + f(n)(0)*xn/n!*
>
> where ' means *derivative* and ! means *factorial*. For example: *3! = 3*2*1*

After working through the math, you can write a function that approximates the distance between two points, *p1* and *p2*, in 2D space (or 3D) with only a few tests and additions. Here are algorithms for both the 2D and 3D cases:

```
// used to compute the min and max of two expressions
#define MIN(a, b)   ((a < b) ? a : b)
#define MAX(a, b)   ((a > b) ? a : b)

#define SWAP(a,b,t) {t=a; a=b; b=t;}

int Fast_Distance_2D(int x, int y)
{
// this function computes the distance from 0,0 to x,y with 3.5% error

// first compute the absolute value of x,y
x = abs(x);
y = abs(y);

// compute the minimum of x,y
int mn = MIN(x,y);

// return the distance
return(x+y-(mn>>1)-(mn>>2)+(mn>>4));

} // end Fast_Distance_2D

////////////////////////////////////////////////////////////////////////

float Fast_Distance_3D(float fx, float fy, float fz)
{
// this function computes the distance from the origin to x,y,z

int temp;  // used for swaping
int x,y,z; // used for algorithm

// make sure values are all positive
x = fabs(fx) * 1024;
y = fabs(fy) * 1024;
z = fabs(fz) * 1024;

// sort values
if (y < x) SWAP(x,y,temp);
if (z < y) SWAP(y,z,temp);
if (y < x) SWAP(x,y,temp);

int dist = (z + 11*(y >> 5) + (x >> 2) );

// compute distance with 8% error
return((float)(dist >> 10));

} // end Fast_Distance_3D
```

The parameters to each function are simply the deltas. For example, to use
Fast_Distance_2D() in the context of your previous algorithm, you would do the following:

```
dist = Fast_Distance_2D(x1-x2, y1-y2);
```

This new technique, based on the function call, uses only three shifts, four additions, a
few compares, and a couple of absolute values—much faster!

NOTE	Notice that both algorithms are approximations, so be careful if exact accuracy is needed. The 2D version has a maximum error of 3.5 percent, and the 3D version is around 8 percent.

One last thing… Astute readers may notice that there's yet another optimization to
take advantage of—and that's not finding the square root at all! Here's what I mean:
Let's say that you want to detect if one object is within 100 units of another. You
know that the distance is dist = sqrt(x*x + y*y), but if you were to square both
sides of the equation, you'd get

```
dist² = (x*x + y*y)
```

And dist in this case was 100, so 100^2 is 10,000. Thus, if you test the RHS and it's
< 10,000, that's equivalent to testing if it's < 100 if you take the square root! Cool, huh?
The only problem with this technique is overflowing, but there is *no* reason whatsoever
to compute the actual distance. Just do all your comparisons in terms of the square of
the distance.

Bounding Box

Although the mathematics of the bounding sphere/circle algorithm are very straightforward, the obvious problem in your case is that the object (polygon) is being
approximated with a circular object. This may or may not be appropriate. For example, take a look at Figure 8.39. It depicts a polygonal object that has general rectangular geometry. Approximating this object with a bounding sphere would induce a lot of
errors, so it's better to use a geometrical entity that's more like the object itself. In
these cases, you can use a bounding box (square or rectangle) to make the collision
detection easier.

Creating a bounding rectangle for a polygon is done in the same manner as for a
bounding sphere, except that you must find four edges rather than a radius. I usually
like to call them (*max_x*, *min_x*, *max_y*, *min_y*) and they're relative to the center of
the polygon. Figure 8.40 shows the setup graphically.

To find the values for (*max_x*, *min_x*, *max_y*, *min_y*), you can use the following simple algorithm:

1. Initialize (*max_x=0*, *min_x=0*, *max_y=0*, *min_y=0*). This assumes that the center of the polygon is at (0,0).

2. For each vertex in the polygon, test the (*x,y*) component against (*max_x*, *min_x*, *max_y*, *min_y*) and update appropriately.

FIGURE 8.39
Using the best bounding geometry for the job.

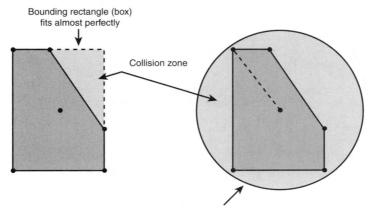

FIGURE 8.40
Bounding rectangle (box) setup.

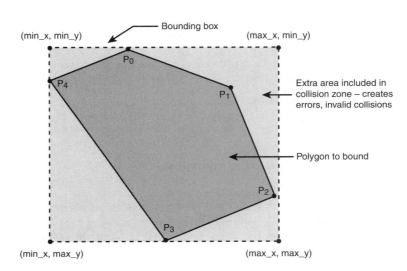

And here's the algorithm coded to work for your standard POLYGON2D structure:

```
int Find_Bounding_Box_Poly2D(POLYGON2D_PTR poly,
                             float &min_x, float &max_x,
                             float &min_y, float &max_y)
{
// this function finds the bounding box of a 2D polygon
// and returns the values in the sent vars

// is this poly valid?
if (poly->num_verts == 0)
    return(0);

// initialize output vars (note they are pointers)
// also note that the algorithm assumes local coordinates
// that is, the poly verts are relative to 0,0
max_x = max_y = min_x = min_y = 0;

// process each vertex
for (int index=0; index < poly->num_verts; index++)
    {
    // update vars - run min/max seek
    if (poly->vlist[index].x > max_x)
      max_x = poly->vlist[index].x;

    if (poly->vlist[index].x < min_x)
      min_x = poly->vlist[index].x;

    if (poly->vlist[index].y > max_y)
      max_y = poly->vlist[index].y;

    if (poly->vlist[index].y < min_y)
      min_y = poly->vlist[index].y;

} // end for index

// return success
return(1);

} // end Find_Bounding_Box_Poly2D
```

NOTE   Notice that the function sends the parameters as "call by reference" using the & operator. This is similar to using a pointer, except that you don't have to dereference. Moreover, unlike a pointer, & references are aliases.

You would call the function like this:

```
POLYGON2D poly; // assume this is initialized

float min_x, min_y, max_x, max_y; // used to hold results
```

```
// make call
Find_Bounding_Box_Poly2D(&poly, min_x, max_x, min_y, max_y);
```

After the call, the min/max rectangle will be built and stored in (*min_x*, *max_x*, *min_y*, *max_y*). With these values, along with the position of the polygon (x0,y0), you can then perform a bounding box collision test by testing two different bounding boxes against each other. Of course, you can accomplish this in a number of ways, including by testing if any of the four corner points of one box are contained within the other box, or by using more clever techniques.

Point Containment

In light of my last statement about testing if a point is contained within a rectangle, I thought it might be a good idea to show you how to figure out if a point is contained within a general convex polygon. What do you think? Obviously, figuring out if a point is within a rectangle is no more than the following:

Given rectangle (*x1,y1*) to (*x2,y2*) and that you want to test (*x0,y0*) for containment:

```
if (x0 >= x1 && x0 <= x2) // x-axis containment
   if (y0 >= y1 && y0 <= y2) // y-axis containment
      { /* point is contained */ }
```

> **NOTE** I could have used a single if statement along with another && to connect the two terms, but this code more clearly illustrates the linear separability of the problem—that is, the x- and y-axes can be processed independently.

Let's see if you can figure out if a point is contained within a convex polygon, as shown in Figure 8.41. At first, you might think that it's an easy problem, but I assure you that it's not. There are a number of ways to approach the problem, but one of the most straightforward is the *half-space test*. Basically, if the polygon you're testing is convex (which it is in this case), you can think of each side as a segment that is colinear with an infinite plane. Each plane divides space into two half-spaces, as shown in Figure 8.42.

If the point you're testing is on the interior side of each half-space, the point must be within the polygon because of the convex property of the polygon. Thus, all you need to do is figure out a way to test if a point in a 2D space is on one side of a line or the other.

This isn't too bad, assuming that you label the lines in some order and convert them to vectors. Then you'll think of each of the line segments as a plane. Using the dot product operator, you can determine if a point is on either side of each plane or on the plane itself. This is the basis of the algorithm.

FIGURE 8.41
The setup for a point in polygon containment testing.

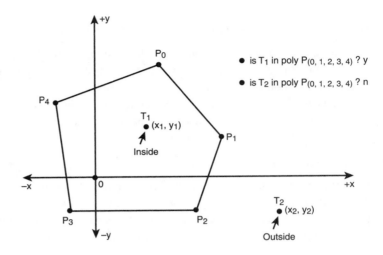

FIGURE 8.42
Using half-spaces to help solve the point in a polygon problem.

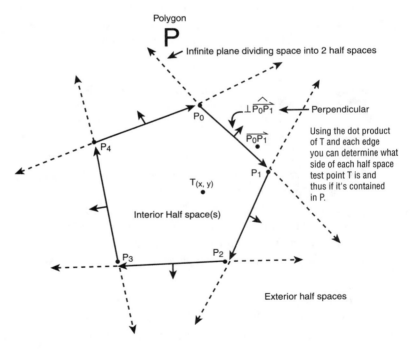

You may not be up to speed on vectors, dot products, and so on, so I'm going to hold off for this test and the accompanying algorithm until we cover 3D math—no need to confuse you here. However, I wanted you to at least understand the geometry of the solution. The details are just math, and any high-level organic or inorganic organism can perform math if taught properly…right?

More on Timing and Synchronization

In most of the programs thus far, I've been using a very cheesy timing system—
Sleep(). That's about as low-tech as you can get <BG>. In real life, you need to lock
your game to some frame rate, such as 30fps. A better way to achieve this lock is to
start a timer at the top of the game loop (or take note of the current time) and then, at
the end of the game loop, test if the amount of time for 30 fps—that is, 1/30 seconds—has elapsed. If so, continue to the next frame. If not, wait until the time has
elapsed (maybe work on the next frame or do some housekeeping so as not to waste
cycles).

In computer code, you would structure your Game_Main() something like this:

```
DWORD Get_Clock(void);
DWORD Start_Clock(void);
DWORD Wait_Clock(DWORD count);


int Game_Main(void *parms = NULL, int num_parms = 0)
{
// this is called each frame


// get the current time in milliseconds since windows
// was started
Get_Clock();

// do work…

// sync to frame rate, 30 fps in this case
Wait_Clock(30);

} // end Game_Mains
```

Simple as that! Oh yeah… what about these phantom functions? Ahhh yes, here they
are—based on Win32 timing functions:

```
DWORD Get_Clock(void)
{
// this function returns the current tick count

// return time
return(GetTickCount());

} // end Get_Clock

///////////////////////////////////////////////////////////

DWORD Start_Clock(void)
{
// this function starts the clock, that is, saves the current
// count, use in conjunction with Wait_Clock()
```

DirectX and 2D Fundamentals

```
return(start_clock_count = Get_Clock());

} // end Start_Clock

////////////////////////////////////////////////////////

DWORD Wait_Clock(DWORD count)
{
// this function is used to wait for a specific number of clicks
// since the call to Start_Clock

while((Get_Clock() - start_clock_count) < count);
return(Get_Clock());

} // end Wait_Clock
```

Notice that they're based on the Win32 function `GetTickCount()`, which returns a `DWORD` equal to the number of milliseconds elapsed since Windows was started. Hence, the time is relative, but who cares? That's all you need. Also, notice the use of the global `start_clock_count` to store the starting time. It's set every time `Get_Clock()` is called and is defined like this in the library:

```
DWORD start_clock_count = 0;      // used for timing
```

| | This is a perfect place for a C++ class; feel free. |

DirectX also has a vertical blank detection function that you can use to determine the state of the electron gun as it renders the image on the CRT. The `IDIRECTDRAW4` interface supports a function called `WaitForVerticalBlank()`, as shown here:

```
HRESULT WaitForVerticalBlank(DWORD dwFlags,
                             HANDLE hEvent);
```

You can use it to determine the various states of the vertical blank. `dwFlags` controls the operation of the function, and `hEvent` is a handle to a Win32 event (advanced stuff). Take a look at Table 8.3 for the valid flag settings.

TABLE 8.3 Flag Settings for `WaitForVerticalBlank()`

Flag	Description
DDWAITVB_BLOCKBEGIN	Returns when the vertical-blank interval begins.
DDWAITVB_BLOCKEND	Returns when the vertical-blank interval ends and the display begins.

Scrolling and Panning

All right, I guess that I think scrolling is easy because I never really put it in my books. (But in my defense, I did put page scrolling in *Sams Teach Yourself Game Programming in 21 Days*, and I put full layered and playfield scrolling in *The Black Art of 3D Game Programming*.) Scrolling games are in a class all their own, and really explaining all the 2D scrolling techniques would take a good chapter or two. Instead, I want to talk to you in a more abstract way about each scrolling method and then show you some demos.

Page Scrolling Engines

Page scrolling basically means that as the player moves around on the screen and crosses some threshold, the entire screen is updated as if the player has walked into another room. This technique is very easy to implement and can be coded in a number of ways. Referring to Figure 8.43, you see a typical game universe consisting of a 4x2 matrix of full screens at 640x480 pixels each. Hence, the entire universe is 2560x960.

The rendering logic is simple for this setup. You load the first screen into memory, and then you can load all adjacent screens into RAM or virtualize them on disk. Either way you do it, the scrolling works the same. As the player's character moves around the screen, you test it for some boundary condition (maybe the screen edges). When the boundary condition is met, you advance to the next "room" or screen and move the player's character to the appropriate position. For example, if you were walking from left to right and you hit the right edge of the screen, the new page would be displayed with the character at the left side of the screen. Of course, this is a bit crude, but it's a start…

FIGURE 8.43
A page scrolling universe setup.

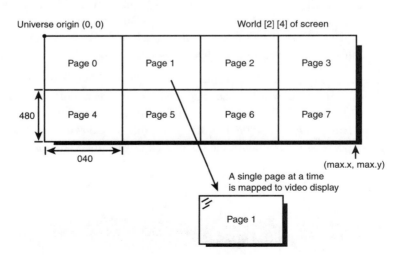

For a demo of this technique, take a look at DEMO8_10.EXE|CPP and
DEMO8_10_16b.EXE|CPP (the 16-bit windowed version, so make sure you are in 16-bit
mode) on the CD. It basically creates a 3x1 universe and lets you move a little character around with the arrow keys. When you hit a screen edge, the image is updated.
Note that I'm using bitmaps for the screen images, but there's no reason why you
couldn't use vector images or a mixture.

Also, I'm cheating a little on this demo by using functions from the final
T3DLIB1.CPP file at the end of this chapter, but you can always look at the source if
you want to. I simply needed more power than what we have so far to make a decent
demo!

Finally, make sure to take a look at the "terrain following" code in the demo. The
character follows the floor as you move right to left by scanning for a specific color
index representing the floor (color index 116, I think for the 8-bit mode, and the
actual RGB value is used in the 16-bit demo). When the scanner detects the color, the
character is pushed up a little, keeping it above the floor line.

Homogeneous Tile Engines

The example of scrolling wasn't really scrolling in the sense of a side-scrolling platform game. That kind of scrolling is a bit smoother—the entire screen image isn't
warped page to page, but is smoothly scrolled up, down, left, or right.

Using DirectX, there are a number of ways to achieve this effect. You could create a
large surface and then display only a portion of it on the primary display surface, as
shown in Figure 8.44.

However, this only works on DirectX 6.0 (and later) and needs heavy acceleration. A
better approach is to break up your worlds into tiles and then represent each screen by
a square matrix of tiles or cells, where each cell represents a bitmap(s) to be displayed
at that position. Figure 8.45 shows this setup.

For example, you might decide to make all your tiles 32x32 pixels and to run in a
640x480 mode, which means that the a single screen will require a tile map of
(640/32) x (480/32) = 20x15. Or if you decide to go 64x64, you would need a tile
map of (640/64) x (480/64) = 10x7.5 or, rounding down, 10x7 (7x64 = 448; the last
48 pixels at the bottom of the screen you'll leave for a control panel).

FIGURE 8.44
Using a large
DirectDraw surface to
achieve smooth
scrolling.

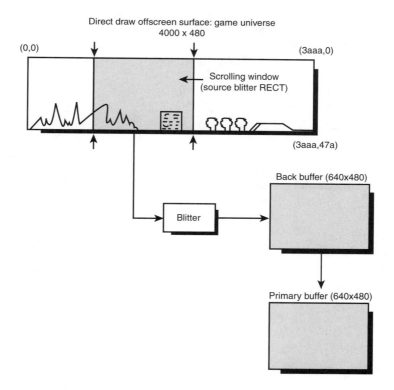

To make this work, you'll need a data structure, like an array or matrix of integers, or maybe structures that each hold the bitmap information (just a pointer or an index) along with anything else you might need. Here's an example of how you might create a tiled image:

```
typedef struct TILE_TYP
{
int x,y;   // position of tile in matrix
int index; // index of bitmap
int flags; // general flags for the cell

} TILE, *TILE_PTR;
```

Then, to hold one screen of information, you would do something like this:

```
typedef struct TILED_IMAGE_TYP
{
TILE image[7][10]; // 7 rows by 10 columns
} TILED_IMAGE, *TILE_IMAGE_PTR;
```

And finally, here's a world that's 3x3 of these large tiled images:

```
TILED_IMAGE world[3][3];
```

DirectX and 2D Fundamentals

Or you might decide to just create a tile array large enough to hold 3x3 screens, 30x21, and forget the array, like this:

```
typedef struct TILED_IMAGE_TYP
{
TILE image[21][30]; // 21 rows by 30 columns
} TILED_IMAGE, *TILE_IMAGE_PTR;

TILED_IMAGE world;
```

> **NOTE**
> You can design the data structure either way, but the single large array is easier to work with because you don't have to deal with jumping screen maps as you scroll past each 10×7 tile map.

FIGURE 8.45
Using a tile-based data structure to represent a scrolling world.

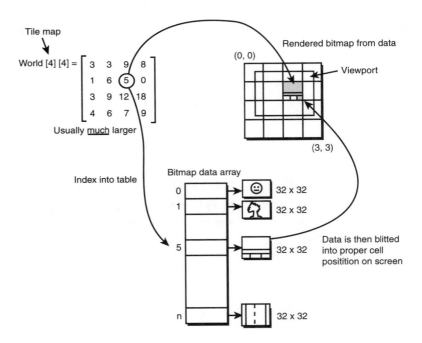

So how do you draw each screen? First, you need to load your bitmaps into a large array of 64x64 surfaces. You may have one or more tiles, and some may be repeatable, such as ships, edges, water, and so on. Figure 8.46 shows an example tile set.

FIGURE 8.46
Bitmap template of a
typical tile set.

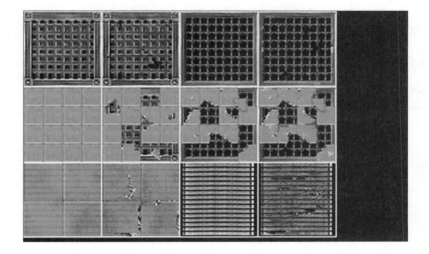

Then you write a tool, or just use an ASCII editor with some conversion software, so
you can generate your tile maps. For example, you might decide to use ASCII data
along with a bit of conversion software, so the numbers 0–9 may be used to indicate
tiles 0 to 9 in the tile set. Given that, you would need to define a tile set composed of
a 30x21 set of cells. Here's what I would do:

```c
// use an array of string pointers, could have used an
// array of chars or int, but harder to initialize
// the characters '0' - '9' represent bitmaps 0-9 in some texture memory
char *map1[21] =
{
"000000000000000000000000000000",
"000000000000000000000000000000",
"000000000000000000000000000000",
"000000000000000000000000000000",
"000000000000000000000000000000",
"000000000000000000000000000000",
"000000000000000000000000000000",
"000000000000000000000000000000",
"000000000000000000000000000000",
"000000000000000000000000000000",
"000000000000000000000000000000",
"000000000000000000000000000000",
"000000000000000000000000000000",
"000000000000000000000000000000",
"000000000000000000000000000000",
"000000000000000000000000000000",
"000000000000000000000000000000",
"000000000000000000000000000000",
"000000000000000000000000000000",
"000000000000000000000000000000",
"000000000000000000000000000000",

};
```

During runtime, you scan the map information into your main structure, and then you're ready to render. To render, you must first have a viewport setup or a mxn window that the user is currently viewing.

In most cases, this window is the same size as the screen—640x480, 800x600, and so forth—but not necessarily. You may have a control panel to the right or something that doesn't scroll. In any case, assuming that the whole screen scrolls and it's 640x480, you must take a couple of things into consideration:

- How the 640x480 viewport overlaps the main tile map of 10x7 cells.
- The boundary conditions.

Let's try and figure out what I'm talking about here. (I think it may help me too—I'm confusing myself!) All right, imagine that the viewport is at (0,0) in the uppermost tile map, as shown in Figure 8.47.

FIGURE 8.47

Boundary problems with scrolling tile maps.

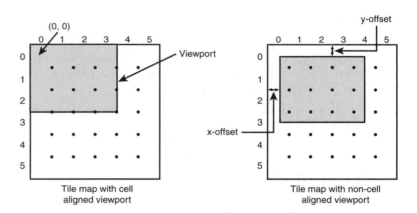

Tile map with cell aligned viewport

Tile map with non-cell aligned viewport

In this case, you must draw only the tiles from map[0][0] to map[6][9]. But the second the map scrolls to the right or down, you're going to have to draw some of the edge tiles from the tile map to the right and directly under the current viewport. Then, as you scroll one entire cell (64x64), you won't draw an entire row and/or column of tile map[0][0].

So, you can see that any time you're going to draw a rectangular collection of tiles that's always 10x7, those tiles will come from one or more tile maps. Moreover, as you scroll +/- from positions that are multiples of 64, you'll only see part of the edge tiles, so clipping is involved. Luckily, DirectDraw clips all bitmap surfaces for you, so if you draw a bitmap that's partially off the screen, it will just be clipped. Hence, your final algorithm only needs to determine the tiles to render, look up the bitmap surfaces that each tile represents, and then send them to the blitter.

For a demo of this, check out DEM08_11.EXE|CPP and DEM08_11b.EXE|CPP (the 16-bit version, make sure the desktop is in 16-bit mode) on the CD. They create the exact world just discussed and allow you to move around in it.

Sparse Bitmap Tile Engines

The only problem with tile engines is that there are a lot of bitmaps to draw. Sometimes you may want to make a scrolling game but you don't have a ton of graphics to scroll around. Moreover, you might not want to make all the tiles the same size. This is true for a lot of space shooters, because those games are mostly blank space. For those types of worlds, you want to create a universe map that's very large (as usual)—let's say 4x4 (or 40x40) screens for argument's sake. Then, instead of having tile maps for each subscreen, you simply place each object or bitmap at any location in world coordinates. Using this method, not only can each object bitmap be any size, but it can be placed anywhere.

The only problem with this scheme is efficiency. Basically, for any position where the current viewport resides, you must find all the objects that are within it so they can be rendered. If you have a small universe with a small number of objects, testing 100 or so objects for inclusion in the current windows isn't going to kill you. But if you have to test thousands of objects, it just *might* kill you!

The solution to the problem is to *sectorize* the game universe. In essence, you create a secondary data structure that tracks all the objects and their relations to a number of cells that you break the universe up into. But wait a minute, aren't you just using a tile map set again? Yes and no. In this case, the sectors can be any size and don't really have any relationship to the screen size. The selection of their size is more related to collision detection and tracking.

Take a look at Figure 8.48, which shows the data structures and their relationships to the screen, world, and viewport.

Note that this is only one method of solving the problem; there are many more, of course. Nevertheless, the point is that you have a collection of objects that are spaced out in a universe that is much larger than the screen—maybe 100000x100000—and you want to be able to move around in it. No problem, just position all the objects with their real-world coordinates and then, based on where the viewport window is (which is 640x480), map or translate all the objects in the window to the screen or video buffer. Of course, I'm again assuming that you have good clipping, because many objects will partially extend off the video display surface when drawn.

FIGURE 8.48
Sparse scrolling
engine data structures.

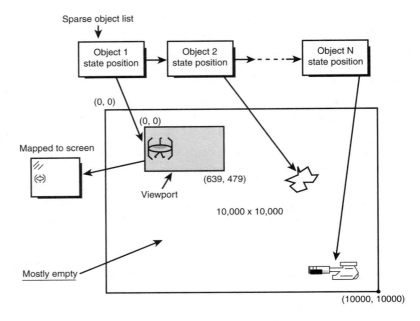

As an example of sparse scrolling, I've created a space demo (this isn't a high-budget production, you know) that allows you to move around in a starfield along with a number of stellar objects. In this demo, there isn't very much data structure support for the sectorizing, and the objects themselves are placed randomly. In real life, you would of course have world maps, sectorizing for collision and rendering optimization, and so on. I've written a demo of sparse scrolling named DEMO8_12.CPP|EXE along with the 16-bit version DEMO8_12_16b.CPP|EXE (as always you must have the desktop in 16-bit mode). Again, they make use of the T3DLIB1.CPP|H files, so make sure to include them in your project.

DEMO8_12.EXE/DEMO8_12_6B.EXE basically loads a number of bitmap objects and then randomly places them in a space that's 10x10 screens in size. Then you navigate around the world with the arrow keys as usual. The beauty of this type of scrolling is that the entire screen doesn't need to be rendered. Only the bitmaps that are visible or partially visible are rendered. Hence, there's a clipping phase in this demo where each object is tested, and if it's totally invisible, it isn't sent to the bitmap rendering code.

Fake 3D Isometric Engines

I have to admit, I've been getting so much email on this topic, I feel like I should have just written a book called *Isometric 3D Games*! What are those, you ask? Well, they're games in which the viewpoint is at some skewed angle, such as 45 degrees. Some of the old isometric (ISO) 3D games include *Zaxxon*, *PaperBoy*, and *Marble Madness*.

These days ISO games are making a comeback—*Diablo*, *Loaded*, and a slew of RPGs and wargames use it. Its popularity stems from that fact that the view allows a lot of cool gameplay and fairly interesting visuals as compared to full 3D. And of course, ISO 3D is about 10 times easier to create than full 3D. So how do you do it?

Well, this is a secret in the game community, and it's not something that anyone writes about too much. What I'm going to do is give you some food for thought and describe a couple of ways to do this. The hints I give you here should be more than enough for you to implement an ISO engine yourself.

> **TIP**
>
> If you really want to learn ISO 3D game programming then check out *Isometric Game Programming with DirectX 7.0* by Ernest Pazera.

There are three ways to approach ISO 3D:

- Method 1—Cell-based, totally 2D.
- Method 2—Full-screen-based, with 2D or 3D collision networks.
- Method 3—Using full 3D math, with a fixed camera view.

Let's talk about each...

Method 1: Cell-Based, Totally 2D

With Method 1, basically you have to decide on your angle of view and then draw all your artwork with that in mind. Usually, you'll draw everything as rectangular tiles, just like you would with a normal scrolling engine. Take a look at the art cells in Figure 8.49.

However, the tricky part comes with the rendering. When you draw the universe, you can't just draw things in any order that you want. You must draw the bitmaps so that the far objects are occluded by near ones. In essence, draw the screen like a painter does, from back to front. Hence, if you have a straight 45-degree view—meaning that the art is tilted 45 degrees from the top view—and you draw the screen from top to bottom, the order should be correct.

FIGURE 8.49
Predrawn isometric 3D artwork.

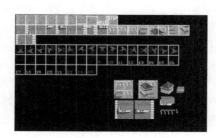

This is important when you have an object like a tree, and a little character walks behind the tree. It had better look like the little guy's behind it. Hence, you must make sure to draw him at the right time in the display list. Take a look at Figure 8.50 to see the problem. This is almost a no-brainer if you just make sure to draw the character at the right time, which is after the row that's slightly behind the character and before the row that's slightly in front. This is also shown in Figure 8.50. So, the bottom line is that you have to work out a little math and sorting to draw moveable objects at the right times.

FIGURE 8.50
Order of drawing is important in isometric 3D rendering.

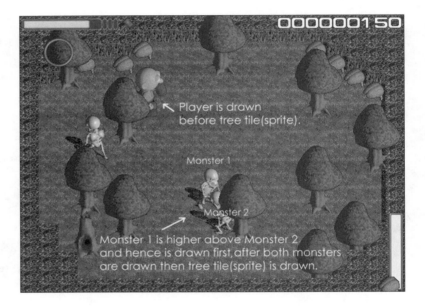

Also, you may have an ISO engine with tiles of varying height. Or in other words, each tile can extend many tiles high. You could just put multiple tiles at multiple row positions, or take height into consideration and think of each row of tiles as varying heights. When you render, you may have to start rendering the current row at a y-position higher than the actual row position.

Figure 8.51 shows this case graphically. There's no difference in drawing this; the only problem is locating the starting y for each block height you add onto the current row. Basically, it's just the height of a cell.

Now, let's make thinks a little harder. What if the angle is 45 tilt and 45 yaw? Or in other words, a standard *Diablo* or *Zaxxon* view? In this case, you just need to order your rendering on the x-axis also. So you must draw from left to right (or right to left, depending on the direction of yaw) and from top to bottom. And again, you'll need to sort your objects on both the x- and y-axis when drawing.

FIGURE 8.51
Drawing large cells in
an isometric 3D
engine.

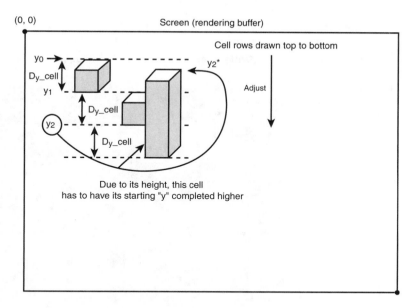

Well, think about it: That's one way to do it. Of course, there are a lot of details when it comes to collision and so forth, and many game programmers use complex coordinate systems based on hexagons or octagons and then map objects into these systems, but this technique will get you going.

Method 2: Full-Screen-Based, with 2D or 3D Collision Networks

The full-screen method is much cooler than using tiles. Basically, what you do is draw an ISO 3D world any way you like (with a 3D modeler or what have you), and you can make each screen any size you want. Then you create a secondary data structure that contains collision information that is overlaid onto the fake 2D world. Using this technique, you augment the 2D information (which has no height or collision data) with extra 2D/3D information, either 2D or 3D, depending on how complex you want to get.

Then you simply draw the background bitmap all at once, but as you draw all your moveable objects, you clip them to the extra geometrical data that is overlaid onto the 2D/pseudo-3D image. Take a look at Figure 8.52 to see this. Here you see a 2D-rendered scene that looks ISO.

In Figure 8.53, you see the same scene with polygon information overlaid on it. This is what you use to clip, do collisions, and so forth.

To generate it, you can do one of two things: Extract it from the 3D modeler, or write a tool that allows you to literally draw the information on each screen full of data. I've used both methods, so it's up to you. However, I suggest you use a 3D modeler to draw your universes and then figure out a way to export only certain important geometry. Drawing the collision geometry by hand with a tool is time-consuming, and one change in the graphics means a redo!

FIGURE 8.52
A fake rendered iso-
metric 3D scene.

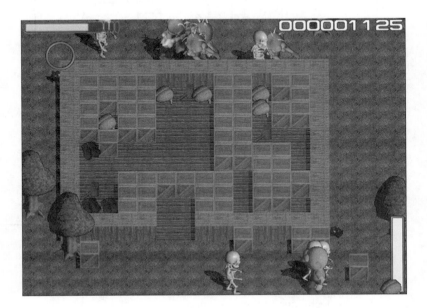

Method 3: Using Full 3D Math, with a Fixed Camera View

This is the easiest of all because there aren't any tricks. Basically, using a full 3D engine, you simply lock the camera at an ISO view and you have an ISO game. Moreover, because you know that the view is always at a certain angle, you can make certain optimizations and assumptions about the drawing order and the scene complexity. This is how many ISO games on the Sony PlayStation I and II work—they're really full 3D, but they're locked in a 45-degree view.

> **NOTE**
>
> As I said, this scrolling stuff is really a 2D topic and could fill up a small book in itself, so I've placed additional articles on the CD if you haven't had enough.

FIGURE 8.53
A polygon collision
geometry overlaid on
a fake rendered
image.

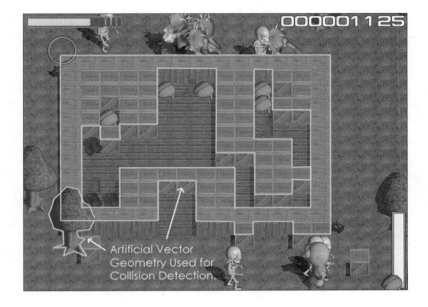

The T3DLIB1 Library

At this point, you're ready to take a look at all the defines, macros, data structures, and functions that you've created throughout the book. Moreover, I've put them all into a single pair of files: T3DLIB1.CPP|H. You can link these into your programs and use everything you've learned so far without hunting down all the code from the dozens of programs you've written.

In addition to all the stuff you've already written, I've created a few more 2D sprite functions to help facilitate 2D game programming. Actually, I used this stuff to create some of the demos at the end of the chapter, so you get to see that code clearly defined. Anyway, I'm not going to take too much time explaining everything here, but I'll give you enough to help you figure it out. Let's take a look at each code element one by one.

The Engine Architecture

Thus far you have a fairly simple 2D engine going, as shown in Figure 8.54. Basically, the engine along with the additions I have made is now a 2D 8/16-bit color back buffered DirectX engine that has support for any resolution, along with clipping to the primary display surface, and has the ability to transparently operate in windowed mode.

To build an application using the library, you'll need to include `T3DLIB1.CPP|H` (from the CD) along with `DDRAW.LIB` (DirectDraw Library), `WINMM.LIB` (Win32 Multimedia Library), and a main game program `T3DCONSOLE2.CPP` which is based on the simpler `T3DCONSOLE.CPP` (you made this earlier in the book). Then you're ready to go.

FIGURE 8.54

The architecture of the graphics engine.

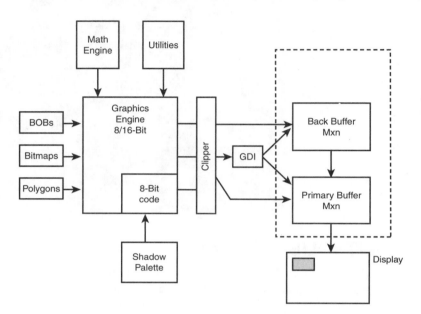

Of course, you wrote a lot of code, and you're free to modify, use, abuse all this stuff, or even burn it if you like. I just thought you might like it all explained and put together in a couple of easy-to-use files.

`T3DCONSOLE2.CPP`: The New Game Programming Console

Before we cover all the functionality and so forth of the engine, take a quick look at the latest incarnation of the console, version 2.0 which now has hooks and support for 8- or 16-bit mode windowed or full screen. Basically, by changing a few `#defines` at the top of the file you can select 8- or 16-bit mode, full screen or windowed display— it's really cool! Here it is for your review:

```
// T3DCONSOLE2.CPP -
// Use this as a template for your applications if you wish
// you may want to change things like the resolution of the
// application, if it's windowed, the directinput devices
// that are acquired and so forth...
// currently the app creates a 640x480x16 windowed display
// hence, you must be in 16 bit color before running the application
// if you want fullscreen mode then simple change the WINDOWED_APP
// value in the #defines below value to FALSE (0). Similarly, if
// you want another bitdepth, maybe 8-bit for 256 colors then
```

```
// change that in the call to DDraw_Init() in the function
// Game_Init() within this file.

// READ THIS!
// To compile make sure to include DDRAW.LIB, DSOUND.LIB,
// DINPUT.LIB, WINMM.LIB in the project link list, and of course
// the C++ source modules T3DLIB1.CPP,T3DLIB2.CPP, and T3DLIB3.CPP
// and the headers T3DLIB1.H,T3DLIB2.H, and T3DLIB3.H must
// be in the working directory of the compiler

// INCLUDES //////////////////////////////////////////////

#define INITGUID       // make sure all the COM interfaces are available
                       // instead of this you can include the .LIB file
                       // DXGUID.LIB

#define WIN32_LEAN_AND_MEAN

#include <windows.h>   // include important windows stuff
#include <windowsx.h>
#include <mmsystem.h>
#include <iostream.h> // include important C/C++ stuff
#include <conio.h>
#include <stdlib.h>
#include <malloc.h>
#include <memory.h>
#include <string.h>
#include <stdarg.h>
#include <stdio.h>
#include <math.h>
#include <io.h>
#include <fcntl.h>

#include <ddraw.h>   // directX includes
#include <dsound.h>
#include <dmksctrl.h>
#include <dmusici.h>
#include <dmusicc.h>
#include <dmusicf.h>
#include <dinput.h>
#include "T3DLIB1.h" // game library includes
#include "T3DLIB2.h"
#include "T3DLIB3.h"

// DEFINES ///////////////////////////////////////////////

// defines for windows interface
#define WINDOW_CLASS_NAME "WIN3DCLASS"  // class name
#define WINDOW_TITLE      "T3D Graphics Console Ver 2.0"
#define WINDOW_WIDTH      640   // size of window
#define WINDOW_HEIGHT     480

#define WINDOW_BPP        16    // bitdepth of window (8,16,24 etc.)
                               // note: if windowed and not
```

```
                                   // fullscreen then bitdepth must
                                   // be same as system bitdepth
                                   // also if 8-bit the a pallete
                                   // is created and attached

#define WINDOWED_APP      1    // 0 not windowed, 1 windowed

// PROTOTYPES ////////////////////////////////////////////

// game console
int Game_Init(void *parms=NULL);
int Game_Shutdown(void *parms=NULL);
int Game_Main(void *parms=NULL);

// GLOBALS ////////////////////////////////////////////////

HWND main_window_handle           = NULL; // save the window handle
HINSTANCE main_instance           = NULL; // save the instance
char buffer[256];                         // used to print text



// FUNCTIONS //////////////////////////////////////////////

LRESULT CALLBACK WindowProc(HWND hwnd,
                                                UINT msg,
                              WPARAM wparam,
                              LPARAM lparam)
{
// this is the main message handler of the system
PAINTSTRUCT ps;                   // used in WM_PAINT
HDC                      hdc;     // handle to a device context

// what is the message
switch(msg)
   {
   case WM_CREATE:
       {
           // do initialization stuff here
           return(0);
           } break;

    case WM_PAINT:
        {
        // start painting
        hdc = BeginPaint(hwnd,&ps);

        // end painting
        EndPaint(hwnd,&ps);
        return(0);
        } break;
```

```
        case WM_DESTROY:
                {
                // kill the application
                PostQuitMessage(0);
                return(0);
                } break;

        default:break;

        } // end switch

// process any messages that we didn't take care of
return (DefWindowProc(hwnd, msg, wparam, lparam));

} // end WinProc

// WINMAIN ///////////////////////////////////////////////////

int WINAPI WinMain(HINSTANCE hinstance,
            HINSTANCE hprevinstance,
            LPSTR lpcmdline,
            int ncmdshow)
{
// this is the winmain function
WNDCLASSEX winclass; // this will hold the class we create
HWND            hwnd;       // generic window handle
MSG             msg;        // generic message
HDC         hdc;        // graphics device context

// first fill in the window class stucture
winclass.cbSize         = sizeof(WNDCLASSEX);
winclass.style                  = CS_DBLCLKS | CS_OWNDC |
                            CS_HREDRAW | CS_VREDRAW;
winclass.lpfnWndProc        = WindowProc;
winclass.cbClsExtra = 0;
winclass.cbWndExtra = 0;
winclass.hInstance  = hinstance;
winclass.hIcon              = LoadIcon(NULL, IDI_APPLICATION);
winclass.hCurso     = LoadCursor(NULL, IDC_ARROW);
winclass.hbrBackground      = (HBRUSH)GetStockObject(BLACK_BRUSH);
winclass.lpszMenuName       = NULL;
winclass.lpszClassName      = WINDOW_CLASS_NAME;
winclass.hIconSm        = LoadIcon(NULL, IDI_APPLICATION);

// save hinstance in global
main_instance = hinstance;

// register the window class
if (!RegisterClassEx(&winclass))
   return(0);

// create the window
if (!(hwnd = CreateWindowEx(NULL,// extended style
```

```
            WINDOW_CLASS_NAME, // class
        WINDOW_TITLE, // title
        WINDOWED_APP ? (WS_OVERLAPPED | WS_SYSMENU | WS_VISIBLE) :
                        (WS_POPUP | WS_VISIBLE)),
        0,0,        // initial x,y
        WINDOW_WIDTH,WINDOW_HEIGHT,  // initial width, height
        NULL,       // handle to parent
        NULL,       // handle to menu
        hinstance,// instance of this application
        NULL)))    // extra creation parms
return(0);

// save the window handle and instance in a global
main_window_handle = hwnd;
main_instance      = hinstance;

// resize the window so that client is really width x height
if (WINDOWED_APP)
{
// now resize the window, so the client area is the
// actual size requested since there may be borders
// and controls if this is going to be a windowed app
// if the app is not windowed then it won't matter
RECT window_rect = {0,0,WINDOW_WIDTH,WINDOW_HEIGHT};

// make the call to adjust window_rect
AdjustWindowRectEx(&window_rect,
     GetWindowStyle(main_window_handle),
     GetMenu(main_window_handle) != NULL,
     GetWindowExStyle(main_window_handle));

// save the global client offsets, they are needed in DDraw_Flip()
window_client_x0 = -window_rect.left;
window_client_y0 = -window_rect.top;

// now resize the window with a call to MoveWindow()
MoveWindow(main_window_handle,
          CW_USEDEFAULT, // x position
          CW_USEDEFAULT, // y position
          window_rect.right - window_rect.left, // width
          window_rect.bottom - window_rect.top, // height
          TRUE);


// show the window, so there's no garbage on first render
ShowWindow(main_window_handle, SW_SHOW);
} // end if windowed

// perform all game console specific initialization
Game_Init();

// enter main event loop
while(1)
```

```
       {
    if (PeekMessage(&msg,NULL,0,0,PM_REMOVE))
          {
          // test if this is a quit
      if (msg.message == WM_QUIT)
          break;

          // translate any accelerator keys
          TranslateMessage(&msg);

          // send the message to the window proc
          DispatchMessage(&msg);
          } // end if

   // main game processing goes here
   Game_Main();

   } // end while

// shutdown game and release all resources
Game_Shutdown();


// return to Windows like this
return(msg.wParam);

} // end WinMain

// T3D II GAME PROGRAMMING CONSOLE FUNCTIONS ////////////////

int Game_Init(void *parms)
{
// this function is where you do all the initialization
// for your game

// start up DirectDraw (replace the parms as you desire)
DDraw_Init(WINDOW_WIDTH, WINDOW_HEIGHT, WINDOW_BPP, WINDOWED_APP);

// initialize directinput
DInput_Init();

// acquire the keyboard
DInput_Init_Keyboard();

// add calls to acquire other directinput devices here...


// initialize directsound and directmusic
DSound_Init();
DMusic_Init();

// hide the mouse
ShowCursor(FALSE);
```

```
            // seed random number generator
            srand(Start_Clock());

            // all your initialization code goes here...


            // return success
            return(1);

            } // end Game_Init

            /////////////////////////////////////////////////////////

            int Game_Shutdown(void *parms)
            {
            // this function is where you shutdown your game and
            // release all resources that you allocated

            // shut everything down

            // release all your resources created for the game here....


            // now directsound
            DSound_Stop_All_Sounds();
            DSound_Delete_All_Sounds();
            DSound_Shutdown();

            // directmusic
            DMusic_Delete_All_MIDI();
            DMusic_Shutdown();

            // shut down directinput
            DInput_Release_Keyboard();

            DInput_Shutdown();

            // shutdown directdraw last
            DDraw_Shutdown();

            // return success
            return(1);
            } // end Game_Shutdown

            /////////////////////////////////////////////////////////

            int Game_Main(void *parms)
            {
            // this is the workhorse of your game it will be called
            // continuously in real-time this is like main() in C
            // all the calls for you game go here!

            int index; // looping var
```

```
// start the timing clock
Start_Clock();

// clear the drawing surface
DDraw_Fill_Surface(lpddsback, 0);

// read keyboard and other devices here
DInput_Read_Keyboard();

// game logic here...

// flip the surfaces
DDraw_Flip();

// sync to 30ish fps
Wait_Clock(30);

// check of user is trying to exit
if (KEY_DOWN(VK_ESCAPE) || keyboard_state[DIK_ESCAPE])
    {
    PostMessage(main_window_handle, WM_DESTROY,0,0);
    } // end if

// return success
return(1);

} // end Game_Main

///////////////////////////////////////////////////////////
```

Basically, by controlling these #defines:

```
#define WINDOW_WIDTH     640    // size of window
#define WINDOW_HEIGHT    480

#define WINDOW_BPP        16    // bitdepth of window (8,16,24 etc.)
                                // note: if windowed and not
                                // fullscreen then bitdepth must
                                // be same as system bitdepth
                                // also if 8-bit the a pallete
                                // is created and attached

#define WINDOWED_APP       1    // 0 not windowed, 1 windowed
```

you can select the screen resolution (for full screen modes), the bitdepth (for full screen modes), and if the display is windowed (windowed displays use the current desktop color depth and resolution, so all you control is the window size).

Basic Definitions

The engine has one header file, T3DLIB1.H, and within it are a number of #defines that the engine uses. Here they are for your reference:

```
// DEFINES ////////////////////////////////////////////////
```

```
// default screen values, these are all overriden by the
// call to DDraw_Init() and are just here to have something
// to set the globals to instead of constant values
#define SCREEN_WIDTH          640  // size of screen
#define SCREEN_HEIGHT         480
#define SCREEN_BPP            8     // bits per pixel
#define MAX_COLORS_PALETTE    256


#define DEFAULT_PALETTE_FILE "PALDATA2.PAL"

// used for selecting full screen/windowed mode
#define SCREEN_FULLSCREEN     0
#define SCREEN_WINDOWED       1

// bitmap defines
#define BITMAP_ID             0x4D42 // universal id for a bitmap
#define BITMAP_STATE_DEAD     0
#define BITMAP_STATE_ALIVE    1
#define BITMAP_STATE_DYING    2
#define BITMAP_ATTR_LOADED    128

#define BITMAP_EXTRACT_MODE_CELL  0
#define BITMAP_EXTRACT_MODE_ABS   1

// directdraw pixel format defines, used to help
// bitmap loader put data in proper format
#define DD_PIXEL_FORMAT8          8
#define DD_PIXEL_FORMAT555        15
#define DD_PIXEL_FORMAT565        16
#define DD_PIXEL_FORMAT888        24
#define DD_PIXEL_FORMATALPHA888   32


// defines for BOBs
#define BOB_STATE_DEAD        0    // this is a dead bob
#define BOB_STATE_ALIVE       1    // this is a live bob
#define BOB_STATE_DYING       2    // this bob is dying
#define BOB_STATE_ANIM_DONE   1    // done animation state
#define MAX_BOB_FRAMES        64   // maximum number of bob frames
#define MAX_BOB_ANIMATIONS    16   // maximum number of animation sequeces

#define BOB_ATTR_SINGLE_FRAME  1   // bob has single frame
#define BOB_ATTR_MULTI_FRAME   2   // bob has multiple frames
#define BOB_ATTR_MULTI_ANIM    4   // bob has multiple animations
#define BOB_ATTR_ANIM_ONE_SHOT 8   // bob will perform the animation once
#define BOB_ATTR_VISIBLE       16  // bob is visible
#define BOB_ATTR_BOUNCE        32  // bob bounces off edges
#define BOB_ATTR_WRAPAROUND    64  // bob wraps around edges
#define BOB_ATTR_LOADED        128 // the bob has been loaded
#define BOB_ATTR_CLONE         256 // the bob is a clone
```

```
// screen transition commands
#define SCREEN_DARKNESS   0          // fade to black
#define SCREEN_WHITENESS  1          // fade to white
#define SCREEN_SWIPE_X    2          // do a horizontal swipe
#define SCREEN_SWIPE_Y    3          // do a vertical swipe
#define SCREEN_DISOLVE    4          // a pixel disolve
#define SCREEN_SCRUNCH    5          // a square compression
#define SCREEN_BLUENESS   6          // fade to blue
#define SCREEN_REDNESS    7          // fade to red
#define SCREEN_GREENNESS  8          // fade to green

// defines for Blink_Colors
#define BLINKER_ADD         0        // add a light to database
#define BLINKER_DELETE      1        // delete a light from database
#define BLINKER_UPDATE      2        // update a light
#define BLINKER_RUN         3        // run normal

// pi defines
#define PI        ((float)3.141592654f)
#define PI2       ((float)6.283185307f)
#define PI_DIV_2  ((float)1.570796327f)
#define PI_DIV_4  ((float)0.785398163f)
#define PI_INV    ((float)0.318309886f)

// fixed point mathematics constants
#define FIXP16_SHIFT     16
#define FIXP16_MAG       65536
#define FIXP16_DP_MASK   0x0000ffff
#define FIXP16_WP_MASK   0xffff0000
#define FIXP16_ROUND_UP  0x00008000
```

You've seen all of these in one place or another.

Working Macros

Next are all the macros you've written thus far. Again, you've seen them all in one place or another, but here they are all at once:

```
// these read the keyboard asynchronously
#define KEY_DOWN(vk_code) ((GetAsyncKeyState(vk_code) & 0x8000) ? 1 : 0)
#define KEY_UP(vk_code)   ((GetAsyncKeyState(vk_code) & 0x8000) ? 0 : 1)

// this builds a 16 bit color value in 5.5.5 format (1-bit alpha mode)
#define _RGB16BIT555(r,g,b) ((b & 31) + ((g & 31) << 5) + ((r & 31) << 10))

// this builds a 16 bit color value in 5.6.5 format (green dominate mode)
#define _RGB16BIT565(r,g,b) ((b & 31) + ((g & 63) << 5) + ((r & 31) << 11))

// this builds a 24 bit color value in 8.8.8 format
#define _RGB24BIT(a,r,g,b) ((b) + ((g) << 8) + ((r) << 16) )

// this builds a 32 bit color value in A.8.8.8 format (8-bit alpha mode)
#define _RGB32BIT(a,r,g,b) ((b) + ((g) << 8) + ((r) << 16) + ((a) << 24))
```

DirectX and 2D Fundamentals

```
// bit manipulation macros
#define SET_BIT(word,bit_flag)   ((word)=((word) | (bit_flag)))
#define RESET_BIT(word,bit_flag) ((word)=((word) & (~bit_flag)))

// initializes a direct draw struct
// basically zeros it and sets the dwSize field
#define DDRAW_INIT_STRUCT(ddstruct) { memset(&ddstruct,0,sizeof(ddstruct));
 ddstruct.dwSize=sizeof(ddstruct); }

// used to compute the min and max of two expresions
#define MIN(a, b)  (((a) < (b)) ? (a) : (b))
#define MAX(a, b)  (((a) > (b)) ? (b) : (a))

// used for swapping algorithm
#define SWAP(a,b,t) {t=a; a=b; b=t;}

// some math macros
#define DEG_TO_RAD(ang)  ((ang)*PI/180.0)
#define RAD_TO_DEG(rads) ((rads)*180.0/PI)

#define RAND_RANGE(x,y) ( (x) + (rand()%((y)-(x)+1)))
```

Data Types and Structures

The next set of code elements includes the types and data structures that the engine uses. I'm going to list them all, but be warned that there are a couple you haven't seen yet that have to do with the *Blitter Object Engine (BOB)*. To be consistent, let's take a look at everything at once:

```
// basic unsigned types
typedef unsigned short USHORT;
typedef unsigned short WORD;
typedef unsigned char  UCHAR;
typedef unsigned char  BYTE;
typedef unsigned int   QUAD;
typedef unsigned int   UINT;


// container structure for bitmaps .BMP file
typedef struct BITMAP_FILE_TAG
        {
        BITMAPFILEHEADER bitmapfileheader;  // this contains the
                                            // bitmapfile header
        BITMAPINFOHEADER bitmapinfoheader;  // this is all the info
                                            // including the palette
        PALETTEENTRY     palette[256];      // we will store
                                            // the palette here
        UCHAR            *buffer;           // this is a pointer
                                            // to the data

        } BITMAP_FILE, *BITMAP_FILE_PTR;

// the blitter object structure BOB
typedef struct BOB_TYP
```

```
        {
        int state;          // the state of the object (general)
        int anim_state;     // an animation state variable, up to you
        int attr;           // attributes pertaining
                            // to the object (general)
        float x,y;           // position bitmap will be displayed at
        float xv,yv;         // velocity of object
        int width, height;  // the width and height of the bob
        int width_fill;     // internal, used to force 8*x wide surfaces
        int counter_1;      // general counters
        int counter_2;
        int max_count_1;    // general threshold values;
        int max_count_2;
        int varsI[16];      // stack of 16 integers
        float varsF[16];    // stack of 16 floats
        int curr_frame;     // current animation frame
        int num_frames;     // total number of animation frames
        int curr_animation; // index of current animation
        int anim_counter;   // used to time animation transitions
        int anim_index;     // animation element index
        int anim_count_max; // number of cycles before animation
        int *animations[MAX_BOB_ANIMATIONS]; // animation sequences

        LPDIRECTDRAWSURFACE7 images[MAX_BOB_FRAMES]; // the bitmap images
                                                     // DD surfaces

        } BOB, *BOB_PTR;

// the simple bitmap image
typedef struct BITMAP_IMAGE_TYP
        {
        int state;          // state of bitmap
        int attr;           // attributes of bitmap
        int x,y;            // position of bitmap
        int width, height;  // size of bitmap
        int num_bytes;      // total bytes of bitmap
        UCHAR *buffer;      // pixels of bitmap

        } BITMAP_IMAGE, *BITMAP_IMAGE_PTR;

// blinking light structure
typedef struct BLINKER_TYP
            {
            // user sets these
            int color_index;      // index of color to blink
            PALETTEENTRY on_color; // RGB value of "on" color
            PALETTEENTRY off_color;// RGB value of "off" color
            int on_time;          // number of frames to keep "on"
            int off_time;         // number of frames to keep "off"

            // internal member
            int counter;    // counter for state transitions
            int state;      // state of light, -1 off, 1 on, 0 dead
            } BLINKER, *BLINKER_PTR;
```

```c
// a 2D vertex
typedef struct VERTEX2DI_TYP
        {
        int x,y; // the vertex
        } VERTEX2DI, *VERTEX2DI_PTR;

// a 2D vertex
typedef struct VERTEX2DF_TYP
        {
        float x,y; // the vertex
        } VERTEX2DF, *VERTEX2DF_PTR;


// a 2D polygon
typedef struct POLYGON2D_TYP
        {
        int state;       // state of polygon
        int num_verts;   // number of vertices
        int x0,y0;       // position of center of polygon
        int xv,yv;       // initial velocity
        DWORD color;     // could be index or PALETTENTRY
        VERTEX2DF *vlist; // pointer to vertex list

        } POLYGON2D, *POLYGON2D_PTR;


// 3x3 matrix /////////////////////////////////////////////
typedef struct MATRIX3X3_TYP
        {
        union
        {
        float M[3][3]; // array indexed data storage

        // storage in row major form with explicit names
        struct
            {
            float M00, M01, M02;
            float M10, M11, M12;
            float M20, M21, M22;
            }; // end explicit names

        }; // end union
        } MATRIX3X3, *MATRIX3X3_PTR;

// 1x3 matrix /////////////////////////////////////////////
typedef struct MATRIX1X3_TYP
        {
        union
        {
        float M[3]; // array indexed data storage

        // storage in row major form with explicit names
        struct
```

```
        {
        float M00, M01, M02;

        }; // end explicit names
    }; // end union
    } MATRIX1X3, *MATRIX1X3_PTR;

// 3x2 matrix //////////////////////////////////////////////
typedef struct MATRIX3X2_TYP
        {
        union
        {
        float M[3][2]; // array indexed data storage

        // storage in row major form with explicit names
        struct
            {
            float M00, M01;
            float M10, M11;
            float M20, M21;
            }; // end explicit names

        }; // end union
    } MATRIX3X2, *MATRIX3X2_PTR;

// 1x2 matrix //////////////////////////////////////////////
typedef struct MATRIX1X2_TYP
        {
        union
        {
        float M[2]; // array indexed data storage

        // storage in row major form with explicit names
        struct
            {
            float M00, M01;

            }; // end explicit names
        }; // end union
    } MATRIX1X2, *MATRIX1X2_PTR;
```

Not bad; nothing new, really. Basic types, all the bitmap stuff, polygon support, and a little matrix math.

Global Domination

You know that I like globals because they're so fast. Moreover, they're really appropriate for a lot of system-level variables (which a 2D/3D engine has a lot of). So here are the globals for the engine. Again, you've seen many of them, but the ones that look alien have comments, so read them:

```
        extern FILE *fp_error;          // general error file
        extern char error_filename[80]; // error file name

        // notice that interface 4.0 is used on a number of interfaces
        extern LPDIRECTDRAW7        lpdd;          // dd object
        extern LPDIRECTDRAWSURFACE7 lpddsprimary; // dd primary surface
        extern LPDIRECTDRAWSURFACE7 lpddsback;    // dd back surface
        extern LPDIRECTDRAWPALETTE  lpddpal;      // dd palette
        extern LPDIRECTDRAWCLIPPER  lpddclipper;  // dd clipper for back surface
        extern LPDIRECTDRAWCLIPPER  lpddclipperwin;  // dd clipper for window
        extern PALETTEENTRY     palette[256];     // color palette
        extern PALETTEENTRY     save_palette[256];// used to save palettes
        extern DDSURFACEDESC2   ddsd;             // a dd surface description struct
        extern DDBLTFX          ddbltfx;          // used to fill
        extern DDSCAPS2         ddscaps;          // a dd surface capabilities struct
        extern HRESULT          ddrval;           // result back from dd calls
        extern UCHAR            *primary_buffer;  // primary video buffer
        extern UCHAR            *back_buffer;     // secondary back buffer
        extern int              primary_lpitch;   // memory line pitch
        extern int              back_lpitch;      // memory line pitch
        extern BITMAP_FILE      bitmap8bit;       // a 8 bit bitmap file
        extern BITMAP_FILE      bitmap16bit;      // a 16 bit bitmap file
        extern BITMAP_FILE      bitmap24bit;      // a 24 bit bitmap file

        extern DWORD            start_clock_count;  // used for timing
        extern int              windowed_mode;      // tracks if dd is windowed or not

        // these defined the general clipping rectangle for software clipping
        extern int min_clip_x,    // clipping rectangle
                max_clip_x,
                min_clip_y,
                max_clip_y;

        // these are overwritten globally by DD_Init()
        extern int screen_width,    // width of screen
                screen_height,   // height of screen
                screen_bpp,      // bits per pixel
                screen_windowed; // is this a windowed app?


        extern int dd_pixel_format;  // default pixel format set by call
                                     // to DDraw_Init

        extern int window_client_x0; // used to track the starting
                                     // (x,y) client area for
        extern int window_client_y0; // for windowed mode dd operations

        // storage for our lookup tables
        extern float cos_look[361]; // 1 extra so we can store 0-360 inclusive
        extern float sin_look[361]; // 1 extra so we can store 0-360 inclusive

        // function ptr to RGB16 builder
        extern USHORT (*RGB16Bit)(int r, int g, int b);
```

```
// root functions
extern USHORT RGB16Bit565(int r, int g, int b);
extern USHORT RGB16Bit555(int r, int g, int b);
```

The DirectDraw Interface

Now that you've seen all the data support, let's take a look at all the DirectDraw support functions that we've written along with some additions that I have made for full 16-bit windowed support. Let's take a quick look at each function.

Function Prototype:

```
int DDraw_Init(int width,  // width of display
               int height, // height of display
               int bpp,    // bits per pixel
               int windowed=0); // controls windowed
```

Purpose:

DDraw_Init() starts up and initializes DirectDraw. You can send any resolution and color depth and select if you desire a windowed mode by setting windowed to 1. If you select a windowed mode then you must have created a window previously that was not full screen. DDraw_Init() must set up DirectDraw differently for windowed modes since the primary buffer is now the entire display, clipping must be performed to just the client area of the window and of course you have no control over the screen resolution or color depth on a windowed mode, so bpp is ignored.

Additionally, this function does a lot for you, it loads in a default palette paldata2.pal for 8-bit modes, sets up the clipping rectangle for both 8 and 16-bit modes windowed or full screen and in 16-bit modes determines the pixel format and tests if it's 5.5.5 or 5.6.5 and based on this points the function pointer:

```
USHORT (*RGB16Bit)(int r, int g, int b) = NULL;
```

At either:

```
USHORT RGB16Bit565(int r, int g, int b)
{
// this function simply builds a 5.6.5 format 16 bit pixel
// assumes input is RGB 0-255 each channel
r>>=3; g>>=2; b>>=3;
return(_RGB16BIT565((r),(g),(b)));

} // end RGB16Bit565

//////////////////////////////////////////////////////////

USHORT RGB16Bit555(int r, int g, int b)
{
// this function simply builds a 5.5.5 format 16 bit pixel
// assumes input is RGB 0-255 each channel
```

```
r>>=3; g>>=3; b>>=3;
return(_RGB16BIT555((r),(g),(b)));
```

which allows you to make the call RGB16Bit(r,g,b) to create a properly formatted RGB word in 16-bit mode and not have to worry about the pixel format. Isn't that nice? And of course R,G,B all must be in the range 0–255. Also, DDraw_Init() is smart enough in windowed mode to set all the clipping up for you, so you don't have to do anything!

Returns TRUE if successful.

Example:

```
// put the system into 800x600 with 256 colors
DDraw_Init(800,600,8);
```

Example:

```
// put the system into a windowed mode
// with a window size of 640x480 and 16-bit color
DDraw_Init(640,480,16,1);
```

Function Prototype:

```
int DDraw_Shutdown(void);
```

Purpose:

DDraw_Shutdown() shuts down DirectDraw and releases all interfaces.

Example:

```
// in your system shutdown code you might put
DDraw_Shutdown();
```

Function Prototype:

```
LPDIRECTDRAWCLIPPER
  DDraw_Attach_Clipper(
    LPDIRECTDRAWSURFACE7 lpdds, // surface to attach to
    int num_rects,      // number of rects
    LPRECT clip_list); // pointer to rects
```

Purpose:

DDraw_Attach_Clipper() attaches a clipper to the sent surface (the back buffer in most cases). In addition, you must send the number of rectangles in the clipping list and a pointer to the RECT list itself. Returns TRUE if successful.

Example:

```
// creates a clipping region the size of the screen
RECT clip_zone = {0,0,SCREEN_WIDTH-1, SCREEN_HEIGHT-1};
DDraw_Attach_Clipper(lpddsback, 1, &clip_zone);
```

Function Prototype:

```
LPDIRECTDRAWSURFACE7
   DDraw_Create_Surface(int width, // width of surface
                        int height, // height of surface
                        int mem_flags, // control flags
                        USHORT color_key_value=0); // the color key
```

Purpose:

DDraw_Create_Surface() is used to create a generic offscreen DirectDraw surface in system memory, VRAM, or AGP memory. The default is DDSCAPS_OFFSCREENPLAIN. Any additional control flags are logically ORed with the default. They're the standard DirectDraw DDSCAP* flags, such as DDSCAPS_SYSTEMMEMORY and DDSCAPS_VIDEOMEMORY for system memory and VRAM, respectively. Also, you may select a color key value, it currently defaults to 0. If the function is successful, it returns a pointer to the new surface. Otherwise, it returns NULL.

Example:

```
// let's create a 64x64 surface in VRAM
LPDIRECTDRAWSURFACE7 image =

        DDraw_Create_Surface(64,64, DDSCAPS_VIDEOMEMORY);
```

Function Prototype:

```
int DDraw_Flip(void);
```

Purpose:

DDraw_Flip() simply flips the primary surface with the secondary surface for full screen modes, or in windowed mode copies the offscreen back buffer to the client area of the windowed display. The call waits until the flip can take place, so it may not return immediately. Returns TRUE if successful.

Example:

```
// flip em baby
DDraw_Flip();
```

Function Prototype:

```
int DDraw_Wait_For_Vsync(void);
```

Purpose:

DDraw_Wait_For_Vsync() waits until the next vertical blank period begins (when the raster hits the bottom of the screen). Returns TRUE if successful and FALSE if something really bad happened.

Example:

```
// wait 1/70th of sec
DDraw_Wait_For_Vsync();
```

Function Prototype:

```
int DDraw_Fill_Surface(LPDIRECTDRAWSURFACE7 lpdds, // surface to fill
                       int color, // color, index or RGB value
                       RECT *client=NULL) // rect to fill
```

Purpose:

DDraw_Fill_Surface() is used to fill a surface or rectangle within a surface with a color. The color must be in the color depth format of the surface, such as a single byte in 256-color mode or a RGB descriptor in high-color modes, if you want to fill the entire surface send set client to NULL which is its default, otherwise, you may send a RECT pointer as client and fill a region only of the surface. Returns TRUE if successful.

Example:

```
// fill the primary surface with color 0
DDraw_Fill_Surface(lpddsprimary,0);
```

Function Prototype:

```
UCHAR *DDraw_Lock_Surface(LPDIRECTDRAWSURFACE7 lpdds,int *lpitch);
```

Purpose:

DDraw_Lock_Surface() locks the sent surface (if possible) and returns a UCHAR pointer to the surface, along with updating the sent lpitch variable with the linear memory pitch of the surface. While the surface is locked, you can manipulate it and write pixels to it, but the blitter will be blocked, so remember to unlock the surface ASAP. In addition, after unlocking the surface, the memory pointer and pitch most likely become invalid and should not be used. DDraw_Lock_Surface() returns the non-NULL address of the surface memory if successful and NULL otherwise. Also, remember if you are in 16-bit mode then there are 2 bytes per pixel, but the pointer returned is still a UCHAR * and value written in lpitch is in bytes not pixels, so beware!

Example:

```
// holds the memory pitch
int lpitch = 0;

// let's lock the little 64x64 image we made
UCHAR *memory = DDraw_Lock_Surface(image, &lpitch);
```

Function Prototype:

```
int DDraw_Unlock_Surface(LPDIRECTDRAWSURFACE7 lpdds);
```

Purpose:

DDraw_Unlock_Surface() unlocks a surface previously locked with
DDraw_Lock_Surface(). You need only send the pointer to the surface. Returns TRUE
if successful.

Example:

```
// unlock the image surface
DDraw_Unlock_Surface(image);
```

Function Prototypes:

```
UCHAR *DDraw_Lock_Back_Surface(void);
UCHAR *DDraw_Lock_Primary_Surface(void);
```

Purpose:

These two functions are used to lock the primary and secondary rendering surfaces.
However, in most cases you'll only be interested in locking the *secondary* surface in
the double buffered system, but the ability to lock the *primary* surface is there if you
need it. Additionally, If you call DDraw_Lock_Primary_Surface(), the following
globals will become valid:

```
extern UCHAR  *primary_buffer;    // primary video buffer
extern int     primary_lpitch;    // memory line pitch
```

Then you're free to manipulate the surface memory as you want; however, the blitter
will be blocked. Also, note that in windowed modes the primary buffer will point to
the entire screen surface, not just your window, however, the secondary buffer will
point to a rectangle exactly the size of the window's client area. Anyway, making the
call to DDraw_Lock_Back_Surface() will lock the back buffer surface and validate the
following globals:

```
extern UCHAR  *back_buffer;       // secondary back buffer
extern int     back_lpitch;       // memory line pitch
```

 NOTE   *Do not* change any of these globals yourself; they're used to track state
changes in the locking functions. Changing them yourself may make the
engine go crazy.

Example:

```
// let lock the primary surface and write a pixel to the
// upper left hand corner
DDraw_Lock_Primary();

primary_buffer[0] = 100;
```

Function Prototype:

```
int DDraw_Unlock_Primary_Surface(void);
int DDraw_Unlock_Back_Surface(void);
```

Purpose:

These functions are used to unlock the primary or back buffer surfaces. If you try to unlock a surface that wasn't locked, there's no effect. Returns TRUE if successful.

Example:

```
// unlock the secondary back buffer
DDraw_Unlock_Back();
```

2D Polygon Functions

The next set of functions make up the 2D polygon system. This is by no means advanced, fast, or cutting-edge, but just your work up to this point. The functions do the job. There are better ways to do all of this stuff, but that's why you're glued to the book, right? <BG> Also, some of the functions have both an 8-bit and 16-bit version, the 16-bit versions are usually denoted by and extra "16" concatenated on the function name.

Function Prototype(s):

```
void Draw_Triangle_2D(int x1,int y1, // triangle vertices
                int x2,int y2,
                int x3,int y3,
                int color,  // 8-bit color index
                UCHAR *dest_buffer, // destination buffer
                int mempitch); // memory pitch

// 16-bit version
void Draw_Triangle_2D16(int x1,int y1, // triangle vertices
                int x2,int y2,
                int x3,int y3,
                int color,  // 16-bit RGB color descriptor
                UCHAR *dest_buffer, // destination buffer
                int mempitch); // memory pitch

// fixed point high speed version, slightly less accurate
void Draw_TriangleFP_2D(int x1,int y1,
                    int x2,int y2,
                    int x3,int y3,
                    int color,
                    UCHAR *dest_buffer,
                    int mempitch);
```

Purpose:

Draw_Triangle_2D*() draws a filled triangle in the given memory buffer with the sent color. The triangle will be clipped to the current clipping region set in the globals, *not* by the DirectDraw clipper. This is because the function uses software, not the blitter, to draw lines. Note: Draw_TriangleFP_2D() does the exact same thing, but it uses fixed-point math internally, is slightly faster, and is slightly less accurate. Both functions return nothing.

Example:

```
// draw a triangle (100,10) (150,50) (50,60)
// with color index 50 in the back buffer surface
Draw_Triangle_2D(100,10,150,50,50,60,
                 50, // color index 50
                 back_buffer,
                 back_lpitch);

// same example, but in a 16-bit mode
// draw a triangle (100,10) (150,50) (50,60)
// with color RGB(255,0,0) in the back buffer surface
Draw_Triangle_2D16(100,10,150,50,50,60,
                 RGB16Bit(255,0,0),
                 back_buffer,
                 back_lpitch);
```

Function Prototype:

```
inline void Draw_QuadFP_2D(int x0,int y0, // vertices
          int x1,int y1,
          int x2,int y2,
          int x3,int y3,
          int color, // 8-bit color index
          UCHAR *dest_buffer, // destination video buffer
          int mempitch); // memory pitch of buffer
```

Purpose:

Draw_QuadFP_2D() draws the sent quadrilateral as a composition of two triangles. Returns nothing.

Example:

```
// draw a quadrilateral, note vertices must be ordered
// either in cw or ccw order
Draw_QuadFP_2D(0,0, 10,0, 15,20, 5,25,
               100,
               back_buffer, back_lpitch);
```

Function Prototype:

```
void Draw_Filled_Polygon2D(
          POLYGON2D_PTR poly, // poly to render
          UCHAR *vbuffer, // video buffer
          int mempitch);  // memory pitch

// 16-bit version
void Draw_Filled_Polygon2D16(
          POLYGON2D_PTR poly, // poly to render
```

```
UCHAR *vbuffer, // video buffer
int mempitch);  // memory pitch
```

Purpose:

`Draw_Filled_Polygon2D*()` draws a general filled polygon with *n* sides. The function simply takes the polygon to render, a pointer to the video buffer, and the pitch, and that's it! Although, the calling parameters are the exact same for the 8-bit and 16-bit versions, internally the functions call different rasterizers, thus you must use the correct call. Note: The function renders relative to the poly's origin (*x0,y0*), so make sure these are initialized. Returns nothing.

Example:

```
// draw a polygon in the primary buffer
Draw_Filled_Polygon2D(&poly,
                      primary_buffer,
                      primary_lpitch);
```

Function Prototype:

```
int Translate_Polygon2D(
          POLYGON2D_PTR poly, // poly to translate
          int dx, int dy); // translation factors
```

Purpose:

`Translate_Polygon2D()` translates the given polygon's origin (*x0,y0*). Note: The function does not transform or modify the actual vertices making up the polygon. Returns TRUE if successful.

Example:

```
// translate polygon 10,-5
Translate_Polygon2D(&poly, 10, -5);
```

Function Prototype:

```
int Rotate_Polygon2D(
            POLYGON2D_PTR poly, // poly to rotate
            int theta); // angle 0-359
```

Purpose:

`Rotate_Polygon2D()` rotates the sent polygon in a counterclockwise fashion about its origin. The angle must be an integer from 0–359. Returns TRUE if successful.

Example:

```
// rotate polygon 10 degrees
Rotate_Polygon2D(&poly, 10);
```

Function Prototype:

```
int Scale_Polygon2D(POLYGON2D_PTR poly, // poly to scale
                    float sx, float sy); // scale factors
```

Purpose:

`Scale_Polygon2D()` scales the sent polygon by scale factors *sx* and *sy* in the x- and y-axes, respectively. Returns nothing.

Example:

```
// scale the poly equally 2x
Scale_Polygon2D(&poly, 2,2);
```

2D Graphic Primitives

This set of functions contains a few of everything; it's kind of a potpourri of graphics primitives. Nothing you haven't seen—at least I don't *think* so, but then I've had so much Snapple Raspberry that I'm freaking out and little purple mechanical spiders are crawling all over me! And once again, some of the functions have both an 8-bit and 16-bit version, the 16-bit versions are usually denoted by and extra "16" concatenated on the function name.

Function Prototype:

```
int Draw_Clip_Line(int x0,int y0, // starting point
                   int x1, int y1, // ending point
                   int color, // 8-bit color
                   UCHAR *dest_buffer,  // video buffer
                   int lpitch); // memory pitch

// 16-bit version
int Draw_Clip_Line16(int x0,int y0, // starting point
                     int x1, int y1, // ending point
                     int color, // 16-bit RGB color
                     UCHAR *dest_buffer,  // video buffer
                     int lpitch); // memory pitch
```

Purpose:

`Draw_Clip_Line*()` clips the sent line to the current clipping rectangle and then draws a line in the sent buffer in either 8 or 16-bit mode. Returns TRUE if successful.

Example:

```
// draw a line in the back buffer from (10,10) to (100,200)
// 8-bit call
Draw_Clip_Line(10,10,100,200,
               5, // color 5
               back_buffer,
               back_lpitch);
```

Function Prototype:

```
int Clip_Line(int &x1,int &y1,    // starting point
              int &x2, int &y2); // ending point
```

Purpose:

Clip_Line() is for the most part internal, but you can call it to clip the sent line to the current clipping rectangle. Note that the function modifies the sent endpoints, so save them if you don't want this side effect. Also, the function does not draw anything; it only clips the endpoints. Returns TRUE if successful.

Example:

```
// clip the line defined by x1,y1 to x2,y2
Clip_Line(x1,y1,x2,y2);
```

Function Prototype:

```
int Draw_Line(int xo, int yo,  // starting point
              int x1,int y1,    // ending point
              int color,       // 8-bit color index
              UCHAR *vb_start, // video buffer
              int lpitch);     // memory pitch

// 16-bit version
int Draw_Line16(int xo, int yo,  // starting point
                int x1,int y1,    // ending point
                int color,       // 16-bit RGB color
                UCHAR *vb_start, // video buffer
                int lpitch);     // memory pitch
```

Purpose:

Draw_Line*() draws a line in 8 or 16 bit mode without any clipping, so make sure that the endpoints are within the display surface's valid coordinates. This function is slightly faster than the clipped version because the clipping operation is not needed. Returns TRUE if successful.

Example:

```
// draw a line in the back buffer from (10,10) to (100,200)
// in 16-bit mode
Draw_Line16(10,10,100,200,
            RGB16Bit(0,255,0), // bright green
            back_buffer,
            back_lpitch);
```

Function Prototype:

```
inline int Draw_Pixel(int x, int y, // position of pixel
                      int color, // 8-bit color
                      UCHAR *video_buffer,  // gee hmm?
                      int lpitch); // memory pitch
```

```
// 16-bit version
inline int Draw_Pixel16(int x, int y, // position of pixel
                        int color, // 16-bit RGB color
                        UCHAR *video_buffer,  // gee hmm?
                        int lpitch); // memory pitch
```

Purpose:

Draw_Pixel() draws a single pixel on the display surface memory. In most cases, you won't create objects based on pixels because the overhead of the call itself takes more time than plotting the pixel. But if speed isn't your concern, the function does the job. At least it's inline! Returns TRUE if successful.

Example:

```
// draw a pixel in the center of the 640x480 screen
// 8-bit example
Draw_Pixel(320,240, 100, back_buffer, back_lpitch);
```

Function Prototype:

```
int Draw_Rectangle(int x1, int y1, // upper left corner
                int x2, int y2, // lower right corner
                int color, // color descriptor, index for
                           // 8-bit modes, RGB value for 16-bit
                           // modes
                LPDIRECTDRAWSURFACE7 lpdds); // dd surface
```

Purpose:

Draw_Rectangle() draws a rectangle on the sent DirectDraw surface. This function works the same in either 8 or 16-bit mode since it's a pure DirectDraw call. Note that the surface must be unlocked for the call to work. Moreover, the function uses the blitter, so it's very fast. Returns TRUE if successful.

Example:

```
// fill the screen using the blitter
Draw_Rectangle(0,0,639,479,0,lpddsback);
```

Function Prototype:

```
void HLine(int x1,int x2, // start and end x points
           int y,         // row to draw on
           int color,     // 8-bit color
           UCHAR *vbuffer, // video buffer
           int lpitch); // memory pitch

// 16-bit version
void HLine16(int x1,int x2, // start and end x points
           int y,         // row to draw on
           int color,     // 16-bit RGB color
           UCHAR *vbuffer, // video buffer
           int lpitch); // memory pitch
```

DirectX and 2D Fundamentals

Purpose:

`HLine*()` draws a horizontal line very quickly as compared to the general line draw-ing function. Works in both 8 and 16-bit modes. Returns nothing.

Example:

```
// draw a fast line from 10,100 to 100,100
// 8-bit mode
HLine(10,100,100,
      20, back_buffer, back_lpitch);
```

Function Prototype:

```
void VLine(int y1,int y2, // start and end row
           int x,         // column to draw in
           int color,     // 8-bit color
           UCHAR *vbuffer,// video buffer
           int lpitch);   // memory pitch

// 16-bit version
void VLine16(int y1,int y2, // start and end row
           int x,         // column to draw in
           int color,     // 16-bit RGB color
           UCHAR *vbuffer,// video buffer
           int lpitch);   // memory pitch
```

Purpose:

`VLine*()` draws a fast vertical line. It's not as fast as `HLine()`, but it's faster than `Draw_Line()`, so use it if you know a line is going to be vertical in all cases. Returns nothing.

Example:

```
// draw a line from 320,0 to 320,479
// 16-bit version
VLine16(0,479,320,RGB16Bit(255,255,255),
      primary_buffer,
      primary_lpitch);
```

Function Prototype:

```
void Screen_Transitions(int effect,    // screen transition
                        UCHAR *vbuffer,// video buffer
                        int lpitch);   // memory pitch
```

Purpose:

`Screen_Transition()` performs various in-memory screen transitions, as listed in the previous header information. Note that the transformations are destructive, so please save the image and/or palette if you need them after the transition. Additionally, the color manipulation transitions only work in 8-bit palettized modes. However, the screen swipes, and scrunches work in either mode. Returns nothing.

Example:

```
// fade the primary display screen to black
// only works for 8-bit modes
Screen_Transition(SCREEN_DARKNESS, NULL, 0);
// scrunch the screen, works in 8/16 bit modes
Screen_Transition(SCREEN_SCRUNCH, NULL, 0);
```

Function Prototype(s):

```
int Draw_Text_GDI(char *text, // null terminated string
          int x,int y, // position
          COLORREF color, // general RGB color
          LPDIRECTDRAWSURFACE7 lpdds); // dd surface

int Draw_Text_GDI(char *text, // null terminated string
            int x,int y, // position
            int color, // 8-bit color index
            LPDIRECTDRAWSURFACE7 lpdds); // dd surface
```

Purpose:

Draw_Text_GDI() draws GDI text on the sent surface with the desired color and position. The function is overloaded to take both a COLORREF in the form of the Windows RGB() macro for 8- or 16-bit modes or a 256-color 8-bit color index for 256-color modes only. Note that the destination surface must be unlocked for the function to operate because it locks it momentarily to perform the text blitting with GDI. Returns TRUE if successful.

Example:

```
// draw text with color RGB(100,100,0);
// note this call would work in either
// 8 or 16-bit modes
Draw_Text_GDI("This is a test",100,50,
            RGB(100,100,0),lpddsprimary);

// draw text with color index 33
// note this call would work ONLY in
// 8-bit modes
Draw_Text_GDI("This is a test",100,50,
            33,lpddsprimary);
```

Math and Error Functions

The math library thus far is almost nonexistent, but that will soon change once you get to the math section of the book. I'll pump your brain full of all kinds of fun mathematical information and functions. Until then, sip the sweet simplicity because it will be your last...

Function Prototype:

```
int Fast_Distance_2D(int x, int y);
```

Purpose:

Fast_Distance() computes the distance from (0,0) to (*x*,*y*) using a fast approximation. Returns the distance within a 3.5 percent error truncated to an integer.

Example:

```
int x1=100,y1=200; // object one
int x2=400,y2=150; // object two

// compute the distance between object one and two
int dist = Fast_Distance_2D(x1-x2, y1-y2);
```

Function Prototype:

```
float Fast_Distance_3D(float x, float y, float z);
```

Purpose:

Fast_Distance_3D() computes the distance from (0,0,0) to (*x*,*y*,*z*) using a fast
approximation. The function returns the distance within an 11 percent error.

Example:

```
// compute the distance from (0,0,0) to (100,200,300)
float dist = Fast_Distance_3D(100,200,300);
```

Function Prototype:

```
int Find_Bounding_Box_Poly2D(
            POLYGON2D_PTR poly, // the polygon
            float &min_x, float &max_x, // bounding box
            float &min_y, float &max_y);
```

Purpose:

Find_Bounding_Box_Poly2D() computes the smallest rectangle that contains the sent
polygon in poly. Returns TRUE if successful. Also, notice that the function takes parameters by reference.

Example:

```
POLYGON2D poly; // assume this is initialized
int min_x, max_x, min_y, max_y; // hold result

// find bounding box
Find_Bounding_Box_Poly2D(&poly,min_x,max_x,min_y,max_y);
```

Function Prototype:

```
int Open_Error_File(char *filename);
```

Purpose:

Open_Error_File() opens a disk file that receives error messages sent by you via the
Write_Error() function. Returns TRUE if successful.

Example:

```
// open a general error log
Open_Error_File("errors.log");
```

Function Prototype:

```
int Close_Error_File(void);
```

Purpose:

Close_Error_File() closes a previously opened error file. Basically, it shuts down the stream. If you call this and an error file is not open, nothing will happen. Returns TRUE if successful.

Example:

```
// close the error system, note no parameter needed
Close_Error_File();
```

Function Prototype:

```
int Write_Error(char *string, ...); // error formatting string
```

Purpose:

Write_Error() writes an error out to the previously opened error file. If there is no file open, the function returns a FALSE and there's no harm. Note that the function uses the variable parameter indicator, so you can use this function as you would printf(). Returns TRUE if successful.

Example:

```
// write out some stuff
Write_Error("\nSystem Starting…");
Write_Error("x-vel = %d", y-vel = %d", xvel, yvel);
```

Bitmap Functions

The following function set makes up the BITMAP_IMAGE and BITMAP_FILE manipulation routines. There are functions to load 8-, 16-, 24-, and 32-bit bitmaps, as well as to extract images from them and create simple BITMAP_IMAGE objects (which are not DirectDraw surfaces). In addition, there's functionality to draw these images in both 8- and 16-bit modes, but there's no clipping support. Hence, you can modify the source yourself if you need clipping or want to step up to the BOB objects, described at the end of the section. And as usual, some of the functions have both an 8-bit and 16-bit version, the 16-bit versions are usually denoted by an extra "16" concatenated on the function name.

Function Prototype:

```
int Load_Bitmap_File(BITMAP_FILE_PTR bitmap, // bitmap file
                     char *filename); // disk .BMP file to load
```

Purpose:

Load_Bitmap_File() loads a .BMP bitmap file from disk into the sent BITMAP_FILE structure where you can manipulate it. The function loads 8-, 16-, and 24-bit bitmaps, as well as the palette information on 8-bit .BMP files. Returns TRUE if successful.

Example:

```
// let's load "andre.bmp" off disk
BITMAP_FILE bitmap_file;

Load_Bitmap_File(&bitmap_file, "andre.bmp");
```

Function Prototype:

```
int Unload_Bitmap_File(BITMAP_FILE_PTR bitmap);
                       // bitmap to close and unload
```

Purpose:

Unload_Bitmap_File() deallocates the memory associated with the image buffer of a loaded BITMAP_FILE. Call this function when you've copied the image bits and/or are done working with a particular bitmap. You can reuse the structure, but the memory must be freed first. Returns TRUE if successful.

Example:

```
// close the file we just opened
Unload_Bitmap_File(&bitmap_file);
```

Function Prototype:

```
int Create_Bitmap(BITMAP_IMAGE_PTR image, // bitmap image
                  int x, int y, // starting position
                  int width, int height // size
                  int bpp=8); // bits per pixel, either 8 or 16
```

Purpose:

Create_Bitmap() creates either an 8- or 16-bit system memory bitmap at the given position with the given size. The bitmap is initially blank and is stored in the BITMAP_IMAGE image. The bitmap is not a DirectDraw surface, so there's no acceleration or clipping available. Returns TRUE if successful.

> **NOTE**
> There's a big difference between a BITMAP_FILE and a BITMAP_IMAGE. A BITMAP_FILE is a disk .BMP file, whereas a BITMAP_IMAGE is a system memory object like a sprite that can be moved and drawn.

Example:

```
// let's create an 8-bit 64x64 bitmap image at (0,0)
BITMAP_IMAGE ship;

Create_Bitmap(&ship, 0,0, 64,64,8);

// and here's the same example in 16-bit mode
BITMAP_IMAGE ship;
Create_Bitmap(&ship, 0,0, 64,64,16);
```

Function Prototype:

```
int Destroy_Bitmap(BITMAP_IMAGE_PTR image); // bitmap image to destroy
```

Purpose:

Destroy_Bitmap() is used to release the memory allocated during the creation of a
BITMAP_IMAGE object. You should call this function on your object when you're all
done working with it—usually during the shutdown of the game, or if the object has
been destroyed in a bloody battle. Returns TRUE if successful.

Example:

```
// destroy the previously created BITMAP_IMAGE
Destroy_Bitmap(&ship);
```

Function Prototype:

```
int Load_Image_Bitmap(
 BITMAP_IMAGE_PTR image, // bitmap to store image in
 BITMAP_FILE_PTR bitmap, // bitmap file object to load from
 int cx,int cy, // coordinates where to scan (cell or abs)
 int mode); // image scan mode: cell based or absolute

// 16-bit version
int Load_Image_Bitmap16(
 BITMAP_IMAGE_PTR image, // bitmap to store image in
 BITMAP_FILE_PTR bitmap, // bitmap file object to load from
 int cx,int cy, // coordinates where to scan (cell or abs)
 int mode); // image scan mode: cell based or absolute


#define BITMAP_EXTRACT_MODE_CELL  0
#define BITMAP_EXTRACT_MODE_ABS   1
```

Purpose:

Load_Image_Bitmap*() is used to scan an image from a previously loaded
BITMAP_FILE object into the sent BITMAP_IMAGE storage area. This is how you get
objects and image bits into a BITMAP_IMAGE. To use the function, you first must load a

BITMAP_FILE and create the BITMAP_IMAGE. Then you make the call to scan an image of the same size out of the bitmap data stored in the BITMAP_FILE. There are two ways the function works, cell mode or absolute mode:

- In cell mode, BITMAP_EXTRACT_MODE_CELL, the image is scanned making the assumption that all the images are in the .BMP file in a template that is some given size, mxn, with a 1-pixel border between each cell. The cells usually range from 8x8, 16x16, 32x32, 64x64, and so on. Take a look at TEMPLATE*.BMP on the CD; it contains a number of templates. Cell numbers range from left to right, top to bottom, and they start with (0,0).

- The second mode of operation is absolute coordinate mode, BITMAP_EXTRACT_MODE_ABS. In this mode, the image is scanned at the exact coordinates sent in *cx*, *cy*. This method is good if you want to load your artwork with various-sized images on the same .BMP; hence, you can't template them.

Also, you must use the correct version of the function based on the bit depth you created the bitmap in and the bit depth of the image you are scanning. Therefore, use Load_Image_Bitmap() for 8-bit bitmaps and Load_Image_Bitmap16() for 16-bit images.

Example:

```
// assume the source bitmap .BMP file is 640x480 and
// has a 8x8 matrix of cells that are each 32x32
// then to load the 3rd cell to the right on the 2nd
// row (cell 2,1) in 8-bit mode, you would do this

// load in the .BMP file into memory
BITMAP_FILE bitmap_file;
Load_Bitmap_File(&bitmap_file,"images.bmp");


// initialize the bitmap
BITMAP_IMAGE ship;
Create_Bitmap(&ship, 0,0, 32,32,8);


// now scan out the data
Load_Image_Bitmap(&ship, &bitmap_file, 2,1,
                  BITMAP_EXTRACT_MODE_CELL);

// same example in 16-bit mode
// assume the source bitmap .BMP file is 640x480 and
// has a 8x8 matrix of cells that are each 32x32
// then to load the 3rd cell to the right on the 2nd
// row (cell 2,1) in 16-bit mode, you would do this
```

```
// load in the .BMP file into memory
BITMAP_FILE bitmap_file;
Load_Bitmap_File(&bitmap_file,"images24bit.bmp");


// initialize the bitmap
BITMAP_IMAGE ship;
Create_Bitmap(&ship, 0,0, 32,32,16);


// now scan out the data
Load_Image_Bitmap16(&ship, &bitmap_file, 2,1,
                BITMAP_EXTRACT_MODE_CELL);
```

To load the exact same image, assuming it's still in the template, but using the absolute mode, you have to figure out the coordinates. Remember that there's a 1-pixel partitioning wall on each side of the image.

```
Load_Image_Bitmap16(&ship, &bitmap_file,
                2*(32+1)+1,1*(32+1)+1,
                BITMAP_EXTRACT_MODE_ABS);
```

Function Prototype:

```
int Draw_Bitmap(BITMAP_IMAGE_PTR source_bitmap, // bitmap to draw
                UCHAR *dest_buffer, // video buffer
                int lpitch,  // memory pitch
                int transparent); // transparency?

// 16-bit version
int Draw_Bitmap16(BITMAP_IMAGE_PTR source_bitmap, // bitmap to draw
                UCHAR *dest_buffer, // video buffer
                int lpitch,  // memory pitch
                int transparent); // transparency?
```

Purpose:

Draw_Bitmap*() draws the sent bitmap on the destination memory surface with or without transparency. If transparent is 1, transparency is enabled and any pixel with a color index of 0 will not be copied. Again, simply use the 16-bit version when you are working with 16-bit modes and bitmaps. Function returns TRUE if successful.

Example:

```
// draw our little ship on the back buffer
// 8-bit mode
Draw_Bitmap( &ship, back_buffer, back_lpitch, 1);
```

Function Prototype:

```
int Flip_Bitmap(UCHAR *image, // image bits to vertically flip
                int bytes_per_line, // bytes per line
                int height); // total rows or height
```

Purpose:

Flip_Bitmap() is usually called internally to flip upside-down .BMP files during loading to make them right-side up, but you might want to use it to flip an image yourself. The function does an in-memory flip and actually inverts the bitmap line by line, so your original sent data will be inverted. Watch out! Works on any bit depth since it works with bytes per line. Returns TRUE if successful.

Example:

```
// for fun flip the image bits of our little ship
Flip_Bitmap(ship->buffer, ship->width, ship_height);
```

Function Prototype:

```
int Scroll_Bitmap(BITMAP_IMAGE_PTR image, // bitmap to scroll
                  int dx,     // amount to scroll on x-axis
                  int dy=0); // amount to scroll on y-axis
```

Purpose:

Scroll_Bitmap() is used to scroll a bitmap horizontally or vertically. The function works on both 8- and 16-bit bitmaps and determines their bit depth internally, so you need only call one function. To use the function simple call it with a pointer to the bitmap you want to scroll along with the x and y scrolling values in pixels. The values can be either positive or negative, positive values mean right and down, while negative values mean left and up. Additionally, you may scroll on both axis simulataneosly, or just one. It's up to you. Function returns TRUE if it was successful.

Example:

```
// scroll an image 2 pixels to the right
Scroll_Bitmap(&image, 2, 0);
```

Function Prototype:

```
int Copy_Bitmap(BITMAP_IMAGE_PTR dest_bitmap, // destination bitmap
                int dest_x, int dest_y,  // destination position
                BITMAP_IMAGE_PTR source_bitmap, // source bitmap
                int source_x, int source_y, // source position
                int width, int height); // size of bitmap chunk to copy
```

Purpose:

Copy_Bitmap() is used to copy a rectangular region the source bitmap to the destination bitmap. The function internally scans the bitdepth of the source and destination, so the function work on either 8- or 16-bit modes with the same call. The bitmaps must of course be the same color depth though. To use the function simply send the destination bitmap, the point you want to copy the bitmap to, along with the source bitmap, the point you want to copy the bitmap from, and finally the width and height of the rectangle you want to copy. The function return TRUE if it's successful.

Example:

```
// copy a 100x100 rectangle from bitmap2 to bitmap1
// from the upper hand corner to the same
Copy_Bitmap(&bitmap1, 0,0,
            &bitmap2, 0,0,
            100,100);
```

Palette Functions

The following functions make up the 256-color palette interface. These functions are only relevant if you have the display set for a 256-color mode—that is, 8-bit color. Additionally, when you start the system up in 8-bit mode via a call to DDraw_Init() it will load in a default palette off disk, or try to at least, the default palette files are palette1.pal, palette2.pal, and palette3.pal—currently palette2.pal is loaded.

Function Prototype:

```
int Set_Palette_Entry(
            int color_index, // color index to change
            LPPALETTEENTRY color); // the color
```

Purpose:

Set_Palette_Entry() is used to change a single color in the color palette. You simply send the color index 0..255, along with a pointer to PALETTEENTRY holding the color, and the update will occur on the next frame. In addition, this function updates the shadow palette. Note: This function is slow; if you need to update the entire palette, use Set_Palette(). Returns TRUE if successful and FALSE otherwise.

Example:

```
// set color 0 to black
PALETTEENTRY black = {0,0,0,PC_NOCOLLAPSE};
Set_Palette_Entry(0,&black);
```

Function Prototype:

```
int Get_Palette_Entry(
            int color_index, // color index to retrieve
            LPPALETTEENTRY color); // storage for color
```

Purpose:

Get_Palette_Entry() retrieves a palette entry from the current palette. However, the function is very fast because it retrieves the data from the RAM-based shadow palette. Hence, you can call this as much as you like because it doesn't disturb the hardware at all. However, if you make changes to the system palette by using Set_Palette_Entry() or Set_Palette(), the shadow palette won't be updated and the data retrieved may not be valid. Returns TRUE if successful and FALSE otherwise.

Example:

```
// let's get palette entry 100
PALETTEENTRY color;
Get_Palette_Entry(100,&color);
```

Function Prototype:

```
int Save_Palette_To_File(
            char *filename,  // filename to save at
            LPPALETTEENTRY palette); // palette to save
```

Purpose:

Save_Palette_To_File() saves the sent palette data to an ASCII file on disk for later retrieval or processing. This function is very handy if you generate a palette on-the-fly and want to store it on disk. However, the function assumes that the pointer in the palette points to a 256-entry palette, so watch out! Returns TRUE if successful and FALSE otherwise.

Example:

```
PALETTEENTRY my_palette[256]; // assume this is built

// save the palette we made
// note file name can be anything, but I like *.pal
Save_Palette_To_file("/palettes/custom1.pal",my_palette);
```

Function Prototype:

```
int Load_Palette_From_File(
        char *filename,  // file to load from
        LPPALETTEENTRY palette); // storage for palette
```

Purpose:

Load_Palette_From_File() is used to load a previously saved 256-color palette from disk via Save_Palette_To_File(). You simply send the filename along with storage for all 256 entries, and the palette is loaded from disk into the data structure. However, the function does *not* load the entries into the hardware palette; you must do this yourself with Set_Palette(). Returns TRUE if successful and FALSE otherwise.

Example:

```
// load the previously ksaved palette
PALETTEENTRY disk_palette[256];

Load_Palette_From_Disk("/palettes/custom1.pal",&disk_palette);
```

Function Prototype:

```
int Set_Palette(LPPALETTEENTRY set_palette);
                // palette to load into hardware
```

Purpose:

Set_Palette() loads the sent palette data into the hardware and updates the shadow palette also. Returns TRUE if successful and FALSE otherwise.

Example:

```
// lets load the palette into the hardware
Set_Palette(disk_palette);
```

Function Prototype:

```
int Save_Palette(LPPALETTEENTRY sav_palette); // storage for palette
```

Purpose:

Save_Palette() scans the hardware palette out into sav_palette so that you can save it to disk or manipulate it. sav_palette must have enough storage for all 256 entries.

Example:

```
// retrieve the current DirectDraw hardware palette
PALETTEENTRY hardware_palette[256];
Save_Palette(hardware_palette);
```

Function Prototype:

```
int Rotate_Colors(int start_index, // starting index 0..255
                  int end_index); // ending index 0..255
```

Purpose:

Rotate_Colors() rotates a bank of colors in a cyclic manner in 8-bit modes. It manipulates the color palette hardware directly. Returns TRUE if successful and FALSE otherwise.

Example:

```
// rotate the entire palette
Rotate_Colors(0,255);
```

Function Prototype:

```
int Blink_Colors(int command, // blinker engine command
                 BLINKER_PTR new_light,  // blinker data
                 int id); // id of blinker
```

Purpose:

`Blink_Colors()` is used to create asynchronous palette animation. The function is too long to explain here, so please refer to Chapter 7, "Advanced DirectDraw and Bitmapped Graphics," for a more in-depth description.

Example:

None

Utility Functions

The next set of functions are just utility functions that I seem to use a lot, so I thought you might want to use them too.

Function Prototype:

```
DWORD Get_Clock(void);
```

Purpose:

`Get_Clock()` returns the current clock time in milliseconds since Windows was started.

Example:

```
// get the current tick count
DWORD start_time = Get_Clock();
```

Function Prototype:

```
DWORD Start_Clock(void);
```

Purpose:

`Start_Clock()` basically makes a call to `Get_Clock()` and stores the time in a global variable for you. Then you can call `Wait_Clock()`, which will wait for a certain number of milliseconds since your call to `Start_Clock()`. Returns the starting clock value at the time of the call.

Example:

```
// start the clock and set the global
Start_Clock();
```

Function Prototype:

```
DWORD Wait_Clock(DWORD count); // number of milliseconds to wait
```

Purpose:

Wait_Clock() simply waits the sent number of milliseconds since the call was made to Start_Clock(). Returns the current clock count at the time of the call. However, the function will *not* return until the time difference has elapsed.

Example:

```
// wait 30 milliseconds
Start_Clock();

// code…

Wait_Clock(30);
```

Function Prototype:

```
int Collision_Test(int x1, int y1, // upper lhs of obj1
                   int w1, int h1, // width, height of obj1
                   int x2, int y2, // upper lhs of obj2
                   int w2, int h2);// width, height of obj2
```

Purpose:

Collision_Test() basically performs an overlapping rectangle test on the two sent rectangles. The rectangles can represent whatever you like. You must send the upper-left-corner coordinates of each rectangle, along with its width and height. Returns TRUE if there is an overlap and FALSE if not.

Example:

```
// do these two BITMAP_IMAGE's overlap?
if (Collision_Test(ship1->x,ship1->y,ship1->width,ship1->height,
                   ship2->x,ship2->y,ship2->width,ship2->height))
   { // hit

   } // end if
```

Function Prototype:

```
int Color_Scan(int x1, int y1, // upper left of rect
               int x2, int y2, // lower right of rect
               UCHAR scan_start, // starting scan color
               UCHAR scan_end,  // ending scan color
               UCHAR *scan_buffer,  // memory to scan
               int scan_lpitch); // linear memory pitch

// 16-bit version
int Color_Scan16(int x1, int y1, // upper left of rect
               int x2, int y2, // lower right of rect
               USHORT scan_start, // scan RGB value 1
               USHORT scan_end,  // scan RGB value 2
               UCHAR *scan_buffer,  // memory to scan
               int scan_lpitch); // linear memory pitch
```

Purpose:

`Color_Scan*()` is another collision-detection algorithm that scans a rectangle for either a single 8-bit value or sequence of values in some continuous range in 8-bit modes or when used in 16-bit modes scans for up to 2 RGB values. You can use it to determine if a color index is present within some area. Returns TRUE if the color(s) was found.

Example:

```
// scan for colors in range from 122-124 inclusive in 8-bit mode
Color_Scan(10,10, 50, 50, 122,124, back_buffer, back_lpitch);

// scan for the RGB colors 10,30,40 and 100,0,12
Color_Scan(10,10, 50, 50, RGB16Bit(10,30,40), RGB16Bit(100,0,12),
back_buffer, back_lpitch);
```

The BOB (Blitter Object) Engine

Although with a bit of programming you can get the BITMAP_IMAGE type to do what you want, it's lacking in a serious way—it doesn't use DirectDraw surfaces, so there's no support for acceleration. Therefore, I've created a new type called a *Blitter Object (BOB)* that's very similar to a sprite. For those of you who've been in a game programming cave, a sprite is nothing more than an object you can move around the screen that usually doesn't disturb the background. In this case that isn't true, so I called my animation object a BOB rather than a sprite—so there!

You haven't seen any of the BOB engine source code so far in this book, but you *have* seen everything that went into making it. I don't have enough space to list the source code, but it's in the file T3DLIB1.CPP along with everything else. What I'm going to do is show you each function that makes up the engine, and you're free to use the code, print it out and burn it, or whatever. I just wanted to give you a good example of using DirectDraw surfaces and full acceleration before you moved on to the remaining non-graphical components of DirectX.

Let's talk briefly about what a BOB is. First, take a look at the data structure for a BOB, which is back in the section "Data Types and Structures," and then come back here…Ready?

A BOB is basically a graphical object represented by one or more DirectDraw surfaces (up to 64). You can move a BOB, draw a BOB, and animate a BOB. BOBs are clipped by the current DirectDraw clipper, so they're clipped as well as accelerated—which is a good thing! Figure 8.55 shows a BOB and its relationship to its animation frames.

FIGURE 8.55
The BOB (blitter object) animation system.

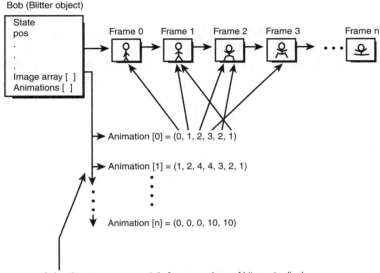

Animation sequences contain frame numbers of bitmap to display

Also, the BOB engine supports animation sequences, so you can load in a set of frames and an animation sequence and the sequence will play by feeding from the frames. This is a very cool feature. Also, all the BOB functions return TRUE if successful and FALSE otherwise. And of course BOBs support both 8 and 16-bit modes. Since BOBs are DirectDraw objects more or less, only a few functions need 16-bit versions (mostly in the loading and drawing calls) since most of the BOB is abstracted enough that it doesn't matter, but where it does there are of course two functions: one for 8-bit and one for 16-bit modes. The 16-bit functions are the exact same as the 8-bit with "16" concatenated on the function name. But, I will take you through this as we go.

So let's take a look at them all...

Function Prototype:

```
int Create_BOB(BOB_PTR bob, // ptr to bob to create
    int x, int y,        // initial position of bob
    int width, int height, // size of bob
    int num_frames, // total number of frames for bob
    int attr,       // attributes of bob
    int mem_flags, // surface memory flags, 0 is VRAM
    USHORT color_key_value=0, // color key value, index for
                            // 8-bit modes or RGB value for
                            // 16-bit modes
    int bpp=8);   // color depth of the requested bob
```

Purpose:

`Create_BOB()` creates a single BOB object and sets it up for either a 8 or 16-bit display. The function sets up all the internal variables in addition to creating a separate DirectDraw surface for each frame. Most of the parameters are self-explanatory; the only value that needs a little explanation is the attribute variable `attr`. Take a look at Table 8.4 to see a better description of each of the attributes you can logically OR together and send in this field.

TABLE 8.4 Valid BOB Attributes

Value	Description
`BOB_ATTR_SINGLE_FRAME`	Creates BOB with a single frame.
`BOB_ATTR_MULTI_FRAME`	Creates BOB with multiple frames, but the animation of the BOB will be a linear sequence through the frames 0..n.
`BOB_ATTR_MULTI_ANIM`	Creates a multiple-frame BOB that supports animation sequences.
`BOB_ATTR_ANIM_ONE_SHOT`	If this is set, an animation sequence will play only once and then stop. At that point the internal variable `anim_state` will be set. To play the animation again, reset this variable.
`BOB_ATTR_BOUNCE`	This flag tells the BOB to bounce off the screen boundaries like a ball. This only works if you use `Move_BOB()`.
`BOB_ATTR_WRAPAROUND`	This flag tells the BOB to wrap around to the other side of the screen as it moves. This only works if you use `Move_BOB()`.

Examples:

Here are some examples of creating BOBs. First, a single-frame 8-bit BOB at (50,100) with a size of 96x64:

```
BOB car; // a car bob

// create the bob
if (!Create_BOB(&car, 50,100,
                96,64,1,BOB_ATTR_SINGLE_FRAME,0))
   { /* error */ }
// note that last two parameters were left out since they
// have default values of 0 for the color key and 8 for bpp
```

And here's a multiple-frame 16-bit BOB with eight frames and a size of 32x32:

```
BOB ship; // a space ship bob

// create the bob
if (!Create_BOB(&ship, 0,0,
                32,32,8,BOB_ATTR_MULTI_FRAME,0,0,16))
   { /* error */ }
```

Finally, a multiple-frame 8-bit BOB that supports animation sequences:

```
BOB greeny; // a little green man bob

// create the bob
if (!Create_BOB(&greeny, 0,0,
    32,32,32,BOB_ATTR_MULTI_ANIM,0,0,0))
    { /* error */ }
```

 It is extremely important that you create BOBs with the correct bit depth or bits per pixel, if you don't then you will probably crash the machine. Remember, the function defaults to 8-bit.

Function Prototype:

```
int Destroy_BOB(BOB_PTR bob); // ptr to bob to destroy
```

Purpose:

Destroy_BOB() destroys a previously created BOB. You would do this when you are done with the BOB and want to release the memory it used back to Windows. This function destroys either 8-bit or 16-bit BOBs with the same call.

Example:

```
// destroy the BOB above, you would do this
Destroy_BOB(&greeny);
```

Function Prototype:

```
int Draw_BOB(BOB_PTR bob,  // ptr of bob to draw
  LPDIRECTDRAWSURFACE7 dest); // dest surface to draw on

// 16-bit version
int Draw_BOB16(BOB_PTR bob,  // ptr of bob to draw
  LPDIRECTDRAWSURFACE7 dest); // dest surface to draw on
```

Purpose:

Draw_BOB*() is a very powerful function. It draws the sent BOB on the DirectDraw surface that you send it. The BOB is drawn in its current position and current frame, as defined by its animation parameters. Use the standard Draw_BOB() function for 8-bit modes and the 16-bit version Draw_BOB16() for 16-bit modes.

 For this function to work, the destination surface must not be locked.

Example:

```
// this is how you would position an 8-bit multiframe BOB at
// (50,50) and draw the first frame of it on the back
// surface:
BOB ship; // a space ship bob

// create the bob
if (!Create_BOB(&ship, 0,0,
                32,32,8,BOB_ATTR_MULTI_FRAME,0))

// load the bob images in..well get to this in a bit
// set the position and frame of bob
ship.x = 50;
ship.y = 50;
ship.curr_frame = 0; // this contains the frame to draw

// draw bob
Draw_BOB(&ship, lpddsback);

// same example with a 16-bit BOB
// this is how you would position an 8-bit multiframe BOB at
// (50,50) and draw the first frame of it on the back
// surface:
BOB ship; // a space ship bob

// create the bob
if (!Create_BOB(&ship, 0,0,
                32,32,8,BOB_ATTR_MULTI_FRAME,0,0,16))

// load the bob images in..well get to this in a bit
// set the position and frame of bob
ship.x = 50;
ship.y = 50;
ship.curr_frame = 0; // this contains the frame to draw

// draw bob
Draw_BOB16(&ship, lpddsback);
```

Function Prototype:

```
int Draw_Scaled_BOB(BOB_PTR bob, // ptr of bob to draw
  int swidth, int sheight, // new width and height of bob
  LPDIRECTDRAWSURFACE7 dest); // dest surface to draw on

// 16-bit version
int Draw_Scaled_BOB16(BOB_PTR bob, // ptr of bob to draw
  int swidth, int sheight, // new width and height of bob
  LPDIRECTDRAWSURFACE7 dest); // dest surface to draw on
```

Purpose:

`Draw_Scaled_BOB*()` works exactly like `Draw_BOB*()`, except that you can send any
width and height to draw the BOB with and the engine will scale the BOB up or
down. This is very cool, and if you have acceleration, it's a great way to scale a BOB
to make it look 3D! Of course, you must use the correct version for your particular bit
depth.

Example:

```
// an example of drawing aship at 128x128 even though
// it was created as only 32x32 pixels
// 8-bit call
Draw_Scaled_BOB(&ship, 128,128,lpddsback);
```

Function Prototype:

```
int Load_Frame_BOB(
  BOB_PTR bob, // ptr of bob to load frame into
  BITMAP_FILE_PTR bitmap,// ptr of bitmap file to scan data
  int frame,    // frame number to place image into 0,1,2...
  int cx,int cy, // cell pos or abs pos to scan from
  int mode);    // scan mode, same as Load_Frame_Bitmap()

// 16-bit version
int Load_Frame_BOB16(
  BOB_PTR bob, // ptr of bob to load frame into
  BITMAP_FILE_PTR bitmap,// ptr of bitmap file to scan data
  int frame,    // frame number to place image into 0,1,2...
  int cx,int cy, // cell pos or abs pos to scan from
  int mode);    // scan mode, same as Load_Frame_Bitmap16()
```

Purpose:

The `Load_Frame_BOB*()` function works identically to the `Load_Frame_Bitmap*()`
function, so refer to that for details. The only additional control parameter `frame` is
the frame to load. If you create a BOB that has four frames, you'll load the frames in
one by one. And of course use the right version for the bit depth you are working in.

Example:

```
// here's an example of loading 4 frames into an 8-bit BOB from a
// bitmap file in cell mode

BOB ship; // the bob
// loads frames 0,1,2,3 from cell position (0,0), (1,0),
// (2,0), (3,0)
// from bitmap8bit bitmap file, assume it has been loaded

for (int index=0; index<4; index++)
    Load_Frame_BOB(&ship,&bitmap8bit,
                    index, index,0,
```

```
                                    BITMAP_EXTRACT_MODE_CELL );
// here's an example of loading 4 frames into an 16-bit BOB from a
// bitmap file in cell mode

BOB ship; // the bob
// loads frames 0,1,2,3 from cell position (0,0), (1,0),
// (2,0), (3,0)
// from bitmap8bit bitmap file, assume it has been loaded

for (int index=0; index<4; index++)
    Load_Frame_BOB16(&ship,&bitmap8bit,
                     index, index,0,
                     BITMAP_EXTRACT_MODE_CELL );
```

Function Prototype:

```
int Load_Animation_BOB(
    BOB_PTR bob,     // bob to load animation into
    int anim_index, // which animation to load 0..15
    int num_frames, // number of frames of animation
    int *sequence); // ptr to array holding sequence
```

Purpose:

Load_Animation() takes a little explaining. This function is used to load one of 16 arrays internal to the BOB that contain animation sequences. Each sequence contains an array of indices or frame numbers to display in sequence.

Example:

You might have a BOB that has eight frames, 0,1,...7, but you might have four animations defined as follows:

```
int anim_walk[]  = {0,1,2,1,0};
int anim_fire[]  = {5,6,0};
int anim_die[]   = {3,4};
int anim_sleep[] = {0,0,7,0,0};
```

Then, to load the animations into a 16-bit BOB, you would do the following:

```
// create a mutli animation bob
// create the bob
if (!Create_BOB(&alien, 0,0, 32,32,8,BOB_ATTR_MULTI_ANIM,0,0,16))
   { /* error */ }

// load the bob frames in... use 16 bit load function!
// load walk into animation 0
Load_Animation_BOB(&alien, 0,5,anim_walk);

// load fire into animation 1
Load_Animation_BOB(&alien, 1,3,anim_fire);

// load die into animation 2
Load_Animation_BOB(&alien, 2,2,anim_die);
```

```
// load sleep into animation 3
Load_Animation_BOB(&alien, 3,5,anim_sleep);
```

After loading the animations, you can set the active animation and play them with functions you'll see in a minute.

Function Prototype:

```
int Set_Pos_BOB(BOB_PTR bob, // ptr to bob to set position
            int x, int y);   // new position of bob
```

Purpose:

Set_Pos_BOB() is a simple way to set the position of the BOB. It does nothing more than assign the internal (x,y) variables, but it's nice to have a function.

Example:

```
// set the position of the alien BOB above
Set_Pos_BOB(&alien, player_x, player_y);
```

Function Prototype:

```
int Set_Vel_BOB(BOB_PTR bob, // ptr to bob to set velocity
        int xv, int yv); // new x,y velocity
```

Purpose:

Each BOB has an internal velocity contained in (xv,yv). Set_Vel_BOB() simply assigns these values the new values sent in the function. The velocity values in the BOB won't do anything unless you use the function Move_BOB() to move your BOBs. However, even if you don't, you can use (xv,yv) to track the velocity of the BOB yourself.

Example:

```
// make the BOB move in a straight horizontal line
Set_Vel_BOB(&alien, 10,0);
```

Function Prototype:

```
int Set_Anim_Speed_BOB(BOB_PTR bob, // ptr to bob
                int speed); // speed of animation
```

Purpose:

Set_Anim_Speed() sets the internal animation rate for a BOB anim_count_max. The higher this number, the slower the animation. The lower the number (0 is the lowest), the faster the animation. However, this function only matters if you use the internal BOB animation function Animate_BOB(). And of course, you must have created a BOB that has multiple frames.

Example:

```
// set the rate to change frames every 30 frames
Set_Anim_Speed_BOB(&alien, 30);
```

Function Prototype:

```
int Set_Animation_BOB(
        BOB_PTR bob,  // ptr of bob to set animation
        int anim_index); // index of animation to set
```

Purpose:

Set_Animation_BOB() sets the current animation that will be played by the BOB. In the earlier example of Load_Animation_BOB(), you created four animations.

Example:

```
// make animation sequence number 2 active
Set_Animation_BOB(&alien, 2);
```

> **NOTE**
>
> This also resets the BOB animation to the first frame in the sequence.

Function Prototype:

```
int Animate_BOB(BOB_PTR bob); // ptr to bob to animate
```

Purpose:

Animate_BOB() animates a BOB for you. Normally, you would call this function once per frame to update the animation of the BOB.

Example:

```
// erase everything...
// move everything...
// animate everything
Animate_BOB(&alien);
```

Function Prototype:

```
int Move_BOB(BOB_PTR bob); // ptr of bob to move
```

Purpose:

Move_BOB() moves the BOB a delta of *xv,yv*, and then, depending on the attributes, it will either bounce the BOB off the walls, wrap it around, or do nothing. Similarly to the Animate_BOB() function, you would place this call once in the main loop right after (or before) Animate_BOB().

Example:

```
// animate bob
Animate_BOB(&alien);

// move it
Move_BOB(&alien);
```

Function Prototype:

```
int Hide_BOB(BOB_PTR bob); // ptr to bob to hide
```

Purpose:

Hide_BOB() simply sets the invisible flag on the BOB so Draw_BOB() won't display it.

Example:

```
// hide the bob
Hide_BOB(&alien);
```

Function Prototype:

```
int Show_BOB(BOB_PTR bob); // ptr to bob to show
```

Purpose:

Show_BOB() sets the visible flag on a BOB so it will be drawn (undoes a Hide_BOB() call). Here's an example of hiding and showing a BOB because you're displaying a GDI object or something and don't want the BOB to occlude it:

Example:

```
Hide_BOB(&alien);
// make calls to Draw_BOB and GDI etc.
Show_BOB(&alien);
```

Function Prototype:

```
int Collision_BOBS(BOB_PTR bob1,  // ptr to first bob
                   BOB_PTR bob2); // ptr to second bob
```

Purpose:

Collision_BOBS() detects if the bounding rectangles of two BOBs overlap. This can be used for collision detection in a game to see if a player BOB hits a missile BOB or whatever.

Example:

```
// check if a missile BOB hit a player BOB:
if (Collision_BOBS(&missile, &player))
   { /* make explosion sound */ }
```

Summary

This chapter has taken forever, huh? There's simply too much material to cover, so I've tried to give you just the most important data on a wide variety of topics. However, don't despair—you're going to hit all this polygon stuff again when you get to 3D in Volume II, so you'll be expert when that's said and done.

Think of this chapter as a primer on a number of topics: rasterization, clipping, line drawing, matrices, collision detection, timing, scrolling, isometric engines, and more. Sometimes you have to take a top-down approach and then follow it up with a bottom-up approach later. Game programming is like that. Anyway, enough philosophy. Now that you have a full bitmap and polygon library, you can do some real damage with the demos during the remaining chapters. And make sure to check out all 16-bit versions of each demo to get familiar with using the 16-bit code. Now, let's have some fun...

CHAPTER 9

Uplinking with DirectInput and Force Feedback

"How's about I pin you?"
—Hot Chick from Pleasantville

I remember a time when I built joystick interfaces out of TTL chips so that games I wrote on my Atari 800 could support up to four players per 9-pin joystick port. Does that make me a sick person? Anyway, input devices have come a long way, and so has the DirectX support for them. In this chapter, we're going to take a look at DirectInput along with some general input algorithms, and I'll throw in a taste of force feedback. Here's what you'll see:

- Overview of DirectInput
- The keyboard
- The mouse
- The joystick
- Input merging
- Force feedback
- The input library

The Input Loop Revisited

This is as good as time as any to review the general structure of a game and the relationship of input to the event loop. Referring to Figure 9.1, you see the generic game loop of erase, move, draw, wait, repeat. That's all there is to a video game. Of course, this is oversimplified. In the world of Win32/DirectX, we already had to add a good amount of setup, termination, and Windows event handling code to get a Windows/ DirectX application up and running. But once that's all taken care of, basically you have erase, move, draw, wait, repeat.

FIGURE 9.1
A generic input loop.

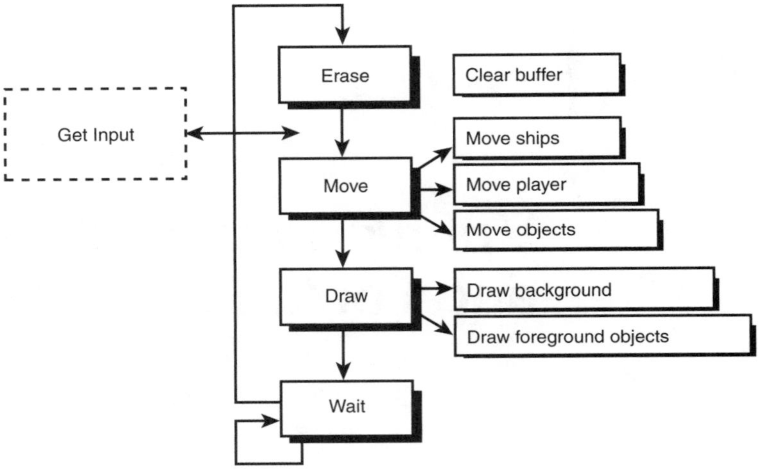

The question is, where does the input go? Good question. It turns out that you could actually put the input in a number of places--at the beginning of the sequence, in the middle, at the end--but most game programmers like to put it right before the *move* section. That way, the last input state set by the player is acted on during the next frame.

Figure 9.2 shows a more detailed game loop with input and all the sections broken down into more detail. Remember, because you're using the game console that you've been working on, you have agreed to do everything for each frame within the Game_Main() function. In essence, your whole world exists within this single function call.

All right, now that I've refreshed your memory on where the input should be scanned or read in, let's see how to do it with DirectInput!

FIGURE 9.2
Detailed input loop.

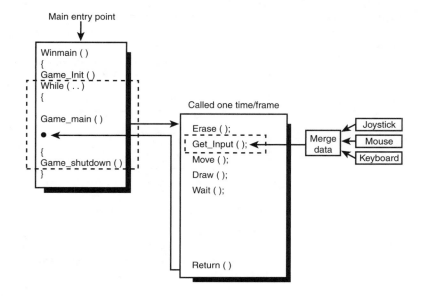

DirectInput Overture

DirectInput is basically a miracle—just like DirectDraw. Without DirectInput, you would be on the phone with every input device manufacturer in the world, begging them for drivers (one for DOS, Win16, Win32, and so on) and having a really bad day--trust me! DirectInput takes all these problems away. Of course, because it was designed by Microsoft, it creates whole new problems, but at least they are localized at one company!

DirectInput is just like DirectDraw. It's a hardware-independent virtual input system that allows hardware manufacturers to create conventional and non-conventional input devices that all act as interfaces in the same way. This is good for you because you don't need a driver for every single input device that your users might own. You talk to DirectInput in a generic way, and the DirectInput driver translates this code into hardware-specific calls, as does DirectDraw.

Take a look at Figure 9.3 to see an illustration of DirectInput as it relates to the hardware drivers and physical input devices.

DirectX and 2D Fundamentals

FIGURE 9.3
DirectInput system-level schematic.

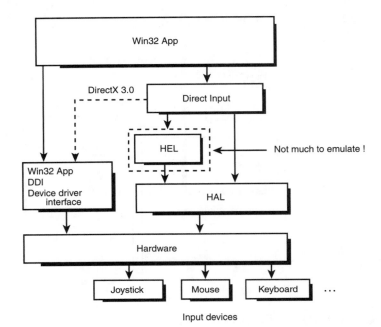

As you can see, you are always insulated by the *HAL (Hardware Abstraction Layer)*. There's not much to emulate with the *HEL (Hardware Emulation Layer)*, so it's not as important as it was with DirectDraw. In any case, that's the basic idea of DirectInput. Let's take a look at what it supports:

Every single input device that exists.

That's pretty much the truth. As long as there is a DirectInput driver for a device, DirectInput can talk to it, and hence you can too. Of course, it's up to the hardware vendor to write a driver, but that's their job. With that in mind, you can expect support for the following devices:

- Keyboards
- Mice
- *Joysticks
- *Paddles
- *Game pads
- *Steering wheels
- *Flight yokes
- *Head-mounted display trackers

- *6-DOF (degree of freedom) space balls
- *Cybersex suits (as soon as they hit the mass market in early 2005)

The devices with asterisks are all considered to be joysticks as far as DirectInput is concerned. There are so many subclasses of joystick-like input devices that DirectInput just decided to call them all *devices*. Each of these devices can have one or more input objects, which might be axial, rotational, momentary, pressure, and so on. Get it? For example, a joystick with two axes (X and Y) and two momentary switches has four input objects—that's it.

DirectInput doesn't really care whether the device in question is a joystick because the device could represent a steering wheel just as easily. However, in reality, DirectInput does subclass a little. Anything that's not a mouse or keyboard is a joystick-like device, whether you hold it, squeeze it, turn it, or step on it. Coolio?

DirectInput differentiates between all these devices by forcing the manufacturer (and hence the driver) to give each device a unique GUID to represent it. This way, at least there is a unique name of sorts for every single device that exists or will exist, and DirectInput can query the system for any device using this name. Once the device is found, however, it's just a bunch of input objects. I'm belaboring this point because it seems to confuse people. Okay, let's move on...

The Components of DirectInput

DirectInput version 8.0 consists of a number of COM interfaces, as do any of the DirectX subsystems. Take a look at Figure 9.4. You can see that there is the main interface, IDirectInput8, and then only one other main interface, IDirectInputDevice8.

FIGURE 9.4
The interfaces of DirectInput.

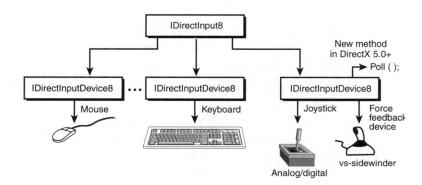

Let's take a look at these interfaces:

- IDirectInput8—This is the main COM object that you must create to start up DirectInput. Luckily there is a wrapper to do DirectInput8Create() that does all the COM stuff for you. Once you have created the IDirectInput8 interface, you will make calls to it to set up the properties of DirectInput and to create and acquire any input devices that you may want to work with.

- IDirectInputDevice8—This interface is created from the main IDirectInput8 interface and is the conduit that you use to communicate with a device, whether it be a mouse, keyboard, joystick, or whatever. They are all IDirectInput8 devices. This latest interface supports joysticks and force feedback devices. In addition, it allows polled devices to be plugged; some joysticks need to be polled.

The General Steps for Setting Up DirectInput

There are a number of steps involved in getting DirectInput up and running, connecting to one or more devices, and finally getting data from the device(s). First is the setup of DirectInput, and next is the setup of each input device. The second part is almost identical for each device, so we can generalize it. That's cool, huh? Here's what you have to do:

1. Create the main DirectInput interface IDirectInput8 with a call to DirectInput8Create(). This returns the IDirectInput8 interface.

2. (Optional) Query for device GUIDs. During this step, you will query DirectInput for input devices belonging to the class keyboard, mouse, joystick, or generic device (one that doesn't fall into the previous list). This is accomplished with (get ready to throw up) a callback function and an enumeration. Basically, you request DirectInput to enumerate all devices of some type/subtype. DirectInput filters them through a callback, which you then build up with a database of GUIDs. Disgusting, huh? Well, luckily this is really only an issue for joystick-like devices, because you can usually bank on a generic mouse and keyboard and there are stock GUIDs for them. I'll show you how this step works when I cover joysticks a little later.

3. For each device that you want to use in your application, you must create it with a call to CreateDevice() passing a GUID. CreateDevice() is an interface function of IDirectInput8, so you must obtain the IDirectInput8 interface before making this call. Also, this step will come after step 2 if you don't know the GUID of the device that you are trying to create. There are two built-in GUIDs, one for the keyboard and one for the mouse:

   GUID_SysKeyboard—This is globally defined and will always work as the primary keyboard device GUID.

GUID_SysMouse—This is globally defined and will always work as the primary mouse device GUID.

> **TIP**
>
> A while ago, an astute reader sent me an email asking about how to detect and use more than one mouse. I hadn't really thought about it, but if the driver supports more than one mouse, you should be able to use it under DirectInput. In this case, you would have to query for the secondary mouse GUID to create it.

4. Once you have created the device, you must set the cooperative level for each. This is accomplished with the call IDirectInputDevice8::SetCooperativeLevel(). Note the C++ syntax here—it simply means that this SetCooperativeLevel() is an interface method or function of IDirectInputDevice8. The cooperation levels are much like those in DirectDraw, but there are fewer of them. We will take a closer look at them when we walk through the keyboard example.

5. Set the data format of each device with a call to SetDataFormat() from the IDirectInputDevice8 interface. This is a bit confusing in practice, but not that bad conceptually. The data format is how you want the data packet for each device event to be formatted. That was nice of DirectInput! This just gives you more flexibility, that's all. Thank goodness, there are some globally predefined data formats that you can use that are reasonably intelligent, so you don't have to set one up yourself.

6. Set any properties of the device that you desire with IDirectInputDevice8:: SetProperty(). This is device context-sensitive, meaning that some devices have some properties and some don't. Thus, you have to know what you're trying to set. In this case, you'll only use this to set some of the range properties of the joystick device, but be aware that in most cases, anything that is configurable on a device is configured with a call to SetProperty(). As usual, the call is fairly horrific, but I'll show you exactly how to do it when we cover the joystick example.

7. Acquire each device with a call to IDirectInputDevice8::Acquire(). This basically attaches or associates the device(s) with your application and tells DirectInput that in the future you'll be requesting data from the device.

8. (Optional) Poll the device(s) with a call to IDirectInputDevice8::Poll(). Some input devices need to be polled rather than you generating interrupts and keeping the input state current. Many joysticks fall into this class, so it's always a good idea to poll joysticks whether they need it or not. Polling doesn't hurt and costs nothing if it isn't needed (the function just returns).

9. Read the device data for each device with a call to
   `IDirectInputDevice8::GetDeviceState()`. The data returned from the call
   will be different for each device, but the call is exactly the same. This call
   retrieves the data from the device and places it into a buffer so you can read it.

That's all there is to it! Seems like a lot, but it's really a small price to pay to access
any input device without having to worry about the device driver for it!

Data Acquisition Modes

Last, but not least, I want to briefly alert you to the existence of *immediate* and
buffered data modes. DirectInput can send you immediate state information or buffer
input, time-stamped in a message format. I haven't had much use for the buffered
input model, but it's there if you want to use it (read the DirectX SDK if you're interested). We'll use the immediate mode of data acquisition, which is the default.

Creating the Main DirectInput Object

Now let's see how to create the main DirectInput COM object `IDirectInput8`. Then
we'll take a look at how to work with the keyboard, mouse, and joystick.

The interface pointer to the main DirectInput object is defined in `DINPUT.H` as follows:

```
LPDIRECTINPUT8 lpdi; // main directinput interface
```

To create the main COM interface, use the standalone function
`DirectInput8Create()`, shown here:

```
HRESULT WINAPI DirectInput8Create(
 HINSTANCE hinst, // the main instance of the app
 DWORD dwVersion, // the version of directinput you want
 REFIID riidltf, // reference id for desired interface
 LPVOID *lplpDirectInput,  // ptr to storage
                                  // for interface ptr
 LPUNKNOWN punkOuter);  // COM stuff, always NULL
```

The parameters are as follows:

`hinst` is the instance handle of your application. This is one of the few function
calls that needs this handle. It's the same handle that is passed into `WinMain()` at
the start of your application, so just save it in a global and stuff it in here.

`dwVersion` is a constant that describes which version of DirectInput you want to be
compatible with. If you assume that some of your game will be played on DirectX
3.0 machines, this will be of concern, but just send `DIRECTINPUT_VERSION` for the
latest version of DirectInput and that will do.

`riidltf` is a constant that selects the version of the interface that you want to create. Normally, this will be `IID_IDirectInput8`.

lplpDirectInput is the address of the interface pointer that will receive the COM interface to DirectInput.

And lastly, punkOuter is for COM aggregation and is not of concern. Set it to NULL.

DirectInput8Create() returns DI_OK (DirectInput OK) if successful, or something else if not. As usual, though, we are going to use the macros SUCCESS() and FAILURE() rather than test for DI_OK because it's now the preferred method under DirectX to test for a problem. But it's pretty safe to use DI_OK if you want.

Here's an example of creating the main DirectInput object:

```
#include "DINPUT.H" // need this and DINPUT.LIB, DINPUT8.LIB

// the rest of your includes, defines etc.

// globals...

LPDIRECTINPUT8 lpdi = NULL; // used to point to com interface

if (FAILED(DirectInput8Create(main_instance,
                              DIRECTINPUT_VERSION,
                              IID_IDirectInput8,
                              (void **)&lpdi,NULL)))
    return(0);
```

> **NOTE**
>
> It's very important that you include DINPUT.H and DINPUT.LIB in your application, or else the compiler and linker won't know what to do. Also, if you've never read my instructions on compiling, please include the .LIB file directly in the application project. Setting a search path in the library search settings is usually not enough.

And that's that. If the function was successful, at this point you'll have a pointer to the main DirectInput object that you can then use to create devices.

As with all COM objects, when your application is complete and you are releasing resources, you must make a call to Release() to decrement the reference count of the COM object. Here's how:

```
// the shutdown
lpdi->Release();
```

And if you want to be technical:

```
// the shutdown
if (lpdi)
    lpdi->Release();
```

Of course, you would do this after releasing the devices created. Remember always to make your calls to `Release()` in the reverse order you created your objects, like unwinding a stack.

The 101-Key Control Pad

Because setting up one DirectInput device is similar to setting up all other devices, I'm going to really go into detail with the keyboard and then speed things up with the mouse and joystick. So make sure to read this section carefully, because it will be applicable to the other devices as well.

Creating the Keyboard Device

The first step in getting any device up and running is creating it with a call to `IDIRECTINPUT8::CreateDevice()`. Remember, this function basically gives you an interface to the particular device that you requested (the keyboard in this first example), which you can then work with. Let's take a look at the function:

```
HRESULT CreateDevice(
 REFGUID rguid, // the GUID of the device to create
 LPDIRECTINPUTDEVICE8 *lplpDirectInputDevice,  // ptr to the
                                               // IDIRECTINPUTDEVICE8
                                               // interface to receive ptr
 LPUNKNOWN pUnkOuter); // COM stuff, always NULL
```

Simple enough, huh, baby? The first parameter, `rguid`, is the `GUID` of the device you want to create. You can either query for the `GUID` of interest or use one of the defaults for the most common devices:

GUID_SysKeyboard—The keyboard.

GUID_SysMouse—The mouse.

> **WARNING**
>
> Danger, Will Robinson! Remember, these are in `DINPUT.H`, so that must be included along with `DINPUT.LIB`, `DINPUT8.LIB`. Furthermore, for all this GUID stuff, you should also place a `#define INITGUID` at the top of your application before all other includes (but only once), as well as including the header `OBJBASE.H` with your application. You can also include the .LIB file `DXGUID.LIB` with your program, but `OBJBASE.H` is preferred. In any case, you can always look at the chapter demos on the CD and see a working example of what to include and what not to include; it's just one of the stupid details.

The second parameter is the receiver of the new interface, and of course the last is just `NULL`. The function returns `DI_OK` if successful and something else if not.

All right, based on your new-found knowledge of `CreateDevice()`, let's see if you can create the keyboard device. The first thing you need is a variable to hold the interface pointer that will be created during the call. All devices are of type `IDIRECTINPUTDEVICE8`:

```
IDIRECTINPUTDEVICE8 lpdikey = NULL; // ptr to keyboard device
```

Now, let's create the device with a call to `CreateDevice()` from the main COM object. Here's all the code, including the creation of the main COM object and all necessary inclusion/defines:

```
// this needs to come first
#define INITGUID


// includes
#include <OBJBASE.H> // need this one for GUIDS
#include "DINPUT.H"  // need this for directinput and
                     // DINPUT.LIB

// globals...

LPDIRECTINPUT8 lpdi = NULL; // used to point to com interface
IDIRECTINPUTDEVICE8 lpdikey = NULL; // ptr to keyboard device

if (FAILED(DirectInput8Create(main_instance,
                              DIRECTINPUT_VERSION,
                              IID_IDirectInput8,
                              (void **)&lpdi,NULL)))
   return(0)



// now create the keyboard device
if (FAILED(lpdi->CreateDevice(GUID_SysKeyboard, &lpdikey, NULL)))
   { /* error */ }

// do all the other stuff....
```

At this point, `lpdikey` points to the keyboard device, and you can call methods of the interface to set the cooperation level, data format, and so on. Of course, when you're done with the device, you release it with a call to `Release()`. However, this call will be before you've released the main DirectInput object `lpdi`, so put something like this in your shutdown:

```
// release all devices
if (lpdikey)
   lpdikey->Release();

// .. more device releases, joystick, mouse etc.
```

```
// now release main COM object
if (lpdi)
    lpdi->Release();
```

Setting the Keyboard's Cooperative Level

Once you've created your device (the keyboard in this case), you must set its cooperation level, just like the main DirectDraw object. But in the case of DirectInput, there isn't as much of a selection. Table 9.1 lists the various possibilities for the cooperation level.

TABLE 9.1 Cooperation Flags for DirectInput `SetCooperativeLevel()`

Value	Description
DISCL_BACKGROUND	Your application can use a DirectInput device when it's either in the background or active in the foreground.
DISCL_FOREGROUND	The application requires foreground access. If foreground access is granted, the device is automatically unacquired when the associated window moves to the background.
DISCL_EXCLUSIVE	Once you acquire the device, no other application can request exclusive access to it. However, other applications can still request non-exclusive access.
DISCL_NONEXCLUSIVE	The application requires non-exclusive access. Access to the device will not interfere with other applications that are accessing the same device.

These give me a headache. It's like, "Background, foreground, exclusive, non-exclusive—you're killing me!" However, after reading the definitions a few times, it becomes clear how the various flags work. In general, if you set DISCL_BACKGROUND, your application will receive input whether it's active or minimized. Setting DISCL_FOREGROUND will only send your application input when it's on top.

The exclusive/non-exclusive setting controls whether your application has total control of the device and no other application can have access. For example, the mouse and keyboard are implicitly exclusive devices; when your application acquires them, no other application can use them until it gains focus. This creates some paradoxes.

First, you can only acquire the keyboard in non-exclusive mode because Windows itself always has to be able to get the Alt-key combinations. Second, you can acquire the mouse in exclusive mode if you want, but you will lose normal mouse messages to your application (this may be your intent) and the mouse cursor will disappear. Like you care, because you will most probably render one yourself. Finally, most force feedback joysticks (and joysticks in general) should be acquired in exclusive mode. However, you can set normal joysticks for non-exclusive.

Thus, the moral of the story is to set the flags to DISCL_BACKGROUND |
DISCL_NONEXCLUSIVE. The only time you'll really need to set exclusive access is for
force feedback devices. Of course, with this setting it's possible that you could lose the
device to something that wants exclusive access when it becomes the active application.
In that case you will have to reacquire the device, but we'll get to that in a moment.

For now, just set the cooperation level with
IDIRECTINPUTDEVICE8::SetCooperativeLevel(...), shown here:

```
HRESULT SetCooperativeLevel(HWND hwnd, // the window handle
      DWORD dwFlags); // cooperation flags
```

And here's the call to set the cooperation level for your keyboard (all devices are done
in the same way):

```
if (FAILED(lpdikey->SetCooperativeLevel(main_window_handle,
    DISCL_BACKGROUND | DISCL_NONEXCLUSIVE)))
    { /* error */ }
```

The only way this won't work is if there is another application that has exclusive/
foreground access and is the current application. Then you just have to wait or tell the
user to kill the application that is hogging the input device.

Setting the Data Format of the Keyboard

The next step to getting the keyboard ready to send input is to set the data format.
This is done with a call to IDIRECTINPUTDEVICE8::SetDataFormat(), shown here:

```
HRESULT SetDataFormat(LPCDIDATAFORMAT lpdf); // ptr to data format structure
```

Bummer... That single parameter is the problem. Here's the data structure:

```
// directinput dataformat
typedef struct
 {
 DWORD dwSize;     // size of this structure in bytes
 DWORD dwObjSize;  // size of DIOBJECTDATAFORMAT in bytes
 DWORD dwFlags;    // flags:either DIDF_ABSAXIS or
                   // DIDF_RELAXIS for absolute or
                   // relative reporting
 DWORD dwDataSize;// size of data packets
 DWORD dwNumObjs; // number of objects that are defined in
                  // the following array of object
 LPDIOBJECTDATAFORMAT rgodf; // ptr to array of objects
  } DIDATAFORMAT, *LPDIDATAFORMAT;
```

This a really complex structure to set up and is overkill for your purposes. Basically,
it allows you to define how the data from the input device will be formatted at the
device object level. Luckily, though, DirectInput comes with some custom-made data
formats that work for just about everything, and you will use one of them. Take a look
at Table 9.2 to see these formats.

TABLE 9.2 Generic Data Formats Available to DirectInput

Value	Description
c_dfDIKeyboard	Generic keyboard
c_dfDIMouse	Generic mouse
c_dfDIJoystick	Generic joystick
c_dfDIJoystick2	Generic force feedback

Once you set the data format to one of these types, DirectInput will send each data packet back in a certain format. DirectInput again has some predefined formats to make this easy, as shown in Table 9.3.

TABLE 9.3 DirectInput Data Structures Used to Send Data When Using Generic Data Formats

Name	Description
DIMOUSESTATE	This data structure holds a mouse message.
DIJOYSTATE	This data structure holds a standard joystick-like device message.
DIJOYSTATE2	This data structure holds a standard force feedback device message.

I'll show you the actual structures when we get to the mouse and the joystick. However, you're probably wondering where the damn keyboard structure is. Well, it's so simple that there isn't a type for it. It's nothing more than an array of 256 bytes, each representing one key, thus making the keyboard look like a set of 101 momentary switches.

Hence, using the default DirectInput data format and data type is very similar to using the Win32 function GetAsyncKeyState(). In any case, all you need is a type like this:

```
typedef _DIKEYSTATE UCHAR[256];
```

  If DirectX is missing something and I want to create a "DirectXish" version of it, I will usually create the missing data structure or function, but with a leading underscore to remind me six months from now that I invented it.

So with all that in mind, let's set the data format for the poor little keyboard:

```
// set data format
if (FAILED(lpdikey->SetDataFormat(&c_dfDIKeyboard)))
   { /* error */ }
```

Notice that I used the & operator to get the address of the global c_dfDIKeyboard because the function wants a pointer to it.

Acquiring the Keyboard

You're getting there! Almost done. You've created the DirectInput main COM object, created a device, set the cooperation level, and set the data format. The next step is to acquire the device from DirectInput. To do this, use the function method `IDIRECTINPUTDEVICE8::Acquire()` with no parameters. Here's an example:

```
// acquire the keyboard
if (FAILED(lpdikey->Acquire()))
   { /* error */ }
```

And that's all there is to it. Now you're ready to get input from the device! It's time to celebrate. I think I'll have a Power Bar. :)

Retrieving Data from the Keyboard

Retrieving data from all devices is mostly the same, plus or minus a couple of details that may be device-specific. In general, you must do the following:

1. (Optional) Poll the device like a joystick.
2. Read the immediate data from the device with a call to `IDIRECTINPUTDEVICE8::GetDeviceState()`.

> **TIP**
>
> Remember, any method you can call with a `IDIRECTINPUTDEVICE` interface can be called with a `IDIRECTINPUTDEVICE2` interface.

Here's what the `GetDeviceState()` function looks like:

```
HRESULT GetDeviceState(
    DWORD cbData,    // size of state data structure
    LPVOID lpvData); // ptr to memory to receive data
```

The first parameter is the size of the receiving data structure that the data will be stuffed into: 256 for keyboard data, `sizeof(DIMOUSESTATE)` for the mouse, `sizeof(DIJOYSTATE)` for the plain joystick, and so on. The second parameter is just a pointer to where you want the data to be stored. Hence, here's how you might read the keyboard:

```
// here's our little helper typedef
typedef _DIKEYSTATE UCHAR[256];

_DIKEYSTATE keystate[256]; // this will hold the keyboard data
```

Now let's read the keyboard:

```
if (FAILED(lpdikey->GetDeviceState(sizeof(_DIKEYSTATE),
        (LPVOID)keystate)))
      { /* error */ }
```

Of course, you would do this once for each game loop at the top of the loop, before any processing has occurred.

Once you have the data, you'll want to test for keypresses, right? Just as there are constants for the GetAsyncKeyState() function, there are constants for the keyboard switches that resolve to their positions in the array. They all start with DIK_ (DirectInput key, I would imagine) and are defined in DINPUT.H. Table 9.4 contains a partial list of them (please refer to the DirectX SDK docs for the complete list).

TABLE 9.4 The DirectInput Keyboard State Constants

Symbol	Description
DIK_ESCAPE	The Esc key
DIK_0-9	Main keyboard 0 through 9
DIK_MINUS	Minus key
DIK_EQUALS	Equals key
DIK_BACK	Backspace key
DIK_TAB	Tab key
DIK_A-Z	Letters A through Z
DIK_LBRACKET	Left bracket
DIK_RBRACKET	Right bracket
DIK_RETURN	Return/Enter on main keyboard
DIK_LCONTROL	Left control
DIK_LSHIFT	Left shift
DIK_RSHIFT	Right shift
DIK_LMENU	Left Alt
DIK_SPACE	Spacebar
DIK_F1-15	Function keys 1 through 15
DIK_NUMPAD0-9	Numeric keypad keys 0 through 9
DIK_ADD	+ on numeric keypad
DIK_NUMPADENTER	Enter on numeric keypad
DIK_RCONTROL	Right control
DIK_RMENU	Right Alt
DIK_HOME	Home on arrow keypad
DIK_UP	Up arrow on arrow keypad
DIK_PRIOR	PgUp on arrow keypad
DIK_LEFT	Left arrow on arrow keypad
DIK_RIGHT	Right arrow on arrow keypad

TABLE 9.4 Continued

Symbol	Description
DIK_END	End on arrow keypad
DIK_DOWN	Down arrow on arrow keypad
DIK_NEXT	PgDn on arrow keypad
DIK_INSERT	Insert on arrow keypad
DIK_DELETE	Delete on arrow keypad

Bolded entries simply mean to follow the sequence. For example, DIK_0-9 means that there are constants DIK_0, DIK_1, DIK_2, and so forth.

To test if any key is down, you must test the 0x80 bit in the 8-bit byte of the key in question; in other words, the uppermost bit. For example, you'd use the following if you wanted to test whether the Esc key was pressed:

```
if (keystate[DIK_ESCAPE] & 0x80)
    { // it's pressed */ }
else
    { /* it's not */ }
```

> **TIP**
>
> You could probably get away without the & and the bit test, but Microsoft doesn't guarantee that other bits won't be high even if the key isn't down. It's a good idea to do the bit test just to be safe.

The and operator is a bit ugly; you can make it look better with a macro like this:

```
#define DIKEYDOWN(data,n) (data[n] & 0x80)
```

Then you can just write this:

```
if (DIKEYDOWN(keystate, DIK_ESCAPE))
    { /* do it to it baby! */ }
```

Much cleaner, huh? And of course, when you're done with the keyboard, you must "unacquire" it with Unacquire() and release it (along with the main DirectInput COM object) like this:

```
// unacquire keyboard
if (lpdikey)
   lpdikey->Unacquire();

// release all devices
if (lpdikey)
   lpdikey->Release();

// .. more device unacquire/releases, joystick, mouse etc.
```

```
// now release main COM object
if (lpdi)
    lpdi->Release();
```

This is the first time that I've talked about the function Unacquire(), but it is so closely tied to releasing the object that I thought it appropriate for use here. However, if you simply want to unacquire a device but not release it, you can surely call Unacquire() on a device and reacquire it later. You might want to do this if you want another application to have access to the device when you aren't using it.

> **WARNING**
>
> Of course, if you want to release the keyboard but keep the joystick (or some other combination), don't release the main COM object until you're completely ready to kill DirectInput.

For an example of using the keyboard, take a look at DEMO9_1.CPP|EXE (DEMO9_1_16B.CPP|EXE 16-bit version) on the CD. Figure 9.5 shows a screen shot of the action. The program uses all the techniques we have covered to set up the keyboard, and it lets you move a character around. To compile the program, remember to include DDRAW.LIB, DINPUT.LIB, and WINMM.LIB for VC++ users. Also, if you look at the header section of the program, you'll notice that it uses T3DLIB1.H. Thus, it obviously needs T3DLIB1.CPP in the project to compile. By the end of the chapter, you will create an entire input library (which I have already completed and named T3DLIB2.CPP|H, but I'll show that to you later in the chapter).

FIGURE 9.5
DEMO09 1.EXE
in action

Problem During Reading: Reacquisition

I hate to talk about problems that can occur with DirectX because there are so many of them. They aren't bugs, but simply manifestations of running in a cooperative OS like Windows. One such problem that can occur with DirectInput is due to a device getting yanked from you or acquired by another application.

In this case, it's possible that you had the device during the last frame of animation, and now it's gone. Alas, you must detect this and be able to reacquire the device. Luckily, there is a way to test for it that is fairly simple. When you read a device, you test to see if it was acquired by another application. If so, you simply reacquire it and try reading the data again. You can tell because the GetDeviceState() function will return an error code.

The real error codes that GetDeviceState() returns are shown in Table 9.5.

TABLE 9.5 Error Codes for GetDeviceState()

Value	Description
DIERR_INPUTLOST	Device has lost input and will lose acquisition on next call.
DIERR_INVALIDPARAM	One of the parms to the function was invalid.
DIERR_NOTACQUIRED	You have totally lost the device.
DIERR_NOTINITIALIZED	The device is not ready.
E_PENDING	Data not yet available: chill.

So what you want to do is test for DIERR_INPUTLOST during a read and then try to reacquire if that error occurs. Here's an example:

```
HRESULT result; // general result

while(result = lpdikey->GetDeviceState(
        sizeof(_DIKEYSTATE),
        (LPVOID)keystate) == DIERR_INPUTLOST)
    {
    // try an re-acquire the device
    if (FAILED(result = lpdikey->Acquire()))
        {
        break; // serious error
        } // end if

    } // end while

// at this point, there is either a serious error or the data is valid
if (FAILED(result))
    { /* error */}
```

Although I'm showing you an example of reacquiring the keyboard, chances are this will never happen. In most cases, you will only lose joystick-like devices.

Trapping the Mouse

The mouse is one of the most amazingly useful input devices ever created. Can you imagine being the guy who invented the mouse and having so many people laugh at how ridiculous they thought it was? I hope the inventor is laughing on some island over margaritas! The point is, sometimes it's the most unusual things that work best, and the mouse is a good example of that. Anyway, let's get serious now... let me take this bra off my head. :)

The standard PC mouse has either two or three buttons and two axes of motion: X and Y. As the mouse is moved around, it builds up packets of information describing state changes and then sends them to the PC serially (in most cases). The data is then processed by a driver and finally sent on up to Windows or DirectX. As far as we are concerned, the mouse is black magic. All we want to know is how to determine when it moves and when a button is pressed. DirectInput does this and more.

There are two ways to communicate with the mouse: *absolute mode* and *relative mode*. In absolute mode, the mouse returns its position relative to the screen coordinates based on where the mouse pointer is. Thus, in a screen resolution of 640x480, you would expect the position of the mouse to vary from 0-639, 0-479. Figure 9.6 shows this graphically.

FIGURE 9.6
The mouse in absolute mode.

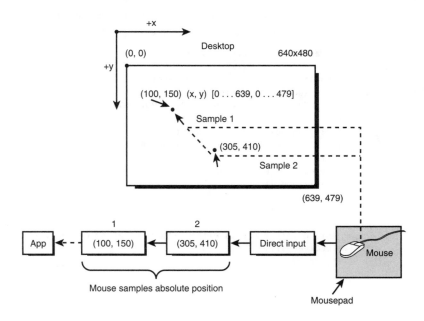

In relative mode, the mouse driver sends the position of the mouse as relative deltas at each clock tick rather than as an absolute position. This is shown in Figure 9.7. In reality, all mice are relative; it's the driver that keeps track of the absolute position of the mouse. Hence, I am going to work with the mouse in relative mode because it's more flexible.

FIGURE 9.7
The mouse in relative mode.

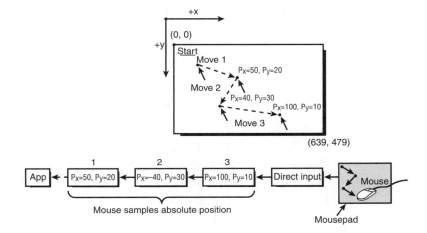

Now that you know a little about the mouse, let's see what you need to do to get it working under DirectInput:

1. Create the mouse device with `CreateDevice()`.

2. Set the cooperation level with `SetCooperativeLevel()`.

3. Set the data format with `SetDataFormat()`.

4. Acquire the mouse with `Acquire()`.

5. Read the mouse state with `GetDeviceState()`.

6. Repeat step 5 until done.

NOTE   If these steps look unfamiliar, please read the previous keyboard section.

Creating the Mouse Device

Looks like bedrock, baby. Let's give it a try. First, you need an interface pointer to receive the device once you create it. Use a `IDIRECTINPUTDEVICE8` pointer for this:

```
// of course you need all the other stuff

LPDIRECTINPUTDEVICE8 lpdimouse = NULL; // the mouse device
```

DirectX and 2D Fundamentals

```
// assuming that lpdi is valid

// create the mouse device
if (FAILED(lpdi->CreateDevice(GUID_SysMouse,
    &lpdimouse, NULL)))
    { /* error */ }
```

Step 1 is handled. Note that you used the device constant GUID_SysMouse for this type. This gives you the default mouse device.

Setting the Cooperation Level of the Mouse

Now, set the cooperation level:

```
if (FAILED(lpdimouse->SetCooperativeLevel(
        main_window_handle,
        DISCL_BACKGROUND | DISCL_NONEXCLUSIVE)))
    { /* error */ }
```

Setting the Data Format of the Mouse

Now for the data format. Remember, there are a number of standard data formats predefined by DirectInput (shown in Table 9.2); the one you want is c_dfDIMouse. Plug it into the function and set the data format:

```
// set data format
if (FAILED(lpdimouse->SetDataFormat(&c_dfDIMouse)))
    { /* error */ }
```

Okay, now you need to take a pause for a moment. With the keyboard data format c_dfDIKeyboard, the data structure returned was an array of 256 UCHARS. However, with the mouse, the data format defines something that is more mouse-like. :) Referring back to Table 9.3, the data structure that you'll be working with is called DIMOUSESTATE and is shown here:

```
// the mouse data structure
typedef struct DIMOUSESTATE
    {
    LONG lX;       // X-axis
    LONG lY;       // Y-axis
    LONG lZ;       // Z-axis (wheel in most cases)
    BYTE rgbButtons[4]; // buttons, high bit means down
    } DIMOUSESTATE, *LPDIMOUSESTATE;
```

Thus, when you make a call to get the device state with GetDeviceState(), this is the structure that will be returned. No surprises here. Everything is what it would seem.

Acquiring the Mouse

The next step is to acquire the mouse with a call to Acquire(). Here it is:

```
// acquire the mouse
if (FAILED(lpdimouse->Acquire()))
    { /* error */ }
```

Cool! This is so easy. Wait until you put a wrapper around all this stuff, which will be even easier!

Reading the Data from the Mouse

At this point, you have created the mouse device, set the cooperation level and the data format, and acquired it. Now you're ready to shake that booty. To make the shake happen, you need to read the data from the mouse with `GetDeviceState()`. However, you must send the correct parameters based on the new data format, `c_dfDIMouse`, and the data structure the data will be placed in, `DIMOUSESTATE`. Here's how you read the mouse:

```
DIMOUSESTATE mousestate; // this holds the mouse data

// .. somewhere in your main loop

// read the mouse state
if (FAILED(lpdimouse->GetDeviceState(sizeof(DIMOUSESTATE),
        (LPVOID)mousestate)))
      { /* error */ }
```

TRICK   Notice how smart the function is. Instead of having multiple functions, the function uses a size and ptr to work with any data format that exists now or that you might think of later. This is a good programming technique to remember, young Jedi.

Now that you have the mouse data, let's work with it. Imagine that you want to move an object around based on the motion of the mouse. If the player moves the mouse left, you want the object to move left by the same amount. In addition, if the user presses the left mouse button, it should fire a missile, and the right button should exit the program. Here's the main code:

```
// obviously you need to do all the other steps...

// defines
#define MOUSE_LEFT_BUTTON    0
#define MOUSE_RIGHT_BUTTON   1
#define MOUSE_MIDDLE_BUTTON  2 // (most of the time)

// globals
DIMOUSESTATE mousestate; // this holds the mouse data

int object_x = SCREEN_CENTER_X, // place object at center
    object_y = SCREEN_CENTER_Y;


// .. somewhere in your main loop
```

```
// read the mouse state
if (FAILED(lpdimouse->GetDeviceState(sizeof(DIMOUSESTATE),
        (LPVOID)mousestate)))
    { /* error */ }


// move object
object_x += mousestate.lX;
object_y += mousestate.lY;

// test for buttons
if (mousestate.rgbButtons[MOUSE_LEFT_BUTTON] & 0x80)
    { /* fire weapon */ }
else
if (mousestate.rgbButtons[MOUSE_RIGHT_BUTTON] & 0x80)
    { /* send exit message */ }
```

Releasing the Mouse from Service

When you're done with the mouse, you need to first unacquire it with a call to
Unacquire() and then release the device as usual. Here's the code:

```
// unacquire mouse
if (lpdimouse)
    lpdimouse->Unacquire();

// release the mouse
if (lpdimouse)
    lpdimouse->Release();
```

As an example of working with the mouse, I have created a little demo called
DEMO9_2.CPP|EXE (DEMO9_2_16B.CPP|EXE 16-bit version). As before, you need to
link in DDRAW.LIB, DINPUT.LIB, and WINMM.LIB (for VC++ users), along with
T3DLIB1.CPP. Figure 9.8 shows a screen shot of the program in action.

Working the Joystick

The joystick is probably the most complex of all DirectInput devices. The term *joystick*
really encompasses all possible devices other than the mouse and keyboard. However,
to keep things manageable, I'm going to primarily focus on devices that look like a
joystick or game paddle, such as the Microsoft Sidewinder, Microsoft Gamepad,
Gravis Flight Stick, and so forth.

Before we get into this, take a look at Figure 9.9. Here you see a joystick and a control
pad. Both devices are considered to be joysticks under DirectInput. The only joystick-
like device that has a class of its own is the *force feedback* device, but I'll get to that
later.

FIGURE 9.8
DEMO09 2.EXE
in action.

FIGURE 9.9
DirectInput devices
are collections of
device objects.

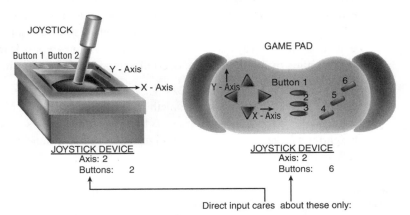

Anyway, the point that I want to make about the joystick and gamepad is that they're
both the same thing as far as DirectInput is concerned. They are both a *collection* of
axes, switches, and sliders. It's just that the axes on the joystick have many positions
(they are continuous), and the gamepad has clamped or extreme positions. The point
is that each device is a collection of *device objects* or *device things* or *input objects,*
depending on your terminology and what reference you use. They're all just input
devices that happen to be on the same physical piece of hardware. Get it? I hope so. :)

The steps for setting up a joystick-like device are the same as for the keyboard and mouse, except that there are a couple of added steps. Let's take a look:

1. Create the joystick device with `CreateDevice()`.

2. Set the cooperation level with `SetCooperativeLevel()`.

3. Set the data format with `SetDataFormat()`.

4. Set the joystick range, dead zone, and other properties with `SetProperties()`. This step is new.

5. Acquire the joystick with `Acquire()`.

6. Poll the joystick with the `Poll()` function. This step basically makes sure that joysticks without interrupt drivers have valid data when `GetDeviceState()` is called. This step is new.

7. Read the mouse state with `GetDeviceState()`.

8. Repeat step 7 until done.

Enumerating for Joysticks

I always hate explaining callback functions and enumeration functions because they seem so complex. However, by the time you get your hands on this book, you will probably be familiar with these types of functions because DOS programming has been falling by the wayside for quite some time. If you are just learning Windows programming, this will seem like overkill, but once you get over it, you won't have to worry about it anymore.

Basically, a callback function is something similar to the `WinProc()` in your Windows programs. It's a function Windows calls that you supply to do something. This is fairly straightforward and understandable. Figure 9.10 shows a standard callback like that of the Windows `WinProc()`.

FIGURE 9.10
A callback function.

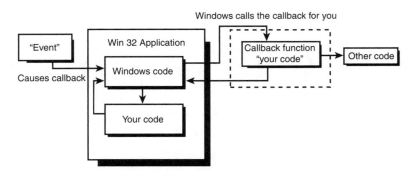

However, Win32/DirectX also uses callback functions for enumeration. *Enumeration* means that Windows (or DirectInput in this case) needs to have the capability to scan the system registry, or whichever database, for something that you're looking for, such as what kind of joysticks are plugged in and available.

There are two ways to do this:

- You could call a DirectInput function that builds a list for you and stores it in a data structure, and you later parse and extrapolate out the important information.

- You could supply DirectInput with a callback/enumeration function that it will call for each new device that it finds. You can be the one who builds up the device list by adding each new entry every time your callback function is called.

The second method is how DirectInput works, so you just have to deal with it. Now, you might wonder why you need to do an enumeration at all. Well, you have no idea what types of joystick devices are plugged in, and even if you did, you need the exact GUID of one or more of them. So you need to scan for them no matter what because you need that GUID for the call to CreateDevice().

The function that does the enumeration is called IDIRECTINPUT8::EnumDevices() and is called directly from the main DirectInput COM object. Here's its prototype:

```
HRESULT EnumDevices(
 DWORD dwDevType,  // type of device to scan for
 LPDIENUMCALLBACK lpCallback, // ptr to callback func
 LPVOID pvRef,   // 32 bit value passed back to you
 DWORD dwFlags); // type of search to do
```

Let's take a look at the parameters. First, dwDevType indicates what kind of devices you want to scan for; the possibilities are shown in Table 9.6.

TABLE 9.6 The Basic Device Types for DirectInput

Value	Description
DIDEVTYPE_MOUSE	A mouse or mouse-like device (such as a trackball).
DIDEVTYPE_KEYBOARD	A keyboard or keyboard-like device.
DIDEVTYPE_JOYSTICK	A joystick or similar device, such as a steering wheel.
DIDEVTYPE_DEVICE	A device that doesn't fall into one of the previous categories.

If you want EnumDevices() to be more specific, you can also give it a subtype that you logically OR with the main type. Table 9.7 contains a partial list of subtypes for mouse and joystick device enumeration.

TABLE 9.7 DirectInput Subtypes (Partial)

Value	Description
DIDEVTYPEMOUSE_TOUCHPAD	Standard touchpad.
DIDEVTYPEMOUSE_TRACKBALL	Standard trackball.
DIDEVTYPEJOYSTICK_FLIGHTSTICK	General flightstick.
DIDEVTYPEJOYSTICK_GAMEPAD	Nintendo-like gamepad.
DIDEVTYPEJOYSTICK_RUDDER	Simple rudder control.
DIDEVTYPEJOYSTICK_WHEEL	Steering wheel.
DIDEVTYPEJOYSTICK_HEADTRACKER	VR head tracker.

NOTE
There are few dozen other subtypes that I haven't listed. The point is, DirectInput can be as general or as specific in the search as you want it to be. However, you're just going to use DIDEVTYPE_JOYSTICK as the value for dwDevType because you just want to find the basic, run-of-the-mill joystick(s).

The next parameter in EnumDevices() is a pointer to the callback function that DirectInput is going to call for each device it finds. I will show you the form of this function in a moment. The next parameter, pvRef, is a 32-bit pointer that points to a value that will be passed to the callback. Thus, you can modify the value in the callback if you want, or use it to pass data back instead of globally.

Finally, dwFlags controls how the enumeration function should scan. That is, should it scan for all devices, just the ones that are plugged in, or just force feedback devices? Table 9.8 contains the scanning codes to control enumeration.

TABLE 9.8 Enumeration Scanning Control Codes

Value	Description
DIEDFL_ALLDEVICES	Scans for all devices that have been installed, even if they aren't currently connected.
DIEDFL_ATTACHEDONLY	Scans for devices that are installed and connected.
DIEDFL_FORCEFEEDBACK	Scans only for force feedback devices.

WARNING
You should use the DIEDFL_ATTACHEDONLY value because it doesn't make sense to allow the player to connect to a device that isn't plugged into the computer.

Now, let's take a more detailed look at the callback function. The way `EnumDevices()` works is that it sits in a loop internally, calling your callback over and over for each device it finds, as shown in Figure 9.11. Hence, it's possible that your callback could be called many times if there are a lot of devices installed or attached to the PC.

FIGURE 9.11
The device enumera-
tion flow diagram.

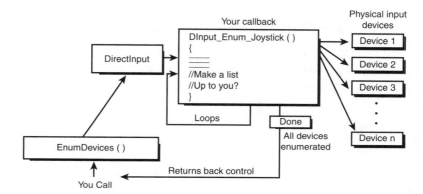

This means that it's up to your callback function to record all these devices in a table or something so you can later review them after the `EnumDevices()` returns. Cool. With that in mind, let's take a look at the generic prototype for the callback function to be compatible with DirectInput:

```
BOOL CALLBACK EnumDevsCallback(
   LPDIDEVICEINSTANCE lpddi, // a ptr from DirectInput
                             // containing info about the
                             // device it just found on
                             // this iteration
   LPVOID data); // the ptr sent in pvRef to EnumDevices()
```

All you need to do is write a function with the previous prototype (but write the control code, of course), pass it as `lpCallback` to `EnumDevices()`, and you're all set. Furthermore, the name can be anything you want because you're passing the function by address.

What you put inside the function is up to you, of course, but you probably want to record or catalog the names of all the devices and their GUIDs as they are retrieved by DirectInput. Remember, your function will be called once for each device found. Then, with the list in hand, you can select one yourself or let the user select one from a list, and then use the associated GUID to create the device.

In addition, DirectInput allows you to continue the enumeration or stop it at any time. This is controlled via the value you return from the callback function. At the end of the function, you can return one of these two constants:

- DIENUM_CONTINUE--Continues enumeration.
- DIENUM_STOP--Stops enumeration.

So if you simply return DIENUM_STOP as the return value of the function, it will enumerate only one device even if more exist. I don't have enough room here to show you a function that catalogs and records all the device GUIDs, but I'm going to give you one that will find the first device and set it up.

The aforementioned enumeration function will enumerate the first device and stop. But before I show it to you, take a quick look at the DIDEVICEINSTANCE data structure that is sent to your callback function for each enumeration. It's full of interesting information about the device:

```
typedef struct
 {
 DWORD dwSize;        // the size of the structure
 GUID guidInstance;   // instance GUID of the device
                      // this is the GUID we need
 GUID guidProduct;    // product GUID of device, general
 DWORD dwDevType;     // dev type as listed in tables 9.1-2
 TCHAR tszInstanceName[MAX_PATH]; // generic instance name
                      // of joystick device like "joystick 1"
 TCHAR tszProductName[MAX_PATH]; // product name of device
                      // like "Microsoft Sidewinder Pro"
 GUID guidFFDriver;   // GUID for force feedback driver
 WORD wUsagePage;     // advanced. don't worry about it
 WORD wUsage;         // advanced. don't worry about it
 } DIDEVICEINSTANCE, *LPDIDEVICEINSTANCE;
```

In most cases, the only fields of interest are tszProductName and guidInstance. Taking that into consideration, here's the enumeration function that you can use to get the GUID of the first joystick device enumerated:

```
BOOL CALLBACK DInput_Enum_Joysticks(
LPCDIDEVICEINSTANCE lpddi, LPVOID guid_ptr)
{
// this function enumerates the joysticks, but stops at the
// first one and returns the instance guid
// so we can create it, notice the cast
*(GUID*)guid_ptr = lpddi->guidInstance;

// copy product name into global
strcpy(joyname, (char *)lpddi->tszProductName);

// stop enumeration after one iteration
return(DIENUM_STOP);
} // end DInput_Enum_Joysticks
```

To use the function to enumerate for the first joystick, you would do something like this:

```
char joyname[80]; // space for joystick name
GUID joystickGUID; // used to hold GUID for joystick

// enumerate attached joystick devices only with
// DInput_Enum_Joysticks() as the callback function
if (FAILED(lpdi->EnumDevices(
            DIDEVTYPE_JOYSTICK,    // joysticks only
            DInput_Enum_Joysticks, // enumeration function
            &joystickGUID,     // send guid back in this var
            DIEDFL_ATTACHEDONLY)))
    { /* error */ }

// notice that we scan for joysticks that are attached only
```

In a real product, you might want to continue the enumeration function until it finds all devices and then, during a setup or options phase, allow the player to select a device from a list. Then you use the GUID for that device to create the device, which is the next step!

Creating the Joystick

Once you have the device GUID of the device that you want to create, the call to create the device is, as usual, CreateDevice(). Assuming that the call to EnumDevices() has occurred and the device GUID has been stored in joystickGUID, here's how you would create the joystick device:

```
LPDIRECTINPUTDEVICE8 lpdijoy; // joystick device interface
// create the joystick with GUID
if (FAILED(lpdi->CreateDevice(joystickGUID, &lpdijoy,
                      NULL)))
    { /* error */ }
```

> **NOTE**
>
> In the demo engines that I create, I tend to use temporary interface pointers to old interfaces to gain access to the latest ones. Thus, in my demos I use a temp pointer, query for the latest, and call it lpdijoy rather than lpdijoy2. I do this because I got sick of having numbered interfaces around. The bottom line is that all of the interfaces used in this book are the latest ones available for the job.

Setting the Joystick's Cooperation Level

Setting the joystick's cooperation level is done in the exact same way as with the mouse and keyboard. However, if you had a force feedback stick, you would want exclusive access to it. Here's the code:

```
if (FAILED(lpdijoy->SetCooperativeLevel(
        main_window_handle,
```

```
                    DISCL_BACKGROUND | DISCL_NONEXCLUSIVE)))
     { /* error */ }
```

Setting the Data Format

Now for the data format. As with the mouse and keyboard, use a standard data format as shown in Table 9.2. The one you want is c_dfDIJoystick (ci_dfDIJoystick2 is for force feedback). Plug it into the function and set the data format:

```
// set data format
if (FAILED(lpdijoy->SetDataFormat(&c_dfDIJoystick)))
    { /* error */ }
```

As with the mouse, you need a specific type of data structure to hold the device state data for the joystick. Referring back to Table 9.3, you see that the data structure you'll be working with is called DIJOYSTATE (DIJOYSTATE2 is for force feedback), shown here:

```
// generic virtual joystick data structure

typedef struct DIJOYSTATE
 {
 LONG 1X;    // x-axis of joystick
 LONG 1Y;    // y-axis of joystick
 LONG 1Z;    // z-axis of joystick
 LONG 1Rx;   // x-rotation of joystick (context sensitive)
 LONG 1Ry;   // y-rotation of joystick (context sensitive)
 LONG 1Rz;   // y-rotation of joystick (context sensitive)
 LONG rglSlider[2];// slider like controls, pedals, etc.
 DWORD rgdwPOV[4]; // Point Of View hat controls, up to 4
 BYTE  rgbButtons[32]; // 32 standard momentary buttons
 } DIJOYSTATE, *LPDIJOYSTATE;
```

As you can see, the structure has a lot of data fields. This generic data format is very versatile; I doubt that you would need to ever make your own data format, because I haven't seen many joysticks that have more than this! Anyway, the comments should explain what the data fields are. The axes are in ranges (that can be set), and the buttons are usually momentary with 0x80 (high bit), meaning that they're pressed.

Thus, when you make a call to get the device state with GetDeviceState(), this is the structure that will be returned and the one that you will query.

Almost done. There is one more detail that you have to take into consideration: the details of the values that are going to be sent back to you in this structure. A button is a button. It's either on or off, but the range entries like 1X, 1Y, and 1Z may vary from one manufacturer to another. Thus, DirectInput lets you scale them to a fixed range for all cases so that your game input logic can always work with the same numbers. Let's take a look at how to set this and other properties of the joystick.

Setting the Input Properties of the Joystick

Because the joystick is inherently an analog device, the motion of the yoke has finite range. The problem is, you must set it to known values so your game code can interpret it. In other words, when you query the joystick for its position and it returns 1X = 2000, 1Y=-3445, what does it mean? You can't interpret the data because you have no frame of reference, so that's what you need to clarify.

At the very least, you need to set the ranges of any analog axis (even if it's digitally encoded) that you want to read. For example, you might decide to set both the X and Y axes to -1000 to 1000 and -2000 to 2000, respectively, or maybe -128 to 128 for both so you can fit them in a byte. Whatever you decide to do, you must do something. Otherwise, you won't have any way of interpreting the data when you retrieve it, unless you have set the range yourself.

Setting any property of the joystick, including the ranges of the joystick, is accomplished with the SetProperty() function. Its prototype is shown here:

```
HRESULT SetProperty(
 REFGUID rguidProp,      // GUID of property to change
 LPCDIPROPHEADER pdiph);// ptr to property header struct
                         // containing detailed information
                         // relating to the change
```

SetProperty() is used to set a number of various properties, such as relative or absolute data format, range of each axis, *dead zone* (or *dead band*; area that is neutral), and so forth. Using the SetProperty() function is extremely complex due to the nature of all the constants and nested data structures.

Suffice it to say that you shouldn't call SetProperty() unless you absolutely must. Most of the default values will work fine. I spent many hours looking at the circular data structures going, "What the heck?" (I didn't really say "What the heck?", but this is a PG-rated book.)

Luckily, you only need to set the range of the X-Y axes (and maybe the dead zone) to make things work, so that's all I'm going to show. If you're interested in learning more, refer to the DirectX SDK on this subject. Nonetheless, the following code should get you started on setting other properties if you need to. The structure you need to set up is as follows:

```
typedef struct DIPROPRANGE
        {
        DIPROPHEADER diph;
        LONG        lMin;
        LONG        lMax;
        } DIPROPRANGE, *LPDIPROPRANGE;
```

This has another nested structure, DIPROPHEADER:

```
typedef struct DIPROPHEADER
        {
        DWORD    dwSize;
        DWORD    dwHeaderSize;
        DWORD    dwObj;
        DWORD    dwHow;
        } DIPROPHEADER, *LPDIPROPHEADER;
```

And both of them have a billion ways of being set up, so please look at the DirectX SDK if you're interested. It would take 10 more pages just to list all the various flags you can send! Anyway, here's the code to set the axes ranges:

```
// this structure holds the data for the property changes
DIPROPRANGE joy_axis_range;

// first set x axis tp -1024 to 1024
joy_axis_range.lMin = -1024;
joy_axis_range.lMax = 1024;

joy_axis_range.diph.dwSize       = sizeof(DIPROPRANGE);
joy_axis_range.diph.dwHeaderSize = sizeof(DIPROPHEADER);

// this holds the object you want to change
joy_axis_range.diph.dwObj  = DIJOFS_X;

// above can be any of the following:
//DIJOFS_BUTTON(n) - for buttons buttons
//DIJOFS_POV(n)    - for point-of-view indicators.
//DIJOFS_RX - for x-axis rotation.
//DIJOFS_RY - for y-axis rotation.
//DIJOFS_RZ - for z-axis rotation (rudder).
//DIJOFS_X - for x-axis.
//DIJOFS_Y - for y-axis.
//DIJOFS_Z - for the z-axis.
//DIJOFS_SLIDER(n) - for any of the sliders.
// object access method, use this way always
joy_axis_range.diph.dwHow = DIPH_BYOFFSET;

// finally set the property
lpdijoy->SetProperty(DIPROP_RANGE,&joy_axis_range.diph);

// now y-axis
joy_axis_range.lMin = -1024;
joy_axis_range.lMax = 1024;
joy_axis_range.diph.dwSize       = sizeof(DIPROPRANGE);
joy_axis_range.diph.dwHeaderSize = sizeof(DIPROPHEADER);
joy_axis_range.diph.dwObj        = DIJOFS_Y;
joy_axis_range.diph.dwHow        = DIPH_BYOFFSET;

// finally set the property
lpdijoy->SetProperty(DIPROP_RANGE,&joy_axis_range.diph);
```

At this point, the joystick would have the X and Y axes set to a range of -1024 to 1024. This range is arbitrary, but I like it. Notice that you use a data structure called DIPROPRANGE. This is the structure that you set up to do your bidding. The bad thing about it is that there are a million ways to set up the structure, so it's a real pain. However, using the previous template, you can at least set the range of any axis—just change the joy_axis_range.diph.dwObj and joy_axis_range.diph.dwHow fields to whatever you need.

As a second example of setting properties, let's set the dead zone (or dead band) of the X and Y axes. The *dead zone* is the amount of neutral area in the center of the stick. You might want the stick to be able to move a bit away from the center and not send any values. This is shown in Figure 9.12.

FIGURE 9.12
The mechanics of the joystick dead zone.

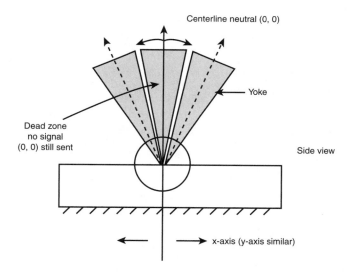

For example, in the previous example you set the X and Y axis range to -1024 to 1024, so if you wanted a 10 percent dead zone on both axes, you would set it for about 102 units in both the + and - directions, right? *Wrong!!!* The dead zone is in terms of an absolute range of 0–10,000, no matter what range you set the joystick to. Thus, you have to compute 10 percent of 10,000 rather than 1024-10% x 10000 — = 1000. This is the number you need to use.

WARNING The dead zone is always in terms of 0-10000 or hundreds of a percent. If you want a dead zone of 50%, use 5000, for 10% use 1000, and so forth.

Because this operation is a little simpler, you need only use the `DIPROPWORD` structure:

```
typedef struct DIPROPDWORD
        {
        DIPROPHEADER     diph;
        DWORD            dwData;
        } DIPROPDWORD, *LPDIPROPDWORD;
```

This is much simpler than the `DIPROPRANGE` structure used in the previous example. Here's how to do it:

```
DIPROPDWORD dead_band; // here's our property word

dead_band.diph.dwSize       = sizeof(dead_band);
dead_band.diph.dwHeaderSize = sizeof(dead_band.diph);
dead_band.diph.dwObj        = DIJOFS_X;
dead_band.diph.dwHow        = DIPH_BYOFFSET;

// 100 will be used on both sides of the range +/-
dead_band.dwData            = 1000;

// finally set the property
lpdijoy->SetProperty(DIPROP_DEADZONE,&dead_band.diph);
```

And now for the Y-axis:

```
dead_band.diph.dwSize       = sizeof(dead_band);
dead_band.diph.dwHeaderSize = sizeof(dead_band.diph);
dead_band.diph.dwObj        = DIJOFS_Y;
dead_band.diph.dwHow        = DIPH_BYOFFSET;

// 100 will be used on both sides of the range +/-
dead_band.dwData            = 1000;

// finally set the property
lpdijoy->SetProperty(DIPROP_DEADZONE,&dead_band.diph);
```

And that's all there is to that. Thank Zeus!

Acquiring the Joystick

Now, let's acquire the joystick with a call to `Acquire()`:

```
// acquire the joystick
if (FAILED(lpdijoy->Acquire()))
   { /* error */ }
```

Of course, remember to `Unacquire()` the joystick when you're through with it, right before calling `Release()` on the interface to release the device itself.

Polling the Joystick

Joysticks are the only devices that need polling (so far). The reason for polling is the following: Some joystick drivers generate interrupts, and the data is always fresh.

Some drivers are less intelligent (or more efficient) and must be polled. Whatever the philosophical viewpoint of the driver developer, you *must* always call `Poll()` on the joystick before trying to read the data. Here's the code for doing so:

```
If (FAILED(lpdijoy->Poll()))
    { /* error */ }
```

Reading the Joystick State Data

Now you're ready to read the data from the joystick (you should be an expert at this by now). Make a call to `GetDeviceState()`. However, you must send the correct parameters based on the new data format, `c_dfDIJoystick` (`c_dfDIJoystick2` for force feedback), and the data structure the data will be placed in, `DIJOYSTATE`. Here's the code:

```
DIJOYSTATE joystate; // this holds the joystick data

// .. somewhere in your main loop

// read the joystick state
if (FAILED(lpdijoy->GetDeviceState(sizeof(DIJOYSTATE),
        (LPVOID)joystate)))
        { /* error */ }
```

Now that you have the joystick data, let's work with it. However, you need to take into consideration that the data is in a range. Let's write a little program that moves an object around, much like the mouse example. And if the user presses the fire button (usually index 0), a missile fires:

```
// obviously you need to do all the other steps...

// defines
#define JOYSTICK_FIRE_BUTTON   0

// globals
DIJOYSTATE joystate; // this holds the joystick data

int object_x = SCREEN_CENTER_X, // place object at center
    object_y = SCREEN_CENTER_Y;

// .. somewhere in your main loop

// read the joystick state
if (FAILED(lpdijoy->GetDeviceState(sizeof(DIJOYSTATE),
        (LPVOID)joystate)))
        { /* error */ }

// move object


// test for buttons
if (mousestate.rgbButtons[JOYSTICK_FIRE_BUTTON] & 0x80)
    { /* fire weapon */ }
```

Releasing the Joystick from Service

When you're done with the joystick, you need to unacquire and release the device as usual. Here's the code:

```
// unacquire joystick
if (lpdijoy)
   lpdijoy->Unacquire();

// release the joystick
if (lpdijoy)
   lpdijoy->Release();
```

> **WARNING** Releasing before unacquiring can be devastating! Make sure to unacquire and *then* release.

As an example of working with the joystick, I have created a little demo called `DEMO9_3.CPP|EXE` (`DEMO9_3_16B.CPP|EXE` 16-bit version). As before, you need to link in `DDRAW.LIB`, `DINPUT.LIB`, and `WINMM.LIB` (for VC++ users), along with `T3DLIB1.CPP`. Figure 9.13 shows a screen shot of the program in action.

FIGURE 9.13
DEMO9 3.EXE
in action.

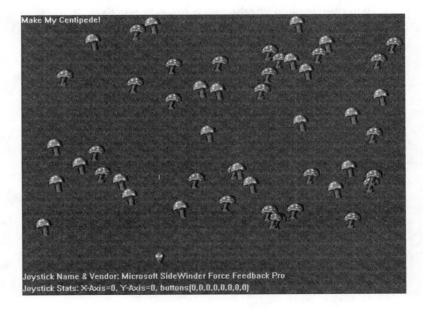

Massaging Your Input

Now that you know how to read each input device, the question becomes one of input system architecture. In other words, you might be obtaining input from a number of input devices, but it would be a pain to have separate control code for each input device.

Thus, you might come up with the idea of creating a generic input record, merging all the input from the mouse, keyboard, and joystick together, and then using this structure to make your decisions. Figure 9.14 shows the concept graphically.

FIGURE 9.14
Merging input data into a virtual input record.

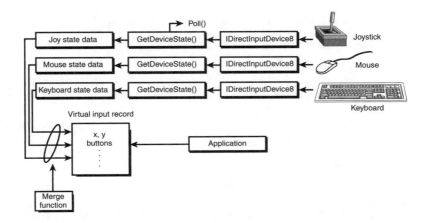

In the case of plain old DirectInput, let's say that you want the player to be able to play with the keyboard, mouse, and joystick all at the same time. The left mouse button might be the fire button, but so is the Ctrl key on the main keyboard and the first button on the joystick. In addition, if the player moves the mouse to the right, presses the right arrow on the keyboard, or moves the joystick to the right, you want all of these events to make the player move right.

As an example of what I'm talking about, let's build a really simple input system that takes a keyboard, joystick, and mouse input record from DirectInput and then merges them into one record that you can query. And when you do query the record, you won't care whether it was the mouse, keyboard, or joystick that was the source of the input because all the input events will be scaled and normalized.

The system you're going to implement will have the following:

- X-axis
- Y-axis
- Fire button
- Special button

And here are the details of the device variables and event mappings:

Mouse Mapping

+x-axis: if (lx > 0)

-x-axis: if (lx < 0)

+y-axis: if (ly > 0)

-y-axis: if (ly < 0)

Fire button: Left mouse button (`rgbButtons[0]`)

Special button: Right mouse button (`rgbButtons[1]`)

Keyboard Mapping

+x-axis: Right arrow key

-x-axis: Left arrow key

+y-axis: Up arrow key

-y-axis: Down arrow key

Fire button: Ctrl key

Special button: Esc key

Joystick Mapping (assume a range of −1024 to +1024 on both axes, with a 10 percent dead zone)

+x-axis: lX > 32

-x-axis: lX < -32

+y-axis: lY > 32

-y-axis: lY < -32

Fire button: `rgbButtons[0]`

Special button: `rgbButtons[1]`

Now that you know the mappings, make up an appropriate data structure to hold the result:

```
typedef struct INPUT_EVENT_TYP
        {
        int dx;        // the change in x
        int dy;        // the change in y
        int fire;      // the fire button
        int special;   // the special button
        } INPUT_EVENT, *INPUT_EVENT_PTR;
```

Using a simple function and logic, you're going to filter all the input into a structure of this type. First, assume that you have retrieved the device data from all input devices with something like this:

```
// keyboard
if (FAILED(lpdikey->GetDeviceState(256,
```

```
            (LPVOID)keystate)))
        { /* error */ }

// mouse
if (FAILED(lpdimouse->GetDeviceState(sizeof(DIMOUSESTATE),
        (LPVOID)mousestate)))
        { /* error */ }


// joystick

If (FAILED(lpdijoy->Poll()))
    { /* error */ }

if (FAILED(lpdijoy->GetDeviceState(sizeof(DIJOYSTATE),
        (LPVOID)joystate)))
        { /* error */ }
```

At this point, you have the structures keystate[], mousestate, and joystate ready
to go. Here's a function that would do the job:

```
void Merge_Input(INPUT_EVENT_PTR event_data, // the result
                 UCHAR *keydata, // keyboard data
                 LPDIMOUSESTATE mousedata, // mouse data
                 LPDIJOYSTATE   joydata) // joystick data
{
// merge all the data together

// clear the record to be safe
memset(event_data,0,sizeof(INPUT_EVENT));

// first the fire button
if (mousedata->rgbButtons[0] || joydata->rgbButtons[0] ||
    keydata[DIK_LCONTROL])
event_data->fire = 1;

// now the special button
if (mousedata->rgbButtons[1] || joydata->rgbButtons[1] ||
    keydata[DIK_ESCAPE])
event_data->special = 1;

// now the x-axis
if (mousedata->lX > 0 || joydata->lX > 32 ||
    keydata[DIK_RIGHT])
event_data->dx = 1;

// now the -x-axis
if (mousedata->lX < 0 || joydata->lX < -32 ||
    keydata[DIK_LEFT])
event_data->dx = -1;

// and the y-axis
if (mousedata->lY > 0 || joydata->lY > 32 ||
```

```
    keydata[DIK_DOWN])
event_data->dy = 1;

// now the -y-axis
if (mousedata->lY < 0 || joydata->lY < -32 ||
    keydata[DIK_UP])
event_data->dy = -1;

} // end Merge_Data
```

Killer, huh? Of course, you can make this much more sophisticated by checking if the device is actually online, scaling the data, and so on, but you get the idea.

Going Deeper with Force Feedback

Force feedback is really a massive topic. I had no idea how complex it was until I tried playing with it. Alas, I'm not going to go into it in any depth. A whole book could be written just about force feedback (and DirectMusic for that matter, but that's another story). However, I am going to give you an idea of what it is, and you'll set up a teeny-weeny force demo.

Force feedback describes the next generation of input devices, which have actuators, motors, and so forth that can exert forces on your hand, or your whole body for that matter. ("Cybersex" is going to take on a whole new meaning in a couple of years.) You've probably seen or may even own a force feedback device, such as the Microsoft Force Feedback joystick or some other similar device.

Programming these devices is very complex. Not only is a good understanding of force, spring, and motion needed, but the devices and the forces events, or *effects*, have a very close relationship to musical notes. That is, they can have an envelope that modulates the forces as they are applied to the various motors and actuators on the joystick. Thus, values like rate, frequency, timing, and so on all play a role in using and programming force feedback. In fact, creating effects to play or command the force feedback device is so complex that there are third-party tools you can use to create them, such as Microsoft's Force Factory. Luckily, you aren't going to need to use anything that fancy for this demo.

The Physics of Force Feedback

Force feedback devices let you set up two types of effects: *motive forces* and *conditions*. Motive forces are like active forces that are always in flux, whereas conditions are in response to an event. In either case, you control the amount of force N (in Newtons) and the properties of the force, such as its direction, duration, and so forth.

Setting Up Force Feedback

The first step in creating a force feedback device is to find one and get its GUID. If you recall how you scanned for standard joystick GUIDs, you're going to do the same thing for force feedback devices. However, when you do the device enumeration, you're going to call it like this:

```
GUID fjoystickGUID; // used to hold GUID for force joystick

// enumerate attached joystick devices only with
// DInput_Enum_Joysticks() as the callback function
if (FAILED(lpdi->EnumDevices(
        DIDEVTYPE_JOYSTICK,     // joysticks only
        DInput_Enum_Joysticks, // enumeration function
        &fjoystickGUID,     // send guid back in this var
        DIEDFL_ATTACHEDONLY | DIEDFL_FORCEFEEDBACK)))
    { /* error */ }
```

Once you have the GUID, you create the device as usual. However, you must make sure that the cooperation level is set for DISCL_EXCLUSIVE mode (no one else can use force feedback while you're using it). Here's all the code:

```
// assume DirectInput has already been created

// version 8 interface pointer
LPDIRECTINPUTDEVICE8 lpdijoy;

// create the joystick with GUID
if (FAILED(lpdi->CreateDevice(joystickGUID, &lpdijoy,
                    NULL)))
    { /* error */ }



if (FAILED(lpdijoy->SetCooperativeLevel(
        main_window_handle,
        DISCL_BACKGROUND | DISCL_EXCLUSIVE)))
    { /* error */ }

// set data format
if (FAILED(lpdijoy->SetDataFormat(&c_dfDIJoystick2)))
    { /* error */ }
```

Okay, now you have a force feedback device set up and ready to go. So what should you do with it?

A Force Feedback Demo

If you like, you can just use the force feedback device like a normal joystick. However, the data packet sent back is now DIJOYSTATE2 rather than DIJOYSTATE. The explanation of the code would take too long, so you're going to have to figure it out based on the comments and the demo program.

However, the code basically sets up an effect that is composed of an envelope and a periodic description. Moreover, the effect is connected to the joystick fire trigger, so it starts when the trigger is held. Here's the code that will set up the force feedback effect, assuming you have the GUID of the device and have set up the force feedback joystick as shown previously:

```
// force feedback setup
DWORD      dwAxes[2] = { DIJOFS_X, DIJOFS_Y };
LONG       lDirection[2] = { 0, 0 };

DIPERIODIC diPeriodic;      // type-specific parameters
DIENVELOPE diEnvelope;      // envelope
DIEFFECT   diEffect;        // general parameters

// setup the periodic structure
diPeriodic.dwMagnitude = DI_FFNOMINALMAX;
diPeriodic.lOffset = 0;
diPeriodic.dwPhase = 0;
diPeriodic.dwPeriod = (DWORD) (0.05 * DI_SECONDS);

// set the modulation envelope
diEnvelope.dwSize = sizeof(DIENVELOPE);
diEnvelope.dwAttackLevel = 0;
diEnvelope.dwAttackTime = (DWORD) (0.01 * DI_SECONDS);
diEnvelope.dwFadeLevel = 0;
diEnvelope.dwFadeTime = (DWORD) (3.0 * DI_SECONDS);

// set up the effect structure itself
diEffect.dwSize = sizeof(DIEFFECT);
diEffect.dwFlags = DIEFF_POLAR | DIEFF_OBJECTOFFSETS;
diEffect.dwDuration = (DWORD) INFINITE; // (1 * DI_SECONDS);

// set up details of effect
diEffect.dwSamplePeriod = 0;               // = default
diEffect.dwGain = DI_FFNOMINALMAX;         // no scaling
diEffect.dwTriggerButton = DIJOFS_BUTTON0; // connect effect
                                           // to trigger button
diEffect.dwTriggerRepeatInterval = 0;
diEffect.cAxes = 2;
diEffect.rgdwAxes = dwAxes;
diEffect.rglDirection = &lDirection[0];
diEffect.lpEnvelope = &diEnvelope;
diEffect.cbTypeSpecificParams = sizeof(diPeriodic);
diEffect.lpvTypeSpecificParams = &diPeriodic;

// create the effect and get the interface to it
lpdijoy->CreateEffect(GUID_Square,  // standard GUID
                      &diEffect,     // where the data is
                      &lpdieffect,   // where to put interface pointer
                      NULL);         // no aggregation
```

For a demo of this in action, check out DEMO9_4.CPP (DEMO9_4_16B.CPP|EXE 16-bit version). It basically takes your little centipede demo and adds a machine gun to it! Of course, you need a force feedback joystick for the demo to work.

> **NOTE** The force feedback code shown previously is based on the example in the DirectX SDK, so you can refer there for a much more in-depth explanation.

Writing a Generalized Input System: T3DLIB2.CPP

Writing a simple set of wrapper functions around DirectInput is almost a no-brainer. Well, it takes *some* brains, but for the most part it's fairly easy. All you need to do is create an API with a very simple interface and very few parameters that

- Initializes the DirectInput system.
- Sets up and acquires the keyboard, mouse, and joystick (or any subset).
- Reads data from any of the input devices.
- Shuts down, unacquires, and releases everything.

I have created such an API, and it's available in T3DLIB2.CPP|H on the CD. The API does everything you need to initialize DirectInput and read any device. However, I didn't do any input merging, as shown in the example a few sections previous. Rather, you will still receive input in terms of standard DirectInput device state(s) structures, and you'll process the various fields within each device state structure (keyboard, mouse, and joystick). However, this gives you the most freedom.

Before reviewing the functions, take a look at Figure 9.15. It depicts the relationship between each device and the data flow.

Here are the globals for the library:

```
LPDIRECTINPUT8       lpdi;       // dinput object
LPDIRECTINPUTDEVICE8 lpdikey;    // dinput keyboard
LPDIRECTINPUTDEVICE8 lpdimouse;  // dinput mouse
LPDIRECTINPUTDEVICE8 lpdijoy;    // dinput joystick
GUID    joystickGUID; // guid for main joystick
char    joyname[80];  // name of joystick

// all input is stored in these records
UCHAR keyboard_state[256]; // contains keyboard state table
DIMOUSESTATE mouse_state;  // contains state of mouse
DIJOYSTATE joy_state;      // contains state of joystick
int joystick_found;        // tracks if stick is plugged in
```

FIGURE 9.15
The DirectInput
software system.

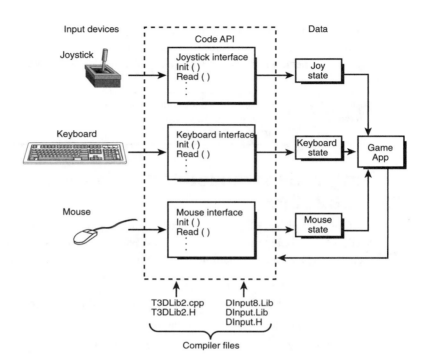

Input from the keyboard is placed in keyboard_state[], the mouse data is stored in mouse_state, and the joystick data is stored in joy_state by the input system. The structures of these records are the standard DirectInput device state structures. But in general, the mouse and joystick are roughly equivalent as far as the x,y position goes. That is, you access them via the fields lX and lY, and the buttons are BOOLEANs in rgbButtons[].

Let's get to the functions. The variable joystick_found is a Boolean that is set when you request joystick access. If a joystick is found, it is True; otherwise, it is False. With it, you can conditionally block out code that uses the joystick. So without further ado, here is the new API.

Function Prototype:

```
int DInput_Init(void);
```

Purpose:

DInput_Init() initializes the DirectInput input system. It creates the main COM object and returns True if successful, False otherwise. And of course, the global lpdi will be valid. The function does not create any devices, though. Here's an example of initializing the input system:

```
if (!DInput_Init())
    { /* error */ }
```

Function Prototype:

```
void DInput_Shutdown(void);
```

Purpose:

`DInput_Shutdown()` releases all the COM objects and any resources allocated during the call to `DInput_Init()`. Normally, you would call `DInput_Shutdown()` at the very end of your application, after you have released all the input devices themselves. We'll get to that shortly. Anyway, here's an example of shutting down the input system:

```
DInput_Shutdown();
```

Function Prototype:

```
DInput_Init_Keyboard(void);
```

Purpose:

`DInput_Init_Keyboard()` initializes and acquires the keyboard. This should always work and return True, unless another DirectX application has taken over in a really uncooperative way. Here's an example:

```
if (!DInput_Init_Keyboard())
    { /* error */ }
```

Function Prototype:

```
int DInput_Init_Mouse(void);
```

Purpose:

`DInput_Init_Mouse()` initializes and acquires the mouse. The function takes no parameters and returns True if successful and False otherwise. But it should always work, unless a mouse isn't plugged in or there's another DirectX application that has totally taken over! If everything goes well, `lpdimouse` becomes the valid interface pointer. Here's an example:

```
if (!DInput_Init_Mouse()) { /* error */ }
```

Function Prototype:

```
int DInput_Init_Joystick(int min_x=-256, // min x range
                int max_x=256,   // max x range
                int min_y=-256,  // min y range
                int max_y=256,   // max y range
                int dead_zone=10); // dead zone in percent
```

Purpose:

`DInput_Init_Joystick()` initializes the joystick device for use. The function takes five parameters, which define the X-Y range of motion of the data sent back from the joystick and the dead zone as a percentage. If you want to use the defaults of -256 to

256 and a 10 percent dead zone for each axis, you need not send parameters because they have default values (it's a C++ thing).

If the call returns back a True, a joystick was found and has been set up, initialized, and acquired. After the call, the interface pointer lpdijoy will be valid if you need it for anything. In addition, the string joyname[] will contain the "friendly" name of the joystick device, such as Microsoft Sidewinder Pro and so on.

Here's an example of initializing the joystick and setting its X-Y ranges to -1024 to 1024, with a 5 percent dead zone:

```
if (!DInput_Init_Joystick(-1024, 1024, -1024, 1024, 5))
    { /* error */ }
```

Function Prototype(s):

```
void DInput_Release_Joystick(void);
void DInput_Release_Mouse(void);
void DInput_Release_Keyboard(void);
```

Purpose:

DInput_Release_Joystick(), DInput_Release_Mouse(), and DInput_Release_Keyboard() release each of those respective input devices when you're done with them. The functions can be called even if you haven't initialized those respective devices, so you can just call them all at the end of your application if you want. Here's a complete example of starting up the DirectInput system, initializing all the devices, and then releasing them and shutting down:

```
// initialize the DirectInput system
DInput_Init();

// initialize all input devices and acquire them
DInput_Init_Joystick();
DInput_Init_Mouse();
DInput_Init_Keyboard();

// input loop ....do work here
// now done...

// first release all devices, order is unimportant
DInput_Release_Joystick();
DInput_Release_Mouse();
DInput_Release_Keyboard();

// shutdown DirectInput
DInput_Shutdown();
```

Function Prototype:

```
int DInput_Read_Keyboard(void);
```

Purpose:

DInput_Read_Keyboard() scans the keyboard state and places the data in keyboard_state[], which is an array of 256 bytes. This is the standard DirectInput keyboard state array, so you must use the DirectInput key constant DIK_* if you want to make sense of it. If a key is pressed, the array value will be 0x80. Here's an example of testing if the right and left keys are down using the manifest constants in DirectInput (which you can look up in the SDK or the abridged Table 9.4):

```
// read the keyboard
if (!DInput_Read_Keyboard())
   { /* error */ }

// now test the state data
if (keyboard_state[DIK_RIGHT]
   { /* move ship right */ }
else
if (keyboard_state[DIK_LEFT]
   { /* move ship left */ }
```

Function Prototype:

```
int DInput_Read_Mouse(void);
```

Purpose:

DInput_Read_Mouse() reads the relative mouse state and stores the result in mouse_state, which is a DIMOUSESTATE structure. The data is in relative delta mode. In most cases you'll only need to look at mouse_state.lX, mouse_state.lY, and rgbButtons[0..2], which are Booleans for the three mouse buttons. Here's an example of reading the mouse and using it to move a cursor around and draw:

```
// read the mouse
if (!DInput_Read_Mouse())
   { /* error */ }

// move cursor
cx+=mouse_state.lX;
cy+=mouse_state.lY;

// test if left button is down
if (mouse_state.rgbButtons[0])
   Draw_Pixel(cx,cy,col,buffer,pitch);
```

Function Prototype:

```
int DInput_Read_Joystick(void);
```

Purpose:

DInput_Read_Joystick() polls the joystick and then reads the data into joy_state, which is a DIJOYSTATE structure. Of course, if there isn't a joystick plugged in, the function returns False and joy_state will be invalid, but you get the idea. If it's successful, `joy_state` contains the state information of the joystick. The data returned will be in the range you previously set for each axis, and the button values are Booleans in `rgbButtons[]`. For example, here's how you would use the joystick to move a ship right and left, and use the first button to fire:

```
// read the joystick data
if (!DInput_Read_Joystick())
    { /* error */ }

// move the ship
ship_x+=joy_state.lX;
ship_y+=joy_state.lY;

// test for trigger
if (joy_state.rgbButtons[0])
    { // fire weapon // }
```

Of course, your joystick may have a lot of buttons and multiple axes. In that case, you can use the other fields of `joy_state` as defined in the `DIJOYSTATE` DirectInput structure.

The T3D Library at a Glance

At this point, you have two main `.CPP|H` modules that make up the T3D library:

- `T3DLIB1.CPP|H`—DirectDraw plus graphics algorithms.
- `T3DLIB2.CPP|H`—DirectInput.

Keep this in mind when you're compiling programs. If you want to compile a demo program, call it `DEMOX_Y.CPP` and then look at its `.H` includes. If it includes either of the related `.H` library modules, you'll obviously need to include the `.CPP` files too.

WARNING	Make sure to link DDRAW.LIB, DINPUT.LIB and DINPUT8.LIB.

As an example of using the new library functions in `T3DLIB2.CPP|H`, I have rewritten the three demos created in this chapter, `DEMO9_1.CPP`, `DEMO9_2.CPP`, and `DEMO9_3.CPP`, as `DEMO9_1a.CPP` (`DEMO9_1a_16B.CPP` 16-bit version), `DEMO9_2a.CPP` (`DEMO9_2a_16B.CPP` 16-bit version), and `DEMO9_3a.CPP` (`DEMO9_3a_16B.CPP` 16-bit version), respectively. Therefore, you can see how much code can be chucked out when you use the library functions.

To compile any of the programs, make sure to include both of the library source files, as well as all of the DirectX .LIB files. And please, for God's sake, set your compiler to Win32 .EXE. I have received over 30 emails today from people asking how to set the compiler! *I'm a scientist, Jim, not a technical support agent for Microsoft!*

Summary

This chapter has been fairly fun, don't you think? It covered DirectInput, keyboards, mice, joysticks, input data massaging, and a little force feedback, and you added another piece to your library. You learned that DirectX supports all input devices through a common interface, and there are just a few steps (all similar) to communicating with any device. Not bad, baby boy (or baby girl). However, you still aren't out of the woods with the DirectX foundation systems. In the next chapter you'll tackle DirectSound and a bit of DirectMusic. After that, you can get to some serious game programming!

CHAPTER 10

Sounding Off with DirectSound and DirectMusic

Historically, creating sound and music on the PC has been a nightmare. However, with the advent of DirectSound and DirectMusic, it's all too easy. This chapter will cover the following topics:

- Fundamentals of sound
- Digital sound versus synthesized sound
- Sound hardware
- DirectSound API
- Sound file formats
- DirectMusic API
- Adding sound support to your library

Sound Programming on the PC

Sound programming is one of those things that always gets put off until the end. Writing a sound system is difficult because not only do you have to understand sound and music, but you have to make sure the sound system works on every single sound card. Here lies the problem. In the past, most game programmers used a third-party sound library such as the Miles Sound System, Diamondware Sound Toolkit, or something similar. Each system has its pros and cons, but the biggest problem is price. A sound library that works for DOS and Windows can cost thousands of dollars.

You don't have to worry about DOS anymore, but you do have to worry about Windows. It's true that Windows has sound and multimedia support, but it was never designed to have the ultra-high performance needed for a real-time video game. Thankfully, DirectSound and DirectMusic solve all these problems and more. Not only are DirectSound and DirectMusic free, but they are extremely high performance, have support for a million different sound cards, and have extensions to do as little or as much as you need.

For example, DirectSound has 3D support under DirectSound3D, and DirectMusic can do a whole lot more than play MIDI files. DirectMusic is a new real-time music composing and playback technology based on DLS (Downloadable Sounds) data. This means that not only will music sound the same on every single sound card, but DirectMusic can create music on-the-fly for your game based on preprogrammed *templates*, *motifs*, and *personalities* that you supply. Getting DirectMusic's AI to compose for you takes a lot of work, but it may be worth it for games in which you want to change the mood based on the gameplay but don't want to compose 10-20 different versions of each song yourself. And of course in DirectX 8.0 there is a much tighter integration of DirectSound and DirectMusic under DirectX Audio. Before version 8.0, these two interfaces were semi-separate and communication between them was difficult to accomplish. With that in mind, let's learn a little about sound.

And Then There Was Sound...

Sound is one of those physical manifestations that has a circular definition. If you went out on the street and asked people what sound is, most of them would probably reply with, "Hmmm, stuff you hear with your ears, like sounds and noises." (Go ahead, try it...) That's true, but it still doesn't get you closer to the actual physics of sound, and that's important if you're going to record, manipulate, and play sound.

Sound is a mechanical pressure wave emitted from a source, as shown in Figure 10.1. Sound can exist only in an environment such as our atmosphere, which is filled with gases such as nitrogen, oxygen, helium, etc. Sound can travel in water also, but it moves at a much higher velocity than in air because the medium's increased density makes it more conductive. Sort of. Close enough. :)

FIGURE 10.1
A sound wave.

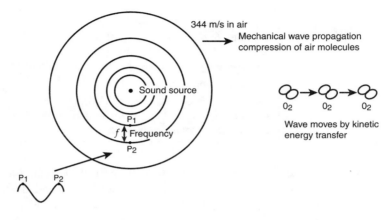

Frequency

A sound wave is really the motion of molecules. When a speaker moves in and out, it moves the surrounding air in and out mechanically, that is, by contact with the molecules, and at some point the sound wave makes its way to your ears. However, because sound travels by a wave propagating through the air via mechanical collisions, it takes time to get to you. That's why sound travels so slowly, relatively speaking. You can see something happen, such as a car crash, and not hear it for a second or two if it's happening far enough away. This is because a mechanical wave in air, or sound wave, can only travel at about 750 MPH or 344 m/s (meters per second), more or less depending on the density and temperature of the air. Table 10.1 lists the velocities of sound in air, seawater, and steel, for average temperatures.

TABLE 10.1   Velocity of Sound in Various Materials

Material/Medium	Approximate Velocity of Sound
Air	344 m/s
Seawater	1,478 m/s
Steel	5,064 m/s

Looking at Table 10.1, you can see why sonar works so well underwater but sucks in air (it's too slow, for one thing). A sonar pulse, or *ping*, travels underwater at 1,478 m/s or, roughly, 14.78 m/s x 3.2 ft/m x 1 mi/5280 ft x 3,600 seconds/1 hour = 3,224.7 miles per hour! This, compared to the average of 750 miles per hour for sound in air, should tell you why sonar scans are almost instantaneous for objects that are moving underwater and within reasonable distance.

MATH	If you're interested, the velocity of sound c (not to be confused with C the note, or c the speed of light) is equal to the frequency × wavelength, or $f*\lambda$. In addition, the velocity can be computed based on factors like tension and density of the medium with this equation:

$$c = sqrt(tension\ factor/density\ factor)$$

where the tension and density are context-sensitive and only a loose starting point. In real life, there are a number of versions of this equation for gases, solids, and liquids.

Moving on, sound is a mechanical wave that travels through air at a constant velocity—the speed of sound. There are two parameters a traveling sound wave can have: *amplitude* and *frequency*. The amplitude of the sound is how much air volume is moved. A large speaker (or someone with a big mouth) moves a lot of air, so the sounds are stronger or more intense. The frequency of the sound is how many complete waves or cycles per second are emanating from the source, and is measured in hertz, or Hz. Most humans can hear in the range of 20-20,000Hz.

Furthermore, the average male has a voice that ranges from 20-2,000Hz, while a female voice ranges from 70-3,000Hz. Men have more bass, and women have more treble. Figure 10.2 shows the amplitude and frequency of some standard waveforms.

FIGURE 10.2
Various waveforms.

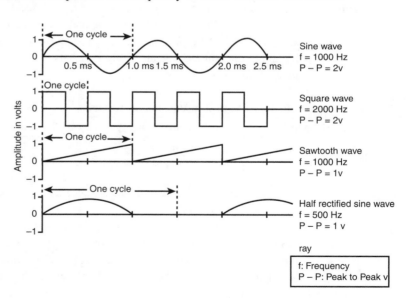

A waveform can be thought of as the shape of a sound's amplitude changes. Some sounds change smoothly, while other sounds rise up and then sharply fall off. Even if two sounds have the same amplitude and frequency, their particular shapes will make them sound different to us.

Lastly, we hear sound with our ears, which may seem simple enough, but here's the real story (like I'm going to lie). Your ears have a sensing array of little hair-like structures called *cilia*. Each of these cilia can detect a different frequency range. When a sound enters your ear as a wave train of pressure pulses, these cilia oscillate and resonate based on the sound and send signals to your brain. Your brain then processes these signals into the conscious perception of sound. However, on some planets the creatures might "see" sound, so remember that this whole sound thing is totally subjective. The only thing that is constant in the universe is how sound travels and the physics of sound. However, this is only true for regions of space that aren't warped, like near a black hole or on the freeways in California.

In review, a sound is a pressure wave that is expanding or contracting and moves air around. The rate of these contractions or expansions is called the *frequency*, and the amount of air moved is related to the relative *amplitude* or volume of the sound. Also, there are different waveforms of sound, such as sine waves, square wave, saw tooth waves, and so on. Humans can hear in the range of 20-20,000Hz, and the average human voice is about 2,000Hz. However, this is not the whole truth.

A single pure tone will always have the shape of a sine wave, but it can have any frequency and amplitude. Single tones sound like electronic toys or touch-tone phone tones (technically, touch-tone phones make two tones per button or DTMF, but close enough). The point is that in the real world, most sounds, like voices, music, and the ambient noises of the outdoors, are composed of hundreds or even thousands of pure tones all mixed together. Hence, sounds have a *spectrum*.

MATH   The most basic waveform in the universe is the sine wave—SIN(t). All other waveforms can be represented by a linear combination or collection of one or more sine waves. This can be proven mathematically with the Fourier Transform, which is a method of breaking a waveform down into its sinusoidal components. And it's also a way of giving math majors serious headaches!

The spectrum of a sound is its *frequency distribution*. Figure 10.3 shows the frequency distribution for my voice. As you can see, my voice has many different frequencies in it, but most of them are low. The point is, to make truly realistic sounds, you must understand that sounds are composed of many simple pure tones at different frequencies and amplitudes.

FIGURE 10.3

Frequency spectrum for the average male voice.

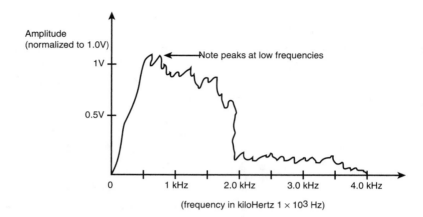

(frequency in kiloHertz 1×10^3 Hz)

That's all great, but your goal is to make the computer produce sounds. No problem; the computer can control a speaker with electrical signals, forcing it to move in and out at any rate, with any force (within reason). Let's see how.

Digital Versus MIDI—Sounds Great, Less Filling

There are two kinds of sounds that a computer can make: *digital* and *synthesized*. Digital sounds are basically recordings of sounds, while synthesized sounds are programmed reproductions of sounds based on algorithms and hardware tone generators. Digital sounds are usually used for sound effects, like explosions and people talking, while synthesized sounds are used for music. And in most cases these days, synthesized sounds are only used for music and not sound effects. However, back in the '80s, game programmers used FM synthesizers and tone generators to make the sounds of engines, explosions, gunshots, drums, sirens, and so forth. Granted, they didn't sound as good as digitized sound effects, but they worked back then.

Digital Sound—Let the Bits Begin

Digital sound involves *digitization*, which means to encode data in the digital form of ones and zeros, such as 110101010110. Just as an electrical signal can create sounds by causing a magnetic field to move the speaker's cone magnet, talking into a speaker creates the opposite effect. That is, the speaker generates an electrical signal based on the vibrations it senses. This electrical signal has the sound information encoded in it as an analog or linear voltage, as shown in Figure 10.4.

FIGURE 10.4

The conversion of sound.

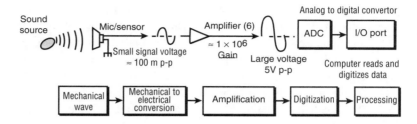

With the proper hardware, this linear voltage with the sound information encoded in it can be sampled and digitized. This is exactly how your CD player works. The information on CDs is in digital form, whereas information on tapes is analog. Digital information is much easier to process and is the only information that digital computers can process (there's a surprise). So for a computer to process sound, that sound must be converted into a digital data stream with an analog-to-digital converter, as shown in section A of Figure 10.5.

Once the sound is recorded into the memory of the computer, it can be processed or played back with a digital-to-analog converter (D/A), as shown in section B of Figure 10.5. The point is, you need to convert the sound information to digital format before you can work with it. But recording digital sound is a bit tricky. Sound has a lot of information in it. If you want to sample sound realistically, there are two factors that you must consider: *frequency* and *amplitude*.

FIGURE 10.5

A/D and D/A conversion (16-bit).

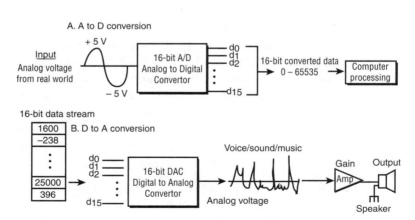

The number of samples you record of a sound per second is called the *sample rate.* It must be at least twice the frequency of the original sound if you want to reproduce it exactly. In other words, if you're sampling a human voice that has a range of 20-2,000Hz, you must sample the sound at 4,000Hz!

The reasoning for this is mathematical and based on the fact that all sounds are composed of sine waves. Thus, if you can sample the highest frequency sine wave contained in a sound, you can sample all the lower ones that compose that sound. But to sample a sine wave of frequency f, you must sample it at a rate of $2*f$. At a rate of only f, you can't tell if you're on the upward crest of a wave or the downward crest of a wave per cycle. In other words, it takes two points to reconstruct any sine wave. This is called *Shannon's Theorem*, and the minimal sampling rate is called the *Nyquist frequency*—were they roommates or something?

Anyway, the second sampling parameter is the *amplitude resolution*—meaning, how many different values are there for the amplitude? If you have only eight bits per sample, that means there are only 256 different possible amplitudes. This is enough for games, but for reproduction of professional sounds and music you need at least 16 bits of resolution, giving 65,536 different possible values.

So that's digital sound for you. Basically, it is a recording or sampling of sound that has been converted to digital form from an analog signal. Digital sound is great for sound effects and short sounds, but it's bad for long sounds because of its memory requirements—a 16-bit, 44.1 KHz, CD-quality sound uses about 88KB a second. On the other hand, if your game is going on CD, you can spare a couple hundred megs for pure digital music. Finally, digital sound sounds far better than synthesized sound 99 percent of the time, but under DirectMusic, synthesized music sounds almost as good.

Synthesized Sound and MIDI

Although digital sound is currently the best-sounding, synthesized sound has been around a long time and is getting better and better. Synthesized sound isn't digitally recorded; it's a mathematical reproduction of a sound based on a description. Synthesizers use hardware and algorithms to generate sounds on-the-fly from a description of the desired sound. For example, let's say you wanted to hear a 440Hz pure concert A note. You could design a piece of hardware that generated a pure analog sine wave of any frequency from 0-20,000Hz and then instruct it to create a 440Hz tone. This is the basis of synthesis.

The only problem is that most people want to hear more than a single tone (unless you're listening to a musical birthday card), so hardware is needed that supports at least 16–32 different tones at the same time, as shown in Figure 10.6. This isn't bad, and a number of different video game consoles used something like this back in the '70s and '80s. But people still weren't satisfied. The problem is that most sounds have many frequencies in them; they have undertones, overtones, and harmonics (multiples of each frequency). This is what makes them sound textured and full.

Normally, I wouldn't use the words *textured* and *full* to describe sound because it lowers my public cool factor, but I had to because they're common terms used by music people. So please bear with me.

FIGURE 10.6
Crude sound synthesis with multiple channels.

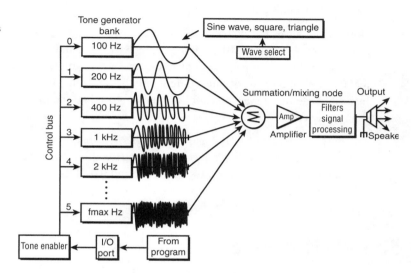

The first attempt at better sound was *FM synthesis*. Remember the old Ad-Lib card? It was the precursor of the Sound Blaster and the first PC card to support multiple-channel FM synthesis. (The *FM* stands for *frequency modulation*.) An FM synthesizer can alter not only the amplitude of a sine wave sound, but also the frequency of the wave.

FM synthesis operates on the mathematical basis of feedback. An FM synthesizer feeds the output of the signals back into themselves, thereby modulating the signals and creating harmonics and phase-shifted tones from the original single sine wave. The bottom line is that they sound very real compared to single tones.

It's MIDI Time!

At about the same time all this FM synthesis stuff came out, a file format for music synthesis was catching on called *MIDI (Musical Instrument Digital Interface)*. MIDI is a language that describes musical compositions as a function of time. Instead of digitizing a sound, a MIDI piece describes it as keys, instruments, and special codes. For example, a MIDI file might look like this:

```
Turn on Channel 1 with a B flat.
Turn on Channel 2 with a C sharp.
Turn off Channel 1.
   .
   .
   .
Turn all channels off.
```

Of course, this information is encoded in a binary serial stream, but you get the picture. Moreover, each channel in the MIDI specification is connected to a different instrument or sound. You might have 16 channels, each one representing a different instrument such as piano, drums, guitar, bass, flute, trumpet, and so on. So MIDI is an indirect method of encoding music.

However, it leaves the synthesis up to the hardware and records only the actual musical notes and timing. Alas, MIDI on one computer may sound completely different than on another, due to the method of synthesis and the instrument data. On the other hand, a MIDI file for an hour of music might only be a few hundred kilobytes of memory, instead of requiring megabytes for the same music in digital form! So it's been worth it, in many cases.

The only problem with MIDI and FM synthesis is that they are only good for music. Sure, you can design FM synthesizers to create white noise for explosions or laser blasts, but the sounds will always be simple and won't have the organic feel that digitized sound has. So more advanced methods of hardware synthesis have been created, such as *wave table* and *wave guide* technology.

Sound Hardware

There are three major classes of sound synthesis these days: FM, wave table (software versions, too), and wave guide. You've already learned about FM, so let's take a look at the wave table and wave guide models for a minute.

Wave Table Synthesis

Wave table synthesis is a mix between synthesis and digital recording. It works like this: The wave table has a number of real, sampled digital sounds within it. This data is then processed by a DSP (Digital Signal Processor), which takes the real sample and plays it back at any frequency and amplitude that you need. Hence, you can sample a real piano and then play any note on that piano using wave table synthesis. It sounds almost as good as digital, but you still have to have the original sources sampled. Again, that takes memory. The Creative Labs AWE32 is a good example of this.

In addition to the hardware wave table, there are software synthesizer-based wave table systems, such as the MOD format for Amigas and the DLS system used in DirectMusic. Computers are so fast now that if you just have a D-to-A converter that plays digital sound, you can use it to synthesize digital sound based on software samples of real instruments much like the wave table does. As long as you can make the DSP happen in real-time and can perform frequency, amplitude, and other processing functions, you don't need any hardware! This is exactly how DirectMusic works.

Wave Guide Synthesis

Wave guide synthesis is the ultimate synthesis technology. Through the use of DSP chips and very special hardware, the sound synthesizer can actually generate a mathematical model of an instrument virtually and then simply play it! This may seem like science fiction, but it's a fact. With this technology, the human ear can't perceive the difference between a sampled instrument, the real one, and the wave guide simulated instrument. Thus, you can create MIDI files that control a wave table or wave guide synthesizer and get great results. The Creative Labs AWE64 Gold and greater have this technology.

So the verdict is, a synthesizer can create music as real as real can get, but the musical piece still must be encoded as MIDI. Also, if you want speech or special sound effects, they're hard to do with synthesizers, and even with wave guide technology you'll need special software.

However, with DirectMusic you can program instruments with digitized sounds and play them like notes, so that problem is solved. Thus, you can use digital sound for all your sound effects and DirectMusic for the music. Granted, there may be a little more work involved than just playing a wave file, but DirectMusic sounds the same on *all* machines, is free, can read standard MIDI files, and has a ton of features if you want to use them. Therefore, you may decide to use a mix of both: DirectSound for sound effects and DirectMusic for music.

Digital Recording: Tools and Techniques

Before I finish off the sound and music preceptor program, I want to give you some hints on recording sound and music for your games because I get millions of emails on the topic all the time. There are at least three ways to create digital samples:

- Sample them from the real world with a microphone or outside input.
- Buy sampled sounds in digital or analog format and download or record them for use.
- Synthesize digital sounds with a waveform synthesizer like Sound Forge.

The third method may seem a little backwards, but it's useful if you want to create pure tones with digital hardware and you don't have a sound source that you can record. But the first two methods are the most important for us.

If you're making a game that has a lot of speech in it, you're probably going to have to sample your own voice (or the voice of a friend), tweak it with a piece of software, and then use it in your game. For games that use standard explosions, doors, growls, and so on, you can probably get away with generic sound clips. For example, just about everybody in this business has a copy of the Sound Ideas General 6000/7000+

sound library. It's about 40 CDs full of thousands of sound effects, and it's used for movies, so it has it all. But if I hear the DOOM/Quake door sound one more time in a full release movie, I'm going to rip my ears off!

The only problem with professional sound libraries is the cost—about $2,500 for a decent license. So what should you do? Any computer store will have $5 CDs of sound effects. You may have to buy a few, but two or three will usually give you enough samples to work with—some cars, spaceships, monsters, and so on. However, since I'm a nice guy, I'm going to supply you with a complete set of cool sounds from one of my games. They're on this book's CD in the directory called SOUNDS\. They're all in .WAV format, so you can use them directly in your games, but you might want to resample and tweak them because they're mutant sounds from a number of different game products.

Recording Sounds

If you record your own sounds, I suggest the following settings: Create your originals with 16 bits per sample in 22KHz mono. Remember, *no stereo*. DirectSound works best with mono sound, so recording in stereo won't help. Also, most sounds you can make or record will be mono anyway, so recording in stereo will be a waste of memory.

If you're recording from a microphone plugged into your sound card, buy a good one. A good one will feel heavy. There is truth to the old saying, "If it's heavy, then it's good." Also, do your recording in an enclosed room without background noise or interruptions. If you're recording direct from a device, such as a CD player or radio, make sure that the connections are good and use high-quality audio connectors.

Finally, give your sound files reasonable names. Don't be cryptic; you'll never remember what's what unless you're organized. And for God's sake, it's the 21st century—use long filenames!

Processing Your Sounds

Once you've sampled your sounds with Sound Forge or a similar piece of software, you'll probably want to post-process those sounds. Again, Sound Forge or a similar package can do all the processing. During processing you'll want to crop out all the dead air, normalize the volumes, remove noise, add echoes, etc. However, I suggest that when you perform this step, you make backups of your sounds and don't mess with the originals. Rename the processed sounds with numbers appended at the end or something. Once they're gone, they're gone!

While you're processing sound, experiment with frequency shifting, echoes, distortion, and various other effects. When you find a cool effect, make sure to write down the *formula* to reproduce the effect. I can't tell you how many times I had the perfect female computer voice (processed from mine) and I lost the formula.

Finally, when you're done with all your sounds, write them all out in the same format, such as 22- or 11KHz mono with 8- or 16-bit. This will help DirectSound tremendously when it's processing your sounds. If you have sounds with different sample rates and bits per sample, DirectSound will always have to convert to its native rate of 22KHz 8-bit.

> **TIP**
>
> Technically, DirectSound's native format is 22 KHz 8-bit stereo. But most sounds are mono in nature, and sending stereo data to DirectSound is a waste unless you're recording with two microphones placed at different locales or have real stereo data.

DirectSound on the Mic

DirectSound is composed of a number of components or interfaces, just like DirectDraw. However, this is a book on game programming, so we only have time to look at the most important ones. Hence, I won't be discussing the 3D sound component, DirectSound3D, or the sound capturing interface, DirectSoundCapture. I'm going to focus on the primary interfaces of DirectSound and that's it. Believe me, that's enough to keep you busy.

Figure 10.7 illustrates the relationship of DirectSound to the rest of the Windows subsystems. Notice that it is very similar to DirectDraw. However, DirectSound has a really cool feature that DirectDraw doesn't—if you don't have a DirectSound driver for your sound card, DirectSound will still work, but it will use emulation and the Windows DDI instead. So as long as you ship your product with the DirectSound .DLLs, your code will work even if the user doesn't have DirectSound drivers for his card. It won't be as fast, but it will still work. This is very cool.

FIGURE 10.7
DirectSound's place in Windows.

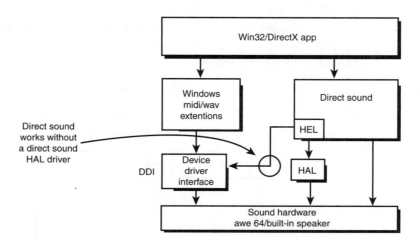

DirectSound has two components as far as we are concerned:

- A run-time .DLL that is loaded when you use DirectSound.
- A compile-time library and header named DSOUND.LIB and DSOUND.H, respectively.

To create a DirectSound application, all you need to do is include these files in your application and everything should be fine.

To use DirectSound, you must create a DirectSound COM object and then request the various interfaces from the main object. Figure 10.8 illustrates the main interfaces of DirectSound:

- **Iunknown**—The base COM object of all COM objects.
- **IDirectSound**—The main COM object of DirectSound. This represents the audio hardware itself. If you have one or more sound cards in your computer, you'll need a DirectSound object for each of them.
- **IDirectSoundBuffer**—This represents the mixing hardware and actual sounds. There are two kinds of DirectSound buffers: *primary* and *secondary* (see how DirectSound is similar to DirectDraw?). There is only a single primary buffer, and it represents the sound that is currently playing and is mixed either by hardware (hopefully) or software. Secondary buffers represent sounds that are stored for playback. They may exist in system memory or SRAM (sound RAM) on the sound card. In either case, you can play as many secondary buffer sounds as you want as long as you have the horsepower and memory to do so. Figure 10.9 represents the relationship between the primary sound buffer and secondary sound buffers.
- **IDirectSoundCapture**—You're not going to use this interface, but like I said, it's used to record and capture sounds. You could use it to allow the player to record his name, or, if you're more of a techno-freak, it can be used to capture speech in real-time for voice recognition.
- **IDirectSoundNotify**—This interface is used to send messages back to DirectSound. You might need this in a game with a complex sound system, but you can get along without it.

FIGURE 10.8
The interfaces of DirectSound.

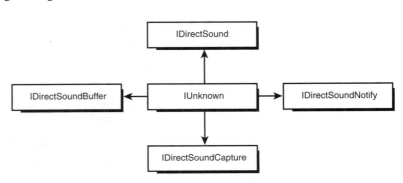

FIGURE 10.9
Sound buffers.

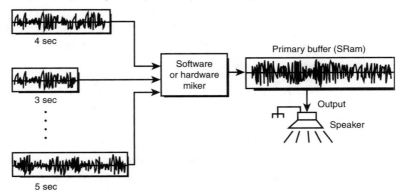

Direct sound secondary buffers (SRam or system memory)

4 sec

3 sec

5 sec

Software or hardware mixer

Primary buffer (SRam)

Output

Speaker

To use DirectSound, you first create the main DirectSound object, create one or more secondary sound buffers, load them with sounds, and then play any sound you want. DirectSound will take care of the details, such as mixing. So let's start with creating the main DirectSound object itself.

NOTE

> Although with DirectX 8.0 there is a new DirectSound interface, `IDirectSound8`, basically Microsoft skipped versions 2, 3, 4, 5, 6, 7. However, it brings nothing to the table for us, so we are going to use the standard DirectSound interfaces that have been available since DirectX 3.0.

Starting Up DirectSound

The main DirectSound object represents a sound card(s). If you have more than one sound card, you'll have to enumerate, detect, and request their GUIDs (Globally Unique Identifiers). But if you just want to connect to the default sound device, you don't have to mess with detection; you can simply create a DirectSound object that represents the main sound card. Here's the interface pointer that represents a DirectSound object:

```
LPDIRECTSOUND  lpds; // directsound interface pointer
```

To create a DirectSound object, you must make a call to `DirectSoundCreate()`, prototyped here:

```
HRESULT DirectSoundCreate(
        LPGUID lpGuid, // guid of sound card
                       // NULL for default device
        LPDIRECTSOUND *lpDS,    // interface ptr to object
        IUnknown FAR *pUnkOuter) // always NULL
```

The preceding call is very similar to the one used to create the main DirectDraw object. In general, this stuff all looks alike; once you've mastered one part of DirectX, you've mastered them all. The problem is that Microsoft keeps adding new interfaces as fast as you can learn them! Anyway, to create a DirectSound object, do this:

```
LPDIRECTSOUND lpds; // pointer to directsound object

// create DirectSound object
if (DirectSoundCreate(NULL, &lpds, NULL)!=DS_OK )
   { /* error */ }
```

Notice that the success value is now DS_OK (DirectSound OK) rather than DD_OK (DirectDraw OK). However, that was just an example to show you the new OK code. Check for success/failure like you've been doing using the FAILURE() and SUCCESS() macros, like this:

```
// create DirectSound object
if (FAILED(DirectSoundCreate(NULL, &lpds, NULL)))
   { /* error */ }
```

And of course, when you're done with the DirectSound object, you must release it like this:

```
lpds->Release();
```

This step occurs during the shutdown stage of your application.

Understanding the Cooperation Level

After you create the main DirectSound object, it's time to set the cooperation level of DirectSound. DirectSound is a little trickier than DirectDraw as far as cooperation level is concerned. You can't be as brutal when taking over the sound system as you can with graphics. Well, you can if you want, but Microsoft advises that you don't, so take their advice.

There are a number of cooperation levels that DirectSound can be set to. They are divided into two groups: settings that give you control over the primary sound buffer, and settings that don't. Remember, the primary sound buffer represents the actual mixing hardware (or software) that is mixing sounds at all times and sending them out to the speaker. If you mess with the primary buffer, DirectSound will want you to make sure you know what you're doing because it could crash or distort not only your application's sound, but others as well. Here's a general briefing on each cooperation level:

- **Normal Cooperation**—This is the most cooperative of all the settings. While your application has the focus, it will be able to play sounds, but so will other applications. Furthermore, you don't have write permission to the primary buffer, and DirectSound will create a default primary buffer of 22 KHz, stereo, 8-bit for you. I suggest using this setting most of the time.

- **Priority Cooperation**—With this setting you have first access to all the hardware, you can change the setting of the primary mixer, and you can request the sound hardware to perform advanced memory operations such as compaction. This setting is only necessary if you must change the data format of the primary buffer—which you might do if you wanted to play 16-bit samples, for example.

- **Exclusive Cooperation**—Same as Priority, but your application will be audible only when it's in the foreground.

- **Write_Primary Cooperation**—This is the highest priority. You have total control and must control the primary buffer yourself to hear anything. You would only use this mode if you were writing your own sound mixer or engine—I think only John Miles uses this one. :)

Setting the Cooperation Level

In my opinion, you should use the normal priority level until you get the hang of DirectSound. It's the easiest to get working and has the smoothest operation. To set the cooperation level, use the SetCooperativeLevel() function from the interface of the main DirectSound object. Here's the prototype:

```
HRESULT SetCooperativeLevel(HWND hwnd, // window handle
                 DWORD dwLevel); // cooperation level setting
```

The function returns DS_OK if successful and something else otherwise. But make sure to check for errors because it's more than possible that another application has taken control of the sound card. Table 10.2 lists the flag settings for the various cooperation levels.

TABLE 10.2 Settings for DirectSound SetCooperativeLevel()

Value	Description
DSSCL_NORMAL	Sets normal cooperation.
DSSCL_PRIORITY	Sets priority cooperation level, allowing you to set the data format of the primary buffer.
DSSCL_EXCLUSIVE	Gives you priority cooperation, in addition to exclusive control when your application is in the foreground.
DSSCL_WRITEPRIMARY	Gives you total control of the primary buffer.

Here's how you would set the cooperation level to normal after creating the DirectSound object:

```
if (FAILED(lpds->SetCooperativeLevel(main_window_handle,
                DSSCL_NORMAL)))
   { /* error setting cooperation level */ }
```

Cool, huh? Take a look at DEMO10_1.CPP|EXE on the CD. It creates a DirectSound object, sets the cooperation level, and then releases the object on exit. It doesn't make any sound, though—that's next!

 TIP When you're compiling programs from this chapter, make sure to include DSOUND.LIB in your project.

Primary and Secondary Sound Buffers

The DirectSound object that represents the sound card itself has a single primary buffer. The primary buffer represents the mixing hardware (or software) on the card and processes all the time, like a little conveyor belt. Manual primary buffer mixing is very advanced, and luckily you don't have to do it. DirectSound takes care of the primary buffer for you as long as you don't set the cooperation level to the highest priority. In addition, you don't need to create a primary buffer because DirectSound creates one for you, as long as you set the cooperation level to one of the lower levels, such as DSSCL_NORMAL.

The only drawback is that the primary buffer will be set for 22 KHz stereo in 8-bit. If you want 16-bit sound or a higher playback rate, you'll have to at least set the cooperation level to DSSCL_PRIORITY and then set a new data format for the primary buffer. But for now, just use the default because it makes life much easier.

Working with Secondary Buffers

Secondary buffers represent the actual sounds that you want to play. They can be any size that you want, as long as you have the memory to hold them. However, the SRAM on the sound card can only hold so much sound data, so be careful when you're requesting sounds to be stored on the sound card itself. But sounds that are stored on the sound card itself will take much less processing power to play, so keep that in mind.

Now there are two kinds of secondary buffers—*static* and *streaming*. Static sound buffers are sounds that you plan to keep around and play over and over. These are good candidates for SRAM or system memory. Streaming sound buffers are a little different. Imagine that you want to play an entire CD with DirectSound. I don't think you have enough system RAM or SRAM to store all 650MB of audio data in memory, so you'd have to read the data in chunks and stream it out to a DirectSound buffer. This is what streaming buffers are for. You continually feed them with new sound data as they are playing. Sound tricky? Take a look at Figure 10.10.

FIGURE 10.10
Streaming audio data.

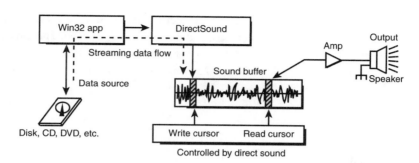

In general, all secondary sound buffers can be written to static or streaming. However, because it's possible that the sound will be playing as you're trying to write to it, DirectSound uses a scheme to take this into consideration: *circular buffering.* This means that each sound is stored in a circular data array that is continually read from at one point by the *play cursor* and written to at another point (slightly behind the first point) by the *write cursor.* Of course, if you don't need to write to your sound buffers as they are playing, you don't have to worry about this, but you will when you're streaming audio.

To facilitate this complex, buffered real-time writing capability, the data access functions for sound buffers might return a memory space that's broken up into two pieces because the data block you're trying to write exists at the end of the buffer and overflows into the beginning of the buffer. The point is, you need to know this fact if you're going to stream audio. However, in most games all this is moot, because as long as you keep all the sound effects to a few seconds each and the musical tracks are all loaded on demand, you can usually fit everything into a few megabytes of RAM. Using 2–4MB of storage for sound in a 32MB+ machine isn't too much of a problem.

Creating Secondary Sound Buffers

To create a secondary sound buffer, you must make a call to `CreateSoundBuffer()` with the proper parameters. If successful, the function creates a sound buffer, initializes it, and returns an interface pointer to it of this type:

```
LPDIRECTSOUNDBUFFER lpdsbuffer; // a directsound buffer
```

However, before you make the call to `CreateSoundBuffer()`, you must set up a DirectSoundBuffer description structure, which is similar to a DirectDrawSurface description. The description structure is of the type `DSBUFFERDESC` and is shown here:

```
typedef struct
{
DWORD   dwSize;       // size of this structure
DWORD   dwFlags;      // control flags
DWORD   dwBufferBytes; // size of the sound buffer in bytes
DWORD   dwReserved;   // unused
LPWAVEFORMATEX  lpwfxFormat; // the wave format
} DSBUFFERDESC, *LPDSBUFFERDESC;
```

The `dwSize` field is the standard DirectX structure size, `dwBufferBytes` is how big you want the buffer to be in bytes, and `dwReserved` is unused. The only fields of real interest are `dwFlags` and `lpwfxFormat`. `dwFlags` contains the creation flags of the sound buffer. Take a look at Table 10.3, which contains a partial list of the more basic flag settings.

TABLE 10.3 DirectSound Secondary Buffer Creation Flags

Value	Description
DSBCAPS_CTRLALL	The buffer must have all control capabilities.
DSBCAPS_CTRLDEFAULT	The buffer should have default control options. This is the same as specifying the DSBCAPS_CTRLPAN, DSBCAPS_CTRLVOLUME, and DSBCAPS_CTRLFREQUENCY flags.
DSBCAPS_CTRLFREQUENCY	The buffer must have frequency control capability.
DSBCAPS_CTRLPAN	The buffer must have pan control capability.
DSBCAPS_CTRLVOLUME	The buffer must have volume control capability.
DSBCAPS_STATIC	Indicates that the buffer will be used for static sound data. Most of the time you'll create these buffers in hardware memory if possible.
DSBCAPS_LOCHARDWARE	Use hardware mixing and memory for this sound buffer if memory is available.
DSBCAPS_LOCSOFTWARE	Forces the buffer to be stored in software memory and use software mixing, even if DSBCAPS_STATIC is specified and hardware resources are available.
DSBCAPS_PRIMARYBUFFER	Indicates that the buffer is a primary sound buffer. Only set this if you want to create a primary buffer and you're a sound god.

In most cases you'll set the flags to DSBCAPS_CTRLDEFAULT | DSBCAPS_STATIC | DSBCAPS_LOCSOFTWARE for default controls, static sound, and system memory, respectively. If you want to use hardware memory, use DSBCAPS_LOCHARDWARE instead of DSBCAPS_LOCSOFTWARE.

> **NOTE**
>
> The more capabilities you give a sound, the more stops (software filters) it has to go through before being heard. This means more processing time. Alas, if you don't need volume, pan, and frequency shift ability, forget DSBCAPS_CTRLDEFAULT and just use the capabilities that you absolutely need.

Now let's move on to the `WAVEFORMATEX` structure. It contains a description of the sound that you want the buffer to represent (it's a standard Win32 structure also). Parameters like playback rate, number of channels (1-mono or 2-stereo), bits per sample, and so forth are recorded in this structure. Here it is for your review:

```
typedef struct
{
WORD  wFormatTag;       // always WAVE_FORMAT_PCM
WORD  nChannels;        // number of audio channels 1 or 2
DWORD nSamplesPerSec;   // samples per second
DWORD nAvgBytesPerSec;  // average data rate
WORD  nBlockAlign;      // nchannels * bytespersmaple
WORD  wBitsPerSample;   // bits per sample
WORD  cbSize;           // advanced, set to 0
} WAVEFORMATEX;
```

Simple enough. Basically, `WAVEFORMATEX` contains the description of the sound. In addition, you need to set up one of these as part of `DSBUFFERDESC`. Let's see how to do that, beginning with the prototype of the `CreateSoundBuffer()` function:

```
HRESULT CreateSoundBuffer(
 LPCDSBUFFERDESC lpcDSBuffDesc,    // ptr to DSBUFFERDESC
 LPLPDIRECTSOUNDBUFFER lplpDSBuff,// ptr to sound buffer
 IUnknown FAR *pUnkOuter);         // always NULL
```

And here's an example of creating a secondary DirectSound buffer at 11KHz mono 8-bit with enough storage for two seconds:

```
// ptr to directsound
LPDIRECTSOUNDBUFFER lpdsbuffer;

DSBUFFERDESC dsbd;   // directsound buffer description
WAVEFORMATEX  pcmwf; // holds the format description

// set up the format data structure
memset(&pcmwf, 0, sizeof(WAVEFORMATEX));
pcmwf.wFormatTag     = WAVE_FORMAT_PCM; // always need this
pcmwf.nChannels      = 1; // MONO, so channels = 1
pcmwf.nSamplesPerSec = 11025; // sample rate 11khz
pcmwf.nBlockAlign    = 1; // see below

// set to the total data per
// block, in our case 1 channel times 1 byte per sample
// so 1 byte total, if it was stereo then it would be
// 2 and if stereo and 16 bit then it would be 4

pcmwf.nAvgBytesPerSec =
                pcmwf.nSamplesPerSec * pcmwf.nBlockAlign;

pcmwf.wBitsPerSample = 8; // 8 bits per sample
pcmwf.cbSize         = 0; // always 0
```

```
// set up the directsound buffer description
memset(dsbd,0,sizeof(DSBUFFERDESC));
dsbd.dwSize = sizeof(DSBUFFERDESC);
dsbd.dwFlags= DSBCAPS_CTRLDEFAULT | DSBCAPS_STATIC |
              DSBCAPS_LOCSOFTWARE ;

dsbd.dwBufferBytes    = 22050; // enough for 2 seconds at
                               // a sample rate of 11025

dsbd.lpwfxFormat      = &pcmwf; // the WAVEFORMATEX struct

// create the buffer
if (FAILED(lpds->CreateSoundBuffer(&dsbd,&lpdsbuffer,NULL)))
   { /* error */ }
```

If the function call is successful, a new sound buffer is created and passed in
`lpdsbuffer`, which is ready to be played. The only problem is that there isn't anything
in it! You must fill the sound buffer with data yourself. You can do this by reading in a
sound file data stored in `.VOC`, `.WAV`, `.AU`, or whatever, and then parse the data and fill
up the buffer. Or you could generate algorithmic data and write into the buffer yourself for a test. Let's see how to write the data into the buffer, and later I'll show you
how to read sound files from disk.

Writing Data to Secondary Buffers

As I said, secondary sound buffers are circular in nature, and hence are a little more
complex to write to than a standard linear array of data. For example, with DirectDraw
surfaces, you just locked the surface memory and wrote to it. (This is only possible
because there is a driver living down there that turns nonlinear memory to linear.)
DirectSound works in a similar fashion: You lock it, but instead of getting one pointer
back, you get two! Therefore, you must write some of your data to the first pointer
and the rest to the second. Take a look at the prototype for `Lock()` to understand what
I mean:

```
HRESULT Lock(
  DWORD dwWriteCursor,     // position of write cursor
  DWORD dwWriteBytes,      // size you want to lock
  LPVOID lplpvAudioPtr1,   // ret ptr to first chunk
  LPDWORD lpdwAudioBytes1, // num bytes in first chunk
  LPVOID lplpvAudioPtr2,   // ret ptr to second chunk
  LPDWORD lpdwAudioBytes2, // num of bytes in second chunk
  DWORD dwFlags);          // how to lock it
```

If you set `dwFlags` to `DSBLOCK_FROMWRITECURSOR`, the buffer will be locked from the
current write cursor of the buffer. If you set `dwFlags` to `DSBLOCK_ENTIREBUFFER`, the
entire buffer will be locked. This is the way to go. Keep it simple.

For example, say you create a sound buffer that has enough storage for 1,000 bytes. When you lock the buffer for writing, you'll get two pointers back along with the length of each memory segment to write to. The first chunk might be 900 bytes long, and the second might be 100 bytes long. The point is that you have to write your first 900 bytes to the first memory region and the second 100 bytes to the second memory region. Take a look at Figure 10.11 to clarify this.

And here's an example of locking the 1,000-byte sound buffer:

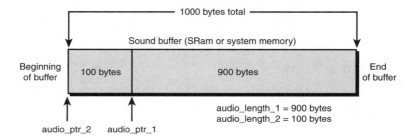

```
UCHAR *audio_ptr_1,  // used to retrieve buffer memory
      *audio_ptr_2;

int audio_length_1, // length of each buffer section
    audio_length_2;

// lock the buffer
if (FAILED(lpdsbuffer->Lock(0,1000,
    (void **)&audio_ptr_1, &audio_length_1,
    (void **)&audio_ptr_2, &audio_length_2,
    DSBLOCK_ENTIREBUFFER )))
    { /* error / }
```

Once you've locked the buffer, you're free to write into the memory. The data can be from a file or can be generated algorithmically. When you're done with the sound buffer, you must unlock it with Unlock(). Unlock() takes both pointers and both lengths, like this:

```
if (FAILED(lpdsbuffer->Unlock(audio_ptr_1,audio_length_1,
                        audio_ptr_2,audio_length_2)))
    { /* problem unlocking */}
```

And as usual, when you're done with the sound buffer, you must destroy it with Release(), like this:

```
lpdsbuffer->Release();
```

However, don't destroy the sound until you don't need it anymore. Otherwise you'll have to load it again.

Now let's see how to play sounds with DirectSound.

Rendering Sounds

Once you've created all your sound buffers and loaded them with sounds, you're ready to rock. (Of course, you're allowed to create and destroy sounds on-the-fly if you want.) DirectSound has a number of control functions to play sounds and alter their parameters as they play. You can change the volume, frequency, stereo panning, and so forth.

Playing a Sound

To play a sound buffer, use the `Play()` function as prototyped here:

```
HRESULT Play(
  DWORD dwReserved1, DWORD dwReserved2,   // both 0
  DWORD dwFlags); // control flags to play
```

The only flag that is defined is `DSBPLAY_LOOPING`. Setting this value will cause the sound to loop. If you want it to play only once, set `dwFlags` to 0. Here's an example of playing a sound over and over:

```
if (FAILED(lpdsbuffer->Play(0,0,DSBPLAY_LOOPING)))
   { /* error */ }
```

Use looping for music and other stuff you want to repeat.

Stopping a Sound

Once you've started a sound, you may want to stop it before it's finished playing. The function to do this is `Stop()`. Here's its prototype:

```
HRESULT Stop(); // that's easy enough
```

Here's how you would stop the sound you just started in the previous example:

```
if (FAILED(lpdsbuffer->Stop()))
   { /* error */ }
```

Now you have enough for a complete demo of DirectSound. Check out `DEMO10_2.CPP|EXE` on the CD. It creates a DirectSound object and a single secondary sound buffer, and then loads the buffer with a synthesized sine wave and plays it. It's simple, but it effectively shows you everything you need to know to play a sound.

Controlling the Volume

DirectSound lets you manipulate the volume or amplitude of a sound. However, this isn't free. If your hardware doesn't support volume changes, DirectSound will have to remix the sound with the new amplitude. This can require a little more processing power. In any case, here's the prototype:

```
HRESULT SetVolume(LONG lVolume); // attenuation in decibels
```

SetVolume() works differently than you would expect. Instead of instructing DirectSound to increase or decrease the amplitude, SetVolume() controls the attenuation (or anti-gain, if you will). If you send a 0, which is equal to DSBVOLUME_MAX, the sound will be played without attenuation—that is, at full volume. A value of -10,000 or DSBVOLUME_MIN will set the attenuation to maximum -100dB (decibels) and you won't hear a thing.

The best thing to do is create a wrapper function around this so you can send a value from 0-100 or something more natural. The following macro transformation will do the job:

```
#define DSVOLUME_TO_DB(volume) ((DWORD)(-30*(100 - volume)))
```

Here, volume is from 0-100, with 100 being full volume and 0 being totally silent. Here's an example that will play sound at 50 percent of full volume:

```
if (FAILED(lpdsbuffer->SetVolume(DSVOLUME_TO_DB(50))))
    { /* error */ }
```

> **NOTE**
>
> If you're wondering what a decibel is, it's a measure of sound or power based on the *bel,* named after Alexander Graham Bell. In electronics, many things are measured *logarithmically*, and the decibel scale is one example. In other words, 0 dB means no attenuation, -1 dB means the sound is 1/10 its original value, -2 dB means it's 1/100 the original value, and so on. Therefore, a sound that's attenuated -100 dB couldn't be heard by an ant!
>
> Note that on some scales, dB is also scaled by a factor of 10 (or even 2). So -10 dB would be 1/10 and -20 dB would be 1/100. It's one of those things that everybody has their own version of: engineers, mathematicians, physicists...

Freaking with the Frequency

One of the coolest manipulations you can apply to a sound is to change its playback frequency. This changes the sound's pitch (sort of), and you can make it slow and evil or fast and happy (yuck). You can make yourself sound like a chipmunk or Darth Vader in real-time! To change the frequency of playback, use the SetFrequency() function as shown below:

```
HRESULT SetFrequency(
    DWORD dwFrequency); // new frequency from 100-100,000Hz
```

Here's how you would make a sound play faster:

```
if (FAILED(lpdsbuffer->SetFrequency(22050)))
    { / * error */ }
```

If the original sound was sampled at 11,025Hz (11KHz), the new sound would play twice as fast and have twice the pitch and play for half as long. Get it? Got it? Then get rid of it!

Panning in 3D

The next killer thing you can do with a sound is change the stereo pan, or the amount of power coming from each speaker. For example, if you play a sound at the same volume in both speakers (or headphones), it will seem like it's right in front of you. But if you shift the volume to the right speaker, the sound will seem like it's moving to the right. This is called *panning* and can help you create localized 3D sounds (in a crude manner).

The function to set the stereo panning is called SetPan(), and here's its prototype:

```
HRESULT SetPan(LONG lPan); // the pan value -10,000 to 10,000
```

The pan value is logarithmic again: A value of 0 is dead center, a value of -10,000 means the right channel is attenuated by -100 dB, and a value of 10,000 means that the left channel is attenuated by -100 dB. Stupid, huh? Anyway, here's how you would attenuate the right channel by -5 dB:

```
if (FAILED(lpdsbuffer->SetPan(-500)))
    { /* error */ }
```

Making DirectSound Talk Back

You may be wondering if there is any way to query DirectSound for information about the sound system or a sound that is playing, like finding out whether the sound is done. Of course there is! DirectSound has a number of functions to do stuff like that. First, here's the general DirectSound capability function to determine the capabilities of your hardware:

```
HRESULT GetCaps(LPDSCAPS lpDSCaps); // ptr to DSCAPS structure
```

The function simply takes a pointer to a DSCAPS structure and fills it in. Here's the DSCAPS structure for your reference (you'll have to refer to the DirectX SDK for more complete descriptions of these fields, but most of them are decipherable by their names):

```
typedef {
    DWORD   dwSize;
    DWORD   dwFlags;
    DWORD   dwMinSecondarySampleRate;
    DWORD   dwMaxSecondarySampleRate;
    DWORD   dwPrimaryBuffers;
    DWORD   dwMaxHwMixingAllBuffers;
```

```
   DWORD   dwMaxHwMixingStaticBuffers;
   DWORD   dwMaxHwMixingStreamingBuffers;
   DWORD   dwFreeHwMixingAllBuffers;
   DWORD   dwFreeHwMixingStaticBuffers;
   DWORD   dwFreeHwMixingStreamingBuffers;
   DWORD   dwMaxHw3DAllBuffers;
   DWORD   dwMaxHw3DStaticBuffers;
   DWORD   dwMaxHw3DStreamingBuffers;
   DWORD   dwFreeHw3DAllBuffers;
   DWORD   dwFreeHw3DStaticBuffers;
   DWORD   dwFreeHw3DStreamingBuffers;
   DWORD   dwTotalHwMemBytes;
   DWORD   dwFreeHwMemBytes;
   DWORD   dwMaxContigFreeHwMemBytes;
   DWORD   dwUnlockTransferRateHwBuffers;
   DWORD   dwPlayCpuOverheadSwBuffers;
   DWORD   dwReserved1;
   DWORD   dwReserved2;
} DSCAPS, *LPDSCAPS;
```

You would call the function like this:

```
DSCAPS dscaps; // hold the caps

if (FAILED(lpds->GetCaps(&dscaps)))
    { /* error */ }
```

Then you can test any of the fields you want and determine what capabilities your sound hardware has. There's also a similar function for a DirectSound buffer that returns a DSBCAPS structure:

```
HRESULT GetCaps(LPDSBCAPS lpDSBCaps); // ptr to DSBCAPS struct
```

Here, a DSBCAPS structure looks like this:

```
typedef struct {
 DWORD dwSize;  // size of structure, you must set this
 DWORD dwFlags; // flags buffer has
 DWORD dwBufferBytes;       // size of buffer
 DWORD dwUnlockTransferRate; // sample rate
 DWORD dwPlayCpuOverhead;   // percentage of processor needed
                            // to mix this sound
} DSBCAPS, *LPDSBCAPS;
```

Here's how you would check out the sound buffer lpdsbuffer that you've been using in the examples:

```
DSBCAPS dsbcaps; // used to hold the results

// set up the struct
dsbcaps.dwSize = sizeof(DSBCAPS); // ultra important

// get the caps
if (FAILED(lpdsbuffer->GetCaps(&dsbcaps)))
   { /* error */ }
```

That's all there is to it. Of course, there are functions to retrieve the volume, pan setting, frequency, etc. of any sound buffer, but I'll let you look those up yourself.

The last `get` function I want to show you is used to determine the status of a playing sound buffer:

```
HRESULT GetStatus(LPDWORD lpdwStatus); // ptr to result
```

Just call the function from the interface pointer of the sound buffer you're interested in with a pointer to the `DWORD` where you want the status to be stored, like this:

```
DWORD status; // used to hold status

if (FAILED(lpdsbuffer->GetStatus(&status)))
  { / * error */ }
```

The data in the status will be one of the following:

- `DSBSTATUS_BUFFERLOST`—Something happened to the buffer. Very bad.
- `DSBSTATUS_LOOPING`—The sound is playing in looped mode.
- `DSBSTATUS_PLAYING`—The sound is currently playing. If this bit isn't set, the sound is not playing at all.

Reading Sounds from Disk

Unfortunately, DirectSound has no support for loading sound files. I mean *no* support. No `.VOC` loader, no `.WAV` loader, no nothing! It's a darn shame. So, you'll have to write one yourself. The problem is that sound files are extremely complex, and it would take half a chapter to do a good job of explaining them. So what I'm going to do is give you a `.WAV` loader and explain how it works in general.

> The guys at Microsoft got sick of writing their own `.WAV` loaders, along with a lot of other utility functions, so they wrote one that you can use if you want. The only problem is, the API isn't standard and will probably change. But if you're interested, check out all the goodies in `DDUTIL*.CPP|H`, located in one of the `SOURCE` directories of the SDK install, usually in the `SAMPLES` or `EXAMPLES` directory.

The .WAV Format

The `.WAV` format is a Windows sound format based on the `.IFF` format originally created by Electronic Arts. *IFF* stands for *Interchange File Format*. It's a standard that allows many different file types to be encoded using a general header/data structure with nesting. The `.WAV` format uses this encoding, and although it's very clean and logical, it's a pain to read the files in. You must parse a lot of header information, which takes a lot of code, and then you have to extract the sound data.

The parsing is so difficult that Microsoft created a set of functions called the *multimedia I/O interface (MMIO)* to help you load .WAV files and other similar types. All the functions of this library are prefixed with mmio*. The moral of the story is that writing a .WAV file reader isn't that easy, and it's tedious programming that has nothing to do with game programming. So, I'm just going to give you a heavily commented .WAV loader and a little explanation. If you want more, find a good reference on sound file formats.

Reading .WAV Files

The .WAV file format is based on *chunks*—ID chunks, format chunks, and data chunks. In essence, you need to open up a .WAV file and read in the header and format information, which then tells you how many channels there are, the bits per channel, the playback rate, and so forth, along with the length of the sampled sound. Then you load the sound.

Now, to help facilitate loading and playing sounds, you're going to create a sound library API, and hence a set of globals and wrapper functions around all this DirectSound stuff to make things easy. Let's begin with a data structure that will hold a virtual sound, which you'll use instead of the lower-level DirectSound stuff:

```
// this holds a single sound
typedef struct pcm_sound_typ
{
LPDIRECTSOUNDBUFFER dsbuffer;   // the ds buffer containing the sound
int state;                       // state of the sound
int rate;                        // playback rate
int size;                        // size of sound
int id;                          // id number of the sound
} pcm_sound, *pcm_sound_ptr;
```

This nicely contains the DirectSound buffer associated with a sound, along with a copy of the important information about the sound. Now let's create an array to hold all the sounds in the system:

```
pcm_sound sound_fx[MAX_SOUNDS];   // the array of secondary sound buffers
```

So, when you load a sound, the idea is to find an open space and set up a pcm_sound structure. This is exactly what the following DSound_Load_WAV() function does:

```
int DSound_Load_WAV(char *filename, int control_flags = DSBCAPS_CTRLDEFAULT)
{
// this function loads a .wav file, sets up the directsound
// buffer and loads the data into memory, the function returns
// the id number of the sound

HMMIO         hwav;    // handle to wave file
MMCKINFO      parent,  // parent chunk
              child;   // child chunk
WAVEFORMATEX  wfmtx;   // wave format structure
```

```c
int    sound_id = -1,        // id of sound to be loaded
    index;                   // looping variable

UCHAR *snd_buffer,           // temporary sound buffer to hold voc data
      *audio_ptr_1=NULL,     // data ptr to first write buffer
      *audio_ptr_2=NULL;     // data ptr to second write buffer

DWORD audio_length_1=0,      // length of first write buffer
      audio_length_2=0;      // length of second write buffer

// step one: are there any open id's ?
for (index=0; index < MAX_SOUNDS; index++)
    {
    // make sure this sound is unused
    if (sound_fx[index].state==SOUND_NULL)
        {
        sound_id = index;
        break;
        } // end if

    } // end for index

// did we get a free ID?
if (sound_id==-1)
    return(-1);

// set up chunk info structure
parent.ckid         = (FOURCC)0;
parent.cksize       = 0;
parent.fccType      = (FOURCC)0;
parent.dwDataOffset = 0;
parent.dwFlags      = 0;

// copy data
child = parent;

// open the WAV file
if ((hwav = mmioOpen(filename, NULL, MMIO_READ | MMIO_ALLOCBUF))==NULL)
    return(-1);

// descend into the RIFF
parent.fccType = mmioFOURCC('W', 'A', 'V', 'E');

if (mmioDescend(hwav, &parent, NULL, MMIO_FINDRIFF))
    {
    // close the file
    mmioClose(hwav, 0);

    // return error, no wave section
    return(-1);
    } // end if

// descend to the WAVEfmt
child.ckid = mmioFOURCC('f', 'm', 't', ' ');
```

```
if (mmioDescend(hwav, &child, &parent, 0))
   {
   // close the file
   mmioClose(hwav, 0);

   // return error, no format section
   return(-1);
   } // end if

// now read the wave format information from file
if (mmioRead(hwav, (char *)&wfmtx, sizeof(wfmtx)) != sizeof(wfmtx))
   {
   // close file
   mmioClose(hwav, 0);

   // return error, no wave format data
   return(-1);
   } // end if

// make sure that the data format is PCM
if (wfmtx.wFormatTag != WAVE_FORMAT_PCM)
   {
   // close the file
   mmioClose(hwav, 0);

   // return error, not the right data format
   return(-1);
   } // end if

// now ascend up one level, so we can access data chunk
if (mmioAscend(hwav, &child, 0))
  {
  // close file
  mmioClose(hwav, 0);

  // return error, couldn't ascend
  return(-1);
  } // end if

// descend to the data chunk
child.ckid = mmioFOURCC('d', 'a', 't', 'a');

if (mmioDescend(hwav, &child, &parent, MMIO_FINDCHUNK))
   {
   // close file
   mmioClose(hwav, 0);

   // return error, no data
   return(-1);
   } // end if

// finally!!!! now all we have to do is read the data in and
// set up the directsound buffer
```

```
// allocate the memory to load sound data
snd_buffer = (UCHAR *)malloc(child.cksize);

// read the wave data
mmioRead(hwav, (char *)snd_buffer, child.cksize);

// close the file
mmioClose(hwav, 0);

// set rate and size in data structure
sound_fx[sound_id].rate  = wfmtx.nSamplesPerSec;
sound_fx[sound_id].size  = child.cksize;
sound_fx[sound_id].state = SOUND_LOADED;

// set up the format data structure
memset(&pcmwf, 0, sizeof(WAVEFORMATEX));

pcmwf.wFormatTag     = WAVE_FORMAT_PCM;  // pulse code modulation
pcmwf.nChannels      = 1;               // mono
pcmwf.nSamplesPerSec = 11025;             // always this rate
pcmwf.nBlockAlign    = 1;
pcmwf.nAvgBytesPerSec = pcmwf.nSamplesPerSec * pcmwf.nBlockAlign;
pcmwf.wBitsPerSample = 8;
pcmwf.cbSize         = 0;

// prepare to create sounds buffer
dsbd.dwSize          = sizeof(DSBUFFERDESC);
dsbd.dwFlags         = control_flags | DSBCAPS_STATIC |
                       DSBCAPS_LOCSOFTWARE;
dsbd.dwBufferBytes   = child.cksize;
dsbd.lpwfxFormat     = &pcmwf;

// create the sound buffer
if (lpds->CreateSoundBuffer(&dsbd,
                &sound_fx[sound_id].dsbuffer,NULL)!=DS_OK)
   {
   // release memory
   free(snd_buffer);

   // return error
   return(-1);
   } // end if

// copy data into sound buffer
if (sound_fx[sound_id].dsbuffer->Lock(0,
                   child.cksize,
                   (void **) &audio_ptr_1,
                   &audio_length_1,
                   (void **)&audio_ptr_2,
                   &audio_length_2,
                   DSBLOCK_FROMWRITECURSOR)!=DS_OK)
      return(0);
```

```
// copy first section of circular buffer
memcpy(audio_ptr_1, snd_buffer, audio_length_1);

// copy last section of circular buffer
memcpy(audio_ptr_2, (snd_buffer+audio_length_1),audio_length_2);

// unlock the buffer
if (sound_fx[sound_id].dsbuffer->Unlock(audio_ptr_1,
                     audio_length_1,
                     audio_ptr_2,
                     audio_length_2)!=DS_OK)
              return(0);

// release the temp buffer
free(snd_buffer);

// return id
return(sound_id);

} // end DSound_Load_WAV
```

You simply pass the filename and the standard DirectSound control flags to the function, such as DSBCAPS_CTRLDEFAULT or whatever. After that, here's what happens:

1. The function opens up the .WAV file from the disk and extracts the important information about it.

2. The function proceeds to create a DirectSound buffer and fills it in.

3. The function stores the information in an open slot in the sound_fx[] array and returns the index, which I refer to as the ID of the sound.

4. Finally, the rest of your API will use the ID number to refer to the sound, and you can do whatever you want with it, such as play it. Here's an example:

```
// load the sound
int id = DSound_Load_WAV("test.wav");

// manually play the sound buffer, later we will wrapper this
sound_fx1.lpdsbuffer->Play(0,0,DSBPLAY_LOOPING);
```

Make sure to check out DEMO10_3.CPP on the disk. (Remember to link with DSOUND.LIB, and WINMM.LIB.) It's a complete demo of DirectSound and the Dsound_Load_WAV() function. In addition, the program lets you manipulate the sound in real-time with scrollbars, so not only is it cool, but you can see how to add scrollbar controls to your applications!

Of course, I'm going to take all this DirectSound stuff and show you the complete library (T3DLIB3.CPP|H), but first let's take a look at DirectMusic.

DirectMusic: The Great Experiment

DirectMusic is one of the most exciting components of DirectX and became available in Version 6.0. As I said before, writing digital sound software is hard, but writing software that plays MIDI files is gnarly! DirectMusic plays MIDI files, and it does a whole lot more. Here's a list of its capabilities:

- Supports DLS instruments (downloadable sounds). This means that when you play a MIDI file using DirectMusic, it will always sound the same no matter what kind of hardware you have.

- Supports on-the-fly composition of music using the Interactive Music Engine. DirectMusic allows you to set up templates, personalities, and variations of mood for your songs. Then DirectMusic will take your song data and rewrite the music in real-time and generate more music!

- Supports an unlimited number of MIDI channels, limited only by the processing power of your PC. Normal MIDI supports 16 channels, or 16 individual sounds, at once. There are 65,536 channel groups under DirectMusic, so you have almost unlimited tracks that can be played at the same time.

- Uses hardware acceleration if available, but the Microsoft software synthesizer is default and sounds as good as wave table or wave guide synthesis.

The only bad news about DirectMusic is that it is as complex as Direct3D! I have read the online documents for it (around 500 pages), and I can tell you one thing: They didn't have simplicity in mind, but they did have power in mind. Luckily, all you want to do is play a darn MIDI file, so I'm going to show you exactly how to do that and create an API around DirectMusic so you can load and play MIDI files. Also, as I mentioned before, with DirectX 8.0, DirectSound and DirectMusic have been integrated (but not removed) into DirectX Audio. The results of which are a new IDirectSound8 interface and a new DirectMusic interface, but these interfaces add nothing for our purposes, less make things more complex. Hence, we are going to forgo them.

DirectMusic Architecture

DirectMusic is rather large, so I'm not going to go into any detail about it. It's a topic for an entire book. However, I'm going to talk about the interfaces that you're going to work with. Take a look at Figure 10.12 for DirectMusic's main interfaces.

FIGURE 10.12
The main interfaces
of DirectMusic.

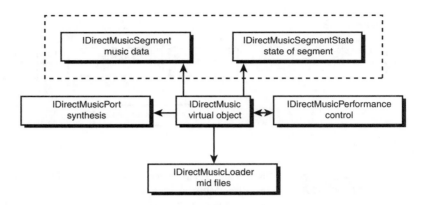

The descriptions of these interfaces are as follows:

IDirectMusic—This is the main interface of DirectMusic, but unlike DirectDraw and DirectSound, you don't necessarily need it to use DirectMusic. It is created by default and hidden away when you create a DirectMusic performance object—thank God.

IDirectMusicPerformance—This is the main interface as far as you're concerned. The performance object controls and manipulates the playback of all musical data. In addition, it creates an IDirectMusic object when it is created.

IDirectMusicLoader—This is used to load all data, including MIDI, DLS, and so forth. You use this to load your MIDI files from disk. So you have a MIDI loader—what a relief!

IDirectMusicSegment—This represents a chunk of musical data; each MIDI file you load will be represented by this interface.

IDirectMusicSegmentState—This is linked to a segment, but it's related to the current state of the segment rather than the data.

IDirectMusicPort—This is where the digital data representing your MIDI music is streamed out to. In most cases it will be the Microsoft Software Synthesizer, but you can always enumerate other possible ports that are hardware-accelerated.

Generally speaking, DirectMusic is a MIDI-to-digital real-time converter with DSP (Digital Signal Processing) abilities. As I mentioned in the DirectSound discussion on MIDI, the problem with MIDI is that it can sound different from one machine to the next based on the hardware and the instrument patches. DirectMusic gets around this by using pure digital samples of the instruments in the form of DLS files. Therefore, whenever you make a song, you can use the default DLS file or create your own instrument file. The catch is that the instruments are digital in nature and come with your music. Digital sound always plays the same through a D/A, so the music always sounds the same. Take a look at Figure 10.13 to see this.

FIGURE 10.13
DirectMusic relies on
digital samples rather
than synthesis.

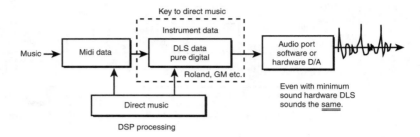

The default DLS instruments that are available on every machine loaded
with DirectMusic are the Roland GM/GS (General MIDI). They sound
great, but you can't modify them in any way—Roland doesn't want you
making them look bad!

You're probably going "What the heck?" right about now. I know, I know, it always
seems that everything is more complicated than it needs to be. But complexity is good
because it allows future technology and innovation to fit in. That is the basis of
DirectMusic.

Starting Up DirectMusic

DirectMusic is the first component of DirectX that is totally pure COM (Component
Object Model), meaning that there aren't any helper functions in an import library to
create the COM objects for you. Alas, you must create the COM objects yourself with
calls to the COM library. So the only files any application needs are the DirectMusic
header files. There isn't any import .LIB file. The header files are

```
dmksctrl.h
dmusici.h
dmusicc.h
dmusicf.h
```

Just make sure to include these in your applications, and COM will take care of the
rest. Let's take a look at the entire sequence.

Initializing COM

First you have to initialize COM with a call to CoInitialize():

```
// initialize COM
if (FAILED(CoInitialize(NULL)))
    {
    // Terminate the application.
    return(0);
    }   // end if
```

This should happen at the beginning of your application, before you make any direct COM calls. If you have other pure COM calls and already have called it, don't worry about it.

Creating the Performance

The next step is to create the master interface, which is the DirectMusic performance. Creation of this interface will also create an internal `IDirectMusic` interface, but you won't need it, so it's hidden away. To create an interface based on pure COM, use the `CoCreateInstance()` function with the interface ID and the class ID, along with storage for the new interface pointer. Take a look at the following call:

```
// the directmusic performance manager
IDirectMusicPerformance     *dm_perf = NULL;

// create the performance
if (FAILED(CoCreateInstance(CLSID_DirectMusicPerformance,
                            NULL,
                            CLSCTX_INPROC,
                            IID_IDirectMusicPerformance,
                            (void**)&dm_perf)))
   {
   // return null
   return(0);
   } // end if
```

Looks a bit cryptic, but within reason. After this call, `dm_perf` is ready to go and you can make calls to the interface functions. The first call you need to make is to initialize the performance with `IDirectMusicPerformance::Init()`. Here's the prototype for it:

```
HRESULT Init(IDirectMusic** ppDirectMusic,
             LPDIRECTSOUND pDirectSound,
             HWND hWnd);
```

`ppDirectMusic` is the address of the IDirectMusic interface if you explicitly created one. You haven't, so make it `NULL`. `pDirectSound` is a pointer to the IDirectSound object.

This is important, so read carefully: If you want to use DirectSound and DirectMusic together, you must start up DirectSound first and then pass the IDirectSound object in the call to `Init()`. However, if you're using DirectMusic alone, pass NULL and DirectMusic will create an IDirectSound object itself. This is needed because DirectMusic ultimately goes through DirectSound, as shown in Figure 10.14.

FIGURE 10.14
Relationship between
DirectMusic and
DirectSound.

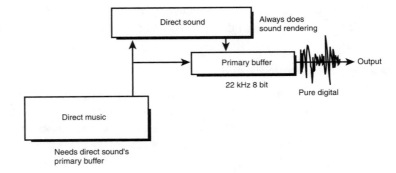

The moral of the story is that you must pass the main DirectSound object pointer, or NULL if you aren't using DirectSound. You'll do the later for illustrative purposes. Finally, you must send the window handle. That's pretty easy—here's the code:

```
// initialize the performance, check if directsound is on-line if so, use
// the directsound object, otherwise create a new one
if (FAILED(dm_perf->Init(NULL, NULL, main_window_handle)))
   {
   return(0);// Failure -- performance not initialized
   } // end if
```

Adding a Port to the Performance

The next step to get DirectMusic up and running is creating a *port* for the digital data to be streamed to. If you like, you can query DirectMusic via enumeration for all valid ports, or you can just use the Microsoft Software Synthesizer as the default. That's my style—keep it simple. To add a port to the performance, use the IDirectMusicPerformance::AddPort(). Its prototype is shown here:

```
HRESULT AddPort(IDirectMusicPort* pPort);
```

Here, pPort is a pointer to a previously created port that you want to play from. However, just use NULL and the default software synthesizer will be used:

```
// add the port to the performance
if (FAILED(dm_perf->AddPort(NULL)))
   {
   return(0);// Failure -- port not initialized
   } // end if
```

Loading a MIDI Segment

The next step in setting up DirectMusic is creating a IDirectMusicLoader object so that you can load your MIDI files. This is accomplished with a low-level COM call again, but it's not bad.

Creating the Loader

The following code creates the loader:

```
// the directmusic loader
IDirectMusicLoader*dm_loader = NULL;

// create the loader to load object(s) such as midi file
if (FAILED(CoCreateInstance(
        CLSID_DirectMusicLoader,
        NULL,
        CLSCTX_INPROC,
        IID_IDirectMusicLoader,
        (void**)&dm_loader)))
    {
    // error
    return(0);
    } // end if
```

Interestingly enough, a number of interfaces have been created internally—including an `IDirectMusic` object and an `IDirectMusicPort` object—and you didn't even know. In most cases, you would never need to make calls to the functions of these interfaces, so it's cool, baby.

Loading the MIDI File

To load the MIDI file, you have to tell the loader where to look and what to look for (type of file), and then tell it to create a segment and load the file into it. I have created a function to do this along with some data structure, so I might as well show it to you now. First, the data structure that's going to hold each musical MIDI segment (DirectMusic likes to call data chunks *segments*) is called `DMUSIC_MIDI` and is shown here:

```
typedef struct DMUSIC_MIDI_TYP
{
IDirectMusicSegment       *dm_segment;  // the directmusic segment
IDirectMusicSegmentState  *dm_segstate; // the state of the segment
int                       id;           // the id of this segment
int                       state;        // state of midi song

} DMUSIC_MIDI, *DMUSIC_MIDI_PTR;
```

This is used to hold each MIDI segment. But you may have more than a few songs for a whole game, so let's make an array of them:

```
DMUSIC_MIDI              dm_midi[DM_NUM_SEGMENTS];
```

Here, `DM_NUM_SEGMENTS` is defined as

```
#define DM_NUM_SEGMENTS 64 // number of midi segments that can be cached in memory
```

Okay, with that all in mind, take a look at the `DMusic_Load_MIDI()` function that follows. It's heavily commented, so take your time, and also pay attention to the funky *wide* character strings that the DirectMusic functions use:

```
int DMusic_Load_MIDI(char *filename)
{
// this function loads a midi segment

DMUS_OBJECTDESC ObjDesc;
HRESULT hr;
IDirectMusicSegment* pSegment = NULL;

int index; // loop var

// look for open slot for midi segment
int id = -1;

for (index = 0; index < DM_NUM_SEGMENTS; index++)
    {
    // is this one open
    if (dm_midi[index].state == MIDI_NULL)
        {
        // validate id, but don't validate object until loaded
        id = index;
        break;
        } // end if

    } // end for index

// found good id?
if (id==-1)
   return(-1);

// get current working directory
char szDir[_MAX_PATH];
WCHAR wszDir[_MAX_PATH];

if(_getcwd( szDir, _MAX_PATH ) == NULL)
  {
  return(-1);;
  } // end if

MULTI_TO_WIDE(wszDir, szDir);

// tell the loader were to look for files
hr = dm_loader->SetSearchDirectory(GUID_DirectMusicAllTypes,
                                   wszDir, FALSE);

if (FAILED(hr))
    {
    return (-1);
    } // end if
```

```
// convert filename to wide string
WCHAR wfilename[_MAX_PATH];
MULTI_TO_WIDE(wfilename, filename);

// setup object description
DD_INIT_STRUCT(ObjDesc);
ObjDesc.guidClass = CLSID_DirectMusicSegment;
wcscpy(ObjDesc.wszFileName, wfilename );
ObjDesc.dwValidData = DMUS_OBJ_CLASS | DMUS_OBJ_FILENAME;

// load the object and query it for the IDirectMusicSegment interface
// This is done in a single call to IDirectMusicLoader::GetObject
// note that loading the object also initializes the tracks and does
// everything else necessary to get the MIDI data ready for playback.

hr = dm_loader->GetObject(&ObjDesc,IID_IDirectMusicSegment,
                          (void**) &pSegment);

if (FAILED(hr))
   return(-1);

// ensure that the segment plays as a standard MIDI file
// you now need to set a parameter on the band track
// Use the IDirectMusicSegment::SetParam method and let
// DirectMusic find the trackby passing -1
// (or 0xFFFFFFFF) in the dwGroupBits method parameter.

hr = pSegment->SetParam(GUID_StandardMIDIFile,-1, 0, 0, (void*)dm_perf);

if (FAILED(hr))
   return(-1);

// This step is necessary because DirectMusic handles program changes and
// bank selects differently for standard MIDI files than it does for MIDI
// content authored specifically for DirectMusic.
// The GUID_StandardMIDIFile parameter must
// be set before the instruments are downloaded.

// The next step is to download the instruments.
// This is necessary even for playing a simple MIDI file
// because the default software synthesizer needs the DLS data
// for the General MIDI instrument set
// If you skip this step, the MIDI file will play silently.
// Again, you call SetParam on the segment,
// this time specifying the GUID_Download parameter:

hr = pSegment->SetParam(GUID_Download, -1, 0, 0, (void*)dm_perf);

if (FAILED(hr))
   return(-1);

// at this point we have MIDI loaded and a valid object
```

```
dm_midi1.dm_segment  = pSegment;
dm_midi1.dm_segstate = NULL;
dm_midi1.state       = MIDI_LOADED;

// return id
return(id);

} // end DMusic_Load_MIDI
```

The function isn't too bad. It basically looks for an open slot in your dm_midi[] array to load the new MIDI segment, sets the search path, creates the segment, loads the segment, and bails. The function takes the filename of the MIDI file and then returns an ID to the array index containing the segment in your data structure.

Manipulating MIDI Segments

A number of interface functions (methods) are available to the IDirectMusicSegment interface that represents a loaded MIDI segment. You can look them up in the SDK if you're interested, but the two functions that should seem most important to you are the ones that play and stop a segment, right? Ironically, these are part of the IDirectMusicPerformance interface rather than the IDirectMusicSegment interface. This makes sense if you think about it: The performance object is like the ringmaster, and everything has to go through him. Like my girlfriend says, "Whatever."

Playing a MIDI Segment

Assuming that you've loaded a segment using the DMusic_Load_MIDI(), or done so manually, let dm_segment be the interface pointer to the segment. Then, to play it with the performance object, use IDirectMusicPerformance::PlaySegment(), prototyped here:

```
HRESULT PlaySegment(
 IDirectMusicSegment* pSegment,  // segment to play
 DWORD dwFlags,                  // control flags
 _int64 i64StartTime,            // when to play
 IDirectMusicSegmentState** ppSegmentState); // state holder
```

In general, set the control flags and start time to 0. The only parameters to worry about are the segment and segment state. Here's an example of playing dm_segment and storing the state in dm_segstate:

```
dm_perf->PlaySegment(dm_segment, 0, 0, &dm_segstate);
```

Here, dm_segstate is of the type IDirectMusicSegmentState and is used to track the segment playing. There is a copy of this in each array element of the dm_midi[], but if you do all this yourself, remember to send one yourself.

Stopping a MIDI Segment

To stop a segment during play, use the `IDirectMusicPerformance::Stop()` function shown here:

```
HRESULT Stop(
  IDirectMusicSegment* pSegment, // segment to stop
  IDirectMusicSegmentState* pSegmentState,   // state
  MUSIC_TIME mtTime,    // when to stop
  DWORD dwFlags);       // control flags
```

Similar to `Play()`, you don't need to worry about most of the parameters, but just the segment itself. Here's an example of stopping `dm_segment`:

```
dm_perf->Stop(dm_segment, NULL, 0, 0);
```

If you want to stop *all* segments that are playing, make `dm_segment` `NULL`.

Checking the Status of a MIDI Segment

Many times you want to know if a song is done playing. To test this, use the `IDirectMusicPerformance::IsPlaying()` function. It simply takes the segment to test and returns `S_OK` if the segment is still playing. Here's an example:

```
if (dm_perf->IsPlaying(dm_segment,NULL) == S_OK)
    { /* still playing */ }
else
    { /* not playing */ }
```

Releasing a MIDI Segment

When you're done with a segment, you have to release the resources. The first step is to unload the DLS instrument data with a call to `IDirectMusicSegment::SetParam()` and then release the interface pointer itself with `Release()`. Here's how:

```
// unload the instrument data
dm_segment->SetParam(GUID_Unload, -1, 0, 0,(void*)dm_perf);

// Release the segment and set to null
dm_segment->Release();
dm_segment  = NULL; // for good measure
```

Shutting Down DirectMusic

When you're all done with DirectMusic, you have to close down and release the performance object, release the loader, and release all the segments (see the preceding code). Finally, you must close down COM unless it's done elsewhere. Here's an example of the process:

```
// If there is any music playing, stop it. This is
// not really necessary, because the music will stop when
// the instruments are unloaded or the performance is
// closed down.
```

```
if (dm_perf)
   dm_perf->Stop(NULL, NULL, 0, 0 );

// *** delete all the midis if they already haven't been

// CloseDown and Release the performance object.
if (dm_perf)
   {
   dm_perf->CloseDown();
   dm_perf->Release();
   } // end if

// Release the loader object.
if (dm_loader)
   dm_loader->Release();

// Release COM
CoUninitialize();
```

A Little DirectMusic Example

As an example of using DirectMusic without DirectSound or any other DirectX component, I have created a program called DEMO10_4.CPP|EXE on the CD. It basically loads a single MIDI file and then plays it. Take a look at it and experiment. When you're done, come back and see how easy all this is with the latest installment of the library, T3DLIB3.CPP|H.

The T3DLIB3 Sound and Music Library

I have taken all the sound and music technology that we've been building and used it to create the next component to your game engine, T3DLIB3. It is composed of two main source files:

- T3DLIB3.CPP—The main C/C++ source
- T3DLIB3.H—The header file

You'll also need to include the DirectSound import library, DSOUND.LIB, to make anything link. However, DirectMusic doesn't have an import library because it's pure COM, so there isn't a DMUSIC.LIB. On the other hand, you still need to point your compiler to the DirectSound and DirectMusic .H header files so it can find them during compilation. Just to remind you, they are

```
DSOUND.H
DMKSCTRL.H
DMUSICI.H
DMUSICC.H
DMUSICF.H
```

With all that in mind, let's take a look at the main elements of the T3DLIB3.H header file.

The Header

The header file T3DLIB3.H contains the types, macros, and externals for T3DLIB3.CPP. Here are the #defines you'll find in the header:

```
// number of midi segments that can be cached in memory
#define DM_NUM_SEGMENTS 64


// midi object state defines
#define MIDI_NULL      0    // this midi object is not loaded
#define MIDI_LOADED    1    // this midi object is loaded
#define MIDI_PLAYING   2    // this midi object is loaded and playing
#define MIDI_STOPPED   3    // this midi object is loaded, but stopped

#define MAX_SOUNDS      256 // max number of sounds in system at once

// digital sound object state defines
#define SOUND_NULL     0 // " "
#define SOUND_LOADED   1
#define SOUND_PLAYING  2
#define SOUND_STOPPED  3
```

Not much for macros; just a macro to help convert from 0–100 to the Microsoft decibels scale and one to convert multibyte characters to wide:

```
#define DSVOLUME_TO_DB(volume) ((DWORD)(-30*(100 - volume)))

// Convert from multibyte format to Unicode using the following macro
#define MULTI_TO_WIDE( x,y )  MultiByteToWideChar( CP_ACP,MB_PRECOMPOSED,
y,-1,x,_MAX_PATH)
```

WARNING The column width of this book is too small to fit the whole macro, so the definition is on two lines. This is a no-no in real life. Macros must be on a single line!

Next are the types for the sound engine.

The Types

First is the DirectSound object. There are only two types for the sound engine: one to hold a digital sample, and the other to hold a MIDI segment:

```
// this holds a single sound
typedef struct pcm_sound_typ
   {
   LPDIRECTSOUNDBUFFER dsbuffer;  // the directsound buffer
                  // containing the sound
   int state;   // state of the sound
   int rate;    // playback rate
   int size;    // size of sound
   int id;      // id number of the sound
   } pcm_sound, *pcm_sound_ptr;
```

And now the DirectMusic segment type:

```
// directmusic MIDI segment
typedef struct DMUSIC_MIDI_TYP
{
IDirectMusicSegment       *dm_segment;  // the directmusic segment
IDirectMusicSegmentState  *dm_segstate; // the state of the segment
int                       id;           // the id of this segment
int                       state;        // state of midi song

} DMUSIC_MIDI, *DMUSIC_MIDI_PTR;
```

Both sounds and MIDI segments, respectively, will be stored by the engine in the preceding two structures. Now let's take a look at the globals.

Global Domination

T3DLIB3 contains a number of globals. Let's take a look. First are the globals for the DirectSound system:

```
LPDIRECTSOUND      lpds;     // directsound interface pointer
DSBUFFERDESC   dsbd;    // directsound description
DSCAPS        dscaps;  // directsound caps
HRESULT        dsresult; // general directsound result
DSBCAPS        dsbcaps; // directsound buffer caps

pcm_sound    sound_fx[MAX_SOUNDS]; // array of sound buffers
WAVEFORMATEX    pcmwf;   // generic waveformat structure
```

And here are the globals for DirectMusic:

```
// direct music globals
// the directmusic performance manager
IDirectMusicPerformance    *dm_perf;
IDirectMusicLoader *dm_loader;  // the directmusic loader

// this hold all the directmusic midi objects
DMUSIC_MIDI dm_midi[DM_NUM_SEGMENTS];
int dm_active_id;   // currently active midi segment
```

NOTE	The highlighted lines show the arrays that hold sounds and MIDI segments.

You shouldn't have to mess with any of these globals, except to access the interfaces directly if you want to do so. In general, the API will handle everything for you, but the globals are there if you want to tear them up.

There are two parts to the library: DirectSound and DirectMusic. Let's take a look at DirectSound first, and then DirectMusic.

The DirectSound API Wrapper

DirectSound can be simple or complicated, depending on how you use it. If you want a "do it all" API, you're going to end up using most of the DirectSound functions themselves. But if you want a simpler API that allows you to initialize DirectSound and load and play sounds of a specific format, that's a lot easier to wrap up into a few functions.

So what I've done is take much of your work in the DirectSound part of this chapter and formalize it into functions for you. In addition, I've created an abstraction around the sound system, so you refer to a sound with an ID (same for the DirectMusic part) that is given to you during the loading process. Thus, you can use this ID to play the sound, check its status, or terminate it. This way there aren't any ugly interface pointers that you have to mess with. The new API supports the following functionality:

- Initializing and shutting down DirectSound with single calls.
- Loading .WAV files with 11 KHz 8-bit mono format.
- Playing a loaded sound file.
- Stopping a sound.
- Testing the play status of a sound.
- Changing the volume, playback rate, or stereo panning of a sound.
- Deleting sounds from memory.

Let's take a look at each function one by one.

> **NOTE** Unless otherwise stated, all functions return TRUE (1) if successful and FALSE (0) if not.

Function Prototype:

```
int DSound_Init(void);
```

Purpose:

DSound_Init() initializes the entire DirectSound system. It creates the DirectSound COM object, sets the priority level, and so forth. Just call the function at the beginning of your application if you want to use sound. Here's an example:

```
if (!DSound_Init(void))
   { /* error */ }
```

Function Prototype:

```
int DSound_Shutdown(void);
```

Purpose:

`DSound_Shutdown()` shuts down and releases all the COM interfaces created during `DSound_Init()`. However, `DSound_Shutdown()` will not release all the memory allocated to all the sounds. You must do this yourself with another function. Anyway, here's how you would shut down DirectSound:

```
if (!DSound_Shutdown())
    { /* error */ }
```

Function Prototype:

```
int DSound_Load_WAV(char *filename);
```

Purpose:

`DSound_Load_WAV()` creates a DirectSound buffer, loads the sound data file into memory, and prepares the sound to be played. The function takes the complete path and filename of the sound file to be loaded (including the extension `.WAV`) and loads the file from the disk. If successful, the function returns a non-negative ID number. You must save this number because it is used as a handle to reference the sound. If the function can't find the file, or too many sounds are loaded, it will return -1. Here's an example of loading a `.WAV` file named `FIRE.WAV`:

```
int fire_id = DSound_Load_WAV("FIRE.WAV");

// test for error
if (fire_id==-1)
    { /* error */}
```

Of course, it's up to you how you want to save the IDs. You might want to use an array or something else.

Finally, you might wonder where the sound data is and how to mess with it. If you really must, you can access the data within the `pcm_sound` array `sound_fx[]`, using the ID you get back from either load function as the index. For example, here's how you would access the DirectSound buffer for the sound with ID `sound_id`:

```
sound_fx[sound_id].dsbuffer
```

Function Prototype:

```
int DSound_Replicate_Sound(int source_id); // id of sound to copy
```

Purpose:

`DSound_Replicate_Sound()` is used to copy a sound without copying the memory used to hold the sound. For example, let's say you have a gunshot sound and you want to fire three gunshots, one right after another. The only way to do this right now would be to load three copies of the gunshot sound into three different DirectSound memory buffers, which would be a waste of memory.

Alas, there is a solution—it's possible to create a duplicate (or replicant, if you're a *Blade Runner* fan) of the sound buffer, excluding for the actual sound data. Instead of copying it, you just point a pointer to it, and DirectSound is smart enough to be used as a "source" for multiple sounds using the same data. If you wanted to play a gunshot up to eight times, for example, you would load the gunshot once, make seven copies of it, and acquire a total of eight unique IDs. Replicated sounds work exactly the same as normal sounds, except that instead of using DSound_Load_WAV() to load and create them, you copy them with DSound_Replicate_Sound(). Get it? Good! I'm starting to get dizzy! Here's an example of creating eight gunshots:

```
int gunshot_ids[8]; // this holds all the id's

// load in the master sound
gunshot_ids[0] = Load_WAV("GUNSHOT.WAV");

// now make copies
for (int index=1; index<8; index++)
    gunshot_ids[index] = DSound_Replicate_Sound(gunshot_ids[0]);

// use gunshot_ids[0..7] anyway you wish, they all go bang!
```

Function Prototype:

```
int DSound_Play_Sound(int id,       // id of sound to play
                      int flags=0,  // 0 or DSBPLAY_LOOPING
                      int volume=0, // unused
                      int rate=0,   // unused
                      int pan=0);   // unused
```

Purpose:

DSound_Play_Sound() plays a previously loaded sound. You simply send the ID of the sound along with the play flags—0 for a single sound, or DSBPLAY_LOOPING to loop—and the sound will start playing. And if the sound is already playing, it will restart at the beginning. Here's an example of loading and playing a sound:

```
int fire_id = DSound_Load_WAV("FIRE.WAV");
DSound_Play_Sound(fire_id,0);
```

Or, you can leave out the 0 for flags entirely because its default parameter is 0:

```
int fire_id = DSound_Load_WAV("FIRE.WAV");
DSound_Play_Sound(fire_id);
```

Either way the FIRE.WAV sound will play once and then stop. To make it loop, send DSBPLAY_LOOPING for the flags parameter.

Function Prototype:

```
int DSound_Stop_Sound(int id);
int DSound_Stop_All_Sounds(void);
```

Purpose:

DSound_Stop_Sound() is used to stop a single sound from playing (if it's playing already). You simply send the ID of the sound and that's it. DSound_Stop_All_Sounds() will stop all the sounds currently playing. Here's an example of stopping the fire_id sound:

```
DSound_Stop_Sound(fire_id);
```

And at the end of your program, it's a good idea to stop all the sounds from playing before exiting. You could do this with separate calls to DSound_Stop_Sound() for each sound, or a single call to DSound_Stop_All_Sounds(), like this:

```
//...system shutdown code
DSound_Stop_All_Sounds();
```

Function Prototype:

```
int DSound_Delete_Sound(int id); // id of sound to delete
int DSound_Delete_All_Sounds(void);
```

Purpose:

DSound_Delete_Sound() deletes a sound from memory and releases the DirectSound buffer associated with it. If the sound is playing, the function will stop it first. DSound_Delete_All_Sounds() deletes all previously loaded sounds. Here's an example of deleting the fire_id sound:

```
DSound_Delete_Sound(fire_id);
```

Function Prototype:

```
int DSound_Status_Sound(int id);
```

Purpose:

DSound_Status_Sound() tests the status of a loaded sound based on its ID. All you do is pass the ID number of the sound to the function, and the function will return one of these values:

- DSBSTATUS_LOOPING—The sound is currently playing and is in loop mode.
- DSBSTATUS_PLAYING—The sound is currently playing and is in single-play mode.

If the value returned from DSound_Status_Sound() is neither of the these constants, the sound is not playing. Here's a complete example that waits until a sound has finished playing and then deletes it:

```
// initialize DirectSound
DSound_DSound_Init();
```

```
// load a sound
int fire_id = DSound_Load_WAV("FIRE.WAV");

// play the sound in single mode
DSound_Play_Sound(fire_id);

// wait until the sound is done
while(DSound_Sound_Status(fire_id) &
            (DSBSTATUS_LOOPING | DSBSTATUS_PLAYING));

// delete the sound
DSound_Delete_Sound(fire_id);

// shutdown DirectSound
DSound_DSound_Shutdown();
```

Pretty cool, huh? A lot better than the couple hundred or so lines of code required to do it manually with DirectSound!

Function Prototype:

```
int DSound_Set_Sound_Volume(int id,    // id of sound
                        int vol); // volume from 0-100
```

Purpose:

DSound_Set_Sound_Volume() changes the volume of a sound in real-time. Send the ID of the sound, along with a value from 0–100, and the sound will change instantly. Here's an example of reducing the volume of a sound to 50 percent of what it was loaded as:

```
DSound_Set_Sound_Volume(fire_id, 50);
```

You can always change the volume back to 100 percent, like this:

```
DSound_Set_Sound_Volume(fire_id, 100);
```

Function Prototype:

```
int DSound_Set_Sound_Freq(
            int id,    // sound id
            int freq); // new playback rate from 0-100000
```

Purpose:

DSound_Set_Sound_Freq() changes the playback frequency of the sound. Because all sounds must be loaded at 11 KHz mono, here's how you would double the perceived playback rate:

```
DSound_Set_Sound_Freq(fire_id, 22050);
```

And to make you sound like Darth Vader, do this:

```
DSound_Set_Sound_Freq(fire_id, 6000);
```

Function Prototype:

```
int DSound_Set_Sound_Pan(
    int id,    // sound id
    int pan); // panning value from -10000 to 10000
```

Purpose:

DSound_Set_Sound_Pan() sets the relative intensity of the sound on the right and left speakers. A value of -10,000 is hard left, and 10,000 is hard right. If you want equal power, set the pan to 0. Here's how you would set the pan all the way to the right side:

```
DSound_Set_Sound_Pan(fire_id, 10000);
```

The DirectMusic API Rapper—Get It?

The DirectMusic API is even simpler than the DirectSound API. I have created functions to initialize DirectMusic and created all the COM objects for you to allow you to focus on loading and playing MIDI files. Here's the basic functionality list:

- Initializing and shutting down DirectMusic with single calls.
- Loading MIDI files from disk.
- Playing a MIDI file.
- Stopping a MIDI that is currently playing.
- Testing the play status of a MIDI segment.
- Automatically connecting to DirectSound if it's already initialized.
- Deleting MIDI segments from memory.

Let's take a look at each function one by one.

NOTE	Unless otherwise stated, all functions return TRUE (1) if successful and FALSE (0) if not.

Function Prototype:

```
int DMusic_Init(void);
```

Purpose:

DMusic_Init() initializes DirectMusic and creates all necessary COM objects. You make this call before any other calls to the DirectMusic library. In addition, if you want to use DirectSound, make sure to initialize DirectSound before calling DMusic_Init(). Here's an example of using the function:

```
if (!DMusic_Init())
    { /* error */ }
```

Function Prototype:

```
int DMusic_Shutdown(void);
```

Purpose:

DMusic_Shutdown() shuts down the entire DirectMusic engine. It releases all COM objects in addition to unloading all loaded MIDI segments. Call this function at the end of your application, but before the call to shut down DirectSound (if you have DirectSound support). Here's an example:

```
if (!DMusic_Shutdown())
    { /* error */ }

// now shutdown DirectSound…
```

Function Prototype:

```
int DMusic_Load_MIDI(char *filename);
```

Purpose:

DMusic_Load_MIDI() loads a MIDI segment into memory and allocates a record in the midi_ids[] array. The function returns the ID of the loaded MIDI segment, or -1 if unsuccessful. The returned ID is used as a reference for all other calls. Here's an example of loading a couple MIDI files:

```
// load files
int explode_id = DMusic_Load_MIDI("explosion.mid");
int weapon_id  = DMusic_Load_MIDI("laser.mid");

// test files
if (explode_id == -1 || weapon_id == -1)
    { /* there was a problem */ }
```

Function Prototype:

```
int DMusic_Delete_MIDI(int id);
```

Purpose:

DMusic_Delete_MIDI() deletes a previously loaded MIDI segment from the system. Simply supply the ID to delete. Here's an example of deleting the previously loaded MIDI files in the preceding example:

```
if (!DMusic_Delete_MIDI(explode_id) ||
    !DMusic_Delete_MIDI(weapon_id) )
{ /* error */ }
```

Function Prototype:

```
int DMusic_Delete_All_MIDI(void);
```

Purpose:

`DMusic_Delete_All_MIDI()` simply deletes all MIDI segments from the system in one call. Here's an example:

```
// delete both of our segments
if (!DMusic_Delete_All_MIDI())
    { /* error */ }
```

Function Prototype:

```
int DMusic_Play(int id);
```

Purpose:

`DMusic_Play()` plays a MIDI segment from the beginning. Simply supply the ID of the segment you want to play. Here's an example:

```
// load file
int explode_id = DMusic_Load_MIDI("explosion.mid");

// play it
if (!DMusic_Play(explode_id))
    { /* error */ }
```

Function Prototype:

```
int DMusic_Stop(int id);
```

Purpose:

`DMusic_Stop()` stops a currently playing segment. If the segment is already stopped, the function has no effect. Here's an example:

```
// stop the laser blast
if (!DMusic_Stop(weapon_id))
    { /* error */ }
```

Function Prototype:

```
int DMusic_Status_MIDI(int id);
```

Purpose:

`DMusic_Status()` tests the status of any MIDI segment based on its ID. The status codes are

```
#define MIDI_NULL      0    // this midi object is not loaded
#define MIDI_LOADED    1    // this midi object is loaded
#define MIDI_PLAYING   2    // this midi object is loaded and playing
#define MIDI_STOPPED   3    // this midi object is loaded, but stopped
```

Here's an example of changing state based on a MIDI segment completing:

```
// main game loop
while(1)
```

```
   {
   if (DMusic_Status(explode_id) == MIDI_STOPPED)
      game_state = GAME_MUSIC_OVER;

   } // end while
```

For a demo of using the library, check out DEMO10_5.CPP|EXE and DEMO10_6.CPP|EXE. The first program is a demo of DirectMusic using the new library, which allows you to pick a MIDI file from a menu and instantly play it. The second demo is a mixed-mode application that uses both DirectSound and DirectMusic at the same time. The important detail of the second demo is that DirectSound must be initialized first. The sound library detects this and then connects to DirectSound. Otherwise, the sound library would create its own DirectSound object.

 Both DEMO10_5.CPP and DEMO10_6.CPP use external cursor, icon, and menu resources contained in DEMO10_5.RC and DEMO10_6.RC, respectively. So make sure to include these files in the projects when you're trying to compile. And you need to include T3DLIB3.CPP|H to compile, but you knew that!

Summary

This chapter has covered a lot of ground. You learned a bit about the nature of sound and music, how synthesis works, and how to record sound. Then you learned about DirectSound and DirectMusic, created a library, and saw a lot of demos. I would have loved to have gone into DirectSound3D, not to mention more advanced DirectMusic, but that's up to you. Now you know everything you need to make a game, and that's the mission for the next chapter!

PART III

Hardcore Game Programming

Algorithms, Data Structures, Memory Management, and Multithreading

"You think I can get a hug after this?"
—Bear, Armageddon

This chapter is going to talk about all those little details that slip through the cracks in any game programming book (even mine). We're going to discuss everything from writing games so they can be saved, to making demos, to optimization theory! This chapter will help you with some of those lingering details. Then, when we cover artificial intelligence in the next chapter, you should have all the general game programming concepts under control so the 3D math doesn't make you crack!

Here's what's in store in this chapter:

- Data structures
- Algorithm analysis
- Optimization theory
- Mathematical tricks

- Mixed-language programming
- Saving games
- Implementing multiple players
- Multithreaded programming techniques

Data Structures

Probably one of the most frequent questions I'm asked is, "What kind of data structures should be used in a game?" The answer is: the fastest and most efficient data structures possible. However, in most cases you won't need the most advanced, complex data structures that computer science has to offer. Rather, you should try to keep things simple. And speed is more important than memory these days, so you should sacrifice memory before you sacrifice speed!

With that in mind, I want to take a look at a few of the most common data structures used in games and give you some insight into when and how to use them.

Static Structures and Arrays

The most basic of all data structures is, of course, a single occurrence of a data item such as a single structure or class. For example:

```
typedef struct PLAYER_TYP // tag for forward references
        {
        int state; // state of player
        int x,y; // position of player
        // ...
        } PLAYER, *PLAYER_PTR;
```

In C++, you no longer need to use `typedef` on structure definitions to create a type; a type is automatically created for you when you use the keyword `struct`. In addition, C++ `struct`s can have methods and even public and private sections.

```
PLAYER player_1, player_2; // create a couple players
```

In this case, a single data structure along with two statically defined records does the job. On the other hand, if there were three or more players, it would probably be a good idea to use an array like this:

```
PLAYER players[MAX_PLAYERS]; // the players of the game
```

Here you can process all the players with a simple loop. Okay, great, but what if you don't know how many players or records there are going to be until the game runs?

When this situation arises, I figure out the maximum number of elements that the array would have to hold. If it's reasonably small number, like 256 or less, and each element is also reasonably small (less than 256 bytes), I will usually statically allocate it and use a counter to count how many of the elements are active at any time.

You may think that this is a waste of memory, and it is, but a preallocated array of a fixed size is easier and faster to traverse than a linked list or more dynamic structure. The point is, if you know the number of elements ahead of time and there aren't that many of them, go ahead and preallocate an array statically by making a call to `malloc()` or `new()` during startup.

 WARNING | Don't get carried away with static arrays. For example, if you have a structure that is 4KB and there may be from 1 to 256 static arrays, you definitely need a better strategy than allocating 1MB in case there may be 256 of them at some point. In this case, it might be better to use a linked list or to dynamically reallocate the array and increase its size on demand.

Linked Lists

Arrays are fine for simple data structures that can be precounted or estimated at compilation or startup, but data structures that can grow or shrink during run-time should use some form of *linked lists*. Figure 11.1 depicts a standard abstract linked list. A linked list consists of a number of nodes, each node containing information and a link to the next node in the list.

FIGURE 11.1
A linked list.

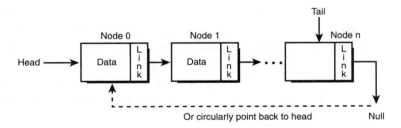

Linked lists are cool because you can insert a node anywhere in the list, and you can delete a node from anywhere in the list. Take a look at Figure 11.2 to see this graphically. The capability to insert and delete nodes (and hence, information) during run-time makes linked lists very attractive as data structures for games.

Hardcore Game Programming

FIGURE 11.2
Inserting into a
linked list.

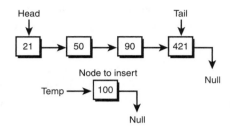

A. Before insertion

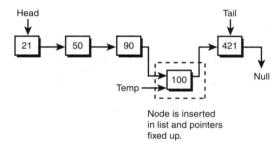

B. After insertion (in order)

The only bad thing about linked lists is that you must traverse them node by node to find what you're looking for (unless other secondary data structures are created to help with the searching). For example, say that you want the 15th element in an array. You would access it like this:

```
players[15]
```

But with linked lists, you need a traversal algorithm to traverse the list to find the 15th element. This means that the searching of linked lists can take a number of iterations equal to the length of the list (in the worst case). That is, $O(n)$—read "Big O of n." This means that there are *on the order of* n *operations* for n elements. Of course, there are optimizations and secondary data structures that you can employ to maintain a sorted indexed list that allows access almost as fast as the simple array.

Creating a Linked List

Let's take a look at how you would create a simple linked list, add a node, delete a node, and search for an item with a given key. Here's the basic node:

```
typedef struct NODE_TYP
    {
    int id;        // id number of this object
    int age;       // age of person
    char name[32]; // name of person
    NODE_TYP *next; // this is the link to the next node
                    // more fields go here
    } NODE, *NODE_PTR;
```

To start the list off, you need a *head* pointer and a *tail* pointer that point to the head and tail of the list, respectively. However, the list is empty, so the pointers start off pointing to NULL:

```
NODE_PTR    head = NULL,
            tail = NULL;
```

> **NOTE** Some programmers like to start off a linked list with a *dummy* node that's always empty. This is mostly a choice of taste. However, this changes some of the initial conditions of the creation, insertion, and deletion algorithms, so you might want to try it.

Traversing a Linked List

Ironically, traversing a linked list is the easiest of all operations:

1. Start at the head pointer.
2. Visit the node.
3. Link to the next node.
4. If it's not NULL, repeat step 2.

And here's the code:

```
void Traverse_List(NODE_PTR head)
{
// this function traverses the linked list and prints out
// each node

// test if head is null
if (head==NULL)
    {
    printf("\nLinked List is empty!");
    return;
    } // end if

// traverse while nodes
while (head!=NULL)
        {
        // visit the node, print it out, or whatever...
        printf("\nNode Data: id=%d", head->id);
        printf("\nage=%d,head->age);
        printf("\nname=%s\n",head->name);

        // advance to next node (simple!)
        head = head->next;
        } // end while

print("\n");

} // end Traverse_List
```

Pretty cool, huh? Next, let's take a look at how you would add a node.

Adding a Node

The first step in adding a node is creating it. There are two ways to approach this: You could send the new data elements to the insertion function and let it build up a new node, or you could build up a new node and then pass it to the insertion function. Either way is basically the same.

Furthermore, there are a number of ways to insert a node into a linked list. The brute-force method is to add it to the front or the end. This fine if you don't care about the order, but if you want the list to remain sorted, you should use a more intelligent insertion algorithm that maintains either ascending or descending order—an insertion sort of sorts. This will make searching much faster.

For simplicity's sake, I'm going to take the easy way out and insert at the end of the list, but inserting with sorting is not that much more complex. You first need to scan the list, find where the new element should be inserted, and insert it. The only problem is keeping track of the pointers and not losing anything.

Anyway, here's the code to insert a new node at the end of the list (a bit harder than inserting at the front of the list). Notice the special cases for empty lists and lists with a single element:

```
// access the global head and tail to make code easier
// in real life, you might want to use ** pointers and
// modify head and tail in the function ???

NODE_PTR Insert_Node(int id, int age, char *name)
{
// this function inserts a node at the end of the list
NODE_PTR new_node = NULL;

// step 1: create the new node
new_node = (NODE_PTR)malloc(sizeof(NODE)); // in C++ use new operator

// fill in fields
new_node->id  = id;
new_node->age = age;
strcpy(new_node->name,name); // memory must be copied!
new_node->next = NULL; // good practice

// step 2: what is the current state of the linked list?

if (head==NULL) // case 1
   {
   // empty list, simplest case
   head = tail = new_node;

   // return new node
   return(new_node);
```

```
    } // end if
else
if ((head != NULL) && (head==tail)) // case 2
    {
    // there is exactly one element, just a little
    // finesse...
    head->next = new_node;
    tail = new_node;

    // return new node
    return(new_node);
    } // end if
else // case 3
    {
    // there are 2 or more elements in list
    // simply move to end of the list and add
    // the new node
    tail->next = new_node;
    tail = new_node;

    // return the new node
    return(new_node);
    } // end else

} // end Insert_Node
```

As you can see, the code is rather simple. But it's easy to mess up because you're dealing with pointers, so be careful! Also, the astute programmer will very quickly realize that with a little thought, cases two and three can be combined, but the code here is easier to follow. Now let's remove a node.

Deleting a Node

Deleting a node is more complex than inserting a node because pointers and memory have to be shuffled. The problem with deletion is that, in most cases, you want to delete a specific node. The node might be at the head, tail, or middle, so you must write a very general algorithm that takes all these cases into consideration. If you're careful, deletion isn't a problem. If you don't take all the cases into consideration and test them, though, you'll be sorry!

In general, the algorithm must search the linked list for the key in question, remove the node from the list, and release its memory. In addition, the algorithm has to fix up the pointers that pointed to the node and that the node pointed to. Take a look at Figure 11.3 to see this.

FIGURE 11.3
Removing a node
from a linked list.

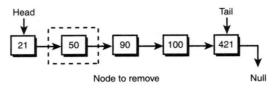

A. Before removal of key "50"

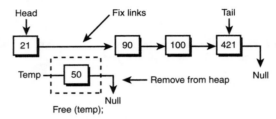

B. After removal of key "50"

In any event, here's the code that implements the deletion based on removing the node with key ID:

```
// again this function will modify the globals
// head and tail (possibly)

int Delete_Node(int id) // node to delete
{
// this function deletes a node from
// the linked list given its id
NODE_PTR curr_ptr = head, // used to search the list
         prev_ptr = head; // previous record

// test if there is a linked list to delete from
if (!head)
    return(-1);

// traverse the list and find node to delete
while(curr_ptr->id != id && curr_ptr)
    {
    // save this position
    prev_ptr = curr_ptr;
    curr_ptr = curr_ptr->next;
    } // end while

// at this point we have found the node
// or the end of the list
if (curr_ptr == NULL)
    return(-1); // couldn't find record
```

```
// record was found, so delete it, but be careful,
// need to test cases
// case 1: one element
if (head==tail)
   {
   // delete node
   free(head);

   // fix up pointers
   head=tail=NULL;

   // return id of deleted node
   return(id);
   } // end if
else // case 2: front of list
if (curr_ptr == head)
   {
   // move head to next node
   head=head->next;

   // delete the node
   free(curr_ptr);

   // return id of deleted node
   return(id);

   } // end if
else // case 3: end of list
if (curr_ptr == tail)
   {
   // fix up previous pointer to point to null
   prev_ptr->next = NULL;

   // delete the last node
   free(curr_ptr);

   // point tail to previous node
   tail = prev_ptr;

   // return id of deleted node
   return(id);

   } // end if
else  // case 4: node is in middle of list
   {
   // connect the previous node to the next node
   prev_ptr->next = curr_ptr->next;

   // now delete the current node
   free(curr_ptr);

   // return id of deleted node
   return(id);
```

```
        } // end else

    } // end Delete_Node
```

Note that there are a lot of special cases in the code. Each case is simple, but you have to think of everything—which I hope I did!

Finally, you may have noticed the dramarama involved with deleting nodes from the interior of the list. This is due to the fact that once a node is traversed, you can't get back to it. Hence, I had to keep track of a previous NODE_PTR to keep track of the last node. This problem, along with others, can be solved by using a *doubly linked list,* as shown in Figure 11.4.

FIGURE 11.4
A doubly linked list.

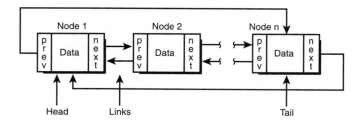

The cool things about doubly linked lists are that you can traverse them in both directions from any point and insertions and deletions are much easier. And the only change to the data structure is another link field, as shown here:

```
typedef struct NODE_TYP
    {
    int id;        // id number of this object
    int age;       // age of person
    char name[32]; // name of person
    // more fields go here
    NODE_TYP *next; // link to the next node
    NODE_TYP *prev; // link to previous node

    } NODE, *NODE_PTR;
```

With a doubly linked list, you always move forward or backward from any node, so the tracking code is simplified for insertions and deletions. For an example of implementing a simple linked list, take a look at the console application DEMO11_1.CPP|EXE. It allows you to add, delete, and traverse a linked list.

NOTE

DEMO11_1.CPP is a console application, rather than the standard Windows .EXE application that you've been working with, so make sure to set the compiler for Console Application before trying to compile it. And obviously, there is no DirectX, so you don't need any of the DirectX .LIB files.

Algorithmic Analysis

Algorithm design and algorithmic analysis are usually senior-level computer science material. However, we can at least touch upon some common-sense techniques and ideas to help you when you start writing more complex algorithms.

First, a good algorithm is better than all the assembly language or optimization in the world. For example, you saw that just changing the order of your data can reduce the amount of time it takes to search for a data element by orders of magnitude. So the moral of the story is to select a solid algorithm that fits the problem and the data, but at the same time to pick a data structure that can be accessed and manipulated with a good algorithm.

For example, if you always use linear arrays, you're never going to get better than linear search time (unless you use secondary data structures). But if you use sorted arrays, you can get logarithmic search time.

The first step in writing good algorithms is having some clue about how to analyze them. The art of analyzing algorithms is called *asymptotic analysis* and is usually calculus-based. I'm not go to go into it too much, but I'll skim some of the concepts.

The basic idea of analyzing an algorithm is computing how many times the main loop is executed for n elements, whatever n happens to be. This is the most important idea. Of course, how long it takes for each execution, plus the overhead of setup, can also be important once you have a good algorithm, but the place to start is the general counting of how many times the loop executes. Let's take a look at two examples:

```
for (int index=0; index<n; index++)
    {
    // do work, 50 cycles
    } // end for index
```

In this case, the loop is going to execute for n iterations, so the execution time is of the order n, or $O(n)$. This is called *Big O notation* and is an upper bound, or very rough upper estimate, of execution time. Anyway, if you want to be more precise, you know that the inner computation takes 50 cycles, so the total execution time is

```
n*50 cycles
```

Right? Wrong! If you're going to count cycles, you'd better count the cycles that it takes for the loop itself. This consists of an initialization of a variable, a comparison, and increment, and a jump each iteration. Adding these gives you something like this:

$$Cycles_{initialization}+(50+Cycles_{inc}+Cycles_{comp}+Cycles_{jump})*n$$

This is a much better estimate. Of course, $Cycles_{inc}$, $Cycles_{comp}$, and $Cycles_{jump}$ are the number of cycles for the increment, comparison, and jump, respectively, and are each around 1-2 on a Pentium-class processor. Therefore, in this case the loop itself contributes just as much to the overall time of the inner loop as the work the loop does! This is a key point.

For example, many game programmers write a pixel-plotting function as a function instead of a macro or inline code. Because a pixel-plotting function is so simple, the call to the function takes more time than the pixel plotting! So make sure that you do enough work in your loop to warrant one, and that the work "drowns out" the loop mechanics themselves.

Now let's see another example that has a much worse running time than n:

```
// outer loop
for (i=0; i<n; i++)
    {
    // inner loop
    for (j=1; j<2*n; j++)
     {
        // do work
      } // end for j
    } // end for i
```

This time, I'm assuming the work part takes much more time than the actual code that supports the loop mechanics, so I'm not interested in it. What I *am* interested in is how many times this loop executes. The outer loop executes n times and the inner loop executes 2*n-1 times, so the total amount of time the inner code will be executed is

```
n*(2*n-1) = 2*n2-n
```

Let's look at this for a moment, because there are two terms. The $2*n^2$ term is the dominate term and will drown out the n term as n gets large. Take a look at Figure 11.5 to see this.

For a small n, say 2, the n term *is* relevant:

```
2*(2)2 - 2 = 6
```

In this case, the n term contributes to subtracting 25 percent of the total time away, but take a look when n gets large. For example, n = 1000:

```
2*(1000)2 - 1000 = 1999000
```

In this case, the n term contributes a decrease of only .05 percent; hardly important. You can see that the dominant term is indeed the $2*n^2$ term, or more simply the n^2 itself. Hence, this algorithm is $O(n^2)$. This is very bad. Algorithms that run in n^2 time will just kill you, so if you come up with an algorithm like this, try, try again!

That's it for asymptotic analysis. The bottom line is that you must be able to roughly estimate the run-time of your loops, which will help you pick out the algorithms and recode areas that need work.

FIGURE 11.5

Rates of growth for the term of 2*n2-n.

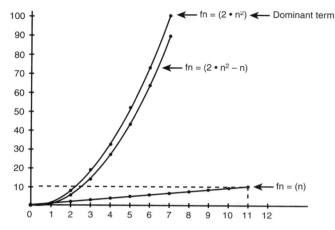

n	n	2 • n²	2 • n² − n
0	0	0	0
1	1	2	1
2	2	8	6
3	3	18	15
4	4	32	28
5	5	50	45
6	6	72	66
7	7	98	91
8	8	128	120
9	9	102	153
10	10	200	190

Recursion

The next subject I want to talk about is *recursion*—did you just get a stomach ache? This may or may not be familiar to you. Recursion is simply a technique of solving a problem by induction—sorta. The basis of recursion is that many problems can be broken down into simpler problems of the same form, until at some point you can actually solve the problem. Then you assemble the large problem by combining the smaller problems. Sounds good, huh?

In computer programming, we usually use recursive algorithms for searching, sorting, and some mathematical operations. The premise is simple: You write a function that has the potential to call itself to solve the problem. Sound weird? Well, the key is that when a function calls itself, a new set of local variables are created on the stack, so it's really like another function is being called. The only things you have to worry about are that the function doesn't overflow the stack and that there is a terminal case at which the function terminates, whereby it can "unwind" the stack via multiple return()s. Let's jump into it with a standard example: the computation of a *factorial*.

The factorial of a number written as n! ("n bang") has the following meaning:

```
n! = n*(n-1)*(n-2)*(n-3)*...(2)*(1)
```

And 0! = 1! = 1,

Thus, 5! is 5*4*3*2*1.

Let's code this the normal way:

```
// assume integers
int Factorial(int n)
{
int sum = 1; // hold result

// accumulate product
while(n >= 1)
    {
    sum*=n;

    // decrement n
    n--;

    } // end while

// return the result
return(sum);

} // end Factorial
```

Looks pretty basic. If you send in a 0 or 1, you get 1. If you send it a 3, the following sequence occurs:

```
sum = sum * 3 = 1 * 3 = 3
sum = sum * 2 = 3 * 2 = 6
sum = sum * 1 = 6 * 1 = 6
```

Which is correct because 3! = 3*2*1.

Now here's the recursive version:

```
int Factorial_Rec(int n)
{
// test for terminal cases
if (n==0 || n==1) return(1);
else
    return(n*Factorial_Rec(n-1));

} // end Factorial_Rec
```

Tell me that isn't cool, my little leprechaun! So let's see what happens here when n is equal to 0 or 1. In these cases, the first if statement is TRUE, 1 is returned, and the function exits. But the cool stuff happens when n > 1. In this case, the else executes and the value returned is n times the function itself called with (n-1). This is recursion.

The state of the current function's variables remains on the stack, and the call is made to the function again as if it were another function with a new working set of variables. The code of the first `return` statement can't be completed until another call is made, and that `return` can't be completed until that call is made, and so on, until the terminal *case* is hit.

With that in mind, let's take a look at the n = 3 case with actual numbers replacing the variable n each iteration:

1. Initial Call to `Factorial_Rec(3)`

   The function falls to the `return` statement:

   ```
   return(3*Factorial_Rec(2));
   ```

2. Second call to `Factorial_Rec(2)`

   The function again falls to the `return` statement:

   ```
   return(2*Factorial_Rec(1));
   ```

3. Third call to `Factorial_Rec(1)`

   This time the terminal case is true and a 1 is returned:

   ```
   return(1);
   ```

Now for the magic. The 1 is returned to the second call of `Factorial_Rec()` that looked like this:

```
return(2*Factorial_Rec(1));
```

This resolves to

```
return(2*1);
```

This then returns to the first call of `Factorial_Rec()` that looked like this:

```
return(3*Factorial_Rec(2));
```

This resolves to

```
return(3*2);
```

And presto, the function can finally return with 6—which is indeed 3! That's recursion. Now, you might ask which method is better—recursion or non-recursion? Obviously, the straightforward method is faster because there aren't any function calls or stack manipulation, but the recursive way is more elegant and better reflects the problem. This is the reason why we use recursion. Some algorithms are recursive in nature, trying to write non-recursive algorithms is tedious, and in the end they become recursive simulations that use stacks themselves! So use recursion if it's appropriate and simplifies the problem. Otherwise, use straight linear code.

For an example of recursion, take a look at DEMO11_2.CPP|EXE. It implements the factorial algorithm. Note how quickly factorial can overflow! See if the computer can beat your calculator's max factorial. Most calculators can compute up to 69! No lie.

MATH For you math people, try implementing a recursive Fibonacci algorithm. Remember, the nth Fibonacci number $f_n = f_{n-1} + f_{n-2}$, $f_0=0$, and $f_1=1$. Hence, $f_2 = f_1 + f_0 = 1 + 0 = 1$, and $f_3 = f_2 + f_1 = 1 + 1 = 2$. Therefore, the Fibonacci sequence looks like 0, 1, 1, 2, 3, 5, 8, 13... Count the number of seeds in each of the consecutive rings of a sunflower plant, and they will be the Fibonacci sequence!

Trees

The next class of advanced data structures, *trees*, are processed by recursive algorithms, so that's why I took the preceding detour. Anyway, take a look at Figure 11.6 to see a number of different tree-like data structures.

Trees were invented to help with the storage and searching of large amounts of data. The most popular kind of tree is the binary tree, AKA B-tree or BST (Binary Search Tree), a tree data structure emanating from a single root that is composed of a collection of nodes. Each node has one or two children nodes (siblings) descending from it; hence the term *binary*. Moreover, we can talk of the *order* or number of levels of a tree, meaning how many layers it has. The B-trees in Figure 11.7 are shown with their various orders.

FIGURE 11.6
Some tree topologies.

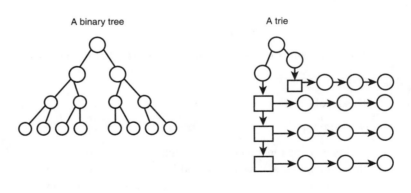

FIGURE 11.7
Some binary trees and
their orders.

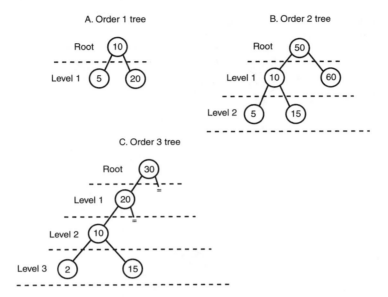

The interesting thing about trees is how fast the information can be searched. Most B-trees use a single search key to order the data. Then a searching algorithm searches the tree for the data. For example, say you wanted to create a B-tree that contained records of game objects, each with a number of properties. You could use the time of creation as the key, or you could make each node represent a person in a database. Here's the data structure that you would use to hold a single person node:

```
typedef struct TNODE_TYP
    {
    int age;        // age of person
    char name[32];  // name of person
    NODE_TYP *right; // link to right node
    NODE_TYP *left;  // link to left node
    } TNODE, *TNODE_PTR;
```

Notice the similarity between the tree node and the linked list node! The only difference is the way you use the data structure and build up the tree. Continuing with the example, let's say that you have five objects (people) with the following ages: 5, 25, 3, 12, and 10. Figure 11.8 depicts two different B-trees that contain this data. However, there are more you could create that would maintain the properties of a B-tree depending on the order that the data is presented to the insertion algorithm.

NOTE   Of course, the data in this example can be anything you want.

FIGURE 11.8
B-tree encoding
of data set
age{5,25,3,12,10}.

A. One possible tree

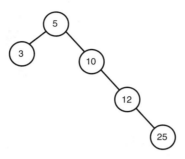

B. Another possible tree

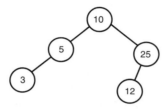

Notice that I have used the convention that any right child is greater than or equal to its parent and any left child is less than its parent. You can use a different convention, as long as you stick to it.

Binary trees can hold enormous amounts of data, and that data can be searched very quickly with a *binary search*. This is a manifestation of the binary structure of the tree. For example, if you have a tree with one million nodes, at most it will take about 20 comparisons to find the data! Is that crazy or what? The reason for this is that during each iteration of your search, you cut half the nodes out of the search space. Basically, if there are n nodes, the average search will take $\log_2 n$; the run-time is $O(\log_2 n)$.

| NOTE | The statement about search time is only true for balanced trees—trees that have an equal number of right and left children per level. If a tree is unbalanced, it degrades into a linked list and search time degrades into a linear function. |

The next cool thing about B-trees is that if you take a branch (sub-tree) and process it separately, it maintains the properties of a B-tree. Hence, if you know where to look, you can search a sub-tree just for whatever it is you're looking for. Thus, you can create trees of trees or index tables that contain sub-trees so you don't need to process the whole tree. This is important in 3D world modeling. You might have one large tree of the entire world, but there are hundreds of sub-trees that represent rooms in the world. Thus, you might have yet another tree that represents a spatially sorted list of pointers into the sub-trees, as shown in Figure 11.9. More on this later in the book....

FIGURE 11.9
Using a secondary index table on a B-tree.

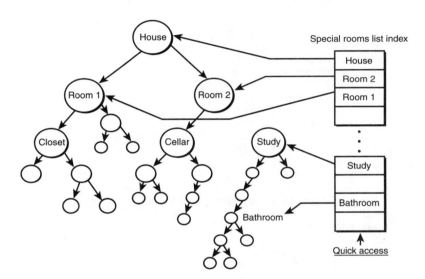

Finally, let's address when to use trees. I suggest using tree-like structures when the problem or data is tree-like to begin with. If you find yourself drawing out the problem and you see branches to the left and right, a tree is definitely for you.

Building BSTs

This subject is rather complex due to the recursive nature of all the algorithms that apply to B-trees. Let's take a quick look at some of the algorithms, write some code, and finish with a demo.

Similar to linked lists, there are a couple of ways to start off a BST: You can have a dummy root or a real root. I'll pick the real root because I prefer it. Hence, an empty tree has nothing in it but a root pointer pointing to NULL:

```
TNODE_PTR root = NULL;
```

Okay, to insert data into the BST, you have to decide what you're going to use as the insertion key. In this case, you can use the person's age or name. Use the person's age because these examples have been using age. However, using the name is just as easy; you would just use a lexicographic comparison function such as strcmp() to determine the order of the names. In any event, here's the code to insert into the BST:

```
TNODE_PTR root = NULL; // here's the initial tree

TNODE_PTR BST_Insert_Node(TNODE_PTR root, int id, int age, char *name)
{
// test for empty tree
if (root==NULL)
   {
   // insert node at root
   root        = new(TNODE);
   root->id    = id;
   root->age   = age;
   strcpy(root->name,name);

   // set links to null
   root->right = NULL;
   root->left  = NULL;

   printf("\nCreating tree");

   } // end if

// else there is a node here, lets go left or right
else
if (age >= root->age)
   {
   printf("\nTraversing right...");
   // insert on right branch

   // test if branch leads to another sub-tree or is terminal
   // if leads to another subtree then try to insert there, else
   // create a node and link
   if (root->right)
      BST_Insert_Node(root->right, id, age, name);
   else
      {
      // insert node on right link
      TNODE_PTR node  = new(TNODE);
      node->id    = id;
      node->age   = age;
      strcpy(node->name,name);

      // set links to null
      node->left   = NULL;
      node->right  = NULL;

      // now set right link of current "root" to this new node
      root->right = node;
```

```
          printf("\nInserting right.");

          } // end else

     } // end if
else // age < root->age
     {
     printf("\nTraversing left...");
     // must insert on left branch

     // test if branch leads to another sub-tree or is terminal
     // if leads to another subtree then try to insert there, else
     // create a node and link
     if (root->left)
        BST_Insert_Node(root->left, id, age, name);
     else
        {
        // insert node on left link
        TNODE_PTR node   = new(TNODE);
        node->id       = id;
        node->age      = age;
        strcpy(node->name,name);

        // set links to null
        node->left    = NULL;
        node->right   = NULL;

        // now set right link of current "root" to this new node
        root->left = node;

        printf("\nInserting left.");
        } // end else

} // end else

// return the root
return(root);

} // end BST_Insert_Node
```

Basically, you first test for an empty tree and then create the root, if needed, with this first item. Hence, the first item or record inserted into the BST should represent something that is in the middle of the search space so that the tree is nicely balanced. Anyway, if the tree has more than one node, you traverse it, taking branches to the right or left depending on the record that you're trying to insert. When you find a leaf or terminal branch, you insert the new node there:

```
root = BST_Insert_Node(root, 4, 30, "jim");
```

Figure 11.10 shows an example of inserting "Jim" into a tree.

FIGURE 11.10
Inserting into a BST.

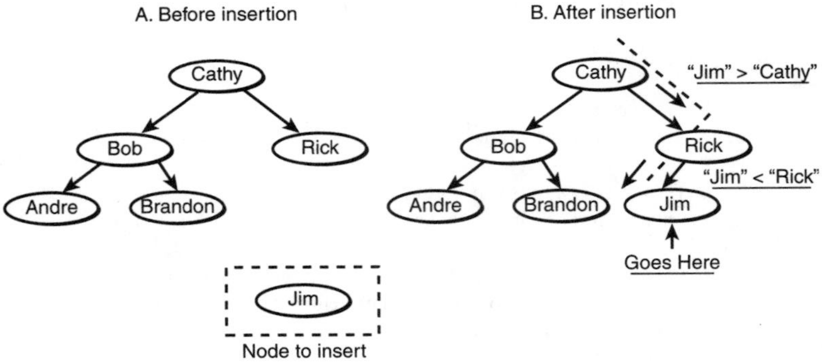

A. Before insertion

B. After insertion

The run-time performance of an insertion into the BST is the same as searching it, so an insertion will take $O(\log_2 n)$ on average and $O(n)$ in the worst case (when the keys happen to fall in linear order).

Searching BSTs

Once the BST is generated, searching it is a snap. However, this is where you need to use a lot of recursion, so watch out, dog. There are three ways to search a BST:

- **Preorder**—Visit the node, search the left sub-tree preorder, and then search the right sub-tree preorder.
- **Inorder**—Search the left sub-tree in order, visit the node, and then search the right-sub tree in order.
- **Postorder**—Search the left sub-tree postorder, search the right sub-tree postorder, and then visit the node.

NOTE

Right and left are arbitrary; the point is the order of visiting and searching.

Take a look at Figure 11.11. It shows a basic tree and the three search orders.

With that in mind, you can write very simple recursive algorithms to perform the traversals. Of course, the point of traversing a BST is to find something and return it. However, the following function just performs the traversals. You could add stopping code to the functions to stop them when they found a desired key; nevertheless, the way you search for the key is what you're interested in at this point:

```
void BST_Inorder_Search(TNODE_PTR root)
{
// this searches a BST using the inorder search

// test for NULL
if (!root)
```

```
        return;

// traverse left tree
BST_Inorder_Search(root->left);

// visit the node
printf("name: %s, age: %d", root->name, root->age);

// traverse the right tree
BST_Inorder_Search(root->right);

} // end BST_Inorder_Search
```

And here's the preorder search:

```
void BST_Preorder_Search(TNODE_PTR root)
{
// this searches a BST using the preorder search

// test for NULL
if (!root)
    return;

// visit the node
printf("name: %s, age: %d", root->name, root->age);

// traverse left tree
BST_Inorder_Search(root->left);

// traverse the right tree
BST_Inorder_Search(root->right);

} // end BST_Preorder_Search
```

And finally, the postorder search:

```
void BST_Postorder_Search(TNODE_PTR root)
{
// this searches a BST using the postorder search

// test for NULL
if (!root)
    return;

// traverse left tree
BST_Inorder_Search(root->left);

// traverse the right tree
BST_Inorder_Search(root->right);

// visit the node
printf("name: %s, age: %d", root->name, root->age);

} // end BST_Postorder_Search
```

FIGURE 11.11
The order of node
visitation for preorder,
inorder, and post-
order searches.

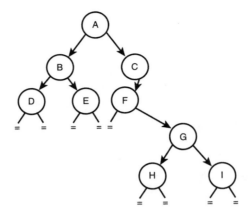

Pre-order: A B D E C F G H I
In order: D B E A F H G I C
Post order: D E B H I G F C A

That's it—like magic, huh? So if you had a tree, you would do the following to traverse it in order:

```
BST_Inorder_Search(my_tree);
```

> **TIP**
>
> I can't tell you how important tree-like structures are in 3D graphics, so
> make sure you understand this material. Otherwise, when you build
> binary space partitions to help solve rendering problems, you're going
> to be in pointer-recursion hell. :)

You'll note that I have conveniently left out how to delete a node. This was intentional.
It's a rather complex subject because you could kill a sub-tree's parent and disconnect
all the children. Alas, deletion of nodes is left as an exercise for you to discover on your
own. I suggest a good data structures text, such as *Algorithms in C++* by Sedgewick,
published by Addison Wesley, for a more in-depth discussion of trees and the associated algorithms.

Finally, for an example of BSTs, check out DEMO11_3.CPP|EXE. It allows you to create
a BST and traverse it using the three algorithms. Again, this is a console application,
so compile it appropriately.

Optimization Theory

No other programming has the kind of performance requirements that games do. Video
games have always pushed the limits of hardware and software and will continue to do

so. Enough is never enough. Game programmers always want to add more creatures, effects, and sounds, better AI, and so on. Hence, optimization is of utmost importance.

In this section, I'm going to cover some optimization techniques to get you started. If you have further interest, there are a number of good books on the subject, such as *Inner Loops* by Rick Booth, published by Addison Wesley; *Zen of Code Optimization* by Mike Abrash, published by Coriolis Group; and *Pentium Processor Optimization* by Mike Schmit, published by AP Press.

Using Your Head

The first key to writing optimized code is understanding the compiler, the data types, and how your C/C++ is finally transformed into executable machine language. The idea is to use simple programming and simple data structures. The more complex and contrived your code is, the harder it will be for the compiler to convert it into machine code, and thus the slower it will execute (in most cases). Here are some basic rules to keep in mind:

- Use 32-bit data as much as possible. 8-bit data may take up less space, but Intel processors like 32-bit data and are optimized to access it.

- Use inline functions for small functions that you call a lot.

- Use globals as much as possible, without making ugly code.

- Avoid floating-point numbers for addition and subtraction because the integer unit is generally faster for these operations.

- Use integers whenever possible. Although the floating-point processor is almost as fast as the integer processor, integers are exact. So if you don't need decimal accuracy, use integers.

- Align all data structures to 32-byte boundaries. You can do this manually, with compiler directives on most compilers, or within code using #pragmas.

- Never pass data to functions as value if it is anything other than a simple type. Always use a pointer.

- Don't use the register keyword in your code. Although Microsoft says it makes faster loops, it starves the compiler of registers and ends up making the worst code.

- If you're a C++ programmer, classes and virtual functions are okay. Just don't go crazy with inheritance and layers of software.

- The Pentium-class processors use an internal data and code cache. Be aware of this, and try to keep the size of your functions relatively small so they can fit into the cache (16KB–32KB+). In addition, when you're storing data, store it in the way it will be accessed. This will minimize cache thrashing and main memory or secondary cache access, which is 10 times slower than the internal cache.

- Be aware that Pentium class processors have RISC-like cores, so they like simple instructions and allow two or more instructions to execute in more than one execution unit. Don't write contrived code on a single line; it's better to write simpler code that's longer, even though you can mash the same functionality into the same line.

Mathematical Tricks

Because a great deal of game programming is mathematical in nature, it pays to know better ways to perform math functions. There are a number of general tricks and methods that you can use to speed things up:

- Always use integers with integers and floats with floats. Conversion from one to another kills performance. Hence, hold off on the conversion of data types to the very last minute.

- Integers can be multiplied by any power of two by shifting to the left. And likewise, they can be divided by any power of two by shifting to the right. Multiplication and division by numbers other than powers of two can be accomplished by using sums or differences of shifts. For example, 640 is not a power of two, but 512 and 128 are, so here's the best way to multiply a number by 640 using shifts:

```
product=(n<<7) + (n<<9); // n*128 + n*512 = n*640
```

However, if the processor can multiply in 1–2 cycles, this optimization is worthless.

- If you use matrix operations in your algorithms, make sure to take advantage of their sparseness—that is, zero entries.

- When you're creating constants, make sure that they have the proper casts so that the compiler doesn't reduce them to integers or interpret them incorrectly. The best idea is to use the new C++ const directive. For example:

```
const float f=12.45;
```

- Avoid square roots, trigonometric functions, or any complex mathematical functions. In general, there is always a simpler way to do it by taking advantage of certain assumptions or making approximations. However, if worse comes to worst, you can always make a look-up table, which I'll get to later.

- If you have to zero out a large array of floats, use a memset(), like this:

```
memset((void  *)float_array,0,sizeof(float)*num_floats);
```

However, this is the only time that you can do this, because floats are encoded in IEEE format and the only integer and float values that are the same are 0.

- When you're performing mathematical calculations, see if you can reduce the expressions manually before coding them. For example, n*(f+1)/n is equivalent to (f+1) because the multiplication and division of n cancel out.

- If you perform a complex mathematical operation and you know you'll need it again a few lines down, cache it. For example:

```
// compute term that is used in more than one expression
float n_squared = n*n;

// use term in two different expressions
pitch = 34.5*n_squared+100*rate;
magnitude = n_squared / length;
```

- Last, but not least, make sure to set the compiler options to use the floating-point processor and create code that is fast rather than small.

Fixed-Point Math

A couple of years ago, most 3D engines used fixed-point mathematics for much of the transformation and mathematical operations in 3D. This was due to the fact that the floating-point support wasn't as fast as the integer support, even on the Pentium. However, these days the Pentium II, III, and Katmai have much better floating-point capabilities, and fixed-point is no longer as important.

However, in many cases the conversion from floating-point to integers for rasterization still is slow, so sometimes it's still a good idea to try fixed-point in inner loops that use addition and subtraction operations. These operations are still faster than floating-point operations on the lower-level Pentiums, and you can use tricks to quickly extract the integral part of a fixed-point number rather than making a conversion from `float` to `int`, as you would if you stuck to floating-point.

In any case, this is all very iffy, and using floating-point for everything is usually the best way to do things these days. But it doesn't hurt to know a little about fixed-point math. My philosophy is to use floating-point for all data representations and transformations, and then to try both floating- and fixed-point algorithms for low-level polygon rasterization to see which is fastest. Of course, this is even more irrelevant if you're using pure hardware acceleration. If so, just stick to floating-point all the way.

With all that in mind, let's take a look at fixed-point representations.

Representing Fixed-Point Numbers

All fixed-point math really is based on scaled integers. For example, let's say that you want to represent the number 10.5 with an integer. You can't; there isn't a decimal place. You could truncate the number to 10.0 or round it to 11.0, but 10.5 isn't an integer. But what if you scale the number by 10? Then 10.5 becomes 105.0, which *is* an integer. This is the basis of fixed-point. You scale numbers by some factor and that make sure to take this scale into consideration when doing mathematics.

Because computers are binary, most game programmers like to use 32-bit integers, or `ints`, to represent fixed-point numbers in a 16.16 format. Take a look at Figure 11.12 to see this graphically.

FIGURE 11.12
A 16.16 fixed-point
representation.

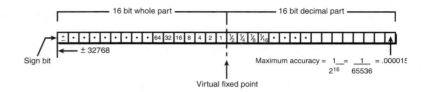

You put the whole part in the upper 16 bits and the decimal part in the lower 16 bits. Hence, you're scaling all numbers by 2^{16}, or 65,536. Moreover, to extract the integer portion of a fixed-point number, you shift and mask the upper 16 bits, and to get to the decimal portion, you shift and mask the lower 16 bits.

Here's some working types for fixed-point math:

```
#define FP_SHIFT 16     // shifts to produce a fixed-point number
#define FP_SCALE 65536  // scaling factor

typedef int FIXPOINT;
```

Conversions to and from Fixed-Point

There are two types of numbers you need to convert to fixed-point: integers and floating-point numbers. You must consider each one differently. For integers, the binary representation is in straight 2's complement, so you can use shifts to multiply the number and convert it to fixed-point. On the other hand, floats use a IEEE format, which has a mantissa and an exponent stored in those four bytes, so shifting will destroy the number. You must use standard floating-point multiplication to make the conversion.

> **MATH**
>
> 2's complement is a method of representing binary integers so that both positive and negative numbers can be represented and mathematical operations are closed on the set—that is, they work! The 2's complement of a binary number means computing by inverting the bits and adding 1. Mathematically, let's say you want to find the 2's complement of 6—that is, –6. It would be –6+1 or ~0110 + 0001 = 1001 + 0001 = 1010, which is 10 in normal binary but –6 in 2's complement.

Here's a macro that converts an integer to fixed-point:

```
#define INT_TO_FIXP(n) (FIXPOINT((n << FP_SHIFT)))
```

For example:

```
FIXPOINT speed = INT_TO_FIXP(100);
```

And here's a macro to convert floating-point numbers to fixed-point:

```
#define FLOAT_TO_FIXP(n) (FIXPOINT((float)n * FP_SCALE))
```

For example:

```
FIXPOINT speed = FLOAT_TO_FIXP(100.5);
```

Extracting a fixed-point number is simple too. Here's a macro to get the integral portion in the upper 16 bits:

```
#define FIXP_INT_PART(n) (n >> 16)
```

And to get the decimal portion in the lower 16 bits, you simply need to mask the integral part:

```
#define FIXP_DEC_PART(n) (n & 0x0000ffff)
```

Of course, if you're smart, you might forget the conversions and just use pointers that are SHORTs to access the upper and lower parts instantly, like this:

```
FIXPOINT fp;
short *integral_part = &(fp+2), *decimal_part = &fp;
```

The pointers integral_part and decimal_part always point to the 16 bits that you want.

Accuracy

A question should be popping up in your head right now: "What the heck does the decimal part mean?" Well, usually you won't need it; it's just there to be used in the computations. Normally, you just want the whole part in a rasterization loop or something, but because you're in base 2, the decimal part is just a base 2 decimal, as shown in Figure 11.12. For example, the numbers

```
1001.0001 is 9 + 0*1/2 + 0*1/4 + 0*1/8 + 1*1/16 = 9.0625
```

This brings us to the concept of accuracy. With four digits of base 2, you're only accurate to about 1.5 decimals base 10 digits, or +-.0625. With 16 digits, you're accurate to $1/2^{16} = 1/65536 = .000015258$, or about one part in 10,000. That's not bad and will suffice for most purposes. On the other hand, you only have 16 bits to hold the integer part, meaning that you can hold signed integers -32767 to +32768 (or nonsigned up to 65535). This might be an issue in a large universe or numerical space, so watch out for overflow!

Addition and Subtraction

Addition and subtraction of fixed-point numbers is trivial. You can use the standard + and − operators:

```
FIXPOINT f1 = FLOAT_TO_FIX(10.5),
         f2 = FLOAT_TO_FIX(-2.6),
         f3 = 0; // zero is 0 no matter what baby

// to add them
f3 = f1 + f2;
```

```
// to subtract them
f3 = f1 - f2;
```

> **NOTE** You can work with both positive and negative numbers without a prob-
> lem because the underlying representation is 2's complement.

Multiplication and Division

Multiplication and division are a little more complex than addition and subtraction.
The problem is that the fixed-point numbers are scaled; when you multiply them, you
not only multiply the fixed-point numbers but also the scaling factors. Take a look:

```
f1 = n1 * scale
f2 = n2 * scale
f3 = f1 * f2 = (n1 * scale) * (n2 * scale) = n1*n2*scale²
```

See the extra factor of scale? To remedy this, you need to divide or shift out the one
factor of scale^2. Hence, here's how to multiply two fixed-point numbers:

```
f3 = ((f1 * f2) >> FP_SHIFT);
```

Division of fixed-point numbers has the same scaling problem as multiplication, but
in the opposite sense. Take a look at this math:

```
f1 = n1 * scale
f2 = n2 * scale
```

Given this, then

```
f3 = f1/f2 = (n1*scale) / (n2*scale) = n1/n2 // no scale!
```

Note that you've lost the scale factor and thus turned the quotient into a non-fixed-
point number. This is useful in some cases, but to maintain the fixed-point property,
you must prescale the numerator like this:

```
f3 = (f1 << FP_SHIFT) / f2;
```

> **WARNING** The problem with both multiplication and division is overflow and
> underflow. In the case of multiplication, the result might be 64-bit in the
> worst case. Similarly, in the case of division, the upper 16 bits of the
> numerator are always lost, leaving only the decimal portion. The solu-
> tion? Use a 24.8-bit format or use full 64-bit math. This can be accom-
> plished with assembly language because the Pentium+ processors
> support 64-bit math. Or, you can alter the format a little and use 24.8.
> This will allow multiplication and division to work better because you
> won't lose everything all the time, but your accuracy will fall apart.

For an example of fixed-point mathematics, try `DEMO11_4.CPP|EXE`. It allows you to enter two decimal numbers and then perform fixed-point operations on them and view the results. Pay attention to how multiplication and division seem not to work at all. This is a result of using 16.16 format without 64-bit math. To fix this, you can recompile the program to use 24.8 format rather than 16.16. The conditional compilation is controlled by two #defines at the top of the code:

```
// #define FIXPOINT16_16
// #define FIXPOINT24_8
```

Uncomment the one you want to use and the compiler will do the rest. Finally, this is a console application, so like Spike says, do the right thing...

Unrolling the Loop

The next optimization trick is loop unrolling. This used to be one of the best optimizations back in the 8/16-bit days, but today it can backfire on you. *Unrolling the loop* means taking apart a loop that iterates some number of times and manually coding each line. Here's an example:

```
// loop before unrolling
for (int index=0; index<8; index++)
    {
    // do work
    sum+=data[index];
    } // end for index
```

The problem with this loop is that the work section takes less time than the loop does for the increment, comparison, and jump. Hence, the loop code itself doubles or triples the amount of time the code takes! You can unroll the loop like this:

```
// the unrolled version
sum+=data[0];
sum+=data[1];
sum+=data[2];
sum+=data[3];
sum+=data[4];
sum+=data[5];
sum+=data[6];
sum+=data[7];
```

This is much better. There are two caveats:

- If the loop body is much more complex than the loop mechanics itself, there is no point in unrolling it. For example, if you're computing square roots in the work section of the loop, a few more cycles each iteration isn't going to help you.

- Because the Pentium processors have internal caches, unrolling a loop too much might prevent it from fitting in the internal cache anymore. This is disastrous and will bring your code to a halt. I suggest unrolling 8–32 times, depending on the situation.

Look-Up Tables

This is my personal favorite optimization. Look-up tables are precomputed values of some computation that you know you'll perform during run-time. You simply compute all possible values at startup and then run the game. For example, say you needed the sine and cosine of the angles from 0–359 degrees. Computing them using sin() and cos() would kill you if you used the floating-point processor, but with a look-up table your code will be able to compute sin() or cos() in a few cycles because it's just a look-up. Here's an example:

```
// storage for look up tables
float SIN_LOOK[360];
float COS_LOOK[360];

// create look-up table
for (int angle=0; angle < 360; angle++)
    {
    // convert angle to radians since math library uses
    // rads instead of degrees
    // remember there are 2*pi rads in 360 degrees
    float rad_angle = angle * (3.14159/180);

    // fill in next entries in look-up tables
    SIN_LOOK[angle] = sin(rad_angle);
    COS_LOOK[angle] = cos(rad_angle);
    } // end for angle
```

As an example of using the look-up table, here's the code to draw a circle of radius 10:

```
for (int ang = 0; ang<360; ang++)
    {
    // compute the next point on circle
    x_pos = 10*COS_LOOK[ang];
    y_pos = 10*SIN_LOOK[ang];

    // plot the pixel
    Plot_Pixel((int)x_pos+x0, (int)y_pos+y0, color);
    } // end for ang
```

Of course, look-up tables take up memory, but they are well worth it. "If you can pre-compute it, put it in a look-up table," that's my motto. How do you think *DOOM*, *Quake*, and my personal favorite, *Half-Life*, work?

Assembly Language

The final optimization I want to talk about is assembly language. You've got the killer algorithm and good data structures, but you just want a little bit more. Handcrafted assembly language doesn't make code go 1,000 times faster like it did with 8/16-bit processors, but it can get you 2 – 10 times more speed, and that's definitely worth it.

However, make sure to only convert sections of your game that need converting. Don't mess with the menu program, because that's a waste of time. Use a profiler or something to see where all of your game's CPU cycles are being eaten up (probably in the graphics sections), and then target those for assembly language. I suggest Vtune by Intel for profiling.

In the old days (a few years ago), most compilers didn't have inline assemblers, and if they did, they sucked! Today, the inline assemblers that come with the compilers from Microsoft, Borland, and Watcom are just about as good as using a standalone assembler for small jobs that are a few dozen to a couple hundred lines. Therefore, I suggest using the inline assembler if you want to do any assembly language. Here's how you invoke the inline assembler when using Microsoft's VC++:

```
_asm
{
.. assembly language code here
} // end asm
```

The cool thing about the inline assembler is that it allows you to use variable names that have been defined by C/C++. For example, here's how you would write a 32-bit memory `fill` function using inline assembly language:

```
void qmemset(void *memory, int value, int num_quads)
{
// this function uses 32 bit assembly language based
// and the string instructions to fill a region of memory
_asm
   {
   CLD                    // clear the direction flag
   MOV EDI, memory        // move pointer into EDI
   MOV ECX, num_quads     // ECX hold loop count
   MOV EAX, value         // EAX hold value
   REP STOSD              // perform fill
   } // end asm

} // end qmemset
```

To use the new function, all you would do is this:

```
qmemset(&buffer, 25, 1000);
```

And 1,000 quads would be filled with the value 25 starting at the address of `buffer`.

NOTE If you're not using Microsoft VC++, take a look at your particular compiler's Help to see the exact syntax needed for inline assembly. In most cases, the changes are nothing more than an underscore here and there.

Making Demos

So you've got this killer game, and you need a *demo mode*. There are two main ways to implement a demo mode: You can play the game yourself and record your moves, or you can use an AI player. Recording your own gameplay turns out to be the most common choice. Writing an AI player that can play as good as a human is difficult, and it's hard to tell the AI that it needs to play the game in a "cool" way because it needs to make a good impression on potential buyers. Let's take a brief look at how each of these methods is implemented.

Prerecorded Demos

To record a demo, basically you record the states of all the input devices each cycle as you create the demo, write the data to a file, and then play back the demo as if it were the input of the game. Take a look at Figure 11.13 to see this graphically. The idea is that the game doesn't know whether the input is from the keyboard (input device) or from a file, so it simply plays the game back.

FIGURE 11.13
Demo playback.

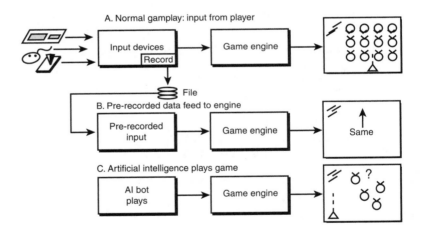

For this to work, you have to have a *deterministic* game: If you play the game again and do the exact same things, the game creatures will do the exact same things. This means that as well as recording the input devices, you must record the initial random number seed so that the starting state of a recording game is recorded as well as the input. This ensures that the game will play back the exact same way as you recorded it.

The best approach to recording a game is not to sample the input at timed intervals, but at each frame. Hence, if the game is played on a slower or faster computer, the playback data won't get out of synchronization with the game. What I usually do is merge all the input devices into a single record, one for each frame, and then make a file of these records. At the beginning of the file, I place any state information or random numbers that I played the demo with so that these values can be loaded back in. Therefore, the playback file might look something like this:

```
Initial State Information

Frame 1: Input Values
Frame 2: Input Values
Frame 3: Input Values
   .
   .
   .
Frame N: Input Values
```

Once you have the file, simply reset the game and start it back up. Then read the file as if it were the input devices. The game doesn't know the difference!

 WARNING   The single worst mistake that you can make is sampling the input at the wrong time when you're writing out records. You should make absolutely certain that the input you sample and record is the actual input that the game uses for that frame. A common mistake that newbies make is to sample the input for the demo mode at a point in the event loop before or after the normal input is read. Hence, they're sampling different data! It's possible that the player might have the fire button down in one part of the event loop and not in another, so you must sample at the same point you read the input for the game normally.

AI-Controlled Demos

The second method of recording a game is by writing an AI *bot* to play it, much like people do for Internet games like Quake. The bot plays the game while in demo mode, just like one of the AI characters in the game. The only problem with this method (other than the technical complexity) is that the bot might not necessarily show off all the cool rooms, weapons, and so on, because it doesn't know that it's making a demo. On the other hand, the cool thing about having a bot play is that each demo is different and the "attract mode" of the game will never get boring.

Implementing a bot to play your game is the same as with any other AI character. You basically connect it to the input port of your game and override the normal input stream, as shown in Figure 11.13. Then you write the AI algorithms for the bot and give it some main goals, like finding its way out of the maze, killing everything in sight, or whatever. Then you simply let the bot loose to demonstrate the game until the player wants to play.

Strategies for Saving the Game

One of the biggest pains in the butt is writing a save game feature. This is one of those things that all game programmers do last, and do by the seat of their pants in most cases. The key is to write your game with the idea that you're going to want to give the player a save game option at some point. That way you won't paint yourself into a corner.

To save at any point in the game means to record the state of every single variable and every single object in the game. Hence, you must record all global variables in a file along with the state of every single object. The best way to approach this is with an object-oriented thought process. Instead of writing a function that writes out the state of each object and all the global variables, a better idea is to teach each object how to write and read its own state to a disk file.

To save a game, all you need to do is write the globals and then create a simple function that tells each game object to write out its state. Then, to load the game back in, all you need to do is read the globals back into the system and then load the states of all the objects back into the game.

This way, if you add another object or object type, the loading/saving process is localized in the object itself rather than strewn about all over the place.

Implementing Multiple Players

The next little bit of game programming legerdemain is implementing multiple players. Of course, if you want to implement a networked game, that's a whole other story, although DirectPlay makes the communication part easy, at least. However, if all you want to do is let two or more players play your game at the same time or take turns, that requires nothing more than some extra data structures and a bit of housekeeping.

Taking Turns

Implementing turn-taking is easy and hard at the same time. It's easy because if you can implement one player, implementing two or more only requires having more than one player record. It's hard because you must save the game for each player when switching players. Hence, usually you need to implement a save game option if you want to have turn-taking. Obviously, the players shouldn't know that the game is being saved as they take turns, but that's what's really going on.

With that in mind, here's a list of the steps that you would follow to allow two players to play, one after another:

1. Start game; player 1 starts.
2. Player 1 plays until she dies.

3. The state of player 1's game is saved; player 2 starts.

4. Player 2 plays until he dies.

5. The state of player 2's game is saved (here comes the transition).

6. The previously saved player 1 game is reloaded, and player 1 continues.

7. Go back to step 2.

As you can see, step 5 is where the action starts happening and the game starts pinging back and forth between players. If you want more than two players, simply play them one at a time until you're at the end of the list, and then start over.

Split-Screen Setups

Enabling two or more players to play on the same screen is a little harder than swapping because you have to write the game a little more generally as far as gameplay, collision, and interaction between the players are concerned. Moreover, with multiple players in the game at the same time, you must allocate a specific input device for each player. This usually means a joystick for each player, or maybe one player uses the keyboard and one uses the joystick.

The other problem with putting multiple players in the game at the same time is that some games just aren't good for it. In a scrolling game, for example, one player might want to go one way while the other wants to go another way. This can cause a conflict, and you'll have to plan for this. Thus, the best games for multiple players are single-screen fighting games, or games in which the players stay relatively near each other for one reason or another.

But if you want to allow the players to roam around freely, you can always create a split-screen display, as shown in Figure 11.14.

FIGURE 11.14
Split-screen game display.

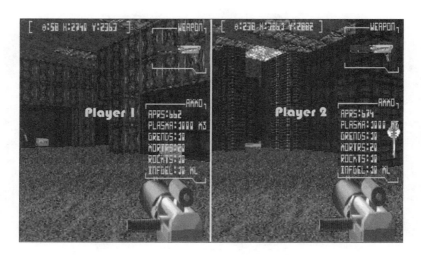

The only problem with the split-screen display is—the split-screen display! You must generate two or more views of the game, which can be technically challenging. Moreover, there might not be enough room on the screen to fit the two or more views, and the players might find it hard to see what's going on. But the bottom line is, if you can pull it off, it's a cool option…

Multithreaded Programming Techniques

Up to this point, all the demos in this book have used a single threaded event loop and programming model. The event loop reacts to the player's input and renders the game at a rate of 30+ fps. Along with reacting to the player, the game performs millions of operations per second, along with processing dozens if not hundreds of small tasks, such as drawing all the objects, retrieving input, making music, and so on. Figure 11.15 shows the standard game loop that you've been using.

As you can see from Figure 11.15, the game logic performs all the tasks of the game in a serial/sequential manner. Of course, there are exceptions to this, including interrupts that can perform simple logic such as music and input control, but for the most part, a game is one long sequence of function calls that repeat forever.

FIGURE 11.15
Standard DOS single-tasking game loop.

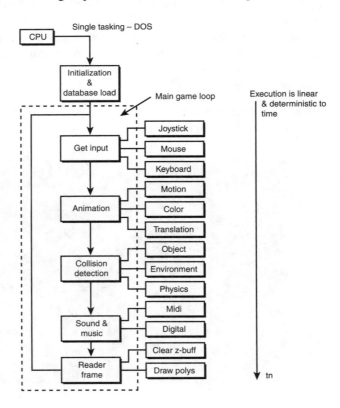

What makes a game seem fluid and real is the fact that even though everything is performed in sequence, step by step, the computer is so fast that it all seems as if it's happening at once. Hence, the model that most game programmers use is a single tasking execution thread that performs many operations in series to arrive at the desired output for each frame. This is one of the best ways to do things and is a side effect of DOS game programming.

However, the days of DOS are over, so it's time that you start using the multithreaded abilities of Windows 95/98/ME/XP/NT/2000 and, well, liking it!

This section is going to cover the *threads of execution* under Windows 95/98/NT. These threads allow you to run multiple tasks within the same application with very little drama. Now, before you get started, let's cover a little terminology so that this simple subject isn't alien to you.

Multithreaded Programming Terminology

There are a number of "multi-" words in the computer lexicon that mean various things. Let's begin by talking about multiprocessors and multiprocessing, and then finish up with multithreading.

A multiprocessor computer is one that has more than one processor. The Cray and the Connection Machine are both good examples. The Connection Machine can have up to 64,000 processing cores (a hypercube network), and each one can be executing code.

Back down on Earth, you can purchase a quad processor Pentium III+ machine and run Windows NT on it. These are usually SMP (symmetrical multiprocessing) systems, meaning that all four processors will run tasks symmetrically. Actually, that is not totally true because the OS kernel will only run only one of the processors (sorta), but as far as processes go, they will run equally well on either processor. So the idea of a multiprocessor computer is to have more than one processor to split the workload.

On some systems, only one task or process can run on each processor, while on other systems, such as Windows NT, thousands of tasks can run on each processor. This is basically multiprocessing, the running of multiple tasks on a single- or multiple-processor machine.

The last concept is multithreading, which is the what you're interested in today. A process under Windows 95/98/NT/2000 is really a whole program; although it may or may not run by itself, most of the time it *is* an application. It can have its own address space and context, and it exists by itself.

A *thread*, on the other hand, is a much simpler entity. Threads are created by processes and have very little identity of their own. They run in the address space of the process that created them, and they are very simple. The beauty of threads is that they get as much processor time as anything else does, and they exist in the same address space as the parent process that created them.

This means that communicating to and from threads is very simple. In essence, they are exactly what you want as a game programmer: a thread of execution that does something in parallel with your other main program tasks, that you don't have to babysit, and that has access to the variables in your program.

Along with the "multi-" words, there are a few more concepts that you need to know about. First, Windows 95, 98, NT, and 2000 are multitasking/preemptive operating systems. This means that no task, process, or thread can take control of the computer; each one will be preempted at some point and blocked, and the next thread of execution will get to run. This is completely different from Windows 3.1, which was *not* pre-emptive. If you didn't call `GetMessage(...)` each cycle, other processes didn't run. In Windows 95/98/NT/2000, you can sit in a FOR loop forever if you like and do nothing, and the OS will still run the other tasks.

Also, under Win95/98/NT/2000, each process or thread has a priority that dictates how long it gets to run before being preempted. So, if there are 10 threads that all have the same priority, they will all get equal time or be processed in a round-robin fashion. However, if one thread has kernel-level priority, it will of course run for more time in each cycle. Take a look at Figure 11.16 to see this.

FIGURE 11.16
Round robin thread execution with equal and unequal thread priorities.

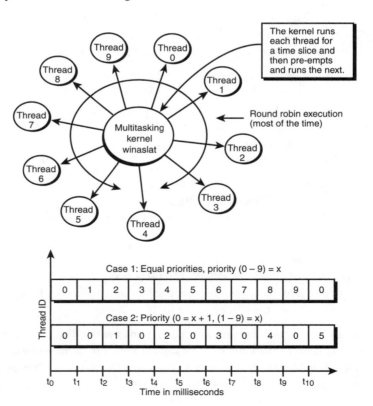

Finally, this question arises: "What are the differences between Windows 95/98/NT/ 2000 multithreading?" Well, there are some differences, but for the most part you can use the Windows 95 OS model and be safe on all platforms. It's the lowest common denominator. Although 98 and NT are much more robust, I'll use a Windows 95 machine for most of the examples in this section.

Why Use Threads in a Game?

The answer to this question should be obvious by now. As a matter of fact, I think you could create a list of about 1,000 things that you could do with threads right off the bat. However, if you're just coming down from a Mountain Dew high (or Sobe, which is my new poison), here are some common uses for threads:

- Updating animation
- Creating ambient sound effects
- Controlling small objects
- Querying input devices
- Updating global data structures
- Creating pop-up menus and controls

That last use is one of my favorites. It's always a pain to put up menus and let the user make changes while the game is running, but with threads it's much simpler.

Now, I still haven't answered the question of why you should use threads in a game, as opposed to just making a huge loop and calling functions. Well, threads do the same thing, basically, and when you start creating more and more object-oriented software, at some point you'll come up with structures that are like *automatons*. These are objects that represent game characters that you want to be able to create and destroy without having logical side effects on the main game loop. This can be accomplished in the coolest way with C++ classes along with threads.

Before you get started creating your first thread, let's make something totally clear here: On a single processor computer, only one thread can execute at a time. So you still get nothing for free, but it seems that way from a software point of view, so just assume you do to make your programming easier and more correct. Figure 11.17 shows an example of a main process and three threads that are executing along with it.

The timetable in the figure shows the various threads that have control of the processor, in milliseconds. As you can see, the threads run one at a time, but they can run out of order and for different amounts of time based on their priority.

Enough foreplay. Let's get to the code!

FIGURE 11.17
Primary process
spawning three
secondary threads.

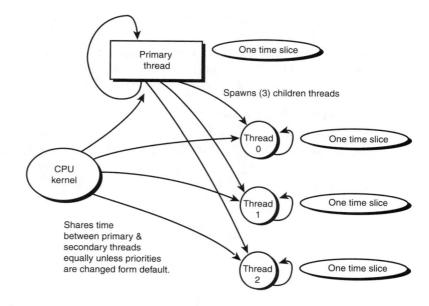

Conjuring a Thread from the Plasma Pool

You'll be using console applications for the examples that follow, so once again, please compile the programs correctly. (I'm only belaboring this because every hour I get 30-60 emails on various books I've written from people using the VC++ compiler wrong. Doesn't anyone read the introductions?)

However, there is one more caveat: You must use the *multithreaded* libraries for these examples. You do this by going into the main menu in MS DEV Studio, under Project, Settings, then under the C/C++ tab go to Category: Code Generation, and set the Use Run-time Library to multithreaded. This is also shown in Figure 11.18. Also, make sure to turn optimization off. It can confuse the multithreaded synchronization code sometimes, so better safe than sorry.

> **NOTE**
>
> I just had deja vu. Or was it really deja vu, or just a glitch in the simulation? If you didn't get that, you won't know what it was you didn't get so it won't matter anyway. :)

All righty then, let's get started. Creating a thread is easy; it's keeping it from destruction that's the hard part! The Win32 API call is as follows:

```
HANDLE CreateThread(
LPSECURITY_ATTRIBUTES  lpThreadAttributes,
        // pointer to thread security attributes
```

```
DWORD   dwStackSize,  // initial thread stack size, in bytes
LPTHREAD_START_ROUTINE  lpStartAddress,
            // pointer to thread function
LPVOID  lpParameter,     // argument for new thread
DWORD   dwCreationFlags,  // creation flags
LPDWORD  lpThreadId );    // pointer to returned thread identifier
```

FIGURE 11.18
Creating a console
application with
multithreaded
libraries.

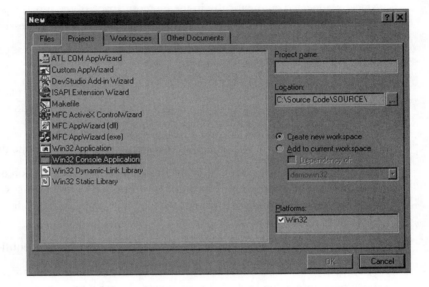

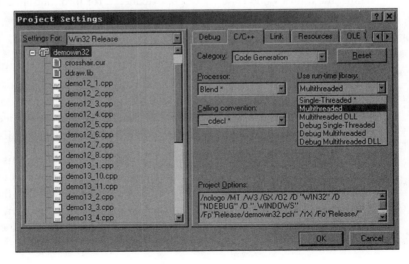

lpThreadAttributes points to a SECURITY_ATTRIBUTES structure that specifies the security attributes for the thread. If lpThreadAttributes is NULL, the thread is created with a default security descriptor and the resulting handle is not inherited.

dwStackSize specifies the size, in bytes, of the stack for the new thread. If 0 is specified, the stack size defaults to the same size as that of the primary thread of the process. The stack is allocated automatically in the memory space of the process, and it is freed when the thread terminates. Note that the stack size grows, if necessary.

CreateThread tries to commit the number of bytes specified by dwStackSize, and fails if the size exceeds available memory.

lpStartAddress points to the application-supplied function to be executed by the thread and represents the starting address of the thread. The function accepts a single 32-bit argument and returns a 32-bit exit value.

lpParameter specifies a single 32-bit parameter value passed to the thread.

dwCreationFlags specifies additional flags that control the creation of the thread. If the CREATE_SUSPENDED flag is specified, the thread is created in a suspended state and will not run until the ResumeThread() function is called. If this value is zero, the thread runs immediately after creation.

lpThreadId points to a 32-bit variable that receives the thread identifier.

If the function succeeds, the return value is a handle to the new thread. If the function fails, the return value is NULL. To get extended error information, call GetLastError().

The function call might look a bit complex, but it's really not. It just allows a lot of control. You won't use much of its functionality in most cases.

When you're done with a thread, you need to close its handle; in other words, let the operating system know that you're done using the object. This is done with the CloseHandle() function call, which uses the handle returned by CreateThread() and reduces the reference count in the kernel object that refers to the thread by 1.

You need to do this for every thread when you're done with it. This does *not* kill the thread; it just *tells* the OS that the thread is dead. The thread must terminate itself, be told to terminate (with TerminateThread()), or be terminated by the OS when the main thread or primary thread terminates. We'll get to all that later, but for now, just realize that this is a clean-up call that needs to be done before you exit a multi-threaded app. Here is the function prototype:

```
BOOL CloseHandle(HANDLE  hObject );      // handle to object to close
```

`hObject` identifies an open object handle. If the function succeeds, the return value is TRUE. If the function fails, the return value is FALSE. To get extended error information, call `GetLastError()`. Furthermore, `CloseHandle()` closes handles to the following objects:

- Console input or output
- Event files
- File mappings
- Mutexes
- Named pipes
- Processes
- Semaphores
- Threads

Basically, `CloseHandle()` invalidates the specified object handle, decrements the object's handle count, and performs object retention checks. Once the last handle to an object is closed, the object is removed from the operating system.

WARNING

The new thread handle is created with full access to the new thread. If a security descriptor is not provided, the handle can be used in any function that requires a thread object handle. When a security descriptor is provided, an access check is performed on all subsequent uses of the handle before access is granted. If the access check denies access, the requesting process cannot use the handle to gain access to the thread.

Now let's take a look at some code that could represent a thread you would pass for processing to `CreateThread()`:

```
DWORD WINAPI My_Thread(LPVOID data)
{
// .. do work

// return an exit code at end, whatever is appropriate for your app

return(26);
} // end My_Thread
```

Now you have everything you need to create your first multithreaded app. The first example will illustrate the creation of a single thread, along with the primary thread of execution (the main program). The secondary thread will print out the number 2, and the primary thread will print out the number 1. DEMO11_5.CPP contains the complete program and is shown here for reference:

```
// DEMO11_5.CPP - Creates a single thread that prints
// simultaneously while the Primary thread prints.
```

Hardcore Game Programming

```
// INCLUDES ////////////////////////////////////////////

#define WIN32_LEAN_AND_MEAN  // make sure win headers
                             // are included correctly

#include <windows.h>    // include the standard windows stuff
#include <windowsx.h>   // include the 32 bit stuff
#include <conio.h>
#include <stdlib.h>
#include <stdarg.h>
#include <stdio.h>
#include <math.h>
#include <io.h>
#include <fcntl.h>

// DEFINES /////////////////////////////////////////////

// PROTOTYPES //////////////////////////////////////////

DWORD WINAPI Printer_Thread(LPVOID data);

// GLOBALS /////////////////////////////////////////////

// FUNCTIONS ///////////////////////////////////////////

DWORD WINAPI Printer_Thread(LPVOID data)
{
// this thread function simply prints out data
// 25 times with a slight delay

for (int index=0; index<25; index++)
    {
    printf("%d ",data); // output a single character
    Sleep(100);         // sleep a little to slow things down
    } // end for index


// just return the data sent to the thread function

return((DWORD)data);

} // end Printer_Thread

// MAIN ////////////////////////////////////////////////////////////

void main(void)
{
HANDLE thread_handle;  // this is the handle to the thread
DWORD  thread_id;      // this is the id of the thread

// start with a blank line
printf("\nStarting threads...\n");
```

```
// create the thread, IRL we would check for errors
thread_handle = CreateThread(NULL,          // default security
                    0,                  // default stack
                    Printer_Thread,  // use this thread function
                    (LPVOID)1,          // user data sent to thread
                    0,                  // creation flags, 0=start now.
                    &thread_id);    // send id back in this var

// now enter into printing loop, make sure this takes longer than thread,
// so thread finishes first
for (int index=0; index<50; index++)
    {
    printf("2 ");
    Sleep(100);
    } // end for index

// at this point the thread should be dead
CloseHandle(thread_handle);

// end with a blank line
printf("\nAll threads terminated.\n");

} // end main
```

Sample output:

```
Starting threads...
2 1 2 1 2 1 2 1 1 2 2 1 1 2 2 1 1 2 2 1 1 2 2 1 1 2
2 1 1 2 2 1 1 2 2 1 1 2 2 1 1 2 2 1 1 2 2 1 1 2 2 2
2 2 2 2 2 2 2 2 2 2 2 2 2 2 2 2 2 2 2 2 2 2 2
All threads terminated.
```

As you can see from the sample output, each thread of execution runs for a short time, and then the OS switches context to the next waiting thread. In this case, the OS simply toggles back and forth between the primary thread and the secondary thread.

Now let's try to create multiple threads. You can make a slight modification to DEMO11_5.CPP to add this functionality. All you need to do is call the CreateThread() function multiple times, once for each thread. Also, the data sent to the thread will be the value to print out each time so you can differentiate each thread from one another.

DEMO11_6.CPP|EXE contains the new modified multithreaded program and is listed here for reference. Notice the use of arrays to hold the thread handles and IDs:

```
// DEMO11_6.CPP - A new version that creates 3
// secondary threads of execution
// INCLUDES //////////////////////////////////////////////////

#define WIN32_LEAN_AND_MEAN   // make sure certain headers
                              // are included correctly

#include <windows.h>         // include the standard windows stuff
#include <windowsx.h>        // include the 32 bit stuff
```

Hardcore Game Programming

```c
#include <conio.h>
#include <stdlib.h>
#include <stdarg.h>
#include <stdio.h>
#include <math.h>
#include <io.h>
#include <fcntl.h>

// DEFINES /////////////////////////////////////////////

#define MAX_THREADS 3

// PROTOTYPES ///////////////////////////////////////////

DWORD WINAPI Printer_Thread(LPVOID data);

// GLOBALS //////////////////////////////////////////////

// FUNCTIONS ////////////////////////////////////////////

DWORD WINAPI Printer_Thread(LPVOID data)
{
// this thread function simply prints out data
// 25 times with a slight delay
for (int index=0; index<25; index++)
    {
    printf("%d ",(int)data+1); // output a single character
    Sleep(100);                // sleep a little to slow things down
    } // end for index

// just return the data sent to the thread function
return((DWORD)data);

} // end Printer_Thread

// MAIN /////////////////////////////////////////////////////////////////

void main(void)
{

HANDLE thread_handle[MAX_THREADS];  // this holds the
                                    // handles to the threads
DWORD  thread_id[MAX_THREADS];      // this holds the ids of the threads

// start with a blank line
printf("\nStarting all threads...\n");

// create the thread, IRL we would check for errors
for (int index=0; index<MAX_THREADS; index++)
    {
    thread_handle[index] = CreateThread(NULL, // default security
                       0,                 // default stack
                    Printer_Thread,  // use this thread function
                     (LPVOID)index, // user data sent to thread
```

```
                        0,        // creation flags, 0=start now.
                        &thread_id[index]); // send id back in this var
        } // end for index

// now enter into printing loop, make sure
// this takes longer than threads,
// so threads finish first, note that primary thread prints 4
for (index=0; index<75; index++)
    {
    printf("4 ");
    Sleep(100);
    } // end for index

// at this point the threads should all be dead, so close handles
for (index=0; index<MAX_THREADS; index++)
    CloseHandle(thread_handle[index]);

// end with a blank line
printf("\nAll threads terminated.\n");

} // end main
```

Sample output:

```
Starting all threads...
4 1 2 3 4 1 2 3 4 1 2 3 1 4 2 3 4 1 2 3 1 4 2 3 4
1 2 3 1 4 2 3 4 1 2 3 1 4 2 3 4 1 2 3 4 1 2 3 4 1
2 3 4 1 2 3 4 1 2 3 4 1 2 3 4 1 2 3 4 1 2 3 4 1 2
3 4 1 2 3 4 1 2 3 4 1 2 3 4 1 2 3 4 1 2 3 4 1 2 3
4 4 4 4 4 4 4 4 4 4 4 4 4 4 4 4 4 4 4 4 4 4 4 4 4
4 4 4 4 4 4 4 4 4 4 4 4 4 4 4 4 4 4 4 4 4 4 4 4 4
All threads terminated.
```

Wow! Isn't that cool? It's so easy to create multiple threads. Now, if you're astute, you should be a little weary at this point, and you should question the fact that you used the same function each time for the thread callback. The reason why this works correctly is that all the variables in the code are created on the stack, and each thread has its own stack. So it all works out. Take a look at Figure 11.19 to see this.

Figure 11.19 overlooks something that is very important: *termination*. Both threads terminated on their own, but the primary thread had no control over this. In addition, the primary thread really had no way to tell if the threads were complete and had terminated (that is, if they had returned).

What you need is a way to communicate between threads and check the status of threads from one another or from the primary thread itself. There is a brute-force way to terminate a thread using TerminateThread(), but I suggest that you don't use this.

FIGURE 11.19

Primary and secondary thread memory and code space allocation.

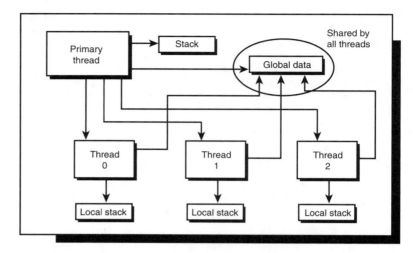

Application process

Sending Messages from Thread to Thread

Let's say that you want the primary thread to have control over the spawned threads that it creates. For example, the primary thread may want to kill all the secondary threads. How can you do this? Well, there are a couple of methods to terminate a thread:

- Sending a message to the thread to tell it to terminate itself (the right way).
- Simply making a kernel-level call and killing the thread (the wrong way).

Although the wrong way might be needed in some cases, it is not safe because it simply pulls the carpet right from under the thread. If the thread needs to perform any clean-up, it never will. This can create memory and resource leaks, so be careful. Figure 11.20 illustrates the different methods to instruct a thread to terminate.

FIGURE 11.20

Thread termination methods.

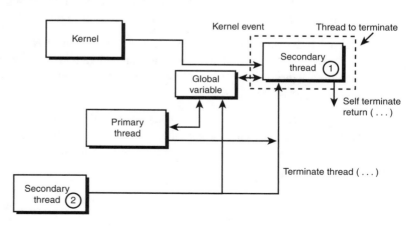

Before you see an example of sending messages to the threads to notify them that they should terminate, take a look at the `TerminateThread()` function call so you know how to use it if the need arises:

```
BOOL TerminateThread(HANDLE  hThread,       // handle to the thread
               DWORD  dwExitCode );     // exit code for the thread
```

`hThread` identifies the thread to terminate. The handle must have `THREAD_TERMINATE` access.

`dwExitCode` specifies the exit code for the thread. Use the `GetExitCodeThread()` function to retrieve a thread's exit value.

If the function succeeds, the return value is `TRUE`. If the function fails, the return value is `FALSE`. To get extended error information, call `GetLastError()`.

`TerminateThread()` is used to cause a thread to exit. When this occurs, the target thread has no chance to execute any user-mode code and its initial stack is not deallocated. DLLs attached to the thread are not notified that the thread is terminating, and that's a bad thing. :)

To use `TerminateThread()`, simply call it with the handle to the thread you want to terminate, along with a return code override, and it will be history. Now, don't get me wrong; the function wouldn't exist if there wasn't a use for it. Just make sure that you know what you're doing when you use it and that you've thought of everything.

Let's move on to the message-passing method of terminating a thread. It works by setting a global variable that the secondary threads watch. Then, when the secondary threads see that the global termination flag has been set, they all terminate. But how does the primary thread know when all the secondary threads have terminated? Well, one way to accomplish the task is have another global variable that the threads decrement when they terminate—a reference counter of sorts.

This counter can be tested by the primary thread, and when it's equal to 0, all the secondary threads have terminated and the primary thread can be confident that it's okay to proceed with work and close the handles to the threads. This is *almost* true... We'll get to the "almost" part after you see a full example of this new message passing system. `DEMO11_7.CPP|EXE` illustrates global message passing and is shown here:

```
// DEMO11_7.CPP - An example of global message passing to control
// termination of threads.

// INCLUDES //////////////////////////////////////////////////

#define WIN32_LEAN_AND_MEAN    // make sure certain headers
                               // are included correctly

#include <windows.h>           // include the standard windows stuff
#include <windowsx.h>          // include the 32 bit stuff
```

```
#include <conio.h>
#include <stdlib.h>
#include <stdarg.h>
#include <stdio.h>
#include <math.h>
#include <io.h>
#include <fcntl.h>

// DEFINES //////////////////////////////////////////////////////

#define MAX_THREADS 3

// PROTOTYPES ///////////////////////////////////////////////////

DWORD WINAPI Printer_Thread(LPVOID data);

// GLOBALS //////////////////////////////////////////////////////

int terminate_threads = 0;  // global message flag to terminate
int active_threads    = 0;  // number of active threads

// FUNCTIONS ////////////////////////////////////////////////////

DWORD WINAPI Printer_Thread(LPVOID data)
{
// this thread function simply prints out data until it is told to terminate

for(;;)
    {
    printf("%d ",(int)data+1); // output a single character
    Sleep(100);                // sleep a little to slow things down

                               // test for termination message
    if (terminate_threads)
       break;

    } // end for index

// decrement number of active threads
if (active_threads > 0)
   active_threads--;

// just return the data sent to the thread function
return((DWORD)data);

} // end Printer_Thread

// MAIN /////////////////////////////////////////////////////////

void main(void)
{

HANDLE thread_handle[MAX_THREADS];  // this holds the
                                    // handles to the threads
```

```
DWORD  thread_id[MAX_THREADS];        // this holds the ids of the threads

// start with a blank line
printf("\nStarting Threads...\n");

// create the thread, IRL we would check for errors
for (int index=0; index < MAX_THREADS; index++)
    {
    thread_handle[index] = CreateThread(NULL, // default security
             0,                // default stack
           Printer_Thread,     // use this thread function
            (LPVOID)index,       // user data sent to thread
           0,                // creation flags, 0=start now.
           &thread_id[index]);// send id back in this var

    // increment number of active threads
    active_threads++;

    } // end for index

// now enter into printing loop, make sure this
// takes longer than threads,
// so threads finish first, note that primary thread prints 4

for (index=0; index<25; index++)
    {
    printf("4 ");
    Sleep(100);
    } // end for index

// at this point all the threads are still running,
// now if the keyboard is hit
// then a message will be sent to terminate all the
// threads and this thread
// will wait for all of the threads to message in

while(!kbhit());

// get that char
getch();

// set global termination flag
terminate_threads = 1;

// wait for all threads to terminate,
// when all are terminated active_threads==0
while(active_threads);

// at this point the threads should all be dead, so close handles
for (index=0; index < MAX_THREADS; index++)
    CloseHandle(thread_handle[index]);
```

```
// end with a blank line
printf("\nAll threads terminated.\n");

} // end main
```

Sample output:

```
Starting Threads...
4 1 2 3 4 2 1 3 4 3 1 2 4 2 1 3 4 3 1 2 4 2 1 3 4 2
 3 1 4 2 1 3 4 2 3 1 4 2 3 1 4 2 3 1 4 2 3 1 4 2 3 1
 4 2 3 1 4 2 3 1 4 2 3 1 4 2 3 1 4 2 3 1 4 2 3 1 4 2
 3 1 4 2 3 1 4 2 3 1 4 2 3 1 4 2 3 1 4 2 3 1 2 3 1 3 2
 1 1 2 3 3 2 1 1 2 3 3 2 1 1 2 3 3 2 1 1 2 3 3 2 1 1 2
 3 3 2 1 2 3 1 3 2 1 2 3 1 3 2 1 2 3 1 3 2 1 2 3 1 3 2
 1 3 1 2 3 2 1 3 1 2 3 2 1
All threads terminated.
```

As you can see from the sample output, when the user hits a key, all threads are terminated and the primary thread then terminates. There are two problems with this
method. The first problem is subtle. Here's the scenario; read it a couple of times to
make sure you see the problem:

1. Assume that all but one of the secondary threads has terminated.

2. Assume that the last thread has processor control, and it decrements the global
   variable that tracks the number of active threads.

3. At the instant this happens, there is a context switch to the primary process. It
   tests the global variable and thinks that all the threads have terminated, but the
   last thread still hasn't *returned*!

In most cases this is not a problem, but it can be if there's anything between the
decrement code and the return code. What you need is a function that can query if a
thread is terminated. This would help in many cases. There is a function group that
waits for signals, referred to as the Wait*() group, that can help.

The second problem is that you've created what is called a *busy loop*, or a polling loop.
This is normally fine in Win16/DOS, but in Win32 it's a bad thing. Sitting in a tight
loop, waiting on a variable, puts a lot of strain on the multitasking kernel and makes
the CPU usage shoot way up.

To see this, you can use SYSMON.EXE (part of the Windows 95/98/ME/XP accessories
usually), PERFMON.EXE (part of Windows NT/2000), or a similar third-party CPU
usage utility. These utilities help you see what is happening with the threads and
processor usage. Anyway, let's look at how the Wait*() class of functions can help
you determine if a thread has terminated.

Waiting for the Right Moment

Get ready for the most confusing explanation you've ever heard... but it's not my
fault, really! Whenever any thread terminates, it becomes *signaled* to the kernel, and

when it is running, it is *unsignaled*. Whatever that means. And what is the price of plastic zippers tomorrow? You don't care! But what you *do* care about is how to test for the signaling.

You can test for this event using the `Wait*()` class of functions, which allow you to test for a single signal (tongue twister) or multiple signals (does that sound sexual to you?). In addition, you can call one of the `Wait*()` functions to wait for the signal(s) until it happens, but without a busy loop. Much better than polling a global, in most cases. Figure 11.21 illustrates the mechanics of the `Wait*()` functions and their relationship to the running application and the OS kernel.

FIGURE 11.21

A timeline of signaling using `Wait*()`.

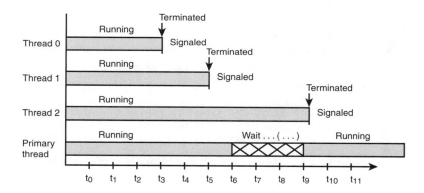

- At t₃ Thread 0 becomes signaled
- At t₅ Thread 1 becomes signaled
- At t₆ primary thread enters wait ... (...)
- At t₉ Thread 2 becomes signaled and primary thread is released.

The two functions that you're going to use are called `WaitForSingleObject()` and `WaitForMultipleObjects()`, which are used to wait for a single signal or multiple signals, respectively. Their definitions are

```
DWORD WaitForSingleObject(HANDLE  hHandle,     // handle of object to wait for
             DWORD  dwMilliseconds );     // time-out interval in milliseconds
```

`hHandle` identifies the object.

`dwMilliseconds` specifies the time-out interval, in milliseconds. The function returns if the interval elapses, even if the object's state is nonsignaled. If `dwMilliseconds` is zero, the function tests the object's state and returns immediately. If `dwMilliseconds` is infinite, the function's time-out interval never elapses.

If the function succeeds, the return value indicates the event that caused the function to return. If the function fails, the return value is `WAIT_FAILED`. To get extended error information, call `GetLastError()`.

The return value on success is one of the following values:

- WAIT_ABANDONED—The specified object is a mutex object that was not released by the thread that owned it before the thread terminated. Ownership of the mutex object is granted to the calling thread, and the mutex is set to nonsignaled.
- WAIT_OBJECT_0—The state of the specified object is signaled.
- WAIT_TIMEOUT—The time-out interval has elapsed, and the object's state is nonsignaled.

Basically, the WaitForSingleObject() function checks the current state of the specified object. If the object's state is nonsignaled, the calling thread enters an efficient wait state. The thread consumes very little processor time while waiting for one of the conditions of the wait to be satisfied. And here is the function used to wait for multiple signals, or in this case multiple threads, to terminate:

```
DWORD WaitForMultipleObjects(DWORD  nCount, // number of handles
                                          // in handle array
         CONST HANDLE *lpHandles, // address of object-handle array
         BOOL  bWaitAll,        // wait flag
         DWORD  dwMilliseconds ); // time-out interval in milliseconds
```

nCount specifies the number of object handles in the array pointed to by lpHandles. The maximum number of object handles is MAXIMUM_WAIT_OBJECTS.

lpHandles points to an array of object handles. The array can contain handles of objects of different types. Note for Windows NT: The handles must have SYNCHRONIZE access.

bWaitAll specifies the wait type. If TRUE, the function returns when all objects in the lpHandles array are signaled at the same time. If FALSE, the function returns when any one of the objects is signaled. In the latter case, the return value indicates the object whose state caused the function to return.

dwMilliseconds specifies the time-out interval, in milliseconds. The function returns if the interval elapses, even if the conditions specified by the bWaitAll parameter are not satisfied. If dwMilliseconds is zero, the function tests the states of the specified objects and returns immediately. If dwMilliseconds is infinite, the function's time-out interval never elapses.

If the function succeeds, the return value indicates the event that caused the function to return. If the function fails, the return value is WAIT_FAILED. To get extended error information, call GetLastError(). The return value upon success is one of the following values

- WAIT_OBJECT_0 **to** (WAIT_OBJECT_0 + nCount - 1)—If bWaitAll is TRUE, the return value indicates that the state of all specified objects is signaled. If bWaitAll is FALSE, the return value minus WAIT_OBJECT_0 indicates the lpHandles array index of the object that satisfied the wait. If more than one object became signaled during the call, this is the array index of the signaled object with the smallest index value of all the signaled objects.

- WAIT_ABANDONED_0 **to** (WAIT_ABANDONED_0 + nCount — 1)—If bWaitAll is TRUE, the return value indicates that the state of all specified objects is signaled and at least one of the objects is an abandoned mutex object. If bWaitAll is FALSE, the return value minus WAIT_ABANDONED_0 indicates the lpHandles array index of an abandoned mutex object that satisfied the wait.

- WAIT_TIMEOUT—The time-out interval elapsed and the conditions specified by the bWaitAll parameter are not satisfied.

WaitForMultipleObjects() determines whether the conditions exist that satisfy the wait. If the wait is not satisfied, the calling thread enters an efficient wait state, consuming very little processor time, while waiting for one of the conditions of the wait to be satisfied.

Using Signaling to Synchronize Threads

These explanations are very technical. So, as an example of how to use these functions, you're going to make another slight change to the program you've been working with. For the next version, you're going to remove the global termination signal flag and create a main loop that simply calls WaitForSingleObject().

The only reason that you're removing the global terminate message is to make the program simpler. This is still the best way to tell threads to terminate; it's just that sitting in a busy loop is not the best way to test if they've actually terminated.

And that is why you're going to use the WaitForSingleObject() call. This call sits in a virtual wait loop that eats very little processor time. Also, because WaitForSingleObject() can only wait for one signal, and thus one thread, to terminate, this example will only have one secondary thread.

In a moment, you'll rewrite the program to contain three threads, and you'll use WaitForMultipleObjects() to wait for all of them to terminate. Anyway, DEMO11_8.CPP|EXE uses WaitForSingleObject() and creates one extra thread. Take a look at the code:

```
// DEMO11_8.CPP - A single threaded example of
// WaitForSingleObject(...).

// INCLUDES /////////////////////////////////////////////////////////
```

Hardcore Game Programming

```
#define WIN32_LEAN_AND_MEAN  // make sure certain
                             // headers are included correctly

#include <windows.h>         // include the standard windows stuff
#include <windowsx.h>        // include the 32 bit stuff
#include <conio.h>
#include <stdlib.h>
#include <stdarg.h>
#include <stdio.h>
#include <math.h>
#include <io.h>
#include <fcntl.h>

// DEFINES ///////////////////////////////////////////////////////

// PROTOTYPES ////////////////////////////////////////////////////

DWORD WINAPI Printer_Thread(LPVOID data);

// GLOBALS ///////////////////////////////////////////////////////

// FUNCTIONS /////////////////////////////////////////////////////

DWORD WINAPI Printer_Thread(LPVOID data)
{ // this thread function simply prints out data 50
// times with a slight delay
for (int index=0; index<50; index++)
    {
    printf("%d ",data); // output a single character
    Sleep(100);         // sleep a little to slow things down
    } // end for index

// just return the data sent to the thread function
return((DWORD)data);

} // end Printer_Thread

// MAIN //////////////////////////////////////////////////////////

void main(void)
{
HANDLE thread_handle;  // this is the handle to the thread
DWORD  thread_id;      // this is the id of the thread

// start with a blank line
printf("\nStarting threads...\n");

// create the thread, IRL we would check for errors
thread_handle = CreateThread(NULL, // default security
              0,              // default stack
              Printer_Thread, // use this thread function
              (LPVOID)1,      // user data sent to thread
              0,              // creation flags, 0=start now.
              &thread_id);    // send id back in this var
```

```
// now enter into printing loop, make sure
// this is shorter than the thread,
// so thread finishes last
for (int index=0; index<25; index++)
    {
    printf("2 ");
    Sleep(100);
    } // end for index

// note that this print statement may get
// interspliced with the output of the
// thread, very key!

printf("\nWaiting for thread to terminate\n");

// at this point the secondary thread so still be working,
// now we will wait for it
WaitForSingleObject(thread_handle, INFINITE);

// at this point the thread should be dead
CloseHandle(thread_handle);

// end with a blank line
printf("\nAll threads terminated.\n");

} // end main
```

Sample output:

```
Starting threads...
2 1 2 1 2 1 1 2 2 1 1 2 2 1 1 2 2 1 1 2 2 1
1 2 2 1 1 2 2 1 1 2 2 1 1 2 2 1 1 2 2 1 1 2 2 1 1 2 2 1 1
Waiting for thread to terminate
1 1 1 1 1 1 1 1 1 1 1 1 1 1 1 1 1 1 1 1 1 1 1 1 1
All threads terminated.
```

The program is very simple. As usual, you create the secondary thread and then, right away, you enter into the printing loop. When it terminates, the WaitForSingleObject() is called. If you had more work to do in the primary thread, you would do it. But in this case you don't, so you just enter into the wait function and wait. If you run the program with SYSMON.EXE active, you'll see that there is almost no processor usage when the wait function is entered, whereas there would be if you used a busy loop.

Before moving on to the next example and multiple threads, there is a little trick you can do with WaitForSingleObject(). Let's say that you want to know the status of a thread at this moment, but you don't want to wait for it to terminate. This can be done by making a NULL call to WaitForSingleObject(), shown here:

```
//...code

DWORD state = WaitForSingleObject(thread_handle, 0);  // get the status
```

```
// test the status
if (state==WAIT_OBJECT_0) { // thread is signaled, i.e. terminated }
else
   if (state==WAIT_TIMEOUT) { // thread is still running }

//...code
```

Simple enough. This is a great way to test if a particular thread has terminated. This, coupled with the global termination message, is a very robust method to terminate a thread and check if it was actually terminated in a real-time loop when you don't want to wait for the termination until it happens.

Waiting for Multiple Objects

You're almost done. The last Wait*() class function waits on multiple objects or threads to signal. Let's make a program that uses this function. All you need to do is create an array of threads and then pass the array of handles to WaitForMultipleObjects(), along with a couple of parameters.

When the function returns, if all went well, all the threads will have terminated. DEMO11_9.CPP|EXE is similar to DEMO11_8.CPP|EXE, except that it creates multiple threads and then the primary thread waits for all of them to terminate. Again, you don't use a global termination flag because you already know how to. Each secondary thread simply runs a few cycles and then terminates. The source for DEMO11_9.CPP is listed here for your review:

```
// DEMO11_9.CPP -An example use of
// WaitForMultipleObjects(...)

// INCLUDES ////////////////////////////////////////////////

#define WIN32_LEAN_AND_MEAN   // make sure certain headers
// are included correctly

#include <windows.h>         // include the standard windows stuff
#include <windowsx.h>        // include the 32 bit stuff
#include <conio.h>
#include <stdlib.h>
#include <stdarg.h>
#include <stdio.h>
#include <math.h>
#include <io.h>
#include <fcntl.h>

// DEFINES /////////////////////////////////////////////////

#define MAX_THREADS 3

// PROTOTYPES //////////////////////////////////////////////

DWORD WINAPI Printer_Thread(LPVOID data);
```

```
// GLOBALS ///////////////////////////////////////////////

// FUNCTIONS /////////////////////////////////////////////

DWORD WINAPI Printer_Thread(LPVOID data)
{
// this thread function simply prints out data 50
// times with a slight delay
for (int index=0; index<50; index++)
    {
    printf("%d ",(int)data+1); // output a single character
    Sleep(100);                // sleep a little to slow things down
    } // end for index

// just return the data sent to the thread function
return((DWORD)data);

} // end Printer_Thread

// MAIN //////////////////////////////////////////////////

void main(void)
{
HANDLE thread_handle[MAX_THREADS]; // this holds the
                                   // handles to the threads
DWORD  thread_id[MAX_THREADS];     // this holds the ids of the threads

// start with a blank line
printf("\nStarting all threads...\n");

// create the thread, IRL we would check for errors
for (int index=0; index<MAX_THREADS; index++)
    {
    thread_handle[index] = CreateThread(NULL, // default security
                         0,         // default stack
                Printer_Thread,// use this thread function
                (LPVOID)index, // user data sent to thread
                0,         // creation flags, 0=start now.
                &thread_id[index]);     // send id back in this var
    } // end for index

// now enter into printing loop,
// make sure this takes less time than the threads
// so it finishes first
for (index=0; index<25; index++)
    {
    printf("4 ");
    Sleep(100);
    } // end for index

// now wait for all the threads to signal termination
WaitForMultipleObjects(MAX_THREADS, // number of threads to wait for
                  thread_handle,  // handles to threads
                  TRUE,           // wait for all?
```

```
                    INFINITE);        // time to wait,INFINITE = forever

// at this point the threads should all be dead, so close handles
for (index=0; index<MAX_THREADS; index++)
    CloseHandle(thread_handle[index]);

// end with a blank line
printf("\nAll threads terminated.\n");

} // end main
```

Sample output:

```
Starting all threads...
4 1 2 3 4 1 2 3 1 4 2 3 2 4 1 3 1 4 2 3 2 4 1 3
1 4 2 3 2 4 1 3 1 4 2 3 2 4 1 3 1 4 2 3 2 4 1 3
1 4 2 3 2 4 1 3 1 4 2 3 2 4 1 3 1 4 2 3 2 4 1 3
1 4 2 3 2 4 1 3 1 4 2 3 2 4 1 3 1 4 2 3 2 4 1 3
1 4 2 3 2 1 3 2 1 3 2 1 3 2 1 3 2 1 3 2 1 3 2 1
3 2 1 3 2 1 3 2 1 3 2 1 3 2 1 3 2 1 3 2 1 3 2 1
3 2 1 3 2 1 3 2 1 3 2 1 3 2 1 3 2 1 3 2 1 3 2 1 3 2 1 3 2 1 3 2 1 3
All threads terminated.
```

The sample output is what you'd expect. All threads print along with the primary thread (which prints 4's for a bit), but when the loop in the primary thread is complete, the secondary threads continue until they all finish. Once all the threads terminate, the primary thread terminates because it is blocked from termination via the WaitForMultipleObjects().

Multithreading and DirectX

Now you know something about multithreading. The next question is how you can really use it in game programming and DirectX programs. Just do it—that's all there is to it. Of course, you must make sure to use the multithreaded libraries rather than the single-threaded libraries when compiling. In addition, there are a lot of "critical section" problems that might arise when you're mucking with DirectX resources.

Make sure that you use a global strategy for resources so that if more than one thread accesses a resource, nothing will blow up. For example, let's say that one thread locks a surface, and then another thread executes and tries to lock the same surface. This will cause a problem. These kinds of problems can be solved using *sempahores*, *mutexes*, and *critical sections*. I don't have time to cover any of these, but you can always pick up a good book on the subject, like *Multithreading Applications in Win32* by Jim Beveridge and Robert Weiner, published by Addison Wesley. This is the best book I've seen on the topic.

To implement these types of resource management applications and to share threads properly, you simply create variables that track if another thread is using the resource. Then, any thread that wants a resource that other thread might be using tests this variable before mucking with it. Of course, this can also be a problem unless the variable can be tested and changed *atomically*, because you could be halfway through changing a variable and another thread could gain control.

You can minimize this by making these variables of the type `volatile`, which tells the compiler not to make memory copies, for one thing. However, in the end you'll have to use *semaphores* (a simple counter like the global variable, but implemented with atomic code in assembly that can't be interrupted), *mutexes* (allows only one thread to enter a critical section; a binary semaphore), *critical sections* (sections that you indicate to the compiler with Win32 calls that are only supposed to allow one thread at a time), and so forth, so read up on them. On the other hand, if each thread is fairly independent in what it does, you won't have to worry about this stuff as much.

For an example of a DirectX application that uses threads, check out `DEMO11_10.CPP|EXE`. (16-bit version, `DEMO11_10_16B.CPP|EXE`). It creates a number of alien BOBs (blitter objects) and moves them around in the mainline. Mutlithreading is used to animate the colors of the BOBs for the 8-bit version and move the BOBs in the 16-bit version. This is a very simple and safe example of multithreading. Make sure to link with all the DirectX `.LIB` files.

However, if you had many threads all calling the same functions, the problem of reentrancy would come into play. Functions that are reentrant need to have state information and can't use globals that can be corrupted by preemptive threads coming in and out of the code.

In addition, if you use threads to animate the DirectX blitter objects themselves, surface contingency, timing, and synchronization will really wreak havoc on your code. I suggest restricting the use of threads to processes that are for the most part independent of others, exist in their own "state space," and don't have to run at a precise rate.

Advanced Multithreading

Well, this is a good place to stop because the next set of topics has to do with race conditions, deadlocks, critical sections, mutexes, semaphores, and really big headaches. All of these things (except the last one) help you write multithreaded programs that don't step on each other. However, even without knowing about them, you can still accomplish a lot of safe multithreaded programming just by using common sense and remembering that any thread can interrupt any other thread. Just be careful with how your threads access shared data structures.

Try to do everything as automatically as possible. Make sure that one thread doesn't alter a variable and then another thread uses this half-altered version! Also, there were a few function calls left out of this chapter that are fairly basic, such as `ExitThread()` and `GetThreadExitCode()`, but they're fairly simple to understand and you can look them up in your favorite API bible.

Summary

This has been a refreshing chapter, don't you think? :) Nothing too technical; just a potpourri of invaluable information in a scintillating format. Okay, I think I've had one too many Power Bars! Seriously, though, we've covered a lot of ground: data structures, memory management, recursion, analysis, fixed-point math, and multi-threading.

These things may not seem to be game-related, but they are. To make a game, you need to know every single topic in programming—it's that complex! Anyway, go out and rent *2001: A Space Odyssey,* because it's time to talk about artificial intelligence....

CHAPTER 12

Making Silicon Think with Artificial Intelligence

"I'm sorry, Dave. I'm afraid I can't do that..."
—HAL 9000, 2001: A Space Odyssey

This chapter is going to answer a lot of questions about the black art of artificial intelligence. In fact, depending on how you look at things, artificial intelligence is not artificial at all. It is an intelligence of sorts based on logic, mathematics, probability, and memory—and isn't that all *we* are?

By the end of this chapter, you'll be able to write code and algorithms to make game creatures perform in a reasonable manner and do almost anything that you want them to do. Here's what's covered:

- Artificial intelligence primer
- Simple deterministic algorithms
- Patterns and scripts
- Behavioral state systems
- Memory and learning
- Planning and decision trees

- Pathfinding
- Advanced scripting languages
- Neural network basics
- Genetic algorithms
- Fuzzy logic

Artificial Intelligence Primer

Artificial intelligence, in the most academic sense of the phrase, has come to mean a piece of hardware or software that enables a computer to "think" or process information in a fashion somewhat similar to our own.

Applications in AI just started to surface a few years ago, but today AI and other related fields, such as *a-life (artificial life)* and *intelligent agents*, are maturing at an exponential rate. In fact, that little MS Word paper clip agent keeps annoying me as I write this sentence!

Today, systems exist that are "alive," as far as anyone can define life. A number of companies have created artificial lifeforms within the virtual domain of the computer that live, die, explore, get sick, reproduce, evolve, get depressed, get hungry, and so on.

This kind of technology has been made possible with *artificial neural networks, genetic algorithms*, and *fuzzy logic*. Neural networks are crude approximations of a human brain, and genetic algorithms are a set of techniques and suppositions used for the evolution of software systems based on biological paradigms. Fuzzy logic is set theory based on *non-crisp* suppositions, like "It's sort of hot out."

Sound far out? It is. But it's real, and it's only going to get better. Remember, cloning used to be science fiction, but now it's science fact.

Coming back down to Earth, you aren't going to create anything as complex as state-of-the-art AI for your games. Instead, you're going to look at the most simplistic and fundamental techniques that game programmers use to create intelligent creatures— or at least creatures that *seem* intelligent. In fact, many game programmers are still very behind on AI and haven't begun to really embrace all that's available in the field. I suspect that AI and related technologies are going to make the same kind of impact on the gaming world that the *DOOM* graphics technology made many years ago.

Truthfully, 3D graphics are starting to slow down. Things are *looking* pretty real these days, but they still *act* pretty dumb. The next killer game is going to look good, but more importantly, it's going to be as cunning and devious as the best of us.

Finally, as you read the following pages and experiment with the accompanying programs, remember that all these techniques are just that—techniques. There isn't a right way or a wrong way, just a way that works. If the computer-operated tank can kick your butt, that's all you need. If it can't, you need to do more.

Regardless of how primitive the underlying AI techniques are, the human players will always project personalities onto their virtual opponents. This is key—the player will believe that the objects in the game really *are* plotting, planning, and thinking, as long as they *look* like they are…Get it?

Deterministic AI Algorithms

Deterministic algorithms are behaviors that are predetermined or preprogrammed. For example, if you take a look at the AI for the polygon Asteroids demo introduced in Chapter 8, "Vector Rasterization and 2D Transformations" (shown in Figure 12.1), it's very simple.

FIGURE 12.1
The Asteroids AI.

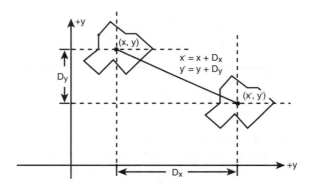

The AI creates an asteroid and then sends it in a random direction with a random velocity. This is a type of intelligence as shown here:

```
asteroid_x += asteroid_x_velocity;
asteroid_y += asteroid_y_velocity;
```

The asteroids have one goal: to follow their course. That's it. The AI is simple—the asteroids don't process any outside input, make course changes, and so on. In a sense they're intelligent, but their intelligence is rather deterministic and predictable. This is the first kind of AI I want to look at—the simple, predictable, programmable kind. In this class of AI, there are a number of techniques that were born in the *Pong/Pac-Man* era.

Random Motion

Just one step above moving an object in a straight line or curve is moving an object or changing its properties randomly, as shown in Figure 12.2.

FIGURE 12.2
Random-motion AI.

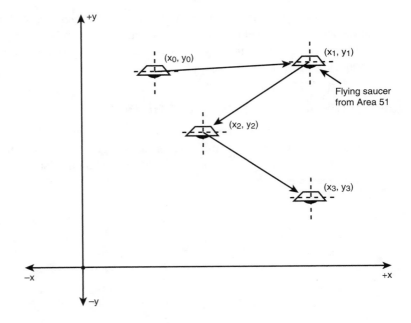

For example, let's say you wanted to model an atom, fly, or something similar that doesn't have a lot of brains, but does have a fairly predictable behavior—it bounces around in an erratic way. Well, at least it *looks* that way.

For a starting AI model, you might try something like this to model a fly's brain:

```
fly_x_velocity = -8 + rand()%16;
fly_y_velocity = -8 + rand()%16;
```

Then you could move the fly around for a few cycles:

```
int fly_count = 0; // fly new thought counter

// fly in the same direction for 10 ticks of time
while(++fly_count < 10)
    {
    fly_x+=fly_x_velocity;
    fly_y+=fly+y_velocity;
    } // end while

// .. pick a new direction and loop
```

In this example, the fly would pick a random direction and velocity, move that way for a moment, and then pick another. That sounds like a fly to me! Of course, you might want to add even more randomness, such as changing how long the motion occurs instead of fixing it at 10 cycles. In addition, you might want to weigh certain directions more heavily than others. For example, you might want to lean toward westward directions to simulate the breeze or something.

In any case, I think you can see that it's possible to make something seem intelligent with very little code. As a working example, check out DEMO12_1.CPP|EXE (16-bit version, DEMO12_1_16B.CPP|EXE) on the CD. It's an example of the artificial fly in action.

Random motion is a very important part of the behavioral modeling of intelligent creatures. I live in Silicon Valley, and I can attest that the people who drive on the roads around here make random lane changes and even drive the wrong direction, which is pretty similar to the fly's brainless motion....

Tracking Algorithms

Although random motion can be totally unpredictable, it's rather boring because no matter what, it works the same way—that is, randomly. The next step up in the AI evolutionary ladder are algorithms, which take into consideration something in the environment and then react to it. As an example of this, I have chosen *tracking* algorithms. A tracking AI takes into consideration the position of the object being tracked, and then it changes the trajectory of the AI object so that it moves toward the object being tracked.

The tracking can be literally vectored directly toward the object, or it can be a more realistic model, turning toward the object much like a heat-seeking missile would do. Take a look at Figure 12.3.

FIGURE 12.3
Tracking methods.

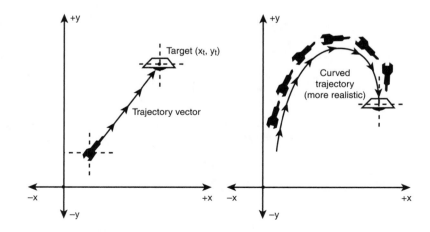

A. Direct vector tracking

B. Curved tracking

For an example of the brute-force method, take a look at this algorithm:

```
// given: player is at player_x, player_y
// and game creature is at
// monster_x, monster_y

// first test x-axis
if (player_x > monster_x)
   monster_x++;
if (player_x < monster_x)
   monster_x--;

// now y -axis
if (player_y > monster_y)
   monster_y++;
if (player_y < monster_y)
   monster_y--;
```

If you dropped this AI into a simple demo, it would track you down in Terminator-like fashion! The code is simple but effective. Pac-Man's AI was written in much the same way. Of course, Pac-Man could only make right-angle turns and had to move in a straight line and avoid obstacles, but it's in the same ballpark. For an example, check out DEMO12_2.CPP|EXE (16-bit version, DEMO12_2_16B.CPP|EXE) on the CD. In it, you control a ghost with the keyboard arrow keys while a bat tries to hunt you down.

This kind of tracking is great, but it's a little artificial because the AI-controlled object tracks the target precisely. A more natural approach to tracking might be to change the trajectory vector of the tracking object in the direction defined from the center of the tracking object to the center of the object being tracked. Take a look at Figure 12.4 to see this.

FIGURE 12.4

Tracking an object based on trajectory vectoring.

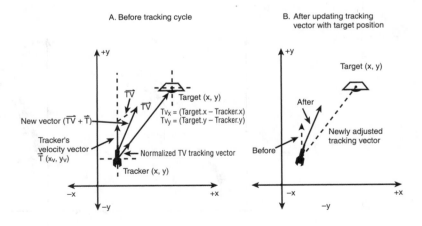

The algorithm works as follows: Assume that the AI-controlled object is called `tracker` and has the following properties:

```
Position:(tracker.x, tracker.y)
Velocity:(tracker.xv, tracker.yv)
```

The object to be tracked is called `target` and has the following properties:

```
Position:(target.x, target.y)
Velocity:(target.xv, target.yv)
```

Based on those definitions, here is the general logic cycle that adjusts the velocity vector of the tracker:

1. Compute the vector from the tracker to the target:

TV =(target.x – tracker.x, target.y – tracker.y) = (tvx, tvy), normalize **TV**—in other words, divide (tvx, tvy)/`Vector_Length`(tvx,tvy) so that the max length is 1.0, and call this **TV***. Note that `Vector_Length()` just computes the length of a vector from the origin (0,0), or in other words the $sqrt(x^2 + y^2)$.

2. Adjust the current velocity vector of the tracker by adding TV* scaled by a `rate`:

```
tracker.x+=rate*tvx;
tracker.y+=rate*tvy;
```

Note that as `rate` becomes larger than 1.0, the track vectoring converges more swiftly, and the tracking algorithm tracks the target more closely and makes changes to the target's movements more quickly.

3. After the tracker's velocity vector has been modified, there's a possibility that the vector velocity has overflowed a maximum rate. In other words, the tracker continues to speed up in the direction of the target once it has a lock. As a result, you should put an upper bound on this and slow the tracker down at some point. Here's an example:

```
// get magnitude of velocity vector
tspeed = Vector_Length(tracker.xv, tracker.yv);

// moving too fast?
if (tspeed > MAX_SPEED)
    {
    // shrink the velocity vector
    tracker.xv*=0.75;
    tracker.yv*=0.75;
    } // end if
```

There are other choices—0.5 or 0.9—whatever. It's even possible to compute the exact overflow and then shrink the vector by that amount, if perfection's your goal.

Hardcore Game Programming

I know we haven't hit vector math yet, and yet I've been using the terminology in this example, so I thought I would give an example of some tracking code that uses this algorithm, ripped right out of a real game. This code makes these little mines track the player. Look at how the real code performs all the previous steps in a real example:

```
// mine tracking algorithm

// compute vector toward player
float vx = player_x - mines[index].varsI[INDEX_WORLD_X];
float vy = player_y - mines[index].varsI[INDEX_WORLD_Y];

// normalize vector (sorta :)
float length = Fast_Distance_2D(vx,vy);

// only track if reasonable close
if (length < MIN_MINE_TRACKING_DIST)
   {
   vx=MINE_TRACKING_RATE*vx/length;
   vy=MINE_TRACKING_RATE*vy/length;

   // add velocity vector to current velocity
   mines[index].xv+=vx;
   mines[index].yv+=vy;

   // add a little noise
   if ((rand()%10)==1)
      {
      vx = RAND_RANGE(-1,1);
      vy = RAND_RANGE(-1,1);
      mines[index].xv+=vx;
      mines[index].yv+=vy;
      } // end if

   // test velocity vector of mines
   length = Fast_Distance_2D(mines[index].xv, mines[index].yv);

   // test for velocity overflow and slow
   if (length > MAX_MINE_VELOCITY)
      {
      // slow down
      mines[index].xv*=0.75;
      mines[index].yv*=0.75;
      } // end if
   } // end if
else
   {
   // add a random velocity component
   if ((rand()%30)==1)
      {
      vx = RAND_RANGE(-2,2);
      vy = RAND_RANGE(-2,2);
```

```
        // add velocity vector to current velocity
        mines[index].xv+=vx;
        mines[index].yv+=vy;

        // test velocity vector of mines
        length = Fast_Distance_2D(mines[index].xv, mines[index].yv);

        // test for velocity overflow and slow
        if (length > MAX_MINE_VELOCITY)
            {
            // slow down
            mines[index].xv*=0.75;
            mines[index].yv*=0.75;

            } // end if

        } // end if

    } // end else
```

Although it's obvious that this code was hijacked from a `for` loop or something that processed a number of mines, that's irrelevant. It's a good example of a clean implementation of the algorithm, but it also has some areas I want to bring to your attention. For example, there's a section of the code that tests if the mine is within a certain distance of the player. If not, the mine doesn't track the player but has its trajectory slightly modified with some random noise. In addition, even when the mine tracks the player, I add some random noise to the result. This adds more realism to the tracking. In space, water, air, or whatever, there are going to be changes in gravity, density, and so forth that would slightly alter the physics. Thus, adding the noise makes things more realistic.

For an example of this trajectory tracking algorithm, check out `DEMO12_3.CPP|EXE` (16-bit version not available) on the CD. It allows you to move a little ship around in a scrolling universe. Within this universe are mines that follow you by using the previous algorithm. The controls are

Arrow Keys	Controls ship
Ctrl	Fires ship's weapons
+/-	Changes the tracking rate
H	Toggles HUDS
S	Toggles scanner

Notice how decreasing the tracking rate makes the tracking object look like it's on ice.

This is a good example of a small game, so there's a lot to learn. Study it well.

TIP   Because I'm using GDI to draw text, the text printing slows the game down tremendously. I wanted you to see this. In a real game, you would make your own font engine to draw text.

Anti-Tracking: Evasion Algorithms

Starting to get little quantum disturbances in your brain—that is, ideas? Good! The next AI technique is to enable creatures in the game to get away from you. Remember how the ghosts in Pac-Man fled when you ate the powerups? Making an evasion AI do the same thing is simple. In fact, you already have the code! The previous tracking code is the exact opposite of what you want; just take the code and flip the equalities around. Presto! You'll have an evasion algorithm. Here's the code after the inversions:

```
// given: player is at player_x, player_y
// and game creature is at
// monster_x, monster_y

// first test x-axis
if (player_x  < monster_x)
   monster_x++;
if (player_x > monster_x)
   monster_x--;

// now y -axis
if (player_y <  monster_y)
   monster_y++;
if (player_y > monster_y)
   monster_y--;
```

NOTE   If you have a heartbeat, you should have noticed that there is no conditional for equal to (==). This is because I don't want the object to move in this case. I want it to sit on the player. If you want, you can make the == case do something else.

Now you can create a fairly impressive AI system with just random motion, chasing, and evasion. In fact, you have enough to make a Pac-Man brain. Not much, but good enough to sell 100 million or so copies, so that's not too bad! To check out evasion in action, run DEMO12_4.CPP|EXE (16-bit version, DEMO12_4._16BCPP|EXE) on the CD. It's basically the same as DEMO12_2.CPP, but with the evasion AI instead of the tracking AI. Now let's move on to patterns.

Patterns and Basic Control Scripting

Algorithmic and deterministic algorithms are great, but sometimes you need to make a game object follow a sequence of steps, or a script of sorts. For example, when you start your car, there is a specific sequence of steps that you perform:

1. Get the keys out of your pocket.
2. Put the key in the door.
3. Open the door.
4. Get in the car.
5. Close the door.
6. Put the key in the ignition.
7. Turn the key.
8. Start the car.

The point is that there's a sequence of steps that you don't think much about. You just replay them every time. Of course, if something goes wrong, you might change your sequence, like pressing the gas pedal or jump-starting the car because you left the lights on last night. Patterns are an important part of intelligent behavior, and even humans, the epitome of intelligent life on this planet (yeah, right), use them.

Basic Patterns

Creating patterns for game objects can be simple, depending on the game object itself. For example, motion control patterns are very simple to implement. Let's say you're writing a shoot-'em-up game similar to *Phoenix* or *Galaxian*. The alien attackers must follow a left-right pattern and then at some point attack you with a specific attack pattern. This kind of pattern or scripted AI can be achieved using a number of different techniques, but I think the easiest technique is based on interpreted motion instructions, as shown in Figure 12.5.

Each motion pattern is stored as a sequence of directions or instructions, as shown in Table 12.1.

TABLE 12.1 A Hypothetical Pattern Language Instruction Set

Instruction	Value
GO_FORWARD	1
GO_BACKWARD	2
TURN_RIGHT_90	3
TURN_LEFT_90	4
SELECT_RANDOM_DIRECTION	5
STOP	6

Hardcore Game Programming

FIGURE 12.5
The pattern engine.

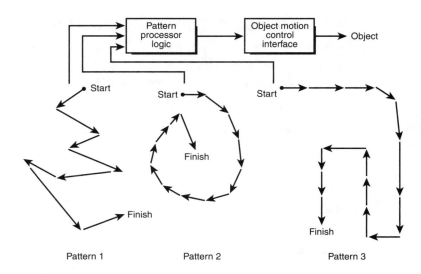

Each pattern consists of a sequence of opcodes:
op-1, op-2, op-3, . . . , op-n
that define the pattern

Along with each directional instruction might be another operand or piece of data that further qualifies the instruction, such as how long to do it. As a result, the pattern language instruction format might look like the following:

INSTRUCTION OPERAND

INSTRUCTION is from the previous list (usually encoded as a single number), and OPERAND is another number that helps further define the behavior of the instruction. With this simple instruction format, you create a program (sequence of instructions) that defines the pattern. Then you write an interpreter that feeds from a source pattern and controls the game creature appropriately.

For example, let's say your pattern language is formatted so that the first number is the instruction itself and the second number indicates how long to perform the motion, in cycles. Creating a square pattern with a spin and stop, as shown in Figure 12.6, would be trivial.

Here's an example of that in coded [INSTRUCTION, OPERAND] format:

```
int num_instructions = 6; // number of instructions in script pattern

// this holds the actual pattern script
int square_stop_spin[
    1,30, 3,1,     // go forward then turn right
    1,30, 3,1,     // go forward then turn right
    1,30, 3,1,     // go forward then turn right
    1,30,          // go forward and finish square
```

```
    6,60,          // stop for 60 cycles
    4,8, ];        // spin for 8 cycles
```

To process the pattern instructions, all you need is a big `switch()` statement that interprets each instruction and tells the game creature what it's supposed to do, like this:

```
// points to first instruction (2 words per instruction)
int instruction_ptr = 0;

// first extract the number of cycles
int cycles = square_stop_spin[instruction_ptr+1];

// now process instruction
switch(square_stop_spin[instruction_ptr])
{
case GO_FORWARD: // move creature forward...
    break;
case GO_BACKWARD: // move creature backward...
    break;
case TURN_RIGHT_90: // turn creature 90 degrees right...
        break;
case TURN_LEFT_90: // turn creature 90 degrees left...
        break;
case SELECT_RANDOM_DIECTION: // select random dir...
        break;
case STOP: // stop the creature
        break;
} // end switch

// advance instruction pointer (2 words per instruction)
instruction_ptr+=2;

// test if end of sequence has been detected...
if (instruction_ptr > num_instructions*2)
   { /* sequence over */ }
```

And, of course, you would add the logic to track the cycle counter and make the motion happen.

There's one catch to all this pattern stuff: *reasonable motion*. Because the game object is feeding off a pattern, it might decide to select a pattern that forces the object to smash into something. If the pattern AI doesn't take this into consideration, patterns will be followed blindly. As a result, you must have a feedback loop with your pattern AI (as with any AI) that instructs the AI that it has done something illegal, impossible, or unreasonable, and it must reset to another pattern or strategy. This is shown in Figure 12.7.

FIGURE 12.6
A detailed square
pattern.

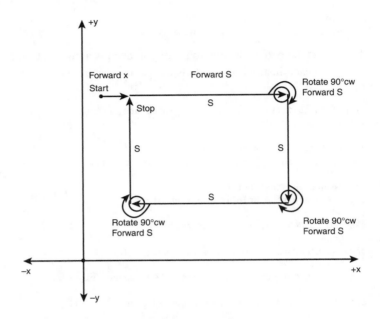

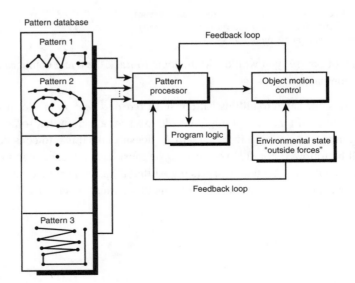

NOTE

Of course, you might want to use a better data structure than an array.
For example, try using a class or structure containing a list of records in
[INSTRUCTION, OPERAND] format, along with the number of instructions.
That way you could very easily create an array of these structures, each
containing a different pattern, and then select a pattern and pass it to
the pattern processor.

FIGURE 12.7
Pattern engine with
feedback control.

Stop for a minute and think about the power of patterns. With them, you could record hundreds of moves and flight patterns. Patterns that would be nearly impossible to create in any reasonable amount of time using other AI techniques can be created in minutes with a tool (that you would write), recorded in a file, and then played back in your game. Using this technique, you can make a game creature look as if it's extremely intelligent. This technique is used by nearly all games, including most fighting games such as *Dead or Alive*, *Tekken*, *Soul Blade*, *Mortal Kombat*, and so on.

Furthermore, there's no need to stop with motion patterns. You could use patterns to control weapon selection, animation control, and so on. There's no limit to how they can be applied. For an example of patterns in action, take a look at DEMO12_5.CPP|EXE (16-bit version, DEMO12_5_16B.CPP|EXE), which demonstrates a monster that moves around using a number of patterns and selects a new pattern every so often.

Patterns with Conditional Logic Processing

Patterns are cool, but they're extremely deterministic. That is, once the player has memorized a pattern, it's useless. Players can always beat your AI because they know what's going to happen next. The solution to this problem, and to other problems that pop up with patterns, is to add a bit of conditional logic that selects patterns based on more than random selection, taking into account the conditions of the game world and the actual player. Take a look at Figure 12.8 to see this abstractly.

FIGURE 12.8
Patterns with
conditional logic.

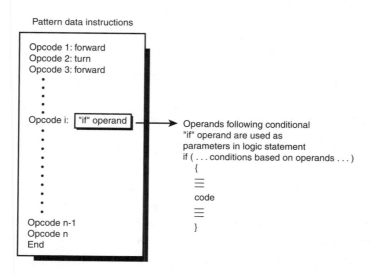

Patterns with conditional logic give you yet one more level of control over your AI models—you can select patterns that contain conditional branches as well as the patterns being selected based on conditional logic. For example, you might add a new instruction to the pattern language that is a conditional logic test:

```
TEST_DISTANCE 7
```

The TEST_DISTANCE conditional might work by testing the distance of the player from the object performing the pattern. If the distance is too close, too far, or whatever, the pattern AI engine might change what it's doing, making for a seemingly more intelligent opponent. For example, you might put a TEST_DISTANCE instruction every so many instructions in a standard pattern, like this:

```
TURN_RIGHT_90, GO_FORWARD, STOP, ...TEST_DISTANCE, ...TURN_LEFT_90,
➥...TEST_DISTANCE, ... GO_BACKWARD
```

The pattern does its thing, but every time a TEST_DISTANCE instruction is encountered, the pattern AI uses the operand following the TEST_DISTANCE instruction as a measure to test the player's position. If the player is getting too far away, the pattern AI stops the current pattern and branches to another pattern. Or possibly better yet, it switches to a deterministic tracking algorithm to get closer to the player. Take a look at the following code:

```
if (instruction_stream[instruction_ptr] == TEST_DISTANCE)
{
// obtain distance, note that on the test
// instructions the operand is no

// longer a time or cycle count
// but becomes context dependent
int min_distance = instruction_stream[instruction_ptr];

// if test if player is too far
if (Distance(player, object) > min_distance)
    {
    // set system state to switch to track
    ai_state = TRACK_PLAYER;

    // .. or you might just switch to
    // another pattern and hope
    // that the object gets closer
    } // end if
} // end if
```

There's no limit to the complexity of the conditional tests that you can perform in the pattern script. In addition, you may want to create patterns on-the-fly and then use them. One such example is to mimic the player's motion. You could sample what the player does each time she kills one of your game characters, and then use the same tactic against her!

In conclusion, technology like this (although much more sophisticated) is used in many sports games, such as football, baseball, and hockey, as well as action and strategy games. It allows the game objects to make predictable moves, while still allowing them to "change their minds."

As an example, DEMO12_6.CPP|EXE (16-bit version, DEMO12_6_16B.CPP|EXE) illustrates the conditional technique. You control a bat creature with the arrow keys, and there is an AI skeleton on the screen. The skeleton follows randomly selected patterns until you get too far away, and then it gets lonely and chases you because it wants your attention. (Reflect on what I just said...I placed an emotional motive on 100 lines of computer code. But isn't that what it seems like, from a spectator's point of view? Mr. Turing, are you there?)

Modeling Behavioral State Systems

At this point, you have seen quite a few *finite state machines* in various forms—code to make lights blink, the main event loop state machines, and so forth. Now I want to formalize how *FSMs* (*finite state machines*) are used to generate AIs that exhibit intelligence.

To create a truly robust FSM, you need two properties:

- A reasonable number of states, each of which represents a different goal or motive.
- Lots of input to the FSM, such as the state of the environment and the other objects within the environment.

The premise of "a reasonable number of states" is easy enough to understand and appreciate. We humans have hundreds, if not thousands, of emotional states, and within each of these we may have further substates. The point is that a game character should be able to move around in a free manner, at the very least. For example, you may set up the following states:

State 1: Move forward.

State 2: Move backward.

State 3: Turn.

State 4: Stop.

State 5: Fire weapon.

State 6: Chase player.

State 7: Evade player.

States 1 to 4 are straightforward, but states 5, 6, and 7 might need substates to be properly modeled. This means that there may be more than one phase to states 5, 6, and 7. For example, chasing the player might involve turning and then moving forward. Take a look at Figure 12.9 to see the concept of substates illustrated. However, don't assume that substates must be based on states that actually exist—they may be totally artificial for the state in question.

The point of this discussion of states is that the game object needs to have enough variety to do "intelligent" things. If the only two states are stop and forward, there isn't going to be much action! Remember those stupid remote-control cars that went forward and then reversed in a left turn? What fun was that?

FIGURE 12.9
A master FSM with substates.

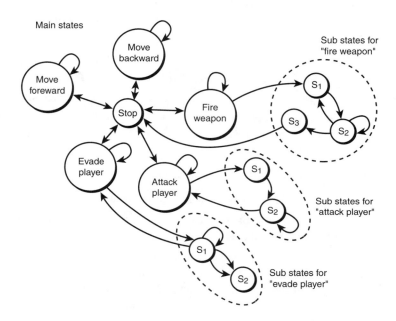

Moving on to the second property of robust FSM AIs, you need to have feedback or input from the other objects in the game world and from the player and environment. If you simply enter a state and run it until completion, that's pretty dumb. The state may have been selected intelligently, but that was 100 milliseconds ago. Now things have changed, and the player just did something that the AI needs to respond to. The FSM needs to track the game state and, if needed, be preempted from its current state into another one.

If you take all this into consideration, you can create an FSM that models commonly experienced behaviors such as aggression, curiosity, and so on. Let's see how this works with some concrete examples, beginning with simple state machines and following up with more advanced personality-based FSMs.

Elementary State Machines

At this point, you should be seeing a lot of overlap in the various AI techniques. For example, the pattern techniques are based on finite state machines at the lowest level which perform the actual motions or effects. What I want to do now is take finite state machines to another level and talk about high-level states that can be implemented with simple conditional logic, randomness, and patterns. In essence, I want to create a virtual brain that directs and dictates to the creature.

To better understand what I'm talking about, let's take a few behaviors and model them with the aforementioned techniques. On top of these behaviors, we'll place a master FSM to run the show and set the general direction of events and goals.

Most games are based on conflict. Whether conflict is the main idea of the game or it's just an underlying theme, the bottom line is that most the time the player is running around destroying the enemies and/or blowing things up. As a result, we can arrive at a few behaviors that a game creature might need to survive given the constant onslaught of the human opponent. Take a look at Figure 12.10, which illustrates the relationships between the following states:

Master State 1: Attack.

Master State 2: Retreat.

Master State 3: Move randomly.

Master State 4: Stop or pause for a moment.

Master State 5: Look for something—food, energy, light, dark, other computer-controlled creatures.

Master State 6: Select a pattern and follow it.

FIGURE 12.10
Building a
better brain.

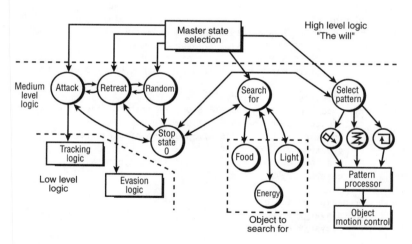

You should be able to see the difference between these states and the previous examples. These states function at a much higher level, and they definitely contain possible substates or further logic to generate. For example, states 1 and 2 can be accomplished using a deterministic algorithm, while states 3 and 4 are nothing more than a couple of lines of code. On the other hand, state 6 is very complex because it dictates that the creature must be able to perform complex patterns controlled by the Master FSM.

As you can see, your AI is getting fairly sophisticated. State 5 could be yet another deterministic algorithm, or even a mix of deterministic algorithms and preprogrammed search patterns. The point is that you want to model a creature from the top down; that is, first think of how complex you want the AI of the creature to be, and then implement each state and algorithm.

If you refer back to Figure 12.10, you also see that in addition to the Master FSM, which selects the states themselves, there's another part of the AI model that's doing the selection. This is similar to the "will" or "agenda" of the creature. There are a number of ways to implement this module, such as random selection, conditional logic, or something else. For now, just know that the states must be selected in an intelligent manner based on the current state of the game.

The following code fragment implements a crude version of the master state machine. The code is only partially functional because a complete AI would take many pages, but the most important structural elements are there. Basically, you fill in all the blanks and details, generalize, and drop it into your code. For now, just assume that the game's world consists of the AI creature and the player. Here's the code:

```
// these are the master states
#define STATE_ATTACK   0    // attack the player
#define STATE_RETREAT  1    // retreat from player
#define STATE_RANDOM   2    // move randomly
#define STATE_STOP     3    // stop for a moment
#define STATE_SEARCH   4    // search for energy
#define STATE_PATTERN  5    // select a pattern and execute it

// variables for creature
int creature_state   = STATE_STOP, // state of creature
    creature_counter = 0,    // used to time states
    creature_x       = 320, // position of creature
    creature_y       = 200,
    creature_dx      = 0,    // current trajectory
    creature_dy      = 0;

// player variables
int player_x = 10,
    player_y = 20;

// main logic for creature
// process current state
switch(creature_state)
    {
    case STATE_ATTACK:
        {
        // step 1: move toward player
        if (player_x > creature_x) creature_x++;
        if (player_x < creature_x) creature_x—;
        if (player_y > creature_y) creature_y++;
```

```
            if (player_y < creature_y) creature_y—;

            // step 2: try and fire cannon 20% probability
            if ((rand()%5)==1)
                Fire_Cannon();

        } break;

    case STATE_RETREAT:
            {
        // move away from player
            if (player_x > creature_x) creature_x—;
            if (player_x < creature_x) creature_x++;
            if (player_y > creature_y) creature_y—;
            if (player_y < creature_y) creature_y++;
            } break;

    case STATE_RANDOM:
        {
            // move creature in random direction
            // that was set when this state was entered
            creature_x+=creature_dx;
            creature_y+=creature_dy;
        } break;

    case STATE_STOP:
            {
            // do nothing!
            } break;

    case STATE_SEARCH:
            {
            // pick an object to search for such as
            // an energy pellet and then track it similar
            // to the player
            if (energy_x > creature_x) creature_x—;
            if (energy_x < creature_x) creature_x++;
            if (energy_y > creature_y) creature_y—;
            if (energy_y < creature_y) creature_y++;
            } break;
    case STATE_PATTERN:
            {
            // continue processing pattern
            Process_Pattern();
            } break;
    default: break;
    } // end switch

// update state counter and test if a state transition is
// in order
if (--creature_counter <= 0)
    {
```

```
// pick a new state, use logic, random, script etc.
// for now just random
creature_state = rand()%6;

// now depending on the state, we might need some
// setup...
if (creature_state == STATE_RANDOM)
    {
    // set up random trajectory
    creature_dx = -4+rand()%8;
    creature_dy = -4+rand()%8;
    } // end if

// perform setups on other states if needed

// set time to perform state, use appropriate method...
// at 30 fps, 1 to 5 seconds for the state
creature_counter = 30 + 30*rand()5;

} // end if
```

Let's talk about the code. To begin with, the current state is processed. This involves local logic, algorithms, and even function calls to other AIs, such as pattern processing. After the state has been processed, the state counter is updated and the code tests to see if the state is complete. If so, a new state is selected. If the new state needs to be set up, the setup is performed. Finally, a new state count is selected using a random number and the cycle continues.

There are a lot of improvements that you can make. You could mix the state transitions with the state processing, and you might want to use much more involved logic to make state transitions and decisions.

Adding More Robust Behaviors with Personality

A personality is nothing more than a collection of predictable behaviors. For example, I have friend with a very "tough guy" personality. I can guarantee that if you say something that he doesn't like, he'll probably let you know with a swift blow to the head. Furthermore, he's very impatient and doesn't like to think that much. On the other hand, I have another friend who's very small and wimpy. He has learned that due to his size, he can't speak his mind because he might get smacked. So he has a much more passive personality.

Of course, human beings are a lot more complex than these examples suggest, but these are still adequate descriptions of those people. Thus, you should be able to model personality types using logic and probability distributions that track a few behavioral traits and place a probability on each. This probability graph can be used to make state transitions. Take a look at Figure 12.11 to see what I'm talking about.

There are four states or behaviors in this model:

State 1: Attack

State 2: Retreat

State 3: Stop

State 4: Random

FIGURE 12.11
Personality distribution for basic behavioral states.

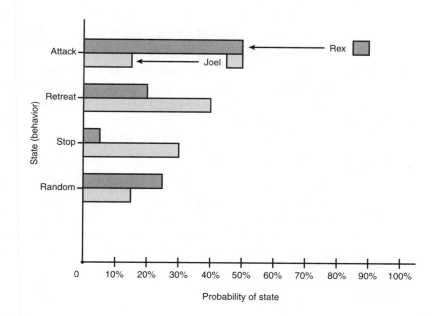

Instead of selecting a new state at random as before, you create a probability distribution that defines the personality of each creature as a function of these states. For example, Table 12.2 illustrates the probability distributions of my friends Rex (the tough one) and Joel (the wimpy one).

TABLE 12.2 Personality Probability Distributions

State	Rex p(x)	Joel p(x)
ATTACK	50%	15%
RETREAT	20%	40%
STOP	5%	30%
RANDOM	25%	15%

Hardcore Game Programming

If you look at the hypothetical data, it seems to make sense. Rex likes to attack without thinking, while Joel thinks much more and likes to run if he can. In addition, Rex isn't that much of a planner, so he does a lot of random things—smashes walls, eats glass, and cheats on his girlfriend—whereas Joel knows what he's doing most of the time.

This entire example has been totally artificial, and Rex and Joel don't really exist. But I'll bet that you have a picture of Rex and Joel in your head, or you know people like them. Hence, my supposition is true—the outward behaviors of a person define their personality as perceived by others (at least in a general way). This is a very important asset to your AI modeling and state selection.

To use this technique of probability distribution, you simply set up a table that has, say, 20–50 entries (where each entry is a state), and then fill the table so that the probabilities are what you want. When you select a new state, you'll get one that has a little personality in it. For example, here's Rex's probability table in the form of a 20-element array—that is, each element has a 5 percent weight:

```
int rex_pers[20] = {1,1,1,1,1,1,1,1,1,1,2,2,2,2,3,4,4,4,4,4}
```

In addition to this technique, you might want to add *radii of influence*. This means that you switch probability distributions based on some variable, like distance to the player or some other object, as shown in Figure 12.12. The figure illustrates that when the game creature gets too far away, it switches to a non-aggressive search mode instead of the aggressive combat mode used when it's in close quarters. In other words, another probability table is used.

FIGURE 12.12

Switching personality probability distribution based on distance.

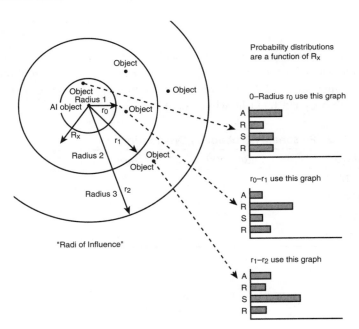

Modeling Memory and Learning with Software

Other elements of a good AI are memory and learning. As the AI-controlled creatures in your game run around, they are controlled by state machines, conditional logic, patterns, random numbers, probability distributions, and so forth. However, they always think on-the-fly. They never look at past history to help make a decision.

For example, what if a creature was in attack mode, and the player kept dodging to the right and the creature kept missing? You'd want the creature to track the player's motions and remember that the player moves right during every attack, and maybe change its targeting a little to compensate.

As another example, imagine that your game forces creatures to find ammo just as the player does. However, every time the creature wants ammo, it has to search randomly for it (maybe with a pattern). Wouldn't it be more realistic if the AI could remember where ammo was found last and try that position first?

These are just a couple of examples of using memory and learning to make game AI seem more intelligent. Frankly, implementing memory is easy to do, but few game programmers ever do it because they don't have time or feel it's not worth it. No way! Memory and learning is very cool, and your players will notice the difference. It's worth trying to find areas where simple memory and learning can be implemented with reasonable ease and can have a visible effect on the AI's decision-making.

That's the general idea of memory, but how exactly do you use it in a game? It depends on the situation. For example, take a look at Figure 12.13.

FIGURE 12.13
Using geographical-temporal memory.

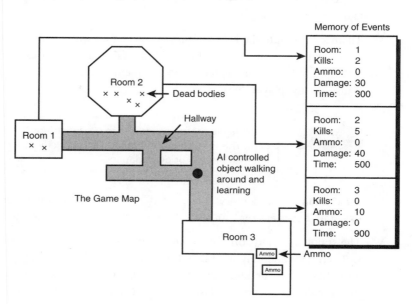

Here you see a map of a game world, with a record attached to each room. These records store the following information:

Kills

Damage from player

Ammo found

Time in room

Every time the creature runs through its AI and you want to have a more robust selection process based on memory and learning, you refer to the record of events—the creature's memory of the room. For example, when the creature enters a room, you might check if the creature has sustained a great deal of damage in that room. If so, it might back out and try another.

For another example, the creature might run out of ammo. Instead of hunting randomly for more ammo, the creature could scan through its memory of all the rooms it has been to and see which one had the most ammo lying around. Of course, the AI has to update the memory every few cycles for this to work, but that's simple to do.

In addition, you can let creatures exchange information! For example, if one creature bumps into another in a hallway, they can merge memory records and learn about each other's travels. Or maybe the stronger creature could perform a force upload on the weaker creature, since the stronger one obviously has a better set of probabilities and experience and is a better survivor. Moreover, if one creature knows the player's last known position, it can influence the other creature's memory with that information and they can converge on the player.

There's no limit to the kinds of things you can do with memory and learning. The tricky part is working them into the AI in a fair manner. For example, it's unfair to let the game AI see the whole world and memorize it. The AI should have to explore it just like the player does.

> **TIP**
>
> Many game programmers like to use bit strings or vectors to memorize data. This is much more compact, and it's easy to flip single bits, simulating memory loss or degradation.

As an example of memory, I've created a little a-life ant simulation, DEMO12_7.CPP| EXE (16-bit version, DEMO12_7_16B.CPP|EXE), shown in Figure 12.14.

The simulation starts off with a number of red ants and piles of blue? food. The ants walk around randomly until they find a pile of food. When they do, they eat the food until they're full, and then they roam around again. When the ants get hungry again, they remember where they last found food and then head for it (if there's any left).

In addition, when two ants bump into each other, they exchange knowledge about their travels. If an ant can't find food in time, it dies a horrible death. (Watch the simulation; it's a trip.) You can change the number of ants according to your system's processing power. Right now there are 16, but there's only enough room to display the state information and memory images for the first 8. This information is shown on the right side of the screen, detailing the current state, hunger level, hunger tolerance, and a couple of the internal counters.

FIGURE 12.14
An ant-based memory demo.

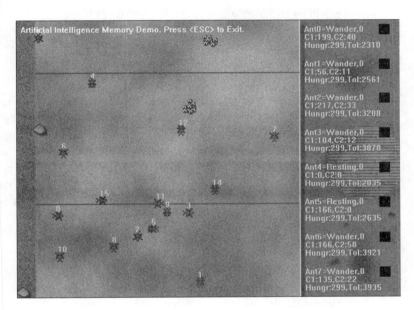

If you want to add something even more involved, enable the ants to leave waste and create a cyclic system that won't run out of food.

Planning and Decision Trees

Thus far, all the AI techniques have been fairly reactionary and immediate—meaning that there isn't much planning or high-level logic going on. Although you've learned how to implement low-level AI, I want to talk about high-level AI. This is usually referred to as *planning*.

A *plan* is simply a high-level set of *actions* that are carried out to arrive at a *goal*. The actions are the steps that are performed in a certain order to arrive at the goal. In addition to the actions, there may be conditionals that must be satisfied before any particular action can be carried out. For example, the following list is an example plan for going to the movies:

1. Look up the movie that you want to see.

2. Get in the car and drive to the theater at least 30 minutes before the movie starts.

3. Once at the theater, buy the tickets.

4. Watch the movie. When it's over, drive home.

Well, that looks like a reasonable plan. However, there are a lot of details I left out. For example, where do you look up the movie? How do you drive the car? What if you don't have any money? And so forth. These details may or may not be needed depending on how complex you want the plan to be, but in general there are conditionals and subplans that you can use to specifically detail this plan so that there's absolutely no question about what to do.

Implementing planning algorithms for game AI is based on the same concept. You have an object that's AI-controlled, and you want it to follow some plan to reach some goal. Therefore, you must model the plan with some kind of language—usually C/C++, but you might use a special high-level script. In any case, in addition to modeling the plan, you must model all the objects that are part of the plan: the actions, the goals, and the conditionals for the actions and goals to take place. Each one of these items might simply be a C/C++ structure or class and have a number of fields in it. For example, a goal might look like this:

```
typedef struct GOAL_TYP
{
int class;      // the class of goal
char *name;     // the name of goal "kill leader"
int time;       // time until goal expires
int *subgoals;  // pointer to sub goal list that must be
                // satisfied
int (* eval)(void); // function pointer to determine if
                    // goal has been satisfied

// more data

} GOAL, *GOAL_PTR;
```

Of course, this definition is just an example and yours might have many more fields, but you get the idea. You have to create a structure that can generically represent any goal in your game, from "blowing up the bridge" to "searching for food."

The next structure you might need is a generic action structure that represents something an object must do as part of a plan to reach a goal. Again, this is up to you, but it must reflect anything and everything you want the AI to be able to do. For example, here's a possible action structure:

```
typedef struct ACTION_TYP
{
int class; // class of action
```

```
int *name; // name of action
int time;  // time allotted to perform action
RESOURCE *resource; // a link to a record that describes
                    // the resources that this action might
                    // need

CONDITIONS *cond;   // a link to a record that describes
                    // all the conditions that must be met
                    // before this action can be made


UPDATES *update;    // a link to a record that describes
                    // all the updates and changes that
                    // should be made when this action is
                    // complete

int (*action_functions)(void); // a function ptr(s) to an
                               // action function that does
                               // the work of the action


} ACTION, *ACTION_PTR;
```

As you can see, we're getting pretty abstract here. The point is that these structures may be completely different in your implementation. As long as they impart the functionality of the plan, action, and goal, that's all that matters.

Coding Plans

There are a number of ways to code a plan. You might code it as pure hard code that implements the actions, the goals, and the plan itself as pure C/C++. This was a very common technique in the old days. A game programmer would just start writing code that performed conditions, set variables, and called functions. This was in essence a *hard-coded* plan.

A more elegant method of encoding a plan is to use *production rules* and decision trees. A production rule is simply a logical proposition with a number of *antecedents* and a *consequence*:

```
IF X OP Y THEN Z
```

X and Y are the antecedents, and Z is the consequence. OP could be any logical operation, like AND, OR, and so on. In addition, X or Y might be composed of other production rules; that is, they might be nested. For example, take a look at the following logic statement:

```
if (P > 20) AND (damage < 100) THEN consequence
```

Or, in C/C++-speak:

```
if (power > 20) && (damage < 100)
   {
   consequence();
   } // end if
```

So a production rule is really a conditional statement. The hard-coded plan was really just a bunch of production statements along with actions and goals, all mashed together. The point of writing a "planner" is to model these things a little more abstractly. Although you could use hard-code C/C++, it would be better to create a structure that can read production rules, contain actions and goals, and represent a plan.

One structure that may help you implement this system is called a *decision tree*. As shown in Figure 12.15, a decision tree is nothing more than a tree structure in which each node represents a production rule and/or an action.

FIGURE 12.15
A decision tree encoding production rules.

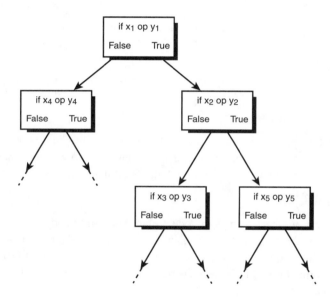

However, instead of using hard code to implement the tree, the tree is built from a file or data that is fed to the AI engine by the game programmer or the level designer. This way the tree is generic and needs no recompilation to work. Let's create a little AI planning language to control a bot with some input variables and a set of actions.

Inputs that can be tested by the AI bot:

DISPLY	Distance to player (0–1000)
FUEL	Fuel left (0–100)
AMO	Ammo left (0–100)
DAM	The current damage (0–100)
TMR	Current game time in virtual minutes
PLAYST	The state of the player (attacking, not attacking)

Actions that the AI bot can perform:

FW	Fire weapons at player
SD	Self-destruct
SEARCH	Search for player
EVADE	Evade player

Now let's make up the decision tree structure. Assume that one or two antecedents can be tested with an AND, OR at each node, and that you can negate them with NOT. And the antecedents themselves can be comparisons with >, <, ==, or != between inputs or a constant. In addition, at any node there is a TRUE branch as well as a FALSE branch, along with an action list that holds eight actions that can be performed. Refer to Figure 12.15 to see this abstractly. Here's a structure that might be used to implement the node:

```
typedef struct DECNODE_TYP
{
int operand1, operand2; // the first operands
int comp1;              // the comparison operator

int operator;           // the conjuctive operator

int operand3, operand4  // the second pair of operands
int comp2;              // the comparison to perform

ACTION *act_true;       // action lists for true and false
ACTION *act_false;

DECNODE_PTR *dec_true;  // branches to take if true or
                        // false
DECNODE_PTR *dec_false;

} DECNODE, *DECNODE_PTR;
```

As you can see, once again there are a lot of little details. If there is only one antecedent:

```
if (DAM <  100) then...
```

Or the difference between variables and constants:

```
if (DAM == FUEL) then...
```

or

```
if (DAM == 20) then...
```

And determining if there are two antecedents or one:

```
if (DAM > 50) and (AMO < 30) then
```

These are all relatively basic programming problems, so I'm not going to go into them. Just be aware that you have to take them into consideration when you make the engine read the decision nodes and process them. Anyway, now that you have your language, write a little decision tree that can determine what to do in a number of settings.

For example, let's make a firing control tree. Remember that you aren't really doing full plans, but you can *think* of the next example as a plan because the implicit goal is to determine when to fire. Granted, there isn't a goal other than the firing itself. In any case, here's my rough plan in plain English:

> *If the player is close **and** damage is low **then** fire at player*
>
> *If the player is far **and** fuel is high **then** search for player*
>
> *If damage is high **and** player is close **then** evade player*
>
> *If damage is high **and** ammo is 0 **and** player is close **then** self destruct*

That's my little AI pseudo-plan for the bot. Of course, a complete plan might have dozens or hundreds of these clauses. But the cool thing is that the game designer enters them with a graphical tool rather than having to program them in code! The results of this plan have been converted into your planning language, and the final decision tree is shown in Figure 12.16.

Isn't that neato? You just write a processor that follows the tree and performs the branches, and that's it. Now that you have an idea about how to create a decision tree that can process decisions and carry out an action, let's finish up with a formal planning algorithm that takes goals into consideration and also performs planning analysis.

Implementing a Real Planner

You've seen how you might implement the conditional part of a planner, and even the action part. The goal part is really nothing more than formalizing that a particular plan has a goal and then assigning the goal as the end point of the plan. Moreover, when a plan is completed, the goal must be tested before any remaining parts of the plan can be executed. You may have subplans that run in parallel with a primary plan, and they must all have their goals met to allow a master goal to be met.

For example, you may have a global plan that "All bots meet at waypoint (x,y,z)." However, this goal can't be reached until each bot executes the plan "Go to waypoint (x,y,z)." Furthermore, if one of the bots can't make it, the planner should figure this out and respond. This is the idea of *plan monitoring* and analysis. I'll talk more about this later in this section. At this point, let's take a look at how you might represent the plans.

FIGURE 12.16
The final decision tree for your planning language.

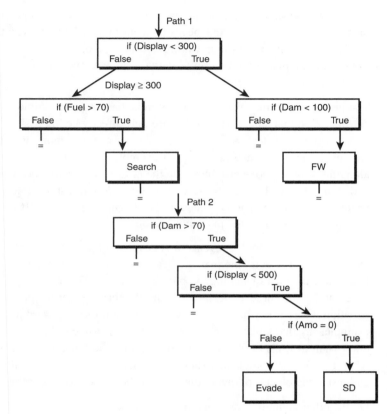

The plan itself might be represented implicitly in the decision/action tree, or it could be a list of decisions/actions, each of which represents a tree or a sequence. It's up to you. The point is that you want to be able to formulate a plan, a sequence of actions, and a goal. The actions themselves usually involve conditional logic and subactions that are low-level, like moving from one (x,y,z) to another or firing a weapon. The term *actions*, in the highest-level sense, means "kill the leader" or "take over the fort," whereas *actions* in a low-level sense are directly executable by the engine. Get it? I hope so—I'm running out of Snapple. :)

So, assuming that a plan is made up of some sort of array or linked list and that you can traverse it, a planner might look like this:

```
while(plan not empty and haven't reached goal)
      {
      get the next action in the plan
      execute the action
      } // end while
```

Of course, you should understand that this is just an abstract implementation of the planner. In a real program, this needs to occur in parallel with everything else. You surely can't sit in a `while` loop waiting for a single plan to reach its goal; you have to implement the planner with a finite state machine or similar structure and keep track of the plan as the game runs.

The problem with this planning algorithm is that it's pretty stupid. It doesn't take into consideration that an action in the future may already be impossible to satisfy, and thus the plan is useless. As a result, the planner needs to monitor or analyze the plan and make sure that it makes sense. For example, if the plan is to blow up a bridge and along the way someone else blows up the bridge, the planner needs to figure this out and stop the plan. This can be accomplished by looking at the goals of the plan and testing if any future goal has been attained by another process. If this goal negates the plan or makes it futile, the plan should stop.

The planner should look at events or states that might make the plan impossible. For example, at some point the plan may call for a blue key, but the blue key has been lost. Thus, the goal of finding the blue key is moot. This kind of problem can be monitored at the current level or the future level, meaning that the planner can look at the situation where it is when it gets there, or it can project forward into the future. For example, say that a plan is to "Walk 1,000 miles east and then blow up the fort." I don't want to walk 1,000 miles to blow up a fort and then realize I'm out of bombs when I get there! The planner should look at the goal, backtrack all the prerequisites, and test if the object following the plan has bombs or could get them along the way.

On the other hand, this can backfire. Even though the bot may not have a bomb right now, it may find one during the 1,000 mile trek, so terminating a plan prematurely because of a lack of resources at the current point may be a bad idea. This leads us to classifying prerequisites with *priorities*. For example, if I need the laser gun in the future, and there's only one in the game and it's been destroyed, there's no need to continue with the plan. On the other hand, if I need 1,000 gold pieces and I only have 50, but I'm going to travel a long distance and there will be a lot of other ways to find gold along the way, I want to keep moving on with my plan.

Finally, when a plan goes awry, you don't necessarily need to terminate it. You can replan, or maybe select a different plan. You might have three plans for each goal so that there are two backup plans if the primary plan fails.

Planning is a very powerful AI tool and is totally applicable to any type of game. Although you may write a *Quake* clone that is mostly shoot-'em-up, you still need a global planner that influences the creatures with a general goal of "Stay in this area and kill the player." On the other hand, in a war simulation like *Command and Conquer*, planning is the only way to write a game that makes any sense at all!

The best way to get planning to work in real game development is to write a planning language and then give the designer a set of variables and objects that can be part of the plans. This allows the designer to come up with things that you never would have thought of—and surely wouldn't want to hard-code!

Pathfinding

In the simplest terms, *pathfinding* is the computation and execution of a path from point *p1* to goal *p2*, as shown in Figure 12.17. If there are no obstacles, the simple AI technique of vectoring toward the goal position will suffice. However, if there are obstacles, obstacle avoidance will have to come into play. This is where things get difficult...

FIGURE 12.17
Finding a path from point to point.

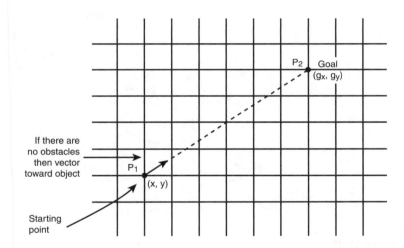

Trial and Error

For simple obstacles that aren't large and are mostly convex, you can usually get away with an algorithm that, when the object hits an obstacle, backs it up, turns it right or left 45-90 degrees, and then moves it forward again for some fixed amount (AVOIDANCE_DISTANCE). When the object has moved that distance, the AI retargets the goal, turns the object toward it, and tries again. The results of this algorithm are traced out in Figure 12.18.

Although this algorithm surely isn't as robust as you'd like, it works because there's a randomness in the avoidance algorithm. It turns randomly each way to try again, so sooner or later the object will find its way around the obstacle.

Contour Tracing

Another method of obstacle avoidance is *contour tracing*. Basically, this algorithm traces the contour of the object that's blocking the object's path. You can implement this by following the outline of the obstacle and periodically testing if a line from your current position to the goal intersects the obstacle anymore. If not, you're clear; otherwise, continue tracing. A sample run of this algorithm is shown in Figure 12.19.

FIGURE 12.18
The "Bump-n-Grind" object avoidance algorithm.

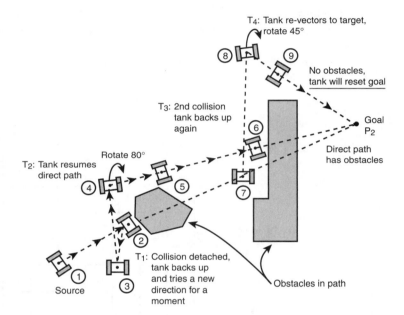

FIGURE 12.19
Contour tracing in action.

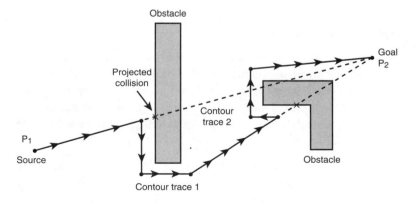

This works, but it looks a little stupid because the algorithm traces around things instead of going through the obvious shortest path. But it works. So what you might do is use the trial-and-error method first, and if that fails after a certain period of time, switch to the contour tracing algorithm and get out!

Of course, the player usually can't get a God's-eye view of a 3D game like *Quake*, so if the creatures don't look that smart when they're avoiding obstacles, it's not going to show up that much. It simply takes them longer than needed. On the other hand, a war game with a top-down view is going to look really bad when the AI-controlled armies look like they're tracing. Let's see if we can do better.

Collision Avoidance Tracks

In this technique, you create virtual *tracks* around objects, consisting of a series of points or vectors that trace out a fairly intelligent path. The path can be computed algorithmically using a shortest-path algorithm (which we will get to later) or manually created by you or your game designers with a tool.

Around each large obstacle you create is an invisible track that only the pathfinding bot AI can see. When a bot wants to get around an object, it asks for the nearest avoidance path for that obstacle and then takes it. This ensures that the pathfinder will *always* know how to get around obstacles. Of course, you might want to have more than one avoidance path for each obstacle or add some tracing "noise" so the bots don't all follow the path perfectly. An illustration of this is shown in Figure 12.20.

FIGURE 12.20
Object avoidance paths.

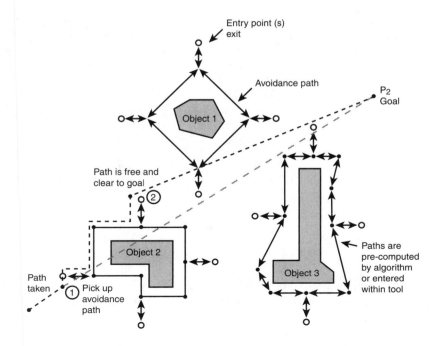

This leads us to another idea: Why not have dozens or hundreds of precomputed paths for all points of interest in the game? Then, when a bot wants to get from point *pi* to *pj*, instead of navigating and performing obstacle avoidance, it just uses a precomputed full path.

Waypoint Pathfinding

Let's say that you have a really complicated world and there are all kinds of obstacles. Sure, you could make a creature with enough intelligence to navigate itself around everything and get to a goal, but is all that necessary? No! You can set up a network of paths that connect all points of interest in the game via a connected network of nodes. Each node represents a *waypoint*, or point of interest, and the edges in the network represent the vector direction and length to get to other nodes in the network.

For example, let's say that you have a plan running and you need to move a bot from its current location over the bridge and into the city. Doesn't that sound like a lot of drama? But if you have a network of paths and you can find a path that goes to the city via the bridge, all you have to do is follow it! The bot is guaranteed to get there and avoid all obstacles. Figure 12.21 shows a top-down view of a world, along with a pathfinding network. The highlighted path is the one that you want to take. Remember, this network not only avoids obstacles, but it also has paths for important destinations. (Sorta like the wormhole network in our universe.)

FIGURE 12.21
A pathfinding network with a path highlighted.

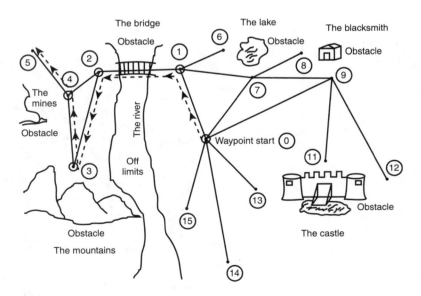

There are two problems with this grand scheme: 1) following the path, and 2) the actual data structure that represents the network can be a bit tricky. First, let's handle following the path itself.

Assume for a moment that you have a path from *p1* to *p2* that consists of *n* nodes, represented by the following structure:

```
typedef struct WAYPOINT_TYP
{
int id;              // id of waypoint
char *name;          // name of waypoint
int x,y;             // the position of waypoint
int distance;        // distance to next waypoint on path
WAYPOINT_TYP *next;  // next waypoint in list
} WAYPOINT
```

This is just an example; you might use something completely different. Now assume that there are five waypoints, including the start and end waypoints *p1* and *p2*, as shown in Figure 12.21. Here they are:

```
WAYPOINT path[5] = { {0,"START", x0, y0, d0 ,&path[1]},
                     {1,"ONPATH", x1, y1,d1 ,&path[2]},
                     {2,"ONPATH", x2, y2,d2 ,&path[3]},
                     {3,"ONPATH", x3, y3,d3 ,&path[4]},
                     {4,"ONPATH", x4, y4,d4 ,NULL}};
```

The first thing to note is that although I statically allocated an array to hold the WAYPOINTs, I still linked their pointers together. Also, the last link is NULL because this is the terminus.

To follow the path, you have a few things to consider. First, you have to get to the first node of the path or a node along it. This can be a problem. Assuming that there are sufficient path entry points on the game grid, you can assume that one of the nodes from a desired path is within range. Therefore, you want to find the node that is closest and vector toward it. During this initial path alignment, you may have to avoid obstacles to get there! Once you're at the starting node or a node on the interior of the path, you're ready to go.

Following the Path

The path is a series of points that are guaranteed to have no obstacles from one point to another. Why? You made that path so you know this! As a result, you can simply move the bot from the current WAYPOINT in the path toward the next one, and keep doing so until you get to the last WAYPOINT, which is the goal:

```
find nearest WAYPOINT in desired path

    while(not at goal)
        {
        compute trajectory from current waypoint to next
        and follow it.

        if reached next waypoint then update current
        waypoint and next waypoint.

        } // end while
```

Basically you're just following a series of points until you run out of points. To find the trajectory vector from one WAYPOINT to the next, you would use something like the following:

```
// start off at beginning of path
WAYPOINT_PTR current = &path[0];

// find trajectory to next waypoint
trajectory_x = path->next.x - path->x;
trajectory_y = path0>next.y - path->y;

// normalize
normalize(&trajectory_x, &trajectory_y);
```

The normalization just makes sure that the length of trajectory is 1.0. This is done by dividing each component by the length of the vector (look at Appendix C, "Math and Trigonometry Review)." Just point the object in the direction of trajectory, wait for it to get to the next WAYPOINT, and continue the algorithm. Of course, I've glossed over the details about what happens when a WAYPOINT is reached. I suggest checking the distance of the object to the WAYPOINT. If it's within some delta, that's close enough, and it's time to select the next WAYPOINT.

There are problems with having paths. First, finding a path to follow might be as difficult as trying to get from point to point! This is an issue, of course, but with the proper network data structure, you can ensure that for any given game cell, a game object needs to travel less than 100 units or so to pick up a path. Granted, the data structure representing the path network will be complex because some links may be used by other paths, but this is more of a data structure problem and depends on how you want to do it. You may simply have 1,000 different paths that don't reuse waypoints even if they're the same for many paths.

Or you might use a connected graph that reuses waypoints, but has logic and data links to follow a path and won't switch tracks. This can be accomplished with clever pointer arithmetic and logic to select the correct links that make up a specific path.

For example, take a look at Figure 12.22, which shows two paths through the same waypoints. You might have to encode in a list the possible waypoints that can be arrived at and the associated link to take—if you're trying to get to goal HOUSE and you're on a path waypoint that has 16 outgoing links, take the one that has HOUSE on its list of stops. Again, this is up to you, and your implementation will depend on the circumstances of the game.

A Racing Example

A good example of using paths is in racing games. Imagine that you want to have a number of cars on a racetrack, and you want them to drive around the track while avoiding the player and looking somewhat intelligent. This is a good place for paths.

What you might do is create, say, eight or 16 different paths that follow the road. Each of the paths might be equidistant or have slightly different properties, like "tight and short" or "long and wide." Each AI car starts off on a different path, and as the game runs, it follows the path by vectoring toward it. If a car gets in a crash, it picks up on the next nearest path, and so on.

FIGURE 12.22
A path network with common waypoints.

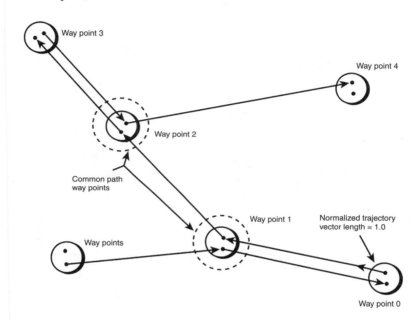

In addition, if a car's AI wants to change lanes to a more aggressive path, it does so. This helps you because you don't have to worry about keeping the cars from bunching up as much, and you don't have to make them steer as much because they're on paths. Controlling their speed and braking time will be more than enough to make them seem real.

For an example of this, take a look at DEMO12_8.CPP|EXE (16-bit version, DEMO12_8_16B.CPP|EXE) on the CD, which creates a little racing demo with a single waypoint path. The cars try to avoid each other, but if they touch they don't crash. This is a DirectX application, so you need to add the libraries and so forth to compile.

Robust Pathfinding

Last but not least, I want to talk a little about *real* pathfinding; in other words, using computer science algorithms to find paths from *p1* to *p2*. There are a number of algorithms that can do this. The problem is that none of them are for real-time and thus don't lend themselves to games easily. However, you can use them in real-time if you employ some tricks, and of course you can use them to compute paths for you in your tools.

All of the algorithms work on graph-like structures, which are representations of your game universe that consist of nodes, along with edges made up of nodes that can be reached from any particular node. There's usually a cost associated with each edge. Figure 12.23 shows a typical graph.

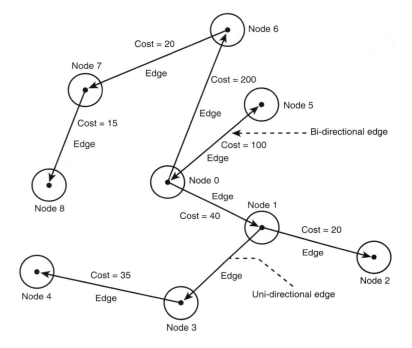

FIGURE 12.23
A typical graph network.

Because you're dealing with 2D and 3D games, you might decide that the graph is just a grid laid down on the game field with each cell implicitly connected to its eight neighbors, and that the cost is just the distance. This is shown in Figure 12.24.

In any case, once you've come up with a way to represent the game world that is graph-like, you can run the algorithm(s) on the problem of finding a short path, or the shortest path, from *p1* to *p2* that avoids obstacles. Obstacles aren't allowed in the graph, so they can't possibly be part of the path—that's a relief <G>.

There are a number of pathfinding algorithms that are well known in computer science. They're shown in the following list and are briefly described in more detail:

- Breadth-first search
- Bidirectional breadth-first search
- Depth-first search
- Dijkstra's search
- A* search

FIGURE 12.24
Creating a graph by
using a regular grid
network on the game
universe.

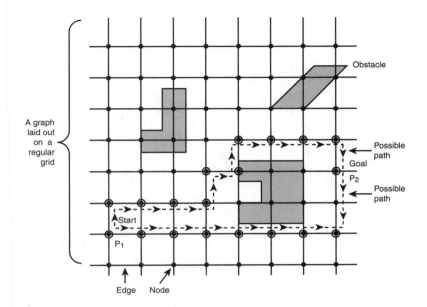

Breadth-First Search

This search fans out in all directions at the same time, visiting each node one unit
away, then two units away, then three units away, and so on—a growing circle. It's
crude because it doesn't focus on the actual direction of the goal. See Figure 12.25
and the algorithm that follows:

```
void BreadthFirstSearch(NODE r)
{
NODE s; // used to scan
QUEUE q; // this is a first in first out structure FIFO

// empty the queue
EmptyQ(q);

// visit the node
Visit(r);
Mark(r);

// insert the node r into the queue
InsertQ(r, q);

// while queue isn't empty loop
while (q is not empty)
    {
    NODE n = RemoveQ(q);

    for (each unmarked NODE s adjacent to n)
        {
        // visit the node
        Visit(s);
```

Hardcore Game Programming

```
                   Mark(s);

                   // insert the node s into the queue
                   InsertQ(s, q);
                   } // end for

          } // end while
     } // end BreadthFirstSearch
```

FIGURE 12.25
Breadth-first search
in action.

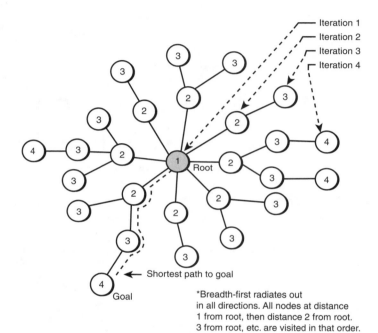

*Breadth-first radiates out
in all directions. All nodes at distance
1 from root, then distance 2 from root.
3 from root, etc. are visited in that order.

Bidirectional Breadth-First Search

The bidirectional breadth-first search is similar to the breadth-first search, except that two different searches are started: one at the start and one at the goal. When they overlap, the shortest path is computed. See Figure 12.26.

Depth-First Search

This is the converse of the breadth-first search. The depth-first search searches one direction all the way until it runs out of space or finds the goal. Then it searches the next direction, and so on. The problem with depth-first is that it needs a stopping limit that says, "If the goal is 100 units away and you've already tried a path that has a cost 1000, it's time to try another path." See Figure 12.27 and the algorithm that follows.

```
void DepthFirstSearch(NODE r)
{
NODE s; // used to scan
```

```
// visit and mark the root node
visit(r);
mark(r);

// now scan along from root all the nodes adjacent
while (there is an unvisited vertex s adjacent to r)
        {
        DepthFirstSearch(s);
        } // end while
} // end DepthFirstSearch
```

FIGURE 12.26
Bidirectional breadth-
first search in action.

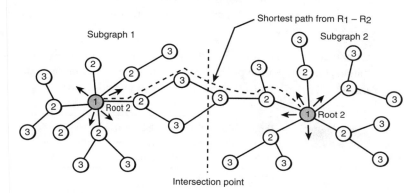

Shortest path from R₁ – R₂

Subgraph 1

Subgraph 2

Root 2

Root 2

Intersection point

Search 1 started from Root 1   Search 2 started from Root 2

Order of visitation: 1, 2, 3, . . .

FIGURE 12.27
Depth-first search
in action.

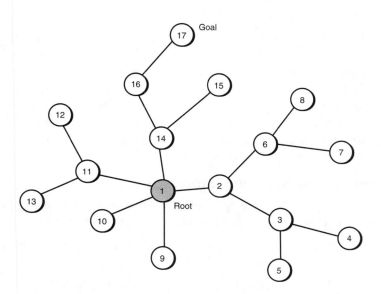

Goal

Root

Search order: 1, 2, 3, . . . 17

Dijkstra's Search

Dijkstra's search stems from the same algorithm used to find the minimum spanning tree of a graph. At each iteration, the algorithm determines what the shortest path to the next point is and then works on it rather than shooting out blindly in a random direction.

A* Search

The A* search (pronounced *A-star*) is similar to Dijkstra's search, except that it uses a heuristic that not only looks at the cost from the start to the current node, but also makes an estimate to the goal from the current node, even though it hasn't visited the nodes along the way.

Of course, there are modifications and mixtures of these algorithms that have mutated names, but you get the picture. Their actual implementations are well documented in many other books, so I'll leave it up to you to find them.

 TIP — Genetic algorithms can also be used to search for a best path. They may not be as real-time as you'd like, but they're definitely more natural than any of these algorithms.

Advanced AI Scripting

At this point, you should be quite the AI expert and things should be starting to gel. I've waited to talk about advanced AI scripting until now so you can see what I'm getting at with more of a foundation.

You already saw that a scripted instruction language can be used for AI when you learned about using a simple [OPCODE OPERAND] language and a virtual interpreter earlier in the chapter. This is a form of scripting, of course. Then I showed you yet another way to create decision trees with a scripted language based on logical productions and a set of inputs, operators, and action functions. This technology can be taken to any limits you want. QUAKE C is a good example, as well as UNREAL Script. Both of these actually allow you to program game code with a high-level English-like language that is processed by the engine.

Designing the Scripting Language

The design of the scripting language is based on the functionality that you want to give it. Here are some questions that you might ask yourself:

- Will the scripting language be used for AI only, or will it be used for the entire game?
- Will the scripting language be compiled or interpreted?

- Will the scripting language be ultra-high-level, with an almost English-like syntax, or will it be a lower-level programming-like language with functions, variables, conditional logic, and so on?

- Will *all* the gameplay be designed using the scripting language? That is, will the programmers do any hard-code game design, or will the entire game run with scripts?

- What level of complexity and power do you want to give the scripters/game designers? Will they have access to system and engine variables?

- What's the level of the game designers who will use the scripting language? Are they HTML coders, entry-level programmers, or professional software engineers?

These are the kinds of questions that you should think about before you start designing the language. Once you've answered these and any other questions, it's time to implement the language and really design the entire game.

This is a very important phase. If your game is going to be completely controlled by a scripting language, you'd better make it really open-ended, robust, extensible, and powerful. For example, the language should be able to model an airplane that flies by every now and then, as well as a monster that attacks you!

In any case, remember that the idea of a scripting language is to create a high-level interface to the engine so that low-level C/C++ code doesn't need to be programmed to control the objects in the game. Instead, an interpreted or compiled pseudo-English language can be used to describe actions in the game. This is shown in Figure 12.28.

FIGURE 12.28
The relationship between the engine and scripting language.

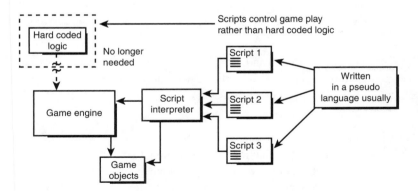

For example, here's a script for an imaginary scripting language to control a street light:

```
OBJECT: "Street Light", SL

VARIABLES:

    TIMER green_timer; // used to track time
```

```
// called when object of this type is created
ONCREATE()
BEGIN

// set animation to green
SL.ANIM = "GREEN"

END

// this is the main script
BEGINMAIN


// is anything near the streetlight
IF EVENT("near","Street Light") AND
    TIMER_STATE(green_timer) EQUAL OFF THEN
    BEGIN
    SL.ANIM = "RED"
    START_TIMER(green_timer,10)
    ENDIF

// has the timer expired yet
IF EVENT(green_timer,10) THEN
    BEGIN
    SL.ANIM = "GREEN"
    ENDIF

ENDMAIN
```

I just threw this together right now, so it may have some holes in it, but the point is that it's very high-level. There are a million little details about setting animations, checking proximity, and so forth, but with this language anyone can make a traffic light program.

The code starts up and sets the light to green with ONCREATE(), and then it tests if anything is close by with the EVENT() test and turns the light red. After the light has been red for awhile, it turns back. The language looks a little like C, BASIC, and Pascal all mixed together—yup!

This is the kind of language you need to design and implement to control a game—something that is neutral and knows how to operate on any object. For example, when you say BLOWUP("whatever"), the language processor better know how to make that work for any object in the game. Even though the call to blow up a blue monster might be TermBMs3(), and the call to blow up a wall might be PolyFractWallOneSide(), you just want to say BLOWUP("BLUE") and BLOWUP("wall"). Get the point?

You're probably wondering how to implement one of these scripting languages. It's not easy. You have to decide whether you want an interpreted or compiled language—is the language going to compile into straight code, be interpreted by an interpreter in the game engine, or something in between? Then you have to write the language, a parser, a code generator, and a P-code interpreter, or make the code generator create straight PentiumX machine code or maybe translate to C/C++. These are all compiler design issues and you're on your own here, but you've already written a couple of baby interpreters.

Some tools to help you are *LEX* and *YACC*, which stand for *Lexical Analyzer* and *Yet Another Compiler Compiler*. These are language parsing and definition tools to help you implement the recursive decent parser and complex state machines needed for a compiler or interpreter. I have a trick that you can use to get started without needing to write a full-blown language compiler/interpreter. Hold onto your hat!

Using the C/C++ Compiler

The nice thing about using an interpreted language is that the engine can read it and the game doesn't need to be recompiled. If you don't mind your game designers compiling (they should know how to anyway), you can use an old trick to make a crude game-scripting language: Use the C/C++ preprocessor to translate your scripting language for you. It takes nothing more than header files and the C/C++ source, which have nothing to do with compiler design.

The C/C++ preprocessor is really an amazing tool. It enables you to perform symbolic referencing, substitutions, comparisons, math, and a lot more. If you don't mind using C/C++ as the root language and compiling your scripts, you might be able to write your scripting language by means of a clever design, a lot of text substitutions, a lot of canned functions, identifiers to refer to objects, and a good object-oriented design.

Of course, under it is going to be real C/C++, but you don't have to tell your game designers that (if you have any). Or you can force them to use *only* the pseudo-language and not use all the real C/C++ functionality.

The best way to show you this is with a very simple example (that's all I have time for). First, the scripting language will be compiled and each script will be run whenever the object it refers to is created. The script will be terminated when the object it refers to dies. The scripting language you're going to write is based on C, so I'm not going to go over everything there. But I *am* going to use text substitutions for a lot of new keywords and data types.

A script consists of these parts:

> **Globals section**—This is where any global variables that are used in the script are defined. There are only two types of data type: REAL and INTEGER. REAL holds real numbers like the C-type `float`, and INTEGER is similar to the C-type `int`.

Functions section—This section is composed of functions. Functions all have this syntax:

```
data_type FUNCNAME(data_type parm1, data_type parm2...)
BEGIN
// code
ENDFUNC
```

Main section—The main of the program is where execution begins, and it will continue to loop here until the object is dead:

```
BEGINMAIN
// code
ENDMAIN
```

As for variable assignment and comparison, only the following operators will be valid:

Assignment	`variable = expression;`
Equality	`(expression EQUALS expression)`
Not Equal	`(expression NOTEQUAL expression)`

Comparisons—Greater than, less than, greater than or equal to, and less than or equal to all use the same C standard, which follows:

```
(expression > expression)
(expression < expression)
(expression >= expression)
(expression <= expression)
```

Conditionals—The form of conditional statements is the same as C, except that the code that executes when the statement is TRUE must be contained within a BEGIN ENDIF block. Look at the following example:

```
if (a EQUALS b)
    BEGIN
    // code
    ENDIF
else
    BEGIN
    // code
    ENDELSE
```

Similarly, the `else` block must be contained within a BEGIN ENDELSE block as well as the `elseif`.

There are no switch statements in this language, and there's only one kind of loop in the language, called a WHILE loop:

```
WHILE(condition)
    BEGIN
    // code
    ENDWHILE
```

Next, there's a `GOTO` keyword that jumps from one point in the code to another. The jump must be labeled with a name of the form:

```
LBL_NAME:
```

where `NAME` can be any character string up to 16 characters in length. See the following example:

```
LBL_DEAD:

if (a EQUALS b) BEGIN
GOTO LBL_DEAD;
ENDIF
```

You probably get the point by now. Of course, you'd want to add dozens or even hundreds of high-level helper functions that could perform tests on objects. For example, for objects that have a health or life state, you could have a function called `HEALTH()`:

```
if (HEALTH("alien1") > 50)
    BEGIN
    // code
    ENDIF
```

Moreover, you might create events that could be tested with a text string parameter:

```
if (EVENT("player dead")
    BEGIN
    // code here
    ENDIF
```

All this magic is accomplished by using clever global state variables and making sure to expose enough generic events to the scripts, along with system state variables (via functions) and a lot of text substitution via the preprocessor. Leaving out some of those details to keep things simple, let's take a look at what you need for text substitutions thus far. Referring to Figure 12.29, each script that is compiled will be processed first through the C/C++ preprocessor.

This is where you're going to make all those text substitutions and convert your little script language back to C/C++. To make it work, you tell the scripter to save all the files with the extension script `.SCR` or something, and when the file is imported into your main C/C++ file for compilation, you make sure to first include the script translation header. Here's the script translator for what you've so far:

```
SCRIPTTRANS.H

// variable translations
#define REAL static float
#define INTEGER static int

// comparisons
#define EQUALS    ==
#define NOTEQUAL !=
```

```
// block starts and ends
#define BEGIN {
#define END   }
#define BEGINMAIN {

#define ENDIF   }
#define ENDWHILE }
#define ENDELSE  }
#define ENDMAIN }

// looping
#define GOTO goto
```

FIGURE 12.29
Using the C/C++ pre-
processor for a script
language interpreter.

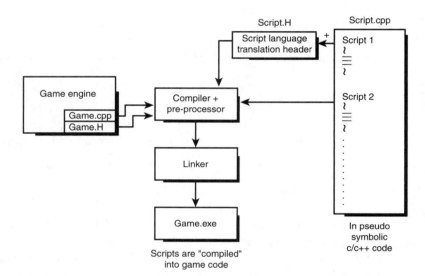

Then you include the following in your game code:

```
#include "SCRIPTTRANS.H"
```

Then you include the actual script file somewhere in your game engine at the proper moment. You can do it at the beginning, or even in a function:

```
Main_Game_Loop()
{
#include "script1.scr"

// more code

} // end main game loop
```

This part is up to you. The point is that the code the scripter writes must be compiled somehow, and it must be able to access the globals, see events, and make calls to the function set you expose. For example, here's a crude script that fires an event (which I didn't define at the count of 10):

```
// the variables
INTEGER index;

index = 0;

// the main section
BEGINMAIN

LBL_START:

if (index EQUALS 10)
   BEGIN
   BLOWUP("self");
   ENDIF

if (index < 10)
   BEGIN
   index = index + 1;
   GOTO LBL_START;
   ENDIF

ENDMAIN
```

Obviously, you would have to define BLOWUP(), but you get the picture. This code
would be translated by the preprocessor into the following:

```
{
static int index;
index = 0;

LBL_START:

if (index == 10)
   {
   BLOWUP("self");
   }

if (index < 10)
   {
   index = index + 1;
   goto LBL_START;
   }
}
```

Cool, huh? Of course, I'm leaving out a lot of details, like problems with variable
names colliding, accessing globals, debugging, making sure the script doesn't sit in
an endless loop, and so forth. However, I think that you have an idea about using the
compiler as a building block of a scripting language.

| TIP | You can tell the Visual C++ compiler to output the preprocessed C/C++ file with the compiler directive /P. |

Artificial Neural Networks

Neural networks are one of those things that you keep hearing about but never seem to show up. Well, I can tell you for a fact that in the past 3–5 years, we've made leaps and bounds in the area of artificial neural networks. Not because there has been any major breakthrough, but because people are taking an interest in them, experimenting with them, and using them. In fact, there are a number of games that use extremely advanced neural networks: *Creatures*, *Dogz*, *Fin Fin*, and others.

A neural network is a model of the human brain. The brain consists of 10–100 billion brain cells. Each of these cells can both process and send information. Figure 12.30 is a model of a human brain cell or neuron.

FIGURE 12.30
A basic neuron.

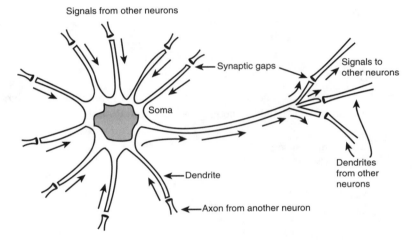

There are three main parts to a neuron: the *soma*, the *axon*, and *dendrites*. The soma is the main cell body and performs the processing, while the axon transmits the signals to the dendrites, which then pass the signals to other neurons.

Each neuron has a fairly simple function: to process input and fire or not fire. *Firing* means sending an electrochemical signal. Neurons have a number of inputs, a single output (which may be distributed), and some rule for processing the inputs and generating an output. The rules for processing are extremely complex, but suffice it to say that a summation of signals occurs and the results of this summation cause the neuron to fire.

Well, that's great, but how can you use this to make games appear to think? Well, instead of trying to create something as bold as thought or consciousness, maybe you can start by modeling simple memory, pattern recognition, and learning with some computer models. Our brains are very good at these tasks, while computers are very bad. It's intriguing to explore the biological computers we have in our heads and see if we can take some ideas from them.

This is exactly what artificial neural networks (or simply neural networks) do. They're simple models that can process information in parallel, just like our brains. Let's take a look at the most basic kinds of artificial neurons or neurodes.

The first artificial neural networks were created in 1943 by McCulloch and Pitts, two electrical engineers who wanted to model electronic hardware after the human brain. They came up with what they called a *neurode,* as shown on the left side of Figure 12.31. Today the form of the neurode hasn't changed much, as shown on the right side of Figure 12.31.

FIGURE 12.31

Basic artificial neurons.

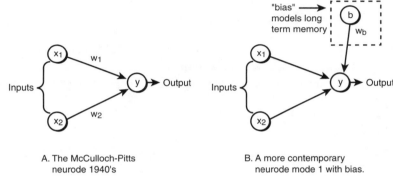

A. The McCulloch-Pitts neurode 1940's

B. A more contemporary neurode mode 1 with bias.

A neurode consists of a number of inputs, $X(i)$, that are scaled by weights, $w(i)$, summed up, and then processed by an activation function. This activation function may be a simple threshold, as in the McCulloch-Pitts (MP) model, or a more complex step, linear, or exponential function. In the case of the MP model, the sum is compared to a threshold value. If the sum is greater than a threshold theta, the neurode fires. Otherwise it doesn't. Mathematically, we have the following:

McCulloch-Pitts Neurode Summation Function

```
         n
Output Y = Σ Xᵢ * wᵢ
        i=1
```

General Neurode with Bias

```
             n
Output Y = B*b + Σ Xᵢ * wᵢ
            i=1
```

To see how a basic neurode works, assume that you have two inputs, X_1, and X_2, that can take on the binary values 0 and 1. Then set your threshold at 2 and $w_1=1$ and $w_2=1$. The summation function looks like this:

$$Y = X_1 * w_1 + X_2 * w_2$$

Compare the result to the threshold theta of 2. If Y is greater than or equal to 2, the neurode fires and outputs a 1.0. Otherwise, it outputs a 0. Table 12.3 is a truth table that shows what this single-neurode network does.

TABLE 12.3 Truth Table for Single Neurode Network

X1	X2	Sum Y	Final Output
0	0	0	0
0	1	1	0
1	0	1	0
1	1	2	1

If you stare at this for a moment, you'll realize it's an AND circuit. Cool, huh? So a simple little neurode can perform an AND operation. In fact, with neurodes you can build any logic circuit you want. For example, Figure 12.32 shows an AND, an OR, and an XOR.

FIGURE 12.32
Basic logic circuits.

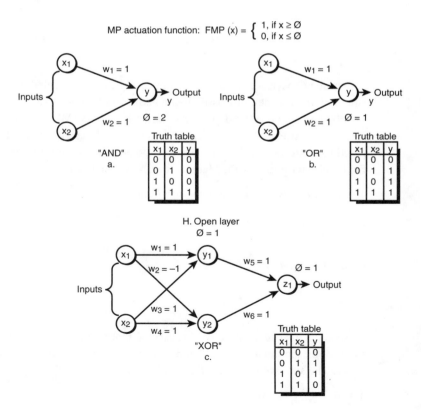

Real neural networks are much more complex, of course. They can have multiple layers, complex activation functions, and hundreds or thousands of neurodes. But now at least you understand their fundamental building blocks. Neural networks are bringing a new level of competition and AI to games that you've never seen before. Soon games will be able to make decisions and learn!

This is an important area of interest, but I have to watch my page count so I don't have time to cover it properly here. However, the ARTICLES\NETWARE\ directory on the CD contains an article on neural networks that will give you a more solid foundation on the topic. It covers all the various types of networks, shows you learning algorithms, and illustrates just what they can do. You'll find all the source code, an executable, and both an MS Word .DOC version and an Adobe Acrobat .PDF version of the text.

Genetic Algorithms

Genetic algorithms are a method of computing that relies on biological models to evolve solutions (if you're reading this, Dr. Koza, don't have a heart attack based on my loose definitions). Nature is great at evolution, and genetic algorithms try to capture some of the essence of natural selection and genetic evolution in computer models to help solve problems that normally couldn't be solved by standard means of computing.

Basically, genetic algorithms work like this: You take a number of informational indicators and string them all together into a bit vector, just like a strand of DNA, as shown in Figure 12.33.

FIGURE 12.33
Binary encoding of genetic information.

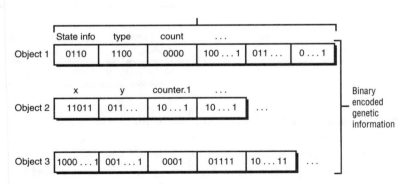

This bit vector represents the strategy or coding of an algorithm or solution. You need a few of these bit vectors to start with. Then you process the bit string and whatever it represents by some objective function that scores its *fitness*. The results are its score. The bit vector is really a concatenation of various control variables or settings for some algorithm, and you manually come up with a few experimental sets of values to start with based on intuition or prior knowledge (if available). Then you run each set and you get the score of each. You may find that out of the five you created manually, two of them did really well and the other three did really poorly. Here's where the genetic algorithm comes in.

You could tweak the solution from there, knowing that you're on the right track, or you could let genetic algorithms do it for you. Mix the two solutions or control vectors together to create two new offspring, as shown in Figure 12.34.

FIGURE 12.34
Digital sex.

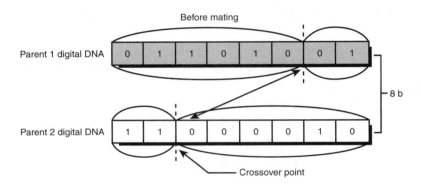

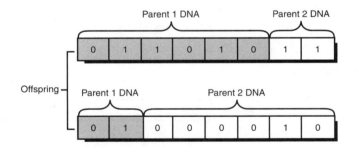

To add a little bit of uncertainty, during the crossover process you flip a bit here and there to simulate mutation. Try your new solutions, along with the last generation's best solutions, and see what happens with the scores. Pick the best results out of this generation and do it again. This is the process of *genetic evolution*. Amazingly, the best possible solution will slowly evolve, and the result might be something you never imagined.

The key things about genetic algorithms are that they try new ideas (patterns) and they can search a very large search space that normally couldn't be searched if you went one by one. This is due to mutation, which represents completely random evolutionary events that may or may not lead to better adaptation.

So how do you use this in a game? There are millions of ways, but I'm going to give you just one to get you started. You can use the probability settings of your AI as the genetic source for digital DNA, and then take the creatures in your game that have survived the longest and merge and evolve their probabilities, thus giving the best traits to future generations. Of course, you would only do this when you needed to spawn a new creature, but you get the idea.

Fuzzy Logic

Fuzzy logic is the last technology I'm going to cover and perhaps one of the most interesting. It has to do with making deductions about the *fuzzy set theory*. In other words, fuzzy logic is a method of analyzing sets of data such that the elements of the sets can have partial inclusion. Most people are used to *crisp logic,* where something is either included or not. For example, if I created the sets *child* and *adult*, I would fall into the *adult* category and my three-year-old nephew would be part of the *child* category. That's crisp logic.

Fuzzy logic, on the other hand, allows objects to be contained within a set even if they aren't *totally* in the set. For example, I might say that I'm 10% part of the child set and 100% part of the adult set. Similarly, my nephew might be 2% part of the adult set and 100% part of the child set. These are fuzzy values. Also, you'll notice that they don't have to add up to 100%—they can be more or less—because they don't represent probabilities, but rather inclusion in different classes. However, the probabilities of an event or state in different classes still must add up to 1.0.

The cool thing about fuzzy logic is that it enables you to make decisions based on fuzzy or error-ridden data that are usually correct. You can't do this with a crisp logic system: If you're missing a variable or input, it won't work. But a fuzzy logic system can still function well with missing variables, just like a human brain. I mean, how many decisions do you make each day that feel fuzzy to you? You don't have all the facts, but you're still fairly confident about the decisions.

That's the two-cent tour of fuzzy logic. Its applications to AI in the areas of decision making, behavioral selections, and input/output filtering should be obvious. With that in mind, let's take a look at the various ways fuzzy logic is implemented and used.

Normal Set Theory

A normal set is simply a collection of objects. To write a set, use a capital letter to represent it and then place the elements contained in it between braces, separated by commas. Sets can consist of anything: names, numbers, colors, whatever. Figure 12.35 illustrates a number of normal sets.

Hardcore Game Programming

FIGURE 12.35
Some simple sets.

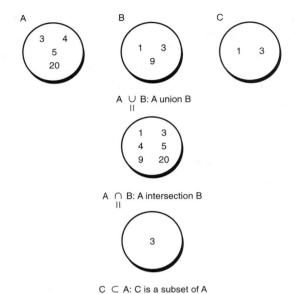

For example, set A = {3,4,5,20} and set B = {1,3,9}. There are many operations that you can perform on these sets:

Element of (ε)—When talking about a set, you might want to know if an object is contained within the set. This is called *set inclusion*. Hence, if you wrote "is 3 ε A," or "is 3 an element of *A*," that would be true. But "2 ε B" is not.

Union (∪)—This operator takes all the objects that exist in both sets and adds them into a new set. If an object appears in both sets initially, it is only added to the new set once. As a result, A ∪ B = {1,3,4,5,9,20}.

Intersection (∩)—This operator takes only the objects that the two sets have in common. Therefore, A ∩ B = {3}.

Subset of (⊂)—Sometimes you want to know if one set is wholly contained in another. This is called *set inclusion* or *subset of*. Therefore, {1,3} ⊂ B, which reads "the set {1,3} is a subset of B." However, A⊄B, which reads "A is not a subset of B."

NOTE	Usually a slash (/) or prime (') symbol means NOT or complement, invert, etc.

Okay, that's a little set theory for you. Nothing complicated, just some terminology and symbols. Everyone works with set theory every day; they just don't know it. The one thing I want you to get from this section is that normal sets are exact. It's either a fruit or it's not. Either 5 is in the set or it's not. This is not the case with fuzzy set theory.

Fuzzy Set Theory

The problem with computers is that they're exact machines, yet we continually use them to solve inexact or fuzzy problems—or at least we *try* to. In the '70s, computer scientists started applying a technique of mathematics called *fuzzy logic*, or *uncertainty logic*, to software programming and problem solving. The fuzzy logic that we're talking about here is really the application of fuzzy set theory and its properties. Let's take a look at the fuzzy set theory version of everything you just learned about with normal set theory.

With fuzzy set theory, you don't focus so much on the objects in the set anymore; the objects *are* in the set, but you focus on the degree of membership a particular object has within a certain class. For example, let's create a fuzzy class or category called *Computer Special FX*. Then take a few of your favorite movies (mine, at least) and estimate how much each of them fits in this fuzzy class. See Table 12.4.

TABLE 12.4   Degree of Membership for **Computer Special FX** class

Movie	Degree of Membership in Class
Antz	100%
Forrest Gump	20%
The Terminator	75%
Aliens	50%
The Matrix	90%

Do you see how fuzzy all this is? Although *The Matrix* had some really killer computer-generated effects, the entire movie *Antz* was computer-generated, so I have to be fair. However, do you agree with all these percentages? *Antz* is totally computer-generated and is an hour and 20 minutes, and *Forrest Gump* has only five minutes total of computer-enhanced imagery. Is it fair to rate *Gump* at 20 percent? I don't know. That's why we're using fuzzy logic.

Anyway, you write each fuzzy degree of membership as an ordered pair of the form "{candidate for inclusion, degree of membership}". Therefore, for the movie example you would write "{ANTZ, 1.00}, {Forrest Gump, 0.20}, {Terminator, 0.75}, {Aliens, 0.50}, {The Matrix, 0.9}". Finally, if you had the fuzzy class *Rainy*, what would you include today as? Where I live, for example, it's "{today, 1.00}"!

Now you can add a little more abstraction and create a *full fuzzy set*. In most cases, this is an ordered collection of the *degrees of membership (DOM)* of a set of objects in a specific class. For example, in the class *Computer Special FX*, you have the set composed of the degrees of membership: A = {1.0, 0.20, 0.75, 0.50, 0.90}. There's one entry for each movie—each variable represents the DOM of each movie as listed in Table 12.4, so the order counts!

Now, suppose that you have another set of movies that all have their own degrees of membership: B = {0.2, 0.45, 0.5, 0.9, 0.15}. Let's apply some of the set operations you've learned about and see the results. Before you do, there's one caveat: Because we're talking about fuzzy sets that represent degrees of membership, or fitness vectors of a set of objects, many set operations must have the same number of objects in each set. This will become more apparent when you see what the fuzzy set operators do below.

Fuzzy union ($\cup$)—The union of two fuzzy sets is the MAX of each element from the two sets. For example, with fuzzy sets:

```
A={1.0, 0.20, 0.75, 0.50, 0.90}
B={0.2, 0.45, 0.5, 0.9, 0.15}
```

The resulting fuzzy set would be the MAX of each pair:

```
A ∪ B  = {MAX(1.0,0.2), MAX(0.20,0.45),
           MAX(0.75,0.5), MAX(0.90,0.15)} = {1.0,0.45,0.75, 0.90}
```

Fuzzy intersection ($\cap$)—The intersection of two fuzzy sets is just the MIN of each element from the two sets. For example, with fuzzy sets:

```
A={1.0, 0.20, 0.75, 0.50, 0.90}
B={0.2, 0.45, 0.5, 0.9, 0.15}
A ∩ B  = {MIN(1.0,0.2), MIN(0.20,0.45),
           MIN(0.75,0.5), MIN(0.90,0.15)} = {0.2,0.20,0.5, 0.15}
```

Subsets and elements have less meaning with fuzzy sets than with standard sets, so I'm skipping them. However, the *complement* of a fuzzy value or set is of interest. The complement of a fuzzy variable with degree of membership x is *(1-x)*, so the complement of A, written A', is computed as

```
A = {1.0, 0.20, 0.75, 0.50, 0.90}
```

Therefore:

```
A' = {1.0 - 1.0, 1.0 - 0.20, 1.0 - 0.75, 1.0 - 0.50, 1.0 - 0.90}
   = {0.0, 0.8, 0.25, 0.5, 0.1}
```

I know this is killing you, but bear with me.

Fuzzy Linguistic Variables and Rules

All righty, then! Now that you have an idea about how to refer to fuzzy variables and sets, let's take a look at how you're going to use them in game AI. You're going to create an AI engine that uses fuzzy rules, applies fuzzy logic to inputs, and outputs fuzzy or crisp outputs to the game object being controlled. Take a look at Figure 12.36 to see this graphically.

FIGURE 12.36
The fuzzy I/O system.

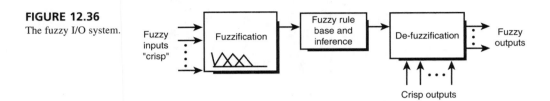

When you put together normal conditional logic, you create a number of statements, or a tree with propositions of the form

```
if X AND Y then Z
```

or

```
if X OR Y then Z
```

The X and Y variables are called the *antecedents*, and Z is called the *consequence*. However, with fuzzy logic, X and Y are *fuzzy linguistic variables*, or *FLVs*. Furthermore, Z can also be an FLV or a crisp value. The key to all this fuzzy stuff is that X and Y represent fuzzy variables, so they're not crisp. Fuzzy propositions of this form are called *rules*, and ultimately they're evaluated in a number of steps. You don't evaluate them like this:

```
if EXPLOSION AND DAMAGE then RUN
```

and execute the RUN consequence if EXPLOSION is TRUE and DAMAGE is TRUE. With fuzzy logic, the rules are only part of the final solution. The *fuzzification* and *defuzzifaction* are what produce the final result.

FLVs represent fuzzy concepts that have to do with a range. For example, let's say that you want to classify the distance between the player and the AI object with three different fuzzy linguistic variables (names, basically). Take a look at Figure 12.37. It shows a *fuzzy manifold* or surface, which is composed of three different triangular regions that I have labeled as follows:

NEAR   Domain range (0 to 300)

CLOSE   Domain range (250 to 700)

FAR   Domain range (500 to 1000)

The input variable is shown on the x-axis and can range from 0 to 1000. This is called the *domain*. The output of the fuzzy manifold is the y-axis and ranges from 0.0 to 1.0. For any input value x_i (which represents range to player in this example), you compute the degree of membership (DOM) by striking a line vertically, as shown in Figure 12.38, and computing the Y value(s) at the intersection(s) with each fuzzy linguistic variable's triangular area.

FIGURE 12.37
A fuzzy manifold
composed of
range FLVs.

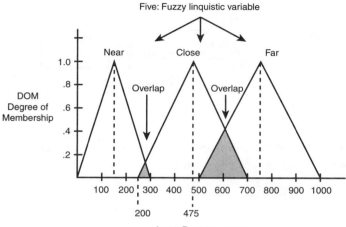

FIGURE 12.38
Computing the degree
of membership of a
domain value in one
or more FLVs.

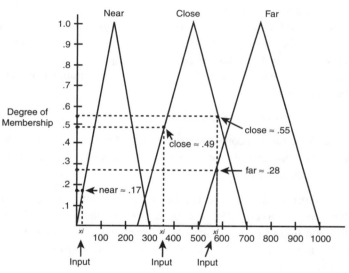

Each triangle in the fuzzy surface represents the area of influence of each fuzzy linguistic variable (NEAR, CLOSE, FAR). In addition, the regions overlap a little—usually 10-50 percent. This is because when NEAR becomes CLOSE and CLOSE becomes FAR, you don't want the value to instantly switch. There should be a little overlap to model the fuzziness of the situation. This is the idea of fuzzy logic.

NOTE You've already seen a similar technique used to select states in a previous FSM example (in the section *Patterns with Conditional Logic Processing*, earlier in this chapter). The range to a target was checked, which forced the FSM to switch states, but in the example with FSMs you used crisp values without overlap or fuzzy computations. There was an exact range where the crisp FSM AI switched from EVADE to ATTACK or whatever. But with fuzzy logic, it's a bit blurry.

Let's recap for a moment. We have rules that are based on fuzzy inputs from the game engine, environment, and so on. These rules may look like normal conditional logic statements, but they must be computed using fuzzy logic because they're really FLVs that classify the input(s) with various degrees of membership.

Furthermore, the final results of the fuzzy logic process may be converted into discrete crisp values, such as "fire phasers," "run," or "stand still," or converted into a continuous value such as a power level from 0–100. Or you might leave it fuzzy for another stage of fuzzy processing.

Fuzzy Manifolds and Membership

It's all coming together, so just hang in there. Now you know that you're going to have a number of inputs in your fuzzy logic AI system. These inputs are going to be classified into one or more (usually more) fuzzy linguistic variable FLVs (which represent some fuzzy range), and then you're going to compute the degree of membership for each input in each of the FLV's ranges. In general, at range input x_i, what is the degree of membership in each fuzzy linguistic variable NEAR, CLOSE, and FAR?

Thus far, the fuzzy linguistic variables are areas defined by symmetrical triangles. However, you can use asymmetrical triangles, trapezoids, sigmoid functions, or whatever. Take a look at Figure 12.39 to see other possible FLV geometries.

FIGURE 12.39
Typical fuzzy linguistic variable geometries.

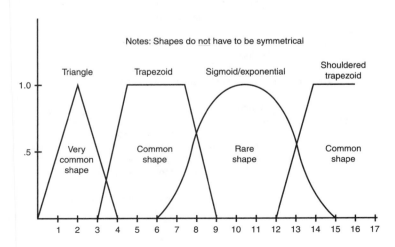

In most cases, symmetrical triangles (symmetrical about the x-axis) work fine. You might want to use trapezoids, though, if you need a range in the FLV that is always 1.0. In any case, to compute the degree of membership (DOM) for any input x_i in a particular FLV, you take the input value x_i and then project a line vertically and see where it intersects the triangle representing the FLV on the y-axis. This is the DOM.

Computing this value in software is easy. Let's assume that you're using a triangular geometry for each FLV, with the left and right starting points defining the triangle labeled min_range, max_range, as shown in Figure 12.40.

FIGURE 12.40
The details of computing DOM for an FLV.

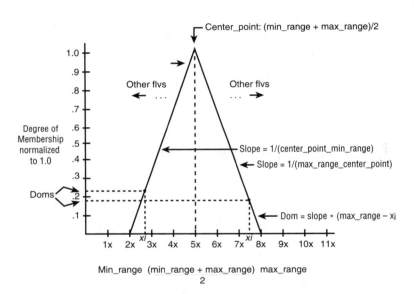

To compute the DOM of any given input x_i, the following algorithm can be used:

```
// first test if the input is in range
if (xi >= min_range && xi <= max_range)
    {
    // compute intersection with left edge or right
    // always assume height of triangle is 1.0

    float center_point = (max_range + min_range)/2;

    // compare xi to center
    if (xi <= center_point)
        {
        // compute intersection on left edge
        // dy/dx = 1.0/(center - left)
        slope = 1.0/(center_point - min_range);

        degree_of_membership = (xi - min_range) * slope;
```

```
    } // end if
else
    {
    // compute intersection on right edge
    // dy/dx = 1.0/(center - right)
    slope = 1.0/(center_point - max_range);

    degree_of_membership = (xi - max_range) * slope;

    } // end else

  } // end if
else // not in range
   degree_of_membership = 0.0;
```

Of course, the function can be totally optimized, but I wanted you to see what was going on. If you had used a trapezoid instead, there would be three possible intersection regions to compute: the left edge, the plateau, and the right edge.

In most cases, you should have at least three fuzzy linguistic variables. If you have more than three, try to keep the number odd so there's always one variable that is centered. Otherwise you might have a *trough* or hole in the center of the fuzzy space.

In any case, let's take a look at some examples of computing the degree of membership of your previous fuzzy manifold, shown in Figure 12.37. Basically, for any input x_i, you project a line vertically and determine where it intersects each of the FLVs in the fuzzy manifold. The line might intersect more than one FLV, and this needs to be resolved. But first, let's get some DOMs.

Assume that you have input ranges x_i = {50,75,250,450, 550,800}, as shown in Figure 12.41.

In that case, the degrees of membership for each FLV—NEAR, CLOSE, FAR—can be computed with the algorithm or read off graphically. They're listed in Table 12.5.

TABLE 12.5   Computations of Degree of Membership for Range Manifold

Degree of Membership Input "Range to target" xi	NEAR	CLOSE	FAR
50	0.33	0.0	0.0
75	0.5	0.0	0.0
250	0.33	0.0	0.0
450	0.0	0.88	0.0
550	0.0	0.66	0.20
800	0.0	0.0	0.80

Hardcore Game Programming

FIGURE 12.41

Your range manifold with a number of inputs.

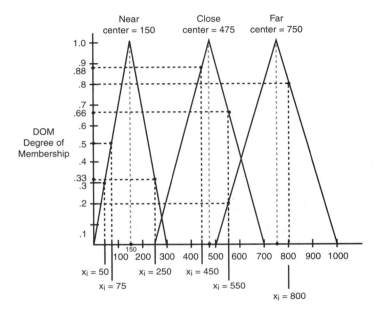

Studying the values, there are a number of interesting properties. First, note that for any input value x_i, the results of membership don't add up to 1.0. Remember, these are degrees of membership, not probabilities, so this is okay.

Secondly, for some x_i's the DOM falls within one or two different fuzzy variables. There could have easily been cases where an input fell into all three regions (if I made the triangles big enough). The process of selecting the size (range) of each triangle is called *tuning*, and sometimes you may have to do this repeatedly to get the results you want. I tried to pick ranges that worked out nicely for examples, but in real life you may need more than three FLVs. And they may not have nice endpoints that are all multiples of 50!

For an example of creating a fuzzy manifold for some input and a number of FLVs, check out DEMO12_9.CPP|EXE on the CD. It enables you to create a number of fuzzy linguistic variables—that is, categories for some input domain. Then you can input numbers and it gives you the degree of membership for each input. It's a console application, so compile appropriately. The data printed for membership is also normalized to 1.0 each time. This is accomplished by taking each DOM and dividing by the sum of DOMs for each category.

At this point you know how to create a fuzzy manifold for an input x_i that is composed of a number of ranges, each of which is represented by a fuzzy linguistic variable. Then you select an input in the range, compute the degree of membership for each FLV in the manifold, and come up with a set of numbers for that particular input. This is called *fuzzifaction*.

The real power of fuzzy logic comes into play when you fuzzify two or more variables, connect them with *if* rules, and see the output. To accomplish this step, first you have to come up with another input to fuzzify—let's call it the power level of the AI bot that you're moving around. Figure 12.42 shows the fuzzy manifold for the power level input.

FIGURE 12.42
The fuzzy manifold for the power level.

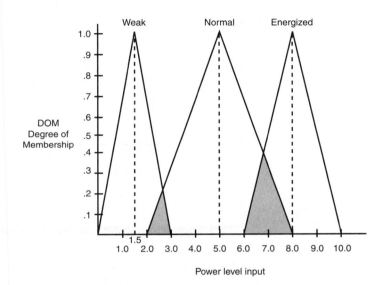

The fuzzy linguistic variables are as follows:

WEAK	Domain range (0.0 to 3.0)
NORMAL	Domain range (2.0 to 8.0)
ENERGIZED	Domain range (6.0 to 10.0)

Notice that this fuzzy variable domain is from 0 to 10.0, rather than 0 to 1000 as is the range to player variable. This is totally acceptable. You could have added more than three FLVs, but three makes the problem symmetrical. To process both fuzzy variables, you need to construct a rule base and then create a fuzzy associative matrix, so let's talk about that next.

Fuzzy Associative Matrices

Fuzzy associative matrices, or *FAMs*, are used to infer a result from two or more fuzzy inputs and a given rule base and output a fuzzy or crisp value. Figure 12.43 shows this graphically.

FIGURE 12.43

Using a fuzzy
associative matrix.

Input x

	x_1	x_2	x_3
y_1	If x_1 and y_1 then z_{11}	If x_2 and y_2 then z_{21}	If x_3 and y_3 then z_{31}
y_2	If x_1 and y_2 then z_{21}	If x_2 and y_2 then z_{22}	If x_3 and y_2 then z_{32}
y_3	If x_1 and y_3 then z_{31}	If x_2 and y_3 then z_{32}	If x_2 and y_3 then z_{33}

Input y

In most cases, FAMs deal with only two fuzzy variables because this can be laid out in a 2D matrix; one variable represents each axis. Each entry in the matrix is the logical proposition "if Xi AND Yi then Zi," where Xi is the fuzzy linguistic variable on the x-axis, Yi is the fuzzy linguistic variable on the y-axis, and Zi is the outcome—which may be a fuzzy variable or crisp value.

To build the FAM, you need to know the rules and the outputs to put in each of the matrix entries. In other words, you need to make a rule base and decide on an output variable that is either crisp or linear. A crisp output would be {"ATTACK", "WANDER", "SEARCH"}, while a linear output might be a thrust level from (0 to 10). Obtaining either one is relatively the same; in both cases, you have to defuzzify the output of the FAM and find the output.

You're going to see examples of both a crisp singular output that selects a class and one that simply outputs a value in a range. Much of the setup is the same. First, let's see the example that computes a range as the final output:

1. Select your inputs, define the FLVs, and build your manifolds.

    The inputs to your fuzzy system are going to be the range to the player and the power level of the AI-controlled bot.

    Input X Range to player.

    Input Y Power level of self.

Refer again to Figures 12.37 and 12.42—these are the fuzzy manifolds that you're using.

2. Create a rule base for the inputs that tie them to an output.

   The *rule base* is nothing more than a collection of logical propositions of the form "if X AND Y then Z" or "if X OR Y then z." This makes a difference when you're computing the FAM outputs. A logical AND means "minimum of the set," while a logical OR means "maximum of the set" when dealing with fuzzy set theory. For now, use all ANDs, but I'll explain how to use ORs later.

In general, if you have two fuzzy inputs and each input has *m* FLVs, the fuzzy associative matrix will have dimension *mxm*. And since each element represents a logical proposition, this means you need nine rules (3x3 = 9) that define all possible logical combinations and the output for each.

However, this is not necessary. If you only have four rules, the other outputs are just set to 0.0 in the FAM. Nevertheless, I will use up all nine slots in our example to make it more robust. For an output, I'm going to use the fuzzy output thrust level, which I'm going to make a fuzzy variable that is made up of the following fuzzy categories (FLVs):

OFF	Domain range (0 to 2)
ON HALF	Domain range (1 to 8)
ON FULL	Domain range (6 to 10)

The fuzzy manifold for these FLVs is shown in Figure 12.44.

FIGURE 12.44

The output fuzzy manifold for the thrust level.

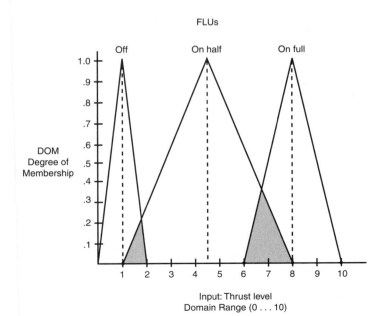

Note that the output could have more categories, but I decided to pick three. Here are my somewhat arbitrary rules:

Input 1: Distance to player.

```
NEAR

CLOSE

FAR
```

Input 2: Power level of self.

```
WEAK

NORMAL

ENERGIZED
```

Output: Internal navigational thrust level (speed).

```
OFF

ON HALF

ON FULL
```

Rules: Somewhat made up (I'm a doctor, not a magician).

```
if NEAR AND WEAK then ON HALF
if NEAR AND NORMAL then ON HALF
if NEAR AND ENERGIZED then ON FULL

if CLOSE AND WEAK then OFF
if CLOSE AND NORMAL then ON HALF
if CLOSE AND ENERGIZED then ON HALF

if FAR AND WEAK then OFF
if FAR AND NORMAL then ON FULL
if FAR AND ENERGIZED then ON FULL
```

These rules are heuristic in nature, imparting knowledge from an "expert" about what the AI should do in these conditions. Although the rules may seem somewhat contradictory, I did think about them for about two minutes! Seriously, now that you have the rules, you can finally fill in the fuzzy associative matrix completely, as shown in Figure 12.45.

FIGURE 12.45
The FAM, complete
with all the rules.

Input 1 = Distance to player

	Near	Close	Far
Weak	And On half	And Off	And Off
Normal	And On half	And On half	And On full
Energized	And On full	And On half	And On full

Input 2: Power level of self

Processing the FAM with the Fuzzified Inputs

To use the FAM, do the following:

Get the crisp inputs for each fuzzy variable and fuzzify them by computing their
DOM for each FLV. For example, let's say that you have the following inputs:

Input 1   Distance to player = 275

Input 2   Power level = 6.5

To fuzzify these, input them into the two fuzzy manifolds and compute the degree
of membership for each fuzzy variable for each input. Refer to Figure 12.46.

For Input 1 = 275, the degree of membership of each FLV is as follows:

NEAR	0.16
CLOSE	0.11
FAR	0.0

For Input 2 = 6.5, the degree of membership of each FLV is as follows:

WEAK	0.0
NORMAL	0.5
ENERGIZED	0.25

FIGURE 12.46

Some inputs plugged into the fuzzy variables.

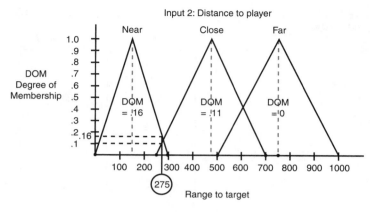

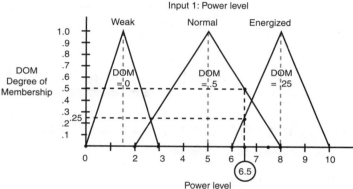

At this point, refer to the fuzzy associative matrix and test the rule in each cell to see what its output value is based on in the preceding fuzzy values. Of course, many of the FAM's cells will be 0.0 because two of the FLVs (one from each input) are 0.0. Anyway, take a look at Figure 12.47, which depicts your FAM along with all the cells that have non-zero outputs shaded in.

Now here comes the tricky part… Each one of those cells in the FAM represents a rule. For example, the upper-left cell represents

```
if NEAR AND WEAK then ON HALF
```

To evaluate this rule, take the antecedents and test them using a MIN() rule for the logical AND. In this case, you have that NEAR = 0.16 and WEAK = 0.0, hence:

```
if (0.16) AND (0.0) then on HALF
```

This is computed using the MIN() function as

```
(0.16) _ (0.0) = (0.0)
```

FIGURE 12.47
The fuzzy associative matrix showing active cells and their values.

Input 2 = 275

	Near = .16	Close = .11	Far = 0
Weak = 0	0 and .16 = 0 0 ^ .16 = 0 min (0, .16) = 0 Output: On half Value: 0	0 and .11 = 0 0 ^ .11 = 0 min (0, .11) = 0 Output: Off Value: 0	0 and 0 = 0 0 ^ 0 = 0 min (0, 0) = 0 Output: Off Value: 0
Normal = .5	.5 and .16 = .16 .5 ^ .16 = .16 min (.5, .16) = .16 Output: *On half Value: .16	.5 and .11 = .11 .5 ^ .11 = .11 min (.5, .11) = .11 Output: *On half Value: .11	.5 and 0 = 0 .5 ^ 0 = 0 min (.5, 0) = 0 Output: On full Value: 0
Energized = .25	.25 and .16 = .16 .25 ^ .16 = .16 min (.25, .16) = .16 Output: *On full Value: .16	.25 and .11 = .11 .25 ^ .11 = .11 min (.25, .11) = .11 Output: *On half Value: .11	.25 and 0 = 0 .25 ^ 0 = 0 min (.25, 0) = 0 Output: On full Value: 0

Input 2 = 6.5

* – means this rule fire S

Thus, the rule doesn't fire at all. On the other hand, let's take a look at the rule

```
if CLOSE AND ENERGIZED then ON HALF
```

This means

```
if (0.11) AND (0.25) then ON HALF
```

which, computed using the MIN() function, is

```
(0.11) _ (0.25) = (0.11)
```

A-ha! The rule ON HALF fires at a level of 0.11, so you place that value in the FAM associated with the rule ON HALF at the intersection of CLOSE and ENERGIZED. Continue this process for the whole matrix until you've found all nine entries. This is shown in Figure 12.47.

At this point, you're finally ready to defuzzify the FAM. This can be accomplished in a number of ways. Basically, you need a final crisp value that represents the thrust level from (0.0 to 10.0). There are two main ways to compute this: You can use the disjunction or MAX() method to find the value, or you can use an averaging technique based on the *fuzzy centroid*. Let's take a look at the MAX() method first.

Method 1: The MAX Technique

If you look at the FAM data, you have the following fuzzy outputs:

OFF   (0.0)

ON HALF   {0.16, 0.11, 0.16}, use sum which is 0.43

ON FULL   (0.16)

Note that the rule ON HALF has fired within three different outputs, so you have to decide what you want to do with the results. Should you add them, average them, or max them? It's really up to you. For this example, choose sum: 0.16+0.11+0.16 = .43.

This is still fuzzy, but looking at the data, it looks like ON HALF has the strongest membership. So it makes sense to just go with that:

```
output = MAX(OFF, ON HALF, ON FULL)
       = MAX(0.0, 0.43, 0.16) = 0.43
```

Using the disjunction operator v:

$(0.0) v (0.43) v (0.16) = (0.43)$

And that's it. Simply multiply (0.43) times the scale of the output, and that's the answer:

```
(0.43) * (10) = (4.3)
Set the thrust to (4.3).
```

The only problem with this method is that even though you're taking the variable that has the highest membership, its total area of influence in the fuzzy space may be very small. For example, a 40% NORMAL is definitely stronger than a 50% WEAK. See my point? It might be better to plug some of the values into the output fuzzy manifold for (OFF, ON HALF, ON FULL), compute the area of influence, and then compute the centroid of the whole thing and use that as the final output.

Method 2: The Fuzzy Centroid

To find the fuzzy centroid, you take the fuzzy values for each FLV in the output:

OFF   (0.0)

ON HALF   (0.14) {average}

ON FULL   (0.16)

Plug them into the y-axis of the FLV diagram and fill in the area for each. This is shown in Figure 12.48.

FIGURE 12.48

Finding the area and the centroids of the fuzzy manifold graphically.

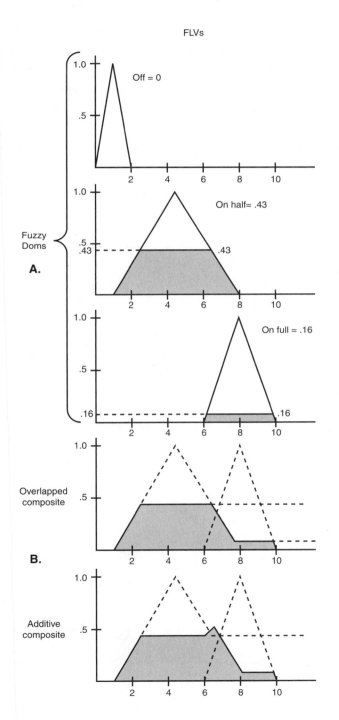

Add the areas up and find the centroid of the resulting geometric shape. As you can see, there are two ways to add the areas up: overlap and additive. Overlapping loses a bit of information, but it's easier sometimes. The additive technique is more accurate.

The centroids of each method have been computed and are shown in Figure 12.48. That's great, but the computer isn't a piece of graph paper. How do you compute the centroid?

To compute a centroid, perform a numerical *integration* (that's a calculus term). All this means is that to find the center of area of this fuzzy area object you need to sum up each piece of the object and its contribution to the total and then divide by the total area:

```
Domain
Σ d_i * dom_i
i
```

_____

```
Domain
Σ dom_i
i
```

d_i is the input value for the domain, and dom_i is the degree of membership of that value. This is much easier to explain with real examples. In this example, the output domain is from 0.0 to 10.0. This represents the thrust level.

You need a loop variable d_i that loops from 0 to 10. At each interval of the loop, you're going to compute the degree of membership that this particular d_i is in the merged geometry shown in Figure 12.49.

FIGURE 12.49

Computing the final crisp output from the fuzzy centroid.

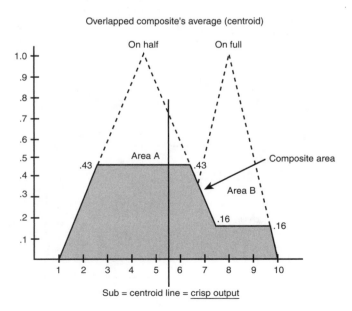

Because each triangle has a certain height now that was cut off by the original values, you have to compute the degree of membership with a trapezoid rather than a triangle (but that's not too bad):

OFF   (0.0)

ON HALF   (0.14)

ON FULL   (0.16)

Here's the pseudo-code:

```
sum        = 0.0;
total_area = 0.0;

for (int di = 0; di<=10; di++)
   {
   // compute next degree of membership and add to
   // total area
   total_area = total_area + degree_of_membersip(di);

   // add next contribution of the shape at position di
   sum = sum + di * degree_of_membersip(di);

   } // end for

// finally compute centroid
centroid = sum/total_area;
```

The thing to remember is that the function degree_of_membership() is taking the generic values (0..10) and plugging them into the merged output fuzzy manifold, which results from plugging the following fuzzy values into the output variable and finding the area of influence of each one:

OFF   (0.0)

ON HALF   (0.14)

ON FULL   (0.16)

As you can see, using the MAX() method sure is a lot easier, and most of the time it works just as well as the centroid.

As for computing a crisp value for the final output rather than a linear value, that's easy. Just use the MAX() method and pigeonhole the output. Or you could select the output domain to be 0,1,2,3,4 and have exactly five crisp output commands. It's all about scale.

Warm and Fuzzy

That about wraps up the topic of fuzzy logic. The idea of fuzzy logic is simple; it's the actual implementation that's detailed. There's no demo this time, but look on the Internet. There are lots of commercial fuzzy logic experimentation programs. They're a lot better than anything I can write in 20 minutes, which is all the time I have left to write this chapter!

Building Real AI for Games

That's about all there is to the basic AI techniques used in games. I've shown you a few techniques to get you started, but you might not be totally sure about which techniques to use and how to mix different techniques to make new models. Here are some basic guidelines:

- Use simple deterministic AIs for objects that have simple behaviors, like rocks, missiles, and so on.
- For objects that are supposed to be smart but are part of the environment rather than the main action (such as birds that fly around or a space ship that flies by once), use deterministic AI coupled with patterns and a bit of randomness.
- For your important game characters that interact with the player, you definitely need FSMs coupled with the other supporting techniques. However, some creatures don't have to be as smart as others, such as the FSMs for your basic creatures, and they don't need to have probability distributions for personality coupled with memory for learning.
- Finally, the main character(s) in the game should be very smart. You should integrate everything together. The AI should be state-driven, with a lot of conditional logic, probability, and memory for controlling state transitions. In addition, the AI should be able to change from one state to another if conditions exist that make the change necessary (even if the state hasn't come to completion).

You don't need to go all out on a randomly moving rock, but for a tank that plays against the player, you should. A model that works well for me is an AI that has at its highest level a set of conditionals and probabilities that select states. The states emulate a number of behaviors, usually about 5–10. I like to use a memory to track key elements in the game and make better decisions. Also, I like to throw in random numbers in a lot of the decisions, even if they're totally simple. This adds a little uncertainty to the AI.

Next, I definitely like to have scripted patterns available to create the illusion of complex thought. However, again I throw random events in the patterns themselves. For example, if my AI moved into a pattern state and selected a circle, fine. But sometimes as it's doing the circle, it makes an egg shape! The point is, people aren't perfect, and sometimes we make mistakes. This quality is very important in game AI, so coin-tossing helps to shake things up.

Finally, a very complex system can evolve from very simple constituents. In other words, even though the AI for each individual creature might not be that complex, their interaction will create an emergent behavioral system that seems to go beyond its programming. Just look at your own brain, where each cell is hardly aware of itself. It's important to help facilitate this with some kind of sharing or merging of information between creatures, such as when they get close enough or at specific intervals. This helps with the sharing of "knowledge" in the simulation.

Summary

This chapter has been an eye-opener, huh? We covered a lot of ground. A lot of weird stuff, too. Makes you wonder about intelligence, doesn't it? Anyway, you should have a good grasp of AI now. Both ad hoc and robust techniques have been covered. We talked about deterministic algorithms, decision trees, planning, scripting languages, neural networks, genetic algorithms, and fuzzy logic. And I would venture to say that you could give any professional game programmer a run for his/her money on the subject of AI, if not blow them away!

CHAPTER 13

Playing God: Basic Physics Modeling

"Follow the white rabbit."
—Morpheus, The Matrix

There wasn't a whole lot of physics involved in the video games in the '70s and '80s. For the most part, games were shoot-'em-ups, search-and-destroy games, adventure games, and so on. However, beginning with the '90s and the "3D era," physics modeling became much more important. You simply can't get away with having objects in games move in non-realistic ways—the motion of the objects has to at least approximate what you'd expect in the real world. This chapter covers fundamental non-calculus-based physics modeling. Then, in the second volume I'll cover more rigid, calculus-based 2D and 3D modeling. Here are the topics you'll see in this chapter:

- Fundamental laws of physics
- Gravity
- Friction
- Collision response

- Forward kinematics
- Particle systems
- Playing God

If the universe is just a simulation in some unbelievably advanced computer, God is one heck of a programmer! The point is, the laws of physics work perfectly at all levels, from the quantum level to the cosmological level. The beauty of physics is that there aren't that many laws that govern the whole universe. Granted, our knowledge of physics and mathematics is that of a Cabbage Patch doll, but we do know enough to create computer simulations that can fool just about anyone.

Most computer simulations and games that use physics models use models based on standard Newtonian physics—a class of physics that works reasonably well on motion and objects that are within reasonable limits of size and mass. That is, speeds much less than the speed of light, and objects that are much bigger than a single atom, but much smaller than a galaxy. However, even modeling reality with basic Newtonian-based physics can take a lot of computing power. A simple simulation like rainfall or a pool table (if done correctly) would bring a Pentium IV to its knees.

Nonetheless, we have all seen rainfall and pool games on everything from the Apple II to the PC. So how did they do it? The programmers of these games understand the physics that they're trying to model and within the budget of the system they're programming on, create models that are close enough to what the player would expect in real life. This programming consists of a lot of tricks, optimizations, and most of all assumptions and simplifications about the systems that are being modeled. For example, it's a lot easier figuring out how two spheres will react after collision than it is to calculate the result of the collision of two irregular asteroids, thus a programmer might approximate all the asteroids in a game with simple spheres (as far as the physics calculations go).

In a state-of-the-art game, physics would take about 10,000 pages because it's not only the physics, but the math that needs to be learned, so I'm just going to cover some of the most fundamental physics models. From them you should be able to model everything you need in your first 2D/3D games. Most of this stuff should be more than familiar from High School physics—or Junior High School!

Fundamental Laws of Physics

Let's begin our physics journey by covering some of the basic concepts of physics and the properties of time, space, and matter. These fundamental concepts will give you a vocabulary to understand the more advanced topics that follow.

WARNING

Everything that I am about to say is not entirely true at the quantum or the cosmological level. However, the statements I'm going to make are true enough for our discussions. In addition, I'm going to lean toward the metric system since the English system is about 200 years antiquated and the only people that use it are the general population of the United States. The scientific community and the rest of the world all use the metric system. Seriously; 12 inches to a foot, 3 feet to a yard, 2 yards to a fathom, 5,280 feet to a mile. Was somebody smoking crack or what?

Mass (m)

All matter has mass. Mass is a measure of how much matter or actual atomic mass units. It doesn't have anything to do with weight. Many people have mass and weight confused. For example, they might incorrectly say that they weigh 75 kilograms (165 pounds) on Earth. First, kilograms (kg) are a metric measure of mass, that is, how much matter an object has. Pounds is a measure of force, or, more loosely, weight (mass in a gravity field). The measure of weight or force in the English system is a *pound (lb.)* and in the metric system is called a *Newton (N)*. Matter has no weight per se; it only can be acted upon by a gravitational field to produce what we refer to as weight. Hence, the concept of mass is a much more pure idea than weight (which changes planet to planet).

In games, the concept of mass is only used abstractly (in most cases) as a relative quantity. For example, I might set the spaceship equal to 100 mass units and the asteroid equal to 10,000. I could use kilograms, but unless I'm doing a real physics simulation it really doesn't matter. All I need to know is an object that has a mass of 100 has twice as much matter as an object that has 50 mass units. I'll revisit mass in a bit when I talk about force and gravity. Mass is the measure of how much matter an object is made of and is measured in kilograms in the metric system or—ready for this—*slugs* in the English system.

NOTE

Mass is also thought of as a measure of the resistance an object has to change in its velocity[md]Newton's First law. Basically, Newton's First law states that an object at rest remains at rest, and an object in motion remains in motion (at a constant velocity) until an exterior force acts on the object.

Time (t)

Time is an abstract concept. Think about it. How would you explain time without using time itself in the explanation? Time is definitely an impossible concept to convey without using circular definitions and a lot of hand waving. Luckily, everyone knows what time is, so I won't go into it, but I do want to talk about how it relates to time in a game.

Time in real life is usually measured in seconds, minutes, hours, and so forth. Or if you need to be really accurate then it's measured in milliseconds (ms 10^{-3} seconds), microseconds (μs 10^{-6}), nano (10^{-9}), pico (10^{-12}), femto (10^{-15}), etc. However, in a video game (most games), there isn't a really close correlation to real-time. Algorithms are designed more around the frame rate than real time and seconds (except for time modeled games). For example, most games consider one frame to be one virtual second, or in other words, the smallest amount of time that can transpire. Thus, most of the time, you won't use real seconds in your games and your physics models, but virtual seconds based on a single frame as the fundamental time step.

On the other hand, if you're creating a really sophisticated 3D game then you probably will use real time. All the algorithms in the game track in real time, and invariant of the frame rate, they adjust the motion of the objects so that a tank can move at, say, 100 feet per second even if the frame rate slows down to 2 frames per second or runs at 60 frames per second. Modeling time at this level of accuracy is challenging, but absolutely necessary if you want to have ultra-realistic motion and physical events that are independent of frame rate changes. In any case, we'll measure time in seconds (s) in the examples or in virtual seconds, which simply means a single frame.

Position (s)

Every object has an (x,y,z) position in 3D space or an (x,y) position in 2D space or an x in 1D or linear space (also sometimes referred to as an s). Figure 13.1 shows examples of all these dimensional cases. However, sometimes it's not clear what the position of an object is even if you know where it is. For example, if you had to pick one single point that locates the position of a sphere then you would probably pick its center as shown in Figure 13.2. But what about a hammer? A hammer is an irregular shape, so most physicists would use its *center of mass,* or balancing point, as the position to locate it, as shown in Figure 13.3.

FIGURE 13.1
The concept of position.

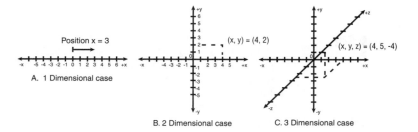

A. 1 Dimensional case

B. 2 Dimensional case

C. 3 Dimensional case

FIGURE 13.2
Picking the center.

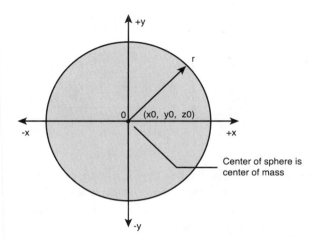

Center of sphere is
center of mass

FIGURE 13.3
Picking the center of
an irregular object.

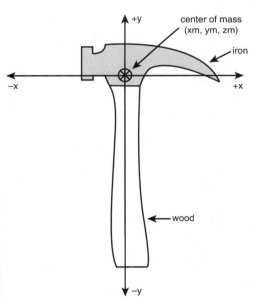

The concept of position and the physically correct location of the position when it comes to games is usually rather lax. Most game programmers place a bounding box, circle, or sphere around all the game objects as shown in Figure 13.4 and simply use the center of the bounding entity as the center of the object. This works for most cases, where most of the mass of the object is located at the center of the object by luck, but if that's not the case then any physics calculations that use this artificial center will be incorrect.

FIGURE 13.4
Collision contour
shapes.

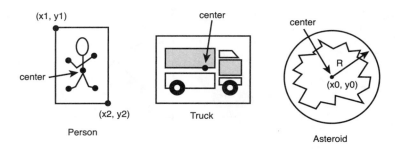

The only way to solve the problem is to pick a better center that takes the virtual mass of the object into consideration. For example, you could create an algorithm that scanned the pixels making up the object and the more pixels that were in an area, the more that area would be weighted to be the center. Or if the object is a polygon-based object then you could attach a weight to each vertex and compute the real center of mass of the object. Assuming that there are n vertices and each vertex position is labeled by (x_i,y_i) with a mass of m_I, then the center of mass is

$$X_c = \frac{\sum_{i=0}^{n} x_i{}^* m_i}{\sum_{i=0}^{n} m_i}$$

$$Y_c = \frac{\sum_{i=0}^{n} y_i{}^* m_i}{\sum_{i=0}^{n} m_i}$$

MATH	The $\sum f_i$ symbol just means "sum of." It's like a for loop that sums the values f_i for each value of i.

Velocity (v)

Velocity is the instantaneous rate of speed of an object and is usually measured in meters per second (m/s) or in the case of the automobile, miles per hour, or mph. Whatever units you prefer, velocity is the change in position per change in time. Stated mathematically in a 1 dimensional case, this reads:

Velocity = $v = ds/dt$.

In other words, the instantaneous change in position (ds) with respect to time (dt). As an example, say you are driving down the road and you just drove 100 miles in one hour, then your average velocity would be

v = ds/dt = 100 miles/1 hour = 100 mph.

In a video game the concept of velocity is used all the time, but again the units are arbitrary and relative. For example, in a number of the demos I have written I usually move objects at 4 units in the x- or y-axis per frame with code something like the following:

```
x_position = x_position + x_velocity;
y_position = y_position + y_velocity;
```

That translates to 4 pixels/frame. But frames aren't time, are they? Actually, they are as long as the frame rate stays constant. In the case of 30 fps, which is equal to $1/30^{th}$ of a second per frame, the 4 pixels per frame translate to:

```
Virtual Velocity = 4 pixel / (1/30) seconds
                 = 120 pixels per second.
```

Hence, the objects in our game have been moving with velocities measured in pixels/second. If you wanted to get crazy then you could estimate how many virtual meters were in one pixel in your game world and perform the computation in meters/second in cyberspace. In either case, now you know how to gauge where an object will be at any given time or frame if you know the velocity. For example, if an object was currently at position x_0 and it was moving at 4 pixels/frame, and 30 frames go by, the object would be at

```
new position = x₀ + 4 * 30 = x₀ + 120 pixels.
```

This leads us to our first important basic formula for motion:

```
New Position = Old Position + Velocity * Time
             = xₜ = x₀ + v*t.
```

This formula states that an object moving with velocity v that starts at location x_0 and moves for t seconds will move to a position equal to its original position plus the velocity times the time. Take a look at Figure 13.5 to see this more clearly. As an example of constant velocity I have created a demo DEMO13_1.CPP|EXE (16-bit version, DEMO13_1_16B.CPP|EXE) that moves a fleet of choppers from left to right on the screen.

FIGURE 13.5
Constant velocity
motion.

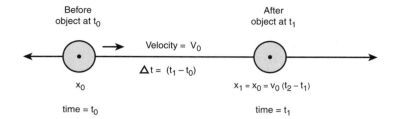

TRICK

I always amaze my friends by telling them how long it will take to get to an off-ramp or some other location when we're in the car. The trick is simple; just look at the speed and use the fact that at 60 mph it takes 1 minute to go 1 mile. So if the driver is driving 60 and the off ramp is in 2 miles then it will take 2 minutes. On the other hand, if the on ramp is in 3.5 miles then it would take 3 minutes and 30 seconds. And if the driver isn't driving 60 mph then use the closest plus or minus 30 mph. For example, if they're going 80 then do you calculations with 90 mph (1.5 miles per minute) and then shrink your answer a bit.

Acceleration (a)

Acceleration is similar to velocity, but it is the measure of the rate of change of velocity rather than the velocity itself. Take a look at Figure 13.6; it illustrates an object moving with a constant velocity and one with a changing velocity. The object moving with a constant velocity has a flat line (slope of 0) for its velocity as a function of time, but the accelerating object has a slope of non-zero because its velocity is changing as a function of time.

FIGURE 13.6
Velocity vs.
acceleration.

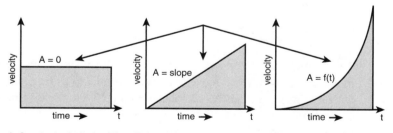

A. Constant velocity (a = 0)   B. Acceleration (A = constant)   C. Non-constant acceleration

Figure 13.6 illustrates constant acceleration. There is also non-constant acceleration. In this case the line would be a curve in part C of Figure 13.6. Pressing the accelerator in your car will give you the feeling of non-constant acceleration and jumping off a cliff will give you the feeling of constant acceleration. Mathematically, acceleration is the rate of change of velocity with respect to time:

```
Acceleration = a = dv/dt.
```

The units of acceleration are a little weird. Since velocity is already in units of distance per second, acceleration is in units of distance per second*second, or in the metric system, m/s^2. If you think about this it makes sense because acceleration is the change of velocity (m/s) per second. Furthermore, our second motion law relates the velocity, time, and acceleration, which states that the new velocity at some time, t, in the future equals the starting velocity plus the acceleration times the amount of time the object has been accelerating for:

```
New Velocity  = Old Velocity + Acceleration * Time
              = vt = v0 + a*t.
```

Acceleration is a fairly simple concept and can be modeled in a number of ways, but let's take a look at a simple example. Imagine that an object is located at (0,0) and it has a starting velocity of 0. If you were to accelerate it at a constant velocity of 2 m/s, you could figure out the new velocity each second simply by adding the acceleration to the last velocity, as shown in Table 13.1.

TABLE 13.1   Velocity as a Function of Time for Acceleration 2 m/s^2

Time (t = s)	Acceleration (v = m/s)	Velocity (a = m/s^2)
0	2	0
1	2	2
2	2	4
3	2	6
4	2	8
5	2	10

Taking the data in the table into consideration, the next step is to figure out the relationship between position, velocity, acceleration, and time. Unfortunately, this takes a bit of calculus, so I'll just give you the results in terms of position at some time t:

```
xt = x0 + v0*t + 1/2*a*t2
```

This equation states that the position of an object at some time t is equal to its initial position, plus its initial velocity, times time, plus one half the acceleration, times time squared. The $1/2*a*t^2$ term is basically the time integral of the velocity. Let's see if you can use the equation in your game world of pixels and frames. Refer to Figure 13.7.

FIGURE 13.7
An acceleration in
pixels/frame^2.

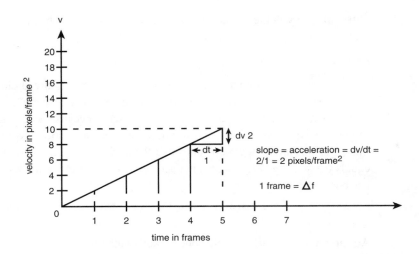

Position of K:

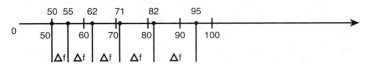

Assume these initial conditions: The object is at x=50 pixels, the initial velocity is 4 pixels/frame, and the acceleration is 2 pixels/frame^2. Finally, assume that these are the conditions at frame 0. To find the position of the object at any time in C/C++, use the following:

```
x = 50 + 4*t + (0.5)*2*t*t;
```

Where t is simply the frame number. Table 13.2 lists some examples for t = 0,1,2...5.

TABLE 13.2 An Object Moving with Constant Acceleration

Time/Frame (t)	Position (x)	Delta (x)=x_t-x_{t-1}
0	50	0
1	50+4*1+(0.5)*2*1^2 = 55	5
2	50+4*2+(0.5)*2*2^2 = 62	7
3	50+4*3+(0.5)*2*3^2 = 71	9
4	50+4*4+(0.5)*2*4^2 = 82	11
5	50+4*5+(0.5)*2*5^2 = 95	13

There's a lot of interesting data in Table 13.2, but maybe the most interesting data is the change in position each time the frame is constant and equal to 2. Now this doesn't mean that the object moves 2 pixels per frame, it means that the change in motion each frame gets larger or increases by 2 pixels. Thus on the first frame the object moves 5 pixels, then on the next frame it moves 7, then 9, 11, then 13, and so on. And the delta between each change in motion is 2 pixels, which is simply the acceleration!

The next step is to model acceleration with C/C++ code. Basically, here's the trick: You set up an acceleration constant and then with each frame you add it to your velocity. This way you don't have to use the long equation shown earlier—you simply translate your object with the given velocity. Here's an example:

```
int acceleration = 2, // 2 pixels per frame
    velocity      = 0, // start velocity off at 0
    x             = 0; // start x position of at 0 also
// ...
// then you would execute this code each
// cycle to move your object
// with a constant acceleration

// update velocity
velocity+=acceleration;

// update position
x+=velocity;
```

> **NOTE**   Of course this example is one-dimensional. You can upgrade to two dimensions simply by adding a y position (and y velocity and acceleration if you wish).

To see acceleration in action, I have created a demo named DEMO13_2.CPP|EXE (16-bit version, DEMO13_2_16B.CPP|EXE) that allows you to fire a missile that accelerates as it moves forward. Press the spacebar to fire the missile, the up and down arrow keys to increase and decrease the acceleration factor, and the A key to toggle the acceleration on and off. Look at the difference acceleration makes to the motion of the missile and how acceleration gives the missile a sense of "mass."

Force (F)

One of the most important concepts in physics is *force*. Figure 13.8 depicts one way to think of force. If an object with mass *m* is sitting on a table with gravity pulling it toward the center of the Earth, the acceleration is a=g (force of gravity). This gives the mass *m* weight and if you try to pick it up you will feel a pain in your lower back.

FIGURE 13.8
Force and weight.

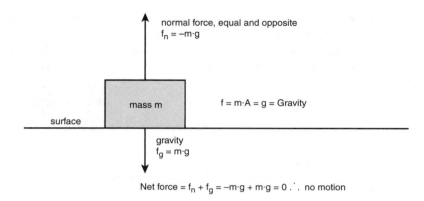

The relationship between force, mass, and acceleration is Newton's Second Law:

F=m*a

In other words, the force exerted on an object is equal to its mass times the acceleration of the object. Or, rearranging terms:

a = F/m

This states that an object will accelerate an amount equal to the force you place on it divided by its mass. Now let's talk about the units of measure. But instead of just blurting it out, let's see where it comes from in the metric system. Force is equal to mass times acceleration or kilograms multiplied by m/s^2 (m stands for meters, not mass). Hence, a possible unit of force is

$F = kg*m/s^2$—kilogram-meters per second squared

This is a bit long, so Newton just called it—a *Newton (N)*. As an example, imagine that a mass m equal to 100 kg is accelerating at a rate of 2 m/s^2. The force that is being applied to the mass is exactly equal to F = m*a = 100 kg * 2 m/s^2 = 200N.

This gives you a bit of a feel for a Newton. A 100 kg mass is roughly equivalent to the force of 220 lbs. on Earth, and 1 m/s^2 is a good accelerating run.

In a video game the concept of force is used for many reasons, but a few that come to mind are

- You want to apply artificial forces like explosions to an object and compute the resulting acceleration.
- Two objects collide and you want to compute the forces on each.
- A game weapon only has a certain force, but it can fire different virtual mass shells and you want to find the acceleration the shells would experience when fired.

Forces in Higher Dimensions

Of course forces can act in all three dimensions, not just in a straight line. For example, take a look at Figure 13.9, which depicts three forces acting on a particle in a 2D plane. The resulting force that the particle p "feels" is simply the sum of the forces that are acting on it. However, in this case it's not as simple as adding scalar numbers together since the forces are vectors. Nevertheless, vectors can be decomposed into their x, y, and z components and then the forces acting in each axis can be computed. The result is the sum of the forces acting on the particle.

FIGURE 13.9

Forces acting on a particle in 2D.

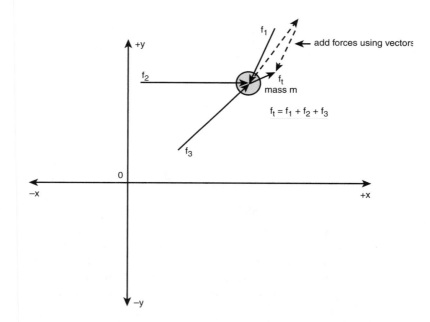

In the example shown in Figure 13.9 there are three forces; F_1, F_2, and F_3. The final force F_{final}=<fx, fy> that object p feels is simply the sum of these forces:

```
fx = f1x + f2x + f3x
fy = f1y + f2y + f3y
```

Plugging in the values from the example in the figure, you get

```
fx = (x+x+x) = x.x
fy = (y+y+y) = y.y
```

With that in mind, it doesn't take much to deduce that in general the final force F on an object is just the vector sum of forces, or mathematically:

$$F_{final} = F_1+F_2+...+F_n$$

Where each force F_i can have 1, 2, or 3 components, that is, each vector can be a 1D (scalar), 2D, or 3D.

Momentum (P)

Momentum is one of those quantities that's hard to define verbally. It's basically the property that objects in motion have. Momentum was invented as a measure of both the velocity and mass of an object. Momentum is defined as the product of mass (m) and the velocity (v) of an object:

$P = m*v$

And the units of measure are kg*m/s, kilogram-meters per second. Now the cool thing about momentum is its relationship to force—watch this:

$F = m*a$

or substituting, p for m:

$F = (p*a)/v$

But, a = dv/dt, thus:

$$F = \frac{p*dv/dt}{v} = \frac{d(p)*v}{dt*v} = dp/dt$$

Or in English, force is the time rate change of momentum per unit time. Hmmm... interesting. That means if the momentum of an object changes a lot then so must the force acting on the object. Now here's the clincher. A pea can have as much momentum as a train—how? A pea may have mass of 0.001 kg and a train have a mass of 1,000,000 kg. But if the train is going 1 m/s and the pea is going 100,000,000,000 m/s (that's one fast pea) then the pea will have more momentum:

$m_{pea}*v_{pea}$ = 0.001 kg * 10,000,000,000 m/s = 10,000,000 kg*m/s
$m_{train}*v_{train}$ = 1,000,000 kg * 1 m/s = 1,000,000 kg*m/s

And thus if either of these objects came to an abrupt stop, hit something for example, that object would feel a whole lot of force! That's why a bee hitting you on a motorcycle is so dangerous. It's not the mass of the bee, but the velocity of the bee that gets you in this example. The resulting momentum is huge and can literally throw a 200-pound guy off the bike.

This brings us to *conservation of momentum* and *momentum transfer*.

> **NOTE**   I was on an FZR600 one time, going about 155 mph, and a bee hit my visor. Not only did it crack the visor, but it felt like someone threw a baseball at me! Lesson to be learned—only speed in designated bee-free areas!

The Physics of Linear Momentum: Conservation and Transfer

Now that you have an idea about what momentum is, let's talk briefly about some of the physics involved when an object strikes another. Later I will go into true collision response in more depth, but for now let's keep it simple.

Remember in the game *DOOM* when you shot a barrel, it would explode and cause the barrels and/or bad guys in the area to move and/or explode? Wasn't that cool splattering a bad guy against a wall! That was just momentum transfer, but believe me, doing it correctly is no picnic!

In general, if two objects collide there are two things that can happen: a perfectly elastic collision and a not so perfectly elastic collision. In a perfectly elastic collision, as shown in Figure 13.10, a ball hits a wall with velocity v_i, and when it bounces off it still has velocity v_i. Thus, the momentum was conserved. Therefore, the collision was totally elastic. However, in real life this isn't usually the case. Most collisions aren't elastic, they are less than perfect. When collisions that are less than perfectly elastic occur, some energy is converted into heat, work to deform the objects colliding, etc. Thus the resulting momentum of the object(s) after collision is less than when the collision started.

FIGURE 13.10
A perfectly elastic collision of a ball and wall.

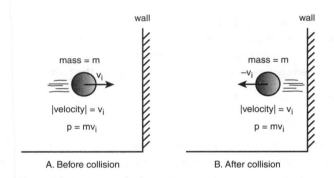

However, I'm not interested in this kind of imperfect world. Since we are gods of the virtual world, we might as well make things easy. Hence, I'm going to talk about perfectly elastic collisions in 1-dimension right now, then later we'll do it in 2D and get medieval with the math! Let's begin.

Figure 13.11 has two block objects A, B with mass m_a and m_b and velocity v_{ai} and v_{bi}, respectively. The question is what happens after they hit, assuming no friction (we'll get to that later) and a perfectly elastic collision? Well, let's start with the *conservation of momentum*. It states that the total momentum before the collision will be the same as after the collision. Or mathematically:

Equation 1: Conservation of momentum

$$m_a*v_{ai} + m_b*v_{bi} = m_a*v_{af} + m_b*v_{bf}$$

FIGURE 13.11
The collision response
of two blocks in 1D.

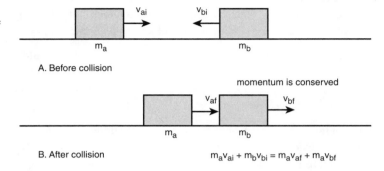

A. Before collision

momentum is conserved

B. After collision $m_a v_{ai} + m_b v_{bi} = m_a v_{af} + m_a v_{bf}$

All right, you know m_a, m_b, v_{ai}, and v_{bi}, but you want the final velocities v_{af} and v_{bf}. The problem is that you only have one equation and two unknowns. This is obviously a bad thing. If you knew the velocity of one of the masses, you could figure the other one out. But, is there a way to figure out both velocities without any further knowledge? The answer is yes! You can use another property of physics to come up with another equation. The property is the *conservation of kinetic energy.*

Kinetic energy is like momentum, but is independent of direction. It's like a magnitude of sorts that gauges the amount of total energy that a system has. Now, energy is the ability to do work and that's all I'm going to say, we are getting a little too quantum here. However, computing kinetic energy is trivial, the formula is

Equation 2: Kinetic energy

$$ke = 1/2*m*v^2$$

Momentum was just $m*v$, so you should see that kinetic energy is very similar, but it's always positive and measured in $kg*m^2/s^2$, which in the Meter-Kilogram-Second system we just call Joules (J). The cool part is that the kinetic energy of any system is always the same before and after a collision, elastic, or not. Of course you would have to compute the energies lost due to deformation, heat, etc. to account for all the energy, but when assuming a perfectly elastic collision, the kinetic energy before and after can be computed by just knowing the velocities of the objects:

Equation 3: Total kinetic energy of collision

$$*m_a*v_{ai}^2 + 1/2*m_b*v_{bi}^2 = 1/2*m_a*v_{af}^2 + 1/2*m_b*v_{bf}^2$$

Combining this with equation 1 results in:

$$m_a*v_{ai} + m_b*v_{bi} = m_a*v_{af} + m_b*v_{bf}$$
$$*m_a*v_{ai}^2 + \_*m_b*v_{bi}^2 = 1/2*m_a*v_{af}^2 + 1/2*m_b*v_{bf}^2$$

At this point, you have two equations and two unknowns and both v_{af} and v_{bf} can be computed; however, the math is rather complex, so I will just give you the results:

Equation 4: The final velocities of each ball

```
vaf = (2*mb*vbi + vai*(ma - mb))/(ma + mb)
vbf = (2*ma*vai - vbi*(ma - mb))/(ma + mb)
```

Finally, referring back to Figure 13.11, you can figure out the final velocities after the collision of the blocks:

```
ma = 2 kg
mb = 3 kg

vai = 4 m/s
vbi = -2 m/s
```

Therefore,

```
vaf
    = (2*mb*vbi + vai*(ma - mb))/(ma + mb)
= (2*3*(-2) + 4*(2 - 3))/(2 + 3)
    = -3.2 m/s

vbf = (2*ma*vai - vbi*(ma - mb))/(ma + mb)
    = (2*2*4 - (-2)*(2 - 3))/(2 + 3)
    =  2.4 m/s
```

Interestingly enough, object A had so much momentum it turned object B around and they both went off in the positive X direction as shown in part B of Figure 13.11.

What you just did shows how to use momentum and kinetic energy to help solve kinetic/dynamic problems. However, they get much more complex in two and three dimensions. The study of such collisions is called *collision response*, and it's covered later in the chapter, along with the complete 2D results for perfect and imperfect collisions! For now, though, just think about momentum.

Modeling Gravity Effects

One of the most common effects that a game programmer needs to model in a game is that of gravity. Gravity is the force that attracts every object in the universe to every other. It is an invisible force and unlike magnetic fields can't be blocked.

In reality, gravity isn't really a force. That's simply how we perceive it. Gravity is caused by the curvature of space. When any object is positioned in space it creates a bending of the surrounding space, as shown in Figure 13.12. This bending creates a potential energy difference and hence any object near the gravity well "falls down" toward the object—weird, huh? That's really what gravity is. It's a manifestation of the bending of the space-time fabric.

FIGURE 13.12
Gravity and
space-time.

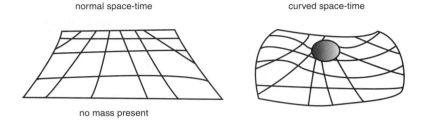

You won't need to worry about space-time curvature and what gravity really is; you just want to model it. There are really two cases that you need to consider when modeling gravity, as shown in Figure 13.13:

- Case 1: Two or more objects with relatively the same mass.
- Case 2: Two objects where the mass of one object is much greater than the other.

FIGURE 13.13
The two general cases
of gravity.

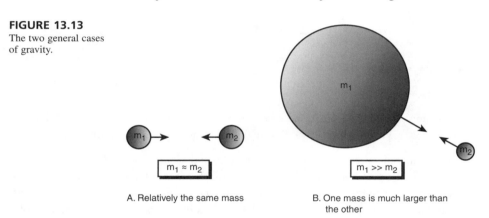

Case 2 is really a sub-case of Case 1. For example, in school you may have learned that if you drop a baseball and a refrigerator off a building they both fall at the same rate. The truth of the matter is they don't, but the difference is so infinitesimal (on the order 10^{-24}) that you could never see the difference. Of course, there are other forces that might make a difference, like wind shear and friction, hence a baseball is going to fall faster than a piece of paper because the paper is going to feel a lot of wind resistance.

Now that you know a little bit about what gravity is, let's take a look at the math behind it. The gravitational force between any two objects with mass m_1 and m_2 is

```
F = G*m_2*m_2 / r^2.
```

where G is the gravitational constant of the universe equal to 6.67×10^{-11} N*m^2 * kg^{-2}. Also, the masses must be in kilograms and the distance r in meters. Say that you want to find out what the gravitational attraction is between two average sized people of 70 kg (155 lbs.) at a distance of 1 meter:

```
F = 6.67x10-11*70kg*70kg/(1 m)2 = 3.26x10-7 N.
```

That's not much is it? However, let's try the same experiment with a person and the planet Earth at 1 meter given that the Earth has a mass of $5.98x10^{24}$ kg:

```
F = 6.67x10-11*70 kg*5.98x1024 kg/(1 m)2 = 2.79x1016 N.
```

Obviously, 10^{16} Newtons would crush you into a pancake, so you must be doing something wrong. The problem is that you're assuming that the Earth is a point mass that is 1.0 meters away. A better approximation would be to use the radius of the Earth (the center of mass) as the distance, which is $6.38x10^6$ m:

MATH	You may assume that any spherical mass of radius r is a point mass as long as the matter the sphere is made of is homogenous and any calculations must place the other object at a distance greater than or equal to r.

```
F = 6.67x10-11 * 70 kg * 5.98x1024 kg / (6.38x106 m)2
  =  685.93 N.
```

Now that seems more reasonable. As a sanity check, on Earth 1 lb. is equal to 4.45 N, so converting the force to lbs. produces

```
685.93 N / (4.45 N / 1 lb.) = 155 lbs.
```

And this was the starting weight! Anyway, now that you know how to compute the force between two objects you can use this simple model in games. Or course, you don't have to use the real gravity constant G = $6.67x10^{-11}$, you can use whatever you like—remember, you are god. The only thing that's important is the form of the equation that states that the gravity between two objects is proportional—to a constant times the product of their masses divided by the distance squared between the objects' centers.

Modeling a Gravity Well

By using the formulation explained in the preceding section, you might, say, model a black hole in a space game. For example, you might have a ship that is flying around on the screen near a black hole, and want the ship to get sucked in if it gets too close. Using the gravitational equation is a snap. You would make up a constant G that worked well in the virtual game world (based on screen resolution, frame rate, etc.) and then simply set an arbitrary mass for the ship and one for the black hole that was much larger. Then you would figure out the force and convert the force to acceleration with F=m*a. You would simply vector or fly the ship directly toward the black hole each frame. As the ship got closer the force would increase until the player couldn't get free!

As an example of a black hole simulation (which is nothing more than two masses, one much larger than another) take a look at DEMO13_3.CPP|EXE (16-bit version, DEMO13_1_16B.CPP|EXE). It's a space simulator that allows you to navigate a ship around the screen, but there's a black hole in the middle that you have to deal with! Use the arrows keys to control the ship. Try to see if you can get into an orbit!

The next use of gravity in games is to simply make things fall from the sky or off buildings at the proper rate. This is really the special case that we talked about before, that is, one object has a mass much greater than the other. However, there's one more constraint and that is that one object is fixed—the ground. Take a look at Figure 13.14; it depicts the situation that I'm describing.

FIGURE 13.14
Gravitational
attraction.

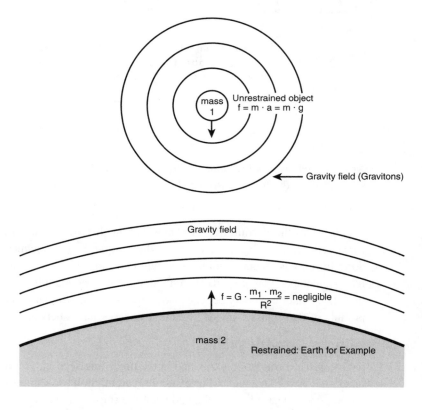

In this case, there are a number of assumptions that we can make that will make the math work out simpler. The first is that the acceleration due to gravity is constant for the mass that is being dropped, which is equal to 9.8 m/s² or 32 ft/s². Of course, this isn't really true, but is true to about 23 decimal places. If we know that the acceleration of any object is simply 9.8 m/s² then we can just plug that into our old motion equation for velocity or position. Thus, the formula for velocity as a function of time with Earth gravity is

$V(t) = v_0 + 9.8 \text{ m/s}^2 * t$.

And position is

$y(t) = y_0 + v_0 * t + 1/2 * 9.8 \text{m/s}^2 * t^2$.

In the case of a ball falling off a building we can let the initial position x_0 be equal to 0 and the initial velocity v_0 also equal 0. This simplifies the falling object model to

$y(t) = 1/2 * 9.8 \text{m/s}^2 * t^2$.

Furthermore, you are free to change the constant 9.8 to anything you like and t represents the frame number (virtual time) in a game. Taking all that into consideration, here's how you would make a ball fall from the top of the screen:

```
int y_pos       = 0, // top of screen
    y_velocity = 0, // initial y velocity
    gravity     = 1; // do want to fall too fast

// do  gravity loop until object hits
// bottom of screen at SCREEN_BOTTOM
while(y_pos < SCREEN_BOTTOM)
    {
    // update position
    y_pos+=y_velocity;

    // update velocity
    y_velocity+=gravity;
    } // end while
```

TIP   I used the velocity to modify the position rather than modifying the position directly with the position formula. This is simpler.

You may be asking how to make the object fall with a curved trajectory. This is simple—just move the x position at a constant rate each cycle and the object will seem like it was thrown off rather then just dropped. The code to do this follows:

```
int y_pos       = 0, // top of screen
    y_velocity = 0, // initial y velocity
    x_velocity = 2, // constant x velocity
    gravity     = 1; // do want to fall too fast
// do  gravity loop until object hits
// bottom of screen at SCREEN_BOTTOM
while(y_pos < SCREEN_BOTTOM)
    {
    // update position
    x_pos+=x_velocity;
    y_pos+=y_velocity;
```

```
// update velocity
y_velocity+=gravity;
} // end while
```

Modeling Projectile Trajectories

Falling objects are fairly exciting, but let's see if we can do something a little more appropriate for video game programming! How about computing trajectory paths? Take a look at Figure 13.15, which shows the general setup for the problem. We have a ground plane, call it y=0, and a tank located at x=0, y=0, with a barrel pointed at an angle of inclination θ (theta) with the x-axis. The question is, if we fire a projectile with mass m at a velocity v_I, what will happen?

FIGURE 13.15
The trajectory problem.

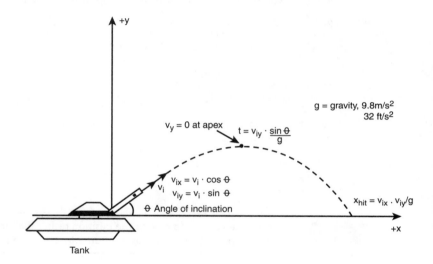

We can solve the problem by breaking it up into its x,y components. First, let's break the velocity into an (x,y) vector:

$$v_{ix} = v*\cos \theta$$
$$v_{iy} = v*\sin \theta$$

Trust me.

Okay, now forget about the x part for a minute, and think about the problem. The projectile is going to go up and down and hit the ground. How long will this take? Take a look at our previous gravity equations:

$$V(t) = v_0 + 9.8 \text{ m/s}^2 * t.$$

The position for the y-axis is

$$y(t) = y_0 + v_0*t + 1/2 * 9.8\text{m/s}^2 * t^2.$$

The first one tells us the velocity relative to time. That's what we need. We know that when the projectile reaches its maximum height, the velocity will be equal to 0. Furthermore, the amount of time that the projectile takes to reach this height will be the same amount of time it takes to fall to the ground again. Take a look at Figure 13.15. Plugging in our values for initial y velocity of our projectile and solving for time t, we have

```
Vy(t) = Viy - 9.8 m/s²*t
```

Note that I flipped the sign of the acceleration due to gravity because down is negative and matters in this case, and in general, when the velocity equals 0:

```
0 = V*sin θ - a*t (a is just the acceleration)
```

Solving for time t, we get

```
t = Viy * (sin θ)/a
```

Now the total time of flight is just time up + time down which equals t+t=2*t since the projectile must go up, then down. Therefore, we can revisit the x component now. We know that the total flight time is 2*t and we can compute t from $(V_{iy} * (\sin \theta)/a)$. Therefore, the distance that the projectile travels in the x-axis is just

```
X(t) = vix*t
```

Plugging in our values, this results in

```
xhit = (V*cos θ) * (V*(sin θ)/a)
```

or

```
xhit = Vix * Viy/a
```

Neat, huh?

MATH	Note that I replaced the 9.8 value of acceleration with a. I did this to re-enforce that the acceleration is just a number, and you can make it whatever you wish.

That's the physics behind everything, but how do you model it in a program? Well, all you do is apply constant x-axis velocity to the projectile and gravity in the y-axis and test for when the projectile hits the ground or something else. Of course, in real life the X and Y velocities would diminish due to air resistance, but throwing that out the algorithm I just described works great. Here's the code to do it:

```
// Inputs
float x_pos      = 0, // starting point of projectile
      y_pos      = SCREEN_BOTTOM, // bottom of screen
      y_velocity = 0, // initial y velocity
      x_velocity = 0, // constant x velocity
      gravity    = 1, // do want to fall too fast
```

```
        velocity    = INITIAL_VEL, // whatever
        angle       = INITIAL_ANGLE; // whatever, must be in radians

// compute velocities in x,y
x_velocity = velocity*cos(angle);
y_velocity = velocity*sin(angle);


// do projectile loop until object hits
// bottom of screen at SCREEN_BOTTOM
while(y_pos < SCREEN_BOTTOM)
    {
    // update position
    x_pos+=x_velocity;
    y_pos+=y_velocity;

    // update velocity
    y_velocity+=gravity;
    } // end while
```

That's all there is to it! If you want to add a wind force, just model it as a small acceleration in the direction opposing the X-motion, and assume that the wind force creates a constant acceleration against the projectile. As a result, you simply need to add this line of code in the projectile loop:

```
x_velocity-=wind_factor;
```

Where `wind_factor` would be something like 0.01—something fairly small.

As a demo of all this trajectory stuff, check out DEMO13_4.CPP|EXE (16-bit version, DEMO13_1_16B.CPP|EXE) on the CD. A screen shot is shown in Figure 13.16. The demo allows you to aim a virtual cannon and fire a projectile.

Here are the controls:

Key	Action
Up, down	Controls the angle of the tank's cannon.
Right, left	Controls the velocity of the projectile.
G, B	Controls the gravity.
W, E	Controls the wind speed.
Ctrl	Fires the cannon!

The Evil Head of Friction

The next topic of discussion is friction. Friction is any force that retards or consumes energy from another system. For example, automobiles use internal combustion to operate; however, a whopping 30–40 percent of the energy that is produced is eaten up by thermal conversion or mechanical friction. On the other hand, a bicycle is about 80–90 percent efficient and is probably the most efficient mode of transportation in existence.

FIGURE 13.16
The projectile demo.

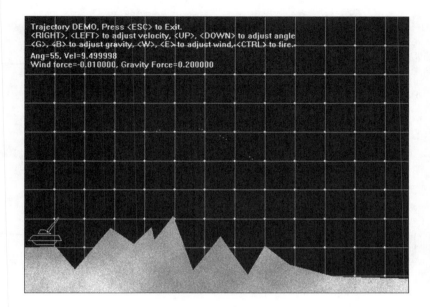

Trajectory DEMO, Press <ESC> to Exit.
<RIGHT>, <LEFT> to adjust velocity, <UP>, <DOWN> to adjust angle
<G>, <B> to adjust gravity, <W>, <E> to adjust wind, <CTRL> to fire.
Ang=55, Vel=9.499998
Wind force=-0.010000, Gravity Force=0.200000

Basic Friction Concepts

Friction is basically resistance in the opposite direction of motion and hence can be modeled with a force usually referred to as the frictional force. Take a look at Figure 13.17; it depicts the standard frictional model of a mass m on a flat plane.

If you try to push the mass in a direction parallel to the plane you will encounter a resistance or frictional force that pushes back against you. This force is defined mathematically as

$F_{fstatic} = m*g*\mu_s$.

where m is the mass of the object, g is the gravitational constant (9.8 m/s^2) and $_s$ is the static frictional coefficient of the system that depends on the conditions and materials of the mass and the plane. If the force F you apply to the object is greater than F_f, then the object will begin to move. Once the object is in motion its frictional coefficient usually decreases to another value, which is referred to as the coefficient of kinetic friction, μ_k.

$F_{fkinetic} = m*g*\mu_k$.

FIGURE 13.17
Basic friction model.

A. Static case, no motion

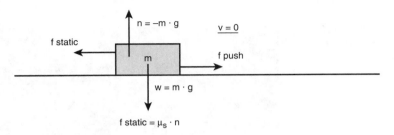

$$n = -m \cdot g \qquad \underline{v = 0}$$

f static

m

f push

$$w = m \cdot g$$

$$f \text{ static} = \mu_s \cdot n$$

B. Kinetic case, block is moving

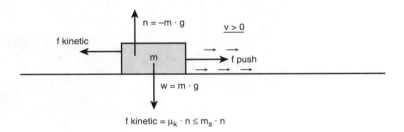

$$n = -m \cdot g \qquad \underline{v > 0}$$

f kinetic

m

f push

$$w = m \cdot g$$

$$f \text{ kinetic} = \mu_k \cdot n \le m_s \cdot n$$

When you release the force, the object slowly decelerates and comes to rest because friction is always present.

To model friction on a flat surface all you need do is apply a constant negative velocity to all your objects that is proportional to the friction that you want. Mathematically, this is

```
Velocity New = Velocity Old - friction.
```

The result is objects that slow down at a constant rate once you stop moving them. Of course, you have to watch out for letting the sign of the velocity go negative or in the other direction, but that's just a detail. Here's an example of an object that is moved to the right with an initial velocity of 16 pixels per frame and then slowed down at a rate of 1 pixel per frame due to virtual friction:

```
int x_pos     = 0,  // starting position
    x_velocity = 16, // starting velocity
    friction   = -1; // frictional value

// move object until velocity <= 0
while(x_velocity > 0)
    {
    // move object
    x_pos+=x_velocity;
```

```
// apply friction
x_velocity+=friction;
} // end while
```

The first thing you should notice is how similar the model for friction is to gravity. They are almost identical. The truth is that both gravitational forces and frictional forces act in the same way. In fact, all forces in the universe can be modeled in the exact same way. Also, you can apply as many frictional forces to an object as you want. Just sum them up.

As an example of friction I have written a little air hockey demo named DEMO13_5.CPP|EXE (16-bit version, DEMO13_5_16B.CPP|EXE), shown in Figure 13.18. The program lets you fire a hockey puck on a virtual air hockey table in a random direction every time you press the spacebar. The puck then bounces around off the borders of the table until it comes to rest due to friction. If you want to change the frictional coefficient of the table, use the arrow keys. See if you can add a paddle and a computer controlled opponent to the simulation!

FIGURE 13.18
The hockey demo.

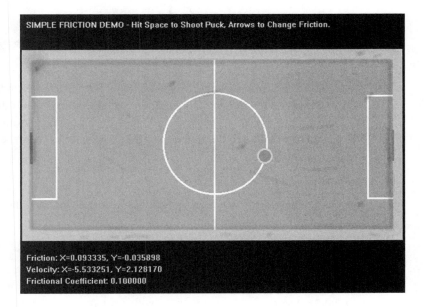

SIMPLE FRICTION DEMO - Hit Space to Shoot Puck, Arrows to Change Friction.

Friction: X=0.093335, Y=-0.035898
Velocity: X=-5.533251, Y=2.128170
Frictional Coefficient: 0.100000

Friction on an Inclined Plane (Advanced)

That wasn't too bad huh? The bottom line is that friction can be modeled as a simple resistive force or a negative velocity on an object each cycle. However, I want to show you the math and derivation of friction on an inclined plane since this will give you the tools you need to analyze much more complex problems. Be warned, though: I'm going to use a lot of vectors, so if you're still rusty or having trouble then take a look back when I talked about them in Chapter 8, "Vector Rasterization and 2D Transformations," or pick up a good linear algebra book.

Figure 13.19 shows the problem we're trying to solve. Basically, there is a mass m on an inclined plane. The plane has frictional coefficients μ_s and μ_k for the static and kinetic (moving) cases respectively. The first thing we need to do is write the formulas that describe the mass in its equilibrium position, that is, not moving. In this case, the sum of the forces in the x-axis are 0 and the sum of the forces in the y-axis are 0.

FIGURE 13.19
The inclined plane problem.

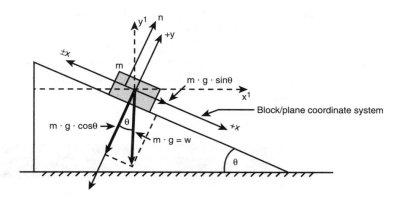

To begin the derivation we must first touch on a new concept called the *normal force*. This is nothing more than the force that the inclined plane pushes the object back with, or in other words, if you weigh 200 lbs., then there is a normal force of –200 lbs. pushing back (due to the surface tension of ground you're standing on) at you. We usually refer to the normal force as η, and it is equal in magnitude to

```
η = m*g.
```

Interesting huh? But if you lay a coordinate system down, then the gravity force must be opposite the normal force, or

```
η - m*g = 0.
```

This is why everything doesn't get sucked into the ground. Okay, now that we know that, let's derive the motion equations of this block mass. First, we lay down an x,y coordinate system on the incline plane with +X parallel to the plane and in the downward sliding direction; this helps the math. Then we write the equilibrium equations for the x and y axes. For the x-axis we know that the component of gravity pushing the block is

```
force due to gravity = m*g*sin θ.
```

And the force due to friction holding the block from sliding is

```
force due to friction = -η*μs.
```

The negative sign is because the force acts in the opposite direction. When the object isn't sliding we know that the sum of these forces are equal to 0. Mathematically, we have

```
force due to gravity + force due to friction = 0
```

Or, the sum of forces in the x-axis is

$$\Sigma\ F_x\ =\ m*g*\sin\ \theta\ -\ \eta*\mu_s\ =\ 0.$$

MATH | Note that I use sine and cosine to resolve the x,y components of the force. I'm basically just breaking the force vectors into components, nothing more.

We have to do the same for the y-axis, but this is fairly easy because the only forces are the weight of gravity and the normal force:

$$\Sigma\ F_y\ =\ \eta\ -\ m*g*\cos\ \theta$$

All right, so all together we have

$$\Sigma\ F_x\ =\ m*g*\sin\ \theta\ -\ \eta*\mu_s\ =\ 0.$$

$$\Sigma\ F_y\ =\ \eta\ -\ m*g*\cos\ \theta\ =\ 0.$$

But, what is η? From $\Sigma\ F_y$, we once again see that:

$$\eta\ -\ m*g*\cos\ \theta\ =\ 0.$$

Hence,

$$\eta = m*g*\cos\ \theta,$$

therefore we can write:

$$\Sigma\ F_x\ =\ m*g*\sin\ \theta\ -\ (m*g*\cos\ \theta)*\mu_s\ =\ 0.$$

This is what we need. From it we can derive the following results:

$$m*g*\sin\ \theta\ =\ (m*g*\cos\ \theta)*\mu_s$$

$$\mu_s\ =\ (m*g*\sin\ \theta)/(m*g*\cos\ \theta)\ =\ \tan\ \theta$$

Or canceling out the m*g and replacing sin/cos by tan,

$$\theta_{critical}\ =\ \tan^{-1}\ \mu_s$$

Now listen carefully. This tells us that there is an angle called the *critical angle* ($\theta_{critical}$) at which the mass starts to slide. It is equal to the inverse tangent of the static coefficient of friction. If we didn't know the frictional coefficient of a mass and some incline plane, we could find it this way by tilting the plane until the mass starts to move. But this doesn't help us with the x-axis, or does it? The equation tells us that the mass won't slide until the angle $\theta_{critical}$ is reached. When it is reached the mass will slide governed by:

Σ F$_x$ = m*g*sin θ - (m*g*cos θ)*μ_s

Well, almost... There is one detail. When the mass starts to slide, the difference is m*g*sin θ – (m*g*cos θ)*$_s$ > 0, but in addition we need to change the frictional coefficient to $_k$ (the coefficient of kinetic friction) to be totally correct!

F$_x$ = m*g*sin θ - (m*g*cos θ)*μ_k

TRICK   You can just average μ_k and μ_s and use that value in all the calculations. Because you're making video games and not real simulations, it doesn't matter if you oversimplify the two frictional cases into one, but if you want to be correct, you should use both frictional constants at the appropriate times.

With all that in mind let's compute the final force along the x-axis. We know that F=m*a, therefore:

F$_x$ = m*a = m*g*sin θ - (m*g*cos θ)*μ_k

And dividing by m we get

```
a = g*sin θ - (g*cos θ)*μk
a = g*(sin θ - μk*cos θ)
```

You can use this exact model to move the block mass, that is, each cycle you can increase the velocity of the block in the positive X-direction by g*(sin θ – μ_k*cos θ). There's only one problem: This solution is in our rotated coordinate system! There's a trick to getting around this: You know the angle of the plane, and hence you can figure out a vector along the downward angle of the plane:

```
xplane = cos θ
yplane = -sin θ

Slide_Vector = (cos θ, -sin θ)
```

The minus sign is on the Y-component because we know it's in the –Y direction. With this vector we can then move the object in the correct direction each cycle—this is a hack, but it works. Here's the code to perform the translation and velocity tracking:

```
// Inputs
float x_pos      = SX, // starting point of mass on plane
      y_pos      = SY,
      y_velocity = 0,   // initial y velocity
      x_velocity = 0,   // initial x velocity
      x_plane    = 0,   // sliding vector
      y_plane    = 0,
```

```
    gravity     = 1,  // do want to fall too fast
    velocity    = INITIAL_VEL, // whatever

    // must be in radians and it must be greater
    // than the critical angle
    angle       = PLANE_ANGLE, // compute velocities in x,y

    frictionk   = 0.1; // frictional value

// compute trajectory vector
x_plane = cos(angle);
y_plane = sin(angle); // no negative since +y is down

// do slide loop until object hits
// bottom of screen at SCREEN_BOTTOM
while(y_pos < SCREEN_BOTTOM)
    {
    // update position
    x_pos+=x_velocity;
y_pos+=y_velocity;

    // update velocity
    x_vel+=x_plane*gravity*(sin(angle) - frictionk *cos(angle));
    y_vel+=y_plane*gravity*(sin(angle) - frictionk *cos(angle));

    } // end while
```

The point of physics modeling sometimes is just to understand what the underlying physics are so you can model them in a somewhat convincing manner. In the case of the incline plane, basically all that math just boiled down to the concept that acceleration is a function of the angle (we knew this from common sense). However, in Volume II of the book I'm going to cover much more realistic physics using numerical integration, and in those cases, you need to know the real models and real forces on everything.

Basic Ad Hoc Collision Response

As I explained earlier in the chapter, two kinds of collisions exist: *elastic* and *non-elastic*. Elastic collisions are collisions where both kinetic energy and momentum are conserved in the colliding objects while non-elastic collisions don't conserve these values and energy is converted to heat and/or used for mechanical deformations.

Most video games don't even try to mess with non-elastic collisions and stick to simplified elastic collisions since they themselves are hard enough to compute. Before I show you the real way to do it let's use the other side of our brains. Game programmers that don't know anything about elastic or inelastic collisions have been faking collisions for years and we can do the same.

Simple x,y Bounce Physics

Take a look at Figure 13.20. It depicts a fairly common collision problem in games, that is, bouncing an object off the boundaries of the screen. Given the object has initial velocity (xv,yv), the object can hit any of the four sides of the screen. If one object collides with another object that has mass much greater than the colliding object, then the collision is much simplified since we only need to figure out what happened to the single object that's doing the colliding rather than two objects. A pool table is a good example of this. The balls have very small mass in comparison to the pool table.

FIGURE 13.20
The bouncing ball.

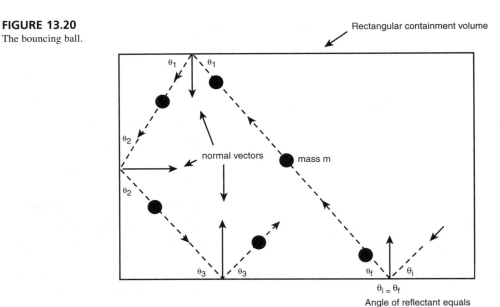

When a ball hits one of the sides then it always reflects off the side at an angle equal and opposite to its initial trajectory, as shown in Figure 13.20. Thus all we need to do to bounce an object off a pool table-like environment that consists of hard edges that have large mass is to compute the normal vector direction, the direction that the object struck at, and then reflect the object at the same angle as shown in Figure 13.21.

Although this isn't as complex as the general elastic collision, it still takes a bit of trigonometry, so there's got to be a simpler way! And of course there is. The trick is to understand the physics model that you're trying to model. Then the idea is to see if you can solve the problem in some other way since you have exact knowledge of all the conditions. Here's the trick: Instead of thinking in terms of angles and all that, think in terms of results. The bottom line is if the object hits a wall to the east or west then you want to reverse its X velocity while leaving its Y velocity alone. And similarly on the north and south walls, you want to reverse the Y velocity and leave the X velocity alone. Here's the code:

```
// given the object is at x,y with a velocity if xv,yv
// test for east and west wall collisions
if (x >= EAST_EDGE || x <= WEST_EDGE)
   xv=-xv; // reverse x velocity

// now test for north and south wall collisions
if (y >= SOUTH_EDGE || y <= NORTH_EDGE)
   yv=-yv; // reverse y velocity
```

FIGURE 13.21
Bouncing a ball off an irregular object with flat facets.

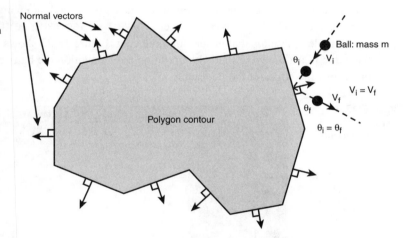

And amazingly the object will bounce off the walls. Of course, this simplification only works well for horizontal and vertical barriers. You'll have to use the more general angle calculation for walls or barriers that aren't co-linear with the x and y axes.

> **TRICK**
>
> If you want to use the preceding technique as a quick cheat to make objects bounce off of each other, simply assume that each object is a bounding rectangle from the other object's point of view. Enact the collision and then re-compute the velocities. Figure 13.22 illustrates this.

FIGURE 13.22
A simple cheat for
object-to-object
collisions.

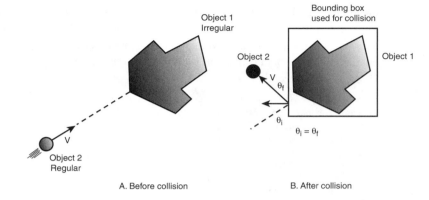

A. Before collision   B. After collision

As an example of using these techniques, I have created a demo named
`DEMO13_6.CPP|EXE` (16-bit version, `DEMO13_6_16B.CPP|EXE`) that models
a pool table with balls that never stop bouncing. Figure 13.23 shows a screen shot of
the game in action. Note that when running the simulation the balls don't hit each
other, just the edges of the pool table.

FIGURE 13.23
Simple collision
pool table model.

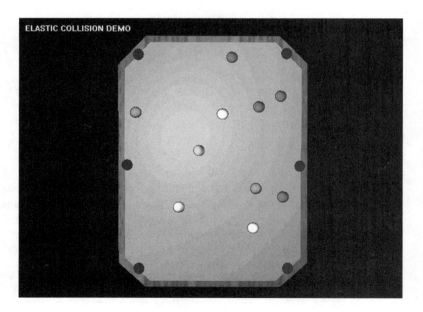

Computing the Collision Response with Planes of Any Orientation

Using rectangles as bounding collision volumes works okay if you write pong games,
but this is the 21st century, baby, and we need just a little bit more! What we need to
do is derive the reflection equations for a vector reflecting off a flat plane. This is

shown in part A of Figure 13.24 in 2D (the 3D case is the same). To solve the problem, first we have to make an assumption about what will happen when an object that's very small and perfectly elastic hits a wall. I think we can already come to the conclusion that it will bounce off the wall at the same angle it arrived at. Therefore, the *angle of reflection* (the angle of departure by the object after the collision) equals the *angle of incidence* (the incoming angle before the collision) relative to the *normal,* or perpendicular to the wall. Now, let's see the math…

FIGURE 13.24
The vector reflection problem illustrated.

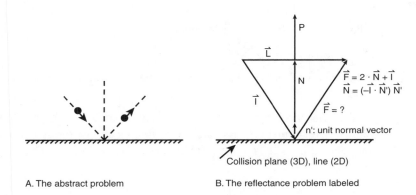

A. The abstract problem   B. The reflectance problem labeled

Solving the problem requires nothing more than a vector geometry construction, but it's not totally trivial.

TIP	If you ever try to get a game programming job, I can almost guarantee they will ask you this question on the interview because it's deceptively complex. Luckily, you can just read this section and blurt out the answer, and they'll think you're a genius! Let's get started.

Part B of Figure 13.24 depicts the problem. Note that there isn't an x,y axis. It's unnecessary since we're using vectors and I want the problem to be totally general.

The problem can be stated like this:

Given the initial vector direction **I** and the normal to the plane **N'**, find **F**.

Before we get crazy, let's talk about the normal vector. The normal vector **N'** is just the normalized version of **P**, but what is **P**? **N** is just the perpendicular to the plane or line that the ball is hitting that we want the ball to bounce off of. We can determine **P** in a number of ways; we might have pre-computed it and stored it in a data structure or we can figure it out on-the-fly.

There are a number of ways to do this depending on the representation of the "wall." If the wall is a plane in 3D then we can extract **P** based on the point-normal form of a plane:

$$n_x(x - x_0) + n_y(y - y_0) + n_z(z - z_0) = 0$$

The normal vector is just $\mathbf{P}=<n_x, n_y, n_z>$. To make sure the normal is normalized or a unit vector then you divide each element by the total length—remember?

$$\mathbf{N'} = <n_x, n_y, n_z >/|\mathbf{P}|$$

Where $|\mathbf{P}|$ is the length and is computed like this:

$$|\mathbf{P}| = sqrt(n_x^2 + n_y^2 + n_z^2)$$

In general, the length of a vector is the square root of the sum of squares of its components.

On the other hand if your collision line is a line in 2D or a segment then you can compute the normal or perpendicular by finding any vector that is perpendicular to the line. Thus if the line is in the form of two endpoints in 2D as shown in Figure 13.25 like this:

Given: $p_1(x_1,y_1)$, $p_2(x_2,y_2)$

$$\mathbf{V_{12}} = <x_2 - x_1, y_2 - y_1> = <v_x, v_y>$$

The perpendicular can be found with this trick:

$$\mathbf{P_{12}} = <n_x, n_y> = <-v_y, v_x>$$

FIGURE 13.25

Computing the per-
pendicular to a line.

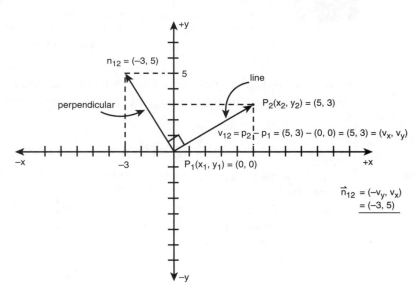

The vector from p1 to p2 (remember endpoint minus initial) is

This trick is based on the definition of dot product, which states that a vector dotted with its normal equals 0, thus:

```
V12 . N12 = 0
<vx, vy> . <nx, ny> = 0
```

or

```
vx*nx + vy*ny = 0
```

And what makes this true is $n_x = -v_y$, $n_y = v_x$:

```
vx*(-vy) + vy*(vx) = -vx*vy+vx*vy = 0
```

Nice, huh?

All right, so you know how to get the normal vector and of course you need to normalize it and make sure it has length 1.0, so **N'**, = **P**/|**P**| which is equal to:

```
N' = <-vy, vx>/sqrt((-vy)² + vx²)
```

Now back to the derivation… At this point we have the normal vector **N'**, which shouldn't be confused with N in the figure since **N** is along **N'**, but not related to the length of **P** in any way. **N** *is the projection of* **I** *along* **N'**. Okay, that sounds like voodoo—and it is. A projection is like a shadow. If I were to shine light from the left side of the figure in the left to right direction then **N** would be the shadow or projection that **I** casts on the **N'** axis. This projection is the **N** we need. Once we have **N** then we can find **F** with a little vector geometry. First, here's **N**:

```
N = (-I . N')*N'
```

This states that **N** (which is the vector projection of I on **N'**) is equal to the dot product of **–I** and **N'** and then multiplied by the vector **N'**. Let's take this apart in two chunks. First the term (**-I** . **N'**) is just a scalar length like 5; it's not a vector. This is a handy thing about dot products: If you want to find the shadow of one vector (projection) then you can dot it with the unit version of the vector in question, thus you can resolve the components of a vector into any direction you want. Basically, you can ask, "What's **R** in the **V'** direction?" Where **V'** is normalized. Therefore, the first part (**-I** . **N'**) gives you a number (the −1 is just to flip the direction of **I**). But, you need a vector **N**, so all you do is multiply the number by the unit vector **N'** (vector multiplication) and, whammo, you have **N**.

Once you have **N** it's all bedrock, baby, just do some vector geometry and you can find **F**:

```
L = N + I
```

and

F = N + L

substituting **L** into **F**,

F = N + (N + I)

Therefore,

F = 2*N + I

Burn that last line into your skull. It could be the difference between Burger King and DreamWorks Interactive—right, Rich?

An Example of Vector Reflection

When I used to study mathematics, I used to read things like "R is a closed ring with an isomorphism on Q's kernel." I wouldn't be as nutty as I am today if they just gave me an example once in a while! Alas, I don't want you to end up running naked in the streets with a cape—one naked super hero game programmer is enough, so let's try a real example.

Figure 13.26 shows the setup of the problem. I have made the bounce plane co-linear with the x-axis to make things easier.

FIGURE 13.26

A numerical example of vector reflection.

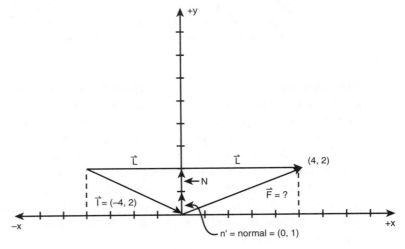

$$\vec{F} = 2 \cdot \vec{N} + \vec{I}$$
$$= 2 * (-\vec{I} \cdot n') * n' + I$$
$$= -2 * (<4, -2> - <0, 1>) * (0, 1) + (4, -2)$$
$$= 4 \cdot (0, 1) + (4, -2)$$
$$= (4, 2)$$

The initial velocity vector of our object is $\mathbf{I}$=<4,-2>, $\mathbf{N'}$=<0,1>, and we want to find $\mathbf{F}$. Let's plug everything into our equation:

```
F =   2*N + I
  =   2*(-I . N')*N' + I
  =  -2*(<4,-2> . <0,1>)*<0,1> + <4,-2>
  =  -2*(4*0 + -2*1)*<0,1> + <4,-2>
  =  4*<0,1> + <4,-2>
  =  <0,4> + <4,-2>
  =  <4,2>
```

Lo and behold, if you look at Figure 13.26, that's the correct answer! Now, there's only one detail that we've left out of all this: determining when the ball or object actually hits the plane or line.

Intersection of Line Segments

You could probably figure this one out, but I'll give you a hand. The problem is basically a line intersection computation. But the surprise is that we are intersecting line segments, not lines; there's a difference. A line goes to infinity in both directions, while a line segment is finite, as shown in Figure 13.27.

FIGURE 13.27
Lines and line segments are very different.

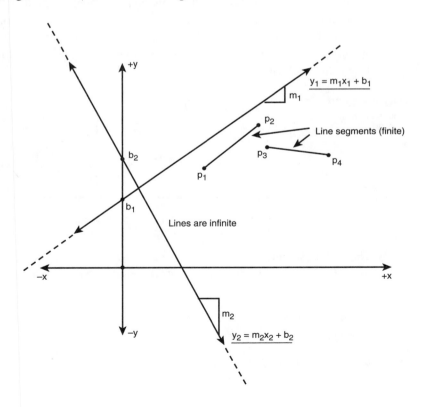

The problem boils down to this: As an object moves with some velocity vector V_i, we want to detect whether the vector pierces through the collision plane or line. Why? Well, if an object is moving at velocity V_i then one frame or time click later it will be located at its current position $(x_0,y_0)+V_i$, or in terms of components:

$$x_1 = x_0 + v_{ix}$$
$$y_1 = y_0 + v_{iy}$$

Therefore, you can think of the velocity vector as a line segment that leads the way to wherever the object we are drawing is going. In other words, we want to determine whether there is an intersection point (x,y) of the line segments. Here's the setup:

> Object Vector Segment: $S_1 = \,<p_1(x_1,y_1) - p_0(x_0,y_0)>$
>
> Boundary Line Segment: $S_2 = \,<p_3(x_3,y_3) - p_2(x_2,y_2)>$

You need the exact intersection point (x,y), so that when you compute the reflection vector **F** you start its initial position at (x,y). This is shown in Figure 13.28. The problem seems simple enough, but it's not as easy as you think. Intersecting two lines is as easy as solving a system of 2 equations, but determining if two line segments intersect is a little harder. That's because that although the segments are lines, they are finite, so even if the lines that the segments run along intersect, the segments may not. This is shown in Figure 13.29. Therefore, you need to not only determine where the lines that the segments define intersect, you need to see if this point is within both segments! This is the hard part.

FIGURE 13.28

Intersection and reflection.

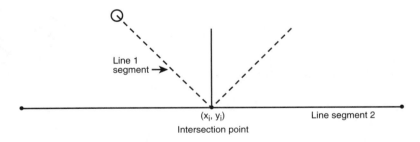

Line 1 segment →

(x_i, y_i)
Intersection point

Line segment 2

The trick to solving the problem is using a *parametric* representation of each line segment. I'll call **U** the position vector of any point on S_1 and **V** the position vector of any point on S_2:

> Equation 1: $U = p_0 + t*S_1$
>
> Equation 2: $V = p_2 + s*S_2$

with the constraint that $(0 <= t <= 1)$, $(0 <= s <= 1)$.

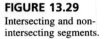

FIGURE 13.29
Intersecting and non-
intersecting segments.

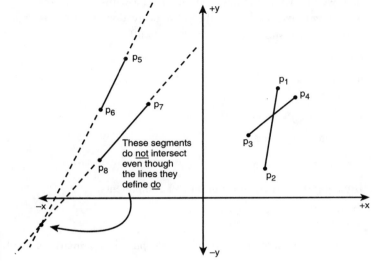

Figure 13.30 shows what these two equations represent.

FIGURE 13.30
The parametric repre-
sentation of U and V.

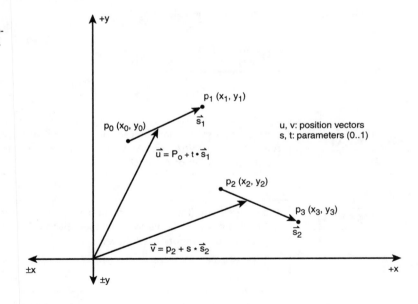

Referring to the figure, we see that as t varies from 0 to 1 the line segment from p_0 to p_1 is traced out and similarly as s varies from 0 to 1, the line segment from p_2 to p_3 is traced out. Now we have all we need to solve the problem. We solve equations 1 and 2 for s,t and then plug the values back in to either equation and find the (x,y) of the intersection. Moreover, when we find (s,t) if either of them is not in the range (0 to 1)

then we know that the intersection was not within the segments. Pretty neat, huh? I'm not going to every detail of the entire derivation since this is in about 100,000 math books, but I'll show you the important stuff:

Given:

$$U = p_0 + t*S_1$$
$$V = p_2 + s*S_2$$

solve for (s,t) when $U = V$,

$$p_0 + t*S_1 = p_2 + s*S_2$$

$$s*S_2 - t*S_1 = p_0 - p_2$$

Breaking the last equation into (x,y) components,

$$s*S_{2x} - t*S_{1x} = p_{0x} - p_{2x}$$
$$s*S_{2y} - t*S_{1y} = p_{0y} - p_{2y}$$

We have two equations, two unknowns, push into a matrix and solve for (s,t):

$$\begin{vmatrix} S_{2x} & -S_{1x} \\ S_{2y} & -S_{1y} \end{vmatrix} \begin{vmatrix} s \\ t \end{vmatrix} = \begin{vmatrix} (p_{0x} - p_{2x}) \\ (p_{0y} - p_{2y}) \end{vmatrix}$$

$$A \qquad\qquad X \quad = \qquad B$$

Using Cramer's Rule we have the following:

$$s = \frac{Det \begin{vmatrix} (p_{0x}-p_{2x}) & -S_{1x} \\ (p_{0y}-p_{2y}) & -S_{1y} \end{vmatrix}}{Det \begin{vmatrix} S_{2x} & -S_{1x} \\ S_{2y} & -S_{1y} \end{vmatrix}} \qquad t = \frac{Det \begin{vmatrix} S_{2x} & (p_{0x}-p_{2x}) \\ S_{2y} & (p_{0y}-p_{2y}) \end{vmatrix}}{Det \begin{vmatrix} S_{2x} & -S_{1x} \\ S_{2y} & -S_{1y} \end{vmatrix}}$$

MATH

Cramer's rule states that you can solve a system of equations **AX=B**, by computing xi = Det(A_i)/Det(**A**). Where A_i is the matrix formed by replacing the ith column of **A** with **B**.

MATH

The determinate (Det) of a matrix in general is rather complex, but for a 2×2 or 3×3 it is very simple to remember. Given a 2×2 matrix the determinate can be computed as follows:

```
A = |a b|   Det(A) = (a*d - c*b)
    |c d|
```

Multiplying all this stuff out, you get

$$s = (-S_{1y}*(p_{0x}-p_{2x}) + S_{1x}*(p_{0y}-p_{2y}))/(-S_{2x}*S_{1y} + S_{1x}*S_{2y})$$
$$t = (S_{2x}*(p_{0y}-p_{2y}) - S_{2y}*(p_{0x}-p_{2x}))/(-S_{2x}*S_{1y} + S_{1x}*S_{2y})$$

Then once you have found (s,t), you can plug either of them into

$$U = p_0 + t*S_1$$
$$V = p_2 + s*S_2$$

and solve for $U(x,y)$ or $V(x,y)$. However, for s,t to be valid both of them must be in the range of (0..1). If either of them is out of range then there is NO intersection. Referring to the worked example in Figure 13.31, let's see if the math works:

> **TRICK**   There's no need to test for intersections of two lines segments if their bounding boxes don't overlap.

FIGURE 13.31
A worked line segment intersection example.

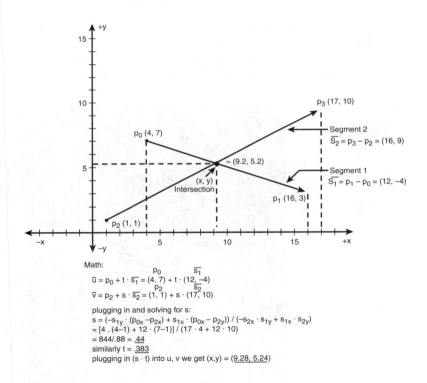

Math:
$$\bar{u} = p_0 + t \cdot \overline{s_1} = (4, 7) + t \cdot (12, -4)$$
$$\bar{v} = p_2 + s \cdot \overline{s_2} = (1, 1) + s \cdot (17, 10)$$

plugging in and solving for s:
$$s = (-s_{1y} \cdot (p_{0x} - p_{2x}) + s_{1x} \cdot (p_{0x} - p_{2y})) / (-s_{2x} \cdot s_{1y} + s_{1x} \cdot s_{2y})$$
$$= [4 \cdot (4-1) + 12 \cdot (7-1)] / (17 \cdot 4 + 12 \cdot 10)$$
$$= 844/.88 = \underline{.44}$$
similarly $t = \underline{.383}$
plugging in (s · t) into u, v we get (x,y) = (9.28, 5.24)

$p_0=(4,7)$, $p_1=(16,3)$, $S_1=p_1-p_0=<12,-4>$
$p_2=(1,1)$, $p_3=(17,10)$, $S_2=p_3-p_2=<16,9>$

And we know that

$$s = (-S_{1y}*(p_{0x}-p_{2x}) + S_{1x}*(p_{0y}-p_{2y}))/(-S_{2x}*S_{1y} + S_{1x}*S_{2y})$$
$$t = (S_{2x}*(p_{0y}-p_{2y}) - S_{2y}*(p_{0x}-p_{2x}))/(-S_{2x}*S_{1y} + S_{1x}*S_{2y})$$

Plugging in all the values we get

```
s = (4*(4-1) + 12*(7-1))/(17*4 + 12*10)   = 0.44
t = (17*(7-1) - 10*(4-1))/ (17*4 + 12*10) = 0.383
```

Since both 0<=(s,t)<=1, we know that we have a valid intersection and thus either s or t can be used to find the intersection point (x,y). Let's use t, shall we?

```
U(x,y) = p₀ + t*S₁
       = <7,7> + t*<12,-4>
```

Plugging in t=.44, we get

```
       = <7,7> + 0.44*<12,-4> = (9.28, 5.24)
```

which is indeed the intersection. Isn't math fun?

As for using all this technology, I have created a demo of a ball bouncing off the interior of an irregularly shaped polygonal 2D object. Take a look at DEMO13_7.CPP|EXE (16-bit version, DEMO13_7_16B.CPP|EXE). A screen shot is shown in Figure 13.32. Try editing the code and changing the shape of the polygon.

FIGURE 13.32

A bouncing ball trapped in an irregularly shaped polygon demo.

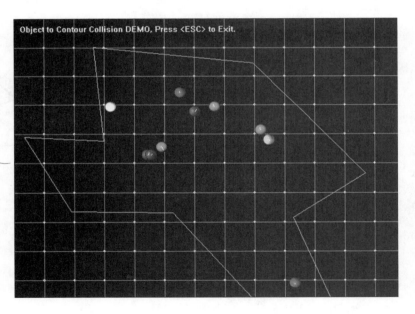

Finally, you may want to try another heuristic when finding a collision trajectory vector. In the previous example we used the velocity vector as one test segment. However, it may make more sense to create a vector that is the length of the radius of the ball and then drop it from the center perpendicular to the edge being tested. This way you catch scathing collisions, but it's a bit more complex and I'll just leave it as an exercise.

Real 2D Object-to-Object Collision Response (Advanced)

I put this section off a bit and moved it down here because I wanted you to really get a handle on momentum and collision and the mathematics needed to work with both. But like Dr. Brown said in *Back to the Future*, "Roads? Where we're going, we don't need roads..." Alas, object-to-object collisions with a fairly realistic collision response aren't the easiest thing in the world to figure out. The final results aren't bad, but coming up with them is no picnic. Anyway, let's get started.

Figure 13.33 depicts the general problem that we want to solve. There are two objects modeled by 2D circles or 3D spheres, and each has a mass and an initial trajectory. When they make contact we want to compute the final trajectory or velocity after the collision. We've touched on this already in the section "The Physics of Linear Momentum: Conservation and Transfer" when we came up with the following equations:

FIGURE 13.33
The central impact of two masses problem.

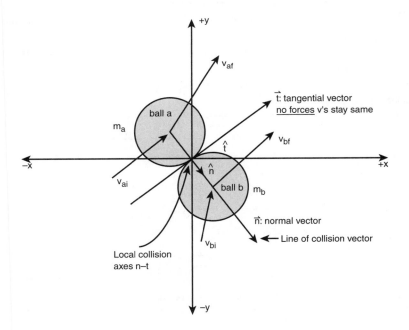

Hardcore Game Programming

Conservation of linear momentum:

$$m_a*v_{ai} + m_b*v_{bi} = m_a*v_{af} + m_b*v_{bf}$$

Conservation of kinetic energy:

$$1/2*m_a*v_{ai}^2 + 1/2*m_b*v_{bi}^2 = 1/2*m_a*v_{af}^2 + 1/2*m_b*v_{bf}^2$$

After combining them and solving for the final velocities, we get

$$v_{af} = (2*m_b*v_{bi} + v_{ai}*(m_a - m_b))/(m_a + m_b)$$
$$v_{bf} = (2*m_a*v_{ai} - v_{bi}*(m_a - m_b))/(m_a + m_b)$$

These equations are true for perfectly elastic collisions. However, there's a little problem—as they stand they are only 1-dimensional. What we need to do is come up with the 2D solution to the problem (something like a pool table) and this is a bit more complex. Let's start with what we know.

We know that each ball (2D representation) has some mass m; furthermore, the balls are made of the same material throughout, so the center of mass is at the center of the ball body. Next, we know that when real balls hit each other, the balls deform for a moment, some of the kinetic energy is converted to heat, and mechanical work to deform the balls, then the balls separate. This is called the impact event, which is shown in Figure 13.34.

FIGURE 13.34
The phases of the impact event.13.34.

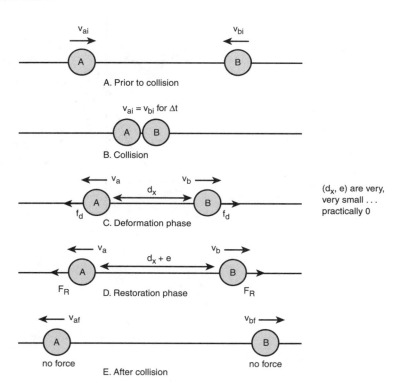

(d_x, e) are very, very small . . . practically 0

The impact event consists of two separate phases. The first phase: *Deformation*, occurs when the balls make first contact and the balls move at the same velocity. At the end of the deformation phase the *restoration* phase begins and continues until the balls separate. The bottom line is that during the collision event a lot of really complex physics happen that we can't possibly model with a computer, so we have to make some assumptions about the collision. The cool thing is that even with the assumptions, when you see the simulation it will look pretty real! The assumptions are the following:

1. The time it takes for the collision event is very small; call it *dt*.
2. During the collision the positions of the balls do not change.
3. *The velocity of the balls may change significantly.*
4. There are no frictional forces acting during the collision.

Assumption 3 is the only one I need to clarify since I think the others are easy to swallow. For assumption 3 to be true, a force has to be applied during the collision that is almost instantaneous. This type of force is called an *impulse force*. This is the key to solving the problem. When the balls hit there will be a very large, short timed force that is created—an impulse. We can compute the impulses and from them come up with another equation to help solve the problem in 2D. The math is advanced and calculus based, so I will forgo it. The results are the generation of a coefficient that models all the physics during the impact event:

Equation 1: Coefficient of restitution

$$e = \frac{v_{bf} - v_{af}}{v_{bi} - v_{ai}}$$

Equation 1 is referred to by e and called the *coefficient of restitution*. It models the velocity before and after the collision and the loss of kinetic energy. If you set e=1 then the model is a perfectly elastic collision. On the other hand, e < 1 models a less than perfect collision and the velocity of each ball after the collision and the linear momentum will be less. Now where do you get e? e is something you set or look up. The interesting thing is that if you combine the equation for e along with the conservation of momentum equation:

$$m_a*v_{ai} + m_b*v_{bi} = m_a*v_{af} + m_b*v_{bf}$$

you get the following results:

Equation 2: Final velocities

$$v_{af} = ((e+1)*m_b*v_{bi} + v_{ai}*(m_a - e*m_b))/(m_a + m_b)$$
$$v_{bf} = ((e+1)*m_a*v_{ai} - v_{bi}*(m_a - e*m_b))/(m_a + m_b)$$

Isn't that interesting? It's almost identical to the formulas we got when we combined the kinetic energy equations with the linear momentum equations. And in fact the assumption we made when we combined the kinetic energy equations with the linear momentum equations was that kinetic energy was conserved. If we assume that now then we set e=1 and we get

```
vaf = ((1+1)*mb*vbi + vai*(ma - 1*mb))/(ma + mb)
vbf = ((1+1)*ma*vai - vbi*(ma - 1*mb))/(ma + mb)
```

or

```
vaf = (2*mb*vbi + vai*(ma - mb))/(ma + mb)
vbf = (2*ma*vai - vbi*(ma - mb))/(ma + mb)
```

These indeed are the equations with both kinetic energy and linear momentum conserved! So it looks like we're on the right track. We have equations 1 and 2, so we should be able to solve the problem. But there's a catch; the equations are still in 1D, so we need to write them in 2D and then find a solution.

Referring back to Figure 13.33, you see there are two extra axes labeled—the **n** and **t** axes. The **n** axis is in the direction of the line of collision and the **t** axis or tangential axis is perpendicular to **n**. Assuming we have computed the vectors representing these axes (I'll show how a little later) then we can write some equations.

The first set of equations we're going to write relates the tangential component of the velocities before and after the collision. Since there are no frictional forces and no impulsive forces acting tangentially to the line of collision (trust me), the tangential linear momentum (and therefore the velocities) must be the same before and after, right? If there are no forces then this must be true, thus we can write

Equation 3: Relationship between initial and final tangential momentum/velocities

```
ma*(vai)t = ma(vaf)t
mb*(vbi)t = mb(vbf)t
```

And if you wish you can combine them like this:

```
ma*(vai)t + mb*(vbi)t = ma(vaf)t + mb(vbf)t
```

MATH	My notation is simple; (a,b) refers to the ball, (i,f) refers to initial or final, and (n,t) refers to the component along the **n** or **t** axes.

Since the masses are the same before and after the collision we can deduce that the velocities are the same by dividing the masses out:

Equation 4: Velocities after collision are equal in tangential direction

```
(vai)t = (vaf)t
(vbi)t = (vbf)t
```

Cool. Now that we have half the problem solved we know the final velocities of the tangential components. Let's find the final velocities of the normal components, or the velocities in the line of collision **n**. We know that linear momentum is conserved always because there are no outside forces acting on the balls when they hit, so we can write:

Equation 5: Linear momentum is conserved in the **n** axis or line of collision

$m_a*(v_{ai})n + m_b*(v_{bi})n = m_a*(v_{af})n + m_b*(v_{bf})n$

And we can also write e in terms of the **n** axis:

Equation 6: The coefficient of restitution in the **n** axis

$$e = \frac{(v_{bf})n - (v_{af})n}{(v_{bi})n - (v_{ai})n}$$

Now let's take a look at what we have. If you look at equations 5 and 6, I have highlighted the variables that we don't have: $(v_{af})n$, and $(v_{bf})n$. Just the normal components of the final velocity. Bingo! We have two equations and two unknowns, so we can solve for them. But we already have the answer! Equation 2 still holds for any particular axis, so I can rewrite it for the component along n:

Equation 7: Final velocities in the normal direction

$v_{af} = ((e+1)*m_b*(v_{bi})n + (v_{ai})n*(m_a - e*m_b))/(m_a + m_b)$
$v_{bf} = ((e+1)*m_a*(v_{ai})n - (v_{bi})n*(m_a - e*m_b))/(m_a + m_b)$

That's it!

Resolving the n-t Coordinate System

Now that we have the final collision response, we need to figure out how to get the initial values for $(v_{ai})n$, $(v_{ai})t$, $(v_{bi})n$, $(v_{bi})t$ and then when the problem is solved we have to convert the values in the **n-t** axes back into values in the x,y axes. Let's begin by first finding the vectors **n** and **t**.

To find **n** we want a vector that is unit length (length equal to 1.0) and along the line from the center of ball $A(x_{a0},y_{a0})$ to the center of ball $B(x_{b0},y_{b0})$. Let's begin by finding a vector from ball A to B, calling it **N**, and then normalizing it:

Equation 8: Computation of **n** and **t**

$N = B - A = <x_{b0} - x_{a0}, y_{b0} - y_{a0}>$

Normalizing **N** to find **n**, we get

$n = N/|N| = <n_x,n_y>$

Now we need the tangential axis **t** which is perpendicular to **n**. We could find it again using vector geometry, but there's a trick we can use; if we rotate n 90 degrees clockwise, that's what we want. However, when a 2D vector <x,y> is rotated in a plane 90 degrees clockwise, the rotated vector is just $t=<-y, x>=<t_x, t_y>$. Take a look at Figure 13.35.

FIGURE 13.35

Rotating a vector 90 degrees to find its perpendicular.

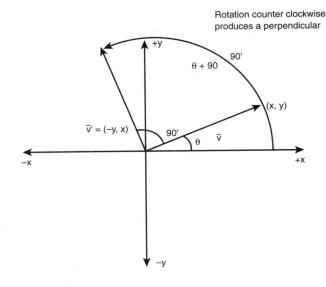

Rotation counter clockwise produces a perpendicular

Now that we have both n and t and they are both unit vectors (since **n** was unit, t is unit also) we're ready to go. We want to resolve the initial velocities of each ball into terms of n and t for ball A and B, respectively:

$$v_{ai}=<x_{vai}, y_{vai}>$$
$$v_{bi}=<x_{vbi}, y_{vbi}>$$

This is nothing more than a dot product. To find $(v_{ai})\mathbf{n}$, the component of the initial velocity of ball A along axis **n**, here's what you do:

$$(v_{ai})n = v_{ai} \cdot n = <x_{vai}, y_{vai}> \cdot <n_x,n_y>$$
$$= (x_{vai}*n_x + y_{vai}* n_y).$$

Note the result is a scalar, as it should be. Computing the other initial velocities is the same as shown in Equation 9.

Equation 9: Components of v_{ai} along **n** and **t**:

$$(v_{ai})\mathbf{n} = \mathbf{v_{ai}} \cdot \mathbf{n} = <x_{vai}, y_{vai}> \cdot <n_x,n_y>$$
$$(x_{vai}*n_x + y_{vai}* n_y)$$
$$=$$
$$(v_{ai})\mathbf{t} = \mathbf{v_{ai}} \cdot \mathbf{t} = <x_{vai}, y_{vai}> \cdot <t_x,t_y>$$
$$= (x_{vai}*t_x + y_{vai}* t_y)$$

Components of v_{bi} along **n** and **t**:

```
(vbi)n = vbi . n = <xvbi, yvbi> . <nx,ny>
       = (xvbi*nx + yvbi* ny)

(vbi)t = vbi . t = <xvbi, yvbi> . <tx,ty>
       = (xvbi*tx + yvbi* ty)
```

Now we're ready to solve the problem completely. Here are the steps:

1. Compute **n** and **t** (use equation 8).

2. Resolve all the components of v_{ai} and v_{bi} into magnitudes along n and t (use equation 9).

3. Plug values into final velocity shown in equation 7 and remember the tangential components of the final velocities are the same as the initial.

4. The results to the problem are in terms of the coordinate axes **n** and **t**, so you must transform back into x,y.

I'll leave step 4 up to you. Now let's talk about tensors. Just kidding, just kidding. Let's finish this bad boy off. At this point we have the final velocities:

Final velocity for Ball A in terms of **n,t**:

```
(vaf)nt=<(vaf)n,(vaf)t>
```

Final velocity for Ball B in terms of **n,t**:

```
(vbf)nt=<(vbf)n,(vbf)t>
```

Now, let's forget about collisions and think about vector geometry. Take a look at Figure 13.36; it illustrates the problem we have.

Stated in plain Vulcan, we have a vector in one coordinate system **n-t** that we want to resolve into x,y. But how? Again, we are going to use dot products. Take a look at the vector $(v_{af})_{nt}$ in Figure 13.36, forgetting about the **n,t** axes. We just want $(v_{af})_{nt}$ in terms of the axis x,y. To compute this we're going to need the contribution of $(v_{af})_{nt}$ along both the x- and y-axes. This can be found with dot products. All we need to do are the following dot products:

For Ball A, v_a in terms of **n,t** is

```
va = (vaf)n * n + (vaf)t * t
     (vaf)n * <nx,ny> + (vaf)t * <tx,ty>
```

Therefore writing with dot products,

```
xaf = <nx,0> . (vaf)n + <tx,0> . (vaf)t
    = nx*(vaf)n + tx*(vaf)t

yaf = <0,ny> . (vaf)n + <0,ty> . (vaf)t
    = ny*(vaf)n + ty*(vaf)t
```

FIGURE 13.36

Transforming a vector
from basis to basis.

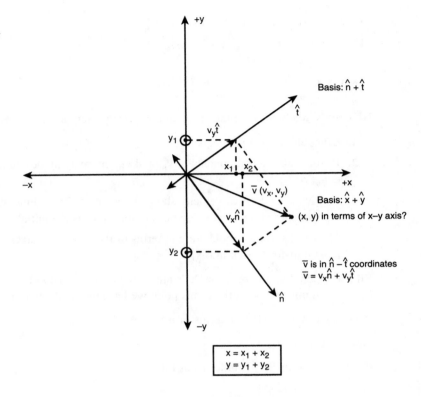

$$x = x_1 + x_2$$
$$y = y_1 + y_2$$

For Ball B:

```
vb = (vbf)n * n + (vbf)t * t
     (vbf)n *<nx,ny> + (vbf)t * <tx,ty>
```

Therefore,

```
xbf = <nx,0> . (vbf)n + <tx,0> . (vbf)t
    = nx*(vbf)n + tx*(vbf)t
```

```
ybf = <0,ny> . (vbf)n + <0,ty> . (vbf)t
    = ny*(vbf)n + ty*(vbf)t
```

Send the balls off with the above velocities and you're done! Wow, that was a whopper,
huh? Now, since I think that the code is a lot easier to understand than the math, I
have listed the collision algorithm here from an upcoming demo:

```
void Collision_Response(void)
{
// this function does all the "real" physics to determine if there has
// been a collision between any ball and any other ball; if there is a
// collision, the function uses the mass of each ball along with the
// initial velocities to compute the resulting velocities
```

Playing God: Basic Physics Modeling

```
// from the book we know that in general
// va2 = (e+1)*mb*vb1+va1(ma - e*mb)/(ma+mb)
// vb2 = (e+1)*ma*va1+vb1(ma - e*mb)/(ma+mb)

// and the objects will have direction vectors co-linear to the normal
// of the point of collision, but since we are using spheres here as the
// objects, we know that the normal to the point of collision is just
// the vector from the centers of each object, thus the resulting
// velocity vector of each ball will be along this normal vector direction

// step 1: test each object against each other object and test for a
// collision; there are better ways to do this other than a double nested
// loop, but since there are a small number of objects this is fine;
// also we want to somewhat model if two or more balls hit simultaneously

for (int ball_a = 0; ball_a < NUM_BALLS; ball_a++)
    {
    for (int ball_b = ball_a+1; ball_b < NUM_BALLS; ball_b++)
        {
        if (ball_a == ball_b)
            continue;

        // compute the normal vector from a->b
        float nabx = (balls[ball_b].varsF[INDEX_X] -
                      balls[ball_a].varsF[INDEX_X] );
        float naby = (balls[ball_b].varsF[INDEX_Y] -
                      balls[ball_a].varsF[INDEX_Y] );
        float length = sqrt(nabx*nabx + naby*naby);

        // is there a collision?
        if (length <= 2.0*(BALL_RADIUS*.75))
            {
            // the balls have made contact, compute response

            // compute the response coordinate system axes
            // normalize normal vector
            nabx/=length;
            naby/=length;

            // compute the tangential vector perpendicular to normal,
            // simply rotate vector 90
            float tabx =  -naby;
            float taby =  nabx;

            // draw collision
            DDraw_Lock_Primary_Surface();

            // blue is normal
            Draw_Clip_Line(balls[ball_a].varsF[INDEX_X]+0.5,
                balls[ball_a].varsF[INDEX_Y]+0.5,
                balls[ball_a].varsF[INDEX_X]+20*nabx+0.5,
                balls[ball_a].varsF[INDEX_Y]+20*naby+0.5,
                252, primary_buffer, primary_lpitch);
```

```
                // yellow is tangential
                Draw_Clip_Line(balls[ball_a].varsF[INDEX_X]+0.5,
                    balls[ball_a].varsF[INDEX_Y]+0.5,
                    balls[ball_a].varsF[INDEX_X]+20*tabx+0.5,
                    balls[ball_a].varsF[INDEX_Y]+20*taby+0.5,
                    251, primary_buffer, primary_lpitch);

                 DDraw_Unlock_Primary_Surface();

                // tangential is also normalized since
                // it's just a rotated normal vector

                // step 2: compute all the initial velocities
                // notation ball: (a,b) initial: i, final: f,
                // n: normal direction, t: tangential direction

                float vait = DOT_PRODUCT(balls[ball_a].varsF[INDEX_XV],
                                         balls[ball_a].varsF[INDEX_YV],
                                         tabx, taby);

                float vain = DOT_PRODUCT(balls[ball_a].varsF[INDEX_XV],
                                         balls[ball_a].varsF[INDEX_YV],
                                         nabx, naby);

                float vbit = DOT_PRODUCT(balls[ball_b].varsF[INDEX_XV],
                                         balls[ball_b].varsF[INDEX_YV],
                                         tabx, taby);

                float vbin = DOT_PRODUCT(balls[ball_b].varsF[INDEX_XV],
                                         balls[ball_b].varsF[INDEX_YV],
                                         nabx, naby);


                // now we have all the initial velocities
                // in terms of the n and t axes
                // step 3: compute final velocities after
                // collision, from book we have
                // note: all this code can be optimized, but I want you
        // to see what's happening :)

                float ma = balls[ball_a].varsF[INDEX_MASS];
                float mb = balls[ball_b].varsF[INDEX_MASS];

                float vafn = (mb*vbin*(cof_E+1) + vain*(ma - cof_E*mb))
                             / (ma + mb);
                float vbfn = (ma*vain*(cof_E+1) - vbin*(ma - cof_E*mb))
                             / (ma + mb);

                // now luckily the tangential components
                // are the same before and after, so
                float vaft = vait;
                float vbft = vbit;
```

```
            // and that's that baby!
            // the velocity vectors are:
            // object a (vafn, vaft)
            // object b (vbfn, vbft)

            // the only problem is that we are in the wrong coordinate
            // system! we need to
        // translate back to the original x,y
            // coordinate system; basically we need to
            // compute the sum of the x components relative to
            // the n,t axes and the sum of
            // the y components relative to the n,t axis,
            // since n,t may both have x,y
            // components in the original x,y coordinate system

            float xfa = vafn*nabx + vaft*tabx;
            float yfa = vafn*naby + vaft*taby;

            float xfb = vbfn*nabx + vbft*tabx;
            float yfb = vbfn*naby + vbft*taby;

            // store results
            balls[ball_a].varsF[INDEX_XV] = xfa;
            balls[ball_a].varsF[INDEX_YV] = yfa;

            balls[ball_b].varsF[INDEX_XV] = xfb;
            balls[ball_b].varsF[INDEX_YV] = yfb;

            // update position
        balls[ball_a].varsF[INDEX_X]+=
                    balls[ball_a].varsF[INDEX_XV];
            balls[ball_a].varsF[INDEX_Y]+=
                    balls[ball_a].varsF[INDEX_YV];

            balls[ball_b].varsF[INDEX_X]+=
                    balls[ball_b].varsF[INDEX_XV];
            balls[ball_b].varsF[INDEX_Y]+=
                    balls[ball_b].varsF[INDEX_YV];

            } // end if

        } // end for ball2

    } // end for ball1

} // end Collision_Response
```

The code follows the algorithm almost identically. However, the code is from a demo that simulates a pool table system, so added loops test all collision pairs. Once inside the loop the code follows the math. To see the algorithm in action check out DEMO13_8.CPP|EXE (16-bit version, DEMO13_8_16B.CPP|EXE). A screen shot from it is shown in Figure 13.37. The demo starts up with a number of randomly moving balls and then the physics takes over. At the bottom of the screen the total kinetic energy is displayed. Try changing the coefficient of restitution with the right and left arrows keys and watch what happens. For values less than 1, the system loses energy, for values equal to 1, the system maintains energy, and for values greater than 1, the system gains energy—I wish my bank account did that!

FIGURE 13.37

The hyper-realistic collision response model.

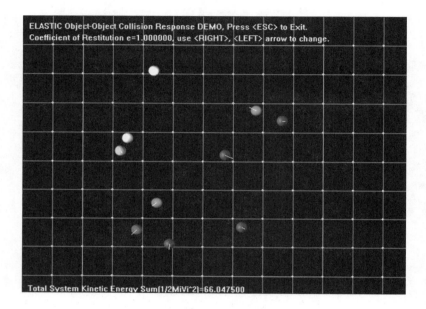

Simple Kinematics

The term *kinematics* means a lot of things. To a 3D artist it means one thing, to the 3D game programmer it means another, and to a physicist it means yet another. However, in this section of the book it means the mechanics of moving linked chains of rigid bodies. In computer animation there are two kinematic problems. The first is called *forward kinematics* and the second is *inverse kinematics*. The forward kinematic problem is shown in Figure 13.38; here you see a 2D serially linked chain of rigid bodies (straight arms). Each joint can freely rotate in the plane, thus there are 2 degrees of freedom in this example, θ_1, and θ_2. In addition, each arm has length l_1 and l_2, respectively. The forward kinematic problem can be stated as follows:

Given θ_1, θ_2, l_1, and l_2, find the position of p_2.

Why are we interested in this? Well, if you are going to write a 2D or 3D game and want to have real-time models that have links that move around, then you better know how to do this. For example, 3D animation is accomplished in two ways. The quick and dirty method is to have a set of meshes that represent the 3D animation of an object. The more flexible method is to have a single 3D mesh that has a number of joints and arms and then to "play" motion data through the 3D model. However, to do this you must understand the physics/mechanics of how to move a hand in relation to the wrist, in relation to the elbow, in relation to the shoulder, in relation to the hips, and so forth—see the problem?

FIGURE 13.38
The forward kine-matic problem.

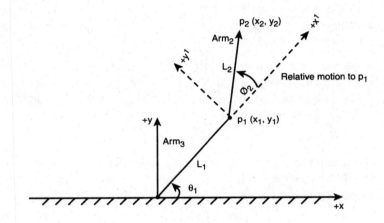

The second kinematic problem is the converse of the first:

Given the position of p_2, find values θ_1, θ_2 that satisfy all the constraints l_1 and l_2 of the physical model. This is much harder than you can imagine. Figure 13.39 shows an example of why this is true.

FIGURE 13.39
The inverse kinematic problem.

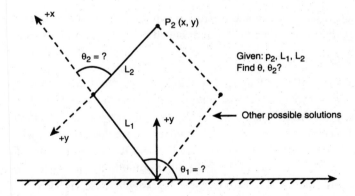

Referring to the figure, you see that there are two possible solutions that satisfy all the constraints. I'm not going to tackle this problem in general since in most cases we never need to solve it, and the math is gnarly, but I will give an example later in the section of how to go about it.

Solving the Forward Kinematic Problem

What I want to do is show you how to solve the forward kinematic problem because it's almost trivial. Referring back to Figure 13.38, the problem is nothing more than relative motions. If you look at the problem from joint 2, then locating p_2 is nothing more than a translation of l_2 and a rotation of θ_2. However, the point p_2 itself is just located as a translation from p_1 of l_1 and a rotation of θ_1. Thus, the solution of the problem is nothing more than a series of translations and rotations from frame to frame or link to link. Let's solve the problem in pieces.

Forget about the first arm and just focus on the second, that is, let's work our way backward. The starting point is p_1 and we want to move a distance l_2 out on the x-axis and then rotate an angle θ_2 around the x,y plane (or the z-axis in 3D) to locate the point p_2. This is easy—all we need to do is the following transformation from p_1:

$p_2 = p_1 * T_{12} * R_{\theta 2}$

But we don't have p_1? That's okay—we assume that we do for the derivation. Anyway, $\mathbf{T}_{12}$ and $\mathbf{R}\theta_2$ are the standard 2D translation and rotation matrices you learned about in Chapter 8, "Vector Rasterization and 2D Transformations." Therefore, we have

$$T_{12} = \begin{vmatrix} 1 & 0 & 0 \\ 0 & 1 & 0 \\ 1_1 & 0 & 1 \end{vmatrix} \quad R_{\theta 2} = \begin{vmatrix} \cos_{\theta 2} & \sin_{\theta 2} & 0 \\ -\sin_{\theta 2} & \cos_{\theta 2} & 0 \\ 0 & 0 & 1 \end{vmatrix}$$

Therefore, p_2 is the product:

$$p_2 = p_1 * \begin{vmatrix} 1 & 0 & 0 \\ 0 & 1 & 0 \\ 1_2 & 0 & 1 \end{vmatrix} * \begin{vmatrix} \cos_{\theta 2} & \sin_{\theta 2} & 0 \\ -\sin_{\theta 2} & \cos_{\theta 2} & 0 \\ 0 & 0 & 1 \end{vmatrix}$$

Okay, if we can compute p_2 from p_1, then p_1 should be p_0 transformed in the same way, that is, translated by l_1 and rotated by θ_1. Or mathematically:

$p_2 = p_0 * T_{12} * R_{\theta 2} * T_{11} * R_{\theta 1}$

where $p_0 = [0,0,1]$, that is, the origin in homogenous 2D coordinates (we could use any point if we wanted, but basically this represents the base of the kinematic chain). The reason for three components in a 2D system is so we can use homogenous transforms and accomplish translation with matrices, hence that last 1.0 is a place holder. All points are in the form (x,y,1). Furthermore, $\mathbf{T}_{11}$ and $\mathbf{R}\theta_1$ are of the same form as T_{12} and $R\theta_2$, but with different values. Note the order of multiplication—since we're working backward, we must first transform p_0 by $\mathbf{T}_{12} * \mathbf{R}\theta_2$ then by $\mathbf{T}_{11} * \mathbf{R}\theta_1$, so order counts!

With all that in mind, we see that the point p_2 is really just the starting point p_0 multiplied by the matrices $(\mathbf{T}_{12} * \mathbf{R}_{\theta 2}) * (\mathbf{T}_{11} * \mathbf{R}_{\theta 1})$. This holds for as many links as needed, or in general:

$p_n = p_0 * T_n * R_n * T_{n-1} * R_{n-1} * T_{n-2} * R_{n-2} * \ldots * T_1 * R_1$

for n links.

This works because each matrix multiplication pair T*R transforms the coordinate system relative to the link, hence, the products of these transforms is like a sequence of changing coordinate systems that you can use to locate the end point. As an example, let's see if this mumbo jumbo works. Figure 13.40 depicts a carefully worked out version of the problem on graph paper.

FIGURE 13.40

A kinematic chain worked out on paper.

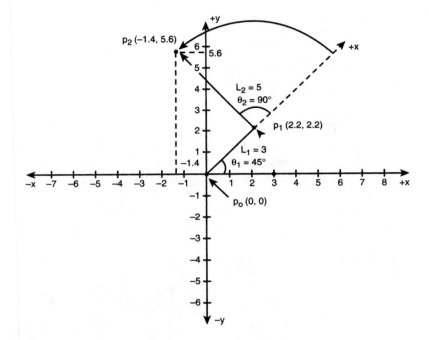

I have labeled the points, angles, and so on, and using a compass and ruler computed the position of p_2 given the input values:

$l_1 = 3, \ l_2 = 5$

$\theta_1 = 45, \ \theta_2 = 90$

$p_0 = (0,0)$

I roughly estimate from the figure that

$p_2 = (-1.4, 5.6)$

Now, let's see if the math gives us the same answer.

$$
p_2 = [0,0,1] * \begin{vmatrix} 1 & 0 & 0 \\ 0 & 1 & 0 \\ 5 & 0 & 1 \end{vmatrix} * \begin{vmatrix} 0 & 1 & 0 \\ -1 & 0 & 0 \\ 0 & 0 & 1 \end{vmatrix} * \begin{vmatrix} 1 & 0 & 0 \\ 0 & 1 & 0 \\ 3 & 0 & 1 \end{vmatrix} * \begin{vmatrix} .707 & .707 & 0 \\ -.707 & .707 & 0 \\ 0 & 0 & 1 \end{vmatrix}
$$

$$
\quad p_0 \qquad T_{12} \qquad \quad R\_2 \qquad \quad T_{11} \qquad \qquad R\_1
$$

$$= [0\ 0\ 1]*\begin{vmatrix} 0 & 1 & 0 \\ -1 & 0 & 0 \\ 0 & 5 & 1 \end{vmatrix} * \begin{vmatrix} .707 & .707 & 0 \\ -.707 & .707 & 0 \\ 2.121 & 2.121 & 1 \end{vmatrix}$$

$$\qquad p_0 \qquad T_{12}*R_{\theta 2} \qquad\qquad T_{11}*R_{\theta 1}$$

$$= [0\ 0\ 1]*\begin{vmatrix} -.707 & .707 & 0 \\ .707 & .707 & 0 \\ -1.414 & 5.656 & 1 \end{vmatrix}$$

$$\qquad p_0 \qquad T_{12}*R_{\theta 2}*T_{11}*R_{\theta 1}$$

$p_2 = [-1.414, 5.656, 1]$

Discarding the 1.0 since [x,y,1] really means, x' = x/1, y'=y/1, or x'=x, y'=y, we have:

$p_2 = (-1.414, 5.656)$.

If you look at Figure 13.40, it looks pretty close! That's all there is to forward kinematics in 2D. Of course, doing it in 3D is a bit more complex due to the z-axis, but as long as you pick a rotation convention then it all works out. I created DEMO13_9.CPP|EXE (16-bit version, DEMO13_9_16B.CPP|EXE) shown in Figure 13.41, as an example of forward kinematics. It lets you change the angle of the two links and then computes the positions p1, p2 and displays them. The keys A, S, D, and F control the angles of link 1 and link 2, respectively. See if you can add a restraint to the program, so the end effector at p_2 can't drop below the y=0 axis, shown by the green line.

FIGURE 13.41
The kinematic chain demo.

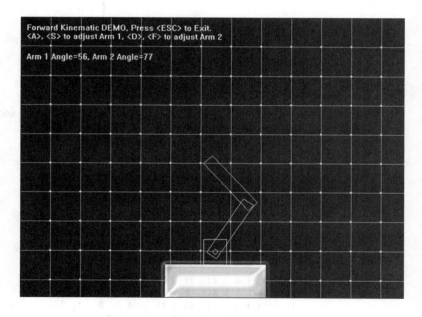

Solving the Inverse Kinematic Problem

Solving inverse kinematics is rather complex in general, but I want to give you a taste of it so you can at least know where to start. The previous section solved for p_2 knowing p_0, l_1, l_2, θ_1, θ_2. But what if you didn't know θ_1, and θ_2, but knew p_2? The solution of the kinematic problem can be found by setting up a system of restraint equations and then solving for the unknown angles. The problem is that you may have an under-determined system, meaning that there is more than one solution. Thus, you must add other heuristic or constraints to find the solution you want.

As an example, let's try a simpler problem with only one link, so you can see the process. Figure 13.42 shows one link l_1 making an angle θ_1 with the x-axis. Given $p_1(x_1, y_1)$, what is θ_1?

FIGURE 13.42
A single link inverse
kinematic problem.

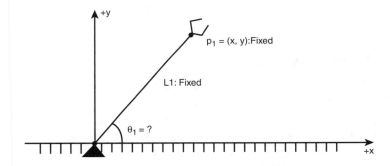

We can use the forward kinematic matrices to solve the problem like this:

```
p₁ = p₀*T₁₁*Rθ₁
                  |1  0  0|  | cos θ₁  sin θ₁  0|
p₁(x₁,y₁) =[0 0 1]*|0  1  0|*|-sin θ₁  cos θ₁  0|
                  |1₁ 0  1|  |  0        0     1|
          p₀         T₁₁             Rθ₁

                    | cos θ₁  sin θ₁  0|
          =[1₁ 0 1]*|-sin θ₁  cos θ₁  0|
                    |  0        0     1|
            p₀*T₁₁            Rθ₁

p₁(x₁,y₁)  =  (1₁*cos θ₁,  1₁*sin θ₁,  1)
```

Therefore,

```
x₁ = 1₁*cos θ₁
y₁ = 1₁*sin θ₁

θ₁ = cos ⁻¹ x₁/1₁
```

or,

```
θ₁ = sin ⁻¹ y₁/1₁
```

| MATH | I could have kept the entire problem in matrix form, but this is more illustrative. |

Okay, this system is overdetermined; in other words, once you select x or y then the other is determined via θ_1. This is interesting, but if you think about it then it makes sense—the arm link l_1 causes us to lose a degree of freedom therefore, you can't locate any point you wish (x,y) anymore, in fact, the only points that are valid anymore are of the form:

```
x₁ = l₁*cos θ₁
y₁ = l₁*sin θ₁
```

If this had two links, then you would see that for any x,y there would be more than one solution set θ_1, θ_2 that satisfied the equations along with a relationship between θ_1, and θ_2.

Particle Systems

This is *the* hot topic. Everyone is always saying, "So, does it have particle systems?" Well, particle systems can be very complex or very simple. Basically, particle systems are physics models that model small particles. They are great for explosions, vapor trails, and general light shows in your game. You have already learned a lot about physics modeling and I'm sure can create your own particle system. However, just to get you started, I'm going to show you how to create a very quick and simple system based on pixel-sized particles.

Let's say that we want to use particles for explosions, and maybe vapor trails. Since a particle system is nothing more than *n* particles, let's just focus on the model of a single particle.

What Every Particle Needs

If you wanted, you could model collision response, momentum transfer, and all that stuff, but most particle systems have extremely simple models. The following are the general features of a garden variety particle:

- Position
- Velocity
- Color/animation
- Life span
- Gravity
- Wind force

When you start a particle, you will want to give it a position, initial velocity, color, and a life span at the very least. Also, the particle might be a glowing cinder, so there might be color animation involved. Additionally, you may want to have some global forces that act on all particles, like gravity and wind. You may want to have functions that create collections of particles with the desired initial conditions that you're looking for, like explosions or vapor trails. And of course, you may want to give particles the ability to bounce off objects with some physical realism. However, most of the time particles just tunnel through everything and no one cares!

Designing a Particle Engine

To design a particle system you need three separate elements:

- The particle data structure.
- The particle engine that processes each particle.
- Functions to generate particular particle initial conditions.

Let's begin with the data structure. I'll assume an 8-bit display since, in animation, it's easier to work with *bytes* than RGB colors. Also, color effects are easier to implement in 8-bit color. Converting the particle engine to 16-bit isn't bad, but lots of the effects will be lost, so I have decided to keep it 8-bit for illustrative purposes. Anyway, here's a first attempt at a single particle:

```
// a single particle
typedef struct PARTICLE_TYP
        {
        int state;          // state of the particle
        int type;           // type of particle effect
        float x,y;          // world position of particle
        float xv,yv;        // velocity of particle
        int curr_color;     // the current rendering color of particle
        int start_color;    // the start color or range effect
        int end_color;      // the ending color of range effect
        int counter;        // general state transition timer
        int max_count;      // max value for counter

        } PARTICLE, *PARTICLE_PTR;
```

Let's add in some globals to handle external effects such as gravity in the Y direction and wind force in the X direction.

```
float particle_wind = 0;    // assume it operates in the X direction
float particle_gravity = 0; // assume it operates in the Y direction
```

Let's define some useful constants that we might need to accomplish some of the effects:

```
// defines for particle system
#define PARTICLE_STATE_DEAD         0
#define PARTICLE_STATE_ALIVE        1
```

```
// types of particles
#define PARTICLE_TYPE_FLICKER            0
#define PARTICLE_TYPE_FADE               1

// color of particle
#define PARTICLE_COLOR_RED               0
#define PARTICLE_COLOR_GREEN             1
#define PARTICLE_COLOR_BLUE              2
#define PARTICLE_COLOR_WHITE             3

#define MAX_PARTICLES                    128

// color ranges (based on my palette)
#define COLOR_RED_START                  32
#define COLOR_RED_END                    47

#define COLOR_GREEN_START                96
#define COLOR_GREEN_END                  111

#define COLOR_BLUE_START                 144
#define COLOR_BLUE_END                   159

#define COLOR_WHITE_START                16
#define COLOR_WHITE_END                  31
```

Hopefully, you can see my thinking here. I want to have particles that are either red, green, blue, or white, so I took a palette and figured out the color indices for the ranges. If you wanted to use 16-bit color then you would have to manually interpolate RGB from the starting value to some ending value—I'll keep it simple. Also, you see that I'm counting on making two types of particles: fading and flickering. The fading particles will just fade away, but the flickering ones will flicker away, like sparks.

Finally, I'm happy with our little particles, so let's create storage for them:

```
PARTICLE particles[MAX_PARTICLES]; // the particles for the particle engine
```

So let's start writing the functions to process each particle.

The Particle Engine Software

We need functions to initialize all the particles, start a particle, process all the particles, and then clean up all the particles when we're done. Let's start with the initialization functions:

```
void Init_Reset_Particles(void)
{
// this function serves as both an init and reset for the particles

// loop thru and reset all the particles to dead
for (int index=0; index<MAX_PARTICLES; index++)
    {
    particles[index].state = PARTICLE_STATE_DEAD;
    particles[index].type  = PARTICLE_TYPE_FADE;
```

```
      particles[index].x        = 0;
      particles[index].y        = 0;
      particles[index].xv       = 0;
      particles[index].yv       = 0;
      particles[index].start_color = 0;
      particles[index].end_color   = 0;
      particles[index].curr_color  = 0;
      particles[index].counter     = 0;
      particles[index].max_count   = 0;
      } // end if

} // end Init_Reset_Particles
```

Init_Reset_Particles() just makes all particles zeros and gets them ready for use. If you wanted to do anything special, this would be the place to do it. The next function we need is something to start a particle with a given set of initial conditions. We will worry how to arrive at the initial conditions in a moment, but for now I want to hunt for an available particle, and if found, start it up with the sent data. Here's the function to do that:

```
void Start_Particle(int type, int color, int count,
                    float x, float y, float xv, float yv)
{
// this function starts a single particle

int pindex = -1; // index of particle

// first find open particle
for (int index=0; index < MAX_PARTICLES; index++)
    if (particles[index].state == PARTICLE_STATE_DEAD)
       {
       // set index
       pindex = index;
       break;
       } // end if

// did we find one
if (pindex==-1)
   return;

// set general state info
particles[pindex].state = PARTICLE_STATE_ALIVE;
particles[pindex].type  = type;
particles[pindex].x     = x;
particles[pindex].y     = y;
particles[pindex].xv    = xv;
particles[pindex].yv    = yv;
particles[pindex].counter   = 0;
particles[pindex].max_count = count;

// set color ranges, always the same
   switch(color)
       {
```

```
        case PARTICLE_COLOR_RED:
            {
            particles[pindex].start_color = COLOR_RED_START;
            particles[pindex].end_color   = COLOR_RED_END;
            } break;

        case PARTICLE_COLOR_GREEN:
            {
            particles[pindex].start_color = COLOR_GREEN_START;
            particles[pindex].end_color   = COLOR_GREEN_END;
            } break;

        case PARTICLE_COLOR_BLUE:
            {
            particles[pindex].start_color = COLOR_BLUE_START;
            particles[pindex].end_color   = COLOR_BLUE_END;
            } break;

        case PARTICLE_COLOR_WHITE:
            {
            particles[pindex].start_color = COLOR_WHITE_START;
            particles[pindex].end_color   = COLOR_WHITE_END;
            } break;

        break;

        } // end switch

// what type of particle is being requested
if (type == PARTICLE_TYPE_FLICKER)
    {
    // set current color
    particles[index].curr_color
     = RAND_RANGE(particles[index].start_color,
                particles[index].end_color);

    } // end if
else
    {
    // particle is fade type
    // set current color
    particles[index].curr_color  = particles[index].start_color;
    } // end if

} // end Start_Particle
```

| NOTE | There is no error detection or even a success/failure sent back. The point is that I don't care; if we can't create one teenie-weenie particle, I think I'll live. However, you might want to add more robust error handling. |

To start a particle at (10,20) with an initial velocity of (0, -5) (straight up), a life span of 90 frames, colored a fading green, this is what you would do:

```
Start_Particle(PARTICLE_TYPE_FADE,    // type
               PARTICLE_COLOR_GREEN, // color
               90,                    // count, lifespan
               10,20,                 // initial position
               0,-5);                 // initial velocity
```

Of course, the particle system has both gravity and wind that are always acting, so you can set them anytime you want and they will globally affect all particles already online as well as new ones. Thus if you want no wind force but a little gravity, you would do this:

```
particle_gravity = 0.1; // positive is downward
particle_wind    = 0.0; // could be +/-
```

Now we have to decide how to move and process the particle. Do we want to wrap them around the screen? Or, when they hit the edges, should we kill them? This depends on the type of game; 2D, 3D, scrolling, and so on. For now let's keep it simple and agree that when a particle goes off a screen edge it's terminated. In addition, the movement function should update the color animation, test if the life counter is expired, and kill particles that are off the screen. Here's the movement function that takes into consideration all that, along with the gravity and wind forces:

```
void Process_Particles(void)
{
// this function moves and animates all particles

for (int index=0; index<MAX_PARTICLES; index++)
    {
    // test if this particle is alive
    if (particles[index].state == PARTICLE_STATE_ALIVE)
        {
        // translate particle
        particles[index].x+=particles[index].xv;
        particles[index].y+=particles[index].yv;

        // update velocity based on gravity and wind
        particles[index].xv+=particle_wind;
        particles[index].yv+=particle_gravity;

        // now based on type of particle perform proper animation
        if (particles[index].type==PARTICLE_TYPE_FLICKER)
            {
            // simply choose a color in the color range and
            // assign it to the current color
            particles[index].curr_color =
              RAND_RANGE(particles[index].start_color,
                        particles[index].end_color);
```

```
                    // now update counter
                    if (++particles[index].counter >= particles[index].max_count)
                       {
                       // kill the particle
                       particles[index].state = PARTICLE_STATE_DEAD;

                       } // end if

                    } // end if
              else
                 {
                 // must be a fade, be careful!
                 // test if it's time to update color
                 if (++particles[index].counter >= particles[index].max_count)
                    {
                     // reset counter
                     particles[index].counter = 0;

                     // update color
                     if (++particles[index].curr_color >
                                     particles[index].end_color)
                        {
                        // transition is complete, terminate particle
                        particles[index].state = PARTICLE_STATE_DEAD;

                        } // end if

                     } // end if

                 } // end else

              // test if the particle is off the screen?
              if (particles[index].x > screen_width ||
                 particles[index].x < 0 ||
                 particles[index].y > screen_height ||
                 particles[index].y < 0)
                 {
                 // kill it!
                 particles[index].state = PARTICLE_STATE_DEAD;
                 } // end if

           } // end if

      } // end for index

} // end Process_Particles
```

The function is self-explanatory—I hope. It translates the particle, applies the external forces, updates the counters and color, tests whether the particle has moved offscreen, and that's it. Next we need to draw the particles. This can be accomplished in a number of ways, but I'm assuming simple pixels and a back buffered display, so here's a function to do that:

```
void Draw_Particles(void)
{
// this function draws all the particles

// lock back surface
DDraw_Lock_Back_Surface();

for (int index=0; index<MAX_PARTICLES; index++)
    {
    // test if particle is alive
    if (particles[index].state==PARTICLE_STATE_ALIVE)
        {
        // render the particle, perform world to screen transform
        int x = particles[index].x;
        int y = particles[index].y;

        // test for clip
        if (x >= screen_width || x < 0 || y >= screen_height || y < 0)
           continue;

        // draw the pixel
        Draw_Pixel(x,y,particles[index].curr_color,
                   back_buffer, back_lpitch);

        } // end if

    } // end for index

// unlock the secondary surface
DDraw_Unlock_Back_Surface();

} // end Draw_Particles
```

Getting exited, huh? Want to try it out, don't you? Well, we're almost done. Now we need some functions to create particle effects like explosions and vapor trails.

Generating the Initial Conditions

Here's the fun part. You can go wild with your imagination. Let's start off with a vapor trail algorithm. Basically, a vapor trail is nothing more than particles that are emitted from a source positioned at (emit_x, emit_y) with slightly different life spans and starting positions. Here's a possible algorithm:

```
// emit a particle every with a change of 1 in 10
if ((rand()%10) == 1)
{
Start_Particle(PARTICLE_TYPE_FADE,    // type
               PARTICLE_COLOR_GREEN, // color
               RAND_RANGE(90,150),    // count, lifespan
               emit_x+RAND_RANGE(-4,4),  // initial x
               emit_y+RAND_RANGE(-4,4),  // initial y
```

```
            RAND_RANGE(-2,2),    // initial x velocity
            RAND_RANGE(-2,2));   // initial y velocity
```

```
} // end if
```

As the emitter moves, so does the emitter source (emit_x, emit_y) and therefore a vapor trail is left. If you want to get really real and give the vapor particles an even more realistic physics model you should take into consideration that the emitter could be in motion and thus any particle emitted would have final velocity = emitted velocity + emitter velocity. You would need to know the velocity of the emitter source, (call it (emit_xv, emit_yv)) and simply add it to the final particle velocity like this:

```
// emit a particle every with a change of 1 in 10
if ((rand()%10) == 1)
{
Start_Particle(PARTICLE_TYPE_FADE,    // type
          PARTICLE_COLOR_GREEN, // color
          RAND_RANGE(90,150),   // count, lifespan
          emit_x+RAND_RANGE(-4,4),  // initial x
          emit_y+RAND_RANGE(-4,4),  // initial y
          emit_xv+RAND_RANGE(-2,2),   // initial x velocity
          emit_yv+RAND_RANGE(-2,2));  // initial y velocity
```

```
} // end if
```

For something a little more exciting, let's model an explosion. An explosion looks something like Figure 13.43. Particles are emitted in a spherical shape in all directions.

FIGURE 13.43
The particles of an explosion.

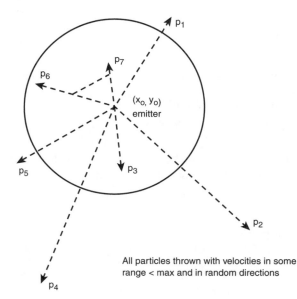

All particles thrown with velocities in some range < max and in random directions

That's easy enough to model. All we need do is start up a random number of particles from a common point with random velocities that are equally distributed in a circular radius. Then if gravity is on, the particle will fall toward Earth and either go off the screen or die out due to its individual life span. Here's the code to create a particle explosion:

```
void Start_Particle_Explosion(int type, int color, int count,
                              int x, int y, int xv, int yv,
                              int num_particles)
{
// this function starts a particle explosion
// at the given position and velocity
// note the use of look up tables for sin,cos

while(--num_particles >=0)
    {
    // compute random trajectory angle
    int ang = rand()%360;

    // compute random trajectory velocity
    float vel = 2+rand()%4;

    Start_Particle(type,color,count,
                   x+RAND_RANGE(-4,4),y+RAND_RANGE(-4,4),
                   xv+cos_look[ang]*vel, yv+sin_look[ang]*vel);

    } // end while

} // end Start_Particle_Explosion
```

Start_Particle_Explosion() takes the type of particle you want (PARTICLE_TYPE_FADE, PARTICLE_TYPE_FLICKER), the color of the particles, the desired number of particles, along with the position and velocity of the source. The function then generates all the desired particles.

To create other special effects, just write a function. For example, one of the coolest effects that I like in movies is the ring-shaped shock wave when a spaceship is blown away. Creating this is simple. All you need to do is modify the explosion function to start all the particles out with exactly the same velocity, but at different angles. Here's that code:

```
void Start_Particle_Ring(int type, int color, int count,
                         int x, int y, int xv, int yv,
                         int num_particles)
{
// this function starts a particle explosion at the
// given position and velocity
// note the use of look up tables for sin,cos

// compute random velocity on outside of loop
float vel = 2+rand()%4;
```

```
while(--num_particles >=0)
    {
    // compute random trajectory angle
    int ang = rand()%360;

    //start the particle
    Start_Particle(type,color,count,
                   x,y,
                   xv+cos_look[ang]*vel,
                   yv+sin_look[ang]*vel);

    } // end while

} // end Start_Particle_Ring
```

Putting the Particle System Together

You now have everything you need to put together some cool particle effects. Just make a call in the initialize phase of your game to `Init_Reset_Particles()`, then in the main loop make a call to `Process_Particles()`. Each cycle and the engine will do the rest. Of course, you have to call one of the generator functions to create some particles! Lastly, if you want to improve the system you might want to add better memory management so you can have infinite particles, and you might want to add particle-to-particle collision detection and particle-to-environment collision detection—that would be really cool.

As a demo of using the particle system, take a look at `DEMO13_10.CPP|EXE` (16-bit version not available) on the CD. It is a fireworks display based on the tank projectile demo. Basically, the tank from the previous demo fires projectiles now. Also, note in the demo I jacked the number of particles up to 256.

Playing God: Constructing Physics Models for Games

This chapter has given you a lot of information and concepts to sift through. The key is to use the concepts and some of the hard math to make working models that look good. No one will ever know if they accurately simulate reality 100 percent, nor will they care. If you can make an approximation then do it—as long as it's worth it. For example, if you're trying to make a racing game and you want to race on road, ice, and dirt, then you better have some frictional effects, otherwise, your cars will drive like they're on rails!

On the other hand, if you have an asteroid field that the player blows up and each asteroid splits into two or more smaller asteroids then I don't think the player is going to care or know for that matter the exact trajectory that the smaller asteroids would take—just pick them in a deterministic way so they look good.

Data Structures for Physics Modeling

One of the questions that I'm asked continuously (in addition to how to compile DirectX programs with VC++) is what data structures to use for physics modeling. There are no physics-data structures! Most physics models are based on the game objects themselves—you simply need to add enough data elements to your primary data structures to figure the physics out—get it? Nonetheless, you should keep track of the following parameters and values in any physics engine for the universe and objects:

- Position and velocity of the object.
- Angular velocity of the object.
- Mass, frictional coefficient, and any other physical properties of the object.
- Physics engine geometry for the object. This is simply a geometry that can be used for the physics calculations. You may use rectangles, spheres, or whatever, rather than the actual object geometry.
- External universal forces such as wind, gravity, and so on.

Now it's up to you to represent all these values with whatever structures or types are appropriate. For example, the realistic collision response demo used a model something like this:

Each Ball Object

```
float x,y; // position
float xv,yv; // velocity
float radius; // guess?
float coefficient_of_restitution; // just what it says
```

Of course the data was hidden a little in some internal arrays in each of the BOBs (blitter objects) that represented the balls, but the abstract data structure is what we're interested in.

Frame-Based Versus Time-Based Modeling

This is the final topic I want to talk about since it's becoming more and more important in 3D games. Thus far in the book, we have had a game loop that looks like Figure 13.44. We have been assuming that the game will run at a constant rate of R fps. If it doesn't, then no big deal, everything will slow down on the screen. But what if you didn't want things to slow down on the screen? What if you wanted a ship to move from a to b in two seconds no matter what the frame rate was? This is called *time-based modeling*.

FIGURE 13.44

The game loop you've learned to love.

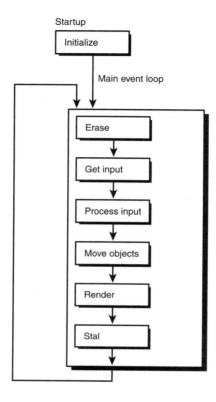

Time-based modeling differs from frame-based modeling in that time t is used in all the kinematic equations that move objects. For example, in a frame-based game if you have the chunk of code:

```
x = 0, y = 0;

x = x + dx;
y = y + dy;
```

and the game runs at 30 fps, then in 30 frames or 1 second, x,y will equal

```
x = 30*dx;
y = 30*dy;
```

If dx=1 and dy=0 then the object would move exactly 30 pixels in the x-direction. And this is fine if you can always guarantee a constant frame rate. But what if the frame rate drops to 10 fps? Then in 1 second, you will have

```
x = 10*dx = 10
y = 10*dy = 0
```

x only changed one-third of what you wanted it to! If visual continuity is what you are going for then this is unacceptable. In addition, this can wreak havoc on a network game. In a network game you can either sync to the slowest machine and stay frame-based, or you can let all the machines run free and use time modeling, which is the more realistic and fair thing to do. I shouldn't have to pay for someone else owning a 486 when I have a PIV 2.4GHz.

To implement time-based motion and kinematics, you have to use time in all of your motion equations. Then, when it's time to move objects, you have to test the difference in time from the last movement and use this as the input into your equations. Thus, as the game slows down a lot, it won't matter because the time parameter will convey this and cause a larger motion. Here's an example game loop:

```
while(1)
{
t0 = Get_Time(); // assume this is in milliseconds

// work, work, work

// move objects
t1 = Get_Time();

// move all the objects
Move_Objects(t1 - t0);

// render
Render();

} // end while
```

With this loop we use the change in time or $(t_1 - t_0)$ as an input to the motion code. Normally there would be no input; the motion code would just move. Let's assume that we want our object to move at 30 pixels per second, but since our time base is in milliseconds, or 1×10^{-3} seconds, we need to scale this:

```
dx = 30 pixels/1 sec = .03 pixels/1 millisecond
```

Can you see where I'm going? Let's write the motion equation for x:

```
x = x + dx*t
```

Plugging everything in we get

```
x = x +.03*(t₁ - t₀)
```

That's it. If a single frame takes one second then $(t_1 - t_0)$ will be 1000 milliseconds and the motion equation will equal

```
x = x + .03*1000 = 30, which is correct!
```

On the other hand, if the time for this frame takes three milliseconds then the motion equation will look like

`x = x + .03*3 = .09, which is also correct!`

Obviously you need to use floating-point values for all this to work since you are going to be tracking fractions of pixel motion, but you get the idea. This is so cool because even if your game starts bogging down hardcore due to rendering, the motion will stay the same.

As an example, check out DEMO13_11.CPP|EXE   (16-bit version, DEMO13_11_16B.CPP|EXE); it basically moves a little ship (with a shadow!) from left to right and allows you to alter the delay of each frame using the arrow keys to simulate processor load.

Notice that the ship moves at a constant rate. It may jump, but it will always travel a total distance of 50 pixels/sec no matter what the frame rate. As a test, the screen is 640 pixels wide, plus the off-screen overlap of 160 pixels, thus the entire travel is 800 pixels. Since the ship is traveling at 50 pixels/sec that means that it should take 800/50=16 seconds to make one pass. Try changing the delay and note that this is always true. If your game was designed to run at 60 fps and it slows to 15–30 then the jumping won't be that apparent and the game will look the same, but less smooth. Without time modeling your game WILL slow down and look like it's in slow motion— I'm sure you have seen this many times. :)

Summary

I'm sure this chapter has been somewhat enlightening whatever your background is. It gave me a headache writing it! We covered a lot of ground and learned various ways to look at things. For example, we tried an ad hoc collision response algorithm that worked great for a ball bouncing off a rectangle. This technique is perfect for any kind of pong or breakout game. Then we looked more closely at the mathematics of reflection and derived the correct way to do it in general. This is the point of physics modeling in games—and you just learned how to do it.

CHAPTER 14

The Text Generation

"I'll be back!"
—You know who

In this bonus chapter we will learn about the oldest games around, known as "text adventures" or text-based games. A long time ago (the 70s and early 80s), computers didn't have the graphics capabilities that they have today. Because of this, most games were descriptive in nature rather than graphic. The games would use text to convey the state of the game and, conversely, the player would enter in plain English sentences to command the character in the game. One of the most notable games created in the early 80's was a game called Zork by Infocom. It was incredibly successful because the language interpreter was very advanced and the game environment was very robust. Furthermore, the user could type in almost any sentence and the game would be able to figure out what the player was trying to say.

The material we will cover isn't hard, but it is different from what we have been covering. There will be a lot of new terms and many of them have meanings that aren't well defined. But, by the end of this chapter, you will be able to make your own text adventure! Here are the topics we'll cover:

- What is a text game?
- How do text games work?
- Getting input from the outside world
- Language analysis and parsing
- Lexical analysis
- Syntactical analysis
- Semantic analysis
- Putting all the pieces together
- Representing the universe
- Placing objects in the world
- Making things happen
- Moving around
- The inventory system
- Implementing sight, sound, and smell
- Making it real-time
- Error handling
- Creeping around with Shadow Land
- The language of Shadow Land
- Building and playing Shadow Land
- Shadow's game loop
- Winning the game

What Is a Text Game?

A text game is a video game without the video! Well, at least without all the cool graphics. Text games are like interactive books that are written as you play. The user gets to use his own imagination to make up what he/she thinks the universe that is being played in looks like. You may have never seen a text game because you are a product of the "GUI age." The interface to a text game is a simple as this:

What do you want to do? Eat the apple.

Yum, that tasted good!

What do you want to do?

What you see here is a short dialog with the computer and player. In most text games, the computer prompts the player to tell it to do something. Then the computer will break the sentence down to its components and see if the action is legal and proceed with it if possible.

The thing to remember is that there are no images or sounds. The only image is in the player's mind. And the only thing that creates this image is the description given by the game. Therefore, the English language used to describe the game universe should be as "fluffy" and poetic as possible. As an example, say that you were designing a text game that had a bathroom in it. When the player asks to "see" what it looks like, one possible description might be

…you see a white bathroom with towels hanging on the racks…

This is fine, but it's boring. A better response would be

…you are stunned by the size of the bathing room that surrounds you. To your West, you see a large shower enclosed in rose tinted glass. The entrance is paved with small polished stones. To the East, you see a large wash area with marble basins and silver faucets. From above, you are bathed in sunlight from the three overhead skylights. Finally, at your feet is a pattern of black and white tiles placed with surgical precision….

As you can see, the second version is much better. It creates an image in your mind and this is the key to text adventures. Even though the interface to a text game is usually nothing more than text, the game that is being played is limited only by the imagination of the designers and that of the player. Usually a text game will contain hundreds of pages of descriptive text within the universe database. This text is used as the foundation for the universe when the player asks something about it.

The technology needed for text games is based on compiler techniques coupled with very elegant data structures and algorithms. Remember, computers don't understand English and making them understand what nouns, verbs, adjectives, prepositional phrases, direct objects, and so forth are is a great task to say the least (I wish I would have paid more attention when my teachers were diagramming sentences). Many people may think that creating a text-based adventure is easy, but they are very wrong. Personally, I think that people who write text adventures probably know more about Computer Science, data structures, and Mathematics than the people who write arcade games.

Text game gurus definitely know a lot about compilers and interpreters—which everyone knows is a very difficult subject. Even today text games are still going strong; however, they have been augmented with incredible graphics. The genre of RPG (Role Playing Games) is really the evolved state of text games. Many RPGs have text interfaces so the player can dialog and ask questions to the characters in the game.

Today we aren't going to take a course in compiler design (which you should do to be a complete person), but we will learn some of the basic concepts and techniques used to create a text-based adventure. You will also see a complete game at the end of the day called Shadow Land.

How Do Text Games Work?

That's a good question. And there are many answers, all of which are correct to some degree, but each of these possible answers will have some factors in common. First, the interface to the game will be a bi-directional, text-only communication channel. This means that the computer will only have text to say what it wants to say and, similarly, the player can only dictate his input with text likewise. Also, there are no joysticks, mice, flight sticks, or light pens. Second, the game will consist of some kind of "universe" whether it is the old west, an apartment building, or a space station. But this universe will consist of geometry, descriptions and rules. The geometry is the actual geometry of the universe, the size and placement of the rooms, hallways, ponds, or whatever. The descriptions are the actual text that can be called on to describe what a location looks like, sounds like, or smells like.

The rules of the game are the things that can and can't be done. For example, you may not be able to eat a rock, but you can eat a sandwich. Once the geometry, descriptions, and rules of the game are in place, then the data structures, algorithms, and software to allow the player to interact with the environment need to be created. This will consist mainly of an input parser. The input parser is responsible for translating and making sense of the player's input. The player will communicate to the game using standard English words. These words may create complete sentences, small phrases, or even single commands. The parser and all its components will break the sentence down into separate words, analyze the meaning of the sentence, and then execute the appropriate functions to make happen whatever the player was asking for.

There is one catch here. The computer doesn't understand natural language and giving it a complete understanding of the English language is a Ph.D. thesis at the very least. As game programmers, we just want to give the player a subset of the English language and impose a few rules about how sentences are constructed. For example, the game you will see later today is called **Shadow Land** and has a very limited vocabulary. It can understand only the words in Table 14.1.

TABLE 14.1 The Vocabulary of Shadow Land

Word	Used As
LAMP	Noun
SANDWICH	Noun
KEYS	Noun

TABLE 14.1   Continued

Word	Used As
EAST	Noun
WEST	Noun
NORTH	Noun/Adjective
SOUTH	Noun/Adjective
FORWARD	Noun/Adjective
BACKWARD	Noun/Adjective
RIGHT	Noun/Adjective
LEFT	Noun/Adjective
MOVE	Verb
TURN	Verb
SMELL	Verb
LOOK	Verb
LISTEN	Verb
PUT	Verb
GET	Verb
EAT	Verb
INVENTORY	Verb
WHERE	Verb
EXIT	Verb
THE	Article
IN	Preposition
ON	Preposition
TO	Preposition
DOWN	Preposition

The vocabulary of Shadow Land is very small, but you would be surprised how many legal sentences can be constructed. The problem is making sense of these constructions using some general algorithm. This process is called *syntactical analysis* and is very tedious and complex. Entire books have been written on how to perform syntactical analysis, such as the infamous "Dragon Book" by Aho, Sethi, and Ullman. We don't need (want) to make things too complex, so we will force rules on our vocabulary that create a little "language." This language will be the one that the user must abide by when constructing sentences.

Once the user has typed something in and the game figures out what he/she is trying to say, then the game will proceed to bring the request to fruition and the game will output the results. For example, if the player asks to "look," then the game will access the universe database along with the current position of the player. Together this data can be used to print out the general description of the room, which may be static. If there are movable objects within the game, then there is as a second phase of description. The game logic would test to see if there are any objects within the field of view of the virtual character and then print them out. However, when the final description prints out, it must seem fluid and not choppy. For example, the game software should first test if there are any objects in the room and, if so, make note of it and slightly alter the last sentence of the static description to have a conjunction like "and" so that the objects when listed don't appear from nowhere.

As an example, a room may have this static description:

...You are surrounded by tall walls with Roman art hanging upon them.

And let's say that there are moveable objects in the room, such as a plant. Then the computer's response might be

...You are surrounded by tall walls with Roman art hanging upon them.

There is a plant in the East corner of the room.

A better algorithm for printing out descriptions might take into consideration that there is a moveable object in the room and then print the description out like this:

...You are surrounded by tall walls with Roman art hanging upon them and there is a plant in the East corner of the room.

Although the sentence is slightly artificial, rough, and the computer wouldn't know the difference between a plant and a ogre, at least the sentences are somewhat connected together. This is one of the "tricks" in making good text games. You must "work" the output sentences to make them read as if they aren't being printed out from a static database.

Of course, there is more than parsing the text and trying to satisfy the request. The game must have some kind of data structure to represent the universe and the objects within the universe. This representation, whatever it may be, must also have some kind of valid geometrical coherence because as the player moves around, he/she will expect to find a key where he dropped it. This means that many times the universe will have to be modeled as a 2D/3D vector map or cell map so that the player can be moved around in a data representation that has some geometrical relation to the virtual space the player thinks he's in. Next the game has to have some kind of structure that contains the "state" of the player. This could mean his health, position, inventory, and position in the game universe.

Finally, other aspects of the game have to be implemented, such as a goal and the enemies (if there are any). The goal may be as simple as finding an enchanted chalice and putting it somewhere. Or the goal may be as complex as solving some kind of puzzle with a question and answer dialog between the player and some creature in the game. The creatures in the game will be implemented as data structures only; however, these data structures can move around the universe data structure, move objects, eat food, and attack the player (possibly). All these aspects of the text game must be implemented in a way so that the illusion of a real environment is upheld. This means that you should assume that the player can't see the game, but everything better make sense or else!

Let's re-iterate all the components of a text game by studying Figure 14.1. Referring to the figure, we see that there is an input section that parses the player's commands and then tries to execute these commands. The parser only understands a specific vocabulary and, furthermore, the sentences created with this vocabulary are limited by the "language" designed by the game designer. Next there is a set of data structures holding the representation of the universe, the position of the objects, the description strings for sights, sounds, and smells. Also there is the representation of the player and his inventory along with the representation of the enemies in the game. Finally, there are a million or so functions, rules, and little details that make it all work, let's cover a few of them!

FIGURE 14.1
The components of
a text game.

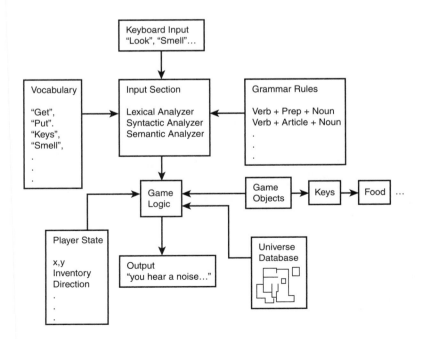

Getting Input from the Outside World

Since a text-based game uses the keyboard as its sole input device, we should take some time to make this as easy as possible. The player will be typing in sentences to command the text game to do something. This seems simple enough, but the problem is how to read these sentences. The standard function scanf() won't work correctly because of the possibility of whitespace and multiple arguments. We need a function that will get a line of input regardless of the characters that make up the line. This input will stop if and only if the user hits the Enter key. At this point, the sentence will be passed to the next piece of software in the parser chain. So the question is how to get a single line of text without the input line editor making decisions for us? The answer is to use single-character input and build up a string until the carriage return is pressed. This can be done using the getch() function with a tests for backspace and carriage return. Listing 14.1 is a typical line input function.

LISTING 14.1 A Single-Line Input Function with Editing Capability

```
char *Get_Line(char *buffer)
{
// this function gets a single line of input and tolerates white space

int c,index=0;

// loop while user hasn't hit return
while((c=getch())!=13)
    {
// implement backspace
    if (c==8 && index>0)
       {

       buffer[--index] = ' ';
       printf("%c %c",8,8);

       } // end if backspace
    else
    if (c>=32 && c<=122)
       {
       buffer[index++] = c;
       printf("%c",c);

       } // end if in printable range

    } // end while

// terminate string
buffer[index] = 0;
```

LISTING 14.1   Continued

```
// return pointer to buffer or NULL
if (strlen(buffer)==0)
   return(NULL);
else
return(buffer);

} // end Get_Line
```

The function takes as a parameter a pointer to a buffer where the inputted string will be placed after the function executes. During execution, `Get_Line()` will allow the user to input a line of text and also to edit errors via the backspace key. As the characters are input, they are echoed out to the screen, so the user can see what he/she is typing. When the user hits the Enter key, the string is terminated with a NULL and the function ends.

Once the user has input the string, the game is ready to parse it. The parsing process has many phases (which we will cover shortly), but before we can parse the sentence and see what it means, we must know what the language is and how it is constructed.

Language Analysis and Parsing

Before the user can type anything, we must define a "language" that he/she must stay within. This language consists of vocabulary and a set of rules (grammar). Together, these conventions create the overall language. Now, the whole idea of a text game is to use the English language. This means that the vocabulary should be English words and the grammar should be legal English grammar. The first request is easy. The second request is much harder. Contrary to the belief of many of my English teachers, the English language is a terribly complex language system. It's full of contradictions, points of view, different ways of doing things, and so on. In general, the English language is not robust and exact like computer languages. This means that as text-game programmers, we may have to allow the user only a very small subset of the possible grammatical constructions that could be made with a given vocabulary.

This may seem like a problem, but it's not. A player of a text game gets very comfortable very quickly with a more robust, well-defined subset of English and finds that the sentences are concise and to the point. With all that in mind, the first thing that any game needs is a vocabulary. This is constructed in an ongoing manner as the game is written. The reason for this is that as the game is being written, the designer may feel that another game object needs to be added such as a "zot." This would mean that "zot" would have to be added to the vocabulary if the player were ever to be able to refer to it. Secondly, the designer might decide that more prepositions are needed to make some sentences more natural. For example, to drop an object, the player might type:

"drop the keys"

The meaning of this is very clear. The word "drop" is a verb, "the" is a worthless article, and "keys" is a noun. However, it might be more natural for the player to type:

"drop down the keys"

or

"drop the keys down"

Regardless of whether these two sentences are as "good," the fact of the matter is this is how people talk and that is all that is important. Therefore, the vocabulary will need words for all the objects in the game (nouns) along with a few good *prepositions*. As a rule of thumb, start with the prepositions of everything you can do to a mountain and that will usually suffice. Table 14.2 is a list of common prepositions used in text games.

TABLE 14.2   Some Good Prepositions

from
on
in
down
up
behind
into
before
at

The next class of words needed in our vocabulary is the *action verbs*. These are the words that mean "do something." They are usually followed by a word or phrase that describes what the action is taking place on. For example, in a text game, the action verb "move" is very useful in navigating the player about the universe. A set of possible sentences using "move" as an action verb might be

1. move north

2. move to the north

3. move northward

Sentence number 1 is simple enough. It says to move to the north. The second sentence also says to move to the north, but it has a prepositional phrase "to the north." Finally, sentence number 3 uses the adjective "northward" to mean the same thing. Technically, it could be argued that each of the sentences could mean different things, but to us as game programmers, they all mean the same thing. And that is to take a step in the direction of north. Therefore, we see that the use of articles such as "the" and prepositions are absolutely needed to make the sentences have a little variety even if they all mean the same thing.

Back to the subject of action verbs. The game should have a large list of action verbs (many of which can be used by themselves with implied objects). For example, say that the vocabulary for your game had the action verb "smell" in it. You might say,

"smell the sandwich"

which is clear. However, the command

smell

isn't so clear. Yes, it's clear what the player wants to do, but what he/she wants to smell is ambiguous. This is where the concept of context comes into play. Since there is no direct or indirect object given to "smell," the game will assume that the player means the exterior environment or the last object acted upon. For example, if the player just picked up a rock, and then requested the game engine to "smell," the game might reply, "the rock?" and then the player would say "yes" and the proper description string would be printed. On the other hand, if the player hadn't recently picked up anything then the single command "smell" might elicit a general description of the smell within the room that the player is standing in.

After you have decided on all the action verbs, nouns, prepositions, and articles that can be used in the language, the rules for the language itself must be generated. These rules describe the possible sentence constructions that are legal, and this information is used by the syntactical analyzer along with the *semantic analyzer* to compute the meaning of the sentence along with its validity. As an example, let's generate a vocabulary along with the rules (grammar) that govern it (see Table 14.3).

TABLE 14.3   A Sample Vocabulary

Word	Used As	Type Name
rock	Noun	OBJECT
food	Noun	OBJECT
table	Noun	OBJECT
key	Noun	OBJECT
get	Verb	VERB

TABLE 14.3 Continued

Word	Used As	Type Name
put	Verb	VERB
the	Article	ARTICLE
on	Preposition	PREP
onto	Preposition	PREP

The "type name" is used to group similar word types, so they can be worked with more efficiently.

Now that we have the vocabulary, let's construct the language with it. This means creating the rules for legal sentences. Not all these sentences may make sense, but they will all be legal. These rules are usually referred to as "the syntax of the language" or the ***productions***. I prefer to call them ***productions*** (see Table 14.4).

TABLE 14.4 The Productions of Glish

OBJECT->"rock"|"food"|"table"|"key"
VERB->"get"|"put"
ARTICLE->"the"|NULL
PREP->"on"|"onto"|NULL
SENTENCE->VERB+ARTICLE+OBJECT+PREP+ARTICLE+OBJECT

Where the "\|" means logical OR, "+" means concatenate, and NULL means NULL string.

Now if you try to build sentences using the production for "SENTENCE," then there are quite a few sentences that can be constructed. However, some of them may not make any semantic sense. For example, the sentence

"put the rock onto the table"

makes perfect sense, but the sentence

"get the rock onto the table"

is unclear; it could mean place the rock on the table. This is where one of two things must be done: Either more productions must be incorporated into the language to separate specific verbs and their constructions, or the game code must test to see if sentences make "sense." To make sure you see how the productions are used, let's do a few examples of legal sentences (see Table 14.5).

TABLE 14.5 Some Sample Sentences and Their Clarity of Meaning Ranked 1–10 (with 10 Meaning Very Clear)

Sentence	Clarity	Legality
"put rock"	4	Yes
"put the rock"	4	Yes
"get the key"	8	Yes
"put down the food"	10	No

(Note: There is no production for placing a preposition after the verb and "down" isn't in the vocabulary.)

"put the food on rock"	7	Yes
"put the rock down onto table"	7	No

(Note: There are two prepositions concatenated after each other following the object; there is no production for this form.)

As you can see from the table, if a production doesn't exist for a particular sentence form, then the sentence is illegal regardless of whether it makes sense. This is because the computer will not know that it is a legal sentence unless there is an implementation of the production or syntactic rule that governs the construction of the desired sentence. To put it another way, you must program in every single sentence type as a logical construction of the elements in the vocabulary, and you must be able to test each sentence to see if it follows the production rules. Of course, I was joking about the "clearly" part!

Once the sentence has been broken down and the meaning is starting to become clear, then comes the semantic checking. This phase tests if a valid sentence makes sense. For example, the sentence

"get the key onto the table"

is a legal construction, but it is unclear what the user wants. It should probably be flagged as unclear and the user should be requested to say it in another way, possibly:

"put the key on table"

The question that should be burning in your mind is, "How do I make the program do what the sentence says to do after I have figured out what the user wanted to say?" The answer is with ***action functions***. Action functions are called based on the action verb of the sentence. These action functions can act as syntax checkers, semantic checkers, or a combination of both or neither (it's up to you). But, one thing the action function should do is make something happen. This is accomplished by having a separate function for each action function. The action functions themselves are responsible for figuring out what object(s) the action verb is supposed to be applied to and then performing the requested action. For example, the action function for the verb "get" might step through the following set of operations:

- Extract the "object" (noun) from the sentence.
- Using "vision" to see if the object that is being requested to be picked up is within the reach of the player.
- If the object is within reach, then it is retrieved. At this point, the universe database and the player's inventory are updated to reflect this action.

The first step (extracting the object) is accomplished by "consuming" words that don't change the meaning of the sentence. For instance, the prepositions and articles in our language Glish don't change the meaning much of any particular sentence. Take a look below:

"put the key"

The article "the" can be taken out of the sentence without changing the meaning. This consumption of irrelevant words is transparent to the player, but allows him/her to write sentences that make more sense from his point of view. Even though our language parser might like

"put key on table"

a human player may feel more comfortable with

"put the key onto the table"

In any case, the action function will take care of this logic. Once the action function has figured out what needs to be done, doing it is easy. In the case of the original example of getting something, the object would be taken out of the universe database and inserted into the player's inventory, where the player's inventory might just be an array of characters or structures that list the objects the player is holding. For example, in the game Shadow Land, the player's inventory and everything about him is contained within the single structure shown in Listing 14.2.

LISTING 14.2   The Structure That Holds the Player in Shadow Land

```
// this structure holds everything pertaining to the player
typedef struct player_typ
        {
        char name[16];    // name of player
        int x,y;          // position of player
        int direction;    // direction of player, east,west north,south
```

LISTING 14.2 Continued

```
        char inventory[8]; // objects player is holding (like pockets)
        int num_objects;   // number of objects player is holding

    } player, *player_ptr;
```

The inventory in this case is an array of characters that represent the objects the player is holding. For example, 's' stands for sandwich. This data structure is just an example; you may want to do it differently.

In essence, all a text game has to do is break a sentence down, figure out the action requested, call the appropriate action function(s), and perform the action. Performing the action is accomplished by updating data structures, changing coordinates, and printing out text. The majority of the problem in a text game is the translation of the input command string into something the computer can deal with, such as numbers (as you have probably surmised). This process is called *tokenization* or *lexical analysis* and is the next topic of discussion.

Lexical Analysis

When the player types in a sentence using the vocabulary we supply him with, the sentence must be converted from strings into tokens (integers) so that syntactic and semantic phases of analysis can proceed. The reason lexical analysis is necessary is due to the fact that working with strings is much more difficult, time consuming, and memory intensive than working with tokens (which are usually integers). Hence, one of the functions of the lexical analyzer is to convert the input sentence from string form to token form. There are three parts to this translation. The first part of lexical analysis is simply separating the "words" in a sentence and extracting them. By words, it is meant strings of characters separated by "white space." White space is usually considered to be the space character (ASCII 32) and the horizontal tab (ASCII 9). For example, the sentence

"This   is   a test."

has four words (tokens). They are

1. "This"
2. "is"
3. "a"
4. "test"

We also see that periods will have to be taken into consideration since they separate sentences. If the user is going to be inputting only a single line at a time, he may or may not put a period at the end of each input sentence. Alas, the period can be thought of as white space. On the other hand, if it is legal for the player to type multiple commands separated by a period or other phrase separator like the colon ":" or semi-colon ";" then extra logic may be needed since the sentences should be parsed separately. For example, if the period is assumed to be white space in a single sentence construction, as in

"This is a test."

then the meaning to the parser is the same as

"This is a test"

However, when two sentences are placed next to each other with the period being interpreted as white space, then the following problem can occur. This sentence

"This is a test. Get the book."

will be interpreted as

"This is a test get the book"

which has no meaning.

The moral of the story is to be careful what you elect to call "white space" and what you don't. Moving on, we need to figure out a way to extract the "words" in a sentence that are separated by white space. The C library actually has a string function to do this, called strtok(), but it doesn't work properly on some compilers and we will summarily dismiss it since we like to re-invent the wheel.

What we need is a function that will separate the words out for us. This is actually a fairly easy function to write as long as you take your time and take all the cases into consideration that can occur, such as NULL terminators, white space, and the return character. Anyway, Listing 14.3 is one such implementation of a token extraction function.

LISTING 14.3   A Function to Extract Tokens from an Input Sentence (Excerpted from Shadow Land)

```
int Get_Token(char *input,char *output,int *current_pos)
{

int index,    // loop index and working index
    start,    // points to start of token
    end;      // points to end of token

// set current positions
index=start=end=*current_pos;
```

LISTING 14.3   Continued

```
// eat white space
while(isspace(input[index]) || ispunct(input[index]))
    {
    index++;
    } // end while

// test if end of string found
if (input[index]==NULL)
   {
   // emit nothing

   strcpy(output,"");
   return(0);

   } // end if no more tokens

// at this point, we must have a token of some kind, so find the end of it
start = index; // mark front of it
end   = index;

// find end of Token
while(!isspace(input[end]) && !ispunct(input[end]) && input[end]!=NULL)
    {
    end++;
    } // end while

// build up output string
for (index=start; index<end; index++)
    {
    output[index-start] = toupper(input[index]);
    } // end copy string

// place terminator
output[index-start] = 0;

// update current string position
*current_pos  = end;

return(end);
} // end Get_Token
```

The function takes three inputs: an input string to be parsed, an output string that holds the token extracted, and the current position in the string that is being processed. For example, let's see how a string can be parsed using the function. First we need to declare a couple of variables:

```
int position=0;  // used as index from call to call
                 // to keep track of current string
                 // position
```

Hardcore Game Programming

```
char output[16]; // output string

// begin program
Get_Token("This is a test",output,&position);
```

After this call, the variable `output` would have a "This" in it and `position` would be equal to 4. Let's do one more call...

```
Get_Token("This is a test",output,&position);
```

Now, the variable `output` would have "is" in it and `position` would now be updated to 7. If `Get_Token()` is repeatedly called in this fashion, each "word" in the sentence will be extracted and be placed in the buffer `output` (of course, each previous string in `output` will be overwritten by the next token word). Consequently, we now have a method of obtaining the "words" that make up a sentence. The next task is to convert these strings into integer tokens so that they can be worked with more easily. This is done with a function that has a table of strings along with the token for each of the vocabulary words. A search through the table is done for each word and when and if the string is found in the table, then it is converted to an integer token (see Figure 14.2).

FIGURE 14.2

A word being tested to see if it's in the vocabulary of the game.

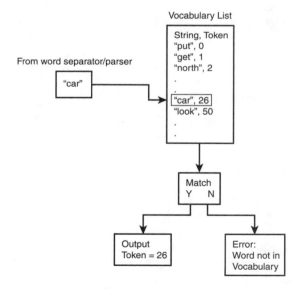

During this phase of lexical analysis is where the vocabulary checking is done. If a word is not in the vocabulary, then it is not in the language and hence is illegal. As an example, the game Shadow Land has the following data structure to hold each word in the vocabulary (see Listing 14.4).

LISTING 14.4 The Data Structure for a Token in Shadow Land

```
// this is the structure for a single token
typedef struct token_typ
       {
       char symbol[16];    // the string that represents the token
       int value;          // the integer value of the token
        } token, *token_ptr;
```

This structure has a place for both the string and a value to be associated with it. The string is the actual vocabulary word, while the value is arbitrary. However, the values for tokens should be mutually exclusive unless you wish to make words synonyms. Using the above structure and some defines, you can create a vocabulary table in very compact form that can be used as a reference in the lexical analysis to convert words to tokens and to check their validity. Listing 14.5 is the vocabulary table used in Shadow Land.

LISTING 14.5 The Static Initialization of the Vocabulary Table for Shadow Land

```
// this is the entire "language" of the language in Shadow Land.
token language[MAX_TOKENS] = {

{"LAMP",       OBJECT_LAMP       },
{"SANDWICH",   OBJECT_SANDWICH },
{"KEYS",       OBJECT_KEYS       },
{"EAST",       DIR_1_EAST        },
{"WEST",       DIR_1_WEST        },
{"NORTH",      DIR_1_NORTH       },
{"SOUTH",      DIR_1_SOUTH       },
{"FORWARD",    DIR_2_FORWARD     },
{"BACKWARD",   DIR_2_BACKWARD    },
{"RIGHT",      DIR_2_RIGHT       },
{"LEFT",       DIR_2_LEFT        },
{"MOVE",     ACTION_MOVE      },
{"TURN",     ACTION_TURN      },
{"SMELL",    ACTION_SMELL       },
{"LOOK",     ACTION_LOOK       },
{"LISTEN",   ACTION_LISTEN       },
{"PUT",        ACTION_PUT        },
{"GET",        ACTION_GET        },
{"EAT",        ACTION_EAT        },
{"INVENTORY", ACTION_INVENTORY},
{"WHERE",    ACTION_WHERE       },
{"EXIT",       ACTION_EXIT        },
{"THE",        ART_THE          },
{"IN",         PREP_IN           },
{"ON",         PREP_ON           },
{"TO",       PREP_TO        },
{"DOWN",       PREP_DOWN         },
};
```

As you see, there are character strings followed by defined symbols (the value of which are irrelevant as long as they are different). You will notice the defined symbols have familiar prefixes such as PREP (preposition), ART (article), and ACTION (verb).

Once a table like this exists in some such form, the token strings can be compared to the elements in the table and the character strings representing the tokens can be converted to integers. At that point, the input sentence will be a string of numbers, which can be processed in a more convenient fashion. A sample *tokenizer* is shown in Listing 14.6. It is also from the game Shadow Land, but if you have seen one, you have seen them all. Don't worry about the defined constants, just concentrate on the overall operation of the function.

LISTING 14.6 A Function That Converts Token Strings of an Input Sentence into Integer Tokens

```
int Extract_Tokens(char *string)
{
// this function breaks the input string down into tokens and fills up
// the global sentence array with the tokens so that it can be processed

int curr_pos=0,     // current position in string
    curr_token=0,   // current token number
    found,          // used to flag if the token is valid in language
    index;          // loop index

char output[16];
// reset number of tokens and clear the sentence out
num_tokens=0;

for (index=0; index<8; index++)
    sentence[index]=0;

// extract all the words in the sentence (tokens)
while(Get_Token(string,output,&curr_pos))
    {
    // test to see if this is a valid token
    for (index=0,found=0; index<NUM_TOKENS; index++)
        {
        // do we have a match?
        if (strcmp(output,language[index].symbol)==0)
            {
            // set found flag
            found=1;

            // enter token into sentence
            sentence[curr_token++] = language[index].value;
            break;
            } // end if
```

LISTING 14.6 Continued

```
        } // end for index

        // test if token was part of language (grammar)
        if (!found)
            {
            printf("\n%s, I don't know what \"%s\" means.",you.name
                                                ,output);

            // failure
            return(0);

            } // end if not found

        // else
        num_tokens++;
    } // end while
} // end Extract_Tokens
```

The function operates with an input string passed to it containing the user's commands. The function then proceeds to break the sentence down into separate "words" using the Get_Token() function. Each word is then scanned for in the vocabulary table, and when a match is made, the word is converted into a token and inserted into a token sentence, which is basically a version of the input sentence in token form (integers instead of strings). If the "word" is not found in the vocabulary table, then there is a problem and the code will emit an error. I have highlighted this section in the function above, so that you may see how easy it is.

Let's take a brief detour for a moment to cover two topics. The first is error handling. This is always an important part of any program, and I can't emphasis how important it is especially in a text-based game where a bad input can "trickle" down into the bowels of the game engine and logic and really mess things up (you Perl scripters should know something about this). Therefore, it can't hurt to have too much error checking in a text game. Even if you are 99% sure an input to a function should be of the correct form, always test that one last case to make sure.

Secondly, you will notice that I use very primitive data structures. Sure, a linked list or binary tree might be a more elegant solution, but is it really worth it for a dozen or so vocabulary words? The answer is no. My rule of thumb is that the data structure should fit the problem and arrays fit a lot of small problems. When the problems get large, then it's time to bring in the big guns such as linked lists, B-trees, graphs, and so forth. But for small problems, get the code working with simple data structures or else you will be forever trying to figure out why you keep getting NULL pointer errors, GP faults, and other bothersome features!

All right, now that we finally know how to convert the sentence into tokens, it's time for the syntactic and semantic analysis phases—let's cover the syntactic phase first.

Syntactical Analysis

Hold on tight because here is where things start getting a bit cloudy. Strictly speaking, syntactic analysis is defined in compiler texts as the phase where the input token stream is converted into grammatical phrases so that these phrases can be processed. Since the languages we have been considering for implementation are fairly simple and have simple vocabularies, this highly general and elusive definition needs to be pruned down to mean something in our context. As far as we are concerned, syntactic analysis will mean "making sense out of the sentence." This means applying the verbs, determining the objects, extracting the prepositions, articles, and so on.

The syntactic analysis phase of our games will occur in parallel with the action(s) processing of the sentence. This is totally acceptable, and many compilers and interpreters are designed in this way. The code is generated or interpreted "on the fly." We have already seen what the syntactic phase of analysis looks like. It is accomplished by calling functions that are responsible for all the action verbs in the language. Then these action functions further process the remainder of the input sentence, which is already in token form, and then try to do whatever is supposed to be done. For example, a syntactic parser for a text game might begin by figuring out which action verb began the sentence and then calling an appropriate action function to deal with the rest of the sentence.

Of course, the rest of the sentence could be processed and tested for validity before the call to the action function, but this isn't necessary. I prefer to place the burden of further processing on the action functions. My philosophy is this: Each action function is like an object that operates on a single kind of sentence. This single sentence is one that starts with a specific word. We shouldn't hold a single function responsible for checking the syntax of all the possible sentences before making the call to the appropriate action function.

As an example, Listing 14.7 is the function used in Shadow Land to dispatch each sentence to the proper action function. The single purpose of this function is to look at the first word in the sentence (which is a token, of course) and then vector to the correct action function. At that point, it's the action function's job to check the rest of the syntax of the sentence. Here is the action dispatcher.

Listing 14.7   The Function Used in Shadow Land to Call the Action Functions Based on the Action Verb Used in the Input Sentence

```
void Verb_Parser(void)
{
// this function breaks down the sentence and based on the verb calls the
```

LISTING **14.7**   Continued

```
// appropriate "method" or function to apply that verb
// note: syntactic analysis could be done here, but I decided to place it
// in the action verb functions, so that you can see the way the errors are
// detected for each verb (even though there is a lot of redundancy)

// what is the verb?

switch(sentence[FIRST_WORD])
      {
      case ACTION_MOVE:
            {
            // call the appropriate function
            Verb_MOVE();
            } break;

      case ACTION_TURN:
            {
            // call the appropriate function
            Verb_TURN();
            } break;

      case ACTION_SMELL:
            {
            // call the appropriate function

            Verb_SMELL();
            } break;

      case ACTION_LOOK:
            {
            // call the appropriate function
            Verb_LOOK();
            } break;

      case ACTION_LISTEN:
            {
            // call the appropriate function
            Verb_LISTEN();
            } break;

      case ACTION_PUT:
            {
            // call the appropriate function
            Verb_PUT();
            } break;

      case ACTION_GET:
            {
            // call the appropriate function
            Verb_GET();
            } break;
```

LISTING 14.7 Continued

```
    case ACTION_EAT:
        {
        // call the appropriate function
        Verb_EAT();

        } break;

    case ACTION_WHERE:
        {
        // call the appropriate function
        Verb_WHERE();
        } break;

    case ACTION_INVENTORY:
        {
        // call the appropriate function
        Verb_INVENTORY();
        } break;

    case ACTION_EXIT:
        {
        // call the appropriate function
        Verb_EXIT();
        } break;

    default:
        {
        printf("\n%s, you must start a sentence with an action verb!",
                you.name);
        return;
        } break;

    } // end switch

} // end Verb_Parser
```

The function is beautifully simple. It looks at the first word in the sentence (which by definition of the language better be a verb) and then calls the corresponding action function. For a graphical representation of this, take a look at Figure 14.3. The next part of parsing analysis is the semantic analysis phase.

Semantic Analysis

Semantic analysis is where most of the error checking takes place. However, since we are doing the syntactic analysis "on the fly" along with making things happen in the game, this responsibility is merged into the action function during syntactic analysis. Syntactic analysis is supposed to break down the sentence into its meaning and then semantic analysis is used to determine if this meaning makes sense (getting confused yet?!). As you can see, this business of syntactic and semantic analysis seems to be almost circular and therefore, again we will cut to the quick and make a hard and fast rule. In a text-based game, the syntactic and semantic analyses are done simultaneously. In other words, **as the sentence's meaning is being computed, the sentence is tested to make sense.**

FIGURE 14.3
An action verb being dispatched to the proper action function.

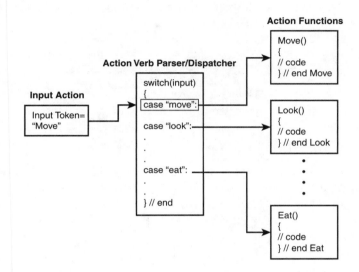

I hope you understand this very subtle concept. If it helps, it's kind of like snow skiing. It easy once you can do it, but until then you have no idea how to do it.

Putting All the Pieces Together

We have all the components of the complete parser and text interpreter engine. Let's see how all the pieces go together to form the backbone of a text game (see Figure 14.4). Referring to the figure, we see that the input stream is broken into words by the front end of the lexical analyzer, then the word strings are converted into integer tokens. The token stream is then fed into the front end of the syntactic parser, which "sends" the sentence of tokens to the proper action function. The action function then tries to apply the action requested by the player to the object(s) in the sentence. As the action is being applied, syntax checking and semantic integrity are also being tested simultaneously by the action function.

The important concept to grasp is that all the input parsing, syntax checking, and so forth are for the single reason of trying to figure out what the player wants to do. Once this is determined, then the coding is straightforward. The only caveat is that the actions performed are acted upon internal data structures. And the only output is text.

Remember, the player only "views" the game universe by way of strings of static or synthesized text that the game outputs as each "move" is made in the game. Hopefully, you have a grasp of how the text input phase of a text game works. If I were to leave the subject now, you should be able to make a text game, but instead let's cover some techniques to control and manipulate other aspects of a text game. However, be warned these techniques are illustrative only and I'm sure there are better, different, and more clever ways of doing them.

FIGURE 14.4

The sections of the input parser.

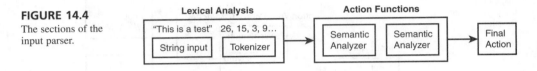

Remember the player only "views" the game universe by way of strings of static or

Representing the Universe

The universe in a text game can be represented in many ways. Whatever representation is used, it should have some kind of geometrical relationship to the virtual environment the player is running around in. For example, if you created a full 3-D space text adventure then you might have a 3-D model in a database. Even though the player would never see the world visually, all collision detection and motion would be done within the 3-D model. Since this book is primarily about 2-D games, we'll make our representations more flat. For a moment, I want you to think of a one-story house. Imagine the roof is removed and you are looking down at the house from above (you're in a hover craft; see Figure 14.5). You could see the rooms of the house, the objects, and the people moving around. This is the kind of representation we want to use for our text games.

FIGURE 14.5

A top-down "blue print" view of an environment.

How do we implement a data structure of such a model? It can be done in two ways. We could use a vector-based model based on lines and polygons. There would be a database of this geometry and the game code would use it to move the game objects around. This technique is fine, but a bit hard to visualize since you would be working in pure "vector space." A better approach would be to have a 2-D matrix of cells that represented the game universe.

Admittedly, you will never "see" the world, but having an actual 2-D floor map that can be accessed very simply will make the game code very simple to write. For example, the game Shadow Land uses a 2-D matrix of characters to represent the game universe (which is my old apartment). Take a look at Listing 14.8 to see the actual data structure used in the game.

LISTING 14.8   The Data Structure Used to Represent the Game Universe of Shadow Land

```
// this array holds the geometry of the universe

// l - living room
// b - bedroom
// k - kitchen
// w - washroom
// h - hall way
// r - restroom
// e - entry way
// o - office


//                              ^
//                           NORTH
// < WEST                    EAST >
//                           SOUTH
//                              v

char *universe_geometry[NUM_ROWS]=
{"******************************",
"*111111111*bbbbbbbbbbbbbbbbbbb*",
"*1111111111*bbbbbbbbbbbbbbbbbb*",
"*11111111111*bbbbbbbbbbbbbbbbb*",
"*111111111111*bbbbbbbbbbbbbbbb*",
"*111111111111*bbbbbbbbbbbbbbbb*",
"*111111111111*bbbbbbbbbbbbbbbb*",
"*111111111111*bbbbbbbbbbbbbbbb*",
"*111111111111*bbbbbbbbbbbbbbbb*",
"*111111111111*bbbbbbbbbbbbbbbb*",
"*111111111111*bbbbbbbbbbbbbbbb*",
"*111111111111*bbbb*rrr*********",
"*11111111111lhhhhh*rrrrrrrrrrr*",
"*11111111111lhhhhh*rrrrrrrrrrr*",
"*111111111lhhh******rrrrrrrrrr*",
"*********hhhh*rrrrrrrrrrrrrrrr*",
```

LISTING **14.8** Continued

```
"*kkkkkkk*hhhh*rrrrrrrrrrrrrrrr*",
"*kkkkkkk*hhhh*rrrrrrrrrrrrrrrr*",
"*kkkkkkk*hhhh*rrrrrrrrrrrrrrrr*",
"*kkkkkkkhhhhh*****************",
"*kkkkkkkhhhhhhhhhhhwwwwwwwwwww*",
"*kkkkkkkhhhhhhhhhhhwwwwwwwwwww*",
"*kkkkkkk*hhhhhhhhhhwwwwwwwwwww*",
"*kkkkkkk*hhhh*ooooo************",
"*kkkkkkk*hhhh*ooooooooooooooooo*",
"*kkkkkkk*hhhh*ooooooooooooooooo*",
"*kkkkkk*hhhhh*ooooooooooooooooo*",
"*******hhhhhh*ooooooooooooooooo*",
"*eeeeeeeeeee*ooooooooooooooooo*",
"*eeeeeeeeeee*ooooooooooooooooo*",
"*eeeeeeeeeee*ooooooooooooooooo*",
"******************************",};
```

It might be a bit hard to see the rooms due to the print font, but if you blur your eyes a little, you will be able to see all the rooms. You will notice that walls are defined by the '*' character and different rooms are defined by placing a single character within the confines of the room, such as 'o' for office. Placing characters in the each room that describe the room type is helpful in determining where the player is at any time. If the player is placed at any (x,y) position in the map, then the code that prints out "where" the player is only has to index into the array and look at the character the player is standing on. Then, using this information, the appropriate text strings can be displayed.

Placing Objects in the World

Objects in the game world can be done using two main techniques. The first technique is to have an array or linked list of objects where each element defines the object, its position, and any other relevant properties. The only problem with this technique is that when a player is in a room and asks to "look," then the object list must be accessed and visibility of each object must be determined. Also, collision detection, "putting," and "getting" are more complex when the objects are stored in this way. An easier method that is related to the way the universe is defined is to have another 2-D matrix of characters with the same geometry as the universe map. However, instead of walls and floor tiles within it, the objects are placed in it. Then you can imagine that both data structures are synthetically overlaid by the game code. For example, Listing 14.9 is the object placement map for Shadow Land.

LISTING 14.9   The Object Placement Database for Shadow Land

```
// this array holds the objects within the universe

// l - lamp
// s - sandwich
// k - keys
//                    ^
//                 NORTH
// < WEST          EAST >
///         SOUTH
//              v

char *universe_objects[NUM_ROWS]=
{"                              ",
 "   l                       k  ",
 "                              ",
 "                              ",
 "                              ",
 "                              ",
 "                              ",
 "                              ",
 "                              ",
 "   l                          ",
 "                              ",
 "                              ",
 "                              ",
 "                              ",
 "                              ",
 "                              ",
 "                              ",
 "                              ",
 "                              ",
 "                              ",
 "                              ",
 "                              ",
 "                              ",
 "    s                         ",
 "                              ",
 "                              ",
 "                              ",
 "                              ",
 "          s                   ",
 "                       l  ",
 "                              ",
 "                         ",};
```

As you can see, the object map is very sparse, and it should be since it contains only
the objects in the universe. However, determining if the player is near an object or
even on top of one is very simple since there is a 1-1 relationship between the geometry
of the universe, the universe of objects, and the position of the player. The only

drawback to using the "cell" technique to represent a game universe for a text game is that the cell world has only a finite number of cells and thus positions within the universe, but this is really a small inconvenience and the player will never know!

Making Things Happen

We previously learned that making things happen merely means to print out some text or change some values in data structures such as the position of the player. A text game is really just a "live" database that is accessed and modified as the game is played. Frankly, an arcade game is also, but there is a more complex output device being used (the screen) and arcade games must be in real time. Text games wait for the user to input a text string before doing anything. When this "waiting" is taking place, the code is stuck in the line input function and the game universe is "motionless" during this period.

Moving Around

Motion in a text game is accomplished by changing the position of the player's character in the game. This is usually as simple as modifying a couple variables. For example, if the player typed

"move north"

the computer would output

"You take a few steps..."

The game code might decrement the Y position of the player's character (north is in the negative Y direction) and then that would be it. Of course, the player's position would be tested to see if the player stepped on something, hit a wall, or fell off a cliff, but the actual motion is accomplished with only a couple variable changes. This simplicity stems from the fact that the player is plopped down in the 2-D map and is just a square that can either move East, West, North, or South.

The Inventory System

The inventory system in a text game is a list that contains a description and tally of all the objects that the player is holding on himself. This list can be an array, a linked list, or whatever. If the objects are complex, then the list might be a list of structures. In Shadow Land, the inventory is so simple that nothing more than an array of characters was used to hold the inventory. The player can have a sandwich 's', a set of keys 'k', and a lamp 'l'. If the player is holding one or more of these objects then, in a character array called inventory[], the characters representing these objects are stored. Then when the player asks to see what he is holding, a simple traversal of this list and a few output strings are all that is needed.

But how does the player get the objects? Well, he picks them up from the game universe. For example, if a player was in a room and "saw" the keys, then he might request the game to "get" the keys. The game would then "pick up" the keys by removing the 'k' from the object universe, replacing the spot the keys were in with a blank, and then inserting a 'k' into the inventory list of the player. Of course, making the computer "see" what's in a room and ascertain if the player is within reach is a bit complex, but you get the idea.

Implementing Sight, Sound, and Smell

The implementation of the human senses in a text game is the most challenging of all since the player can't really see, hear, or smell. This means that apart from the algorithmic considerations, the output descriptions must be full of adjectives, descriptives, qualifiers, and so forth to create mental images. Implementing sounds and smells are the easiest since they are not focused senses. By focused, I mean that if a specific room has a general smell, then the player should smell it at any location of the room. Similarly, the same goes for sounds. If the room has music playing, then the music will be heard in any part of the room. Vision is the most complex because it is more focused than sound and smell and is much harder to implement. Let's take a look at all three senses and see how to implement them.

Sound

There are two types of sounds in a text game: *ambient* and *dynamic*. Ambient sounds are the sounds that are always in a room, and dynamic sounds are sounds that can enter and leave a room. First, let's talk about the ambient sounds. To implement ambient sounds, there should be a data structure that contains a set of descriptive strings for each room. Then when the player asks to "listen," these strings are printed out by testing the room the player is standing within and using this information to select the correct set of strings. For example, if the player types in **listen** in a machine shop, then this might be the monologue he/she is presented with:

What do you want to do? Listen

...You hear the sounds of large machines all around you. The sounds are so strong and piercing you feel them in your teeth. However, beyond all the sounds of the large machines, somewhere in the background you here a peculiar hum, but you're not sure what it is...

The data structure containing these static strings is up to you, but I suggest either an array of strings with a field that describes which room the string is for, or an array of structures with a structure for each room. For example, Listing 14.10 is the ambient sound string data structure used for Shadow Land along with the sounds for the game.

Hardcore Game Programming

LISTING 14.10   The Static Data Structure Used to Contain the Informational Strings in Shadow Land Along with the Ambient Sounds in the Game

```
// this is the structure used to hold a single string that is used to
// describe something in the game like a smell, sight, sound...

typedef struct info_string_typ
        {
        char type;        // the type of info string i.e. what does it describe
        char string[100]; // the actual description string
        } info_string, *info_string_ptr;

// these info strings hold the smells in each room
info_string smells[]={

{'l',"You smell the sweet odor of Jasmine with/
 an undertone of potpourri. "},
{'b',"The sweet smell of perfume dances within/
 your nostrils...Realities possibly. "},
{'k',"You take a deep breath and your senses/
 are tantalized with the smell of"},
{'k',"tender breasts of chicken marinating in/
 a garlic sauce. Also, there is "},
{'k',"a sweet berry smell emanating from the oven./
                          "},
{'w',"You are almost overwhelmed by the smell of/
 bathing fragrance as you"},
{'w',"inhale.                                   /
                  "},
{'h',"You smell nothing to make note of. "},
{'r',"Your nose is filled with steam and the smell/
 of baby oil... "},
{'e',"You smell pine possible from the air coming/
 through a small orifice near"},
{'e',"the front door.                           /
                       "},
{'o',"You are greeted with the familiar odor of /
 burning electronics. As you inhale"},
{'o',"a second time, you can almost taste the/
 rustic smell of aging books.        "},
{'X',""}, // terminate
};
```

As you can see, there are strings for each room in the game and the end of the strings is delineated with an 'X' character. This is just one way to do things, but it works for me!

Dynamic sounds are more complex to implement than static ones since they can move around the environment. Shadow Land has no dynamic objects, but I will explain how to implement dynamic sound. Each object that can move around the universe has a sound attached to it, which is just a string that describes the sound the object makes. Hence, when a player asks to listen to the sounds in a room, first the static sound is printed out, and then it is determined what objects are in the room. Their "sounds" are printed out as well after the static portion of the text. Of course, you should try and make the sentences "connect" together with some kind of conjunction so that the sounds don't look like a bullet list!

Smell

The sense of smell is programmed in the exact same way sounds are, except that the text strings should describe the smells in the room instead of the sounds. Moreover, dynamic smells are implemented in the same way as described above: as an "attachment" to the dynamic objects. For example, an ogre might have a bad smell attached to it that is described along with the static smell of the room. This would be determined by testing if the ogre is in the same room as the player. That is easy since we can look at the position of the ogre and of the player, index into the universe map, and see if they are on the same cell type. Before moving on, there is one artistic aspect of describing smells we should touch on. If something smells bad, try to make it sound as if it smells bad in a good way, get my drift?

Sight

Implementing vision in a text game is an interesting problem. We want to make a virtual character "see" in a virtual world that isn't even visible to the player! Well, being the software sorcerers that we are, this is no problem at all if the correct data structures and approach are used. First, the easiest data structure to implement sight with is the map world since it is a 2-D version of the world the player is walking around in. The algorithm is easy also; all we have to do is understand how we (ourselves) see, and then implement a version of our sight within the text game that is based on the data structures in the game.

To begin with, there is static vision and dynamic object base vision. The static vision is taken care of as we have seen and is very general. If a player asks to "look" at a room, then the first part of the description would be a static one that is always the same. The second part of the description might focus on what's within the player's virtual field of view or VFOV (I like acronyms). This is the hard part. We must somehow scan in front of the player and detect if objects are within this scan space. Unlike the smell and sound test, we just can't check if the dynamic object is within the room since it might be behind the player. We must instead see if it's within the room in conjunction with being within the VFOV.

To test if an object is within the VFOV of view of the player, we need to know five things:

1. The position of the player
2. The direction of the player

3. The positions of all the dynamic objects

4. The depth of the scan (distance)

5. The view angle of the scan

Numbers 1, 2, and 3 are easy. We can find that information by looking at the data structures for the player and all the dynamic objects. The only question arises when we consider numbers 4 and 5. First, the depth means how far should the player be able to see? This is relative, but as a rule of thumb, the player should be able to see at least the length of the largest room. The second factor, "view angle," is really the field of view and simply means the angle at which the scan will take place (see Figure 14.6). Now, since the player can only be facing four directions (North, South, East, and West), the scan becomes very simple. All that is needed are two `for` loops to accomplish the scan.

FIGURE 14.6

The virtual vision system in action.

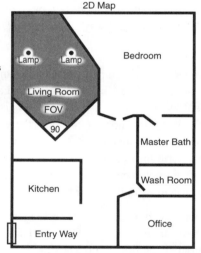

Image scan starts from player's (x, y) position and scans a 90 degree area directly in front of player. In this case, the scan would reveal the two lamps.

The scan will have a shape of an upside-down pyramid, and the view and or field of view will be 90 degrees. This is close enough to a normal human's field of view and is realistic for a game. Hence, the scan will emanate out from the player's position and test each cell in the scan (see Figure 14.7). In general, one `for` loop will control the X-axis deflection of the scan and one `for` loop will control the Y-axis deflection. The scan will continue until a specified depth is reached (which is the distance) and then the vision scan will be complete. Now, as the vision scan is running, tests are made to see if any of the blocks within vision contain a dynamic object. If this is true, then each object is "tagged" and placed in a list. When the vision strings print out, the list is referred to and the specific visual strings for each dynamic object are printed out along with the general static view.

FIGURE 14.7
A close up of the
player's vision scan.

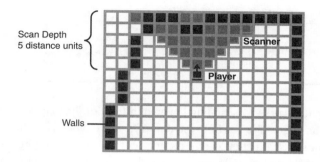

Shadow Land uses this technique to "see" in a room. As an example, Listing 14.11 is
the vision code that takes care of vision in the northern direction. Pay close attention
to the structure of the for loops and the tests. Don't worry if some of the variables or
defines are not visible; just try to understand the overall operation of the code fragment.

LISTING 14.11   A Code Fragment from Shadow Lands That Produces a Vision Scan in
the Northern Direction

```
case NORTH:
{
// scan like this
//   .....
//    ...
//     P
for (y=you.y,scan_level=0; y>=(you.y-depth); y--,scan_level++)
    {
    for (x=you.x-scan_level; x<=you.x+scan_level; x++)
        {
        // x,y is test point, make sure it is within the universe
        // boundaries and within the same room
        if (x>=1 && x<NUM_COLUMNS-1 &&
            y>=1 && x<NUM_ROWS-1 &&
            universe_geometry[y][x]==universe_geometry[you.y][you.x])
            {
            // test to see if square has an object in it
            if (universe_objects[y][x]!=' ')
                {
                // insert the object into object list
                stuff[*num_objects].thing = universe_objects[y][x];
                stuff[*num_objects].x     = x;
                stuff[*num_objects].y     = y;
                // increment the number of objects
                (*num_objects)++;

                } // end if an object was found
            } // end if in boundaries
        } // end for x
    } // end for y
```

LISTING 14.11   Continued

```
// return number of objects found
return(*num_objects);

} break;
```

The function works by scanning the area in front of the player and testing each block
in the scan to see if it is within the universe. If the block is within the universe, then
the object's data structure is referred to see if an object is sitting on the block. If so,
then the object is inserted into a list and the code proceeds until the scan is done. You
should pay close attention to the bounding code that determines if the scanned block
is within the universe. This is absolutely needed since the scan takes place at a given
distance, the code doesn't have any way of determining if it has gone out of bounds of
the array or in the negative direction. This is why a "filter" is needed to condition and
test each test block position that is generated by the double for loops. Finally, when
you print out the dynamic objects after the static visual, make sure that they read in a
fluid manner!

Making It Real-Time

The text game technology we have been considering thus far is not real-time. This is
because the game logic waits for the user to input the text string, the string is processed,
the game logic executes, and the cycle starts over. The problem is that during the text
input phase, the game logic is in a wait state. This has two effects on the game. First,
time stops until the player inputs a string and presses return. Secondly, dynamic objects
in the game can't move around; in essence, the game universe can't evolve while the
player is "thinking." This may or may not be desired. There are some text games that
stop and wait and others run while waiting for text input.

For example, in a real-time text game, the player may sit at the command prompt for
ten minutes, but as he does this, he is being surrounded by orcs! To make a game real-
time is very easy: All you need to do is slightly change the input function so that it
resembles a keyboard handler that only sends the string to the input parser when the
Enter key is hit. So, the game event loop might look like this:

```
while(!done)
   {
   Get_Next_Input_Character();

      if (user has typed in a whole string)
      {
      Parser_Logic();
      } // end if an input was entered
```

```
    // whatever happened above, let's move all the

    // objects in the game universe
    Move_Objects();
    } // end main loop
```

The real-time aspect of this structure is that the input character is not waited for. If there is one, fine; otherwise, game logic continues in real-time.

Error Handling

A text game must have error handling just as arcade games do. However, most of the error handling is done in the text parsing. There are lexical tests, syntax tests, and semantic tests that all must be performed. Lexical tests are easy since they have to do with string comparisons and vocabulary checks. The syntax and semantic tests are more complex since the game logic must start using language productions and rules to check if the sentence is valid. This is complex and there are usually many special cases that have to be considered. Similarly, when writing a compiler or interpreter, the code starts off clean, but has a lot of kludges in it by its completion. Text games are very similar: You may find yourself doing some lexical testing in the string input function and some syntax checking in the lexical analyzer. However, better to be safe than sorry! So, the more filters, traps, and tests the input parser has, the better!

Creeping Around with Shadow Land

Well, I know that you are an expert text game writer at this point, but I wanted to show you an example of such a game. The name of the game is called Shadow Land and it is a fully operational text game that allows you full interaction with the environment. The idea behind the game is simple: You must find your keys and drop them in the office. The environment you will be playing in is my old apartment in Silicon Valley, CA. I have completely modeled my apartment for you along with the sights, sounds, and smells that were usually in it.

The idea behind the game is that you are an invisible shadow that can move freely around without being detected by me or anyone else in the apartment. The vocabulary and grammar of the game is very simple, as are the actions you can perform. But if you understand Shadow Land, then you shouldn't have a problem making something like Zork with the proper planning, data structures, and algorithms. Moreover, if you are interested in creating RPGs at all, then this is something you need to understand!

The Language of Shadow Land

In Table 14.1, we saw the vocabulary of Shadow Land, but now let's take a look at the productions or syntax rules. Instead of stating them in a rigorous manner, let's try and list them in a bit more of a relaxed way. Let's begin by listing all the words in the vocabulary again:

- The objects in the game: LAMP, SANDWICH, KEYS
- Nautical directions: EAST, WEST, NORTH, SOUTH
- Relative directions: FORWARD, BACKWARD, RIGHT, LEFT
- The "actions" or verbs of the language: MOVE, SMELL, LOOK, LISTEN, PUT, GET, EAT, INVENTORY, WHERE, EXIT
- The articles or connectives of the language: THE
- The prepositions of the language: IN, ON, TO, DOWN

Let's begin with the legal form of the action verbs. Some of the verbs need no object to mean something. These are "smell," "listen," "inventory," "where," and "exit." If any action verb is typed by itself, it will work. Furthermore, if prepositional phrases, articles, or objects are placed after the verbs, they will have the effect of causing warnings. The outcome of entering any of these verbs follows:

"smell"—This will describe the smell of the room you are in.

"listen"—This will describe the sounds of the room you are in.

"inventory"—This will tell you what you are carrying.

"where"—This will describe your location in the house along with the direction you are facing.

"exit"—This will end the game.

The next set of action verbs can be further qualified by objects, adjectives, or complete prepositional phrases. These verbs are "move," "put," "get," "look," and "eat." Here are the legal forms using some of the earlier production rule syntax:

"move" + (relative direction) | "move" + "to" + relative direction | "move" + "to the" + relative direction

where the parentheses mean that the word(s) are optional and "|" means logical OR.

Using the above production, the following sentence would be legal:

"move to the right"

This would have the effect of the player parry right (sidestep). Another possibility would be

"move"

This would have the effect making the player walk in the direction he was currently facing. An illegal sentence would be

"move to the east"

This is illegal since "east" is a nautical direction instead of a relative direction. The next interesting action verb is "look." Here is its rule:

"look" +(nautical direction) | "look"+"to"+nautical direction | "look"+"to the"+nautical direction

Using this verb, the player can "see" objects in the room. For example, if the player just typed in "look" without a direction, then the game would print out the static visual only. To see objects in a room, you MUST use "look" combined with a nautical direction. For example, to see the northern part of the room, you would type

"look to the north"

or

"look north"

or

"look to north"

All the above forms are equivalent, and the result of them will be the objects within the player's view being described.

The player will start the game off facing north, so there needs to be a way to turn him. This is done with the "turn" action, which is similar to the "look" verb as far as the production rules go.

"turn" +(nautical direction) | "turn"+"to"+nautical direction | "turn"+"to the"+nautical direction

Hence, to turn East, you can type:

"turn to east"

The next two action verbs relating to object manipulation are "put" and "get." They are used to put down and pick up objects. The only valid objects in the game are the keys, lamp, and sandwich. Here are the production rules for each action verb:

"put"+object | "put" + "down" +"object" | "put"+"down the"+object

"get"+object | "get" + "the" +"object"

You use "put" and "get" to move objects around the environment. For example, imagine that you saw a set of keys in front of you. You might say this:

"get the keys"

Then later you may wish to drop the keys. This would be accomplished with something like this:

"put down the keys"

The final, most important action verb is "eat," and I'm sure you know what it does. It will make you eat whatever you tell it to as long as you have the object in your possession. The rule for "eat" is

"eat"+object |"eat"+"the"+"object"

So, if you wanted to eat the lamp, you would type

"eat the lamp"

after which you will have satisfied your iron requirements for the day!

At first, you will find the grammar and limited vocabulary tedious, but after a few moments of playing the game, it will become very natural to you. You are of course free to add to the vocabulary and grammar rules. One final detail: The input parser is case insensitive, so you can use uppercase and lowercase characters at will.

Building and Playing Shadow Land

Shadow Land is the only game so far that is almost totally portable. This is due to the fact that the game is text only. The only two things that might change this statement are that Shadow Land uses kbhit() and the ANSI color text driver. The ANSI color driver was used back in DOS days to allow special escape sequences to be used to change colors in pure text applications. To enable it, simply add the line

```
DEVICE=C:\WINDOWS\COMMAND\ANSI.SYS
```

to your config.sys file. If there's a problem, then simply search on your system for ANSI.SYS and use the proper path. Other than that, the code is straight C/C++ without any graphics or machine-dependent calls. To build the program, use the source module called SHADOW.CPP, compile it as a CONSOLE application (not a win32 .EXE), and link it with the standard C/C++ libraries and that's all you need to do. I have created an executable called SHADOW.EXE for you already, if you don't want to do this.

You already know just about everything you need to know to play. However, here are a few tips. The game will begin by asking for your name. Then it will ask you what you want to do. At this point in the game, you are standing in the entryway to my apartment. To your left is a kitchen and to the north is a hallway. Move around in the environment with the "move" command and be sure to listen and smell everything. Remember "move" by itself will always move you in the direction you are currently facing, and "look" needs to be qualified by a nautical direction if you wish to see the objects in the room.

Shadow's Game Loop

The game loop for Shadow Land is extremely simple since it's not in real-time. Here it is in Listing 14.12.

LISTING 14.12   The Game Loop of Shadow Land

```
void main(void)
{

// call up intro
Introduction();

printf("\n\nWelcome to the world of  S H A D O W   L A N D...\n\n\n");

// obtain users name to make game more personal
printf("\nWhat is your first name?");
scanf("%s",you.name);

// main event loop,note: it is NOT real-time
while(!global_exit)
    {
    // put up an input notice to user

    printf("\n\nWhat do you want to do?");

    // get the line of text
    Get_Line(global_input);

    printf("\n");
    // break the text down into tokens and build up a sentence
    Extract_Tokens(global_input);

    // parse the verb and execute the command
    Verb_Parser();

    } // end main event loop

printf("\n\nExiting the universe of S H A D O W  L A N D...
see you later %s.\n",you.name);

// restore screen color
printf("%c%c37;40m",27,91);

} // end main
```

The `main()` begins by printing an introduction screen and then asking the player for his name. At this point, the game falls into the main event loop, which is static. The loop will wait for the user to type in a string which is returned from `Get_Line()`. Then the string is tokenized by `Extract_Tokens()` and finally parsed and acted upon the verb parser named `Verb_Parser()`. That's all there is to it. This cycle will occur every time the player enters a line of text until he types "**exit**".

Winning the Game

I think I already told you how to do this, but if I didn't, then good luck figuring it out! Also, try adding features to the game. For example, more objects, verbs, a help system. And if you're really up to it, create a graphical display of the room, player, position, and so forth and update the game to a graphic adventure!

Summary

This chapter has definitely been a burn for both of us. You have taken a crash course in compiler design along with learning the details of implementing a text game. You learned about universe representations, how to implement the senses, and how to make the descriptions in a text game "fluffy" and fun. Finally, you got to see where I used to live!

CHAPTER 15

Putting It All Together: You Got Game!

"He slimed me!"
—Bill Murray, Ghostbusters

This is the last chapter of Volume I, and it's just in time; I'm starting to have a three-way conversation with myself. I admit I talk to myself, but when two different people talk back, it's time to quit! Anyway, in this chapter I'm going to outline the design and implementation of a simple game, *Outpost*, which I wrote using the techniques that you have learned in the book.

The game took about five days to write, so don't expect much. However, it sports 3D-modeled sprites, particles, some gameplay, sound effects, and a few different enemies, and I think it should be really easy for you to mess with if you want to. Here's what I'm going to cover:

- The initial design of *Outpost*
- The tools used to write the game
- The game universe: scrolling in space
- The player's ship: the Wraith

- The asteroid field
- The enemies
- The power-ups
- The HUDs
- The particle system
- Playing the game
- Compiling *Outpost*

The Initial Design of *Outpost*

I wanted to create a game that was easy to write, looked good, had some rudimentary gameplay, and used scrolling (if I had a dollar for every scrolling question I received, I would be a millionaire). Thus, I picked an Asteroids-type space game because the only background is black space. Plus, the artificial intelligence (AI) for Asteroids, along with search-and-destroy AI for the enemies, is pretty simple, so it all sounded like a good idea.

The Story

The story goes something like this: You are the pilot of the top-secret Wraith, a highly armored attack fighter sent to sector Alpha 11 to rid the area of an alien incursion. The aliens have infested the area with outposts that you must destroy. The only problem is that the sector is filled with heavy debris (the asteroids), alien warships, and homing mines protecting each outpost. That's about all there is to the story. (Sounds like a great movie, huh?) Figures 15.1 and 15.2 show the game during startup and gameplay.

FIGURE 15.1
Outpost starting up.

FIGURE 15.2
Outpost during
gameplay.

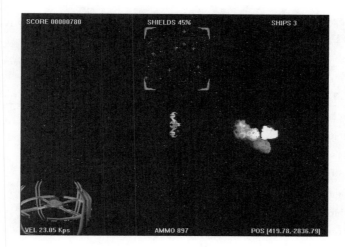

Although in most cases I think that creating the story of a game is one of the least important things about writing a program, it does give you a point of reference to build from and keeps the game semi-coherent.

Designing the Gameplay

Once I had the story down, I started designing the gameplay. This consisted of making up the rules. Which object/control performs which function? What's the goal? And so forth. The game isn't that advanced, so I basically thought up what the player can do, what the enemies can do, how the player wins (or loses), what kind of AI everything has, and so on. Because *Outpost* isn't level-based and doesn't have any kind of strategy, there's not much else to the design.

The Tools Used to Write the Game

I wanted to stick to 256 colors because I've used 256-color modes in the book to keep things simple, but I still wanted a really clean look for the objects. Hence, I decided to render almost everything. I used Caligari TrueSpace IV (TS4), which in my estimation is the best 3D modeler in the world for its price. However, price aside, TS4 can give 3D Studio Max a run for its money. There's a demo copy of TS4 on the CD, so make sure to check it out.

The 2D artwork and touchup was done using JASC Paint Shop Pro 5.1, which is a killer paint package that supports plug-ins and has the easiest interface I have ever seen. Again, there is a demo copy on the CD.

Finally, the sound effects were taken from various sources and processed with Sonic Foundry's Sound Forge XP, which is one of the best sound-editing packages for PCs.

You can also find a demo copy of Sound Forge on the CD. That's just about all the tools I used, in addition to VC++ 5.0, 6.0, and DirectX.

Table 15.1 lists all the game objects and how they were created.

TABLE 15.1 The Objects in **Outpost**

Object	Technique
Asteroids	Rendered with TS4
Player's ship	Hand-drawn with PSP
Outposts	Rendered with TS4
Predator mines	Rendered with TS4
Gunships	Rendered with TS4
Power-ups	Rendered with TS4
Plasma pulses	Hand-drawn with PSP
Star field	Single pixels
Explosions	Digitized Pyrotechnics Stock Media

The meshes for all the 3D models were created by hand, and each took less than an hour with TS4. The hand-drawn images took about an hour each. I rotated the player's ship using the software rotation algorithm in PSP rather than doing it manually. All sounds were sampled down to 11 KHz, 8-bit mono.

The Game Universe: Scrolling in Space

I already covered how to implement scrolling, so I'm not going to cover it again. However, there are a couple of interesting details about the scrolling in *Outpost*. First, the player is always at the center of the screen. This makes things a bit easier, but more importantly it gives the player the biggest game area possible to react in. If you allowed the player's character to get near the edges of the screen in a scrolling game, it's possible that an enemy could pop up and hit the player before he even had a few milliseconds to react. By keeping the player in the center of the screen, you give him good visibility of what's around him at all times.

As for the size of the game universe, I chose 16000x16000, as shown here:

```
// size of universe
#define UNIVERSE_MIN_X   (-8000)
#define UNIVERSE_MAX_X   (8000)
#define UNIVERSE_MIN_Y   (-8000)
#define UNIVERSE_MAX_Y   (8000)
```

Universe size is always a hard thing to decide, but my standard technique is the following: Estimate how many frames per second the game is going to run at, estimate the max speed the player can move, and then, based on that, decide how long you want the player to take to get from one end of the universe to the other:

```
universe_size = player_velocity*fps*desired_time
```

Hence, if the player moves at a max of 32 pixel/frames per second, and you want to run at 30 fps with a time of 10 seconds from one end to another, you have a universe size of

```
universe_size = 32 pixels/frame * 30 fps * 10
              = 9600 units
```

Here, each unit is a pixel. This is basically how I came up with the 16,000. Of course, the final values in the game were slightly different, but this is how I came up with the ballpark figures.

The other issue to consider when you're making a scrolling space game is the sparseness. You may think that a space of 10x10 seconds or 16000x16000 pixels isn't that big, but to populate it, you will need hundreds if not thousands of asteroids. Otherwise, the player will be flying around forever looking for stuff to shoot! My friend Jarrod Davis learned this when writing Astro3D, which you can find on the CD.

As for the scrolling algorithm, there's not much to it. The player's position is used as the center of a window to render from, as shown in Figure 15.3.

FIGURE 15.3

The scrolling window algorithm for Outpost.

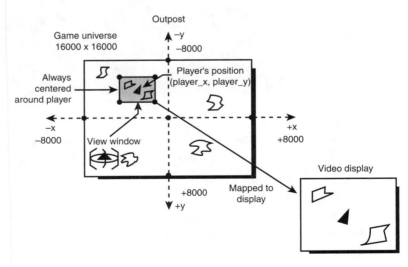

The algorithm works by taking the player's position, and then translating the player to the origin (the screen center) and translating the objects to the player. The objects that are within the window are rendered, and the others are not. The only objects that aren't drawn this way are the stars, which are basically pixels that wrap around as they move off the edges of the screen. Hence, if you look carefully, you can see the same stars in the same positions if you move slowly in the x- or y-axis.

The Player's Ship: "The Wraith"

The player's ship was hand-drawn. I was going to render it, but it had so much detail that I decided to just draw it and then use Paint Shop Pro to light it and make it look real. In addition, I only drew the Wraith facing north and then used PSP's built-in bitmap rotation to rotate the ship in 16 different angles. The artwork is shown in Figure 15.4.

FIGURE 15.4
The artwork for
the Wraith.

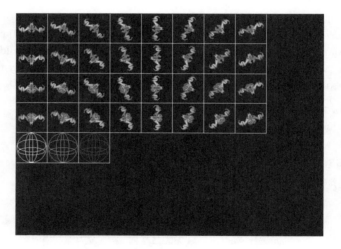

The Wraith doesn't do much except fly around and shoot, but the friction algorithm is interesting. I wanted the Wraith to look like it was flying under gravity, so I wanted some form of friction when it turned. I implemented this with the standard techniques that you learned in previous chapters.

The Wraith has a velocity vector that is modified when the player thrusts in any particular direction. The nice thing about this approach is that you don't have to worry about things like, "If the ship is going east at this speed and the player thrusts north, what should the ship do?" Instead, I let the vector math do it.

Here's a portion of the control code for the Wraith:

```
// test if player is moving
if (keyboard_state[DIK_RIGHT])
    {
    // rotate player to right
    if (++wraith.varsI[WRAITH_INDEX_DIR] > 15)
        wraith.varsI[WRAITH_INDEX_DIR] = 0;

    } // end if
else
if (keyboard_state[DIK_LEFT])
    {
    // rotate player to left
    if (—wraith.varsI[WRAITH_INDEX_DIR] <  0)
        wraith.varsI[WRAITH_INDEX_DIR] = 15;

    } // end if

// vertical/speed motion
if (keyboard_state[DIK_UP])
    {
    // move player forward
    xv = cos_look16[wraith.varsI[WRAITH_INDEX_DIR]];
    yv = sin_look16[wraith.varsI[WRAITH_INDEX_DIR]];

    // test to turn on engines
    if (!engines_on)
        DSound_Play(engines_id,DSBPLAY_LOOPING);

    // set engines to on
    engines_on = 1;

    Start_Particle(PARTICLE_TYPE_FADE, PARTICLE_COLOR_GREEN, 3,
                    player_x+RAND_RANGE(-2,2),
                    player_y+RAND_RANGE(-2,2),
                  (-int(player_xv)>>3), (-int(player_yv)>>3));

    } // end if
else
if (engines_on)
    {
    // reset the engine on flag and turn off sound
    engines_on = 0;

    // turn off the sound

    DSound_Stop_Sound(engines_id);
    } // end if
```

```
// add velocity change to player's velocity
player_xv+=xv;
player_yv+=yv;

// test for maximum velocity
vel = Fast_Distance_2D(player_xv, player_yv);

if (vel >= MAX_PLAYER_SPEED)
   {
   // recompute velocity vector by normalizing then rescaling
   player_xv = (MAX_PLAYER_SPEED-1)*player_xv/vel;
   player_yv = (MAX_PLAYER_SPEED-1)*player_yv/vel;
   } // end if

// move player, note that these are in world coords
player_x+=player_xv;
player_y+=player_yv;
```

> **NOTE**
>
> About the name *Wraith*. A long time ago I saw a movie called *The Wraith* with Charlie Sheen. In the film, Charlie ended up in the trunk of his car, falling off a cliff at 32 ft/sec². He died and came back as a wraith, which is an evil ghost that takes revenge on its killers. Anyway, he had this cool car, a prototype Dodge Interceptor, and the movie is where I got the name. I thought you should know. (Plus, guess who has the Dodge Interceptor?)

Studying the code, you'll notice there is some code to keep the Wraith from going too fast. Basically, I continually check the length of the velocity vector against a MAX length. If it's too long, I shrink it. Another approach could have been to use a unit direction vector and a speed scalar, and then translate the ship each frame an amount equal to the unit vector scaled by the speed. Either way is about the same.

Lastly, the Wraith has a shield and a vapor trail. The shield is nothing more than a bitmap that I overlay on the Wraith when something hits it, and the vapor trail is just particles that I emit out randomly when the thrusters are on. The thruster effect is achieved with two bitmaps for each direction of the Wraith: one with thrusters on and one with thrusters off. When the thrusters are on, I randomly select the on/off image and it looks like a Klingon impulse drive.

The Asteroid Field

The asteroid field consists of a large number of randomly moving asteroids of three different sizes: small, medium, and large. The asteroids were rendered using TS4 with real-time rendering enabled. Figure 15.5 shows the asteroids in the modeler, and Figure 15.6 shows their rendered forms. Once I had the asteroids looking like asteroids and lit properly, I created a rotation animation and then a Targa (.TGA) movie of each asteroid rotating, converting the .TGA movie files, image0000.tga, image0001.tga, and so on, into bitmaps (.bmp) and importing them directly into the game without templating them.

FIGURE 15.5
The 3D models for the asteroids.

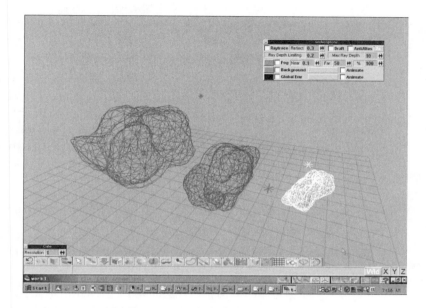

FIGURE 15.6
The rendered asteroids.

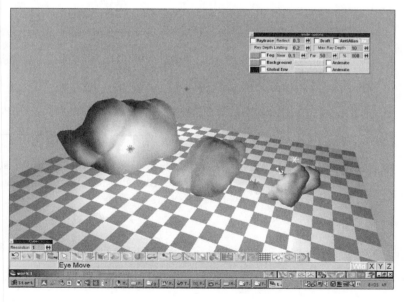

The physics model of the asteroids is rather simple. They just move in the same direction at a constant velocity until they're fired upon. In addition, the asteroids rotate at varying speeds to give a feel of mass. When an asteroid is fired upon, its size and hardness determine how it's blown up. You can hit a large asteroid so hard with a blaster pulse that it's completely obliterated, but sometimes it only splits. Splitting is dictated by two factors: probability and availability. There are only so many medium and small asteroids, so you can't always split all the large ones.

In addition, I didn't like the way that a large asteroid always split into two medium ones, and a medium asteroid always split into two small ones. Therefore, sometimes a large asteroid might split into one medium and two small ones, or two medium and two small ones, and so on. I threw in some extra permutations based on probability to make things more interesting. If you want to add more asteroids, you can change the following `define`:

```
#define MAX_ROCKS          300
```

Try jacking it up to 1,000, or 10,000 if you have a Pentium III 550 MHz!

> **TIP**
>
> I have this love for the game *Asteroids*. I guess it was that $100 I won in college on a bet. Some other computer science students bet me that I couldn't write an *Asteroids* game right in front of them in Pascal on an IBM XT. They had seen other games I'd written and said I'd copied them. Of course, these were your typical comp-sci students who couldn't do anything unless there was an API call for it.
>
> I sat down and wrote Asteroids in about eight hours flat—an exact copy of the vector version by Atari (no sound, though). I won the 100 bucks, and then I slapped them all with a backhand and took their pocket protectors.
>
> The point is that I have memorized the code for Asteroids after doing it so many times, and I always like using it as an example. It's like my "Hello World" for game programming. :)

Finally, when an asteroid hits the edge of the game universe, it just wraps around by resetting the x or y position variable. But what if you want to make it bounce off the edge by reflecting the velocity vector's sign?

The Enemies

The enemies in the game aren't the smartest guys in the universe, but they get the job done. For the most part they use the more introductory AI methods, such as deterministic logic and FSMs (finite state machines). However, there are a couple of cool techniques that I used for tracking algorithms. You'll see this later in the chapter when I show you the code that makes the predator mines home in on the player's position. Anyway, take a look at how each enemy was created and implemented.

The Outposts

The model I used for the outposts was probably the most complex 3D model in the whole game. It took me hours to build the model. The bummer is that the 3D model has a ton of detail, as shown in Figures 15.7 and 15.8, but I lost all that detail when I rendered the model and shrank it down.

FIGURE 15.7
The 3D model for
an outpost.

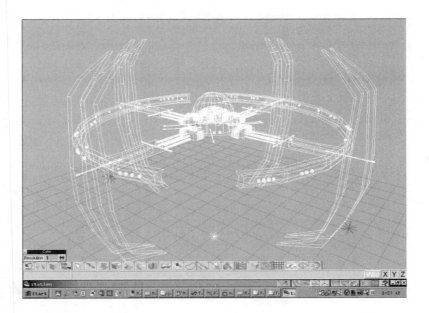

Anyway, the outposts don't do much except sit there and rotate. They have no weapons, no AI, nothing. However, they can detect damage, and when the player fires on them they will start to explode. Particles and secondary explosions will occur until the damage level of the outpost is so great that it explodes!

FIGURE 15.8
A rendered outpost.

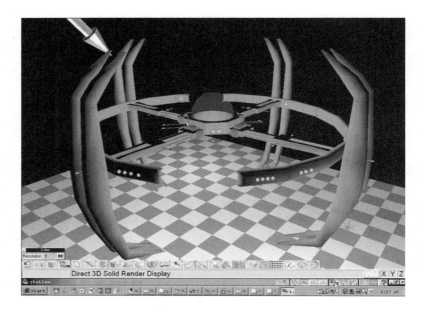

The Predator Mines

The predator mines are the protectors of the outposts. They hold position nearby until you get within a specified range, and then they turn on and track you. The predator mines were rendered with TS4 and are shown in Figures 15.9 and 15.10.

FIGURE 15.9
The 3D model for a predator mine.

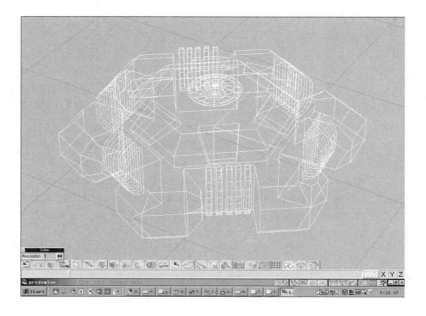

FIGURE 15.10
A rendered predator mine.

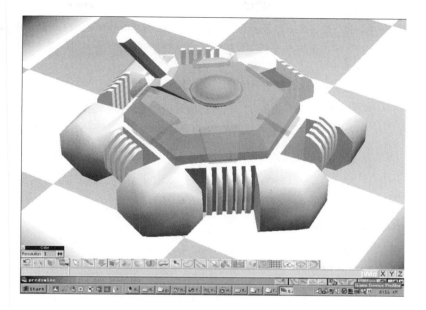

I wasn't very happy with the final 3D model for them. Actually, I created another 3D model, shown in Figure 15.11, but it looked more like a stationary mine than something that could attack you.

FIGURE 15.11
Another predator mine concept.

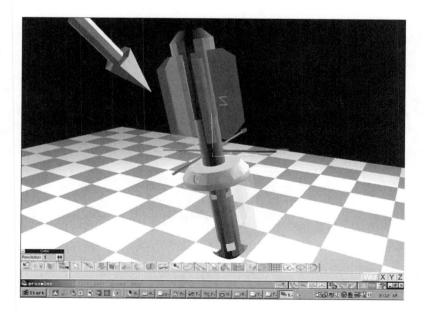

In any case, the AI for the predator mine is simple. It's a finite state machine that starts off in an *idle* or *sleep* state. It's activated when you get within a specified range, based on the following define:

```
#define MIN_MINE_ACTIVATION_DIST 250
```

If the player is within this range of a predator mine, it will activate and track using the vector-tracking algorithm that I described and demonstrated when I covered artificial intelligence and tracking algorithms in Chapter 12, "Making Silicon Think with Artificial Intelligence."

The predator mines don't have any weapons; they simply try to track you and detonate near you, causing damage to your ship.

The Gunships

The gunships were modeled in TS4, as shown in Figures 15.12 and 15.13. They were very detailed and looked great until I shrank them down and converted them to the 256-color palette. But that's life.

FIGURE 15.12
The 3D model for a gunship.

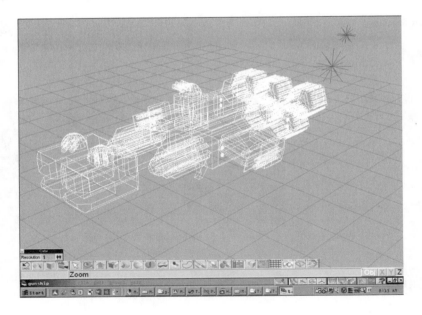

FIGURE 15.13
A rendered gunship.

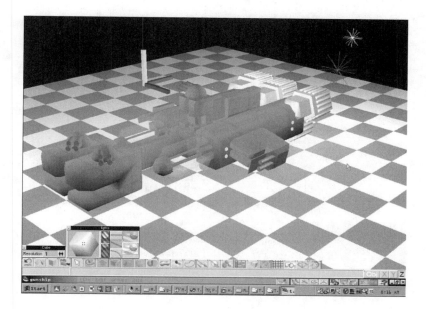

The AI for the gunships is simple. They travel on the x-axis at a constant velocity. If they get within a specified distance to the player, they adjust their y-axis position to track the player, but at a slow rate. Hence, the player can always make a quick directional change to get away. The power of the gunships is in their heavy weapons. Each gunship is equipped with three laser cannons that can be fired independently, as shown in Figure 15.14.

The tracking algorithm for the cannons is rather cool. It works by projecting a vector in the direction that the turret is currently pointing, and another vector from the turret to the player's ship. Then the algorithm wants to minimize the distance from the head of the turret to the player's ship, so it tests both clockwise and counterclockwise rotations to see which rotation minimizes the distance and then performs the rotation that minimizes the distance.

The algorithm was written without trig or any complex vector calculations, just using a distance calculation and a minimization algorithm. I came up with it by taking into consideration how people's heads track an object. We start turning in the direction of the object, and when we feel that we're looking in the right direction, we start slowing our head's rotation rate and come to a stop. But sometimes we may overshoot and have to readjust. This was the inspiration for the algorithm. Take a look here to see the source for the tracking:

```
// first create a vector point in the direction of the turret

        // compute current turret vector
        int tdir1 = gunships[index].varsI[INDEX_GUNSHIP_TURRET];
```

```
float d1x = gunships[index].varsI[INDEX_WORLD_X] +
            cos_look16[tdir1]*32;
float d1y = gunships[index].varsI[INDEX_WORLD_Y] +
            sin_look16[tdir1]*32;

// compute turret vector plus one
int tdir2 = gunships[index].varsI[INDEX_GUNSHIP_TURRET]+1;

if (tdir2 > 15)
    tdir2 = 0;

float d2x = gunships[index].varsI[INDEX_WORLD_X] +
            cos_look16[tdir2]*32;
float d2y = gunships[index].varsI[INDEX_WORLD_Y] +
            sin_look16[tdir2]*32;

// compute turret vector minus one
int tdir0 = gunships[index].varsI[INDEX_GUNSHIP_TURRET]-1;

if (tdir0 < 0)
    tdir0=15;

float d0x = gunships[index].varsI[INDEX_WORLD_X] +
            cos_look16[tdir0]*32;
float d0y = gunships[index].varsI[INDEX_WORLD_Y] +
            sin_look16[tdir0]*32;

// now find the min dist
float dist0 = Fast_Distance_2D(player_x - d0x,
                               player_y - d0y);
float dist1 = Fast_Distance_2D(player_x - d1x,
                               player_y - d1y);
float dist2 = Fast_Distance_2D(player_x - d2x,
                               player_y - d2y);

if (dist0 < dist2 && dist0 < dist1)
    {
    // the negative direction is best
    gunships[index].varsI[INDEX_GUNSHIP_TURRET] = tdir0;

    } // end if
else
if (dist2 < dist0 && dist2 < dist1)
    {
    // the positive direction is best
    gunships[index].varsI[INDEX_GUNSHIP_TURRET] = tdir2;
    } // end if
```

FIGURE 15.14
The turret-tracking
algorithm for the
gunships.

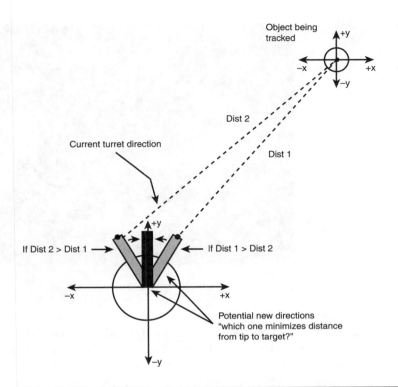

TIP	You'll notice that I am using a lot of distance calculations. However, they're based on the Fast_Distance2D() function, so they're very fast and amount to nothing more than a couple of shifts and adds.

The Power-Ups

The game felt a little "strategy-less" to me with infinite ammo and shields, so I thought, "Why not have some power-ups?" With that in mind, I sat down with TS4 and started modeling power-ups. Then I realized I didn't have a good idea of what to model!

Power-ups usually aren't very realistic. I mean, they say "AMMO" on them, float with some kind of anti-gravity drive, and so on, but still they have to look right. In the end, I decided on simple transparent spheres with the words "AMMO" and "SHLD" glowing inside. The 3D model renderings are shown in Figure 15.15.

Once I had the 3D models down, I rendered the power-ups and got ready to put them in the game. I wanted the power-ups to appear as a result of destroying either an asteroid or an enemy, and I decided that it made more sense to put the power-ups inside the asteroids. My argument was that when you destroy an asteroid, debris and precious minerals (such as dilithium crystals) might be thrown out during the explosion. Sounds reasonable. :)

FIGURE 15.15
The rendered
power-ups.

When an asteroid is destroyed, it's as if a 10-sided die is rolled. If the die lands on the side labeled TRUE, a power-up is created (ammo or shields) and it moves away from the explosion site at a low velocity. When you run through the power-up, you absorb the material and either your shields or ammo increase.

At first, I just created the power-up and let it float off. But I soon realized that space is vast, and the second I lost sight of the power-up, it was really hard to find. Sure, I could have put a blip on the scanner, but it made more sense to give the power-up a lifespan. Hence, when a power-up is spawned, it lives for 3–9 seconds and then dies. This way there are an infinite number of power-ups, and if you lose one, it's sure to get recycled and not just lost in space.

The HUDS

The HUDS (Heads-Up Displays) for *Outpost* consist of two main components: a scanner and some tactical information, including fuel, velocity, shields, ammo, number of ships left, and score. This is shown in Figure 15.16. It's all rendered in a nice alien green—I love green. The tactical information is simply GDI-rendered text, but the scanner is DirectX-rendered via lines, bitmaps, and pixels.

FIGURE 15.16
The HUDs.

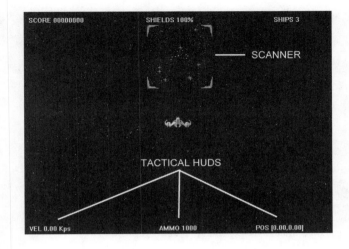

Take a look at the scanner code:

```
void Draw_Scanner(void)
{
// this function draws the scanner

int index,sx,sy; // looping and position

// lock back surface
DDraw_Lock_Back_Surface();

// draw all the rocks
for (index=0; index < MAX_ROCKS; index++)
    {
    // draw rock blips
    if (rocks[index].state==ROCK_STATE_ON)
        {
        sx = ((rocks[index].varsI[INDEX_WORLD_X] -
               UNIVERSE_MIN_X) >> 7) +
               (SCREEN_WIDTH/2) -
               ((UNIVERSE_MAX_X - UNIVERSE_MIN_X) >> 8);
        sy = ((rocks[index].varsI[INDEX_WORLD_Y] -
               UNIVERSE_MIN_Y) >> 7) + 32;

        Draw_Pixel(sx,sy,8,back_buffer, back_lpitch);
        } // end if

    } // end for index


// draw all the gunships
for (index=0; index < MAX_GUNSHIPS; index++)
    {
    // draw gunship blips
```

```
            if (gunships[index].state==GUNSHIP_STATE_ALIVE)
               {
               sx = ((gunships[index].varsI[INDEX_WORLD_X] -
                   UNIVERSE_MIN_X) >> 7) +
                      (SCREEN_WIDTH/2) - ((UNIVERSE_MAX_X -
                      UNIVERSE_MIN_X) >> 8);
               sy = ((gunships[index].varsI[INDEX_WORLD_Y] -
                   UNIVERSE_MIN_Y) >> 7) + 32;

               Draw_Pixel(sx,sy,14,back_buffer, back_lpitch);
               Draw_Pixel(sx+1,sy,14,back_buffer, back_lpitch);

               } // end if

           } // end for index

    // draw all the mines
    for (index=0; index < MAX_MINES; index++)
        {
        // draw gunship blips
        if (mines[index].state==MINE_STATE_ALIVE)
           {
           sx = ((mines[index].varsI[INDEX_WORLD_X] -
               UNIVERSE_MIN_X) >> 7) +
                  (SCREEN_WIDTH/2) - ((UNIVERSE_MAX_X -
                  UNIVERSE_MIN_X) >> 8);
    sy = ((mines[index].varsI[INDEX_WORLD_Y] -
               UNIVERSE_MIN_Y) >> 7) + 32;

           Draw_Pixel(sx,sy,12,back_buffer, back_lpitch);
           Draw_Pixel(sx,sy+1,12,back_buffer, back_lpitch);

           } // end if

       } // end for index


    // unlock the secondary surface
    DDraw_Unlock_Back_Surface();

    // draw all the stations
    for (index=0; index < MAX_STATIONS; index++)
        {
        // draw station blips
        if (stations[index].state==STATION_STATE_ALIVE)
           {
           sx = ((stations[index].varsI[INDEX_WORLD_X] -
               UNIVERSE_MIN_X) >> 7) +
                  (SCREEN_WIDTH/2) - ((UNIVERSE_MAX_X -
                  UNIVERSE_MIN_X) >> 8);
           sy = ((stations[index].varsI[INDEX_WORLD_Y] -
               UNIVERSE_MIN_Y) >> 7) + 32;
```

```
        // test for state
        if (stations[index].anim_state == STATION_SHIELDS_ANIM_ON)
           {
                        stationsmall.curr_frame = 0;
                        stationsmall.x = sx - 3;
                        stationsmall.y = sy - 3;
                        Draw_BOB(&stationsmall,lpddsback);
           } // end if
        else
           {
                          stationsmall.curr_frame = 1;
                    stationsmall.x = sx - 3;
                         stationsmall.y = sy - 3;
                        Draw_BOB(&stationsmall,lpddsback);
           } // end if
        } // end if
    } // end for index

// unlock the secondary surface
DDraw_Lock_Back_Surface();

// draw player as white blip
sx = ((int(player_x) - UNIVERSE_MIN_X) >> 7) + (SCREEN_WIDTH/2) -
     ((UNIVERSE_MAX_X - UNIVERSE_MIN_X) >> 8);
sy = ((int(player_y) - UNIVERSE_MIN_Y) >> 7) + 32;

int col = rand()%256;

Draw_Pixel(sx,sy,col,back_buffer, back_lpitch);
Draw_Pixel(sx+1,sy,col,back_buffer, back_lpitch);
Draw_Pixel(sx,sy+1,col,back_buffer, back_lpitch);
Draw_Pixel(sx+1,sy+1,col,back_buffer, back_lpitch);

// unlock the secondary surface
DDraw_Unlock_Back_Surface();

// now draw the art around the edges
hud.x          = 320-64;
hud.y          = 32-4;
hud.curr_frame = 0;
Draw_BOB(&hud,lpddsback);

hud.x          = 320+64-16;
hud.y          = 32-4;
hud.curr_frame = 1;
Draw_BOB(&hud,lpddsback);

hud.x          = 320-64;
hud.y          = 32+128-20;
```

```
    hud.curr_frame = 2;
    Draw_BOB(&hud,lpddsback);

    hud.x          = 320+64-16;
    hud.y          = 32+128-20;
    hud.curr_frame = 3;
    Draw_BOB(&hud,lpddsback);

    } // end Draw_Scanner
```

I wanted you to see a typical scanner function because they tend to be a little messy. Basically, a scanner represents the position of various objects in a game, usually scaled and centered. The problem is making a huge space into a small space and drawing image elements that look realistic. Thus, the scanner imagery usually consists of a number of heterogeneous image elements.

Also, when you're viewing a scanner, you want to be able to quickly pick out important data such as where you are, the positions of the enemies, and so on, so color and shape is very important. In the end, I decided to use one or more pixels to represent enemies, single gray pixels to represent asteroids, and actual bitmaps to represent the outposts. The player's ship is represented by a glowing blob.

Finally, the scanner itself is supposed to be some kind of holographic imaging system. I wanted it to look cool, so I drew some nice bitmaps for the corners of it.

As for the workings of the scanner algorithm, take a look at the code. It does nothing more than divide the position of each object by some constant so the results fit into the window of the scanner.

The Particle System

The particle system for *Outpost* is exactly like the one from Chapter 13, "Playing God: Basic Physics Modeling." Particles can be created with various velocities and colors, and there are functions to create sets of particles with specific properties to mimic explosions and so forth. The important thing is not how particles work (because you already know), but how I used them.

Particles are used for a lot of things in *Outpost*. I want all the enemies to leave vapor trails when damaged. I want the player to leave plasma behind when flying around. And when something is damaged or blown up, I want a lot of particles to be part of the explosion in addition to the bitmap-animated explosions.

The cool thing about particles is that they're so cheap and add so much to the visual excitement of a game. Not to mention that vapor trails and particles can be used as game elements themselves for tracking, or for other interpretations: food, footprints, whatever.

Playing the Game

Playing *Outpost* is very simple: you just fly around and blow things up. However, if there was a goal to the game, I would say that it's to blow up all the outposts.

Here are the controls:

Right arrow, left arrow	Rotate ship
Up arrow	Thrust
Ctrl, spacebar	Fire weapons
H	Toggle tactical information
S	Toggle scanner
Left Alt+right Alt+A	Special
Esc	Exit

Compiling *Outpost*

Compiling *Outpost* is no different than compiling any other demo you have created so far. Figure 15.17 illustrates the components needed to compile and run the project.

Take a look in the next sections to see these components in more detail.

FIGURE 15.17
The software architecture of Outpost.

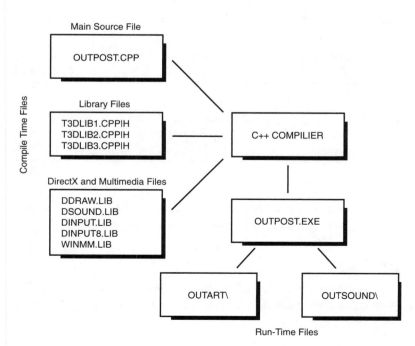

Compilation Files

Source Files:

OUTPOST.CPP	The main game file.
T3DLIB1.CPP|H	The first part of the game engine.
T3DLIB2.CPP|H	The second part of the game engine.
T3DLIB3.CPP|H	The third part of the game engine.

Library Files:

DDRAW.LIB	MS DirectDraw.
DSOUND.LIB	MS DirectSound.
DINPUT.LIB and DINPUT8.LIB	MS DirectInput.
WINMM.LIB	The Win32 Multimedia library extensions.

 TIP You must include the DirectX library files in your project. Setting the search path is not enough. In addition, you must set the search path to find the DirectX .H header files in the DirectX SDK installation directory.

Runtime Files

Main .EXE:

OUTPOST.EXE	This is the main .EXE of the game. It can exist anywhere as long as the media directories are under it.

Runtime Media Directories:

OUTART\	The art directory for the game. You need all of it.
OUTSOUND\	The sound directory for the game. You need all of it.

And of course, you need the DirectX run-time files on your system. Finally, all the 3D models are in OUTMODELS\, so feel free to do what you want with them. But if I see them in a *Star Trek* movie, I want royalties!

Epilogue

I'm speechless... Are we really done? Is it really over? Hell no. There's also Volume II, which covers nothing but 3D information, advanced physics, and really hard math—yumm yumm.

However, the CDs that come with this book have a lot more information about game programming, and even Direct 3D and General 3D. So whether you get Volume II or not, make sure to read all the articles and the small 3D programming cyber-books by Sergei Savchenko and Matthew Ellis contained on the CDs. You can find out more about the CDs in the table of contents and in Appendix A. In addition, you might want to check out the appendices for some cool stuff about resources, C++, and mathematics.

This book has been the hardest project I have ever put together. It started out as a three-volume set on 3D game programming titled *The Necronomicon de Gam*, but we decided to do a single book and bring back *Tricks*. Then, about halfway through the book, we all realized that there was no way it was going to fit into less than 2,000-3,000 pages, so we split it back up into two volumes. In retrospect, I guess I got my way. Everything I wanted to say in this volume and the next is there, with no cuts to save pages, so that's a good thing. :)

Although there aren't any plans for another book after Volume II, there are two more areas that I might want to write about: networked games and console game programming. What do you think? I don't know; the networked game stuff is cool because it's something that's applicable to PCs, but console stuff is so expensive. On the other hand, I think it would be cool to cover programming for PlayStation I and II, Dreamcast, Xbox, and Game Boy Advance—don't you? Maybe I'll do it, and maybe monkeys will fly out of my butt—you never know.

After these two volumes, you may never see anything more out of me because writing this has been a killer. I worked on these books more than 120 hours a week for around a year non-stop. In the end, I think of the smiles on so many new game programmers' faces when they first see the glow of the screen and a little blip moving around. That's the only real satisfaction I get.

I remember when I wrote the first *Tricks of the Game Programming Gurus*, and how bad it was (I wrote it in two months). Now I think about how exciting it was, though. I was flown to id Software in Texas to talk to John Carmack about *DOOM*. I also got to hear John Romero rave about *Quake*. It was unreal, to say the least. I came home and wrote like the wind. I think that book was the catalyst that helped a lot of people discover the possibilities of creating 3D video games.

Although I didn't cover polygon graphics, texture mapping, or a lot of other topics, that book started me off on this crazy, non-stop roller coaster from hell. And to tell you the truth, I guess I've had a good time. Sure beats working at a nine-to-five job! And if there's one piece of advice that I can give you, it would be this:

When you see a roller coaster, get on it, put your hands in the air, and ride it to the very end. Life doesn't remember you unless you kick, scream, and claw your way to the top. There is nothing in the world that is impossible. If you believe that you can do it, you will. See you again in Volume II!

PART IV

Appendixes

APPENDIX A

What's on the CD-ROMs

CD-ROM Disk 1 contains all the source code, executables, sample programs, stock art, software programs, sound effects, online books, graphics engines, and bonus technical articles that make up the book. CD-ROM Disk 2 contains the Introductory version of Microsoft VC++ 6.0. Here's the directory structure of Disk 1:

```
CD-DRIVE:\

T3DGAMER1\

SOURCE\
                T3DCHAP01\
                T3DCHAP02\
                    .
                    .
                T3DCHAP14\
                T3DCHAP15\


APPLICATIONS\

ARTWORK\
                BITMAPS\
                MODELS\

SOUND\
                WAVES\
                MIDI\
```

DIRECTX\

GAMES\

ARTICLES\

ONLINEBOOKS\

ENGINES\

Each main directory contains specific data that you'll need. Here's a more detailed breakdown:

T3DGAMER1	The root directory that contains all other directories. Be sure to read the README.TXT file for any last-minute changes.
SOURCE	Contains all the source directories for the book, in chapter order. Simply drag the entire SOURCE\ directory to your hard drive and work from there.
APPLICATIONS	Contains demo programs that various companies have so graciously allowed me to place on the CD.
ARTWORK	Contains stock artwork that you may use in your games royalty-free.
SOUND	Contains stock sound effects and music that you may use in your games royalty-free.
DIRECTX	Contains the latest version of the DirectX SDK.
GAMES	Contains a number of 2D and 3D shareware games that I think are cool!
ARTICLES	Contains articles for your edification, written by various gurus in the field of game programming.

ONLINEBOOKS   Contains two completely digital online books covering
                               Direct3D and General 3D graphics.

ENGINES   Contains numerous 2D and 3D engines, including the
                               Genesis 3D engine (with full docs), and PowerRender.

There isn't a general installation program for the CD because so many different types
of programs and data exist. I'm leaving the installation to you. However, in most cases
you'll simply copy the SOURCE\ directory to your hard drive and work within it. As for
the other programs and data, you can install them as you need them. Just drag them to
your hard drive or run the various setup or installation programs within each directory.

TIP

In addition, the ONLINEBOOKS\ directory contains complete coverage of
Direct3D and General 3D graphics, so don't forget to check them out to
get a head start on Volume II.

WARNING

When you copy files from a CD-ROM, many times the ARCHIVE bit
and/or the READ-ONLY bit are set. Make sure that any files you copy to
your hard drive have these bits reset. You can reset the bits in Windows
by selecting the files or directory(s) of interest; use the shortcut Ctrl+A
to select all of them, press the right mouse button, and select File
Properties. Once you have the Properties dialog up, reset the READ-
ONLY and ARCHIVE bits, and then press Apply to finish the job.

APPENDIX B

Installing DirectX and Using the C/C++ Compiler

The most important part of the CD that you must install is the DirectX SDK and runtime files. The installation program is located within the DIRECTX\ directory, along with a README.TXT file explaining any last-minute changes.

When you're installing DirectX, pay attention to the location where the installer places the SDK files. You will have to point your compiler's LIB and HEADER search paths appropriately when you want to compile.

In addition, when you install the DirectX SDK, the installer will also ask if you want to install the DirectX runtime files. You need the runtime files as well as the SDK to run the programs. However, there are two versions of the runtime libraries:

Debug—This version has hooks for debugging and is the one that I suggest you install for development. However, your DirectX programs will run a little slower.

Retail—This version is the full release retail consumer version that you would expect a user to have. It's faster than the Debug version. You can always install this one on top of the Debug version later if you want.

> **NOTE**
>
> Attention Borland users (if there are any left): The DirectX SDK does have Borland versions of the `DirectX` `.LIB` import libraries. You will find them in the BORLAND\ directory of the DirectX SDK installation. You must use these files when compiling. Also, make sure to go to Borland's Web site and read the `README.TXT` file in the BORLAND\ directory for any last-minute hints on compiling DirectX programs with Borland compilers

Finally, by the time I finish this book, Microsoft will have approximately six more versions of DirectX. Make sure to keep up-to-date with the SDK by visiting the DirectX site from time to time:

`http://www.microsoft.com/directx/`

Using the C/C++ Compiler

I have received more than 17,000 e-mails in the past three years from people who don't know how to use the C/C++ compiler. I don't want another e-mail about compiler problems unless blood is squirting from the screen and the computer is speaking in tongues! Every single problem was a result of a rookie compiler user. You simply can't expect to use a piece of software as complex as a C/C++ compiler without reading the manual—right, Jules? So please do so before trying to compile programs from this book.

Anyway, here's the deal about compiling: I used MS VC++ 5.0 and 6.0 for this book, so everything works perfectly with those compilers. I'd also imagine that VC++ 4.0 would work, but don't hold me to that (I heard there are some problems with DirectX and VC++ 4.0). If you have a Borland or Watcom compiler, they should work also, but you may have to do a bit of work to get the right setup to compile. My suggestion is to save yourself the headache and get a copy of VC++. Student and Standard editions are usually less than $100.

The bottom line is that the MS compiler is the best for Windows/DirectX programs, and it just makes everything work better. I have used Borland and Watcom for other things, but for Windows applications, I don't know many professional game programmers who don't use MS VC++. It's just the right tool for the right job. (Note to Bill Gates: My Bank of Cayman account number is 412-0300686-21. Thanks.)

Here are some hints for setting up the MS VC++ compilers. Other compilers are similar:

Application Type—DirectX programs are Windows programs. More accurately, they're Win32 .EXE applications. Hence, set your compiler to Win32 .EXE applications for *all* DirectX programs. If I tell you that you're making a *console* application, set the compiler for *console* applications. Also, I suggest that you make a single workspace and compile all your programs in it.

Search Directories—To compile DirectX programs, the compiler needs two things: the .LIB files and the .H files. Now, listen up: Set both search paths in the compiler/linker options to search the DirectX SDK .LIB directory and .H directory so the compiler can find the files during compilation. However, this isn't enough! You must also make absolutely sure the DirectX paths are *first* in the search tree. The reason for placing them first is that VC++ comes with an old version of DirectX, and you will end up linking DirectX 3.0 files if you aren't careful. Furthermore, make sure that you *manually* include the DirectX .LIB files in your projects. I want to see DDRAW.LIB, DSOUND.LIB, DINPUT.LIB, DINPUT8.LIB, and so on in the project! This is very important!!!

Error-Level Setting—Make sure that you turn the error level on your compiler to something reasonable, like level 1 or 2. Don't turn it off, but don't put it on full-blast. The code in this book that I wrote is professional-level C/C++, and the compiler will think that there are a lot of things that I didn't want to do that I intended to do. Hence, turn the warning level down.

Typecast Errors—If the compiler gives you a typecast error on a line of code (VC++ 6.0 users beware), just cast it! I have more than 3,000 e-mails from people who don't know what a typecast is. If you don't, look it up in a C/C++ book. But I will tell you that some of my code may still be missing an explicit typecast here or there. VC++ 6.0 might become belligerent. If you get one of these errors, look at what the compiler expects and just put it in front of the rvalue in the expression to fix it.

Optimization Settings—You aren't making full release products yet, so don't set the compiler to a crazy optimization level. Just set it for standard optimizations that prefer speed over size.

Threading Models—In this book 99% of the examples are single-threaded, so use the single-threaded libraries. If you don't know what that means, read a compiler book. However, when I do use multithreaded libraries, I will tell you. For example, to compile the examples on multithreading from Chapter 11, "Algorithms, Data Structures, Memory Management, and Multithreading," you must switch to the multithreaded libraries.

Code Generation—This controls what kind of code the compiler generates. Set it for Pentium. I haven't seen a 486 in a long time, so don't worry about being compatible.

Struct Alignment—This controls the "filling" between structures. PentiumX processors like things that are in multiples of 32 bytes, so set the alignment as high as possible. It will make the code a bit bigger, but also a lot faster.

Finally, when you're compiling programs, make sure that you include all the source files referenced in the main program. For example, if you see me include T3DLIB1.H, chances are there's a T3DLIB1.CPP that needs to be in the project—get it?

Math and Trigonometry Review

I love math. Do you know why? Because it's indisputable. I don't have to think of the best way to do something. It is what it is, and that's that!

This little math review is divided into sections, so feel free to jump around. It's like a little reference, so you can read it and say, "Oh yeah, that's right!"

Trigonometry

Trigonometry is the study of angles, shapes, and their relationships. Most trigonometry is based on the analysis of a right triangle, as shown in Figure C.1.

Table C.1 lists the radian/degree values.

TABLE C.1   Radians vs. Degrees

360 degrees = 2*PI radians is approximately 6.28 radians

180 degrees = PI radians is approximately 3.14159 radians

Appendixes

TABLE C.1   Continued

360 degrees = 1 radian is approximately 57.296 degrees

2*PI radians

2*PI radians = 1 degree is approximately 0.0175 radians

360 degrees

FIGURE C.1
The right triangle.

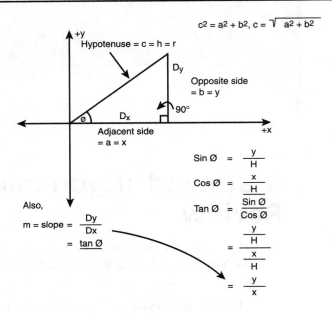

Here are some trigonometric facts:

Fact 1: There are 360 degrees in a complete circle, or 2*PI radians. Hence, there are PI radians in 180 degrees. The computer functions `sin()` and `cos()` work in radians, *not* degrees—remember that! Refer to Table C.1 for a list of common angles in both systems.

Fact 2: The sum of the interior angles *theta1* + *theta2* + *theta3* = 180 degrees or PI radians.

Fact 3: Referring to the right triangle in Figure C.1, the side opposite *theta1* is called the *opposite side*, the side below it is called the *adjacent side*, and the long side is called the *hypotenuse*.

Fact 4: The sum of the squares of the sides of a right triangle equals the square of the hypotenuse. This is called the *Pythagorean theorem*. Mathematically, it's written like this:

```
hypotenuse² = adjacent² + opposite²
```

Or sometimes it's written using a, b, and c for dummy variables:

$c^2 = a^2 + b^2$

Therefore, if you know two sides of a triangle, you can find the third.

Fact 5: There are three main trigonometric ratios that mathematicians like to use: *sine*, *cosine*, and *tangent*. They are defined as

```
                  opposite side        y
sin(theta)   =    ───────────────  =   ─
                   hypotenuse          r
```

```
DOMAIN: 0 <= theta <= 2*PI
RANGE: -1 to 1
```

```
                  adjacent side        x
cos(theta)   =    ───────────────  =   ─
                   hypotenuse          r
```

```
DOMAIN: 0 <= theta <= 2*PI
RANGE: -1 to 1
```

```
                  sin(theta)        opposite/hypotenuse
tan(theta)   =    ───────────   =   ───────────────────
                  cos(theta)        adjacent/hypotenuse

                      opposite        y
                 =    ──────────  =   ─  = slope = M
                      adjacent        x
```

```
DOMAIN: -PI/2 <= theta <= PI/2
RANGE: -infinity to +infinity
```

Figure C.2 shows graphs of all the functions. Notice that they're all periodic (repeating) and that *sin(theta)* and *cos(theta)* have periodicity of 2*PI, while *tangent* has periodicity of PI. Also, notice that *tan(theta)* goes to +-infinity whenever *theta mod PI* is PI/2.

NOTE   You may note the use of the terms *domain* and *range*. They simply mean the input and the output, respectively.

Appendixes

FIGURE C.2

Graphs of basic trigonometric functions.

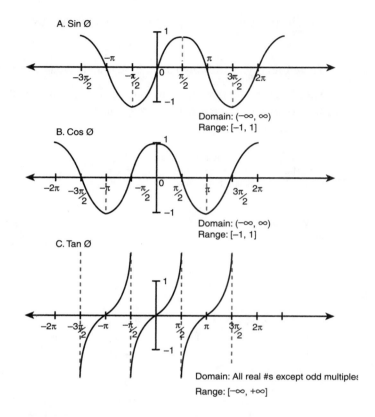

A. Sin Ø

Domain: (−∞, ∞)
Range: [−1, 1]

B. Cos Ø

Domain: (−∞, ∞)
Range: [−1, 1]

C. Tan Ø

Domain: All real #s except odd multiples
Range: [−∞, +∞]

Now, there are about a gazillion trigonometric identities and tricks, and it would take a math book to prove them all. I'm just going to show you the ones that a game programmer should know. Table C.2 lists some trigonometric ratios as well as some neat identities.

TABLE C.2   Useful Trigonometric Identities

Cosecant: csc(theta) = 1/sin(theta)

Secant: sec(theta) = 1/cos(theta)

Cotangent: cot(theta) = 1/tan(theta)

Pythagorean theorem in terms of trig functions:

sin(theta)^2 + cos(theta)^2 = 1

Conversion identity:

sin(theta1) = cos(theta1 − PI/2)

TABLE C.2   Continued

Reflection identities:

sin(-theta) = -sin(theta)

cos(-theta) = cos(theta)

Addition identities:

sin(theta1 + theta2) = sin(theta1)*cos(theta2) + cos(theta1)*sin(theta2)

cos(theta1 + theta2) = cos(theta1)*cos(theta2) – sin(theta1)*sin(theta2)

sin(theta1 – theta2) = sin(theta1)*cos(theta2) – cos(theta1)*sin(theta2)

cos(theta1 – theta2) = cos(theta1)*cos(theta2) + sin(theta1)*sin(theta2)

Of course, you could derive identities until you turned many shades of green. In general, identities help you simplify complex trigonometric formulas into simpler ones so you don't have to do the math. Hence, when you come up with an algorithm based on sin, cos, tan, and so on, always take a look in a trigonometry book to see whether you can simplify your math so that fewer computations are needed to get to the result. Remember: speed, speed, speed!!!

Vectors

Vectors are a game programmer's best friend. They're basically nothing more than line segments and are defined by a starting point and an endpoint, as shown in Figure C.3.

FIGURE C.3

Vectors in the plane.

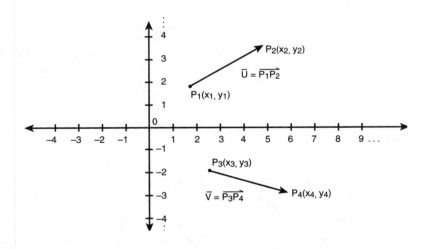

Referring to Figure C.3, you see a vector **U** defined by the two points p1 (the initial point) and p2 (the terminal point). The vector $\mathbf{U} = <u_x, u_y>$ is from p1(x1,y1) to p2(x2,y2). To compute **U**, you simply subtract the initial point from the terminal point:

```
U = p2 - p1 = (x2-x1, y2-y1) = <ux, uy>
```

Also, you usually represent vectors with boldface uppercase letters, like this: **U**. And the components are written within angled brackets, like this: $<u_x, u_y>$.

Okay, so a vector represents a line segment from one point to another, but that segment can represent a lot of concepts, such as *velocity*, *acceleration*, or whatever. Be warned: Vectors, once defined, are always relative to the origin. This means that once you create a vector from p1 to p2, the initial point in vector space is always at (0,0), or (0,0,0) in 3D. This doesn't matter because the math takes care of everything, but if you think about it, it makes sense.

A vector is only two or three numbers in 2D and 3D space, so it really only defines an endpoint in 2D or 3D space. This means the starting point is always thought of as the origin. This doesn't mean that you can't translate vectors around and perform various geometrical operations with the vectors themselves. It just means that you need to keep in mind what a vector really is.

The cool thing about vectors is the operations that you can perform on them. Because vectors are really sets of ordered numbers, you can perform many of the standard mathematical operations on them by performing a mathematical operation on each component independently.

NOTE Vectors can have any number of components. Usually, in computer graphics you'll deal with 2D and 3D vectors, or vectors of the form $\mathbf{A} = <x,y>$, $\mathbf{B} = <x,y,z>$. An *n*-dimensional vector has the form $\mathbf{C} = <c_1, c_2, c_3, ..., c_n>$. *n*-dimensional vectors are used to represent sets of variables rather than geometrical space, because after 3D, you enter *hyperspace*.

Vector Length

The first thing that will pop up time and time again when you're working with vectors is how to compute the length. The length of a vector is called the *norm* and is represented by two vertical bars, like this: |**U**|. This is read as "the length of **U**."

The length is computed as the distance from the origin to the tip of the vector. Hence, you can use the standard Pythagorean theorem to find the length. Therefore, |**U**| is equal to

```
|U| = sqrt(ux2 + uy2)
```

And if **U** happened to be a 3D vector, the length would be

$$|U| = \text{sqrt}(u_x^2 + u_y^2 + u_z^2)$$

Normalization

Once you have the length of a vector, you can do something interesting with it. You can normalize the vector, or shrink it to make sure that its length is 1.0. Unit vectors have a lot of nice properties, just like the scalar 1.0 does, so your intuition probably agrees with me. Given a vector $N=<n_x,n_y>$, the normalized version of **N** is usually written in lowercase as **n** and is computed like this:

$$n = N/|N|$$

Very simple. The normalized version of a vector is simply the vector divided (multiplied by the inverse) by the length of a vector.

Scalar Multiplication

The first operation that you might want to perform on a vector is scaling. You perform this operation by multiplying each component by a single scalar number. For example:

$$\text{Let } U=<u_x, \ u_y>$$
$$k*U = k*<u_x, \ u_y> = <k*u_x, \ k*u_y>$$

Figure C.4 shows the scaling operation graphically.

FIGURE C.4
Vector scaling.

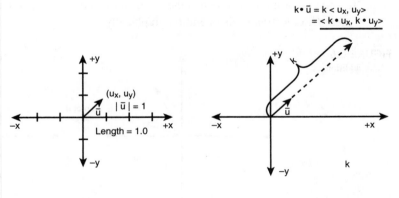

A. Before scaling by k

B After scaling by k

In addition, if you want to invert the direction of a vector, you can multiply any vector by −1. This will invert the vector, as shown in Figure C.5.

FIGURE C.5
Vector inversion.

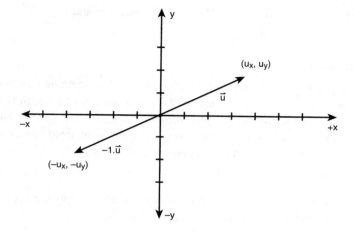

Mathematically:

Let $U=<u_x, u_y>$

The vector in the opposite direction of **U** is

$-1*U = -1*<u_x, u_y> = <-u_x, -u_y>$

Vector Addition

To add two or more vectors together, you simply add the respective components. Figure C.6 illustrates this operation graphically.

FIGURE C.6
Vector addition.

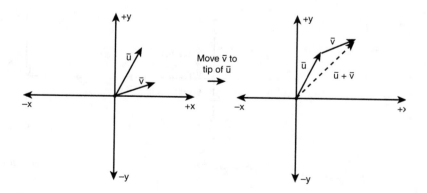

Vector **U** is added to **V**, and the result is **R**. Notice how the addition was performed geometrically. I took **V** and moved it to the terminal point of **U**, and then I drew the other side of the triangle. Geometrically, this is equivalent to the following operation:

$U + V = <u_x, u_y> + <v_x, v_y> = <u_x+v_x, u_y+v_y>$

Thus, to add any number of vectors together on graph paper, you can simply add them "tip to tail." Then, when you add them all up, the vector from the origin to the last tip is the result.

Vector Subtraction

Vector subtraction is really vector addition with the opposite pointing vector. However, it is sometimes helpful to see subtraction graphically also. Take a look at Figure C.7 to see **U–V** and **V–U**.

FIGURE C.7
Vector subtraction.

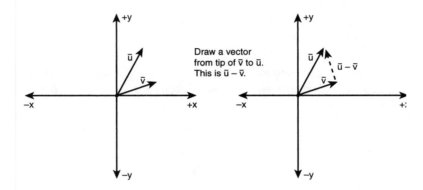

Notice that **U–V** is computed by drawing a vector from **V** to **U**, and **V–U** is computed by drawing a vector from **U** to **V**. Mathematically, it's

U - **V** = <u_x, u_y> - <v_x, v_y> = <u_x-v_x, u_y-v_y>

This expression may be easier to remember, but a piece of graph paper can sometimes be a much better "computer" when you're doing the math manually because you can visualize the data more quickly. Hence, it's a good idea to know how to add and subtract vectors on graph paper when you're rendering algorithms—trust me!

The Inner Product, or the "Dot" Product

At this point you might be asking, "Can you multiply two vectors together?" The answer is yes, but as it turns out, the straight component-wise multiplication isn't very useful. In other words:

U * **V** = <u_x*v_x, u_y*v_y>

This expression doesn't really mean anything in vector space. However, the dot product does. It's defined like this:

U . **V** = u_x*v_x + u_y*v_y

The dot product, usually represented by a dot (.), is computed by adding the products of the individual terms. Moreover, the result is a scalar. Well, heck, how does that help? There aren't even vectors anymore! True, my young Jedi, but the dot product is also equal to this expression:

```
U . V = |U|*|V|*cos θ
```

This expression states that **U** dot **V** is equal to the length of **U** multiplied by the length of **V** multiplied by the cosine of the angle between the vectors. If you combine the two different expressions, you get this:

```
U . V = ux*vx + uy*vy
U . V = |U|*|V|*cos θ
ux*vx + uy*vy = |U|*|V|*cos θ
```

This is a very interesting formula; it basically gives you a way to compute the angle between two vectors, as shown in Figure C.8, and that's a really useful operation.

FIGURE C.8
The dot product.

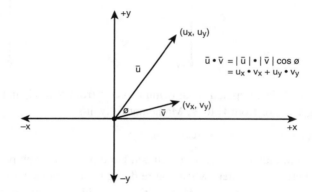

If you can't see how this expression works, take a look at the equation after rearranging and taking the inverse cosine of both sides:

```
θ = cos-1 (ux*vx + uy*vy/|U|*|V|)
```

Or, more compactly, assume that (**U.V**) means ($u_x*v_x + u_y*v_y$) and just write

```
θ = cos-1 (U.V/|U|*|V|)
```

The dot product is a very powerful tool and is the basis of many 3D graphics algorithms. The cool thing is that if the length of **U** and **V** are already 1.0, their product is 1.0 and the formula simplifies even more to

```
θ = cos-1 (U.V), for |U|=|V| = 1.0
```

And here are a couple interesting facts:

Fact 1: If the angle between **U** and **V** is 90 (perpendicular), **U.V** = 0.

Fact 2: If the angle between **U** and **V** is < 90 (acute), **U.V** > 0.

Fact 3: If the angle between **U** and **V** is > 90 (obtuse), **U.V** < 0.

Fact 4: If **U** and **V** are equal, **U.V** = |**U**|^2 = |**V**|^2.

These facts are all shown graphically in Figure C.9.

FIGURE C.9

Angles and their relationships to the dot product.

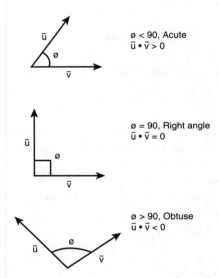

ø < 90, Acute
ū • v̄ > 0

ø = 90, Right angle
ū • v̄ = 0

ø > 90, Obtuse
ū • v̄ < 0

The Cross Product

The next type of multiplication that can be applied to vectors is called the *cross product*. However, the cross product makes sense only on vectors with three or more components, so let's use 3D space vectors as an example. Given **U**=<u_x, u_y, u_z> and **V**=<v_x, v_y, v_z>, the cross product written **U X V** is defined as

```
U X V = |U|*|V|*sin q * n
```

All righty, then! Let's take this expression apart piece by piece. |**U**| denotes the length of **U**, |**V**| denotes the length of **V**, and sin q is the sin of the angle between the vectors. Thus, the product (|**U**|*|**V**|*sin q) is a scalar—that is, a number. Then you multiply it by **n**. But, what is **n**? **n** is a unit vector, which is why it's in lowercase. In addition, **n** is a normal vector, meaning that it's perpendicular to both **U** and **V**. Figure C.10 shows this cross product graphically.

Appendixes

FIGURE C.10
The cross product.

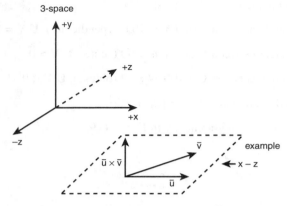

$\bar{u} \times \bar{v}$ is perpendicular to both $\bar{u}_1$ and $\bar{v}$
if both $\bar{u}_1$ and $\bar{v}$ lie in the x – z plane
then $\bar{u} \times \bar{v}$ is parallel to the y axis

So the cross product tells you something about the angle between **U** and **V** and the normal vector to both **U** and **V**. But without another equation, you aren't going to get anywhere. The question is how to compute the normal vector from **U** and **V** so that you can compute the sin q term or whatever. The cross product is also defined as a very special vector product. However, it's hard to show without matrices, so bear with me. Assume that you want to compute the cross product of **U** and **V** written **U X V**. First, you build a matrix like this:

```
|i      j      k  |
|uₓ     u_y    u_z|
|vₓ     v_y    v_z|
```

Here, **i**, **j**, and **k** are unit vectors parallel to the x, y, and z axes, respectively.

Then, to compute the cross product of **U** and **V**, you perform this multiplication:

```
N=(u_y*v_z-v_y*u_z)*i + (-uₓ*v_z+vₓ*u_z)*j + (uₓ*v_y-vₓ*u_y)*k
```

That is, **N** is just a linear combination of three scalars, each multiplied by mutually orthogonal (perpendicular) unit vectors that are each parallel to the x, y, and z axes, respectively. Thus, you can forget the **i**, **j**, and **k** and rewrite the equation as

```
N=<u_y*v_z-v_y*u_z,  -uₓ*v_z+vₓ*u_z,  uₓ*v_y-vₓ*u_y>
```

N is the normal vector to both **U** and **V**. However, it's not necessarily a unit vector (if **U** and **V** were both unit vectors, **N** would be), so you must normalize it to find **n**. Once that's done, you can plug everything into your cross product equation and do what you will.

In practice, though, few people ever use the $\mathbf{U} \times \mathbf{V} = |\mathbf{U}|*|\mathbf{V}|*\sin \theta * \mathbf{n}$ formula. They simply use the matrix form to find the normal vector. Again, normal vectors are very important in 3D graphics, and you will be computing a lot of them in Volume II! Normals are great not only because they are normal to two vectors, but they also are used to define planes and to compare the orientation of polygons—useful for collision detection, rendering, lighting, and so forth.

The Zero Vector

Although you probably won't use the zero vector much, it's still there. The *zero vector* has zero length and no direction. It's just a point, if you want to get technical. Thus, in 2D the zero vector is <0,0>, in 3D it's <0,0,0>, and so on for higher dimensions.

Position Vectors

The next topic I want to talk about is position vectors. They are really useful when you're tracing out geometrical entities like lines, segments, curves, and so on. I used them during clipping and during the computation of segment intersection in Chapter 13, "Playing God: Basic Physics Modeling," so they're important. Take a look at Figure C.11, which depicts a position vector that can be used to represent a line segment.

FIGURE C.11
Position vectors.

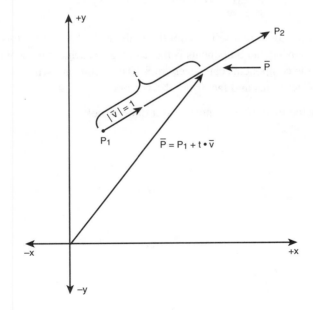

The line segment is from p1 to p2, $\mathbf{V}$ is the vector from p1 to p1, and $\mathbf{v}$ is a unit vector from p1 to p2. You then construct $\mathbf{P}$ to trace out the segment. $\mathbf{P}$ looks like this, mathematically:

```
P = p1 + t*v
```

Here, t is a parameter that varies from 0 to |**V**|. If t=0, you have

```
P = p1 + 0*v = <p1> = <p1ₓ, p1_y>
```

Thus, at t=0, **P** is pointing to the beginning of the segment. On the other hand, when t=|**V**|, you have

```
P = p1 + |V|*v = p1 + V = <p1+V>
              = <p1ₓ+Vₓ, p1_y+V_y>
              = p2 = <p2ₓ, p2_y>
```

Vectors as Linear Combinations

As you saw in the cross product calculation, vectors can also be written in this notation:

```
U = uₓ*i + u_y*j + u_z*k
```

Here, **i**, **j**, and **k** are unit vectors parallel to the x, y, and z axes. There's nothing magical about this notation; it's just another way to write vectors that you might need to know. All the operations still work exactly the same. For example:

```
let U = 3i + 2j + 3k
let V = -3i - 5j + 12k

U + V = 3i + 2j + 3k - 3i - 5j + 12k
      = 0i - 3j + 15k = <0, -3, 15>
```

Nothing but notation, really. The cool thing about thinking of vectors as linear combinations of independent components is that as long as each component has its vector coefficient, the components can never "mix." Thus, you can write very long expressions and then collect terms and factor out the vectors.

That's it for the math review; now read it once more!

APPENDIX D

C++ Primer

First, let's get the pronunciation of "primer" out of the way. For many years I pronounced "primer" so it rhymed with "timer," but the truth is, that's wrong. My friend Mitch Waite (the founder of Waite Group) has made a pretty good living off the word "primer," but he told me one day that a British author working for him said that he was pronouncing the word wrong. "Primer" actually rhymes with "trimmer." "Primer," the way we were pronouncing it, means the stuff you put on something before you paint it, or the first stage in an explosive process. In any case, I don't know if I will ever say it right. "PRIME-ER" just sounds better!

TRICK

If you're a C++ programmer, you might be asking, "Why does André always use C?" The answer is simple—C is easier to understand, and that's all there is to it. C++ programmers obviously know C because it's a subset, and most game programmers learn C before C++.

What Is C++?

C++ is simply C upgraded with *object-oriented* (OO) technology. Really, it's nothing more than a superset of C. C++ has the following major upgrades:

- Classes
- Inheritance
- Polymorphism

Let's take a quick look at each of these features. *Classes* are simply a way of combining data and functions. Normally, when you program in C, you have data structures that hold data and functions that operate on the data, as shown in part A of Figure D.1. However, with C++, both the data and the functions to operate on the data are contained within a class, as shown in part B of Figure D.1. Why is this good? Well, you can think of a class as an *object* that has properties and that can perform actions. It's just a more abstract way of thinking.

FIGURE D.1
The structure of a class.

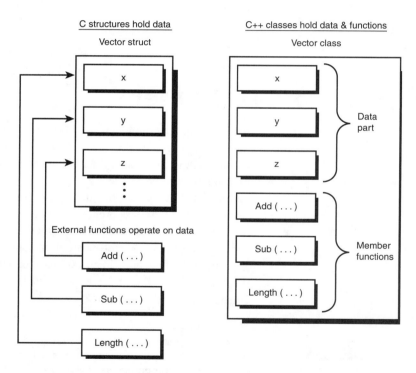

A. In C, the functions that operate on structures are external to the structure.

B. In C++, both data & functions are defined in the class.

The next cool thing about C++ is *inheritance*. Once you create classes, they give you the abstract ability to create relationships between class objects and base one object or class upon another. It's done all the time in real life, so why not in software? For example, you might have a class called person that contains data about the person and maybe some class methods to operate on the data (don't worry about that for now). The point is, a person is fairly generic. But the power of inheritance comes into play when you want to create two different types of people—a software engineer and a hardware engineer, for example. Let's call them sengineer and hengineer.

Figure D.2 shows the relationship between person, sengineer, and hengineer. See how the two new classes are based on person? Both sengineer and hengineer are persons, but with extra data. Thus, you inherit the properties of a person but add new ones to create sengineer and hengineer. This is the basis of inheritance. You build up more complex objects from preexisting ones. In addition, there is *multiple inheritance*, which enables you to build a new object as a set of subclasses.

FIGURE D.2
Class inheritance.

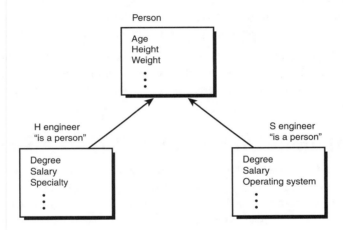

The third and last big deal about C++ and OO programming is *polymorphism*, meaning "many forms." In the context of C++, polymorphism means that functions or operators are different things depending on the situation. For example, you know that the expression (a + b) in straight C means to add a and b together. You also know that a and b *must* be built in types such as int, float, char, and short. In C, you can't define a new type and then say (a + b). In C++, you can! Therefore, you can overload operators like +, -, *, /, [], and so on and make them do different things depending on the data.

Furthermore, you can overload functions. For example, let's say you write a function Compute() like this:

```
int Compute (float x, float y)
{
// code
}
```

The function takes two floats, but if you send it integers, they're simply converted to floats and then passed to the function. Hence, you lose data. However, in C++ you can do this:

```
int Compute (float x, float y)
{
// code
}

int Compute (int x, int y)
{
// code
}
```

Even though the functions have the same names, they take different types. The compiler thinks they're completely different functions, so a call with integers calls the second function, whereas a call with floats calls the first. If you call the function with a float and an integer, things get more complex. Promotion rules come into play, and the compiler decides which one to call using those rules.

That's really all there is to C++. Of course, there's some added syntax and a lot of rules about all this stuff, but for the most part all of it has to do with implementing these three new concepts. Pretty easy explanation of what will become a very complicated concept, huh?

The Minimum You Need to Know About C++

C++ is an extremely complex language, and using the new technologies too much and too fast can create totally unreliable programs with all kinds of memory leaks, performance issues, and so on. The problem with C++ is that it is a language of black boxes. A number of processes go on behind the scenes, and you may never find bugs that you have created. However, if you start off using just a little C++ here and there and then add new features to your repertoire as you need them, you'll be fine.

The only reason that I even wrote this appendix on C++ is that DirectX is based on it. However, most of C++ is encapsulated in wrappers and COM interfaces that you communicate with via function pointer calls—that is, calls of the form `interface->function()`. If you've made it this far in the book, you must have just dealt with that weird syntax. Moreover, Chapter 5, "DirectX Fundamentals and the Dreaded COM," the chapter on COM (Component Object Model) should have eased your nerves on the subject. In any event, I am going to cover just the basics so you can better understand C++, talk about it with your friends, and have a good working knowledge of what's available.

I am going to cover some new types, conventions, memory management, stream I/O, basic classes, and function and operator overloading, and that's about it—but believe me, that's enough! So, let's get started...

New Types, Keywords, and Conventions

Let's start off with something simple—the new comment operator (//). It has become part of C, so you might already use it, but the // operator is a single-line comment in C++.

Comments

```
// this is a comment
```

And you can still use the old comment style, /* */, if you like:

```
/* a C style multiline comment

everything in here is a comment

*/
```

Constants

To create a constant in standard C, you can do one of two things:

```
#define PI 3.14
```

or

```
float PI = 3.14;
```

The problem with the first method is that PI isn't a real variable with a type. It's only a symbol that the preprocessor uses to do a text replacement, so it has no type, no size, and so on. The problem with the second type definition is that it is writeable. Thus, C++ has a new type called const, which is like a read-only variable:

```
const float PI = 3.14;
```

Now, you can use PI anywhere you want—its type is float, and its size is sizeof(float)—but you can't overwrite it. This is really a much better way to make constants.

Referential Variables

In C, you will often want to change the value of a variable in a function, so you pass a pointer like this:

```
int counter = 0;

void foo(int *x)
{
(*x)++;
}
```

And if you make a call to `foo(&counter)`, counter will be equal to 1 after the call. Hence, the function changes the value of the sent variable. This is such a common practice that C++ has a new type of variable to help make it easier to do. It's called a *reference* variable and is denoted by the address operator, &.

```
int counter = 0;

void foo(int &x)
{
x++;
}
```

Interesting, huh? But, how do you call the function? You do it like this:

```
foo(counter);
```

Notice that you don't need to put the & in front of counter anymore. What happens is that x becomes an alias for whichever variable is sent. Therefore, counter is x and no & is needed during the call.

You can also create references outside functions, like this:

```
int x;

int &x_alias = x;
```

x_alias is an alias to x. Wherever and however you use x, you can use x_alias— they are *identical*. I don't see much need for this, though.

Creating Variables On-the-Fly

One of the coolest new features of C++ is the ability to create variables within code blocks and not just at the global or function level. For example, here's how you might write a loop in C:

```
void Scan(void)
{
int index;

// lots of code here...

// finally our loop
for (index = 0; index < 10; index++)
    Load_Data(index);

// more code here...

} // end Scan
```

There's nothing wrong with code. However, index is used as a loop index in only one code segment. The designers of C++ saw this as nonrobust and felt that variables should be defined closer to where they're used. Moreover, a variable that's used in one code block shouldn't be visible to other code blocks. For example, say you have a set of code blocks like this:

```
void Scope(void)
{
int x = 1, y = 2; // global scope
printf("\nBefore Block A: Global Scope x=%d, y=%d",x,y);
    { // Block A
    int x = 3, y = 4;
    printf("\nIn Block A: x=%d, y=%d",x,y);
    } // end Block A
printf("\nAfter Block A: Global Scope x=%d, y=%d",x,y);
    { // Block B
    int x = 5, y = 6;
    printf("\nIn Block B: x=%d, y=%d",x,y);
    } // end Block B
printf("\nAfter Block B: Global Scope x=%d, y=%d",x,y);
} // end Scope
```

There are three different versions of x,y. The first x,y is globally defined. However, once code block A is entered, they go out of scope in light of the locals x and y that come into scope. Then, when code block A exits, the old x and y come back into scope with their old values, and the same process occurs for block B. With block-level scoping, you can better localize variables and their use. Moreover, you don't have to keep thinking up new variable names; you can continue to use x,y or whatever and not worry about the new variables corrupting globals with the same name.

The really cool thing about this new variable scoping is that you can create a variable on-the-fly in code. For example, take a look at the same for() loop based on index, but using C++:

```
// finally our loop
for (int index = 0; index < 10; index++)
    Load_Data(index);
```

Isn't that the coolest? I defined index right as I used it rather than at the top of the function. Just don't get too carried away with it.

Memory Management

C++ has a new memory management system based on the operators new and delete. They are equivalent to malloc() and free() for the most part, but are much smarter because they take into consideration the type of data being requested and/or deleted. Here's an example:

In C, to allocate 1,000 ints from the heap:

```
int *x = (int*)malloc(1000*sizeof(int));
```

What a mess! Here's the same thing in C++:

```
int *x = new int[1000];
```

Much nicer, huh? You see, new already knows to send back a pointer to int—that is, an int*—so you don't have to cast it. Now, to release the memory in C, you would do this:

```
free(x);
```

In C++, you would do this:

```
delete x;
```

They're about the same, but the cool part is the new operator. Also, use either C or C++ to allocate memory. Don't mix calls to new with calls to free(), and don't mix calls to malloc() with calls to delete.

Stream I/O

I love printf(). Nothing is more pure than

```
printf("\nGive me some sugar baby.");
```

The only problem with printf() is all those format specifiers, like %d, %x, %u, and so forth. They're hard to remember. In addition, scanf() is even worse because you can really mess things up if you forget to use the address of a variable for storage. For example:

```
int x;
```

```
scanf("%d",x);
```

This is incorrect! You need the address of x or &x, so the correct syntax is

```
scanf("%d",&x);
```

I'm sure you have made this mistake. The only time you don't have to use the address operator is when you're working with strings, because the name is the address. In any case, this is why the new IOSTREAM class was created in C++. It knows the types of the variables, so you don't need to tell it anymore. The IOSTREAM class functions are defined in IOSTREAM.H, so you need to include it in your C++ programs to use it. Once you do, you will have access to the streams cin, cout, cerr, and cprn, as shown in Table D.1.

TABLE D.1   C++ I/O Streams

Stream Name	Device	C Name	Meaning
cin	Keyboard	stdin	Standard input
cout	Screen	stdout	Standard output
cerr	Screen	stderr	Standard error
cprn	Printer	stdprn	Printer

Using the I/O streams is a bit weird because they're based on the overloaded operators, << and >>. These operators normally signify bit shifting in C, but in the context of the I/O streams, they're used to send and receive data. Here are some examples of using the standard output:

```cpp
int i;
float f;
char c;
char string[80];

// in C
printf("\nHello world!");

// in C++
cout << "\nHello world!";

// in C
printf("%d", i);

// in C++
cout << i;

// in C
printf("%d,%f,%c,%s", i, f, c, string);

// in C++
cout << i << "," << f << "," << c << "," << string;
```

Isn't that cool? You don't need any type specifier because cout already knows the type and does it for you. The only really weird thing about the syntax is the way C++ allows you to concatenate the << operator to the end of each operation. The reason for this is that each operation returns a stream itself, so you can add << forever. The only downside to using streams for simple printing is the way you have to separate variables and string constants, like the "," that separates each variable. However, you can put the << on each line if you wish, like this:

```cpp
cout << i
     << ","
     << f
     << ","
```

```
    << c
    << ","
    << string;
```

Remember, in C and C++, whitespace is discarded, so this coding is legal.

The input stream works in much the same way, but with the >> operator instead. Here are some examples:

```
int i;
float f;
char c;
char string[80];

// in C
printf("\nWhat is your age?");
scanf("%d",&i);

// in C++
cout << "\nWhat is your age?";
cin >> i;

// in C
printf("\nWhat is your name and grade?");
scanf("%s %c", string, &c);

// in C++
cout << "\nWhat is your name and grade?";
cin >> string >> c;
```

A little nicer than C, isn't it? Of course, the IOSTREAM system has a million other functions, so check it out.

Classes

Classes are the most important addition to C++ and give the language its OO zeal. As I discussed before, a *class* is simply a container of both data and the methods (often called *member functions*) that operate on that data.

The New Struct in Town

Let's begin learning classes by starting with standard structures, with a little added twist. In C, you defined a structure like this:

```
struct Point
{
int x,y;
};
```

Then you could create an instance of a structure with this:

```
struct Point p1;
```

This creates an instance or object of the structure `Point` and names it `p1`. In C++, you don't need to use the `struct` keyword anymore to create an instance, hence:

```
Point p1;
```

This creates an instance of the structure `Point` named `p1`. The reason for this is that C++ programmers have been creating types so they didn't have to type `struct` anymore, like this:

```
typedef struct tagPOINT
{
int x,y;
} Point;
```

Thus the syntax

```
Point p1;
```

Classes are similar to the new structures in that you don't have to create a type. The definitions themselves are the types.

Just a Simple Class

A class in C++ is defined with the keyword `class`. Here's an example:

```
class Point
{
public:
int x,y;

};
```

```
Point p1;
```

This is almost identical to the struct version of `Point`; in fact, both versions of `p1` work in the exact same way. For example, to access data, you just use the normal syntax:

```
p1.x = 5;
p1.y = 6;
```

And, of course, pointers work the same way. So, if you defined something like

```
Point *p1;
```

then you would have to allocate memory for it first with `malloc()` or `new`:

```
p1 = new Point;
```

Finally, you could assign values to `x,y` like this:

```
p1->x = 5;
p1->y = 6;
```

The bottom line is that classes and structures are identical when accessing public data elements. The key term is *public*—what does this mean? If you noticed in my previous example of the `Point` class, defined as

```
class Point
{
public:
int x,y;
};
```

the keyword `public:` appears at the top of the definition before any declarations. This defines the visibility of the variables (and member functions). There are a number of visibility options, but usually only two are used—`public` and `private`.

Public Versus Private

If you place the keyword `public` at the top of all your class definitions and have only data in the classes, you have nothing more than a standard structure. That is, structures are classes with public visibility. Public visibility means that anyone can look at the class data elements. As for code in the main, other functions, and member functions, the data is not hidden or encapsulated. Private visibility, on the other hand, lets you hide data that shouldn't be altered by other functions that aren't part of the class. For example, take a look at this class:

```
class Vector3D
{
public:
int x,y,z; // anyone can mess with these

private:
    int reference_count; // this is hidden

};
```

`Vector3D` has two different parts: the public data area and the private data area. The public data area has three fields that can be changed by anyone: `x,y,z`. On the other hand, there is a hidden field called ***reference_count*** in the private section. This field is hidden to everything except the member functions of the class (there aren't any yet). Thus, if you were to write some code like this:

```
Vector3D v;

v.reference_count = 1; // illegal!
```

the compiler would give you an error! So the question is, what good are private variables if you can't access them? Well, they're great for writing something like a black box class when you don't want or need the user to alter internal working variables. In that example, private is the way to go. However, to access the private members, you need to add member functions or methods to the class—this is where we jump off the deep end....

Class Member Functions (a.k.a. Methods)

A member function, or *method* (depending on whom you're talking to), is basically a function within a class that works only with the class. Here's an example:

```
class Vector3D
{
public:
int x,y,z; // anyone can mess with these

    // this is a member function
    int length(void)
        {
        return(sqrt(x*x + y*y + z*z);
        } // end length

private:
    int reference_count; // this is hidden

};
```

Notice the highlighted member function `length()`. I have defined a function right in the class! Weird, huh? Let's see how to use it:

```
Vector3D v; // create a vector

// set the values
v.x = 1;
v.y = 2;
v.z = 3;

// here's the cool part
printf("\nlength = %d",v.length());
```

You call a class member function just like you access an element. And if v were a pointer, you would do this:

```
v->length();
```

Now, you might be saying, "I have about 100 functions that are going to have to access the class data; I can't possibly put them all in the class!" Well, you can if you want, but I agree that it would get messy. However, you can define class member functions outside the class definition. We'll get to that in a minute. Right now, I want to add another member function to show you how you might access that private data member `reference_count`:

```
class Vector3D
{
public:
int x,y,z; // anyone can mess with these

    // this is a member function
    int length(void)
```

```
          {
          return(sqrt(x*x + y*y + z*z);
          } // end length

   // data access member function
    void addref(void)
    {
    // this function increments the reference count
    reference_count++;

    } // end addref

private:
    int reference_count; // this is hidden

};
```

You talk to `reference_count` via the member function `addref()`. This approach may seem odd, but if you think about it, it's a good thing. Now the user can't do anything stupid to the data member. It always goes through your access function, which in this case allows the caller only to increment the `reference_count`, as in

```
v.addref();
```

The caller can't change the reference count, multiply it by a number, and so on because `reference_count` is private. Only member functions of the class can access it—this is data hiding and encapsulation.

At this point, I think you're seeing the power of classes. You can fill them with data-like structure, add functions within the classes that operate on the data, and hide data—pretty cool! But it gets even better!

Constructors and Destructors

If you've been programming C for more than a week, there's something that I'm sure you've had to do about a million times—initialize a structure. For example, say that you create a structure `Person` like this:

```
struct Person
{
int age;
char *address;
int salary;
};

Person people[1000];
```

Now, you need to initialize 1,000 `people` structures. Maybe all you want to do is this:

```
for (int index = 0; index < 1000; index++)
{
```

```
people[index].age     = 18;
people[index].address = NULL;
people[index].salary  = 35000;

} // end for index
```

But what if you forget to initialize the data and then just use the structures? Well, you might wind up seeing your old friend General Protection Fault. Similarly, during the run of your program, what if you allocate memory and point the address field of a person to the memory like this?

```
people[20].address = malloc(1000);
```

And then you use the memory, forget about it, and do this:

```
people[20].address = malloc(4000);
```

Oops! A thousand bytes of memory just went to never-never land. What you needed to do, before allocating more memory, was release the old memory with a call to free() like this:

```
free(people[20].address);
```

I think you've probably made this mistake too. C++ solves these housekeeping problems by giving you two new automatic functions that are called when you create a class: *constructors* and *destructors*.

Constructors are called when a class object is instantiated. For example, when this code is executed:

```
Vector3D v;
```

the default constructor is called, which doesn't do anything in this case. And similarly, when v goes out of scope—that is, when the function that v was defined in terminates, or if v is global when the program terminates—the default destructor is called, which again doesn't do anything. To see any action, you have to write a constructor and destructor. You don't have to if you don't want to, and you can define one or both.

Writing a Constructor

Let's use the person structure converted to a class as an example:

```
class Person
{
public:
int age;
char *address;
int salary;

// this is the default constructor
// constructors can take a void, or any other set of parms
```

Appendixes

```
// but they never return anything, not even a void
Person()
      {
      age     = 0;
      address = NULL;
 salary  = 35000;
      } // end Person
};
```

Notice that the constructor has the same name as the class, in this case `Person`. This is not a coincidence—it's a rule! Also, notice that the constructor returns nothing. This is a must. However, the constructor can take parameters. In this case, there are no parameters, but you can have constructors with parameters. In fact, you can have an infinite number of different constructors, each with a different calling list. This is how you can create various types of `Persons` with different calls. Anyway, to create a `Person` and have it automatically initialized, you just do this:

```
Person person1;
```

The constructor will be called automatically, and the following assignments will occur:

```
person1.age     = 0;
person1.address = NULL;
person1.salary  = 35000;
```

Cool, huh? Now, the power of the constructor comes into play when you code something like this:

```
Person people[1000];
```

The constructor will be called for every single instance of `Person`, and all 1,000 of them will be initialized without a single line of code on your part!

All right, now let's get a little more advanced. Remember how I told you that functions could be overloaded? Well, you can overload constructors too. Hence, if you wanted a constructor for which you could set the age, address, and salary during its creation, you could do this:

```
class Person
{
public:
int age;
char *address;
int salary;

// this is the default constructor
// constructors can take a void, or any other set of parms
// but they never return anything, not even void
Person()
      {
      age     = 0; address = NULL; salary  = 35000;
      } // end Person
```

```
// here's our new more powerful constructor
Person(int new_age, char *new_address, int new_salary)
{
// set the age
age = new_age;

// allocate the memory for the address and set address
address = new char[strlen(new_address)+1];
strcpy(address, new_address);

// set salary
salary = new_salary;

} // end Person int, char *, int

};
```

Now you have two constructors, one that takes no parameters and one that takes three: an `int`, a `char *`, and another `int`. Here's an example of creating a person who is 24 years old, lives at 500 Maple Street, and makes $52,000 a year:

```
Person person2(24,"500 Maple Street", 52000);
```

Isn't that the coolest? Of course, you might think that you can initialize C structures as well with a different syntax, something like:

```
Person person = {24, "500 Maple Street", 52000};
```

However, what about the memory allocation? What about the string copying, and so on? Straight C can do a blind copy, but that's it. C++ gives you the power to also run code and logic when an object is created. This gives you much more control.

Writing a Destructor

After you've created an object, at some point it must die. This is where you might normally call a `cleanup` function in C, but in C++ the object cleans itself up via a call to its destructor. Writing a destructor is even simpler than writing a constructor because you have much less flexibility with destructors—they have only one form:

```
~classname();
```

No parameter, no return type—period. No exceptions! With this in mind, let's add a destructor to your `Person` class:

```
class Person
{
public:
int age;
char *address;
int salary;
```

```
// this is the default constructor
// constructors can take a void, or any other set of parms
// but they never return anything, not even void
Person()
      {
      age     = 0; address = NULL; salary  = 35000;
      } // end Person

// here's our new more powerful constructor
Person(int new_age, char *new_address, int new_salary)
{
// set the age
age = new_age;

// allocate the memory for the address and set address
address = new char[strlen(new_address)+1];
strcpy(address, new_address);

// set salary
salary = new_salary;

} // end Person int, char *, int


// here's our destructor
~Person()
      {
      free(address);
      } // end ~Person

};
```

I've highlighted the destructor. Notice that there's nothing special about the code within it; I could have done anything that I wanted. With this new destructor, you don't have to worry about deallocating memory. For example, in C, if you created a structure with internal pointers in a function and then exited the function without deallocating the memory pointed to by the structure, that memory would be lost forever. That's called a *memory leak* and is shown here with a C example:

```
struct
    {
    char *name;
    char *ext;
    } filename;

foo()
{
filename file; // here's a filename

file.name = malloc(80);
file.ext  = malloc(4);

} // end foo
```

The structure `file` is destroyed, but the 84 bytes you allocated are lost forever! But in C++, with your destructor, this won't happen because the compiler makes sure to call the destructor for you, which deallocates the memory.

I've provided the basics about constructors and destructors, but there's a lot more. There are special constructors called copy constructors, assignment constructors, and so forth. But you have enough to get started. As for destructors, there's just one type, the one I showed you, so you're in good shape there.

The Scope Resolution Operator

There's a new operator in C++ called the *scope resolution operator*, represented by a double colon (`::`). It's used to make reference to class functions and data members at class scope. Don't worry too much about what that means; I'm just going to show you how to use it to define class functions outside the class.

Thus far you've been defining class member functions right inside the class definition. Although this is totally acceptable for small classes, it gets to be a little problematic for large classes. Hence, you're free to write class member functions outside the class, as long as you define them properly and let the compiler know that they're class functions and not normal file-level functions. You do this with the scope resolution operator and the following syntax:

```
return_type class_name::function_name(parm_list)
{
// function body
}
```

Of course, in the class itself, you must still define the function with a prototype (minus the scope resolution operator and class name, of course), but you can hold off on the body until later. Let's try this with your `Person` class and see what you get. Here's the new class with the function bodies removed:

```
class Person
{
public:
int age;
char *address;
int salary;

// this is the default constructor
Person();

// here's our new more powerful constructor
Person(int new_age, char *new_address, int new_salary);
```

```
// here's our destructor
~Person();

};
```

And here are the function bodies, which you would place with all your other functions after the class definition:

```
Person::Person()
{
// this is the default constructor
// constructors can take a void, or any other set of parms
// but they never return anything, not even void
age     = 0;
address = NULL;
salary  = 35000;

} // end Person

//////////////////////////////////////////////////////

Person::Person(int new_age,
               char *new_address,
               int new_salary)
{
// here's our new more powerful constructor
// set the age
age = new_age;

// allocate the memory for the address and set address
address = new char[strlen(new_address)+1];
strcpy(address, new_address);

// set salary
salary = new_salary;

} // end Person int, char *, int

//////////////////////////////////////////////////////

Person::~Person()
{
// here's our destructor
free(address);
} // end ~Person
```

TRICK Most programmers place a capital C before class names. I usually do, but I didn't want to trip you out. Thus, if I was programming, I probably would have called it CPerson instead of Person. Or maybe, CPERSON in all caps.

Function and Operator Overloading

The last topic I want to talk about is *overloading*, which comes in two flavors: *function overloading* and *operator overloading*. I don't have time to explain operator overloading in detail, but I'll give you a general example. Imagine that you have your `Vector3D` class and you want to add two vectors, v1 + v2, and store the sum in v3. You might do something like this:

```
Vector3D v1 = {1,3,5},
         v2 = {5,9,8},
         v3 = {0,0,0};


// define an addition function, this could have
// been a class function
Vector3D Vector3D_Add(Vector3D v1, Vector3D v2)
{
Vector3D sum; // temporary used to hold sum

sum.x = v1.x+v2.x;
sum.y = v1.y+v2.y;
sum.z = v1.z+v2.z;

return(sum);

}// end Vector3D_Add
```

Then, to add the vectors with the function, you would write the following code:

```
v3 = Vector3D_Add(v1, v2);
```

It's crude, but it works. With C++ and operator overloading, you can actually overload the + operator and make a new version of it to add the vectors! So you can write this:

```
v3 = v1+v2;
```

Cool, huh? The syntax of the overloaded operator function follows, but you'll have to read a C++ book for details:

```
class Vector3D
{
public:

int x,y,z; // anyone can mess with these

// this is a member function
int length(void)  {return(sqrt(x*x + y*y + z*z)); }

// overloaded the + operator
Vector3D operator+(Vector3D &v2)
{
Vector3D sum; // temporary used to hold sum
```

```
sum.x = x+v2.x;
sum.y = y+v2.y;
sum.z = z+v2.z;

return(sum);
}

private:
    int reference_count; // this is hidden

};
```

Notice that the first parameter is implicitly the object, so the parameter list has only v2. Anyway, operator overloading is very powerful. With it, you can really create new data types and operators so that you can perform all kinds of cool operations without making calls to functions.

You already saw function overloading when I was talking about constructors. Function overloading is nothing more than writing two or more functions that have the same name but different parameter lists. Let's say you want to write a function called Plot Pixel that has the following functionality: If you call it without parameters, it simply plots a pixel at the current cursor position, but if you call it with an x,y, it plots a pixel at the position x,y. Here's how you would code it:

```
int cursor_x, cursor_y; // global cursor position

// the first version of Plot_Pixel
void Plot_Pixel(void)
{
// plot a pixel at the cursor position
plot(cursor_x, cursor_y);
}


//////////////////////////////////

// the second version of Plot_Pixel
void Plot_Pixel(int x, int y)
{
// plot a pixel at the sent position and update
// cursor
plot(cursor_x=x, cursor_y=y);
}
```

You can call the functions like this:

```
Plot_Pixel(10,10); // calls version 2

Plot_Pixel(); // calls version 1
```

TRICK
The compiler knows the difference because the *real* name of the function is created not only by the function name, but by a mangled version of the parameter list, creating a unique name in the compiler's namespace.

Summary

Well, that's my whirlwind tour of C++. If Robert Lafore (the world's best C++ author) read this appendix, he would probably kill me for being so liberal, but all in all you should have a working knowledge of the language now, and at least be able to follow C++ code, if not write it.

APPENDIX E

Game Programming Resources

The following is a potpourri of resources that you might find useful in your endeavors as a game programmer.

Game Programming Sites

There are hundreds of great game programming sites, so I can't list them all here. The following are some of my favorites:

GameDev.Net

http://www.gamedev.net/

The Official MAME Page

http://www.mame.net/

The Games Domain

http://www.gamesdomain.com/

The Coding Nexus

http://www.gamesdomain.com/gamedev/gprog.html

The Computer Game Developers' Conference

`http://www.gdconf.com`

The Xtreme Game Developers' Conference

`http://www.xgdc.com`

Download Points

A game programmer needs to have access to cool games, tools, utilities, and stuff like that. Here's a list of places that I like to download from:

eGameZone	`http://www.egamezone.net`
Happy Puppy	`http://www.happypuppy.com`
Game Pen	`http://www.gamepen.com/topten.asp`
Ziff Davis Net	`http://www.zdnet.com/swlib/games.html`
Adrenaline Vault	`http://www.avault.com/pcrl/`
Download.Com	`http://www.download.com/pc/cdoor/`
	`0,323,0-17,00.html?st.dl.fd.cats.cat17`
Jumbo.Com	`http://www.jumbo.com/games/g2/`
GT Interactive	`http://www.gtgames.com`
Epic Megagames	`http://www.epicgames.com`
CNet	`http://www.cnet.com`
WinFiles.com	`http://www.winfiles.com`
eGames	`http://www.egames.com`

2D/3D Engines

There's one place on the Web that's the focal point of all 3D engine development. It's called *The 3D Engine List* and contains 3D engines of varying levels of technology. The amazing thing is that many of the authors will let you use their engines for free! Here's the address:

`http://cg.cs.tu-berlin.de/~ki/engines.html`

In addition, here are some links to some specific 2D/3D engines that rock!

Genesis 3D Engine	`http://www.genesis3d.com`
SciTech MGL	`http://www.scitechsoft.com`
Crystal Space	`http://crystal.linuxgames.com/`

Game Programming Books

There are a lot of books on graphics, sound, multimedia, and game development, but buying them all is too expensive. Therefore, here are some sites that review game-related books and give you the lowdown:

Games Domain Bookstore

http://www.gamesdomain.com/gamedev/gdevbook.html

Premier Publishing Game Development Series

http://www.premierpressbooks.com/gamedevseries.asp

Microsoft DirectX Multimedia Exposition

Undoubtedly, Microsoft has the biggest Web site in the world. There are thousands of pages, sections, FTP sites, and so on. However, the page that you should be interested in is the DirectX Multimedia Expo. You can find it at

http://www.microsoft.com/directx/

On this page you'll find the latest news and downloads of the latest versions of DirectX, DirectMedia, and any patches to previous versions. You could do worse than to take an hour each week and read through this information. It will definitely keep you up-to-date with the wonderful world of Microsoft and DirectX. And, of course, let's not leave out the new Xbox site:

http://www.xbox.com/

Usenet Newsgroups

I've never been much into Internet newsgroups because using them is such a slow way to communicate (it's almost as bad as reading hard copy). But here are a few newsgroups that might be worth checking out:

```
alt.games
rec.games.programmer
comp.graphics.algorithms
comp.graphics.animation
comp.ai.games
```

If you've never read newsgroups before, read on…. You'll need a newsreader that can download the information and allow you to read the message threads. Most Web browsers, such as Netscape Navigator and Internet Explorer, have a built-in newsreader. Just read the Help files and figure out how to set up your browser to read newsgroups.

Then log on to any of the newsgroups, such as `alt.games`, download all the messages, and start reading!

Keeping Up with the Industry: Blues News

About 99.9% of the Internet is a complete waste of bandwidth. It's mostly a bunch of people babbling back and forth and communicating flights of fantasy. But there are a couple of places that aren't a total waste of your time. One of them, *Blues News*, is basically a place where various industry icons and poseurs post their thoughts of the day. Just log on to

`http://www.bluesnews.com`

and check out what's happening on a daily basis.

Game Development Magazines

To my knowledge, there are only two game development magazines in the English language. The first and largest is *Game Developer,* which is published monthly and contains articles on game programming, art, 3D modeling, market trends, and more. Its Web site is at

`http://www.gdmag.com`

For a laugh, you can visit its sister site, *Gamasutra* (the game programmer's book of sex), at

`http://www.gamasutra.com`

Game Web Site Developers

The last thing that you may think of when you're creating a game is its Web site! If you're trying to sell a game yourself as shareware, having a mini-site that shows off the game is very important. You may know how to use FrontPage or the simple Web editor in Netscape, but if you want a really cool Web site to show off your game and make it look larger than life, you should have it done professionally. I have seen so many really good games that have a horrible Web presence.

The company that I use is the Belm Design Group, which can help you make a site for your game, usually from $500 to $3,000. Here's the URL:

`http://www.belmdesigngroup.com`

Xtreme Games LLC

The name of my company is Xtreme Games LLC. We develop and publish 2D/3D games for the PC platform. You can check us out on the Web at

```
http://www.xgames3d.com
```

You'll find articles on 3D graphics, artificial intelligence, physics, DirectX, and a lot more. In addition, I'll be posting any changes or additions to this book.

Xtreme Games LLC publishes games as well as develops them. So if you think you have a good game, log on and check out the information about authoring games through Xtreme. *We also provide technical assistance to developers.*

Additionally, I have created two new companies to help developers. The eGameZone.net is targeted as a completely online distribution point for games at

```
http://www.egamezone.net
```

The other company, NuRvE Networks, creates the next generation of globally aware games and network play:

```
http://www.nurve.net
```

And last but not least, here's my e-mail address once more:

```
CEO@xgames3d.com
```

APPENDIX F

ASCII Tables

If there's one thing that I'm always looking for, it's an ASCII chart. I think the only books in existence that have ASCII charts are Peter Norton's PC books! There should be an ASCII chart in every computer book ever printed, and I'm at fault as much as the next guy. But I've changed my evil ways. Behold, here are the fully annotated ASCII charts for the characters 0-127, 127-255.

Dec	Hex	ASCII	Dec	Hex	ASCII
000	00	null	027	1B	←
001	01	☺	028	1C	∟
002	02	☻	029	1D	↔
003	03	♥	030	1E	▲
004	04	♦	031	1F	▼
005	05	♣	032	20	space
006	06	♠	033	21	!
007	07	•	034	22	"
008	08	◘	035	23	#
009	09	○	036	24	$
010	0A	◙	037	25	%
011	0B	♂	038	26	&
012	0C	♀	039	27	'
013	0D	♪	040	28	(
014	0E	♫	041	29	)
015	0F	☼	042	2A	*
016	10	►	043	2B	+
017	11	◄	044	2C	,
018	12	↕	045	2D	-
019	13	‼	046	2E	.
020	14	¶	047	2F	/
021	15	§	048	30	0
022	16	▬	049	31	1
023	17	↨	050	32	2
024	18	↑	051	33	3
025	19	↓	052	34	4
026	1A	→	053	35	5

Dec	Hex	ASCII	Dec	Hex	ASCII
054	36	6	081	51	Q
055	37	7	082	52	R
056	38	8	083	53	S
057	39	9	084	54	T
058	3A	:	085	55	U
059	3B	;	086	56	V
060	3C	<	087	57	W
061	3D	=	088	58	X
062	3E	>	089	59	Y
063	3F	?	090	5A	Z
064	40	@	091	5B	[
065	41	A	092	5C	\
066	42	B	093	5D	]
067	43	C	094	5E	^
068	44	D	095	5F	_
069	45	E	096	60	`
070	46	F	097	61	a
071	47	G	098	62	b
072	48	H	099	63	c
073	49	I	100	64	d
074	4A	J	101	65	e
075	4B	K	102	66	f
076	4C	L	103	67	g
077	4D	M	104	68	h
078	4E	N	105	69	i
079	4F	O	106	6A	j
080	50	P	107	6B	k

Dec	Hex	ASCII	Dec	Hex	ASCII
108	6C	l	135	87	ç
109	6D	m	136	88	ê
110	6E	n	137	89	ë
111	6F	o	138	8A	è
112	70	p	139	8B	ï
113	71	q	140	8C	î
114	72	r	141	8D	ì
115	73	s	142	8E	Ä
116	74	t	143	8F	Å
117	75	u	144	90	É
118	76	v	145	91	æ
119	77	w	146	92	Æ
120	78	x	147	93	ô
121	79	y	148	94	ö
122	7A	z	149	95	ò
123	7B	{	150	96	û
124	7C	¦	151	97	ù
125	7D	}	152	98	ÿ
126	7E	~	153	99	Ö
127	7F	Δ	154	9A	Ü
128	80	Ç	155	9B	¢
129	81	ü	156	9C	£
130	82	é	157	9D	¥
131	83	â	158	9E	₧
132	84	ä	159	9F	ƒ
133	85	à	160	A0	á
134	86	å	161	A1	í

Dec	Hex	ASCII	Dec	Hex	ASCII
162	A2	ó	189	BD	╝
163	A3	ú	190	BE	╛
164	A4	ñ	191	BF	┐
165	A5	Ñ	192	C0	└
166	A6	ª	193	C1	┴
167	A7	º	194	C2	┬
168	A8	¿	195	C3	├
169	A9	⌐	196	C4	─
170	AA	¬	197	C5	+
171	AB	½	198	C6	╞
172	AC	¼	199	C7	╟
173	AD	¡	200	C8	╚
174	AE	«	201	C9	╔
175	AF	»	202	CA	╩
176	B0	▓	203	CB	╦
177	B1	▓	204	CC	╠
178	B2	▓	205	CD	═
179	B3	│	206	CE	╬
180	B4	┤	207	CF	╧
181	B5	╡	208	D0	╨
182	B6	╢	209	D1	╤
183	B7	╖	210	D2	╥
184	B8	╕	211	D3	╙
185	B9	╣	212	D4	╘
186	BA	║	213	D5	╒
187	BB	╗	214	D6	╓
188	BC	╝	215	D7	╫

Dec	Hex	ASCII	Dec	Hex	ASCII
216	D8	╪	241	F1	±
217	D9	⌡	242	F2	≥
218	DA	⌐	243	F3	≤
219	DB	■	244	F4	⌠
220	DC	▄	245	F5	⌡
221	DD	▌	246	F6	÷
222	DE	▐	247	F7	≈
223	DF	▀	248	F8	°
224	E0	α	249	F9	•
225	E1	β	250	FA	·
226	E2	Γ	251	FB	√
227	E3	π	252	FC	ⁿ
228	E4	Σ	253	FD	²
229	E5	σ	254	FE	■
230	E6	μ	255	FF	
231	E7	γ			
232	E8	Φ			
233	E9	θ			
234	EA	Ω			
235	EB	δ			
236	EC	∞			
237	ED	ø			
238	EE	∈			
239	EF	∩			
240	F0	≡			

INDEX

threads

X-Z

Other Related Titles

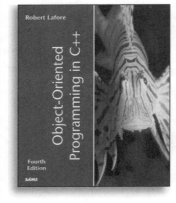
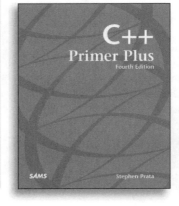